"Augustine calls *City of God* a 'great and arduous work.' It is his magnum opus. But the text's loftiness comes with lofty demands. Gregory W. Lee is an eminently trustworthy guide whose meticulousness, reliability, and accessibility befit the stature and strenuousness of this remarkable text. His judicious selections combined with his superb introduction, annotations, and essays on vexed topics represent the ideal starting point for engaging this greatest work of one of history's greatest authors."

—**Han-luen Kantzer Komline,** Western Theological Seminary

"Augustine is always relevant, and in the twenty-first century even moreso. Gregory W. Lee's selection of passages from Augustine's masterpiece, *City of God*, together with Lee's own astute commentary on those passages, makes for an exceptional work for students and interested general readers. Highly recommended."

—**Charles Mathewes,** University of Virginia

"Augustine notes that his *City of God* is the result of 'great and arduous labor.' As anyone who has tried to read it knows, that can describe the reader's experience too. For those daunted by the prospect, Gregory W. Lee has created this intelligently abbreviated edition. Readers can become familiar with the work, then be tempted to read the whole thing next time!"

—**John C. Cavadini,** University of Notre Dame

"Augustine desperately needs not just an editor but a wingman—someone to track his flight as he deep dives into cultural critique, metaphysical speculation, exegetical acrobatics, and otherworldly musings. Gregory W. Lee, one of the best of the new generation of political theologians, offers readers a framework for reading *City of God*: an introduction to the text and its context within Augustine's political theology, an outline of the book's contents, chapter intros, explanatory notes, expository essays."

—**James Wetzel,** Villanova University

The Essential
City of God

The
Essential
City of God

A READER AND COMMENTARY

GREGORY W. LEE

Ⓑ
Baker Academic
a division of Baker Publishing Group
Grand Rapids, Michigan

Published by Baker Academic
a division of Baker Publishing Group
Grand Rapids, Michigan
BakerAcademic.com

Printed in the United States of America

Library of Congress Cataloging-in-Publication Data
Names: Lee, Gregory W., 1978– author.
Title: The essential City of God : a reader and commentary / Gregory W. Lee.
Description: Grand Rapids, Michigan : Baker Academic, a division of Baker Publishing Group,
  [2025] | Includes bibliographical references.
Identifiers: LCCN 2024045299 | ISBN 9781540967107 (paperback) | ISBN 9781540968357
  (casebound) | ISBN 9781493447695 (ebook) | ISBN 9781493447701 (pdf)
Subjects: LCSH: Augustine, of Hippo, Saint, 354–430. De civitate Dei. | Kingdom of God. |
  Apologetics.
Classification: LCC BR65.A65 L443 2025 | DDC 239/.3—dc23/eng/20241104
LC record available at https://lccn.loc.gov/2024045299

Cover image of Saint Augustine, by Vincenzo Foppa / Magliani, Mauro

25 26 27 28 29 30 31   7 6 5 4 3 2 1

For my parents

Contents

Essays

Acknowledgments

As seems appropriate for a work about Augustine, this book is the fruit of many communities. It originated at Duke with my instruction in Augustine under Geoffrey Wainwright, Warren Smith, Elizabeth Clark, David Aers, and Paul Griffiths; the provocations of Stanley Hauerwas, who made more sense to me after I read *City of God*; and my first undergraduate students, whom I was privileged to teach Augustine. During these years, I shared often about Augustine with friends from Manna Christian Fellowship. I still see these conversations in this work. I continue to reflect on their implications in Chicago with my church family at Lawndale Christian Community Church.

This book was developed at Wheaton College through a seminar for certificate students in early Christian studies. I designed the course as a project-based collaboration toward the publication of this volume. My students talked with me through the book's design, suggested notes to include, and produced initial research and drafts of the essays. I am humbled by the quality of students who participated: Samuel Cho, Sarah Duke, Christopher Iacovetti, Angela Tsarouhis Schott, Brady Woods, Darren Yau; Rebecca Beluk, Collin Flake, Stephen Lee, Ashley Lopez, James Schetelich; Michael Contreras, Henry Prinz, Kathleen Taylor; Christopher Albert, Philip Lindia, Lucy Shafik; Kyle Carter, Avyi Hill, and Sadie Rynbrandt. This experience was possible only because of George Kalantzis, director of The Wheaton Center for Early Christian Studies and the mentor behind this project.

Among these students, Avyi Hill deserves special recognition for her investment in this book. Following her graduation, she served as my research assistant for several months and quickly became a trusted partner on every aspect of the project, from the production of essays to the presentation of controversial matters to minor formatting issues. On many essays, her work was so exceptional that it seemed only appropriate to name her as coauthor. She also extended her support until the submission of the manuscript, well past our original timeline. This book is far better because of her.

This project was supported by the G. W. Aldeen Memorial Grant and the steady leadership of my dean, David Lauber. Keith Johnson offered wisdom throughout my writing, which was inspired by his book *The Essential Karl Barth: A Reader and Commentary*. Tim Larsen and John Walton also shared professional advice. My research assistants Caleb Sprenger, Kathleen Taylor, and Emili Shepperson edited initial versions of the primary source material. Priscilla Logan painstakingly confirmed the citations in all the essays.

Han-luen Kantzer Komline and Tom McGlothlin provided astute revisions on the introduction and several of the essays. Tom also shared a prepublication version of his "Augustine's Resurrection Framework" (*Augustinian Studies*, 2024) that sharpened my treatment of the topic. Veronica Roberts Ogle lent her erudition on multiple elements of the project, including the introduction and the notes on Book 19. I am thankful for Sheryl Overmyer (with whom I first read *City of God*), Toni Alimi, and Young Kim for stimulating feedback and discussion on various essays. Given all the errors these friends have corrected, it seems especially important for me to confess responsibility for those that remain. In general, my study of Augustine has been enriched through conversation with John Bowlin, Luke Bretherton, Patout Burns, Matt Elia, Eric Gregory, Kristen Deede Johnson, Sean Larsen, and Chuck Mathewes.

The production of this book required a unique collaboration between Baker Academic and New City Press, together with the approval of the Augustinian Heritage Institute. That this coordination proved frictionless owes much to Greg Metzger and especially to Jim Wetzel, a longtime source of mentorship and encouragement. I am enormously grateful for permission to use the New City Press translation of *City of God*, without which I may not have continued with this book. Besides Jim, several other friends supported this project during the proposal process: Peter Kaufman, Han-luen Kantzer Komline, Matthew Levering, Veronica Roberts Ogle, Jamie Smith, Warren Smith, and Kevin Vanhoozer. I am indebted to the Baker Academic team for shepherding this project to completion. I am particularly appreciative of

Bob Hosack, for his support and patience with this manuscript, and Alex DeMarco, for wise and incisive editorial direction.

My final thanks are for family. My wife, Jeanette, is my closest friend and best conversation partner about church and society. Nothing makes me feel luckier than being married to her, especially as we marvel at our little miracles, Remy and Audrey. My sister and brother-in-law, Christine and Ryan, continue to encourage my work as their kids, Jonathan and Catherine, continue to inspire us all. I dedicate this book to my parents, Yoon Joo and Sook Ja, who have supported my academic pursuits from the beginning and whose presence in my life grows dearer every year. "Our thoughts, too, will then lie open to each other" (*City of God* 22.29).

Abbreviations

AttA   Fitzgerald, Allan D., ed. *Augustine through the Ages: An Encyclopedia*. Grand Rapids: Eerdmans, 1999

AugLex   Mayer, Cornelius, ed. *Augustinus-Lexikon*. 4 vols. Basel, Switzerland: Schwabe, 1986–2019

Cicero, Republic   Cicero. *On the Commonwealth*. In *"On the Commonwealth" and "On the Laws."* Edited by James E. G. Zetzel. Cambridge: Cambridge University Press, 1999

City of God, Books 1–10   Augustine. *City of God ("De civitate dei"), Books 1–10.* Translated by William Babcock. The Works of Saint Augustine: A Translation for the 21st Century. Hyde Park, NY: New City, 2012

City of God, Books 11–22   Augustine. *City of God ("De civitate dei"), Books 11–22.* Translated by William Babcock. The Works of Saint Augustine: A Translation for the 21st Century. Hyde Park, NY: New City, 2013

Clark, Comm. 1–5   Clark, Gillian. *Commentary on Augustine "City of God," Books 1–5.* Oxford: Oxford University Press, 2021

Clark, Comm. 6–10   Clark, Gillian. *Commentary on Augustine "City of God," Books 6–10.* Oxford: Oxford University Press, 2024

History of Rome   Livy. *The Early History of Rome.* Translated by Aubrey de Sélincourt. London: Penguin, 1960

Meconi, COG   Meconi, David Vincent, ed. *The Cambridge Companion to Augustine's "City of God."* Cambridge: Cambridge University Press, 2021

NCP   New City Press. The Works of Saint Augustine: A Translation for the 21st Century

Vessey, Blackwell Companion   Vessey, Mark, ed. *A Companion to Augustine.* Chichester, UK: Wiley-Blackwell, 2012

Walsh, DCD   Walsh, P. G. *De Civitate Dei ("The City of God").* 9 vols. Oxford: Aris & Phillips, 2005–18

Wetzel, COG   Wetzel, James, ed. *Augustine's "City of God": A Critical Guide.* Cambridge: Cambridge University Press, 2012

Introduction

City of God is arguably Augustine's greatest work, and it is the most important source for his understanding of church and society. After the sack of Rome in 410, many Romans despaired about the future of the empire. Critics blamed the devastation on Rome's conversion to Christianity. *City of God* is Augustine's massive response to these concerns, a theology of the Christian's relation to this world developed through an analysis of Roman culture, a commentary on Scripture, and a philosophy of love. It is the longest work defined by a single argument to have survived from Greco-Roman antiquity.[1]

Augustine's text has inspired over a millennium of political and theological reflection.[2] One of Charlemagne's contemporaries reported that *City of God* was the emperor's favorite book. Medieval theologians cited the text in disputes about war, slavery, political authority, and the relation between imperial and church rulers. Martin Luther, John Calvin, and other reformers drew on the text for their treatments of the fall, their theology of political life, and their interpretations of historical events. In recent years, civic and Christian leaders have turned to Augustine's work for guidance in the midst of political instability.[3] As Western institutions suffer a crisis of trust, Augustine

---

1. James J. O'Donnell, "Augustine, *City of God*," written in 1983 on commission but never published, https://faculty.georgetown.edu/jod/augustine/civ.html. O'Donnell notes the difference between *City of God* and histories, collections of sermons, and other compilations that exceed *City of God* in length but do not require the coherence of design exhibited in Augustine's work.

2. For a survey of this history, see Michael C. Sloan, "*De civitate Dei*," in *The Oxford Guide to the Historical Reception of Augustine*, ed. Karla Pollmann, 3 vols. (Oxford: Oxford University Press, 2013), 1:255–61. See also Michael Lamb, *A Commonwealth of Hope: Augustine's Political Thought* (Princeton: Princeton University Press, 2022), ix–xi.

3. David Gibson, "Is Augustine the Patron Saint of the 2016 Election?," *National Catholic Reporter*, November 3, 2016, https://www.ncronline.org/news/politics/augustine-patron-saint

encourages Christians that their ultimate hope resides in heavenly goods. He also reminds them that earthly institutions are necessary for earthly peace and that institutions require moral commitments to function well.

Despite *City of God*'s influence, it remains, for many, an intimidating and inaccessible book. The most obvious barrier is its size. In English translations, *City of God* runs over one thousand pages, leaving new readers to wonder whether they should tackle the whole text, and if not, where to begin. In addition to being long, *City of God* is highly digressive. Augustine veers from one topic to another, treating some subjects briefly and others in detail before changing topics again—sometimes back to the original subject, sometimes to something different and obscure. He does this with minimal explanation, leaving the uninitiated reader perplexed as to what he is doing. The reader may be left wondering: Why does Augustine treat the topics that he does? Why does he address them at such varying lengths? And what do these discussions have to do with one another?

Another obstacle is the scope of Augustine's project. *City of God* casts a vision of the universe from a Christian perspective, which involves an analysis of Roman history, culture, and society as well as a commentary on Scripture from Genesis to Revelation. Augustine engages the entire literary world known to him as a Roman, and he recounts human history from Adam and Eve to heaven and hell. This narrative does not cover every time period or people group, nor does it detail each topic at equal length. But it is formally comprehensive, and for that reason alone it counts as one of the most ambitious accomplishments of Western literature.

Because of these challenges, many references to *City of God* quote it out of context and misrepresent Augustine's social vision. It is common, for instance, to contrast the two cities according to a distinction between the present and the future. In this reading, Christians are part of the earthly city now, but they will someday enter the heavenly city. The problem with this interpretation is that Augustine's two cities are concurrent realities. Both have existed among humans since the fall of Adam and Eve, and they will continue coexisting until they are separated from each other at final judgment. Moreover, Christians are not members of the earthly city. Citizenship in each city is exclusive; each person can belong to only one city at a given time. Christians reside in

---

-2016-election. President Joe Biden went so far as to quote *City of God* 19.24 in his 2021 inaugural address: https://www.whitehouse.gov/briefing-room/speeches-remarks/2021/01/20/inaugural-address-by-president-joseph-r-biden-jr.

the earthly city, but they are not members of it. Citizens of the earthly city become citizens of the heavenly city by converting to Christianity. To be sure, the cities orient themselves differently toward the present and the future. The earthly city hopes in temporal goods while the heavenly city hopes in eternal goods. But this is different from claiming that the earthly city exists now and the heavenly city will exist in the time to come.

The relation between the two cities determines Christians' posture toward the world. Augustine's defining image for this topic is pilgrimage (*peregrinatio*), a multivalent term that encompasses the ideas of exile, sojourning, journeying, and noncitizenship.[4] Like the Israelites in Babylon, Christians are warned not to adopt the customs of the earthly city or to forget their identity as citizens of the heavenly city. Yet they are also commanded "to pray for Babylon, *because in its peace is your peace* (Jer. 29:7)."[5] Life as an exile is not defined exclusively by resistance or insurrection. It also requires cooperation on goods that both the earthly city and the heavenly city depend on. Christians can support the social and political life of a corrupt order to the extent that it furnishes material blessings necessary for all people. They dissent from the earthly city when it promotes unjust or idolatrous ends. Though this perspective does not resolve the complications of participation in civic life, it establishes two core principles. Since Christians are not citizens of the earthly city, they should consider themselves outsiders to political society. Yet Christians have a stake in earthly peace, so they may cooperate with the earthly city on temporal concerns.

Few readers have the background to understand all the topics Augustine addresses. Even specialists have struggled to produce commentaries on *City of God* because of the breadth of learning required.[6] *City of God* demands

---

4. Sarah Stewart Kroeker, *Pilgrimage as Moral and Aesthetic Formation in Augustine's Thought* (Oxford: Oxford University Press, 2017), 10–17. See also A. Lauras and H. Rondet, "Le thème des deux cités dans l'oeuvre de saint Augustin," in *Études augustiniennes*, ed. H. Rondet, M. Le Landais, A. Lauras, and C. Couturier (Paris: Aubier, 1953), 97–160; Antoine Lauras, "Deux cités, Jérusalem et Babylone: Formation et évolution d'un thème central du 'De Civitate Dei,'" *La Ciudad de Dios* 167 (1954): 117–50; and Johannes van Oort, *Jerusalem and Babylon: A Study into Augustine's "City of God" and the Sources of His Doctrine of the Two Cities* (orig. 1991; Leiden: Brill, 2013), 131–42.

5. *City of God* 19.26.

6. For a history of commentaries on *City of God*, see Gillian Clark, *Commentary on Augustine "City of God," Books 1–5* (Oxford: Oxford University Press, 2021), 27–32. The second volume of this commentary series, covering Books 6 to 10, was published by Oxford University Press in 2024. Besides Clark's work, notable efforts include G. Bardy, ed., *La Cité de Dieu*, trans. G. Combès, Oeuvres de Saint Augustin: Bibliothèque Augustinienne 33–37 (Paris: Desclée de Brower, 1959–60); and P. G. Walsh, *De Civitate Dei (The City of God)* (Oxford: Aris & Phillips), which covers Books 1 to 16.

familiarity with ancient history, religion, and rhetoric alongside knowledge of Scripture, philosophy, and early Christian theology. Scholars typically concentrate on one or two of these areas, not all of them. Most studies of *City of God* are written for academics and assume facility with Latin.[7] Not many works exist for a general reader who wants to understand Augustine's basic perspective on church and society and why it matters today.[8] That is the gap this book seeks to fill.

The Essential "City of God" reflects the conviction that uninitiated readers can engage Augustine's work with the right support and that reading it is a spiritual exercise. My interest in Augustine began when I was a doctoral student at Duke University under the tutelage of early Christianity scholars Warren Smith and Elizabeth Clark. Their courses introduced me to the range of Augustine's writings: his anti-Manichean, anti-Donatist, and anti-Pelagian works as well as his treatises on Scripture, the Trinity, marriage, and sex. Yet we had little time for *City of God*, given its length, and I longed to learn more about it. I thus jumped at the opportunity to take a course on the work when it was offered by the medievalist David Aers.

Reading *City of God* cover to cover was one of the most exhilarating experiences of my life. I consumed much of it on the steps of Duke's chapel in North Carolina's resplendent fall weather. From almost the first paragraph, I sensed that this was the work where Augustine had synthesized his thought, that all his writings came to a head in this single volume. Unlike Thomas Aquinas or John Calvin, Augustine never wrote a systematic theology structured by

7. Important sources include Gerard O'Daly, *Augustine's "City of God": A Reader's Guide*, 2nd ed. (orig. 1999; Oxford: Oxford University Press, 2020); James Wetzel, ed., *Augustine's "City of God": A Critical Guide* (Cambridge: Cambridge University Press, 2012); and David Vincent Meconi, ed., *The Cambridge Companion to Augustine's City of God* (Cambridge: Cambridge University Press, 2021). For earlier studies, see Dorothy F. Donnelly and Mark A. Sherman, eds., *Augustine's "De Civitate Dei": An Annotated Bibliography of Modern Criticism, 1960–1990* (New York: Peter Lang, 1991); Dorothy F. Donnelly, ed., *The City of God: A Collection of Critical Essays* (New York: Peter Lang, 1995); and Christoph Horn, ed., *Augustinus, De civitate dei* (Berlin: Akademie, 1997).

8. Augustine, *The City of God ("De civitate dei"): Abridged Study Edition*, ed. Joseph T. Kelley, The Works of Saint Augustine: A Translation for the 21st Century (Hyde Park, NY: New City, 2018) presents an abbreviated edition of the text with helpful study questions. Two books that present Augustine's political thought for a wider audience are Charles Mathewes, *The Republic of Grace: Augustinian Thoughts for Dark Times* (Grand Rapids: Eerdmans, 2010); and James K. A. Smith, *Awaiting the King: Reforming Public Theology* (Grand Rapids: Baker Academic, 2017). For a stimulating series of lectures, see Charles Mathewes, "Books That Matter: *The City of God*," The Great Courses: Christianity, 2016, https://www.thegreatcourses.com/courses/books-that-matter-the-city-of-god.

doctrinal loci: the doctrine of God, the doctrine of salvation, and so forth. *City of God* offers instead a narrative of Scripture and human history. Though Augustine treats theological topics as they arise, they do not determine the shape of his work. *City of God* is structured by a story, one that forms readers' affections as they follow along.[9]

Augustine is best known for his *Confessions*, in which he recounts his wanderings and conversion as a tale of disorderly and orderly loves. *City of God* is the story of love on a grander, even cosmic, scale. Here the subject is not the individual person but the great realities of history and society: empires, wars, religious institutions, and political intrigue; angels and demons; Israel, Christ, and the church. The heavenly and earthly cities divide according to whether they love God or self, whether they prioritize heavenly or earthly goods. The contrast between these loves plays out in the histories of the two cities—whether in the violence, corruption, and idolatry of the earthly city or in the peace, love, and humility of the heavenly city. As I was reading Augustine's work, I found myself attracted to the virtues of the heavenly city and repulsed by the vices of the earthly city. *City of God* persuaded me, page by page, that love resides at the center of the universe because the world was created by God, and God is love. Arguably, this is the thesis of Augustine's entire corpus.

The force of Augustine's argument cannot be experienced in isolated snippets of his work. The reader must track the whole of his presentation, as with a novel in which the narrative is inherent to understanding its characters and their development. Still, it is not necessary to read all of *City of God* to grasp its vision. The reader can follow the main components of Augustine's narrative by studying extended selections. This book is an abbreviated and annotated edition of his work. It is long enough for readers to grasp Augustine's master argument but short enough not to overwhelm them. It concentrates on Augustine's social and political thought, the primary topic associated with *City of God*, while also including other material to provide a sense for the larger work. Several aids will support readers as they work through the text. As a theologian, I am primarily interested in Augustine's ideas and how they relate to our times. Though the book addresses other areas of inquiry, this material is instrumental to the larger goal of thinking with Augustine about the ideas he cared about. I suspect this is how he would have wanted us to read his work.

9. On Augustine, formation, and love, see James K. A. Smith, *Desiring the Kingdom: Worship, Worldview, and Cultural Formation* (Grand Rapids: Baker Academic, 2009).

Biography

Augustine was born in 354 in Thagaste of Roman Africa and spent most of his life in the areas of modern-day Algeria and Tunisia.[10] His father, Patrick, was a mid-level Roman official who would become a Christian only toward the end of his life. *Confessions* says little about Patrick except to criticize him for caring more about Augustine's worldly success than his soul. Augustine shares much more affectionately about his mother, Monica, a devout Christian who prayed for him throughout his earlier years of rebellion. Scholars sometimes claim that Monica had Berber origins, with roots in an indigenous African population, though this designation is contested.[11] Whatever Augustine's ethnic background, he was legally and culturally a Roman, even as he was aware of his African identity and spoke Latin with an African accent.[12]

Augustine began his classical education in Madauros. He then took a gap year at home before continuing his studies in Carthage, the capital city of Roman Africa. His goal was to become a teacher of rhetoric. Augustine describes his teenage years as a period of self-indulgence. *Confessions* famously recounts an incident in which Augustine and his friends stole pears from a neighbor's tree, a story he uses to analyze the character of temptation and sin. Augustine also laments his sexual immorality, though he would eventually commit himself to one woman (whom he does not name) and remain faithful to her for over a decade. Their son, Adeodatus, would die as a teenager.

At the age of nineteen, Augustine came across a (now lost) text by Cicero called *Hortensius*, which inspired him to pursue wisdom. He first sought it in the Bible but found the text rhetorically inelegant, a judgment he would later attribute to pride. Augustine then turned to Manicheism, a dualistic religion

---

10. For biographies of Augustine, see Peter Brown, *Augustine of Hippo: A Biography*, new ed. (orig. 1967; Berkeley: University of California Press, 2000); Serge Lancel, *St. Augustine*, trans. Antonia Nevill (orig. 1999; London: SCM, 2002); James J. O'Donnell, *Augustine: A New Biography* (New York: Ecco, 2005); Robin Lane Fox, *Augustine: Conversions to Confessions* (New York: Basic Books, 2015). This section is lightly revised from my "Augustine of Hippo," in *Evangelical Dictionary of Theology*, ed. Daniel J. Treier and Walter A. Elwell, 3rd ed. (Grand Rapids: Baker Academic, 2017), 102–4.

11. John J. O'Meara, *The Young Augustine*, 2nd rev. ed. (orig. 1954; New York: Alba House, 2001), 10–11; van Oort, *Jerusalem and Babylon*, 18–21; Lancel, *St. Augustine*, 5–6; O'Donnell, *Augustine*, 116–20, 325, 374n618; Fox, *Augustine*, 23–24; Ramzi Rouighi, *Inventing the Berbers: History and Ideology in the Maghrib* (Philadelphia: University of Pennsylvania Press, 2019).

12. *De Doctrina Christiana* 4.10.24; *Order* 2.17.45. For a modern reflection on these themes, see Justo L. González, *The Mestizo Augustine: A Theologian between Two Cultures* (Downers Grove, IL: IVP Academic, 2016).

that caused him to question the authority of the Old Testament. Augustine became disillusioned with the religion when a celebrated Manichean bishop, Faustus, failed to answer his questions about it. Spiritually homeless, Augustine began exploring other philosophies in search of wisdom.

Augustine's developing career brought him from Carthage to Rome and finally to Milan, the Western imperial capital, where he assumed a prestigious post as its official orator in 384. There Augustine encountered the bishop Ambrose, whose allegorical interpretations of Scripture helped Augustine address Manichean critiques of the Old Testament. Augustine also discovered Neoplatonic writings that provided answers for his questions about God, evil, and the physical world. His new understanding of evil as privation, or nonbeing, would suffuse his later writings, including *City of God*.

After Augustine's intellectual doubts were resolved, his main hindrance to conversion was the desire for sex, which he believed he needed to renounce in order to become a Christian. "Grant me chastity and self-control, but please not yet."[13] After a serendipitous conversation about the emerging monastic movement, Augustine was inspired to follow a similar path but found himself incapable of surrendering his will to God. This interior battle culminated in a storied incident in a garden in Milan.

As *Confessions* recounts, Augustine hears a child's voice repeating, "Pick it up and read [*tolle, lege*]," and he interprets these words as a divine command to open a collection of Paul's epistles that he had with him. The first passage he happens upon, Romans 13:13–14, brings instant resolution and peace: "*Not in dissipation and drunkenness, nor in debauchery and lewdness, nor in arguing and jealousy; but put on the Lord Jesus Christ, and make no provision for the flesh or the gratification of your desires.*"[14] This story of Augustine's conversion would inspire countless conversion stories in subsequent Christian tradition.

After this experience, and partly because of health concerns, Augustine gave up his position as rhetorician and retired with his mother and some companions to a country estate in Cassiciacum, where he wrote some of his earliest philosophical dialogues. In 387, he came back to Milan and was baptized under Ambrose. He then began a return journey to North Africa, where he intended to establish a monastic community. These plans were delayed when Monica became sick and died in Ostia, outside Rome. Her death is the last event narrated in *Confessions*.

13. *Confessions* 8.7.17.
14. *Confessions* 8.12.29.

In 391, Augustine was ordained as a priest in Hippo Regius, an important port city of Roman Africa, and in 396 he became the bishop of the city. This position involved preaching, administering the sacraments, overseeing alms distribution, and adjudicating legal disputes. He wrote his *Confessions* in the late 390s, and his writings thereafter would be marked by emphases on sin and grace. For the next decade and beyond, the chief controversy of Augustine's bishopric concerned the Donatists, a rival Christian community in North Africa. Augustine's campaign against them was the most significant context for his social and political writings. Another major controversy concerned Pelagius and his supporters, who prompted Augustine's most developed treatments of original sin and predestination. Augustine began writing *City of God* in 412/13, following the sack of Rome in 410. He died in 430, a few years after completing the work.

Background

City of God was produced at the decline of the Roman empire, following major shifts in the relationship between the empire and Christianity.[15] In the early 300s, Christians suffered Rome's most aggressive persecution of the church. This persecution occurred under the emperor Diocletian and was sometimes called the Great Persecution. Soon after the edicts against Christians were rescinded, the emperor Constantine converted to the faith. He and his fellow emperor, Licinius, then issued the Edict of Milan (313), establishing religious toleration and the legality of Christianity throughout the empire. Constantine promoted Christianity throughout his reign, though he stopped short of making it the official religion of the empire. His efforts earned the praise of Eusebius of Caesarea, the first church historian, who depicted Constantine as a quasi-messianic figure and conflated the conversion of Rome with the fulfillment of God's purposes in history. This theory of "Christian times" (*tempora christiana*) gained prominence in the late fourth century when the emperor Theodosius I established Christianity as the religion of the empire and banned traditional Roman religion. Though the prohibition

15. John Matthews, *Western Aristocracies and Imperial Court A.D. 364–425* (London: Clarendon, 1975); Gillian Clark, *Christianity and Roman Society* (Cambridge: Cambridge University Press, 2004); Averil Cameron, "Christianity and the 'Peace of the Church,'" in *The Cambridge History of Christianity*, vol. 1, *Origins to Constantine*, ed. Margaret M. Mitchell and Frances M. Young (Cambridge: Cambridge University Press, 2006), 538–51; R. Malcolm Errington, *Roman Imperial Policy from Julian to Theodosius* (Chapel Hill: University of North Carolina Press, 2006).

of Roman religion seems to have been unevenly enforced, this development spurred many Christians to interpret the Christianization of the empire as the mechanism by which God was drawing all nations to Christ. The empire represented the nations, so when Rome became Christian, the nations did too.

In 410, after years of aggression, the Visigoth king Alaric sacked Rome, pillaging the city and brutalizing its inhabitants for three intense days. For Romans across the empire, news of this event was devastating. Writing from Bethlehem, Jerome likened it to the fall of Troy and the destruction of Jerusalem by Babylon.[16] Though Rome was no longer the imperial capital, it remained the symbolic capital of the Roman people. Rome had not experienced such an attack in eight hundred years. Questions soon arose as to the veracity of the Christian faith. Supposedly, Rome had enjoyed peace when it worshiped the traditional gods. Alaric's attack proved the gods were angry at the Roman people for abandoning them. Many aristocrats brought these objections with them from Rome to North Africa, where they fled for their estates in the area. This is the context in which Augustine encountered their criticisms and took up his pen.

City of God rejects the identification of the Roman empire with the people of God. It claims that, since the fall, humanity has been divided into two peoples, the earthly city and the heavenly city. By "city" (*ciuitas*), Augustine is not referring to an urban center or a town with walls but to a community of citizens that extends across generations and geographies.[17] Whereas the Romans associated cities with physical territories, Augustine's two cities span humanity from the time of Adam and Eve through the present day. What distinguishes them is not nation, dress, or custom but their respective loves. Both communities experience temporal goods and temporal evils. Temporal suffering is no argument against the Christian faith, which never guaranteed earthly blessing as the reward of worshiping Jesus. Since Christians hope in eternal, not temporal goods, they remain unshaken by the sack of Rome.

In developing this argument, Augustine advances a comprehensive critique of Roman society and a narration of the heavenly city from the beginning of human history to the end. *City of God* thus goes far beyond the original purpose of addressing objections after the sack of Rome. Given its significance

16. Jerome, *Letter* 127.12. For Augustine's reaction, see *Sermon 397*, "On the Sack of the City of Rome."

17. Clark, *Comm.* 1–5, 1. For background on the theme of the two cities in Augustine, see van Oort, *Jerusalem and Babylon*, 199–359; and O'Daly, *Augustine's "City of God,"* 57–71.

for Augustine's social thought, readers may be surprised to discover how little it offers in the vein of political theory. *City of God* says almost nothing about the nature and purpose of government or how it should be constituted (e.g., as a monarchy, an aristocracy, or a democracy).[18] Readers will find more concentrated treatments of politics in Augustine's letters, including his interventions in concrete situations.[19] *City of God* furnishes a broader, theological account of the world as humanity experiences it. Social reality is determined by people's loves, whether for God or for self, whether for eternal goods or for temporal goods. "Two loves, then, have made two cities. Love of self, even to the point of contempt for God, made the earthly city, and love of God, even to the point of contempt for self, made the heavenly city."[20] This is Augustine's enduring contribution to Christian political thought.

City of God is dedicated to Flavius Marcellinus, tribune and notary of Africa and Augustine's closest contact in high imperial office. This context is important for understanding the work. For multiple decades, Augustine was consumed with what scholars typically call the Donatist controversy.[21] This challenge arose in the early 300s following the Diocletianic persecution. One of the hardest hit

18. Clark, *Comm.* 1–5, 18–21. *City of God* 2.21 mentions these forms of government without expanding on them. *City of God* 19.14–16 is often cited in discussions about political authority, though this section does not concentrate on the topic. For recent discussion, see Eric Gregory and Joseph Clair, "Augustinianisms and Thomisms," in *The Cambridge Companion to Christian Political Theology*, ed. Craig Hovey and Elizabeth Phillips (Cambridge: Cambridge University Press, 2015), 176–95.

19. For primary sources, see Margaret Atkins and Robert Dodaro, eds., *Augustine: Political Writings* (Cambridge: Cambridge University Press, 2001). For studies, see Robert Dodaro, "Between the Two Cities: Political Action in Augustine of Hippo," in *Augustine and Politics*, ed. John Doody, Kevin L. Hughes, and Kim Paffenroth (Lanham, MD: Lexington Books, 2005), 99–115; and Joseph Clair, *Discerning the Good in the Letters and Sermons of Augustine* (Oxford: Oxford University Press, 2016).

20. *City of God* 14.28.

21. For an overview of the Donatist controversy, see Richard Miles, ed., *The Donatist Schism: Controversy and Contexts* (Liverpool, UK: Liverpool University Press, 2016). See also Brent D. Shaw, *Sacred Violence: African Christians and Sectarian Hatred in the Age of Augustine* (Cambridge: Cambridge University Press, 2011); J. Patout Burns Jr. and Robin M. Jensen, *Christianity in Roman Africa: The Development of Its Practices and Beliefs* (Grand Rapids: Eerdmans, 2014). On Marcellinus, see Madeleine Moreau, *Le dossier Marcellinus dans la correspondance de saint Augustin* (Paris: Études Augustiniennes, 1973). The word "Donatist" was an epithet that the followers of Donatus protested. Despite its contestation, it remains the most common term to describe Augustine's opponents. For further discussion, see Brent D. Shaw, "African Christianity: Disputes, Definitions, and 'Donatists,'" in *Orthodoxy and Heresy in Religious Movements: Discipline and Dissent*, ed. Malcolm R. Greenshields and Thomas A. Robinson (Lewiston, NY: Edwin Mellen, 1992), 4–34; and John Whitehouse, "The Course of the Donatist Schism in Late Roman North Africa," in Miles, *Donatist Schism*, 34–53, esp. 14–15.

areas was North Africa, where Augustine would become bishop. During the persecution, some bishops gave up copies of the Bible and other liturgical books to Roman officials. This act was called *traditio*, which literally means "to hand over" and is the root for the English word "traitor." These events occurred when churches might possess only one copy of the Bible, long before the invention of the printing press. *Traditio* was an insidious betrayal of Christ and his people.

After the persecution ended, a debate erupted in Carthage concerning a bishop named Caecilian, who had allegedly been ordained by at least one *traditor*. A group of Christians opposed the ordination on the grounds that it compromised the purity of the church. They installed another individual, Majorinus, as bishop of Carthage. He would soon be succeeded by Donatus, from whom the Donatists received their name. The Donatists protested the ordination of Caecilian before Constantine, who ruled several times against them. Those who remained in fellowship with Caecilian, the "Catholics," thus had the support of the empire, which would persecute the Donatists on the Catholics' behalf.

Augustine stepped into this controversy almost a century after it began, and he was firmly on the Catholic side. He wrote extensively against the Donatists, developed a vision for the universal church around the Mediterranean, and eventually enlisted the support of imperial officials to coerce the Donatists into Catholic communion. His most willing partner was Marcellinus, who was appointed to oversee a conference at Carthage against the Donatists in 411. This conference marked the victory of the Catholics over the Donatists. Augustine coordinated closely with Marcellinus prior to the proceedings to ensure this result. At the conference, Augustine distinguished himself as the leading theologian and polemicist against the Donatists, further cementing his relationship with Marcellinus.

Following the conference at Carthage, Marcellinus wrote Augustine a letter with questions about Christianity from Volusian, former proconsul of Africa and future prefect of the city of Rome.[22] One of these questions concerned the relationship between Christianity and the Roman empire. Does Jesus's command to turn the other cheek forbid the empire from protecting its territories? Marcellinus also asked Augustine to write a longer work in response to these questions.[23] Augustine replied with a couple of letters addressing

---

22. *Letter* 136. See also *Letters* 132; 135; and 137 for correspondence between Volusian and Augustine.

23. *Letter* 136.3.

Volusian's questions.[24] He then began *City of God*, identifying Marcellinus as the dedicatee of this fuller discussion.[25] Shortly after Augustine started the work, Marcellinus was killed in a political insurrection.[26] About fourteen years later, when Augustine completed *City of God*, he described it as the fulfillment of a debt (without mentioning Marcellinus).[27]

It is an awkward fact that Augustine dedicated his greatest political work, *City of God*, to the official who authorized persecuting the Donatists. During the Donatist controversy, Augustine developed Christianity's first major defense of religious coercion.[28] Some scholars have treated this theme as an aberration in Augustine's thought. In my judgment, this approach ignores the centrality of Augustine's campaign against the Donatists for his bishopric and how deeply it formed his political vision.[29] Augustine's defense of coercion illuminates several passages in *City of God* that we might otherwise gloss over, including Augustine's celebration of the ideal emperor in 5.24–26 as someone who stamps out false religion and patronizes Christianity. Augustine's perspective may seem offensive to modern readers who take for granted the separation between church and state. But Roman life fused civic and religious life to a great degree, and Augustine took much of this context for granted. He saw no problem with a Christian emperor ruling as a Christian and promoting the faith in political office. This is one of the challenges of applying Augustine's political vision

24. *Letters* 137; 138.

25. *City of God* 1.*preface*. *Letter* 138.4.20 seems to suggest Augustine's plans for this larger work.

26. Marcellinus was executed in September 413.

27. *City of God* 22.30.

28. See Peter Brown, "Religious Coercion in the Later Roman Empire: The Case of North Africa" (orig. 1963), in *Religion and Society in the Age of St. Augustine* (London: Faber, 1972), 301–31; Brown, "St. Augustine's Attitude to Religious Coercion" (orig. 1964), in *Religion and Society in the Age of St. Augustine*, 260–78; Frederick H. Russell, "Persuading the Donatists: Augustine's Coercion by Words," in *The Limits of Ancient Christianity: Essays on Late Antique Thought and Culture in Honor of R. A. Markus*, ed. William E. Klingshirn and Mark Vessey (Ann Arbor: University of Michigan Press, 1999), 115–30; Brent D. Shaw, "Augustine and Men of Imperial Power," *Journal of Late Antiquity* 8, no. 1 (2015): 32–61; and Peter Van Nuffelen, "Coercion in Late Antiquity: A Brief Intellectual History," in *Religious Violence in the Ancient World: From Classical Athens to Late Antiquity*, ed. Jitse H. F. Dijkstra and Christian R. Raschle (Cambridge: Cambridge University Press, 2020), 266–85.

29. See Gregory W. Lee, "Using the Earthly City: Ecclesiology, Political Activity, and Religious Coercion in Augustine," *Augustinian Studies* 47, no. 1 (2016): 41–63. See also John R. Bowlin, "Augustine on Justifying Coercion," *The Annual of the Society of Christian Ethics* 17 (1997): 49–70; and Michael Lamb, "Augustine and Republican Liberty: Contextualizing Coercion," *Augustinian Studies* 48, no. 1/2 (2017): 119–59.

today. Any appropriation of his thought has to reckon with the differences between his time and ours.

Composition, Audience, and Genre

Augustine wrote *City of God* during an intense season when he was also producing his literal commentary on Genesis, several treatises against the Pelagians, ongoing refutations of the Donatists, his expositions on the Psalms, his homilies on John, and his great work on the Trinity. From various writings, we learn that Augustine was constantly working (including evenings, Saturdays, and Sundays), unable to respond to everyone's requests of him, and repeatedly interrupted from writing *City of God* by time-sensitive demands.[30] Augustine composed his works by dictation, speaking his words to a scribe who wrote them down. He had access to limited sources, often quoted sources from memory, and did not always confirm historical or textual details.[31]

The composition of *City of God* thus proceeded in fits and starts.[32] Books 1–3 were released as a unit in 413/14, circulated widely, and celebrated by the vicar of Africa, Macedonius, who claimed he did not know what to admire in them more, "the perfection of the priesthood, the teachings of philosophy, the ample knowledge of history, or the charm of eloquence."[33] Others, whom Augustine does not name, plotted a critical response.[34] As to the rest of *City of God*, we know that Books 4–5 were completed by 415,[35] and Books 6–10 were completed by 417.[36] We have indications that Book 12 was written around 417, Books 14–16 were written around 418–20, and Book 18

30. For glimpses of Augustine's work schedule, see *Expositions of the Psalms* 118.24.3; *Letters* 13.1; 48.1; 98.8; 110.5–6; 118.1.1–118.1.7; 139.3; 162.1; 169.1; 213.5–6; 224.1–2; 246.3; 261.1; 2*.1; 23A*.3–4; *Revisions* 2.43; *Work of Monks* 29.37; and Possidius, *Life of Augustine* 19, 24. For additional citations, see "Augustine's Lack of Free Time," *Scrinium Augustini*, http://www.scrinium.umk.pl/cloud/details/184.

31. Clark, *Comm. 1–5, 9–12.* See also Harald Hagendahl, *Augustine and the Latin Classics,* 2 vols. (Göteborg, Sweden: Acta Universitatis Gothoburgensis, 1967); and James J. O'Donnell, "Augustine's Classical Readings," *Recherches Augustiniennes* 15 (1980): 144–75.

32. Bardy, "Introduction Générale," in *La Cité de Dieu,* Bibliothèque Augustinienne 33, 22–35; van Oort, *Jerusalem and Babylon,* 62; O'Daly, *Augustine's "City of God,"* 35–37.

33. *Letter* 154.2.

34. *City of God* 5.26. We do not know who these individuals were or whether they published their response.

35. *Letter* 169.1.

36. Orosius, *Histories against the Pagans* 1.prologue.11.

was completed by 424/25.[37] And we are confident Augustine completed *City of God* by 426/27.[38]

City of God was written for an audience of elite Christians and non-Christians.[39] The most immediate recipients were a group of aristocrats in Carthage, including some who had come to Africa after the sack of Rome. Among them was Marcellinus, the Christian tribune and notary of Africa who had ruled against the Donatists during the conference at Carthage. One unnamed landowner from Hippo was vocally critical of Augustine.[40] Others were not Christian but open to the faith. Volusian, whose questions prompted Augustine to write *City of God*, was from a prominent Christian family and would receive baptism at the end of his life. Outside this circle, we discover a similar mix of Christian and non-Christian readers.[41] One catechumen, Firmus, was inspired to read all of *City of God* after hearing Book 18 read aloud on three consecutive afternoons.[42] Augustine urged him to finish reading the work and join the heavenly city. By producing *City of God*, Augustine sought to arm Christians against objections and to persuade non-Christians to become Christians. His audience helps explain the intensity of his polemic. Since most of his readers were Christian or Christian-friendly, he could caricature other Romans without fear of alienating his audience.

37. *De Trinitate* 13.9.12 refers to a completed Book 12. For Book 14, scholars rely on *Answer to an Enemy of the Law and the Prophets* 1.14.18, which was written no earlier than 420, and *Letter* 184A.3.5, which was written about 418. Books 15–16 exhibit dependence on *Questions on the Heptateuch*, which was written no earlier than 419. The evidence in Book 18.54 for its date of composition is complicated. See O'Daly, *Augustine's "City of God,"* 313–14.

38. *Revisions* 2.43.

39. Gillian Clark, "Letters and the City of God," in *"Scrinium Augustini": The World of Augustine's Letters*, ed. Przemysław Nehring, Mateusz Stróżyński, and Rafal Toczko (Turnhout, Belgium: Brepols, 2017), 181–202; Mattias Gassman, "The Ancient Readers of Augustine's *City of God*," *Augustinian Studies* 52, no. 1 (2021): 1–18. See also Gassman, "The Composition of *De consensu euangelistarum* 1 and the Development of Augustine's Arguments on Paganism," *Augustinian Studies* 54, no. 2 (2021): 157–75.

40. *Letter* 136.3.

41. These individuals include Evodius of Uzalis and Possidius of Calama, both fellow bishops (*Letter* 169.1 and *Letter* 23A*.3, respectively); Peter and Abraham, probably monks who needed help addressing criticisms of Christianity (*Letter* 184A.3.5); Firmus, a catechumen reluctant to receive baptism (*Letter* 1A*, 2*); Darius, an imperial officer curious to learn more about the faith (*Letter* 230.4); and Orosius, a presbyter and the author, at Augustine's request, of a companion work to *City of God* (Orosius, *Histories against the Pagans*).

42. *Letter* 2*.3. This detail bears some irony, since Book 18 is twice the length of the other books in *City of God* and has been denigrated by modern scholars for being unstructured and disorganized. I have challenged this perspective in "Republics and Their Loves: Rereading *City of God* 19," *Modern Theology* 27, no. 4 (2011): 553–81.

City of God is the culmination of the Latin apologetic tradition, a body of writings that challenged Roman religion and defended Christianity against critics. Many of Augustine's arguments can be found in earlier writers like Tertullian, Arnobius, and Lactantius.[43] Yet *City of God* is something of an outlier among Augustine's works. Although Augustine engages the Roman tradition in earlier texts, his writings as a bishop tend to focus on theological questions and draw heavily on the Bible.[44] In *City of God*, Augustine returns to his classical education to interrogate Roman history and culture.[45] This material composes much of Books 1–10, the first half of *City of God*.

The second half of *City of God*, Books 11–22, is largely an exposition of Scripture. These books resemble an earlier work called *Instructing Beginners in Faith*, which is a handbook for catechizing those preparing for baptism.[46] As Augustine explains in this text, catechesis should introduce newcomers to the whole storyline of Scripture.[47] Since the Bible is so long, teachers cannot dwell on every detail. They should concentrate instead on major moments: creation, fall, flood, the call of Abraham, and so forth. Each of these events should be explained with reference to Christ and the church, the body of Christ, so as to display God's love for humanity.[48] This love should, in turn, prompt readers' love for God and neighbor, which is the ultimate purpose of Scripture. *Instructing Beginners in Faith* provides two sample expositions that narrate the biblical story from Genesis through Revelation.[49] The structure of these expositions matches *City of God*'s narration of Scripture, though *City of God* expands hugely on the major moments. This suggests that *City of God* should be read not just as a work of apologetics but as an exercise in catechesis. Despite the length, complexity, and digressions of Augustine's work, his goals are simple: to persuade non-Christians of the faith, to instruct believers, and to encourage love for God and neighbor.

43. O'Daly, *Augustine's "City of God,"* 42–56.
44. For Augustine and the Bible, begin with Michael Cameron, *Christ Meets Me Everywhere: Augustine's Early Figurative Exegesis* (Oxford: Oxford University Press, 2012).
45. O'Donnell, "Augustine's Classical Readings," 147.
46. Van Oort, *Jerusalem and Babylon*, 175–98; O'Daly, *Augustine's "City of God,"* 298–306, which also stresses parallels with *True Religion*.
47. *Instructing Beginners in Faith* 3.5.
48. *Instructing Beginners in Faith* 4.8.
49. *Instructing Beginners in Faith* 18.29–24.44; 26.51–27.55.

Interpretation

Given the challenges of interpreting *City of God*, it is no surprise that scholars have differed in their interpretations of the text and its implications.[50] For the last several decades, studies of *City of God* have operated in the shadow of Robert Markus. As Markus argues in *Saeculum: History and Society in the Theology of St. Augustine* (originally published in 1970), Augustine once embraced a theology of *tempora christiana*, but he came to reject it in favor of a theology of ambiguity, even before the sack of Rome.[51] According to Augustine's revised perspective, Christians should not expect any events of final significance before the eschaton. The two cities are ideal types that do not correspond to real communities. No institution can be identified with the earthly city or the heavenly city. Nor does any historical event between the time of the incarnation and Christ's return bear ultimate importance for God's plans for the world. Indeed, Markus argues, Augustine envisioned a pluralistic "state" in which persons of divergent religious commitments could negotiate temporal affairs in relation to one another. He thus invited Christians to consider themselves members of temporal society and to promote temporal goods in which Christians and non-Christians have a common stake.

In recent years, many scholars (including me) have criticized Markus for rendering the two cities invisible and molding Augustine's theology into the image of political liberalism.[52] Augustine did not propose a third sphere of society between the earthly and heavenly cities, nor did he advocate for religious pluralism. Still, debates remain over many aspects of Augustine's political

50. On the history of the interpretation of *City of God*, see Michael J. S. Bruno, *Political Augustinianism: Modern Interpretations of Augustine's Political Thought* (Minneapolis: Fortress, 2014).

51. R. A. Markus, *Saeculum: History and Society in the Theology of St. Augustine*, 2nd ed. (orig. 1970; Cambridge: Cambridge University Press, 1988). See also Markus, *Christianity and the Secular* (Notre Dame, IN: University of Notre Dame Press, 2006); and Markus, *"'Tempora Christiana' Revisited,"* in *Augustine and His Critics: Essays in Honour of Gerald Bonner*, ed. Robert Dodaro and George Lawless (London: Routledge, 2000), 201–13.

52. For analysis of these issues, see Michael J. Hollerich, "John Milbank, Augustine, and the 'Secular,'" in *History, Apocalypse, and the Secular Imagination: New Essays on Augustine's "City of God,"* ed. Mark Vessey, Karla Pollmann, and Allan D. Fitzgerald (Bowling Green, OH: Philosophy Documentation Center, 1999), 311–26; and Robert Dodaro, "*Ecclesia* and *Res Publica*: How Augustinian Are Neo-Augustinian Politics?," in *Augustine and Postmodern Thought: A New Alliance against Modernity?*, ed. L. Boeve, M. Lamberigts, and M. Wisse (Leuven, Belgium: Peeters, 2009), 237–71.

theology and how to appropriate it.[53] Some scholars believe Augustine was optimistic about the possibilities for political change, others that he was pessimistic. Some believe he had a negative attitude toward non-Christian political orders, others that he was more positive. Some scholars believe Augustine was so focused on heavenly reward that he cared little about this temporal life, while others consider his theology world-embracing. Given the scope and complexity of *City of God*, it is perilous for any interpreter to assume they have gotten him exactly right. There are, however, strategies for discerning his intent. The most important is to heed the structure of Augustine's work.[54]

To draw out Augustine's narrative, this book attends closely to introductions, conclusions, transition sentences, and other structural clues. The beginnings and ends of sections are crucial for discerning the shape of the text. In 1.36, for instance, Augustine identifies several points he will cover next: the evils that Rome suffered before Christ, why God allowed Rome to grow, and the uselessness of the gods for benefits after death. The difficulty is that he does not indicate how long he will treat each topic, and he treats each topic at vastly different lengths. The reader might expect all three topics to be treated in the next book. But that is not what happens. Instead, Augustine treats the evils Rome suffered before Christ in Books 2–3, why God allowed Rome to

53. Besides texts cited above, see Oliver O'Donovan, "The Political Thought of *City of God* 19," in *Bonds of Imperfection: Christian Politics, Past and Present*, ed. Oliver O'Donovan and Joan Lockwood O'Donovan (orig. 1987; Grand Rapids: Eerdmans, 2004), 48–72; Rowan Williams, "Politics and the Soul: Reading the *City of God*," in *On Augustine* (orig. 1987; London: Bloomsbury, 2016), 107–29; Robert Dodaro, *Christ and the Just Society in the Thought of Augustine* (Cambridge: Cambridge University Press, 2004); Kristen Deede Johnson, *Theology, Political Theory, and Pluralism* (Cambridge: Cambridge University Press, 2006); Peter Iver Kaufman, *Incorrectly Political: Augustine and Thomas More* (Notre Dame, IN: University of Notre Dame Press, 2007); Charles Mathewes, *A Theology of Public Life* (Cambridge: Cambridge University Press, 2007); Eric Gregory, *Politics and the Order of Love: An Augustinian Ethic of Democratic Citizenship* (Chicago: University of Chicago Press, 2008); Veronica Roberts Ogle, *Politics and the Earthly City in Augustine's "City of God"* (Cambridge: Cambridge University Press, 2021); and Mary M. Keys, *Pride, Politics, and Humility in Augustine's "City of God"* (Cambridge: Cambridge University Press, 2022). Two influential texts that preceded Markus are Reinhold Niebuhr, "Augustine's Political Realism," in *Christian Realism and Political Problems* (New York: Scribner's Sons, 1953), 119–46; and Herbert A. Deane, *The Political and Social Ideas of St. Augustine* (New York: Columbia University Press, 1963).

54. This material is adapted from my "Republics and Their Loves." For other treatments of the structure of *City of God*, see Roy J. Deferrari and M. Jerome Keeler, "St. Augustine's 'City of God': Its Plan and Development," *American Journal of Philology* 50, no. 2 (1929): 109–37; Jean-Claude Guy, *Unité et structure logique de la "Cité de Dieu" de saint Augustin* (Paris: Études Augustiniennes, 1961); O'Daly, *Augustine's "City of God,"* 72–95; John C. Cavadini, "Epilogue: The Architectonic Plan of *The City of God*," in Meconi, *COG*, 297–320.

grow in Books 4–5, and the uselessness of the gods for benefits after death in Books 6–10.

We might think of *City of God* as operating like a toggle list where each line represents content that appears only when the user clicks on it. Without clicking, the user cannot know how much will emerge. Sometimes the content is brief; sometimes it is quite long. It disappears when the user clicks again. The user can then proceed to the next line.

Book 19: The Final Good
- ▸ Varro's six categories of philosophy (1–3)
- ▾ The Christian response (4–20)
  - ▾ Categories 1–2 (4)
    - Text
  - ▾ Category 3 (5–17)
    - Text
    - Text
    - Text
    - Text
    - Text
  - ▾ Category 4 (18)
    - Text
  - ▸ Categories 5–6 (19)
  - ▸ Conclusion (20)
- ▸ Appendix (21–28)

One gains the impression that Augustine began his work with a list of topics and little idea how much space each would require.[55] He proceeds methodically down the list, and he indicates when he is treating the next topic. But these cues are subtle and easily missed, especially when he digresses on minor points. When the reader misses the transitions, Augustine's text looks like a jumbled mess. This volume identifies the shifts, specifying which sections of *City of God* correspond to which topics. By observing where one section ends and another begins, the reader can track Augustine's argument instead of veering off course.

55. See Clark, *Comm.* 1–5, 7–9.

It is also important to understand where each section fits within the larger work. As Augustine explains, *City of God* is composed of two main parts: Books 1–10, which critique the Roman gods, and Books 11–22, which narrate the two cities across human history.[56] Each part is divided into sections. In the first part, Books 1–5 argue that the gods are of no benefit for temporal goods, and Books 6–10 argue that the gods are of no benefit for goods after this life. In the second part, Books 11–14 address the origins of the two cities, Books 15–18 address their development, and Books 19–22 address their ends.

Books 1–10: Against the gods

    Books 1–5: The gods are of no benefit in this life

    Books 6–10: The gods are of no benefit for the life to come

Books 11–22: History of the two cities

    Books 11–14: The origins of the two cities

    Books 15–18: The development of the two cities

    Books 19–22: The ends of the two cities

Though *City of God* generally follows a chronological sequence, there are some discrepancies between the order of the text and the order of the events recounted. While subtle, these discrepancies are illuminating. If we depart from the sequence of pages and track the sequence of events, Augustine's narrative appears as follows:

Earthly City	Heavenly City
Angelic/human origins: Books 11–14	Angelic/human origins: Books 11–14
Cain to flood: Book 15	Abel to flood: Book 15
Flood to Ninus: Book 16.1–11	Flood to early prophets: Books 16–17
Ninus to beginning of Rome: Book 18.2–26	
Beginning of Rome to time of Christ: Book 3	Later prophets: Book 18.27–44
Cessation of prophets to present: Book 18.45–54	Cessation of prophets to present: Book 18.45–54
Judgment: Book 20	Judgment: Book 20
Hell: Book 21	Heaven: Book 22

56. *Revisions* 2.43.1–2.43.2.

There are two unique sections in this narrative, both italicized in the table: Book 18.2–26, which traces the history of the earthly city from Ninus of Assyria to the beginning of Rome, and Book 3, which treats the history of the earthly city from the beginning of Rome to the time of Christ. These sections draw from different sources than the others, and they exhibit some oddities.

For much of his history of the two cities, Augustine relies on the Bible. Genesis 1–11 furnishes Augustine's account of both cities until the time of Abraham. The rest of the Old Testament provides Augustine's account of the heavenly city until the time of Christ. But Augustine cannot rely on the Bible alone for the development of the earthly city. There is too much other history to recount. Book 18.2–26 and Book 3 thus draw from classical and Christian authors like Livy and Eusebius. These sections receive far less space than the biblical material given the duration of history covered, and they treat the developments of the earthly city at varying length and interest. The material from Book 3 also appears at an unexpected place, not in the unit tracing the development of the two cities (Books 15–18) but in Augustine's earlier polemic against the gods.

These features indicate the special role these sections play in *City of God*. By narrating nonbiblical history, Book 18.2–26 and Book 3 substantiate Augustine's diagnosis of the earthly city. Together with Book 4, they detail the history of two offenses, violence and idolatry, both of which arise from a lust for earthly goods. Far from a private matter, this impulse spawns widespread devastation. Nations pursue conquest to secure earthly goods, and they fabricate gods for the same reason. The history of nations is one war after another, buttressed by false religion and incoherent ideology. Book 18.2–26 and Book 3 furnish evidence for a theological point: the lust for earthly goods destroys humanity. They also show that *City of God* is not a chronicle of Roman and Christian history. It is a narrative of human loves and an argument for their social consequence.

How to Use This Book

What follows is a guide for readers new to Augustine's work. First and foremost, this book offers an abridged edition of *City of God*. The selections focus on Augustine's social and political thought while also including other material that may help clarify the work as a whole. To the extent possible, I have included extended sections of text. This is because, in my experience, students gain a better sense of the whole when they read continuous material, as opposed to isolated quotations. My goal has been to provide sufficient text to orient readers without overwhelming them. At the beginning of each book from which selections have been drawn, I provide a summary explaining the structure of the book and signaling important sections. The selections in this book are taken from the translation by William Babcock—a superb rendition for both accuracy and style—in the series The Works of Saint Augustine: A Translation for the 21st Century, by New City Press. All other quotations of Augustine's work have, likewise, been taken from the editions in this series.

Along with the text of *City of God*, this book provides explanatory notes. These notes elucidate Augustine's arguments, flag important quotations, explain issues from the Latin, cross-reference other relevant passages, and offer guidance on his most challenging remarks. For ease of use, the notes sometimes repeat material from other aids in this book. My annotations have been coordinated with the original notes from the New City Press edition of *City of God*. As a rule, I have retained the New City Press notes whenever possible, moving or removing them only when this seemed appropriate for the purposes of the book.[57] I also follow New City Press for titles of Augustine's works. The two exceptions are *De Doctrina Christiana*, whose title does not translate easily into English (it is typically *On Christian Doctrine, On Christian Teaching,* or *Christian Teaching*), and *De Trinitate*, for which I simply prefer the Latin.

This book also includes essays on especially involved topics in *City of God*. The themes covered in the essays merit special attention because they arise several times in the work, they may be unfamiliar for new readers, or they raise challenges that cannot adequately be addressed in the notes. Examples include Augustine's treatment of Roman religion and his writings on war. Each essay is located after a book relevant to the theme. Though the essays treat these topics for their significance in *City of God*, they also sketch Augustine's positions in his wider corpus. For many of the topics, scholars disagree on how to interpret Augustine. In general, I avoid weighing in on these matters,

---

57. Apart from this introduction, unmarked notes are from the New City Press edition of *City of God*. I have marked my notes with the bracketed "[GWL]." In some cases, I have combined my notes and the New City Press notes into a single footnote, putting the latter in quotation marks and identifying them with the abbreviation "NCP." Alterations to internal text references have been indicated with brackets ("[ ]"). Minor typos have been corrected without indication, and titles, citation styles, and formatting have been updated for consistency throughout this volume. I have avoided altering the translation. My notes explain when something might be rendered differently.

directing readers instead to citations from Augustine's writings. I also list sources that have informed the essays and might encourage further research.

Finally, in the appendix I provide an outline for the entirety of *City of God*. The outline will help readers see how the pieces of Augustine's text fit together. It will also show which sections constitute Augustine's main arguments, and which are digressions that can be passed over. Readers can then discern the context for the selections included in this book. Those who want to tackle the entire work on their own can use the outline as a guide for the material not included here.

Here are some suggestions for new readers. First, read with an eye to Augustine's theological concerns. What is Augustine trying to accomplish with a particular argument? Why is he concerned about this or that point? What is at stake if a competing position prevails? How is he trying to shape his audience? Do not get bogged down in details. Readers can understand the gist of Augustine's arguments without grasping the minutiae. When a subtle reference is important, it will be highlighted in the notes. Readers will not stray far from Augustine's meaning if they can relate a given passage to love for God and neighbor or to the contrast between earthly and heavenly goods.

Second, do not take Augustine's descriptions of people, events, or practices at face value. As I mentioned above, Augustine is not always careful with his sources. Sometimes he misquotes them. Sometimes he depends on unreliable texts, repeating historical inaccuracies or trusting authors that modern scholars would not. At other points, Augustine recounts somewhat unbelievable stories of miracles or natural phenomena. Though he occasionally expresses doubts about these stories, he embraces the rare and fantastic more than many readers would today. These issues need not distract us from Augustine's theological insights.

This advice also applies to Augustine's depictions of his opponents. *City of God* includes some of Augustine's sharpest polemics. Like all controversialists, Augustine invokes evidence selectively, and he sometimes distorts points to his advantage.[58] Even the word "pagan," sometimes included in the title of Augustine's work, is a term of derision representing a contested perspective.[59] Those who worshiped the gods considered themselves to be respecting Roman tradition. From their vantage point, it was the Christians who invented new

58. Clark, *Comm.* 6–10, 7–9.
59. The longer title *City of God against the Pagans* is not original to Augustine, who simply called the work *De civitate dei*. See O'Daly, *Augustine's "City of God,"* 307–8.

ideas and despised what had served the Romans for centuries. It was thus the Christians, and not the "pagans," who deserved suspicion. In general, we should not assume Augustine's opponents would have affirmed his depictions of them, even if we agree with his conclusions.

Third, anticipate discomfort in your reading of Augustine. *City of God* includes some of Augustine's richest theological moments, displaying his conceptual and rhetorical gifts at the peak of his abilities. It also includes difficult, even disturbing, passages on several topics: women, rape, slavery, Judaism, original sin, and predestination, to name only a few. The essays in this book indicate the problem areas. In some cases, we can appreciate Augustine's remarks better by understanding his historical context. In other cases, contextual considerations will not mitigate the philosophical or moral difficulties. I have left it to readers to determine how to respond to these challenges—and to Augustine himself. Augustine offers much to admire and much to reject, and there is no simple strategy for deciding which response is appropriate in a given case. Indeed, the same applies for the Western Christian tradition as a whole, so much of which bears Augustine's imprint. It is perhaps best to see these challenges as tensions to engage rather than problems to solve.

Finally, appreciate the personal benefits of reading Augustine. Experiencing a classic work is like traveling to a foreign country. When we immerse ourselves in a different culture, we see how other people eat, talk, work, worship, and order their affairs. This provides fresh perspective on our own context, helping us perceive the distinctions and idiosyncrasies of our native environment. Immersive experiences do not dictate our responses to those experiences. Different travelers can encounter the same cross-cultural phenomenon and react to it in different ways. The same is true with ancient texts. Great texts offer enduring wisdom for our times, even when we differ on the implications.

City of God can sometimes feel like an alternate reality. It takes time to understand Augustine's universe: his concerns, his assumptions, his points of reference, his writing style and patterns of thought. Different readers will react differently to Augustine's writings, attending to disparate details, responding positively or negatively to the same argument, finding the same passage amusing or exasperating or both. This is why reading Augustine works best in community, whether it be a class, a book club, a Sunday school, or an ad hoc group of friends. We gain more from the text by welcoming others' reactions to it. Discussing our disagreements is an exercise in intellectual and personal formation, teaching us humility, patience, and respect toward those with different perspectives. On this matter, we can learn from Augustine's approach to interpreting the Bible. As he contends in *De Doctrina Christiana*, since Christians' ultimate purpose in life is love for God and neighbor, this should be their purpose in reading Scripture too.[60] Though they should correct one another when they err, Christians should receive misinterpretations charitably. Misreadings can still promote love for God and neighbor, and there is no reason to castigate one another for minor mistakes. This is the spirit readers might adopt for reading Augustine as well.

60. *De Doctrina Christiana* 1.35.39–1.37.41.

History of the Romans

Gregory W. Lee and Avyi Hill

Augustine's many references to Roman individuals and events will make more sense with a basic overview of Roman history. This essay sketches the major developments as they figure in *City of God*, concentrating on how the Romans recounted their history and how Augustine interpreted it, even when scholars doubt the veracity of these events. Roman history is commonly divided into three major periods: the monarchy, the republic, and the empire.

The Monarchy (753–509 BCE)

The founding legends of Rome begin with Romulus and Remus, twins who were born of Rhea Silvia and Mars, exposed to die by order of their great uncle, suckled by a she-wolf, and raised by a shepherd. Romulus killed his brother and founded Rome (the traditional date is 753 BCE), becoming the first of its seven kings. During his reign, Romulus offered asylum to fugitives and abducted wives for them from the Sabines, a neighboring people. His successor, Numa Pompilius, was associated with peace and the establishment of Rome's religious institutions. Rome's final king, Tarquin the Proud (Tarquinius Superbus, of whom there is historical evidence), was deposed in 509 BCE after his son, Sextus, raped the noblewoman Lucretia. Tarquin's failed attempts to retake Rome gave way to the beginning of the republic.

According to a separate story, Rome's prehistory begins with Aeneas, a Trojan leader who escaped Troy as it was being destroyed by the Greeks. Aeneas journeyed to Italy, defeated the Latins, and settled in Alba Longa, the city that would found Rome. Romulus and Remus were understood to be descendants of Aeneas. Augustine's treatment of this period questions the veracity of these stories, stresses Rome's violence and idolatry, and critiques Rome's understanding of honor. (See 1.3, 19, 34; 2.17–18; 3.2–16; 5.18; 15.5; 18.24; and essay: "*City of God* 1.16–28: Rape of Christian Women.")

The Republic (509–27 BCE)

The early republic (509–287 BCE) began with the establishment of the consuls, two elected magistrates who ruled together for one-year terms and were advised by the senate. Soon after the establishment of the republic, the plebeians (common citizens) began a long struggle for equality with the patricians (privileged citizens). This Conflict of the Orders (494–287 BCE) resulted in many gains, including the establishment of tribunes to represent plebeian interests. During this time, Rome expanded to become the dominant power in all Italy. Rome was sacked by the Gauls in 390 BCE, the last time it would suffer such an attack until 410 CE.

The middle republic (287–133 BCE) was defined by Rome's expansion around the Mediterranean. In the western Mediterranean, Rome fought Carthage, the major power in North Africa, in three Punic Wars spanning 264–146 BCE. The First Punic War was the context for the general Marcus Regulus's heroic submission to torture by the Carthaginians. The Second Punic War began when the Carthaginian commander Hannibal besieged and conquered Saguntum, a Spanish city and ally of Rome. Hannibal was eventually defeated by the Roman commander Scipio Africanus the Elder. The Third Punic War ended when Rome razed Carthage in 146 BCE. Rome also secured the Hellenistic East through the three Macedonian Wars (217–168 BCE), among other victories.

The late republic (133–27 BCE) was dominated by internal conflicts. This era began when the tribune Tiberius Gracchus proposed reforms to redress economic imbalances between the landowners and the peasants. His proposals prompted severe opposition by the senate, and he was murdered, the first tribune to be killed while in office (133 BCE). His brother, Gaius Gracchus, also served as tribune and proposed reforms that resulted in his death (121 BCE). Some years later, a dispute between Rome and various Italians over their citizenship rights broke into the Social War (91–89 BCE), which devastated Italy and set the stage for decades of further conflicts.

Civil war soon erupted between Gaius Marius, a former consul, and Sulla, who had once served under Marius. In 88, Sulla was elected consul and given command to wage war against Mithridates VI of Pontus, who had massacred thousands of Romans in Asia Minor. When Marius conspired to have this command transferred to him, Sulla returned from Pontus, marched his army on Rome, and drove out his opponents. Marius escaped for a time to Africa. When Sulla pursued further campaigns in the East, Marius returned to Rome, became consul, and killed his enemies before dying in office (86 BCE). In 83 BCE, Sulla returned to Rome, killed *his* enemies, and became dictator. Marked by Sulla's use of proscriptions, this second return was especially brutal. The 70s BCE witnessed another civil war and then a slave revolt (73–71 BCE) led by the former gladiator Spartacus, probably with the support of peasants who had suffered under Sulla.

A couple decades later, following other internal conflicts, Pompey, Marcus Crassus, and Julius Caesar formed what is commonly called the First Triumvirate to rule the republic from 59 to 53 BCE. After Crassus's death, conflict arose between Pompey and Caesar. Caesar defeated Pompey at the Battle of Pharsalus in 48 BCE. In the aftermath of this conflict, when Caesar's rise to power was assured, Marcus Cato (Cato the Younger) opposed him to the point of committing suicide. Later, Caesar established himself as perpetual dictator. He was assassinated on the Ides of March (March 15) in 44 BCE. After a period of turmoil, Lepidus, Mark Antony, and Caesar's grandnephew Octavian formed the Second Triumvirate in 43 BCE. Octavian then ousted Lepidus from the Triumvirate (36 BCE), setting up a conflict between himself and Antony. After Octavian defeated Antony at the Battle of Actium (31 BCE), Antony escaped with his lover, Cleopatra, to Egypt, where he would commit suicide. Octavian assumed undisputed authority over the Romans under the name Augustus Caesar (27 BCE).

In *City of God*, Augustine reckons especially with the historian Sallust's depiction of the Romans. Sallust had praised Roman morality during the early republic and the period spanning the Second and Third Punic Wars (2.18; 3.16–21). According to Augustine, the oppression of the plebeians by the patricians better represented Rome's character. Augustine also stresses Rome's moral degeneration after the destruction of Carthage (1.30–31). These arguments advance Augustine's case that Rome experienced moral suffering before Christ. As for Rome's physical suffering before Christ, Augustine emphasizes the social and civil wars (3.23–30), especially the conflict between Marius and Sulla (3.27–29), and Mithridates's massacre of the Romans (3.22). Though Augustine does not detail the transition from the republic to the empire, he treats Cato and Julius Caesar at important points in *City of God* (1.23; 5.12). Regulus (1.15, 24; 2.23; 3.18, 20; 5.18), Spartacus (3.26; 4.5), and the siege of Saguntum (3.20; 22.6) also feature in notable sections.

The Empire (27 BCE–476 CE)

Augustus's victory marked the beginning of the empire. This era is commonly divided into two periods: the Principate (27 BCE–284 CE), in which an apparent commitment to republican principles was retained, and the Dominate (284–476 CE), in which even this appearance was generally disregarded. Augustine does not treat these periods in much detail; he cites very few authors after the republican period. Still, several events are relevant for his concerns.

In 64 CE, the emperor Nero blamed Christians for a great fire in Rome that he was suspected to have caused. By torturing and killing them, he aroused sympathy for the

Christians and exacerbated his own notoriety. The destruction of the Jerusalem temple occurred in 70 CE under the emperor Vespasian and his son, Titus, a general who would succeed him as emperor. The expulsion of the Jews from Jerusalem and Judea occurred in 135 CE under Hadrian, following the Bar Kokhba revolt. Decius and his successor, Valerian, oversaw the first empire-wide persecution of Christians (249–60). Diocletian (284–305) established the Tetrarchy, in which four emperors ruled different regions of the empire, and oversaw Rome's most aggressive persecution of Christians. Constantine (306–37) was the first emperor to convert to Christianity. Except for Julian "the Apostate" (361–63), all of Constantine's successors were Christian.

Two major dynasties followed: the Valentinian (364–92) and the Theodosian (379–455). These were the main dynasties of Augustine's lifetime, and they feature in 5.25–26, where he treats the emperors after Constantine. Valentinian I (364–75) ruled the West as his brother Valens ruled the East (364–78). After the death of Valentinian I, Gratian ruled the West until he was usurped by Magnus Maximus in 383. In the East, Valens was killed by the Goths at the catastrophic Battle of Adrianople (378). He was succeeded by Theodosius I, the figure Augustine celebrates in 5.26 for his piety and opposition to Roman religion. Theodosius made Nicene Christianity the official religion of the empire in 380. In 391, perhaps under the influence of Ambrose, Theodosius issued a law closing the Roman temples and banning sacrifices. Theodosius was also the emperor who called the Council of Constantinople (381), from which Christians received the updated version of the Nicene Creed, sometimes referred to as the Niceno-Constantinopolitan Creed.

During his rule, Gratian had recognized Valentinian II, Valentinian I's young son, as a junior co-emperor who would rule at the direction of his mother, Justina. Valentinian II was the emperor in Milan during Augustine's career there (*Confessions* 6.6.9). Valentinian II sided with the bishop Ambrose against Symmachus in a controversy over the restoration of the Altar of Victory to the Roman senate house (384). The next year, he capitulated to Ambrose in a conflict about the use of a basilica by Arian Christians (*Confessions* 9.7.15). After Gratian was killed by Maximus's associate, Valentinian II continued as emperor until Maximus invaded Italy in 387. This invasion is the reason Augustine and his mother Monica were delayed in Ostia, a port city outside Rome, from traveling back to Africa (*Confessions* 9.8.17). Valentinian II and his mother fled to Thessalonica for Theodosius's protection. In 388, Theodosius defeated Maximus and reinstalled Valentinian II as emperor of the West. Valentinian II died under suspicious circumstances in 392.

For a brief time, Theodosius ruled the entire empire, the last emperor to do so. After he died in 395, the empire was divided into east and west. Gothic and Germanic invasions weakened the western empire until it collapsed under Romulus Augustulus in 476. The eastern empire continued as the Byzantine Empire until 1453, when it fell to the Ottoman Turks.

Bibliography

Boatwright, Mary T., Daniel J. Gargola, Noel Lenski, and Richard J. A. Talbert. 2014. *A Brief History of the Romans*, 2nd ed. Orig. 2006. Oxford: Oxford University Press.

Cancik, Hubert, Helmuth Schneider, and Christine F. Salazar, eds. 2002–10. *Brill's New Pauly: Encyclopaedia of the Ancient World*. Antiquity: 15 vols. Leiden: Brill.

Gagarin, Michael, ed. 2009. *The Oxford Encyclopedia of Ancient Greece and Rome*. 7 vols. Oxford: Oxford University Press.

Hornblower, Simon, Antony Spawforth, and Esther Eidinow, eds. 2012. *The Oxford Classical Dictionary*, 4th ed. Orig. 1949. Oxford: Oxford University Press.

Book 1

PREFACE, 1–9, 15–36

Book 1 commences the first major unit of City of God, *Books 1–5. These books argue that the gods are of no value for this temporal life. The preface of Book 1 is a condensed summary of the work as a whole. Augustine then confronts those who claimed Rome was sacked because the Romans had abandoned traditional religion for Christianity (1.1–7). Many of these critics took refuge in Christian shrines and basilicas when Rome was being attacked. Augustine next presents a general explanation of suffering, according to which God brings temporal goods and evils on good and evil people for pedagogical purposes (1.8–9). The following chapters walk through specific forms of suffering that Christians endured during the sack of Rome (loss of riches, torture, famine, death, lack of burial, captivity), arguing that none of these experiences ultimately harmed Christians, whose hope is in heavenly goods (1.10–15). As Augustine continues his discussion of suffering, he addresses at length the rape of Christian women who had made a vow of celibacy (1.16–28). After a concluding chapter on suffering (1.29), Augustine again attacks the critics of Christianity. They disparage Christianity, he says, only because they want to indulge vice, especially the theatrical shows (1.30–34). These shows were instituted by demons. Augustine concludes with a chapter on the intermingling of the two cities (1.35) and a summary of topics that he will treat in Books 2–5 (1.36).*

Preface.[1] In this work, my dearest son Marcellinus,[2] I have taken up the task of defending the most glorious city of God, whether in the course of these present times when it is on pilgrimage among the ungodly, living by faith,[3] or in the stability of its eternal home which it now awaits in patience,[4] *until justice returns in judgment* (Ps. 94:15), but will finally attain, by virtue of its surpassing excellence, in ultimate victory and perfect peace.[5] I have undertaken to defend it against those who prefer their own gods to its founder; and, in doing so, I will keep my promise and pay my debt to you. It is a massive work, and arduous, but *God is our helper* (Ps. 62:8).

For I know very well what efforts are needed to persuade the proud how great the power of humility is.[6] But by humility we reach a height—a height not grasped by human arrogance but granted by divine grace—which transcends all these earthly pinnacles that totter with the shifts of time. For the king and founder of the city of which we are going to speak has made known, in the Scripture of his people, a provision of divine law which asserts, *God resists the proud but gives grace to the humble* (James 4:6). This belongs to God alone, but the inflated spirit of human pride strives to claim it for itself and loves to have the same thing said in its own praise, "To spare the conquered

1. [GWL] This first paragraph represents one Latin sentence and digests Augustine's theology of the two cities. Roman authors began sentences with words they wanted to emphasize. Augustine chooses *gloriosissimam* ("most glorious"), signaling the importance of glory. In Augustine's Roman context, glory referred to the praise someone receives from others, particularly because of military exploits. These valorous displays were celebrated by Roman poets and other writers. Later in *City of God*, Augustine will critique the Romans for seeking glory as a final end (5.12–20). He will also describe heaven as a place where there will be true glory and "no one will be praised in error or in flattery" (22.30).

2. [GWL] Marcellinus was the tribune and notary of Roman Africa who oversaw the conference at Carthage in 411 against the Donatists. He was Augustine's closest contact in high imperial power. In *Letter* 136, Marcellinus asked Augustine questions that Roman elites had been raising about Christianity, including questions about its compatibility with the Roman empire. He also requested Augustine write a longer work responding to them (*Letter* 136.3). Augustine writes initial responses in *Letters* 137 and 138 before commencing *City of God*.

3. See Hab. 2:4.

4. See Rom. 8:25.

5. [GWL] Augustine distinguishes between the present and future conditions of the heavenly city. In the future, the heavenly city will enjoy perfect peace and stability. In the present, the heavenly city endures a kind of "pilgrimage" among sinful people. This term, which evokes the Israelites' exile in Babylon (19.26), is Augustine's favorite image for the heavenly city in this fallen world. Christians live as sojourners in a hostile land.

6. [GWL] Augustine declares the polemical character of his work. He will defend the goodness of the heavenly city against those who worship Roman gods and refuse to worship Jesus. Books 1–10 are dedicated to refuting Roman religion.

and subdue the proud."[7] That is why, when the plan of this work requires it and as the opportunity arises, I must also speak of the earthly city—the city which, when it seeks dominion, even though whole peoples are its slaves, is itself under the dominion of its very lust for domination.[8]

Barbarian Respect for Christ's Churches as Places of Sanctuary

1. It is from this earthly city that there emerge the enemies against whom the city of God must be defended. Many of these, once the error of their impiety has been corrected, do become quite worthy citizens of God's city, but many others burn against it with the fires of fierce hatred. They are so ungrateful for the obvious benefits of its redeemer that they forget that they would not be wagging their tongues against it today if they had not, in fleeing the enemy's sword, found in the refuge of its sacred places the life in which they take such pride.[9] Are not the Romans who assail Christ's name the very ones whom the barbarians spared for Christ's sake?[10] The shrines of the martyrs and the basilicas of the apostles bear witness to the fact. During the devastation of the

7. [GWL] Augustine contrasts the humility of the heavenly city with the pride of the earthly city. He does so by juxtaposing James 4:6, which says that "God resists the proud but gives grace to the humble," with Virgil's *Aeneid* (6.853), where it is *Rome* that subdues the proud and spares the conquered. Virgil's *Aeneid* was a defining work of Roman literature. By ascribing to Rome what Scripture ascribes to God, Virgil displays the arrogance of the Roman people. Augustine cites this passage from the *Aeneid* again in 5.12 when he is analyzing Rome's lust for glory.

8. [GWL] The term "lust for domination" (*libido dominandi*) recurs throughout *City of God*. It comes from Sallust, *Cataline Conspiracy* 2, and it refers to a violent impulse to subjugate other peoples. Augustine describes Rome's lust for domination as ironic and self-destructive, for although Rome desires to dominate others, it is dominated by this desire. The lust for domination frequently results in the Romans' conflict with fellow Romans. Augustine details this history in Book 3.

9. [GWL] In the following paragraphs, Augustine stresses the hypocrisy of the Romans in criticizing Christianity for the sack of Rome when they themselves escaped death by hiding in Christian basilicas. The Visigoths who attacked Rome were "Arian" Christians. Though they did not espouse the trinitarian formulations of Nicene Christianity, they respected the basilicas enough to refrain from attacking Romans who were hiding in them. The term "Arian" was an epithet for non-Nicene Christians that modern scholars use with reservation. Augustine alludes to the Visigoths' Christian identity in 5.23; 18.52; and *Sermon* 105.13. See Gillian Clark, "Augustine and the Merciful Barbarians," in *Romans, Barbarians, and the Transformation of the Roman World: Cultural Interaction and the Creation of Identity in Late Antiquity*, ed. Ralph W. Mathisen and Danuta Shanzer (Farnham, UK: Ashgate, 2011), 33–42.

10. [GWL] The term "barbarian" was a Roman epithet for non-Romans who did not speak Latin. The Romans adopted this term from the ancient Greeks, who used it for non-Greeks. Augustine is referring to the Visigoths who sacked Rome. "Barbarian" is a derogatory term that modern English speakers generally avoid as a description of other human beings.

city they gave refuge to those who fled to them, both to their own people and to strangers as well. The bloodthirsty enemy raged just this far but no further. Here the frenzied slaughter came to a halt; here the merciful among the enemy brought those whom they had spared—and had even spared far away from these sacred sites—to save them from the assaults of others who showed no such mercy. Elsewhere these marauders raged and slaughtered as enemies do, but when they reached these places, where a ban had been imposed on acts that were otherwise permitted by the laws of war, all their murderous cruelty was reined in and their fierce desire for prisoners was shattered.

As a result, many escaped who now deride these Christian times and make Christ responsible for the evils that Rome endured. But they do not make Christ responsible for the good that happened to them—the fact that they themselves are still alive due to the honor in which Christ was held. This they ascribe rather to their fate. If they were sensible about it, however, they ought instead to attribute the harsh and bitter blows they suffered at the enemy's hands to the divine providence which often uses wars to correct and destroy the corrupt ways of human beings—or, again, uses such afflictions to put the righteous and the praiseworthy to the test and, once they have been proved, either to convey them to a better world or to keep them here on earth for further service.

And they certainly ought to ascribe it to these Christian times that, contrary to the usages of war, the cruel barbarians spared them anywhere at all for the sake of Christ's name or spared them, more specifically, in the places specially dedicated to Christ's name—vast places, chosen to hold huge throngs, so that mercy might be spread more widely.[11] For this they ought to give thanks to God; for this they ought truly to flee to his name in order to escape the punishment of eternal fire, seeing that so many of them falsely assumed his name in order to escape the punishment of present destruction. For, among those whom you now see insolently and impudently insulting Christ's servants, there are many who would not have eluded that ruin and disaster if they had not pretended to be Christ's servants themselves. And now, in ungrateful pride and the most ungodly folly, they oppose his name with perverse hearts, incurring the punishment of eternal darkness—the very name to which they fled with lying lips, in order to enjoy this mere temporal light.

11. Among these was certainly the old Basilica of Saint Peter, which was more than 340 feet long and designed to hold large crowds of pilgrims visiting the tomb of Saint Peter. Paulinus of Nola, Letter 13.11–14, written about fifteen years before *City of God*, describes an agape sponsored by a wealthy Roman that attracted a throng of poor people to the basilica.

2. So many wars have been recorded, whether waged before Rome was founded or after her rise to power. Let them read the records and produce a single instance of a city captured by invading troops where the enemies who took it spared the people whom they found taking refuge in the temples of their gods, or where some barbarian commander ordered that, once a town was stormed, no one should be killed who was found in this or that temple.[12] Did not Aeneas see Priam before the altars, "staining with his blood the fires he himself had consecrated"?[13] Did not Diomedes and Ulysses "slay the keepers of the topmost citadel, seize the sacred image, and with bloody hands dare to touch the fillets of the virgin goddess"?[14] Nor is there any truth to the words that come next: "The Greeks' hopes thereafter ebbed, slipped back, and failed."[15] Afterward, in fact, the Greeks conquered; they destroyed Troy with sword and flames; and they cut Priam down as he fled to the altars.[16]

Rome's "Conquered Gods"

Nor is it true that Troy perished because it lost Minerva. For what had Minerva herself lost first, with the result that Troy perished? Perhaps it was her guards? That was it, of course. Once her guards were killed, it was possible to take her away. The image was not protecting human beings; human beings were protecting the image. What was the point, then, of worshiping her for the sake of having her guard the country and its people? She could not even guard her own guardians![17]

3. To think that the Romans used to rejoice that they had entrusted the protection of their city to gods such as these![18] What a miserable mistake!

12. [GWL] Augustine contrasts the Visigoths' merciful treatment of those who had taken refuge in Christian shrines and basilicas with the Greeks' ruthlessness during the Trojan War. Augustine mentions two incidents from Virgil. In the first, Aeneas, a Trojan leader and the protagonist of the *Aeneid*, witnesses the Greeks kill Priam, the king of Troy, as he flees to the altar of Jupiter in his own palace. In the second, Diomedes and Ulysses kill Trojan guards and seize the image of Troy's guardian god, Pallas Athena.

13. Virgil, *Aeneid* 2.501–2.

14. Virgil, *Aeneid* 2.166–68.

15. Virgil, *Aeneid* 2.169–70.

16. See Virgil, *Aeneid* 2.663.

17. The image of Minerva, otherwise known as Pallas, goddess of war and wisdom, had been stolen from Troy by the Greeks. See Virgil, *Aeneid* 2.223–67.

18. [GWL] Though the Romans attacked the Christian God for not protecting Rome, their founding myth illustrates the impotence of their own gods. According to Virgil's *Aeneid*, during the Trojan War, the Trojans (predecessors of the Romans) sought to protect their gods but

They are angry with us when we say such things about their gods, and yet they are not angry with their own authors. In fact, they paid a fee to be taught these authors in school, and considered their teachers to be fully worthy of a public stipend and high honors. Their small children read Virgil precisely so that—once their tender minds have soaked up the great poet, the best and most famous of them all—he cannot easily be forgotten or fade into oblivion (as Horace says, "New vessels will long preserve the scent of what they first contained"[19]). But in this Virgil's work, Juno is introduced as hostile to the Trojans, and as she stirs up Aeolus, king of the winds, against them, she is made to say, "A people I hate now sails the Tyrrhenian sea, carrying Troy and her conquered gods to Italy."[20] How wise was it, then, for them to entrust Rome—in order to keep it from being conquered—to these very "conquered gods"? But perhaps Juno was simply speaking like an angry woman here, without knowing what she said. Then what about Aeneas himself, so often called "the pious"?[21] Doesn't he tell us that "Panthus, Othrys' son, priest of the citadel and of Phoebus, snatching up the conquered gods and his small grandson, comes running in a frenzy to my door"?[22] And does he not portray these gods—which he does not hesitate to call conquered gods—as entrusted to his care, not he to theirs, when he is told, "To you Troy entrusts her sacred things and her native gods"?[23] Thus, if Virgil says both that these gods were conquered and that, in order somehow to escape despite the fact that they were conquered, they were entrusted to a man, what sort of madness is it to suppose that it was wise to entrust Rome to such guardians as these or to imagine that, if only she had not lost them, she could not possibly have been brought down! To worship conquered gods as protectors and defenders, what is that but to hold fast

---

failed. They lost the war to the Greeks, and many of their gods were destroyed. They then fled Troy, bringing their "conquered gods" with them as they journeyed to Rome (Virgil, *Aeneid* 1.67–68). Augustine relishes Virgil's use of this phrase, "conquered gods," which proves that Rome's own authors did not consider the gods capable of protecting the Roman people. Since the gods were unable to protect the Romans, the Romans have no grounds to criticize the Christian God for not protecting Rome.

19. *Letter* 1.2.69–1.2.70.

20. Virgil, *Aeneid* 1.67–68.

21. Virgil frequently refers to his hero Aeneas as pious, intending to mean that he was devoted to, among others, the gods. Augustine is sarcastically suggesting that, if Aeneas were so pious, he should not have had to admit that he had protected the gods, rather than they him. See also below at 3.14.

22. Virgil, *Aeneid* 2.319–21.

23. Virgil, *Aeneid* 2.293.

not to good divinities but to bad defaulters? Far wiser to believe not that Rome would not have met disaster if these gods had not perished, but rather that they would have perished long before if Rome had not preserved them as long as it could! A moment's thought is enough to show how silly it is to presume that Rome could not be conquered while under the protection of conquered defenders, and thus that she perished because she lost her guardian gods. In fact, the only cause there could be for her perishing is that she chose to have guardians who were themselves going to perish. Thus, when the poets wrote and sang about conquered gods, it is not that they simply took pleasure in lying; it is rather that the truth compelled them, as men of sense, to make this admission.

But these are matters which it will be more appropriate to treat fully and in detail in another place.[24] Here, rather, I shall briefly set out, as best I can, what I had begun to say about those ungrateful people who blasphemously blame Christ for the evils they deservedly suffer for their own moral perversity. The fact that even such people as these were spared for Christ's sake is something they do not care to acknowledge, and in the madness of their sacrilegious perversity they wag their tongues against his name, the very tongues with which they falsely took on his name in order to save their lives, or at least the very tongues which they silenced in terror in the places consecrated to Christ so that, kept safe and protected where—thanks to him—they were unharmed by their enemies, they might then rush out against him, cursing him as their enemy.

Neither the Greeks nor the Romans Respected the Temples of the Gods as Places of Sanctuary

4. As I said, Troy herself, the mother of the Roman people,[25] was unable to protect her citizens from the fire and steel of the Greeks in the places sacred to her gods, even though the Greeks worshiped those very same gods. In fact, "in Juno's sanctuary, the chosen guards, Phoenix and dread Ulysses, kept watch over the spoils. Here Troy's treasure, torn from burning shrines and altars of

---

24. [GWL] Augustine will return to the fall of Troy in 3.2, where he develops his argument on the physical disasters Rome experienced before Christ.

25. So called because, according to one of the founding legends of Rome (summarized in Virgil, *Aeneid* 1.1–7), a small number of Trojans, when the Trojan army had been defeated by the Greeks, crossed the Mediterranean under the leadership of Aeneas and settled near Rome.

the gods—bowls of solid gold and looted vestments—is brought together. Boys and trembling matrons stand in ranks nearby."[26]

The place consecrated to so great a goddess was chosen, then, not as a place from which it was unlawful to take captives out but rather as a place where captives might at will be locked in. Now compare that sanctuary— not the sanctuary of some common or plebeian god from the crowd, but the sanctuary of Jupiter's own "sister and spouse,"[27] the queen of all the gods—with the memorial shrines of our apostles. To the former were brought spoils stripped from burning temples and their gods, not to be donated to the vanquished but rather to be divided among the victors; to the latter, in contrast, were brought back, with honor and the most scrupulous reverence, even things found elsewhere that belonged to them. There liberty was lost; here it was preserved. There captivity was imposed; here it was forbidden. There people were driven in for slavery by an enemy exercising dominance; here people were led in for freedom by an enemy exercising mercy. Finally, it was the avarice and pride of the fickle little Greeks[28] that chose Juno's temple as their setting, but it was the mercy and humility of still savage barbarians that chose Christ's basilicas as theirs.

Or perhaps the Greeks did, after all, in that great victory of theirs, spare the temples of the gods they shared with Troy? Perhaps they did not really dare to slaughter or enslave the miserable and vanquished Trojans who took refuge there? Perhaps Virgil made all these things up, as poets do? But quite the opposite is true. He simply described the common practice when an enemy sacks a city.

5. As Sallust writes (and he is a historian noted for his truthfulness), Cato himself did not fail to mention this practice in the opinion he delivered in the senate about the conspirators. "Maidens and boys are violated; children torn from the embrace of their parents; mothers of families endure whatever suits the pleasure of the victors; temples and homes are looted; there is slaughter and burning; in short, all is filled with weapons, corpses, gore,

26. Virgil, *Aeneid* 2.761–67.
27. Virgil, *Aeneid* 1.47.
28. "Fickle little Greeks": *levium Graeculorum*. This demeaning reference to the Greeks of mythology perhaps suggests something of Augustine's general feelings toward those of his own time. Dods, however, translates the words as "gentle Greeks" and adds in a note that the phrase is intended to stand in contrast to the "savage barbarians" (*immanium barbarorum*) of the next line; in other words, according to this view, the Greeks were, ironically, more civilized than the barbarians but less merciful. [See *City of God* 1.4, trans. Marcus Dods, *Nicene and Post-Nicene Fathers*, series 1, vol. 2 (Buffalo: Christian Literature, 1887).] See also . . . 2.14.

and lamentation."[29] Now, if Cato had not mentioned the temples here, we might have imagined that enemies customarily spared the seats of the gods. In fact, however, Roman temples had to fear assault not from foreign enemies but from Catiline and his co-conspirators, highly distinguished senators and Roman citizens![30] But these, no doubt, were abandoned men, murderers of their own fatherland.

6. What need is there, then, for our account to range over the many peoples who have waged war against each other without ever sparing the vanquished in the seats of their gods? Let us simply take a look at the Romans themselves. Let us recall and consider those very Romans who, as a special point of praise, are said "to spare the conquered and subdue the proud,"[31] and who "preferred to forgive rather than to avenge a wrong."[32] To extend their dominance, the Romans stormed, captured, and overthrew any number of great cities. Let them tell us, then, which temples they used to exclude so that anyone who fled to them would be free. Is it, perhaps, that they actually used to do this, but their historians say nothing about it? But would writers who were most especially looking for points to praise have passed over what were, to their eyes, such preeminent marks of piety?

Marcus Marcellus, the distinguished Roman who took the magnificent city of Syracuse, is said to have wept before its fall and to have shed his own tears before he shed its blood. He also took great care to preserve the chastity even of an enemy. For before the victor gave the order to enter the city, he issued an edict that no free person should be violated.[33] Nevertheless, the city was sacked according to the customary practice of war, and nowhere is it reported that even this upright and compassionate commander prescribed that anyone who had fled to this or that temple should be kept from harm. And this certainly would not have been omitted, when neither his weeping nor his edict against even the least violation of chastity could be left unreported. Fabius, the conqueror of the city of Tarentum, is praised for having abstained from taking its images as loot. In fact, when his scribe raised the question of the many images of the gods that had been captured, he even spiced his restraint

29. *Catiline Conspiracy* 51.
30. Lucius Sergius Catilina, or Catiline (108–62 BCE), engineered an attempt to overthrow the Roman republic in 63 BCE. He was denounced by Cato, regarding whom see [*City of God, Books 1–10*, 25n74].
31. Virgil, *Aeneid* 6.853.
32. Sallust, *Catiline Conspiracy* 9.
33. See Livy, *History of Rome* 25.24.11. Syracuse was taken in 212 BCE. See also . . . 3.14.

with a joke. For he asked what sort they were, and when he was told that many were not only large but armed, he said, "Let us leave these irate gods to the Tarentines."[34] And since the Roman historians could not keep themselves from reporting either the tears of the one or the laughter of the other, either the chaste compassion of the one or the witty restraint of the other, would they fail to mention it if they had spared any people, in honor of some one of their gods, by forbidding slaughter or enslavement in any temple at all?

7. Any devastation, slaughter, looting, burning, and affliction committed in that most recent calamity at Rome was done, then, according to the customary practice of war. What was quite new, however, and put a whole new face on things, was that barbarian brutality appeared in a guise so gentle that the very largest basilicas were selected and set apart to be filled with people who were spared. Here no one was to be slain; no one was to be dragged out; but many were led in by their merciful enemies to be set free, and none were led away into captivity by cruel foes. Anyone who does not see that this is to be attributed to Christ's name and to these Christian times is blind. Anyone who sees it and does not praise it is ungrateful. Anyone who opposes such praise is insane. Nor will anyone with any sense at all impute this simply to the barbarians' savagery. The one who overawed, reined in, and miraculously softened their utterly ferocious and brutal minds was the one who, long ago, said through the prophet, *I will punish their iniquities with the rod and their sins with scourges; but I will not take my mercy from them* (Ps. 89:32–33).

Divine Providence, Human Suffering, and Temporal Goods and Evils

8. "But why," someone will ask, "was this divine mercy extended even to the ungodly and the ungrateful?"[35] What explanation can there be except that

---

34. Livy, *History of Rome* 27.16.8. Quintus Fabius Maximus Varrucosus Cunctator (ca. 280–203 BCE) took Tarentum, in southern Italy, in 209, during the Second Punic War.

35. NCP: "What follows is a typical argument used by Augustine to explain the apparent arbitrariness of God's dealings with the good and the bad. See also *Expositions of the Psalms* 66.3; *Sermon* 50.5. The argument recurs . . . at 5.21–26 with respect to the distribution of earthly kingdoms to both good and bad rulers, and analogously below at 18.51 regarding the troubles that heretics cause orthodox Christians. Augustine uses basically the same argument . . . at 2.23—but this time to illustrate from the lives of four prominent figures from Roman history (Regulus, Marius, Metellus and Catiline) that the favors of the pagan gods were capricious."

[GWL] For Augustine, temporal goods and evils come upon both righteous and unrighteous people but for different purposes and to different effects. Temporal goods bless the righteous

the one who showed mercy was the one who daily *makes his sun rise on the good and on the evil and sends rain on the just and the unjust* (Matt. 5:45)? For some of them, reflecting on this point, repent of their ungodliness and reform themselves. But others, as the Apostle says, *despise the riches of God's goodness and forbearance and by their hardness of heart and their impenitent heart are storing up wrath for themselves on the day of wrath and of the revelation of the righteous judgment of God, who will repay each according to his deeds* (Rom. 2:4–6). It is still true, however, that God's patience invites the evil to repentance, just as God's scourge trains the good for patience; and so too, God's mercy embraces the good, to cherish them, just as God's severity takes hold of the evil, to punish them. It has pleased divine providence to prepare future goods for the righteous that will not be enjoyed by the unrighteous and future evils for the ungodly that will not torment the good. But God willed the temporal goods and evils of this life to be common to both, so that we would neither avidly desire goods which we see that the evil also possess nor shamefully avoid evils by which the good are also very often afflicted.

The most important point, however, is what sort of use we make of the things that are reckoned either as prosperity or as adversity. For the good are neither lifted up by temporal goods nor beaten down by temporal evils; but the evil, just because they are corrupted by temporal good fortune, feel temporal misfortune as punishment. Yet, even in distributing prosperity and adversity, God often shows his manner of working quite plainly. For if every sin received obvious punishment in the present, people would think that nothing was reserved for the last judgment; but if God's power never openly punished any sin in the present, people would think that there was no such thing as divine providence. In the same way, with regard to prosperity, if God did not grant it with the most open and obvious generosity to some who pray for it, we would claim that it was not his to give. And, on the other hand, if he granted it to all who asked, we would conclude that God was only to be served for

---

and invite the unrighteous to repent. Temporal evils test the righteous and chastise the unrighteous. This diversity of experiences reflects God's providence. Alignments between personal righteousness and temporal blessing (where the righteous receive good things, and the unrighteous suffer) show that God is sovereign over the world. Misalignments between personal righteousness and temporal blessing (where the righteous suffer, and the unrighteous receive good things) demonstrate that temporal goods are not ultimately significant. Augustine interprets the distribution of temporal goods and evils in pastoral terms, as a mechanism God uses to shape people's character. In comparison with non-Christians, Christians should be less elated by temporal goods and less deflated by temporal evils. See essay: "Providence and Suffering."

the sake of this kind of reward—and that sort of service would make us not godly but grasping and avaricious.

This does not mean, however, that when the good and the evil suffer alike, there is no distinction between them simply because there is no distinction in what they suffer. Even when the sufferings are alike, the sufferers remain unlike; and even when virtue and vice undergo the same torment, they are not themselves the same. In one and the same fire, gold glows red but chaff smokes; and under one and the same flail, straw is broken up but grain is separated out; nor is the oil mixed in with the dregs, even though it is extracted by the weight of the same press. By the same token, one and the same force, assailing the good, proves and purifies and cleanses them, but, assailing the evil, condemns and ruins and destroys them. Thus, under the same affliction, the evil detest and blaspheme God, but the good praise and pray to him. What is really important, then, is not the character of the suffering but rather the character of the sufferer. Stirred by the same motion, filth gives out a foul stench, but perfume a sweet fragrance.[36]

Why the Good Also Suffered in the Sack of Rome: Failure to Correct the Evil

9. When all this is considered from the point of view of faith, then, what did Christians suffer in that time of devastation that would not work rather for their advancement? First, when they humbly reflect on the very sins for which God in his anger has filled the world with such terrible calamities, even though they themselves are far from being disgraceful and ungodly criminals, they still do not reckon themselves so entirely free from fault as to judge that they do not deserve to suffer even temporal evils for their failings. Leave aside the fact that each person, no matter how praiseworthy his life may be, sometimes gives in to carnal desire. Even if he does not fall into the atrocity of crime and the depths of shame and the abomination of ungodliness, he still commits some sins either rarely or all the more often the less serious the sins are. But leaving this aside, it is hard to find anyone who treats as they ought to be treated the very people on account of whose horrendous pride, lasciviousness, greed, and detestable wickedness and impiety God now smites the earth, just as he forewarned that he

---

36. Augustine is citing a commonplace proverb.

would.[37] It is hard to find anyone who lives among them as life ought to be lived among such people.

For all too often we wrongly shy away from our obligation to teach and admonish them, and sometimes even to rebuke and correct them. We shy away either because we are unwilling to make the effort or because we hesitate to offend their dignity or because we want to avoid enmities that might impede and harm us with respect to some temporal things which our desire still longs to acquire or which our weakness still fears to lose. It is true that the life of the wicked is displeasing to the good, and therefore the good do not fall with them into the damnation that is prepared for such people after this life. But because they are lenient toward the damnable sins of the wicked so long as— as one of their own sins (although these are light and venial)—they are afraid of them, it is only right that they are scourged along with the wicked here in time, even though they will by no means be punished in eternity.[38] It is only right that they should know bitterness in this life, when they are afflicted by God along with the wicked, for it was due to love of the sweetness of this life that they were unwilling to be bitter to the wicked in their sinning.

If anyone refrains from rebuking and correcting evildoers because he is waiting for a more propitious moment or because he is afraid that, by doing so, he might make them even worse or because he fears that, if he does so, they might start obstructing others who are weak and need guidance to a good and godly life, putting pressure on them and turning them away from the faith, this does not appear to be a pretense of desire but rather the counsel of love. What is blameworthy is that people who live quite differently from the wicked, and abhor their deeds, are nonetheless indulgent towards the sins of others when they ought to teach them otherwise and rebuke them. It is blameworthy, that is, when they do this for fear of offending people who might do them harm with regard to things which the good may certainly use, permissibly and innocently, but which they are pursuing more avidly than is proper for people who are only on pilgrimage in this world, bearing with them the hope of a heavenly homeland. It is not only the weaker ones,[39] who live the married life, who have or wish to

37. See Isa. 24:1–23.

38. [GWL] Against the Stoics, who claimed all sins were of equal gravity, Augustine distinguishes between more and less serious sins. See *Letters* 104.4.17 and 167.2.4. On Augustine's disciplinary responses to different sins, see Allan D. Fitzgerald, "Penance," in *AttA*, 640–46.

39. Note the distinction here and in what follows between the "weaker" married life and the "higher" unmarried life. On the superiority of virginity to marriage see *The Excellence of Marriage* 8.8; *Holy Virginity* 16.16–19.19.

have children, who have houses and families—these are the people whom the Apostle addresses in the churches, teaching and warning them how they ought to live, wives with husbands and husbands with wives, children with parents and parents with children, slaves with masters and masters with slaves[40]—that are glad to acquire many temporal and earthly things and grieve to lose them, and therefore do not dare to offend people whose deeply contaminated and utterly criminal way of life they detest. Even those who hold to a higher order of life—who are not entangled in the bonds of matrimony and do not make much use of food or clothing—often refrain from reproving the wicked because they are fearful that the wicked will plot against them and attack their reputation and welfare. Although they are not so afraid of the wicked that they would ever agree to act in the same way, no matter what threats and villainies they faced, they are often unwilling, all the same, to rebuke actions they would never join the wicked in committing. And they are unwilling to do so, even though their rebukes might put some on the right path. They are fearful that, if they do not succeed, their own reputation and welfare might be endangered or ruined; and this is not because they consider their reputation and welfare to be necessary for use in instructing others, but rather because of the weakness that delights in a flattering tongue and human popularity and is terrified of the judgment of the crowd and the torture or death of the flesh. It is due, that is, to a kind of bondage to desire, not to the obligations of love.

This seems to me, therefore, to be no small reason why the good are scourged along with the evil, when it pleases God to punish abandoned morals by inflicting temporal penalties. They are scourged together not because they both lead an evil life but because they both love this temporal life. They do not love it equally, of course, but they both love it. In truth, however, the good ought to think nothing of temporal life so that the evil, rebuked and corrected, might attain eternal life. But if the evil refuse to join them in attaining it, let the evil at least be endured and loved as enemies, for, as long as they are alive, it always remains uncertain whether their will might not be changed for the better.

In this matter, however, there are some who have not an equal but a far more serious responsibility. They are the ones to whom it is said through the prophet, *He will certainly die in his sin, but his blood I will require at the hand of the watchman* (Ezek. 33:6). For the reason why watchmen—that is, those who are set over the people—were established in the churches is precisely so

40. See Eph. 5:22–6:9; Col. 3:18–22.

that they would not be lenient in rebuking sins.[41] This does not mean, however, that the person is wholly free of blame who, even though he is not set over the people, notices many things deserving of admonition and reproof in those with whom he is linked in the necessities of this life but ignores them—ignoring them because he wants to avoid giving offense, ignoring them for the sake of things which it is not wrong to make use of in this life, but in which it is wrong to take more delight than one should.

Then again, there is another reason why the good are afflicted with temporal evils, as in the case of Job—so that the human spirit may be tested and may learn for itself how strong its devotion really is, how strongly it loves God even without reward.

◆

Captivity: The Example of Regulus and His Loyalty to His Gods

15. But they have, among their own famous men, a supreme example of captivity willingly endured for the sake of religion. Marcus Regulus, a general of the Roman people, was a captive of the Carthaginians. But the Carthaginians preferred an exchange of prisoners to get their own men back rather than to keep their Roman captives; and so, to obtain this end, they sent Regulus back to Rome with their own ambassadors, having first bound him by oath to return to Carthage if he did not accomplish what they wanted. Regulus went, and in the senate he persuaded them to take the opposite course, because he did not judge an exchange of prisoners to be to the advantage of the Roman republic. After persuading them, he was not compelled by his own people to return to the enemy. But because he had taken an oath, he voluntarily fulfilled it, and the Carthaginians put him to death with ingenious and terrible tortures. They shut him in a narrow box in which he was forced to stand upright. The box was studded on all sides with the sharpest nails so that he could not lean in any direction without horrible pain; and so they killed him by keeping him awake.[42]

41. Augustine understands the watchman of whom Ezekiel speaks as the bishop, and he is undoubtedly making a reference here not only to bishops in general but to himself in particular. The Latin word for "watchman" is *speculator*; this translates the Greek *episkopos*, which also carries the meaning of "bishop."

42. NCP: "Marcus Attilius Regulus (before 307–ca. 250 BCE) was often cited by the Romans as an example of honor and fidelity. The account of his death that Augustine gives is recorded in Horace, *Odes* 3.5, but is of doubtful authenticity." [GWL] Augustine uses Regulus's

The Romans are certainly right to praise a virtue greater than such great misfortune. And the gods whom Regulus swore by are the very gods who, in the Roman view, are now inflicting these calamities on the human race because their worship has been prohibited. Now the reason for worshiping these gods was precisely so that they would make this life prosperous. But if they willed or permitted such punishments as these to be imposed on one who kept his oath, what heavier punishment could they possibly inflict in anger on one who broke it?

Why, then, should I not conclude my argument with a dilemma? Regulus plainly worshiped the gods so conscientiously that, to keep his oath, he would not remain in his own country or go anywhere else but without a moment's hesitation went straight back to his bitterest enemies. If he thought that this would be to his benefit in this life, he was very much mistaken, for it earned him a horrible end. In fact, what he taught by his example was that the gods are of no use to their worshipers so far as temporal happiness is concerned. For, even though he was devoted to their worship, he was defeated and taken captive; and, because he was not willing to do anything but what he had sworn by the gods to do, he was tortured and put to death by a new, unprecedented, and horrible form of punishment. But if, on the other hand, worship of the gods brings happiness as its reward only after this life, why do people slander these Christian times? Why do they say that this disaster came upon the city of Rome because she stopped worshiping her gods when, no matter how diligently she worshiped them, she could still have been just as unfortunate as Regulus was? Or perhaps someone will oppose the most obvious truth with such demented and amazing blindness that he dares to argue that if a whole city worships the gods it cannot meet misfortune, even though one person can. Do they think that the power of their gods is better able to protect a multitude than to protect single individuals, despite the fact that a multitude is made up of single individuals?

If, however, they say that M. Regulus, even while in captivity and undergoing that cruel torture of his body, could have been happy due to the virtue of his mind,[43] let them seek rather that true virtue by which a city, too, can be happy. The happiness of a city and the happiness of a person, after all,

---

example to demonstrate that the gods do not spare their own worshipers from suffering. Given his praise for Regulus, this chapter often figures in discussions about Augustine's position on virtue among non-Christians. See essay: "Pagan Virtue."

43. This would have been the Stoic position.

do not have different sources, for a city is nothing other than a multitude of persons in concord.[44] For the moment, I am not calling into question the kind of virtue Regulus had. It is enough, at this point, that they are compelled by his most noble example to admit that it is not for the sake of bodily goods or for the sake of external advantages that the gods are to be worshiped; for Regulus preferred to do without all these rather than to offend the gods by whom he had sworn.

What are we to make, then, of people who glory in having such a citizen but fear to have such a city? And if they do not fear this, let them admit that the sort of thing that happened to Regulus could also happen to a city that worships the gods just as conscientiously as he did, and let them stop slandering these Christian times. And since the whole point at issue began with those Christians who were also taken captive, let those who impudently and foolishly mock our most wholesome religion keep the example of Regulus in mind and hold their tongues. He worshiped the gods most attentively and kept the oath he had sworn by them; but he was deprived of his homeland, the only homeland he had, and, held captive among his enemies, was put to a lingering death by a torture of unprecedented cruelty. If this was no disgrace to their gods, far less should the Christian name be accused for the captivity of its devoted followers who, awaiting a heavenly homeland with true faith, know that they are pilgrims even in their own homes.

Forms of Christian Suffering: Rape; Moral Purity and the Issue of Suicide

16. They certainly think they have a great charge to hurl against Christians when, to dramatize their sufferings in captivity, they add also the rape not only of married women and maidens intending to marry but even of certain women consecrated to the religious life.[45] Here, however, it is not faith, not godliness,

---

44. [GWL] This important sentence offers two points. First, the happiness of individuals and the happiness of communities have the same source (i.e., God). Augustine has an incipient concept of collective identity and character that enables him to speak of the happiness of groups and not just of individuals. Second, a city is a multitude of individuals. Augustine defines collectives as aggregations of persons without reference to the structures or relationships that shape their interactions with one another. A similar perspective appears in his discussion of *res publica* ("republic" or "commonwealth") in 19.21–24.

45. [GWL] During the sack of Rome, Christian women suffered rape. Many of these women had vowed themselves to celibacy. Augustine's explanation for why God permitted them to be

not even the virtue that is called chastity, which faces any problem, but rather our argument, which must find a way to negotiate the narrow line between the claims of modesty and the claims of reason.[46]

Here we are not so much concerned to respond to outsiders as we are to comfort our own.[47] In the first place, then, let it be stated and established that virtue, by which we live rightly, governs the members of the body from its seat in the mind and that the body becomes holy through its use by a holy will; and, so long as the will remains steadfast and unshaken, nothing that anyone else does with the body or to the body—and that cannot be avoided by the person who suffers it without some sin on his own part—brings any blame to the one who undergoes it.[48] Not only acts inflicting pain, however, but also acts gratifying lust can be perpetrated on the body of another; and when something like that happens—even when it does not shatter the chastity to which the supremely constant mind holds fast—it still brings on a sense of shame, for fear that people might think that an act which could not have occurred, perhaps, without some pleasure of the flesh must also have taken place with the consent of the mind.[49]

---

raped extends from 1.16 to 1.28 and raises several challenges. See essay: "*City of God* 1.16–28: Rape of Christian Women."

46. [GWL] According to Augustine, it is easy to defend the chastity of the Christian women. The challenge is doing so with modesty, since it is difficult to discuss sex without embarrassment. For similar sentiments, see 14.23 and 14.26. See also *Confessions* 8.11.26.

47. [GWL] The next sentence articulates the central premise for the discussion that follows. Augustine distinguishes the mind, which is the seat of virtue, from the body, which can be acted upon without the consent of the mind. Despite the violation of their bodies, Christian women can remain pure in their minds. Augustine offers similar remarks in *On Lying* 7.10 and 20.41, written nearly twenty years earlier. Augustine's position reflects the influence of Stoicism, which defended the possibility of virtue regardless of what happens to the body. The Stoics went so far as to claim it was possible to experience intense bodily suffering and still be "happy," since happiness depends on virtue alone. Augustine rejects this position in 19.4, where he says that happiness requires freedom from bodily suffering and thus awaits the future life. See Clark, *Comm.* 1–5, 63–64; and essay: "Stoics and Stoicism."

48. A similar thought is graphically expressed in *Lying* 15–17.

49. [GWL] This sentence involves a Latin wordplay between *uoluptas* ("pleasure") and *uoluntas* ("consent"). According to this translation, because rape can cause "pleasure of the flesh" (*carnis . . . uoluptate*), some might conclude there was "consent of the mind" (*mentis . . . uoluntate*). Scholars have criticized Augustine for claiming that women can experience pleasure while they are being raped, which is to trivialize the trauma of sexual violence and to impose on women a male experience of sex. Melanie Webb has claimed *uoluptas* should be translated as "arousal," rather than as "pleasure." She argues that women can experience sexual stimulation during rape—an involuntary reaction that produces confusion and shame given the incongruity between the physical reaction and the horror of the experience. Following her interpretation, Augustine's point is that physical arousal during rape does not prove that the rape survivor consented to the act. According to Webb, Augustine is indeed offering consolation, and he is

17. And if, for this reason, some of these women took their own lives rather than suffer anything of this kind, who with any human feeling would refuse to forgive them?[50] And if some were not willing to kill themselves, because they did not want to escape another's shameful act by committing a crime of their own, anyone who makes that a charge against them will lay himself open to the charge of being a fool. For if it is not lawful to kill even a guilty person on one's private authority—and no law grants the license to do that—then anyone who kills himself is certainly a murderer; and the more innocent he is with regard to whatever led him to think he ought to kill himself, the more guilty he is for killing himself.[51] We rightly detest what Judas did; and the Truth judges that, when he hanged himself, he added to rather than atoned for his vicious act of betrayal.[52] For, even though he was repentant at the end, by despairing of God's mercy, he left himself no room for a saving repentance.[53] How much the more, then, should a person who has nothing in him to warrant such a punishment refrain from killing himself! When Judas killed himself, he killed a criminal, and yet he ended this life guilty not only of Christ's death but also of his own. Thus he killed himself for one crime by committing another. Why, then, should a person who has done no evil do evil to himself? Why should he, in killing himself, kill an innocent person in order not to suffer the crime of another? Why should he perpetrate on himself a sin of his own to keep another's sin from being perpetrated on him?

---

the first philosopher to see it as an appropriate response to rape. See Melanie Webb, "'On Lucretia Who Slew Herself': Rape and Consolation in Augustine's *De ciuitate dei*," *Augustinian Studies* 44, no. 1 (2013): 37–58.

50. [GWL] An expression of empathy toward women who committed suicide after being raped. This paragraph introduces an extended treatment of suicide. In Augustine's time, suicide was associated with valor. When a Roman soldier faced a humiliating situation, he might kill himself to preserve his honor. Given Roman obsession with glory and shame, Christian victims of rape may have felt pressure to commit suicide in order to prove their chastity. Augustine will urge them not to do so.

51. [GWL] Note Augustine's opposition to private killing. Judas Iscariot, he will continue, was wrong to kill himself even though he betrayed Jesus. How much less appropriate is it for one to kill oneself if one has not done anything wrong? Augustine will return to the question of killing in 1.21 and 1.26, where he claims that killing is justified only if it occurs under proper authority (see also *Sermon* 302.13). Though Augustine's concern is for Christian women, he often uses male pronouns in this discussion, perhaps because of the awkwardness of the topic, or perhaps because the valor of suicide was associated with men. Lucretia was an exception, and the Romans considered her courage "manly." See Clark, *Comm. 1–5*, 62–63.

52. The phrasing of the sentence suggests that "Truth" should be capitalized and thus refer to Christ, although nowhere does either Christ or any other scriptural personage say that Judas's suicide added to his guilt.

53. See Matt. 27:3–5.

18. But there remains the fear that even someone else's lust may bring defilement. It will not defile if it is another's; and if it does defile, it is not another's. Purity is a virtue of the mind,[54] and it has fortitude as its companion, by which it determines to endure any evils rather than consent to evil.[55] No one, no matter how noble-minded and pure, has it in his power to determine what happens to his flesh, but only what his mind will accept or reject.[56] Who of sound mind, then, will suppose that his purity is lost if it happens that his flesh is seized and held down and someone else's lust exercised and satisfied on it? If purity can be lost in this way, then it is certainly not a virtue of the mind. Nor does it belong to those goods by which we live rightly but will rather be reckoned among the goods of the body, such as strength, beauty, good health, and the like. But these are goods which, even if diminished, do not diminish a good and righteous life. If purity is something of this kind, why strive so hard not to lose it, even putting the body at risk? If purity is a good of the mind, however, it is not lost when the body is overpowered. In fact, when the good of holy continence does not yield to the impurity of carnal desires, the body itself is sanctified as well; and, therefore, when this continence persists in its unshaken resolve not to yield, the holiness of the body itself is not destroyed, because the will to use the body in a holy manner remains and, so far as in it lies, so also does the capacity.

What makes the body holy is not that its members are intact or that they have not been defiled by touch. For they can suffer violent injury in various accidents; and sometimes physicians, in trying to heal, do things to them that are gruesome to look at. During a manual examination, a midwife—whether by malice or blunder or accident—destroyed the maidenhead of a certain virgin while inspecting it.[57] But I do not suppose that anyone would be so foolish as to think that the virgin has lost any of her body's holiness, even though the integrity of that member is now gone. Thus, so long as the mind stays firm in its resolve, through which the body also deserved to be sanctified,

54. [GWL] A clear statement of Augustine's position, influenced by the Stoics, that virtue resides in the mind and is not compromised by harm to the body. Humans cannot control what happens to the body, but they can choose how they respond to external suffering.

55. On the connection between fortitude and virginity, or chastity, see Philo, *On the Virtues* 1.34–8.50; Gregory of Nyssa, *On Virginity* 18.3.

56. [GWL] A confusing use of the male pronoun in light of the next sentence, which refers to the rape of women.

57. [GWL] Genital virginity examinations were a familiar but controversial practice during Augustine's time. He invokes this incident to prove that chastity does not reside in the body. On this topic, see Clark, *Comm. 1–5*, 64; and Julia Kelto Lillis, *Virgin Territory: Configuring Female Virginity in Early Christianity* (Oakland: University of California Press, 2023), 52–55, 197–216.

the violence of another's lust does not take away the body's holiness, which is preserved by the mind's own perseverance in continence.

On the other hand, if some woman, already corrupted in mind and in violation of the pledge she vowed to God, is on her way to her seducer to be defiled, do we say that while she is on the way she is still holy, at least in body, despite the fact that the holiness of mind by which her body was sanctified is already lost and destroyed?[58] God forbid any such mistake! Let us rather learn from this that the body's holiness is not lost as long as the mind's holiness remains, even when the body itself is overpowered, just as, in contrast, the body's holiness is lost as soon as the mind's holiness is violated, even if the body itself is still intact.

For this reason, a woman who has been overpowered by force and violated by another's sin without any consent on her part has nothing which she ought to punish in herself by voluntary death. And all the less before it happens! Let no one incur the certain guilt of murder while the shameful act itself—and another's act at that—is still uncertain.

Rape and Suicide: The Example of Lucretia

19. We assert, then, that when the body is overpowered but the resolve to remain chaste stands firm, unaltered by any consent to evil, the crime belongs only to the man who took the woman by force and not at all to the woman who was taken by force, without her consent and against her will. Will those against whom we are defending as holy not only the minds but also the bodies of the Christian women who were raped in captivity dare to contradict this clear reasoning? They certainly extol with high praise the purity of Lucretia, that noble woman of ancient Rome.[59] When the son

58. [GWL] Augustine argues that it is possible for women to be virgins in their bodies but to be impure in their minds. Again, his point is that virtue is in the mind and not the body.

59. [GWL] Lucretia was a noblewoman during the time of Rome's kings, the earliest stage of Roman political history. She was raped by Sextus Tarquin, son of King Tarquin the Proud. Her suicide sparked a revolt against the Tarquin dynasty, resulting in the end of the monarchy and the beginning of the republic. Augustine's interpretation of her action, as either self-murder or a confession of adultery, subverts the traditional reception of Lucretia's story and challenges Roman understandings of honor. See essay: "City of God 1.16–28: Rape of Christian Women."

NCP: "The story of Lucretia is told in Livy, History of Rome 1.57–59 and seems to have had a historical basis. Lucretia's death can be dated to ca. 508 BCE. The amount of space that Augustine devotes to her is a measure of the power of her example, which was considerable in the ancient Roman world. She is mentioned again . . . at 2.17 and 3.15."

of Tarquin the king took her body by force and lustfully used it, she made that most villainous young man's crime known to her husband Collatinus and her kinsman Brutus, men of great distinction and courage, and bound them to take revenge. Then, sick at the vileness of what had been done to her and unable to bear it, she killed herself. What shall we say? Should she be judged adulterous or chaste? Who can think it worth laboring over the issue? In a declamation on the subject, someone put the matter admirably and truthfully: "Wonderful to relate, there were two, but only one committed adultery."[60] Splendidly put, and very true! He saw in this union of two bodies the utterly depraved desire of the one and the wholly pure will of the other, and he directed attention not to the conjunction of the bodies but to the diversity of the minds: "There were two," he said, "but only one committed adultery."

How is it, then, that the one who did not commit adultery was the one more severely punished? He was banished from his fatherland with his father; she suffered the supreme penalty. If it is no impurity for an unwilling woman to be taken by force, then it is no justice for a pure woman to be punished. I appeal to you, O laws and judges of Rome.[61] Even when a crime was committed, you did not want the criminal to be executed without being tried and condemned. For you, that was itself a punishable offence. If someone were to bring this case before your tribunal, then, and it were proved to you that a woman had been put to death who was not only uncondemned but in fact chaste and innocent, would you not punish the person who had done this with all due severity? But this is exactly what Lucretia did; Lucretia—the much celebrated Lucretia—did away with the innocent and chaste Lucretia, the victim of violence. Pronounce your sentence, or, if you cannot do so, because she is not there before you for you to punish, why is it, at any rate, that you praise so fulsomely the murderess of an innocent and chaste woman? You certainly cannot defend her on any rational grounds before those judges of the underworld of whom your poets sing in their verses. For she is clearly numbered among those "who, though innocent,

60. [GWL] Augustine quotes this line multiple times in the following paragraphs. The quotation aligns with Livy's account of Lucretia's words: "My body only has been violated. My heart is innocent, and death will be my witness" (*History of Rome* 1.58). NCP: "The source of the quotation is unknown."

61. [GWL] Augustine presents his arguments as if he were in a court of law, where Roman law required cases concerning capital punishment to be tried. See Clark, *Comm. 1–5*, 65.

did themselves to death and, hating the light, cast out their souls."[62] And if she wants to return to the upper regions, "Fate bars the way, and the dismal swamp's unlovely waters confine them."[63] Or perhaps she is not numbered here, because she did not kill herself in innocence but in awareness of her guilt? What if—and only she could know this—even though the young man set upon her with violence, she herself consented, seduced by her own lust?[64] And what if, in punishing herself for this, she was so remorseful that she thought that death must be its expiation? But even in this case she ought not to have killed herself if there were any possibility that doing penance would bear fruit with false gods.

If this is so, however, and it is false that "there were two, but only one committed adultery," and if, instead, both committed adultery, one by open assault, the other by hidden consent, then she did not kill herself innocent. And, in that case, her learned defenders can say that she is not in the underworld among those "who, though innocent, did themselves to death." But then their case is caught on the horns of a dilemma: if she is cleared of murder, she is convicted of adultery; and if she is cleared of adultery, she is convicted of murder. There is no escape from this dilemma: If she was adulterous, why is she praised? If she was pure, why was she killed?

We are concerned with the example of this noble woman, however, simply for the sake of refuting those who, with no understanding of holiness, jeer at the Christian women who were raped in captivity; and it is enough for our purposes that it was admirably said in her praise, "There were two, but only one committed adultery."[65] For they preferred to believe that Lucretia was not one who could have stained herself with even a hint of consent to adultery. As a consequence, when she killed herself because she had endured an adulterer (even though she was not herself an adulteress), it was not out of the love of purity but out of the weakness of shame.[66] What made her feel shame was the debased act of another committed on her but not with her; and, as a Roman woman too avid for praise, she was afraid that, if she

---

62. Virgil, *Aeneid* 6.434–35.

63. Virgil, *Aeneid* 6.438–39.

64. [GWL] Augustine believes it is possible for a woman to consent to sex as she is being raped. This disturbing suggestion will figure throughout the rest of his treatment of rape.

65. [GWL] Augustine repeats his stated purpose in this section: consoling the Christian women who were raped.

66. [GWL] The pivotal moment in Augustine's discussion of Lucretia. She was "a Roman woman too avid for praise." In 5.12–13, Augustine will treat lust for glory as Rome's defining sin.

continued to live, she would be thought to have suffered with pleasure what she actually suffered by violence when she was still alive. For this reason she thought that she must present her self-punishment to men's eyes in witness to her state of mind, since she could not show them her conscience itself. She blushed at the very thought that, if she were to bear patiently the foul act that another had done to her, she might be considered an accomplice in it.

This is not what those Christian women did who suffered similar things and yet are still alive.[67] They did not avenge another's crime on themselves, not wanting to add crimes of their own to the crimes of others. For that is what they would have done if, when enemies committed rape on them out of lust, they had committed murder on themselves out of shame. They have the glory of chastity within them, the witness of conscience. They have this in the eyes of God, and they need nothing more. In fact, there is nothing more that they can rightly do, for they have no intention of straying from the authority of divine law by doing wrong to avoid the scandal of human suspicion.

20. It is not without significance that, in the holy canonical books, no divinely given precept or permission can be found that allows us to put ourselves to death, either to attain immortality or to avert or avoid evil. In fact, we must understand that the law forbids this, where it says, *You shall not kill* (Exod. 20:13).[68] And this is especially true because here it does not add "your neighbor," as it does when it forbids false witness. There it says, *You shall not bear false witness against your neighbor* (Exod. 20:16). This does not mean, however, that anyone who bears false witness only against himself should consider himself exempt from this crime. For the one who loves takes the rule for love of neighbor from love of self, since Scripture plainly says, *You shall love your neighbor as yourself* (Matt. 22:39). Thus, if a person who bears false witness only against himself is no less guilty of bearing false witness than if he did so against his neighbor (and this is true even though the precept forbidding false witness forbids only false witness against a neighbor and thus might seem, to those who do not understand it rightly, not to have forbidden anyone from serving as a false witness against himself), how

---

67. [GWL] This sentence assumes other women had committed suicide after being raped. Augustine urges the Christian women not to take such action. Their honor does not depend on the opinion of others. God sees their chastity within.

68. [GWL] Augustine is applying the command against killing to the question of suicide. Even though the command does not say, "You shall not kill *yourself*," he claims the prohibition against self-killing is implied. For a similar argument, see *Letter* 204.5–8.

much more must we understand that no one is allowed to kill himself. Where Scripture says, *You shall not kill*, nothing further is added, and so it must be recognized that there are no exceptions, not even for the one to whom the commandment is addressed.

On this basis, some try to extend this commandment even to beasts and cattle and claim that it is not even allowed to kill any of them.[69] But then, why not extend it also to plants and anything else rooted in and fed by the soil? For although things of this kind have no feeling, they are still said to live. Consequently, they can also die and hence, when force is used, be killed. Thus the Apostle himself, when he speaks of seeds of this kind, says, *What you sow does not come to life unless it dies* (1 Cor. 15:36); and in a Psalm it is written, *He killed their vines with hail* (Ps. 78:47). When we hear *You shall not kill*, then, do we conclude for this reason that it is a crime to pull up a bush, and, losing all trace of sanity, acquiesce in the error of the Manicheans?[70] Thus, putting these ravings aside, when we read *You shall not kill*, we do not take this commandment to apply to plants, since they have no feeling. Nor does it apply to the irrational animals which fly, swim, walk, or crawl, since they do not share with us any capacity for reason. It was not given to them to have reason in common with us; and consequently, by the most just ordinance of the creator, both their life and their death are subordinate to our needs. What remains, then, is that we understand this commandment—*You shall not kill*—to apply to human beings, both to others and to oneself, for to kill oneself is nothing else than to kill a human being.

21. The divine authority itself, however, did make certain exceptions to the rule that it is against the law to kill a human being.[71] But these exceptions

69. The Manicheans held this view. See *Heresies* 46.11–12; Epiphanius, *Panarion* 66.28.

70. The Manicheans, founded by the Persian sage Mani (216–77), held that plants contained particles of light that needed to be freed and that, if possible, they should not be eaten or otherwise destroyed. See *The Manichean Way of Life* 17.54–55.62; *Answer to Faustus, a Manichean* 6.4. Augustine was familiar with Manichean doctrine from having been a Manichean "hearer" for about a decade before his embrace of Christianity. See *Confessions* 3.6.10–3.10.18.

71. NCP: "The question of just war and the just taking of another's life is raised here, to be returned to below at 1.26; 4.15; 15.4. See also *Free Will* 1.4.9–1.5.12; *Answer to Faustus, a Manichean* 22.74–76. Augustine's position is briefly summarized in *AttA*, 875–76."

[GWL] According to Augustine, killing is permitted when God commands it. God's command can be communicated through a direct order or through a legal structure. For examples of the former, Augustine cites Abraham, Jephthah, and Samson. See Melanie Webb, "Abraham, Samson, and 'Certain Holy Women': Suicide and Exemplarity in Augustine's *De ciuitate dei* 1.26," in *Sacred Scripture and Secular Struggles*, ed. David Vincent Meconi (Leiden: Brill, 2015), 201–34. Concerning the latter, Augustine is probably referring to war and capital punishment. Though Augustine believes wars can be just, he does not codify a theory of just war. As for

include only those whom God orders to be killed, either by a law he provided or by an express command applying to a particular person at a particular time. In addition, the one who owes this service to his commander does not himself kill; rather he is, like a sword, an instrument in the user's hand.[72] Consequently, those who, by God's authority, have waged wars have in no way acted against the commandment which says, *You shall not kill*; nor have those who, bearing the public power in their own person, have punished the wicked with death according to his laws, that is, according to the authority of the supremely just reason. And Abraham not only was not blamed for a criminal act of cruelty but was even praised in the name of piety, because it was not at all from wickedness but rather from obedience that he resolved to kill his son.[73] And it may rightly be asked whether it was not by God's command that Jephthah killed his daughter, when she ran to meet her father, in that he had vowed to sacrifice to God whatever first met him as he returned home victorious from battle.[74] Nor is Samson, who crushed both himself and his enemies in the collapse of the house, excused on any other ground than that the Spirit, who had been working miracles through him, secretly commanded him to do this.[75] With the exceptions, then, of those commanded to be killed either generally by a just law or specifically by God himself, who is the fount of justice, anyone who kills a human being, whether himself or anyone else, is involved in the crime of murder.

22. But perhaps those who have done this to themselves are to be admired for their greatness of soul, even though they are not to be praised for their good sense and wisdom?[76] If you think about it more carefully, however, it is not even right to call it greatness of soul when someone kills himself because he is not strong enough to endure hardships or other people's sins. Rather, the mind is found to be weak if it cannot bear either the harsh servitude of its

capital punishment, Augustine affirms the authority of earthly rulers to wield the sword, but he consistently opposes the death penalty when he knows someone is at risk of being executed. See essay: "War."

72. [GWL] A striking defense of the soldier's responsibility to obey commands. Augustine says nothing here about whether a soldier should question or disobey unjust commands.

73. See Gen. 22:1–14.

74. See Judg. 11:30–40.

75. See Judg. 16:28–30. Scripture does not speak of any such secret command given to Samson, but Augustine evidently feels obliged to justify an act that Scripture itself does not condemn. Augustine excuses Samson again below at 1.26.

76. [GWL] Augustine turns to a potential objection: perhaps suicide reflects "greatness of soul."

own body or the foolish opinion of the crowd. The soul that is rightly to be called great is the soul that can bear a life of hardship without fleeing from it and, in the light of a pure conscience, can scorn human judgment, especially the judgment of the crowd, which is so often wrapped in a fog of error.

If putting oneself to death is to be considered the act of a great soul, then Theombrotus will be found to be the one who exemplifies this greatness of soul.[77] The story goes that, when he read Plato's book which discusses the immortality of the soul, he threw himself headlong from a wall and so passed from this life to one he believed to be better.[78] He was not driven to do this by any calamity or accusation, whether true or false, which he could not manage to bear and so did away with himself. Rather it was greatness of soul alone that moved him to snatch at death and break the sweet bonds of this life. But Plato himself, whom he had read, could have told him that his was an act of greatness rather than goodness.[79] For Plato would certainly have been the first to do this himself, and to recommend it to others, if he had not concluded— with the same mind by which he saw the soul's immortality—that it should never be done and, in fact, should be forbidden.

And yet many have killed themselves to avoid falling into the hands of an enemy. Our question here, however, is not whether this *was* done but whether it *should* have been done. Sound reason is certainly to be preferred to examples.[80] But some examples are in accord with sound reason, and the more they excel in godliness the more worthy they are of imitation. None of the patriarchs did this, none of the prophets; nor did any of the apostles, even though the Lord Christ himself, instead of admonishing them to flee from city to city if they suffered persecution,[81] could have admonished them to lay hands on themselves to avoid falling into the hands of their persecutors. And if he did not command or admonish them to depart this life in this way, even though he had promised that he would prepare eternal mansions for them on

77. [GWL] Augustine is invoking an example that he does not take seriously. He is more interested in the cases of Lucretia (1.19) and Cato (1.23).

78. The suicide of Theombrotus, a Cynic philosopher who flourished ca. 300 BCE, is recounted in Callimachus, *Epigrams* 23. He is said to have read only one work by Plato, on the soul (Augustine adds the qualification that it was on the immortality of the soul), but since Plato's theory of the soul is scattered throughout his writings, it is not clear what work he might have read.

79. See *Phaedo* 61d.

80. [GWL] A reference to the Roman tradition of exemplarity, according to which the actions of historical figures offer case studies for moral questions. As Augustine argues, Scripture offers no examples to imitate for committing suicide instead of submitting to an enemy.

81. See Matt. 10:23.

their departure,[82] it is obvious that, no matter what examples are put forth by peoples who do not know God,[83] this is not lawful for worshipers of the one true God.

Suicide: The Example of Cato

23. But apart from Lucretia (and I have already said enough about my view of her), it is not easy for them to find an authoritative example to support their teaching, unless it is the famous Cato who killed himself at Utica.[84] It is not, of course, that Cato was the only one who did this. It is rather that he was held to be a man of learning and probity, and so one might have reason to think that what he did could have been done rightly and can still be done rightly.

What can I say about his act that is more telling than this—that his friends, who were also learned men, but more sensible, tried to dissuade him from it? They considered suicide the misdeed of a weak mind, not a strong one, an act showing weakness unable to bear adversity rather than honor on guard against disgrace. And Cato himself thought the same with regard to his dearly beloved son. For if it was shameful to live under Caesar's triumph, why was he the author of this shame for his son, whom he instructed to put all his hope in Caesar's generosity?[85] Why did he not compel his son to die with him? If it was praiseworthy for Torquatus to kill his son for engaging the enemy against orders, even though he came out the victor,[86] why did the vanquished Cato spare his vanquished son when he did not spare himself? Or was it more shameful to be the victor against orders than endure the victor against honor? Actually, then, Cato did not really judge it shameful to live under the victorious Caesar; otherwise he would have freed his son from this shame with a father's sword. What can we say, therefore, except that, as Caesar himself is reported to have said, Cato loved his son, whom he hoped and wished for Caesar to

82. See John 14:3.
83. See 1 Thess. 4:5.
84. [GWL] Cato the Younger (95–46 BCE) was a senator and Stoic who supported Pompey during the civil war between Pompey and Julius Caesar. After Caesar's victory, Cato committed suicide instead of accepting a pardon. At the same time, he told his son to accept Caesar's clemency. In later centuries, Stoics would invoke Cato's example to defend suicide as an alternative to submitting to a tyrant. Augustine challenges this famous example. If it was shameful for Cato to live under Caesar, Cato should have compelled his son to kill himself too.
85. See Livy, *Periochae* 114.
86. Titus Manlius Torquatus, a fourth-century BCE Roman general and political figure, had his son put to death for disobeying orders after a victorious battle. See Livy, *History of Rome* 8.7.

spare, just as much as he hated—or, to say it more gently, was ashamed—to let Caesar have the glory of sparing himself?[87]

24. Our opponents are unwilling to let us give preference over Cato to the holy man Job, who chose to endure horrendous evils in his flesh rather than to rid himself of all these torments by putting himself to death, or to give preference to other saints from our writings—writings raised to the heights by their supreme authority and wholly worthy of belief—who chose to bear captivity and enemy domination rather than to kill themselves.[88] On the basis of their own writings, then, I shall prefer to Marcus Cato the same Marcus Regulus whom we have already mentioned. For Cato had never defeated Caesar, and, when he was defeated by Caesar, he disdained to submit and, rather than submit, chose to kill himself. Regulus, in contrast, had already defeated the Carthaginians, and, as a Roman commander holding a Roman command, he had brought back not a lamentable victory over fellow-citizens but a laudable victory over the enemy. And afterwards, when he was defeated by the Carthaginians, he chose to endure them in servitude rather than to escape from them by dying. Accordingly, he preserved both his patience under Carthaginian domination and his constancy in love for the Romans, taking neither his vanquished body from his enemies nor his unvanquished spirit from his fellow-citizens. Nor was it out of love for this life that he refused to kill himself. He proved this when, to keep his promise and his oath, he returned without hesitation to those same enemies whom he had offended more gravely by his words in the senate than by his arms in battle. Thus, even as one who set no store on this life, he obviously judged it a great crime to kill himself, since he chose to end this life among savage enemies by terrible tortures rather than to do away with himself.

Among all their praiseworthy men, renowned for their outstanding virtue, the Romans offer none better than Regulus. Good fortune did not corrupt him, for he remained a very poor man even in his great victory;[89] and bad fortune did not break him, for he went back undaunted to his terrible end. But if the bravest and most distinguished men, defenders of an earthly homeland and of the gods—false gods, to be sure, but they were not false worshipers, being utterly faithful in keeping their oaths—if these men could by the law

---

87. See Appian, *Civil War* 2.99.

88. [GWL] A counterexample to Cato, Job endured suffering instead of committing suicide. As Augustine will continue, Marcus Regulus, already treated in 1.15, furnishes another example against suicide.

89. See Valerius Maximus, *Memorable Deeds and Sayings* 4.4.1–4.4.6.

and custom of war strike down defeated enemies but refused, when defeated by their enemies, to strike themselves down and, though they had no fear of death, preferred to endure the victors as overlords rather than to inflict death on themselves, how much the more will Christians, who worship the true God and aspire to a supernal homeland, refrain from this crime if ever divine providence subjects them to their enemies for a time, either to test or to correct them![90] They are not abandoned in this humiliation by the Most High, who came in such humility for their sake, and, above all, they are bound by no military authority or oath of military service to strike down even a defeated enemy.[91] What a terrible error sneaks in, then, when it is thought that a person may kill himself either because an enemy has sinned against him or to keep an enemy from sinning against him, even though he may not dare to kill the very enemy who has sinned or who is going to sin against him!

Is Suicide Permissible to Avoid Sin?

25. But we must fear and take care lest the body, when subjected to an enemy's lust, lure the soul by a most enticing pleasure to consent to the sin. And it is for this reason, they say, that one ought to kill oneself—not, now, because of another's sin, but because of one's own, and before one has even committed it.[92] But the mind that is subject to God and his wisdom rather than to the body and its lusts will by no means act in such a way as to consent to any lust in its own flesh aroused by the lust of another. And, in any case, if it is a detestable crime and a damnable evil for a person to kill himself, as manifest truth declares, who is so foolish as to say, "Let us sin now, lest we happen to sin later; let us commit murder now, lest we happen to fall into adultery later"? If wickedness has such a dominant hold on us that we can only choose sinful rather than innocent acts, is not uncertain adultery in the future better than certain murder in the present? Is it not better to commit a shameful act

90. [GWL] This argument foreshadows a longer discussion in 5.17–18 about Romans who displayed valor for the sake of an earthly homeland. Augustine will invoke them for an argument from the lesser to the greater. The Romans displayed great (alleged) virtues for an earthly homeland. Christians should display even greater virtues for a heavenly homeland.

91. [GWL] A striking and, to my knowledge, little discussed remark on Christians' exemption from military responsibilities. See essay: "War."

92. [GWL] Augustine is turning to another question: whether those in danger of being raped should commit suicide to avoid being lured into lust and thus consenting to adultery. As in 1.19, Augustine believes it is possible for a woman to enjoy sex as she is being raped.

which may be healed by repenting than a sordid crime that leaves no room for the healing of repentance?

I say this for the sake of those men or women who think they should do themselves mortal violence in order to avoid not another's sin but their own, for fear that otherwise, under another's lust, they might consent to a lust aroused in themselves. Never let it be said that a Christian mind which trusts in God, puts its hope in him, and relies on his aid—never let it be said, I insist, that such a mind would yield to any pleasures of the flesh to the point of shameful consent. It is true that the lustful disobedience that still dwells in our dying members is moved, so to speak, by a law of its own, quite apart from the law of our will. But if this happens without guilt in the body of one who is sleeping, how much the more does it happen without guilt in the body of one who gives no consent![93]

26. But, they say, in a time of persecution, certain holy women, in order to escape those who were attacking their chastity, threw themselves into a river that would carry them away and drown them.[94] They died in that way, and yet in the Catholic Church they are venerated as martyrs, and great crowds frequent their shrines. I do not presume to make any rash judgment on these women. I do not know whether divine authority convinced the Church, by some trustworthy testimonies, to honor their memories in this way, and it may be that this is so. For what if the women did this not in human delusion but under divine command, not in error but in obedience[95]—as in the case

93. On the involuntary and guiltless arousal of the sexual members see . . . 14.23–26; *Marriage and Desire* 1.6.7.

94. Augustine is referring to Ambrose's treatise *On Virgins* 3.7.32–3.7.36, written four decades before *City of God*, in which Ambrose approvingly recounts the suicide of a certain Pelagia, along with her mother and sisters, who threw themselves into a river during the early-fourth-century persecution of Diocletian, in order to escape violation. The author may have conflated two stories here—that of Pelagia herself and that of three other women (Domnina, Berenice and Prosdocia) who were supposed to have killed themselves in the same way and for the same reason. Although he never mentions Ambrose by name, probably out of respect for the great bishop of Milan with whom he is disagreeing, Augustine's extensive treatment of suicide as a response to possible violation is almost certainly an attempt to offer a reasoned alternative to Ambrose's enthusiastic embrace of suicide (he compares the death of the women to baptism *On Virgins* 3.7.34) in the circumstances. But Ambrose was not the first to speak approvingly of suicide in such circumstances. See Eusebius, *Ecclesiastical History* 8.14.17.

95. [GWL] Augustine suggests that the women received a divine command to kill themselves. This ad hoc proposal indicates the challenge they posed for his position. Augustine condemns suicide for the sake of avoiding rape, but the Catholic Church venerates these women for exactly that. By suggesting they received a special command, Augustine seeks to affirm the church's judgment on the women while claiming their decision was exceptional and not a model for imitation.

of Samson, which it would be utterly wrong for us not to believe?[96] For when God gives a command and makes it unambiguously clear that he gives the command, who will charge obedience with crime? Who will bring an accusation against piety's compliance?

But this does not mean that, if someone decides to sacrifice his son to God, his act is not wicked simply because Abraham was praised for doing the same. For when a soldier kills a man in obedience to the authority under which he is legitimately serving, he is not guilty of murder according to any laws of his city; in fact, he is guilty of dereliction of duty and insubordination if he refuses.[97] But if he had done this of his own accord and on his own authority, he would have been liable to the charge of shedding human blood. Thus the act for which he is punished if he does it without orders is the very act for which he will be punished if he refuses to do it under orders. And if this is true when the command is given by a general, how much more is it true when the command is given by the creator! Anyone who knows that it is not lawful to kill oneself may still do so, then, as long as he is commanded to do so by the one whose commands it is not lawful to despise. Let him make very sure, however, that there is no room for doubt about the divine command.[98]

It is through the ear that we become aware of a person's conscience; we do not presume to judge things hidden from us. *No one knows what goes on in a person except the spirit of the person that is in him* (1 Cor. 2:11). But what we say, what we assert, what we approve in every way is this: no one ought to inflict voluntary death on himself on the pretext of escaping temporal troubles, lest he fall into eternal troubles; no one ought to do this because of another's sins, lest by doing so he incur a most serious sin of his own when he would not have been at all defiled by the other's sin; no one ought to do this because of his own past sins, for he has all the more need of this life so that they can be healed by repentance; and no one ought to do this out of desire for a better life that is hoped for after death, for those who are guilty of their own death are not received into the better life that follows death.

27. There remains one reason, of which I had already begun to speak, for thinking it an advantage to kill oneself, namely, to avoid falling into sin either

---

96. See Judg. 16:28–30.

97. [GWL] This passage aligns with Augustine's remarks on killing in 1.21 and illustrates his commitment to hierarchy and subordination. What legitimates killing in war is the order of a superior—most immediately the human commander, and ultimately God. See essay: "War."

98. [GWL] Augustine warns against appealing glibly to divine command. The women in question may have been commanded to commit suicide, but this is not a common occurrence.

through the lure of pleasure or through the ferocity of pain.[99] If we decide to admit this reason, however, it will carry us along to the point of thinking that people should be urged to kill themselves as soon as they have been washed in the font of holy regeneration and received the forgiveness of all sins.[100] For the moment to avoid all future sins is obviously the moment at which all past sins have been blotted out. And if it is right to avoid sin by voluntary death, why not do it at that moment above all? Once baptized, why spare oneself? Once set free, why thrust one's head back into the dangers of this life, when nothing could be easier than to avoid them all by killing oneself? After all, Scripture says, *Whoever loves danger will fall into it* (Sir. 3:26). Why, then, are so many and such grave dangers loved—or, if not loved, at least accepted—by remaining in this life when one may legitimately abandon it? Does foolish perversity go so far in overturning the heart and diverting it from attention to the truth as to lead it to think that, if a person ought to kill himself to avoid falling into sin under the domination of a single captor, he should still go on living when he must endure this world itself, which is full of trials at every moment—not only trials like the one he fears under a single master but countless others which there is no escaping in this life? Why, then, do we waste time on exhorting the baptized, striving to enflame them for virginal chastity, or for the continence of widowhood, or for the fidelity of the marriage bed? Why do this, when we have a better way, a short-cut removed from all risk of sinning? Let us just persuade everyone that we can to grasp death and inflict it on themselves immediately after the remission of their sins, and so send them to the Lord fully healed and wholly pure!

But if anyone thinks that we should actually take this course, or urge it on others, I do not say that he is simply being foolish but that he is raving mad. How can anyone have the effrontery, then, to tell a person, "Kill yourself, lest you add to your little sins a more serious one, since you are living under a shameless master with the morals of a barbarian," when he cannot say, without being utterly wicked, "Kill yourself, now that all your sins have been forgiven, lest you commit such sins again, or even worse sins, inasmuch as you are living in a world that is so alluring in its impure pleasures, so savage in its

99. [GWL] Back to the question of 1.25: whether those in danger of being raped should commit suicide to avoid the risk of lust.

100. This should be read in the context of the frequent early Christian practice of holding off baptism until later in life, or even until one's deathbed, because baptism provided the forgiveness of sins at a time in the Church's history when only one other opportunity, besides baptism, for sacramental forgiveness (involving an often arduous and humiliating process) was offered.

monstrous cruelties, so menacing in its errors and terrors."[101] And because it is monstrous to say this, it is clearly monstrous to kill oneself. For if there could be any just reason for voluntarily killing oneself, it is beyond doubt that there could be no reason more just than this. But since not even this reason is just, there is no just reason at all.

28. Therefore, Christ's faithful, do not let your lives become a burden to you, even if your enemies have made a plaything of your chastity. You have a great and true consolation if you remain sure in your conscience that you did not consent to the sins of those who were permitted to sin against you.[102] And if you should ask why they were permitted to do so: deep is the providence of the creator and ruler of the world, *and his judgments are inscrutable, and his ways past finding out* (Rom. 11:33).[103]

But even so, question your souls honestly.[104] Perhaps you took too much pride in your virginity and continence or purity.[105] Perhaps you took delight in human praise and even envied others in this regard. I make no accusations where I have no knowledge, and I do not hear what your hearts say in reply to your questioning. If they respond that this is so, however, do not be surprised that you have lost that for which you longed to win human

101. [GWL] For Augustine, it is worse to live under spiritual domination than to live under political domination. If Christians should not kill themselves to avoid temptation and sin, they should not kill themselves to avoid temporal evils either. For similar sentiments, see 4.3; 5.17; and 19.15.

102. [GWL] Augustine insinuates that the women may have consented to sex as they were being raped. While Augustine already broached this idea in earlier chapters, his remarks here—addressing recent victims of rape, and not just reflecting on historical figures or theoretical scenarios—are especially disturbing.

103. [GWL] Augustine's standard response to evil that he cannot explain: the mysteries of divine providence. In the following paragraphs, Augustine repeatedly speaks of God's "permitting" the women to be violated. This word suggests an indirect relationship between God and evil, according to which God lets evil happen but does not cause it. Elsewhere in Book 1, Augustine uses more active language: "God's scourge trains the good for patience" (1.8); God "smites the earth" because of the wicked (1.9); God sees fit "to punish abandoned morals by inflicting temporal penalties" (1.9); God "afflicts" Christians to test their merits or chastise their sins (1.29). See essay: "Providence and Suffering."

104. [GWL] The remarks that follow are perhaps the most objectionable of Augustine's discussion. Augustine indicates that God may have allowed women who had dedicated themselves to celibacy to be raped because they had become spiritually proud or were at risk of becoming spiritually proud. Rape, he suggests, taught the women humility without violating their integrity, since their minds did not consent to the act. If Augustine does not outright blame the women for being raped, he comes very close to doing so.

105. The danger of being proud of one's virginity was frequently stressed in Christian antiquity from the very beginning (see Clement, *1 Corinthians* 38; Ignatius, *Polycarp* 5.2) and is a major theme in *Holy Virginity* 31–52.

approval but have kept that which cannot be displayed to human eyes. If you did not consent to the sinners, divine aid was added to divine grace so that you would not lose the grace, and human glory was followed by human reproach so that you would not love the glory. Take comfort from both, you faint of heart: being proved *and* being chastised, being justified *and* being corrected.

But the hearts of some reply, when questioned, that they have never prided themselves on their virginity or widowhood or marital chastity, but rather, ranking themselves with the lowly, have rejoiced with trembling in God's gift.[106] Nor have they begrudged anyone an equal excellence in holiness and chastity. Rather, indifferent to human praise—which is usually given the more lavishly the rarer the good is that evokes it—they have chosen to have their numbers grow instead of making their preeminence stand out by keeping their numbers small. But let not even women such as these—if barbarian lust forced itself on some of them too—lodge a complaint that this was permitted; let them not believe that, because God permits something that no one commits without punishment, he pays no attention to such matters. For the pull, so to speak, of evil desires is sometimes given rein by the present, hidden judgment of God even while it is stored up for the final, manifest judgment of God. Also, it may be that these women, who are fully sure in their conscience that their heart never swelled with pride at the good of chastity but who still suffered the enemy's violence in their flesh, had some hidden weakness which might have swollen into the arrogance of pride if they had escaped this humiliation during the sack. Just as some people were taken away by death to prevent wickedness from changing their understanding,[107] then, so something was taken away by force from these women to prevent good fortune from changing their humility.

Thus neither those who were already taking pride in the fact that their flesh had suffered no shameful contact nor those who might have taken pride in this fact if their flesh had not been abused by enemy violence were robbed of their chastity. Rather both were led to humility. In the one case, help came for a tumor already growing, in the other, for a tumor ready to grow.

But we should not fail to note a further point: to some of the women who suffered these things, it may have seemed that the good of continence is to be reckoned as a bodily good and thus that it lasts only so long as the body is

106. See Isa. 66:2.
107. See Wis. 4:11.

not touched by anyone's lust.[108] They may not have seen that, in fact, it resides solely in strength of will, as assisted by God, so that the spirit as well as the body may be holy, or that this kind of good cannot be taken away without the mind's consent. Perhaps they have now been freed from this error. For when they consider how conscientiously they have served God, and, with unshaken faith, refuse to think that he could ever abandon those who serve and call upon him in this way, and find it impossible to doubt how much chastity pleases him, they see that it follows that he could never have permitted such things to happen to his saints if holiness could perish in this way—the very holiness which he bestowed on them and which he loves in them.

29. The whole family of the supreme and true God, then, has its own consolation, a consolation which does not deceive and which is not based on hope in anything faltering or unreliable. And even the temporal life that the faithful have in this world is not to be regretted. In this life they are schooled for eternity and, like pilgrims, make use of earthly goods without being taken captive by them, while they are either proved or corrected by evils. Some jeer at their uprightness and, when they happen to fall into temporal evils, say to them, *Where is your God?* (Ps. 42:3) But let such scoffers say where their own gods are when such things happen to them. It is, after all, precisely to avoid such evils that they worship their gods, or claim that they ought to be worshiped.

For the family of God responds: Our God is present everywhere, wholly present everywhere, nowhere confined. He can be present without being seen, absent without moving away. When he afflicts me with adversity, he is either testing my merits or chastising my sins, and he is holding an eternal reward for my faithful endurance of temporal evils. But who are you that we should deign to discuss even your gods with you, let alone our God, *who is to be feared above all gods, for all the gods of the peoples are demons, but the Lord made the heavens* (Ps. 96:4–5)?

The Perils of Unfettered Prosperity: Scipio Nasica against Roman Extravagance

30. If the renowned Scipio Nasica, who was once your pontiff, were still alive, he would put a stop to your impudence.[109] During the terror of the Punic War, when

---

108. [GWL] Augustine offers another possibility for why God permitted the women to be raped. Maybe God wanted to teach the women that chastity resides in the mind and not the body.

109. [GWL] Augustine transitions to a critique of Roman immorality, focusing on greed, theater, and idolatry. Augustine will continue his polemic against Roman mores throughout

a man of the highest qualities was sought, the senate unanimously selected him to bring the sacred objects from Phrygia. But you, perhaps, would hardly dare to look him in the face. For why, when afflicted by adversities, do you complain about these Christian times? Is it not simply because you want to remain secure in your extravagance and to wallow in the most abandoned self-indulgence, exempt from all austerity and hardship? You desire to have peace and all kinds of wealth in abundance, but not so that you may use them honorably—that is, modestly, soberly, moderately, and with godliness. Rather you want them in order to procure an infinite variety of pleasures for your mad excesses, giving rise, in times of prosperity, to moral evils worse than any raging enemies.

It was because he feared just this calamity that Scipio, your chief pontiff, the best of men in the judgment of the whole senate, opposed the destruction of Carthage, then Rome's rival for empire, and spoke against Cato who demanded its destruction.[110] He was afraid that security would be the undoing of frivolous minds, and he saw that terror was needed for the citizens, like a tutor for schoolchildren. Nor was he deceived in his opinion. The event itself proved how truly he had spoken. Once Carthage was destroyed, that is, once the great terror of the Roman republic was repulsed and eliminated, all the evils arising from prosperity immediately followed. First, harmony was corrupted and destroyed by fierce and bloody insurrections. Then, by a chain of evil causes, came the civil wars which brought such great slaughter, so much bloodshed, and such a savage frenzy of desire for proscriptions and plunder, that the Romans themselves—who used to fear evils from their enemies when their lives had greater moral integrity—now, with their integrity in ruins, suffered worse cruelties from their fellow citizens. And the lust for domination—which, of all the human vices, is found in its most undiluted form in the whole Roman

---

Books 1–10. Publius Cornelius Scipio Nasica was *pontifex maximus*, head of Rome's college of priests, and served as consul in 162 BCE. During the Third Punic War (149–46 BCE), he opposed the destruction of Carthage because he feared the absence of a political rival would result in Rome's moral corruption, a natural result of security and prosperity. Augustine conflates this Scipio with his father, who had the same name. The earlier Scipio was chosen in 204 BCE by the senate to retrieve a sacred stone from Phrygia that would help the Romans during the Second Punic War. According to Augustine, (the younger) Scipio's worries were validated by Rome's subsequent history of oppression, political unrest, and civil war. In 2.17, relying on Sallust, Augustine will develop the argument that Rome suffered moral decline after the destruction of Carthage. See Clark, *Comm. 1–5*, 75–76.

110. Marcus Porcius Cato, the Elder (234–149 BCE), opposed Scipio Nasica Corculum, the son of the previous Scipio Nasica (Augustine has confused the two), regarding the treatment of Carthage and was famous for repeating in his speeches in the Roman senate, "Carthage must be destroyed" (*Carthago delenda est*). See Plutarch, Cato 27.

people—after winning the day in a few of the more powerful, oppressed the rest, worn out and exhausted, under the yoke of servitude.

31. For, once it is embedded in arrogant minds, where can the lust for domination come to rest until, by passing from office to office, it has reached despotic power? In fact, there would be no provision for a sequence of offices if ambition were not so prevalent. But ambition would not be so prevalent except in a people corrupted by avarice and extravagance.[111] And what makes a people avaricious and extravagant is prosperity—the very thing that Nasica, with great foresight, voted to guard against when he opposed destroying the enemy's largest, strongest, and wealthiest city. His aim was to keep lust under the restraint of fear so that lust, thus restrained, would not indulge itself in extravagance. And so, with extravagance under control, avarice would not make mischief; and, with these vices barred, virtue would grow and flourish to the city's benefit, and the liberty consistent with such virtue would endure.

It was for the same reason, and from the same farsighted love of country, that this very same chief pontiff of yours—who was selected (it cannot be said too often) as the best man by the senate of that time, without one dissenting vote—restrained the senate from its inclination and desire to build a theater equipped with seats. In a weighty oration, he persuaded them not to allow Greek extravagance to creep into the virile morality of the fatherland, nor to agree to let foreign wickedness undercut and erode Roman virtue. So great was his authority that the senate, moved by his words, had the foresight to prohibit even the setting up of those temporary benches that the citizenry had begun to use at the games.[112]

The Theaters and the Gods

How eagerly a man such as this would also have banished theatrical performances themselves from the city of Rome, if only he had dared to resist the authority of those he imagined to be gods![113] He did not understand that these

111. [GWL] See Sallust, *Catiline Conspiracy* 11–12.

112. This was, once again, Scipio Nasica Corculum. See Valerius Maximus, *Memorable Deeds and Sayings* 2.4.2.

113. [GWL] Augustine despised Roman theater, which depicted the gods' immoral behavior and thus encouraged the audience to imitate their vices. Augustine identifies the gods as demons, and he presents theater as a trick they used to corrupt the Romans. During an intense pestilence, the gods promised to end the disease if the Romans instituted theatrical performances in the gods' honor. The gods were motivated by pride, envy, and spite in their desire to be worshiped

gods are actually pernicious demons;[114] or, if he did, he held that they should be appeased rather than scorned. For the divine teaching which purifies the heart by faith[115] had not yet been revealed to the peoples, the teaching which moves human affections in humble piety to the pursuit of heavenly—or more than heavenly—things and frees them from the domination of prideful demons.

32. Know, then, you who are ignorant of the fact, and you who pretend to be ignorant, and take note, you who mutter complaints against the deliverer who has set you free from such overlords:[116] the theatrical performances, those spectacles of shame and licentious folly, were instituted at Rome not by human vice but at the command of your gods. It would be more tolerable for you to confer divine honors on this Scipio than to worship gods of that sort, for those gods were definitely not as worthy as their priest. Listen here, then, if your minds, drunk from swilling error for so long, will allow you to think sensibly: the gods commanded theatrical performances to be put on for them in order to end a pestilence of the body; their priest, in contrast, prohibited the building of a theater in order to prevent a pestilence of the soul. If by any light of reason you value the soul more than the body, choose whom to worship! For that bodily pestilence did not abate just because a warlike people, previously accustomed only to the games of the circus, suddenly got caught up in a prissy craze for theatrical shows. Rather, the profane spirits in their guile, seeing that the pestilence was already about to reach its appointed end, took the opportunity to introduce another, far graver pestilence, which is their greatest delight—a pestilence not of bodies but of morals.[117] This blinded the minds of the miserable victims with such darkness and sullied them with such decadence that even now, with Rome just sacked, the people infected by this pestilence who were able to reach Carthage in their flight from Rome are in the theaters every day, raving for

---

and to make humans as immoral as they. In this Faustian bargain, Augustine sees the Romans trading their souls for bodily protection, a sign of their lust for earthly goods. See Clark, *Comm.* 6–10, 23–24; and essay: "Roman Spectacles."

NCP: "The polemic against theatrical performances that begins here had a long history in early Christian writing. Tertullian's treatise *On the Spectacles* is an early and powerful example."

114. On the commonly accepted notion that the pagan gods were really demons, see Tertullian, *Apology* 22; Marcus Minucius Felix, *Octavius* 27. This idea recurs throughout *City of God* and forms one of the bases for Augustine's argument against the worship of the pagan gods.

115. See Acts 15:9.

116. I.e., Christ.

117. See Livy, *History of Rome* 7.2–3.

their favorite actors. Those who come after us, if they hear of this, may well find it hard to believe!

33. What insanity! What is this error—or rather not error but madness? As we have heard, the peoples of the East and the greatest cities of the uttermost parts of the earth were bewailing your downfall with public grief and mourning. But you were looking for theaters! You entered them, filled them, and behaved even more insanely than you had before. It was just this ruin and bane of souls, just this subversion of probity and integrity, that Scipio feared for you when he prohibited the building of the theater, when he discerned that you could easily be corrupted and subverted by prosperity, when he did not want you to be secure against the terror of an enemy. For he did not consider a republic happy when its walls were standing but its morals were in ruins. You gave more credit, however, to the seductions of impious demons than to the precautions of farsighted men. This is why you do not want to be blamed for the evils you do; this is why you blame the evils you suffer on Christian times. For, in your security, you are seeking not a republic at peace but unpunished extravagance; you were depraved by prosperity, but you could not be corrected by adversity. Scipio wanted you to live in terror of the enemy, so that you would not sink into extravagant living; but, even when crushed by the enemy, you have not suppressed your extravagance. You have lost the chance of gaining from calamity; you have become utterly wretched while, at the same time, you remained utterly foul.

34. Even so, it is thanks to God that you are still alive—the God who, in sparing you, warns you to correct your ways by repenting. Despite your ingratitude, he allowed you to escape the hands of the enemy, either by taking the name of his servants or by taking refuge in the shrines of his martyrs. It is said that Romulus and Remus[118] established an asylum—anyone who fled there would be safe from all harm—with the aim of increasing the population of the city they were founding.[119] That is a marvelous example, anticipating what was done in honor of Christ: the destroyers of the city established the very thing that the founders of the city had established before. But what is so extraordinary about the latter's doing this to augment

---

118. The twin brothers Romulus and Remus were the legendary founders of Rome.
119. [GWL] To increase the population of Rome, Romulus offered asylum and freedom from criminal charges to refugees from other cities (Livy, *History of Rome* 1.8). Augustine suggests Romulus's actions foreshadowed the mercy the Visigoths displayed during the sack of Rome to those who had taken refuge in Christian shrines and basilicas. See also 4.5 and 5.17.

the numbers of their citizens when the former did it to save even greater numbers of their enemies?

The Intermingling of the Two Cities in This World

35. Let these be the answers—and others, if more fruitful and suitable ones can be found—that the redeemed family of the Lord Christ and the pilgrim city of Christ the king make to their enemies. Remember, however, that among those very enemies are hidden some who will become citizens, and do not think it fruitless to bear their enmity until they come to confess the faith.[120] By the same token, so long as it is on pilgrimage in this world, the city of God has with it, joined to it by participation in the sacraments,[121] some from the number of its enemies who will not be with it in the eternal destiny of the saints. Some of these are hidden, some out in the open, and, along with its enemies, they do not hesitate to murmur against God, whose sacrament they bear.[122] At one moment, they fill the theaters along with our enemies; at the next, they fill the churches along with us. But we have no reason to despair of the correction of at least some of these, for even among our most open adversaries there lie hidden, still unknown even to themselves, some who are predestined to be friends. In this world, in fact, these two cities remain intermixed and intermingled with each other until they are finally separated at the last judgment.[123] With God's help, I will set out what I think should be said about the origin, the course, and the appointed end of the two cities.[124] This will highlight the glory of the city of God, which will stand out the more clearly when set in contrast to the other city.

120. [GWL] The visible church includes individuals who claim to be Christian but do not truly belong to Christ. The reality of false Christians (*ficti*) was a particular worry in Augustine's context, when Christianity had become the official religion of the empire and there were social and material advantages to becoming Christian. Augustine developed this theology of the church as a mixed body against the Donatists.

121. "Joined to it by participation in the sacraments": *connexos communione sacramentorum*. Although Augustine is certainly referring here primarily to baptism and the eucharist, he is probably not excluding other practices characteristic of Christianity, which he also understood as sacraments. See *AttA* 741–47.

122. "Whose sacrament they bear": *cuius sacramentum gerunt*. The reference is to baptism, whose spiritual effect is borne for life.

123. On the notion of the intermingling of the righteous and the unrighteous until the last judgment see also *On Baptism against the Donatists* 4.3.5; 5.27.38; 6.1.1. The idea appears earlier as well in Origen, *Homily on Leviticus* 14.3.

124. This is a summary of Books 11–22 in a single phrase.

Points for Further Discussion

36. There are still some things I must say, however, against those who attribute the disasters of the Roman republic to our religion, which forbids offering sacrifices to their gods.[125] For I must note all the evils that come to mind—or at least as many as seem sufficient—which that city, or the provinces belonging to her empire, suffered before those sacrifices were actually prohibited. No doubt they would attribute all these evils to us too, if our religion had already shed its light on them at that time and so had already forbidden their sacrilegious sacrifices.

Next I must show what their moral qualities were, and why the true God, who holds all kingdoms in his power, deigned to help them expand their empire. I must also show that those whom they suppose to be gods gave them no help at all and, in fact, how much harm they did by deceiving and deluding them.

Finally, I shall reply to those who, even though refuted and disproved by the clearest proofs, still try to assert that the gods should be worshiped not for the sake of any benefits in this present life but for the sake of benefits which will come after death. This, if I am not mistaken, will be a much more difficult issue and far more worthy of nuanced discussion.[126] For in this case I will be arguing against philosophers—and not just any philosophers but against those among them who shine with the most outstanding glory and who agree with us on many points: with regard to the immortality of the soul, that the true God created the world, and with regard to his providence, by which he governs all that he created. But since even these philosophers must be refuted where their views run counter to ours, we must not fail to meet this obligation so that—once their impious counter-arguments have been rebutted, so far as God gives us strength—we may then affirm the city of God and true godliness and the worship of God, in which alone is found the true promise of eternal blessedness. Here, then, let this book end, so that we can make a fresh start in following out this plan.

---

125. [GWL] This chapter outlines Books 2–10 without specifying which books correspond to which points. Books 2–3 will recount "all the evils that come to mind . . . which that city, or the provinces belonging to her empire, suffered before those sacrifices were actually prohibited." Books 4–5 will "show what their moral qualities [*mores*] were, and why the true God, who holds all kingdoms in his power, deigned to help them expand their empire." Finally, Books 6–10 will address those who "assert that the gods should be worshiped not for the sake of any benefits in this present life but for the sake of benefits which will come after death."

126. [GWL] Augustine is referring especially to the Platonists. See essay: "Platonists and Platonism."

Providence and Suffering

Gregory W. Lee and Avyi Hill

Augustine understands providence as God's all-encompassing sovereignty in history, according to which God administers temporal blessing and suffering for pastoral and pedagogical purposes. Though Augustine never wrote a treatise on the topic, his theology of providence is foundational for *City of God*. It also raises many challenging questions.

Augustine's early views of suffering were forged against the Manicheans, who understood suffering to be a result of a dualist, cosmic battle between good and evil forces and affirmed the existence of inherently evil things. In response, Augustine claimed that God created and rules all things and that God made all things good. Augustine also explained suffering in terms of the overall order and harmony of creation. Apparent evils may be good according to their broader purposes. Evil brings good in its contrast with goodness. As with a mosaic, the beauty of the universe can be seen only when one steps back to view the whole (*Order* 1.1.2; see also *City of God* 11.16, 18, 22–23; 12.4; *Enchiridion* 3.11; *True Religion* 40.74–76).

Augustine also affirms God's sovereignty over suffering. The greatest form of suffering is sin itself. God punished Adam and Eve by giving them over to themselves; humanity is now bound by its own propensity to sin (*City of God* 14.15). God inclines evil people toward sin according to their prior disposition toward sin, in response to their negative merits. Thus, God does not cause people to sin in the same way God causes people to do good. Those who fall, fall by their will. Those who stand, stand by God's grace (*Answer to Julian* 5.4.15; *Confessions* 3.8.16; *Expositions of the Psalms* 5.10; 77.30; *Gift of Perseverance* 8.19; *Grace and Free Choice* 20.41–21.43; *Miscellany of Eighty-Three Questions* 79.1; *Nature and Grace* 22.24; *De Trinitate* 13.12.16).

Temporal forms of suffering reflect God's rule too. In some cases, Augustine speaks of God permitting temporal evil, including through the evil actions of evil individuals (*City of God* 1.28; 21.13; 22.22; for additional instances of permission, see *City of God* 14.27; 20.1; *Enchiridion* 26.100). In other cases, Augustine uses more active language, claiming that God inflicts temporal evil on people, rather than simply letting it happen (*City of God* 1.9; 5.23; *Free Will* 1.1.1; *Miscellany of Eighty-Three Questions* 53.2; *Revisions*

1.26, concerning *Miscellany of Eighty-Three Questions* 21). For Augustine, temporal suffering serves remedial purposes, prompting sinners to repent and receive healing for their souls (*Answer to the Letter of Mani* 1.1; see also *Confessions* 2.2.4; *Expositions of the Psalms* 9.10). But not all suffering accomplishes this end (*City of God* 21.13), and Augustine defends retributive punishment in his theology of final judgment. The wicked will suffer everlasting punishment, with no opportunity to repent (*City of God* 21.24).

Following the sack of Rome, Augustine preached several sermons to address his congregants' consternation about the catastrophe (*Sermon* 397: "On the Sack of the City of Rome"; see also *Sermons* 15A; 25; 33A; 81; 105; 113A; 296). These sermons elucidate Augustine's theology of suffering and preview his arguments in *City of God*. Rome is not eternal (nor is any human institution), and it has been burned before. Even with the recent disaster, Rome has been only scourged, not destroyed (*Sermons* 81.9; 105.9–10; 296.9; 397.2, 8). God brings temporal hardship on the good and the evil alike. What separates the two is how they respond to suffering, whether by cursing or by praising God (*Sermons* 15A.2; 81.2; 113A.11; 397.3, 9). The sack of Rome should spur Christians to seek eternal goods. It is better to be corrected now than to suffer eternal punishment (*Sermons* 113A.14; 296.6–7, 10–12; 397.4–6). Christians should consider examples like Job, who endured suffering without complaint (*Sermons* 15A.5–7; 81.2; 397.3), and Lazarus, who suffered earthly tribulation but received a heavenly reward (*Sermons* 15A.2; 397.45). Ultimately, God's providence is inscrutable, and Christians should not question God's will (*Sermon* 296.7–8).

Many of these arguments are restated in *City of God* 1.8–9, a touchstone for the rest of the work. For Augustine, the apparently arbitrary distribution of temporal blessing and suffering serves God's pedagogical purposes for this present time, training humanity to value heavenly goods over earthly goods. Temporal suffering also disciplines sufferers for their wrong desires. In the rest of Book 1, Augustine applies this perspective to the suffering Christians experienced during the sack of Rome. At points, he comes close to blaming sufferers for their suffering, a temptation most vividly displayed in his treatment of rape in 1.16–28 (see essay: "*City of God* 1.16–28: Rape of Christian Women").

Bibliography

Babcock, William. 1993. "Sin and Punishment: The Early Augustine on Evil." In *Augustine: Presbyter Factus Sum*, edited by Joseph T. Lienhard, Earl C. Muller, and Roland J. Teske, 235–48. New York: Peter Lang.

Brachtendorf, Johannes. 2000. "The Goodness of Creation and the Reality of Evil: Suffering as a Problem in Augustine's Theodicy." *Augustinian Studies* 31, no. 1: 79–92.

De Bruyn, Theodore S. 1993. "Ambivalence within a 'Totalizing Discourse': Augustine's Sermons on the Sack of Rome." *Journal of Early Christian Studies* 1, no. 4: 405–21.

Kambo, Kevin M. 2021. "Theories of Divine Punishment in Augustine's *De ciuivate Dei*." *Studia Patristica* 117, no. 14: 61–75.

Thompson, Samantha Elizabeth. 2010. "Augustine on Suffering and Order: Punishment in Context." PhD diss., University of Toronto.

van Egmond, Bart. 2018. *Augustine's Early Thought on the Redemptive Function of Divine Judgement*. Oxford: Oxford University Press.

Pagan Virtue

Gregory W. Lee and Avyi Hill

Like other ancient philosophers, Augustine defines virtue teleologically. Action should be directed toward humanity's final end, happiness, and it should be motivated by proper intentions. In contrast to the philosophers, Augustine understands happiness eschatologically as eternal life with God, he believes grace is necessary for virtue, and he denies the possibility of perfect virtue in this life. He also foregrounds love: "A brief and true definition of virtue is 'rightly ordered love'" (*City of God* 15.22). Temperance, fortitude, justice, and prudence are all forms of love (*The Catholic Way of Life and the Manichean Way of Life* 1.15.25).

Augustine's position on "pagan virtue," or whether non-Christians can act virtuously, has generated persistent debate. Cited frequently on this question, *City of God* offers evidence to support affirmative and negative answers. One important consideration is Augustine's depiction of Marcus Regulus, a Roman general who was taken captive by the Carthaginians during the First Punic War but released to negotiate peace with Rome (*City of God* 1.15, 24; *Letter* 125.3). Out of loyalty to Rome, he sabotaged the negotiations. Then he honored his oath to return to Carthage, where he was tortured and killed, displaying remarkable endurance and fidelity. Augustine uses this story to counter Roman polemic against Christianity. Despite Regulus's devotion to the gods, they did not save him from this fate. The recent sack of Rome is thus no argument for the gods. They might not have saved Rome even if the city had worshiped them.

A broader discussion of Roman virtue arises in *City of God* 5.12–20, where Augustine explores why God allowed Rome's expansion and what this had to do with Roman mores. Augustine concentrates his analysis on Rome's lust for glory, which is a unique vice that tempers other vices for the appearance of virtue (5.12–13). Lust for glory inspired many Roman heroes to suffer admirably for their earthly homeland (5.16–18). Drawing on their examples, Augustine admonishes Christians to display even greater virtue for the sake of their heavenly homeland. At the same time, he questions whether Roman heroism counts as virtue at all. "No one can possibly have true virtue without true godliness—that is, without true worship of the true God—and that virtue is not true virtue when it is put to the service of human glory" (5.19). In another apparent critique of the Romans' character, following a discussion of whether Rome counts as a republic, Augustine claims that the body's submission to the mind requires the mind's submission to God: "For, no matter how laudably the soul may appear to rule the body and reason the vices, if the soul and reason do not themselves serve God as God himself has taught that he is to be served, they do not rule the body and the vices rightly at all" (19.25).

Augustine stresses the power of moral exemplars to inspire imitation. In that vein, as scholar Jennifer Herdt has suggested, it is instructive to contrast Augustine's treatment of Roman heroes with his treatment of Roman theater and its depiction of the gods. While the heroes are role models for Christians to exceed, the gods are to be repudiated as demons seeking to be worshiped and to corrupt the Romans. Though Regulus and the other heroes worshiped false gods, they did not worship the gods in a false manner. They were "the bravest and most distinguished men, defenders of an earthly homeland and of the gods—false gods, to be sure, but they were not false worshipers [*non tamen fallaces cultores*], being utterly faithful in keeping their oaths" (1.24). The most virtuous Romans "preserved a certain goodness of its own kind that was able to suffice for establishing, increasing, and preserving the earthly city" (*Letter* 138.3.17).

Again, though, Augustine compares Roman heroism negatively to Christian morality. While the Roman tradition celebrates military valor, which secures human glory and praise, Christianity honors the apostles and martyrs, who were characterized by humility and suffering, seeking not their own glory but referring it to God (*City of God* 5.14). Cato, who rightly sought virtue over human praise (5.12), was still so obsessed with glory that he senselessly committed suicide to avoid submitting to Julius Caesar (1.24). The Roman heroes sought earthly glory, they have received it, and that is the only reward they will get (5.15).

Many scholarly discussions about Augustine's position on pagan virtue relate the topic to broader concerns. For instance, a positive assessment of pagan virtue might encourage a positive relationship between theology and philosophy, showing that Christians can engage constructively with secular thought as opposed to repudiating it. It might also promote cooperation in civic life, motivating Christians to partner with non-Christians on matters of common concern instead of retreating from the world. Augustine also offers a window into questions of nature and grace. Though Augustine never produced a systematic work on the virtues, scholars of Thomas Aquinas debate whether Augustine had an incipient conception of imperfect but genuine virtues, of virtues oriented toward proximate (but not final) goods.

Bibliography

Burns, Paul C. 2001. "Roles of Roman Rhetorical *Exempla* in Augustine's *City of God*." *Studia Patristica* 38: 31–40.

Dodaro, Robert. 2004. *Christ and the Just Society in the Thought of Augustine*. Cambridge: Cambridge University Press.

Gaul, Brett. 2009. "Augustine on the Virtues of the Pagans." *Augustinian Studies* 40, no. 2: 233–49.

Harding, Brian. 2008. *Augustine and Roman Virtue*. London: Continuum.

Herdt, Jennifer. 2012. "The Theater of the Virtues: Augustine's Critique of Pagan Mimesis." In Wetzel, *COG*, 111–29.

Irwin, T. H. 1999. "Splendid Vices? Augustine for and against Pagan Virtues." *Medieval Philosophy and Theology* 8, no. 2: 105–27.

Lamb, Michael. 2022. "Hope among the Civic Virtues: Genuine Virtues or Splendid Vices?" In *A Commonwealth of Hope: Augustine's Political Thought*, 230–62. Princeton: Princeton University Press.

Tornau, Christian. 2006. "Does Augustine Accept Pagan Virtue? The Place of Book 5 in the Argument of the *City of God*." *Studia Patristica* 43: 263–75.

City of God 1.16–28: Rape of Christian Women

Gregory W. Lee, with Angela Tsarouhis Schott and Darren Yau

This section of *City of God* contains some of the most troubling passages in Augustine's corpus. According to his stated intent, Augustine seeks to console Christian women who were raped during the sack of Rome and to defend them from mockery (1.16, 19, 28–29; 2.2). Many of these women had vowed themselves to virginity. He also seeks to dissuade the women from committing suicide, a serious worry given that others had already committed suicide after being violated (1.17, 19). Augustine attempts a balancing act, conveying empathy for those who committed suicide while rejecting suicide as an appropriate response. In the process, he says the women may have suffered due to their hidden sins—thus, arguably, blaming them for their own suffering.

Augustine's remarks arise in a wider discussion of the calamities Romans experienced during the sack of Rome. In 1.8–9 he offers general remarks on physical suffering, claiming that God allows Christians to suffer for the purpose of teaching and correcting them. In subsequent chapters, he addresses particular forms of suffering during the sack of Rome: the loss of riches (1.10), torture (1.10), famine (1.10), death (1.11), no burial for the dead (1.12–13), and captivity (1.14–15). His treatment of rape extends this discussion, receiving far more attention than the other topics.

Augustine's arguments reflect cultural assumptions very different from those of modern times. Unlike understandings of rape today, which focus on the victim's emotional and physical trauma, Roman law treated rape in terms of its social consequences, especially for men (see Clark, *Comm. 1–5*, 61–62, which notes anachronisms in the term "rape"). There was no legal redress for the rape of an unmarriageable woman. The rape of a married woman was an offense against her husband, who could lose his property to the child of the perpetrator if his wife were impregnated. The rape of a virgin was significant because it compromised her family's ability to choose her husband. The rape of women who had consecrated themselves to a god was an offense against the god. This is the situation closest to what Augustine is addressing in 1.16–28, which requires him to explain why God permitted the crime.

Suicide also carried different significance in the Roman context. Whereas suicide today tends to be associated with isolation, depression, and other mental health challenges, Augustine thinks of it as an alleged display of valor. For the Romans, courageous individuals might kill themselves to protect their own honor. (For an analogy, consider the suicide of samurai warriors.) In Augustine's African context, Donatists were committing suicide to avoid submission to the Catholic Church. *City of God* addresses two celebrated instances of Roman suicide. The first is that of Cato the Younger, a senator and opponent of Julius Caesar who killed himself to avoid the shame of submitting to Caesar's rule (1.23). Augustine considers Cato inconsistent for not killing his son too. Augustine's treatment of the second example, the noblewoman Lucretia, is far more involved (1.19).

The incident concerning Lucretia triggered Rome's transition from a monarchy to a republic, the form of government that would define the Romans for nearly five hundred years. During the reign of Tarquin the Proud, Lucretia was raped by his son Sextus. After the crime, Lucretia summoned her father and her husband, telling each to come with a trusted friend, and relayed what happened: "My body only has been violated. My heart is innocent, and death will be my witness" (Livy, *History of Rome* 1.58). She also charged the men to avenge her. Then, to vindicate her honor, she stabbed herself in the heart. Inspired by her courage, Lucius Junius Brutus led a revolt against Tarquin and the monarchy. Tarquin's expulsion was followed by the establishment of the republic and the elections of Lucretia's husband, Lucius Tarquinius Collatinus, and Brutus as the first consuls.

Lucretia would remain an exemplar of chastity and courage through centuries of Roman literature and tradition, including for Christian writers like Tertullian, Jerome, and Paulinus of Nola. Augustine breaks from this consensus, claiming that Lucretia should not have killed herself if she were innocent and going so far as to suggest that perhaps she was *not* innocent and had consented to adultery. If Lucretia was innocent, Augustine argues, her suicide demonstrated that she was "too avid for praise" (1.19). She killed herself simply to prevent others from thinking she had consented. Augustine positions his arguments against Ambrose, whose *On Virgins* celebrated a group of women who committed suicide to avoid rape. In 1.26, Augustine alludes to Ambrose's work, without naming him as its author, and speculates that these women received a divine command to kill themselves.

In 1.28, Augustine applies his interpretation of Lucretia to the women who had been raped in Rome. Since they have not lost their chastity, he claims, they have no reason for shame. They remain pure in mind despite the violation of their bodies. Like Lucretia, however, they may have been tempted to delight in human praise. By permitting them to be raped, God may have been chastising them for their pride. Perhaps God was also correcting those who defined chastity in terms of the body instead of the mind.

Scholars have criticized these arguments for several reasons. First, Augustine claims that women can lust while they are being raped and thus consent to the act (1.19, 25, 28). This is a psychological impossibility, and it projects on the experiences of raped women a male assumption that sex requires physical arousal. Second, Augustine assigns pedagogical value to rape, claiming that God's purpose in permitting the women to be violated may have been to curb their pride. He thus attributes victims' suffering to their sin, which is hardly a form of consolation. This problem extends beyond Augustine's treatment of rape to his theology of suffering as a whole. Third, Augustine defines consent as the criterion for guilt or innocence in sexual relations. Whether a sexual experience counts as rape thus depends on the invisible state of the victim's mind. This perspective has been assumed in modern legal contexts, and it generates severe pressure to ascertain the victim's chastity and motivations. Forensic scrutiny should not concentrate on victims more than on perpetrators.

Bibliography

Barry, Jennifer. 2020. "So Easy to Forget: Augustine's Treatment of the Sexually Violated in the *City of God.*" *Journal of the American Academy of Religion* 88, no. 1: 235–53.

Burrus, Virginia. 2008. *Saving Shame: Martyrs, Saints, and Other Abject Subjects.* Philadelphia: University of Pennsylvania Press, 125–33.

Clark, Gillian. 1993. *Women in Late Antiquity: Pagan and Christian Lifestyles.* Oxford: Clarendon.

Donaldson, Ian. 1982. *The Rapes of Lucretia: A Myth and Its Transformations.* Oxford: Clarendon.

Glendinning, Eleanor. 2013. "Reinventing Lucretia: Rape, Suicide and Redemption from Classical Antiquity to the Medieval Era." *International Journal of the Classical Tradition* 20, no. 1/2: 61–82.

Miles, Margaret R. 2012. "From Rape to Resurrection: Sin, Sexual Difference, and Politics." In Wetzel, *COG,* 75–92.

Thompson, Jennifer J. 2004. "'Accept This Twofold Consolation, You Faint-Hearted Creatures': St. Augustine and Contemporary Definitions of Rape." *Studies in Media and Information Literacy Education* 4, no. 3: 1–17.

Trout, Dennis E. 1994. "Re-textualizing Lucretia: Cultural Subversion in the *City of God.*" *Journal of Early Christian Studies* 2, no. 1: 53–70.

Webb, Melanie. 2013. "'On Lucretia Who Slew Herself': Rape and Consolation in Augustine's *De ciuitate dei.*" *Augustinian Studies* 44, no. 1: 37–58.

———. 2015. "Abraham, Samson, and 'Certain Holy Women': Suicide and Exemplarity in Augustine's *De ciuitate dei* 1.26." In *Sacred Scripture and Secular Struggles,* edited by David Vincent Meconi, 201–34. Leiden: Brill.

War

Gregory W. Lee

Augustine is often associated with the Western tradition of just war theory. *City of God* is frequently cited for his theology of war, and this volume includes the most-referenced passages: 1.21, 24, 26; 3.10; 4.15; 15.4; 19.7, 12; 22.6. Augustine's fullest treatment of war is *Answer to Faustus* 22.69–79, where he responds to Manichean criticisms of Moses's violence. Other oft-cited passages are *Expositions of the Psalms* 124.7; *Free Will* 1.4.9–1.5.13; *Letters* 47; 138; 189; 220; 229; *Questions on the Heptateuch* 4.44; 6.10; and *Sermon* 302.

Just war theory consists of a collection of principles for governing the ethics of warfare. Common versions of the theory claim that a war is just only if, among other conditions, it is prompted by a just cause, it is conducted under a legitimate authority, it aims toward a just end, its potential goods outweigh its potential harms, and it is the least harmful way to achieve the intended outcome. Though Augustine is sometimes called the founder of just war doctrine, recent scholarship has questioned this characterization. Augustine never wrote a treatise on war, and his writings on the topic are scattered and undeveloped. He was cited heavily in medieval discussions of war (Gratian, *Decretum* Part 2, c. 23; Thomas Aquinas, *Summa Theologiae* II-II.40.1), but medieval theologians had little access to Augustine's full works, given the expense of reproducing them before the invention of the printing press. They thus relied on collections of Augustine's sayings that suggested a more systematic theology of war than he developed. It is perhaps most accurate to describe Augustine as a just war thinker whose writings influenced important articulations on the ethical use of force in medieval and early modern thought.

Though Augustine thought wars could be just, he considered war a result of the fall, and he associated it with the earthly city. His harshest denunciations of war appear in *City of God* 1–5, where he details the savagery the Romans inflicted on other nations and one another. Concerning the appropriate grounds for war, Augustine concentrates less on just cause than on proper authority. For a war to be legitimate, it must be commanded by a human ruler or by God. The soldier's duty is to obey. (For Augustine's emphasis on authority, see *Answer to Adimantus* 17.5; *Answer to Faustus* 22.75; *City of God* 1.21, 26; *Expositions of the Psalms* 124.7; *Free Will* 1.5.11–1.5.13; and *Letter* 204.5. For his treatments of Luke 3:14 and Romans 13, see *Sermon* 302.11–15. For a contrasting passage, see *City of God* 1.24.)

In the only passage where Augustine offers a definition of a just war, he appears to be relying on Cicero, and he leaves unclear the degree of his agreement with the definition: "Just wars are normally defined as those which avenge wrongdoing, as when a nation or city that is to be attacked in war has either failed to punish what its own people have done wrongly or to return what was wrongfully seized" (*Questions on the Heptateuch* 6.10). In *City of God* 22.6, Augustine notes Cicero's position that "the best city will not go to war except in defense of its good faith or its safety." Though Augustine may have agreed with this position (see *City of God* 4.15; 15.4; 19.7), he stresses the heavenly city's refusal to fight for its temporal security, even in the face of martyrdom. In several other passages, Augustine says the aim of war should be peace. War is a matter of necessity and not a final goal, and mercy should be shown to the defeated (*City of God* 15.4; 19.7, 12; *Letters* 189.6; 229.2).

Augustine presents war as a mechanism by which God mercifully chastises sinners for their spiritual good (*Answer to Faustus* 22.75; *Letter* 138.2.14). This affirmation of benevolent severity pervades Augustine's theology, including his writings on religious coercion, slavery, and providence (see "Background" in the introduction, above; and essays: "Slavery"; "Providence and Suffering"). Though war may appear to violate the Sermon on the Mount, where Jesus teaches his disciples to turn the other cheek (Matt. 5:38–48), Augustine distinguishes between external actions and internal motivations. Physical harm, he believes, can be an expression of love (*Answer to Faustus* 22.76, 79; *Letter* 138.2.14; *Lord's Sermon on the Mount* 1.20.63–1.20.65). After the Israelites worshiped the golden calf, Moses loved the Israelites as he executed them in that his actions warned the other Israelites against future idolatry (*Answer to Faustus* 22.79).

Is it possible to love the individuals one is killing? In a few early texts, Augustine answers yes. Killing transgressors can prevent them from sinning worse. It is better to die in the body than to die in the soul (*Answer to Adimantus* 17.1–6; *Answer to the Letter of Parmenian* 3.1.3; *Lord's Sermon on the Mount* 1.20.63–1.20.65, relying on 1 Kings 18:36–40; 2 Kings 1:10; Acts 5:1–11; 1 Cor. 5:1–5; and 1 Cor. 11:28–32). Augustine does not consider physical death the worst consequence of war since everyone dies anyway. He worries more about moral vices like belligerence, cruelty, and the lust for domination (*Answer to Faustus* 22.74).

Letter 138 defends the compatibility of Christianity and war in response to Marcellinus, the eventual dedicatee of *City of God* (see "Background" in the introduction). Marcellinus had relayed to Augustine the concern of Volusian, former proconsul of Africa, that the Sermon on the Mount would undermine the empire by forbidding it from defending its territory. In response, Augustine claims that Jesus was not commanding his disciples literally to turn the other cheek but to cultivate patience and benevolence of will. Wars can be conducted with benevolence toward the conquered (*Letter* 138.2.11–138.2.14). Augustine also cites Sallust and Cicero for their approval of forbearance, which facilitated Rome's early expansion and fosters civic harmony and stability. In its promotion of virtue, Christianity is an asset and not a threat to the empire (*Letter* 138.2.10; cf. *City of God* 2.22, which blames the gods' failure to promote morality for the degeneration of the empire).

Another topic that illuminates Augustine's position on force is capital punishment. In principle, Augustine affirms that judges have a right to wield the sword, but he opposes the death penalty in every case when he knows someone is at risk. Augustine's fullest discussion of capital punishment is *Letter* 153. (See also *Letters* 100; 104.2.5; 104.4.16; 133; 134; 139; and *Sermon* 13.8.) Though Augustine affirms the authority of judges (*Letter* 153.5.19, quoting Rom. 13:1–8), he urges them to exercise mercy, remembering Jesus's admonition, "*Let whoever of you is without sin be the first to throw a stone at her*" (*Letter* 153.4.9, quoting John 8:7). He also defends the responsibility of bishops to intercede for the guilty to preserve the possibility of wrongdoers' repentance. There is no opportunity for correction after this life, and capital punishment would consign the condemned to eternal punishment (*Letter* 153.4.10; 153.5.16–153.5.18). Arguably at least, Augustine's opposition to the death penalty is in tension with his support for war.

Bibliography

Carnahan, Kevin. 2008. "Perturbations of the Soul and Pains of the Body: Augustine on Evil Suffered and Done in War." *Journal of Religious Ethics* 36, no. 2: 269–94.

Dyson, R. W. 2001. *The Pilgrim City: Social and Political Ideas in the Writings of St. Augustine of Hippo*. Woodbridge, UK: Boydell, 131–78.

Holmes, Robert L. 1999. "St. Augustine and the Just War Theory." In *The Augustinian Tradition*, edited by Gareth B. Matthews, 323–44. Berkeley: University of California Press.

Johnson, James Turner. 1987. *The Quest for Peace: Three Moral Traditions in Western Cultural History*. Princeton: Princeton University Press, 50–66.

———. 2018. "St. Augustine (354–430 CE)." In *Just War Thinkers: From Cicero to the 21st Century*, edited by Daniel R. Brunstetter and Cian O'Driscoll, 21–33. Milton Park, UK: Routledge.

Langan, John. 1984. "The Elements of St. Augustine's Just War Theory." *Journal of Religious Ethics* 12, no. 1: 19–38.

Lenihan, David A. 1988. "The Just War Theory in the Work of Saint Augustine." *Augustinian Studies* 19: 37–70.

Markus, R. A. 1983. "Saint Augustine's Views on the 'Just War.'" *Studies in Church History* 20: 1–13.

Mattox, John Mark. 2006. *Saint Augustine and the Theory of Just War*. London: Continuum.

Russell, Frederick H. 1975. *The Just War in the Middle Ages*. Cambridge: Cambridge University Press.

Smith, J. Warren. 2007. "Augustine and the Limits of Preemptive and Preventive War." *Journal of Religious Ethics* 35, no. 1: 141–62.

Swift, Louis J. 1983. *The Early Fathers on War and Military Service*. Wilmington, DE: Michael Glazier, 110–49.

Wynn, Phillip. 2013. *Augustine on War and Military Service*. Minneapolis: Fortress.

Book 2

———

17–21

———

Book 2 begins Augustine's account of the suffering Rome experienced before Christ. Whereas Book 3 treats physical disasters, the suffering the Romans care most about, Book 2 treats the suffering Augustine considers most significant: immorality. Following introductory chapters (2.1–3), Augustine attacks the gods of Roman religion, who never introduced laws to promote morality but instead promoted the theater, which encouraged the people to immorality (2.4–16). Augustine develops his case about Roman immorality through two major Roman thinkers: Sallust, whose analysis of Roman history demonstrates that the Romans were always immoral, even when they appeared to be moral (2.17–20), and Cicero, who claimed Rome had become so unjust that it no longer deserved to be called a republic (2.21). The rest of Book 2 continues Augustine's polemic against the gods (2.22–27) and concludes with an exhortation for the Romans to become Christian (2.28–29).

The Natural "Justice and Goodness" of the Romans

17. Perhaps the reason why the divinities established no laws for the Roman people is that, as Sallust says, "justice and goodness prevailed among them not so much by laws as by nature"?[1] It was from this "justice and goodness,"

---

1. [GWL] Sallust (86–35 BCE) was a Roman historian and politician, and he became a canonical figure in Roman literature. This quotation is from his *Catiline Conspiracy* 9. In the chapters that follow, Augustine will quote this line several times, almost as a refrain. By relying

I suppose, that the rape of the Sabine women came about.[2] For what is more just and good than to use the pretence of a show to lure in another people's daughters and then, instead of receiving them from their parents in marriage, to carry them off by force, each man as he could? For if the Sabines were wrong in refusing the request for their daughters, it was still far more wrong to seize them when they had not been given. And it would have been more just to wage war on a people who had refused a request for their daughters in marriage from a neighboring people, who shared the same country, than on a people who were requesting the return of their abducted daughters. That is how it should have happened, and in that case Mars might have helped his son in his struggle to avenge with arms the wrong done to him by the refusal of marriage and to attain in this way the women he wanted.[3] For some law of war, perhaps, might have justified a victor in carrying off women who had been unjustly refused. No law of peace, however, justified him in snatching away women who had not been given and then waging an unjust war on their parents who were justly enraged. The upshot, however, was more beneficial and fortunate: even though the circus games continued to be held as a memorial of the deception, the precedent of the crime itself found no favor in Rome's city and empire. It proved easier for the Romans to go wrong in consecrating Romulus as a god, even after his injustice, than to go wrong by permitting, in any law or custom, the imitation of his action in abducting women.

From this same "justice and goodness," after the expulsion of King Tarquin and his children—Tarquin's son had violently raped Lucretia—the consul Junius Brutus forced Lucius Tarquinius Collatinus, Lucretia's husband and his own fellow consul, a good and innocent man, to go into exile for no more reason than that he was related to the Tarquins and carried the

---

on Sallust to critique Roman morality, Augustine is signaling his alignment with Rome's most trusted authorities. Typically, in his criticisms of Rome, Augustine does not exceed the severity of these writers. He does, however, challenge some of their arguments, and he offers a distinctly theological account of Rome's immorality. In what follows, Augustine will identify inconsistencies in Sallust's depiction of Rome and argue that Rome was worse than Sallust sometimes acknowledged. Rome is immoral because it rejects heavenly goods for earthly goods.

2. [GWL] After Romulus founded the city of Rome, he sought to grow the population by promoting intermarriage with neighboring peoples (Livy, *History of Rome* 1.9–10). After his overtures were rebuffed, he hosted a festival for Neptune and invited the Sabines to participate. During the festival, the Roman men seized the Sabine women and forced them into marriage. Augustine invokes this incident to display the depravity of the Roman people. He returns to this incident in 3.13.

3. According to legend, Romulus, who helped precipitate the abduction of the Sabine women, was the son of Mars and Ilia.

Tarquin name.[4] Brutus carried out this crime with the support and favor of the people, the very people from whom that same Collatinus had received the consulship, as had Brutus himself.

From this same "justice and goodness," Marcus Camillus, an outstanding man of his era, was put on trial due to the envy of those who disparaged his virtue and the insolence of the tribunes of the people. After ten years of war, during which the Roman army fought poorly and was so gravely afflicted that Rome itself was cast into fear and doubt about its own safety, Camillus easily vanquished the Veians, the most dire of the enemies of the Roman people, and took their city captive with all its wealth. Then, sensing the ingratitude of the city he had liberated and convinced that he would be found guilty, he voluntarily went into exile and, in his absence, was fined 10,000 *asses*, despite the fact that he was soon to deliver his ungrateful country once again, this time from the Gauls.[5]

But it would be burdensome to recall all the foul and unjust actions by which Rome was convulsed during the time when the powerful were trying to subjugate the common people and the people were resisting subjugation. The leaders of both parties, in their zeal, acted far more from love of victory than from any thought for what might be equitable and good.

Roman Morality, the Constraint of Fear, and the Destruction of Carthage

18. I shall hold myself back, therefore, and shall instead simply cite the witness of Sallust.[6] It was his praise of the Romans that gave my discussion its point of departure: "Justice and goodness prevailed among them not so much by

---

4. See Livy, *History of Rome* 1.58; 2.2. See also above at 1.19.

5. See Livy, *History of Rome* 5.21, 32, 46, 49–50. Marcus Furius Camillus (ca. 446–365 BCE) was hailed as the second founder of Rome for his military deeds.

6. [GWL] This chapter examines Sallust's presentation of Roman morality. Sallust's statement about "justice and goodness" presented the beginning of the Roman republic as a time of great virtue. Augustine responds that this period was characterized by the elite's oppression of the common people. Sallust also depicted the period between the Second and Third Punic Wars as the height of Roman morality, and the period after the Punic Wars as a time of moral decline. After it defeated Carthage, Rome had no major enemies and descended into a series of civil wars. Challenging this history, Augustine invokes Sallust's own acknowledgment that Roman virtue during the Punic Wars did not reflect the Romans' love for justice but their fear of Carthage. For Augustine, such morality is only apparent, since it arises from the wrong motives. Rome was never moral, then, even during the periods Sallust celebrated the most. For background, see essay: "History of the Romans."

laws as by nature." He was speaking of the period just after the expulsion of
the kings when, in an unbelievably short space of time, the city experienced
enormous growth. Yet he also admits, at the very start of the first book of his
history, that even then, when government had passed from kings to consuls,
oppressive actions by the powerful soon led to the alienation of the common
people from the patricians, as well as to other discords in the city. He notes
that it was during the period between the second and the last wars against
Carthage that the Roman people conducted themselves with the highest morality and the greatest harmony, and he states that the reason for this moral
goodness was not love of justice but rather sheer fear that no peace could be
trusted so long as Carthage was still standing, which is why Nasica, seeking
to restrain wickedness and to preserve that high moral conduct, opposed the
destruction of Carthage with the aim of keeping vice in check through fear.[7]
Sallust himself immediately adds, "But after the destruction of Carthage,
discord, greed, ambition, and the other evils that ordinarily spring from prosperity increased all the more"[8]—and by saying "all the more" he gives us to
understand that these evils used to arise and increase even before this. Then
he goes on to give the reason why he said this: "For oppression by the more
powerful, leading to the alienation of the people from the patricians and to
other discords in the city, was present right from the beginning, and rule by
equitable and moderate law, after the expulsion of the kings, lasted only so
long as the fear of Tarquin and the draining war with Etruria continued."[9]
You see how he states that, even during this brief period, it was due to fear
that equitable and moderate law ruled for the most part after the kings were
expelled, that is, were banished. And what the Romans feared was the war
that King Tarquin was waging against them, in alliance with the Etruscans,
after he was driven from his throne and from the city. And notice how Sallust
goes on: "From then on, the patricians ordered the common people about like
slaves, devalued their lives and their persons in the manner of the kings, drove
them from their land, and, with the rest excluded, exercised power strictly on
their own. Crushed by this savage treatment and especially by extortionate
interest rates, and at the same time bearing the double burden of taxation
and military service in ceaseless wars, the people finally armed themselves and
took up a position on the Mons Sacer and the Aventine. And so they gained

7. See above at 1.30.
8. *History* 1, fragment 10.
9. *History* 1, fragment 10.

the tribunes of the people and other rights for themselves. The discord and strife only came to an end with the second Punic War."[10] You see, then, what the Romans were like after that time, that is, after the brief interval following the expulsion of the kings. And these are the people of whom Sallust claims that "justice and goodness prevailed among them not so much by laws as by nature"!

And if this is what the times were like when the Roman republic is said to have been at its finest and best, what are we to say or to think now of the following era when "little by little"—to use the words of the same historian—the republic "changed from the finest and best to become the worst and most depraved,"[11] that is, as Sallust records, during the period after the destruction of Carthage. How Sallust himself briefly recalls and describes this era can be read in his history. He shows how the moral evils which arose from prosperity led finally to civil wars. "From that time on," as he says, "the decline of traditional morality no longer took place little by little, as before, but like a rushing torrent. The young were so corrupted by luxury and greed that it would be right to say that this was a generation which could neither preserve their own family property nor bear to have others preserve theirs."[12] Sallust then dwells on the vices of Sulla and other disgraces to the republic,[13] and other writers agree on this point, although they write far less eloquently.

So you see, I take it (and anyone who pays the slightest attention can hardly fail to notice), that Rome had sunk into the dregs of the worst immorality well before the coming of our heavenly king. For this all happened not only before Christ, present in the flesh, had begun to teach, but even before he was born of a virgin. The Romans do not dare to blame their gods for all the terrible moral evils of those times, whether the less serious evils of the earlier period or the more serious and horrible evils that followed the destruction of Carthage, even though it was precisely these gods who, with malignant cunning, sowed in human minds the outlook that produced such a wild tangle of vices. Why, then, do they blame Christ for the evils of the present, when Christ by his saving doctrine forbids the worship of false and deceiving gods? When

10. *History* 1, fragment 10. This passage is also cited . . . at 3.17.
11. *Catiline Conspiracy* 5.
12. *History* 1, fragment 13.
13. See *History* 1, fragment 13. Lucius Cornelius Sulla (ca. 138–78 BCE) was a distinguished Roman statesman and general whose legacy was mixed, but who was generally esteemed for his achievements. Augustine finds much to admire in him, while regretting his eventual descent into violent injustice.

Christ by divine authority denounces and condemns humanity's pernicious and shameful desires? When Christ everywhere withdraws his family by slow degrees from a world wasting and decaying with these evils in order to found with them an eternal and most glorious city—most glorious not as measured by vanity's applause but as measured by truth's own verdict?

19. There you have it: "little by little" the Roman republic "changed from the finest and best to become the worst and most depraved." (I am not the first to say this; their own authors, from whom we learned these things for a fee,[14] said it long ago, long before the coming of Christ.) There you have it: before the coming of Christ, after the destruction of Carthage, "the decline of traditional morality no longer took place little by little as before but like a rushing torrent. The young were so corrupted by luxury and greed. . . ."

Let them read to us any commandments against luxury and greed given to the Roman people by their gods. Would that their gods had simply been silent about chastity and propriety and had not demanded from the people those shameful and disgraceful performances, giving them a baneful authority by means of their spurious divinity! In contrast, let them read all our many commandments against luxury and greed, given through the prophets, through the holy gospel, through the Acts of the Apostles, through the epistles, which are everywhere read out to the people assembled for this purpose.[15] How excellent, how divine they sound, not like the noisy uproar of philosophers' debates but like the tones of God thundering from oracles or from the clouds. But they still do not blame their gods for the luxury and greed and fierce immorality which, well before the coming of Christ, made the republic the worst and most depraved; rather, they berate the Christian religion for any and every affliction suffered by their pride and self-indulgence in these times. If Christianity's commandments on justice and morality were listened to and heeded by *the kings of the earth and all peoples, princes and all judges of the earth, young men and maidens, old and young together* (Ps. 148:11–12), by those of every age capable of reason, male and female, and even by those addressed by John the Baptist, the tax collectors and soldiers,[16] then the Roman republic would adorn its lands with happiness in this present life and ascend the peak of eternal life to reign in ultimate felicity. But because some listen,

14. The mention of a fee suggests a certain contempt for the teachers, although their accepting a fee was completely justified. See *Confessions* 1.13.22.

15. Augustine is referring to the liturgical reading of these texts in church.

16. See Luke 3:12–14.

others scoff, and most find the evil allure of the vices more to their liking than the helpful austerity of the virtues, Christ's servants—whether kings or princes or judges, whether soldiers or provincials, rich or poor, free or slave, men and women alike—are told to endure, if need be, the worst and most depraved republic and, by their endurance, to win for themselves a place of glory in the most holy and majestic senate of the angels, so to speak, in the heavenly republic whose law is the will of God.

20. But the worshipers and lovers of the Roman gods, whom they delight to imitate even in the gods' most wicked and disgraceful acts, have no concern at all that the republic not be the worst and most depraved.[17] "As long as it stands," they say, "as long as it flourishes, rich in its resources and glorious in its victories, or—better yet—secure in its peace, what has any of this to do with us? Our concern is rather for each of us to get richer all the time. It is wealth that sustains daily extravagance. It is through wealth that the powerful subject the weak to themselves. Let the poor fawn on the rich for the sake of filling their bellies and in order to enjoy a life of laziness under their patronage. Let the rich make ill use of the poor to gain clients for themselves and to feed their own arrogance. Let the people applaud not those who look out for their benefit but those who provide for their pleasure. Let nothing harsh be commanded and nothing shameful be prohibited. Let kings care only that their subjects are docile, not that they are good. Let provinces be subject to kings not as directors of conduct but as lords over their fate and providers of their pleasures, and let them honor their rulers not in sincere regard but in servile fear. Let the laws address harm done to another's vineyard rather than harm done to one's own moral character. Let no one be brought to court unless he threatens or actually does harm to another's property, house, or security against that person's will. Otherwise let everyone do whatever he wishes with what belongs to him, whether with his own people or with anyone else who is willing. Let there be plenty of public prostitutes for the sake of all who like to enjoy them and especially for the sake of those who cannot afford private mistresses. Let vast and lavishly furnished houses be built and sumptuous banquets be held where, day and night, anyone who wants can play, drink, vomit, and abandon himself. Let the din of dancing resound on all sides, and let the theaters boil over with cries of indecent delight and with every kind

17. [GWL] This chapter is worth dwelling on for its description of Roman selfishness, greed, licentiousness, and disregard for the poor. It is not difficult to observe parallels with the modern West.

of cruel and shameful pleasure carried to the highest pitch. If anyone disapproves of this kind of happiness, let him be branded a public enemy. If anyone tries to change it or do away with it, let the uninhibited mob stop his mouth, toss him out, kill him off. Let those be considered the true gods who see to it that the people get this sort of happiness and who preserve it for them once they have it. Let these gods be worshiped as they wish; let them demand any shows they want, whatever they can afford with their worshipers—or from them. Just let them make sure that such happiness has nothing to fear from any enemy, any plague, or any kind of calamity at all."

Who in his right mind would not put a republic of this kind on a level not with the Roman empire but with the very palace of Sardanapalus? This king of long ago was so enamored of sensual pleasures that he had it inscribed on his tomb that his only possessions in death consisted of the things his desire had drained to the dregs while he was still alive.[18] If the Romans had such a king as this, one who both indulged himself in all such pursuits and never showed any severity against anyone else in such matters, they would surely consecrate a temple and a flamen to him even more eagerly than the ancient Romans did for Romulus.

The Issue of Justice and Scipio's Definition of a Republic

21. But perhaps they scoff at the one who claimed that the Roman republic was "the worst and most depraved." Perhaps they do not care that it overflows with the shame and infamy of the worst and most depraved immorality, just so long as it continues to exist and endure. In that case, let them hear not Sallust's tale of how it became "the worst and most depraved" but Cicero's argument that in his day it had entirely perished and no republic at all remained.[19] Cicero

---

18. Sardanapalus was a legendary seventh-century BCE king of Assyria who was supposed to have devoted himself completely to a life of hedonism and was especially notorious for his effeminacy. See Diodorus Siculus, *Historical Library* 2.27. Augustine probably knew of his supposed epitaph from Cicero, *Tusculan Disputations* 5.35.

19. [GWL] Having treated Sallust in 2.17–20, Augustine transitions to an important discussion of Cicero. He will return to this discussion in Book 19. Cicero (106–43 BCE) was a Roman statesman and philosopher. He is generally considered the greatest orator in Roman history. In this section, Augustine engages Cicero's work *On the Republic* (here, *Republic*), which has now been lost. We retain it only in fragments, many of which are taken from Augustine's quotations of it in *City of God*. In what follows, Augustine treats a conversation that appears in *Republic* on the relation between justice and the republic (*res publica*; sometimes translated "commonwealth"). In the conversation, Philus contends for the primacy of wisdom (*sapientia*) over justice (*iustitia*). Wisdom promotes power and the expansion of empire, whereas justice cares only about mercy and fair treatment of others (3.24b). As Philus asserts, "There is no

introduces Scipio—the very one who had destroyed Carthage[20]—and presents him as discussing the republic at a time when people were already beginning to sense that it was about to perish due to the corruption that Sallust describes. In fact, the discussion is set at the point when one of the Gracchi had already been put to death (and it was with the Gracchi, as Sallust writes, that the serious seditions began), for his death is recorded in that same work.[21]

At the end of Cicero's second book, Scipio says, "In music for strings or flutes and in song and vocal music, a certain harmony must be maintained among the different sounds, and if this is altered or discordant, the trained ear cannot bear to hear it. This harmony in concord and agreement is achieved by means of the modulation of highly dissimilar voices. And in the same way, from the high, the low, and between them the middle orders of society, as from sounds, a city comes together in agreement by means of a consensus, modulated by reason, of its very different parts. Now what the musicians call harmony in singing corresponds to concord in a city, which is the best and closest bond of well-being in a republic; and, without justice, it cannot exist at all."[22]

After Scipio had gone on to discuss more broadly and fully the great advantage of justice to the city and the great disadvantage of its absence, Philus, another of the participants in the discussion, intervened to ask that this very issue be considered in more detail and that more be said, in particular, on the topic of justice, inasmuch as it was then a commonplace to claim that a republic cannot be governed without injustice. Scipio accordingly agreed that this point should be pursued and explained. He replied that, in his view, nothing they had said so far about a republic provided any basis for continuing unless they first established not only that it is false that a republic cannot be governed without injustice but also that it is true beyond any doubt that a republic cannot be governed without the most supreme justice.[23]

---

state so stupid that it would not prefer to rule unjustly than to be enslaved justly" (3.28). In response, Scipio, the character representing Cicero's position, defends a different conception of republic as a community founded on justice. For Scipio, realpolitik is morally inadequate. A republic counts as a republic only if it exhibits righteousness. For background and analysis, see Malcolm Schofield, "Cicero's Definition of *Res Publica*," in *Cicero the Philosopher: Twelve Papers*, ed. J. G. F. Powell (Oxford: Clarendon, 1995), 63–83.

20. This is the same Scipio who appears above at 1.30, who is also referred to as Africanus.

21. The brothers Tiberius and Gaius Gracchus were second-century BCE figures who attempted to reform the Roman polity; each suffered a violent death. Augustine mentions them again in 3.24 and seems to view them at once cautiously and sympathetically.

22. *Republic* 2.42–43.

23. See *Republic* 2.44.

The discussion of this issue was postponed to the following day; and then, in the third book, the point was debated with great controversy. Philus, for his part, took the position of those who held that a republic cannot be governed without injustice (at the same time, however, he carefully dissociated himself from this view, lest anyone think he really held it himself). He argued vigorously for injustice against justice, trying to show by plausible arguments and examples that the one is useful, the other useless for the republic. Then Laelius, at the request of all, proceeded to defend justice and argued, to the best of his ability, that nothing is so inimical to a city as injustice and that, without a high degree of justice, no republic can possibly be governed or endure.[24]

Scipio's Definition of a Republic

Once this point was treated satisfactorily, Scipio returns to the interrupted theme and recalls and recommends his own brief definition of a republic which, he had said, is the common good of a people.[25] He stipulates, however, that a people is not just any assembly of a multitude but rather an assembly joined together by a common sense for what is right and a community of interest.[26] He then explains the great advantage of definition in debate, and he goes on to conclude from these definitions of his that a republic—that is, the common good of a people—only exists when it is well and justly governed, whether by a single king or by a few of the most prominent men or by the people as a whole.[27] But when the king is unjust (in this case, following the Greeks, he called the king a tyrant), or the most prominent men are unjust (he termed the consensus of such men a faction), or the people itself is unjust (for this case he found no term in common use, although he might also have called the people itself a tyrant), the republic is not simply flawed, as had been argued the day before. Rather, as logical deduction from his definitions

24. See *Republic* 3 passim.

25. See *Republic* 1.25. On translating Cicero's Latin for "republic" (*res publica*), see [William Babcock, introduction to *City of God, Books 1–10*, l].

26. [GWL] This definition is clearer in the Latin. Scipio says that a *res publica* ("republic" or "commonwealth") is a *res populi* ("common good of a people" or "weal of a people"). He then says that a *populus* ("people") is not just any assembly but an assembly characterized by a "common sense for what is right and a community of interest." The phrase "common sense for what is right" translates *consensu iuris*. The key word is *iuris*, a conjugated form of *ius*, the root word for *iustitia* ("justice" or "righteousness"). In short, a republic is not just any people but a people characterized by justice.

27. See *Republic* 1.26.

would show, it does not exist at all. For there is no common good of a people when a tyrant or a faction has taken it over, nor is the people itself any longer a people if it is unjust, since it is no longer a multitude joined together by a common sense for what is right and a community of interest—which was the very definition of a people. Thus, when the Roman republic was in the sorry state Sallust described, it was not simply "the worst and most depraved," as he claimed. In fact, according to the reasoning set out in this discussion of the republic by its great leaders of the time, it did not exist at all.

Cicero: The Republic Has Perished

Again, at the beginning of his fifth book, where he is speaking in his own right, not in the person of Scipio or anyone else, Cicero first quotes a line from the poet Ennius: "The mores and the men of old sustain the Roman state."[28] "This line," he goes on to say, "by virtue of both its brevity and its truth seems to me like something uttered by an oracle. For neither the men, if the mores had not been what they were, nor the mores, if these men had not been in charge, would have been able either to found such a great republic or to preserve it for so long, holding sway over such a vast and broad domain. Thus, long before any time we can remember, our ancestral way of life brought forth outstanding men, and these excellent men maintained the ancient ways and institutions of their elders. But our era received the republic like a magnificent painting that was fading with age, and it not only neglected to renew its original colors but did not even care enough to preserve at least its faint outline and the last remnants of its design. For what is left of the ancient mores which, as Ennius said, sustained the Roman state? We see them so fallen into oblivion that they are not only not cultivated but are scarcely even known. And what about the men? The ancient mores were lost for lack of such men, and we must not only be held accountable for so great an evil but must even somehow plead our case as if we were facing a capital charge. For it is due to our own vices, not to any mere chance or accident, that we now retain the republic in name only, having long ago lost it in reality."[29]

28. [GWL] This quotation is from Ennius, *Annals*, fragment 156, following the numbering system in *The "Annals" of Q. Ennius*, ed. Otto Skutsch (Oxford: Clarendon, 1985). It is quoted in Cicero, *Republic* 5.1 and known only through this passage in *City of God*.

29. [GWL] Cicero's pessimistic assessment of Rome, taken from *Republic* 5.1, relies on his definition of a republic. If Rome lacks justice, it is no longer a republic. Given Cicero's authority for Roman readers, his judgment is crucial to Augustine's case against Rome.

Cicero made this admission long after the death of Africanus, whom he took as one of the participants in the discussion in his work on *The Republic*, but still well before the coming of Christ.[30] If anyone had thought or said such things after the Christian religion had spread and was gaining strength, what Roman would not have claimed that the Christians were the ones to blame for this state of affairs? Why is it, then, that their own gods took no care to prevent the ruin and loss of the republic, whose loss Cicero so lugubriously laments long before Christ came in the flesh? Those who praise the republic should take a second look at its character in the time of "the mores and men of old," asking themselves whether true justice prevailed or whether even then, perhaps, it was not really alive in human conduct but was actually no more than a picture painted in as yet unfaded colors. For Cicero himself unwittingly suggested as much in the way he spoke of it.

God willing, however, we will look into this matter elsewhere.[31] For, in the appropriate place, I will try to show that, according to Cicero's own definitions of a republic and of a people, as briefly expressed through the mouth of Scipio (and as attested by many other statements in the discussion, statements made both by Cicero himself and by the characters he portrays as taking part in the debate), that republic never actually existed, because there was no true justice in it. According to more plausible definitions, of course, it was a republic in a way, and it was better administered by the earlier Romans than by their descendents. True justice, however, exists only in the republic whose founder and ruler is Christ—if indeed we want to call this too a republic, since we cannot deny that it is the common good of a people.[32] But if this use of the term, which is ordinarily employed in other contexts with other meanings, is too remote from our usual way of speaking, true justice certainly exists in the city of which Holy Scripture says, *Glorious things are spoken of you, O city of God* (Ps. 87:3).

---

30. Cicero lived from 106 to 43 BCE, and hence died four decades before the birth of Christ.

31. [GWL] Augustine will return to this discussion in 19.21—some seventeen books, and over a decade, later. According to Augustine's reading of Roman history, Rome was never characterized by justice. According to Cicero's definition, then, Rome was never a republic. This is a very negative judgment. Augustine thus rejects Cicero's definition of *res publica* and promises to explore "more plausible definitions" later, when he will assert that Rome is indeed a *res publica*. He fulfills that promise in 19.24, where he defines *res publica* as a people united by common objects of love. Augustine's return to this discussion signals the importance of the topic and the importance of Book 19.

32. [GWL] An important summary statement. Augustine quotes Ps. 87:3 to claim that the city of God is the only just republic. Augustine also quotes this psalm in 10.7 and 11.1.

Roman Spectacles

Gregory W. Lee and Avyi Hill, with Angela Tsarouhis Schott

Roman spectacles were forms of entertainment that included theatrical performances, athletic competitions, chariot races, circus games, gladiatorial contests, animal hunts, and executions. While most spectacles were held publicly, usually to mark important events, private games were also held for special occasions such as funerals. Spectacles were strongly associated with religious rites. They were funded by wealthy individuals who sought to display their civic generosity.

The frequency and duration of spectacles increased during the republican and imperial periods. According to one fourth-century calendar, spectacles occurred on 175 days of the year. Spectacles remained popular well after the Christianization of the empire, though their association with Roman religion somewhat diminished. Carthage was notorious for its love of spectacles, particularly the animal games of the circus and amphitheater. Many of Augustine's sermons against spectacles were preached in that city. His criticisms developed a long-standing Christian tradition that had been shaped especially by Tertullian, who wrote two centuries earlier, also from Carthage.

Augustine's position on spectacles was informed by his personal experiences. *Confessions* laments his former attraction to theatrical shows, which arouse false grief for fictional tragedies as opposed to mercy for those who actually suffer (*Confessions* 3.2.2–3.2.4; see also *City of God* 2.4). It also recounts Alypius's failure to resist a gladiatorial show in Rome (*Confessions* 6.7.11–6.8.13). The passage about Alypius may be the most extended account in ancient literature of spectacles' intoxicating effects.

In his sermons, Augustine complained frequently about those who skipped church for spectacles, warning his congregants that their souls were in danger (*Expositions of the Psalms* 39.6–11; 50.1; 61.10; 98.5; 99.12; 147.7–8; *Sermons* 46.8; 51.1; 198; 313A.3). He also warned against spectacles in his work on catechesis, *Instructing Beginners in the Faith* (16.25). Like other bishops, Augustine preached that Christian worship and virtue were better spectacles than Roman entertainment and that the martyrs were greater athletes than the victors of Roman games (*Expositions of the Psalms* 39.9–10; *Homilies on the Gospel of John* 7.6; *Sermon* 280.2). He also challenged spectacles as a social practice—chastising Christians who funded them; lobbying for an imperial ban against spectacles on Sundays; and celebrating the example of Simittu, a town between Hippo and Carthage that had shut down its theater (*Expositions of the Psalms* 102.13; *Sermon* 301A.9; *Registri Ecclesiae Carthaginensis* 61).

In *City of God*, Augustine claims spectacles were commanded by demons to manipulate the Romans into worshiping them. The Romans first established the theater to secure divine assistance against a devastating plague (1.32–33; see Livy, *History of Rome* 7.2). They received instead the pestilence of immorality. Augustine opposes the shows because they legitimate immoral content with divine authority, inciting the Romans to mimic the gods' disgraceful deeds (2.25–26; 8.5). Of particular offense is the playwright Terence's story of a man who was inspired by Jupiter's sexual deception of Danae to rape a young girl (2.7, 12; 18.13; see also *Confessions* 1.16.26).

City of God singles out theater as the strongest proof of Rome's moral suffering before Christ. Augustine critiques the Romans' inconsistency on theater by comparing them with the Greeks (2.4–16). Both the Greeks and the Romans permitted the gods to be slandered in the theater. Unlike the Greeks, however, the Romans forbade the slander of humans, and they excluded actors from civic honors. As Augustine argues, these practices indicated the Romans' own reservations about the gods, who should never have been worshiped in the first place. In this discussion and elsewhere, Augustine invokes classical authorities who also raised doubts about the theater, demonstrating that critiques of spectacles were not from Christians alone (Plato: 2.14; 8.13; Cicero: 4.26; Varro: 6.5–9).

Bibliography

Beacham, Richard C. 1991. *The Roman Theater and Its Audience*. London: Routledge.

Herdt, Jennifer. 2012. "The Theater of the Virtues: Augustine's Critique of Pagan Mimesis." In Wetzel, *COG*, 111–29.

Leppin, Hartmut. 2008. "Spectacles." In *Brill's New Pauly: Encyclopaedia of the Ancient World*, edited by Hubert Cancik, Helmuth Schneider, and Christine F. Salazar, 714–21. Leiden: Brill.

Lim, Richard. 2012. "Augustine and Roman Public Spectacles." In Vessey, *Blackwell Companion*, 138–50.

Markus, R. A. 1990. "Secular Festivals in Christian Times?" In *The End of Ancient Christianity*, 107–23. Cambridge: Cambridge University Press.

Munier, C., ed. 1974. *Concilia Africae a. 345–525*. Turnhout, Belgium: Brepols.

Potter, D. S., and D. J. Mattingly, eds. 2010. *Life, Death, and Entertainment in the Roman Empire*. New and expanded ed. Orig. 1999. Ann Arbor: University of Michigan Press.

Van Slyke, Daniel G. 2005. "The Devil and His Pomps in Fifth-Century Carthage: Renouncing Spectacula with Spectacular Imagery." *Dumbarton Oaks Papers* 59: 53–72.

Webb, Ruth. 2008. *Demons and Dancers: Performance in Late Antiquity*. Cambridge, MA: Harvard University Press.

Wiedemann, Thomas. 1992. *Emperors and Gladiators*. London: Routledge.

Book 3

1, 9–12, 23–31

Book 3 continues Augustine's account of the suffering Rome experienced before Christ, focusing on physical disasters. This book surveys Roman history from the destruction of Troy through the time of Augustus Caesar, and it considers how the Romans both suffered violence and inflicted it on others. After an introductory chapter (3.1), the first section concentrates on the destruction of Troy (3.2–8). The next section treats the proliferation of gods under Rome's second king, Numa Pompilius (3.9–12). Augustine then traces how the gods failed to protect the Romans in their wars against external enemies (3.13–22) and in their civil wars against one another (3.23–31). This last section especially stresses the brutality of Rome's wars.

1. I have now said enough, I believe, about those evils of mind and moral character—the evils which we ought most especially to guard against—to show that the Romans' false gods took no care to help the people who worshiped them to be any less weighed down by the burden of these evils but rather took every care to make sure they were as fully weighed down by them as possible. Now, I see, I must speak of those evils which are the only ones these people really want to avoid—such evils as famine, sickness, war, pillage, captivity, slaughter, and any similar disasters already mentioned in the first book.[1] For

---

1. [GWL] God cares about moral disasters more than physical disasters, yet the Romans care only about the latter because they value earthly goods above heavenly goods. Book 3 details Rome's history of wars, illustrating how calamitous they were for the Roman people. This

these are the only things that evil people consider evil, rather than the things which have the effect of making persons evil, and they feel no shame at all in the fact that, surrounded by the goods they praise, they themselves, the very ones who do the praising, remain evil. They are more distressed at having a bad house than at having a bad life, as if a person's greatest good were to have everything good except himself.

But when they were worshiped freely, those gods of theirs did not prevent such evils—the only ones these people fear—from happening to them. At various times and in diverse places before the coming of our redeemer, the human race was ground down by innumerable and sometimes even incredible disasters. But what other gods did the world worship back then (with the exception, of course, of the one Hebrew people and a few other persons, here and there, who were found worthy of divine grace by the most hidden and most just judgment of God)? To keep from going on too long, however, I shall say nothing of the terrible evils that struck other peoples all over the world. I shall speak only of what pertains to Rome and the Roman empire, that is, the city proper and any lands which were either joined to it by alliance or subjected to it by conquest, and specifically of what they suffered before Christ's coming, when they already pertained, so to speak, to the body of the republic.

◆

The Peace of Numa's Reign

9. The gods are also believed to have helped Numa Pompilius,[2] Romulus's successor, to have peace for the whole period of his reign and to shut the gates of Janus which, by custom, are kept open in times of war.[3] He earned

---

history is intended to shape the reader's perception of Rome as a violent people, thereby advancing Augustine's association between violence and the earthly city. The earthly city is driven to violence by its lust for earthly goods. The reader is encouraged to seek heavenly goods instead. Augustine's treatment of Rome's history furnishes an important component in Augustine's narration of the earthly city. Later sections will fill out Augustine's narrative by treating the earthly city before the time of Rome (18.2–26) and after Augustus Caesar through Augustine's time (18.45–54).

2. [GWL] Numa Pompilius was Rome's second king. He is said to have ruled from 715 to 673 BCE, and he was associated with the great proliferation of the Roman gods.

3. According to legend, Janus was a king who reigned in ancient Italy and was numbered among the gods after his death. The doors of his temple in Rome were customarily shut in time of peace and open in time of war.

this help, no doubt, because he instituted many religious rites among the Romans. It would certainly have been in order to congratulate this man for such a period of quiet, if only he had known enough to use it for salutary purposes and, giving up his exceedingly dangerous curiosity,[4] to seek the true God with true piety. In reality, however, it is not that the gods gave him that time of quiet; it is rather that they might have deceived him less if they had found him less at leisure. For the less they found him occupied, the more they themselves occupied his time. Varro tells us what Numa undertook to do and by what arts he was able to ally such gods as these with himself and with his city. God willing, I will discuss all this more fully in its proper place.[5] Here, however, the question has to do with the benefits brought by the gods.

Peace, of course, is a great benefit. But it is a benefit bestowed by the true God, and—like the sun, the rain, and other supports of life—it is commonly bestowed even on the ungrateful and the scurrilous.[6] But if it was the gods who brought this great good to Rome or to Pompilius, why is it that they never granted it to the Roman empire in later times, even in the periods when it was worthy of praise? Were the sacred rites more effective when they were first being instituted than when they were celebrated after they had been instituted? In Numa's time they did not yet exist but rather were added so that they would come to exist. Later, when they already existed, they were kept up so that they might bring benefits. How is it, then, that the forty-three years—or, as some would have it, the thirty-nine years—of Numa's reign passed in such prolonged peace, but afterwards, after the sacred rites had been established and the gods invoked by those rites had become the city's protectors and guardians, during all the long years from the founding of the city to the reign of Augustus, only one year is recorded (the

---

4. "Exceedingly dangerous curiosity": *perniciosissima curiositate.* "Curiosity" is generally a negative term for Augustine, denoting an overweening interest in something inconsequential or even bad. As well as . . . at 4.34 and 10.9 see also *Confessions* 2.6.13; 3.3.5; 10.35.54–10.35.57; *Letter* 118.1.1; *Demonic Divination* 3.7. In the case of Numa Pompilius the curiosity was clearly of a religious nature.

5. [GWL] Augustine returns to this topic in 7.34–35, where he claims, citing Varro, that Numa discovered the falsity of Rome's sacred rites. According to this account, Numa recorded his findings in writing and buried them near his tomb. The senate later discovered Numa's writings and had them burned.

6. [GWL] Augustine is alluding to Matt. 5:45 and his discussion of suffering and providence in 1.8–9. God bestows the sun and the rain (temporal goods) on both moral and immoral people. Thus, the political peace of Numa's reign cannot be assumed to represent divine favor. See essay: "Providence and Suffering."

year immediately following the First Punic War) when the Romans were able to close the gates of war.[7] And that year itself was reckoned a great marvel!

10. Do they reply that the Roman empire simply could not have expanded so far and wide, nor its fame have spread so grandly, without incessant wars, each following immediately upon the other? What a worthy reason! Must an empire be in turmoil in order to be great?[8] In the case of the human body, is it not better to attain a moderate stature with good health than to reach some gigantic bulk with constant afflictions and then, once you reach it, not to find rest but rather to be afflicted with greater evils the larger your limbs are? What evil would have resulted—or, rather, would not all the more good have resulted—if the era had continued which Sallust mentioned where he states, "At first, then, kings—for this was the first name for holders of power on earth—were diverse. Some exercised the mind, others the body. At that time, human life was still lived without greed; each was satisfied with what he had."[9] Or is it true that, in order for empire to grow so much, there had to take place what Virgil deplores when he says, "Until, little by little, there came a baser, drabber age, and rage for war and love of having"?[10]

But the Romans clearly have a just defense for undertaking and waging so many wars: they were compelled to resist the savage incursions of their enemies, and this due not to any avid desire for human glory but rather to the necessity of defending life and liberty. For, as Sallust himself writes, "Once their condition, enhanced by their laws, customs, and territories, was seen to be growing strong and prosperous, wealth gave rise to envy, as often happens in human affairs. Consequently the neighboring kings and peoples put them to the test in war. Only a few friends came to their aid; the rest, unnerved by fear, stayed well out of danger. But the Romans, alert both in peace and in war, were quick to act; they made ready, exhorted each other, went to meet the enemy and defended their liberty, their homeland, and their families with arms. Afterwards, when by their valor they had repelled the danger, they brought help to their friends and allies and won friendships

---

7. I.e., in 235 BCE.

8. [GWL] By definition, empires are large nations. Augustine believes empires are the political expression of the earthly city, which relentlessly seeks more territory and power because of its lust for domination. Under Augustine's ideal scenario, different nations would be moderate in size and interact harmoniously with one another. See 4.3–4 and 4.15 for other places where Augustine criticizes the obsession of nations with the expanse of their rule.

9. *Catiline Conspiracy* 2.

10. *Aeneid* 8.326–27.

more by granting benefits than by receiving them."[11] By these methods Rome achieved her growth with honor.

But what about the long peace of Numa's reign? Were harsh enemies invading and putting the Romans to the test of war at that point, or was the peace able to endure because no such attacks occurred? On the one hand, if Rome was also being provoked by wars back in Numa's time and yet did not meet arms with force of arms, then whatever means she used to pacify her enemies without defeating them in battle or terrifying them with threats of war are means she might always have put to use, and so Rome might always have reigned in peace and kept the gates of Janus closed. On the other hand, if this was not in her power, then it was due not to the will of the gods that Rome had peace but rather to the will of the neighboring peoples on every side. Rome had peace, that is, only as long as the neighboring peoples did not provoke her into war—unless, perhaps, such gods as these would have the gall to sell off to one person what is actually the result of another person's decision about what he is or is not going to do. What interests these demons, of course, is to terrify or to incite, so far as they are permitted to do so, minds that have already been made evil by their own vice. But if they were always able to do this, and if their efforts were not often thwarted by a more hidden and higher power, they would always hold peace and military victory in their power, for these most often come about through the impulses of human minds. As a general rule, however, these actually come about against the will of the gods, and this is attested not only by the myths, which tell many lies and state or hint at hardly any truth at all, but also by Roman history itself.

11. It was for no other reason than this that the renowned Apollo at Cumae was reported to have wept for four days during the war against the Achaeans and King Aristonicus.[12] The soothsayers were terrified at this portent and reached the conclusion that this image should be thrown into the sea.[13] But the old men of Cumae intervened and reported that the same statue had shown just such a

11. *Catiline Conspiracy* 6.
12. See Cicero, *On Divination* 1.43. Aristonicus claimed the throne of Pergamon under the name of Eumenes III; he was defeated by the Romans, who had rights to Pergamon, in 129 BC.
13. [GWL] According to Roman tradition, during Rome's war against Cumae, a Greek colony in Italy, a statue of Apollo wept for four days. The Romans originally thought this was a sign against them. They were then assured that Apollo was weeping for the Greeks and thus signaling the Romans' victory over Cumae. Rome would eventually defeat Cumae, against Apollo's desires. Augustine uses this example to argue that the gods are powerless to ensure military victory. He probably derives this story from a now-lost text by Livy, and his account involves some historical mistakes. See Clark, *Comm. 1–5*, 143; and Walsh, *DCD 3–4*, 193.

portent during the war with Antiochus and Perseus,[14] and they testified that, since that war had gone in Rome's favor, gifts had been sent to this same Apollo by decree of the senate. Then supposedly more expert soothsayers were called in, and they responded that the weeping of Apollo's image was, in fact, favorable to the Romans, since Cumae was a Greek colony and Apollo's tears signified grief and calamity for the lands from which he had been summoned—that is, for Greece itself. Not long afterwards it was announced that King Aristonicus had been defeated and taken captive. But Apollo plainly had not wanted Aristonicus to be defeated, and he showed his grief through the tears of his own stone statue.

Thus the songs of the poets, although made up of fictions, are not entirely out of line; they describe the ways of the demons with some likeness to the truth. In Virgil, for instance, Diana grieved for Camilla,[15] and Hercules wept for Pallas when Pallas was about to die.[16] Perhaps this is the reason why Numa Pompilius, enjoying abundant peace but neither knowing nor asking who bestowed it, when he considered at leisure to what gods he should entrust the protection of Rome's sovereignty and wellbeing—since he had no idea that the true and all-powerful supreme God cares for such earthly matters, and since he remembered that the Trojan gods, whom Aeneas brought, were unable to preserve for very long either the kingdom of Troy or the kingdom of Lavinium founded by Aeneas himself[17]—came to the conclusion that he must provide other gods, in addition to the earlier ones who either had come over to Rome with Romulus or would come over when Alba was overthrown.[18] These new gods, then, were to serve either as guardians for the former who came as fugitives or as helpers for the latter who would come as weaklings.

Gods Brought In after Numa's Reign

12. Even so, however, Rome could not bring itself to rest content with the numerous rites instituted by Pompilius on her behalf.[19] She still did not have her

---

14. During the years 169–168 BCE both Perseus, king of Macedonia, and Antiochus IV, king of Seleucia, were involved in hostilities with Rome.

15. See *Aeneid* 11.836.

16. See *Aeneid* 10.464–65; 11.823–49.

17. According to legend, Aeneas founded Lavinium, south of Rome, and named it after Lavinia, the woman who would be his wife.

18. See . . . 3.14.

19. [GWL] Augustine names several gods in this paragraph. Knowing their background is not crucial for understanding his argument. Augustine wants to illustrate how many gods the Romans added even after Numa's reign. The more the Romans expanded, the more gods

chief temple of Jupiter, and it was King Tarquin, of course, who erected the Capitol there.[20] Aesculapius, too, came over to Rome from Epidaurus so that he might practice his art with greater glory as the most expert physician in the most illustrious city.[21] And the mother of the gods came from Pessinus, wherever that may be,[22] for it was hardly fitting that she should still be lurking in some obscure little place now that her son was presiding over the Capitoline Hill. Even if she is the mother of all the gods, however, she not only followed some of her offspring to Rome but also preceded others who were still to come. But I wonder whether it was she herself who gave birth to Cynocephalus, who came long afterwards from Egypt.[23] And whether she also bore the goddess Fever is a matter for her great-grandson Aesculapius to decide.[24] But whatever the circumstances of Fever's birth may have been, no immigrant gods, I imagine, will dare to call ignoble a goddess who is a Roman citizen.

Who, then, can count all the gods that were protecting Rome? Native and foreign gods, celestial and terrestrial gods, gods of the underworld, of the sea, of springs, of rivers, and, as Varro says, gods "certain and uncertain,"[25] and in every category, just as among the animals, male and female gods. Set under the protection of all these gods, Rome surely should not have been assailed and afflicted by such massive and terrible disasters as the ones I shall mention, listing only a few out of many. For her protection, she had called together all too many gods, drawing them by a great cloud of her smoke as by a given sign; and by instituting and providing temples, altars, sacrifices, and priests for them, she offended the true and supreme God, to whom alone these services are rightly owed. In fact, Rome lived more happily when she had fewer gods, but the greater she became, the more gods she thought she should add, just as a larger ship needs more sailors. She despaired, I believe, of

---

they acquired. These gods were added to secure earthly goods. For Augustine, this history demonstrates the Romans' lust for earthly goods and their lack of confidence in the gods. He develops this critique further in 4.8–32.

20. See Livy, *History of Rome* 1.55.

21. See Livy, *History of Rome* 10.47. Aesculapius was the god of healing, whose most famous temple was located in Epidaurus in Greece.

22. See Livy, *History of Rome* 29.10–11. Pessinus, in Phrygia, was the site of a temple dedicated to Cybele, also known as the mother of the gods. See also . . . 2.4 and [*City of God, Books 1–10*, 40n6].

23. See . . . 2.14 and [*City of God, Books 1–10*, 50n37].

24. See 2.14 and [*City of God, Books 1–10*, 50n38].

25. See . . . 6.3.

those fewer gods—under whom, in comparison with her worse life to come, she had lived better—thinking them insufficient to support her grandeur.

In the first place, even under the kings (with the exception of Numa Pompilius, of whom I have already spoken above), there was the great evil of all that discord and rivalry, which spawned the murder of Romulus's brother.

————————◆————————

Evils Internal to the Republic: Civil Strife and Civil War

23. But now let us at least mention, as briefly as possible, those evils which were all the more heartrending because they were internal to the republic: civil—or, rather, uncivil—discords, which were no longer mere riots but outright urban wars, in which so much blood was shed and factional strife now raged not by squabbles in the assemblies and voices raised against each other but by the open clash of steel and arms.[26] The Social War, the Servile War, the Civil Wars: how much blood they shed, and how much devastation and desolation they brought to Italy!

Before Latium moved against Rome to start the Social War, all the animals tamed for human use—dogs, horses, asses, oxen, and all the other livestock under human dominion—suddenly turned wild, forgot the gentleness of their domestic ways, left their barns, and roamed at large.[27] They shied away at the approach not only of strangers but even of their own masters—and not without risk of death or danger to anyone bold enough to herd them at close range. If this was a sign, what a great evil it signified, especially when, even if it was not a sign, it was such a great evil in itself! If this had happened in our own times, we would surely find our critics more rabid against us than their animals were against them.[28]

26. [GWL] In this chapter, Augustine transitions from treating Rome's wars with external enemies to treating Rome's internal wars. As he narrates the history, following Sallust (2.18), after the Punic Wars and the fall of Carthage, Rome had no more external enemies. Without anyone outside Rome to fight, the Romans turned on one another. And the violence the Romans inflicted on one another was worse than anything they suffered from outside enemies.

27. See Julius Obsequens, *Book of Prodigies* 54.

28. [GWL] Augustine refers to miraculous stories, non-Christian and Christian, several times in *City of God* (3.31; 14.24; 16.8; 21.4–5; 22.8). In some cases, he seems to believe these events happened. In other cases, he is more skeptical of the stories but still uses them to advance his arguments. Here, Augustine is trying to establish the severity of Rome's internal wars. These wars were so momentous that they were preceded by all the domestic animals suddenly turning

24. The civil disorders began with the disturbances sparked by the agrarian laws of the Gracchi.[29] For the Gracchi wanted to distribute among the people the lands wrongly held by the nobility. To dare to undo a long-standing injustice, however, was dangerous in the extreme; or rather, as the event showed, it was utterly ruinous. Think of all the mourning brought on when the elder Gracchus was killed, and again when the other Gracchus, his brother, was killed not long afterwards! High-born and low-born alike were put to death not by the due exercise of authority under law but in the raw conflict of armed mobs. After the younger Gracchus was slain, the consul Lucius Opimius—who had taken up arms against him in the city and, after defeating and killing him, along with his associates, had slaughtered untold numbers of citizens—held an investigation. He now used the mode of judicial inquiry to go after the younger Gracchus's remaining supporters, and he is reported to have had three thousand men put to death.[30] From the fact that what was supposedly a judicial inquiry produced so many deaths, we can begin to grasp what an enormous number of deaths must have come from the unrestrained clash of the armed mobs themselves. The man who killed Gracchus sold his victim's head to the consul for its weight in gold, in accord with an agreement made prior to the slaughter; and it was in this same slaughter that Marcus Fulvius, a man of consular rank, was killed along with his children.

25. There was, it is true, something elegant about the senate's decree that a temple of Concord be built on the very spot where the deadly tumult took place, where so many citizens of all ranks had fallen, precisely so that a testimony to the punishment of the Gracchi would meet the eyes and prod the memory of those who addressed the assembly. But what else was it except a mockery of the gods to build a temple to the very goddess who, if she had actually been present in the city, would never have let it be brought down, torn to shreds by such vicious dissension? Or perhaps Concord herself was guilty of this crime, because she had abandoned the minds of the citizens, and deserved to be shut up in that temple as if in a prison? For, if they really wanted a shrine in keeping with the events, why did they not rather build

---

wild. If this event truly occurred, it shows that Rome suffered great physical evils before Christ, which proves that the sack of Rome cannot be blamed on the conversion of the Roman empire to Christianity.

29. On the Gracchi see also above at 2.21 and [*City of God, Books 1–10*, 57n63 // above, Book 2n21].

30. See Appian, *Civil War* 1.26.

a temple to Discord there?[31] Is there any reason why Concord should be a
goddess, but not Discord, especially when, following Labeo's distinction,[32]
Concord might be ranked as a good goddess and Discord as an evil goddess?
Labeo noticed that there were temples in Rome both to Fever and to Health,
and he seems to have based his distinction on no more than that. On the
same grounds, then, a temple should have been erected not only to Concord
but also to Discord.

It was to their peril, therefore, that the Romans chose to live under the wrath
of such an evil goddess and forgot that Troy's downfall began precisely when
she took offense. It was because Discord was not invited with the other gods
that she contrived a dispute between three goddesses by setting the golden apple
before them. From this arose the quarrel of the divinities, the victory of Venus,
the abduction of Helen, and the destruction of Troy.[33] Perhaps, then, she was
wildly indignant that she alone of all the gods had not been thought worthy
of a temple in the city of Rome and, for that reason, had thrown the city into
turmoil through those deadly tumults. And just think how much more fiercely
irate she might well have been when she saw a temple erected to her rival on
the very spot where that slaughter took place, that is, on the very spot of her
own handiwork!

When we make fun of these absurdities, those wise and learned Romans
get all upset. But, because they do in fact worship both good and evil gods,
they cannot escape this question concerning Concord and Discord: either they
overlooked the worship of these goddesses and put ahead of them Fever and
Bellona, to whom they built shrines far back in time, or they really did worship the two goddesses, even as Concord left them in the lurch and Discord,
in her rage, led them straight into civil wars.

26. The Romans believed, however, that it was a temple to Concord that
should face speakers in the assembly as a reminder of the death and punishment
of the Gracchi and should serve as a block against further sedition. How much
good it did them, the even worse events to follow show well enough. For, from
that time on, speakers made every effort not to avoid the example of the Gracchi but rather to outdo them at their own game. Lucius Saturninus, the tribune

31. [GWL] Augustine mocks the Romans for having constructed a temple to Concord in a
location that was defined by violent conflict. It would have been more fitting to have a temple to
Discord, who appears in Virgil's *Aeneid* (6.280; 8.702) but otherwise does not figure in Roman
religion. See Walsh, *DCD* 3–4, 212.
32. See . . . 2.11 and . . . 8.13; on Cornelius Labeo see [*City of God, Books 1–10*, 46n26].
33. See Homer, *Iliad* 24; 28–30.

of the people, Gaius Servilius, the praetor, and, much later, Marcus Drusus:[34] all three of these, by their seditions, first sparked bloody riots—which was already serious enough at the time—and then fanned into flame the Social Wars, which inflicted terrible damage on Italy and reduced her to an appalling state of devastation and desolation.[35] Then came the Servile War and the Civil Wars.[36]

What battles were fought, what blood was shed, for the sole purpose of bringing almost all the peoples of Italy into subjection like savage barbarians—and these the very peoples on whom Roman dominion most especially depended for its strength! The writers of history have hardly been able to find a satisfactory way of explaining how the Servile War, begun by a tiny band of gladiators (fewer than seventy, in fact), came to expand to such a vast number of such bitter and ferocious men who went on to defeat so many generals of the Roman people and to devastate so many cities and regions.[37] Nor was this the only Servile War. Earlier, bands of slaves had depopulated the province of Macedonia, and then Sicily and the coast of Italy.[38] Who could find the words to match the magnitude of the events, the sheer horror of the pirates' initial acts of banditry and then the fierce wars they waged?

Civil War: Marius and Sulla

27. Marius[39] already bore the stains of civic blood when, having killed off many from the opposing faction, he was defeated and fled from the city.[40] And the city scarcely had time to catch its breath when, to use Cicero's words, "Cinna,[41] with Marius, later got the upper hand. Then, in truth, the most illustrious men

34. [GWL] Lucius Saturninus served as tribune of the people twice between 103 and 100 BCE. He and Gaius Servilius Glaucia sought various land and citizenship reforms. They were opposed by the senate and assassinated in 100 BCE. Marcus Drusus, tribune of the people from 92 to 91 BCE, also sought reforms and challenged the senate. He was assassinated in 91 BCE, an event that sparked the Social War of 90–88 BCE between the Italians and the Romans.

35. See Appian, Civil War 1.31–38.

36. [GWL] By "Servile War," Augustine is referring to an uprising in 73 BCE by the former gladiator Spartacus (see 4.5). By "Civil Wars," Augustine is referring especially to the conflict between Marius and Sulla, treated in 2.22–24 and 3.27–29. For more context, see essay: "History of the Romans."

37. See Appian, Civil War 1.116–20.

38. See Florus, Epitome of Roman History 2.7 (3.19).

39. On Marius see also . . . 2.22 and [City of God, Books 1–10, 60n73].

40. [GWL] This extended section details the cruelty of Marius and Sulla's war against each other. Augustine's goal is to elicit the reader's horror and persuade the reader of Rome's folly.

41. On Cinna see also . . . 2.22 and [City of God, Books 1–10, 60n74].

were slain, and the lights of the city snuffed out. Sulla[42] afterwards avenged this
ruthless victory; and there is really no need to mention what a loss of citizens
it involved or what a disaster it was for the republic."[43] Speaking of Sulla's vengeance, which was more destructive than if the crimes it punished had been left
to go unpunished, Lucan also says, "The remedy overstepped all measure, and
went much too far, since it was the diseased who guided its hand. The guilty
perished, but by then it was no longer possible for any but the guilty to survive."[44]

In that war between Marius and Sulla—leaving aside those who fell in
battle outside the walls—within the city itself the streets, squares, markets,
theaters, and temples were so full of dead bodies that it was hard to tell at
which point the victors did more killing, whether prior to the victory in order
to achieve it or after the victory because they had achieved it. For as soon as
Marius triumphed and gained his return from exile—leaving aside the general
slaughter perpetrated on all sides—the head of the consul Octavius was put on
display on the speakers' platform in the forum; the Caesars were murdered by
Fimbria in their own homes; the two Crassi, father and son, were killed before
each other's eyes; Baebius and Numitorius died when they were dragged on
hooks and their entrails ripped out; Catulus evaded the hands of his enemies
by drinking poison; and Merula, the flamen of Jupiter, slit his veins and so
poured out an offering to Jupiter of his own blood. And, in addition, anyone
whose greeting Marius refused to acknowledge by extending his right hand
was immediately cut down before his very eyes.[45]

28. Then came Sulla's victory, which certainly avenged all this cruelty but
was purchased at the price of terrible bloodshed among the citizenry. Even
though the war was now over, its antagonisms lived on, and his victory was even
more cruel in peace. Even before Sulla's triumph, after the first and still very
recent butcheries perpetrated by the elder Marius, others even more dire were
added by the younger Marius and Carbo,[46] who belonged to the same faction
as Marius. At Sulla's approach they despaired not only of victory but even of
surviving at all, and they filled the whole area with new butcheries of their own.
For over and above the widespread slaughter spread on all sides, they even laid
siege to the senate, and the senators were led out from the senate house, as if

42. On Sulla see also above at 2.18, 22–24; and [*City of God, Books 1–10*, 54n57 // above,
Book 2n13].
43. *Catiline Conspiracy* 3.
44. *Pharsalia* 2.142–46.
45. See Appian, *Civil War* 1.95–96.
46. On Carbo see also . . . 2.22 and [*City of God, Books 1–10*, 60n75].

from a prison, and put to the sword. Since the Romans hold nothing to be more sacred than the temple of Vesta, the pontiff Mucius Scaevola clung to its very altar, but he was killed all the same, and with his blood he nearly put out the flame which is kept ever burning under the perpetual care of the virgins. Then Sulla entered the city victorious, and in the Villa Publica, not in the course of battle but simply by his command, he had seven thousand men cut down, men who had already surrendered and therefore were certainly unarmed. Now it was no longer war but peace itself that was raging like a savage.

All through the city, any supporter of Sulla struck down anyone he pleased. The deaths were beyond counting, until someone finally suggested to Sulla that a few ought to be allowed to live, so that there would be some people left for the victors to rule. Then the furious license to kill—which was spreading here, there, and everywhere—was restrained, and to great thanksgiving that notorious list was published which named two thousand men from the highest ranks (that is, from the equestrian and senatorial orders) who were to be killed and proscribed.[47] There was grief at the number on the list, but consolation in the limit it put on those to be killed, and the sorrow that so many were to die was overshadowed by the joy that the rest had nothing to fear. But, in the case of some of those condemned to die, even the stone-hearted security of the rest cringed in pity at the exquisite ways in which their deaths were contrived. One man was torn to pieces by the bare hands of his executioners, using no weapon—men tearing at a living man more brutally than beasts usually tear at dead meat left out for them! Another had his eyes gouged out and his limbs cut off one by one, and so was forced to end his lingering life—or, rather, his lingering death—in unspeakable tortures. Certain illustrious cities were auctioned off as if they were so many country estates, and one was sentenced to be executed whole, as if a single criminal were being sentenced to death. All this was done in peacetime, after the war was over, and done not to gain victory more quickly but simply to keep the victory gained from being regarded too lightly. Peace vied with war in cruelty, and peace won! War struck down the armed, but peace the unarmed. War allowed those who were being struck to strike back if they could, but peace did not allow those who survived to live but only to die without fighting back at all.[48]

47. See Appian, *Civil War* 1.95–96.
48. [GWL] The last sentences of this paragraph display Augustine's rhetorical gifts and his polemical sarcasm. Marius and Sulla's civil war occurred during a time of "peace," after Rome's victory in the Punic Wars. Yet this peace was more violent than the time of war.

29. Is there any fury of foreign nations or any savagery on the part of barbarians that can be compared to this victory of citizens over fellow-citizens?[49] Which was the more deadly, the more hideous, the more heart-rending for Rome to see: the incursion of the Gauls long ago and the more recent incursion of the Goths,[50] or the sheer ferocity of Marius and Sulla and other distinguished men in their factions? It was as if Rome's own bright eyes were on a rampage against her own limbs. The Gauls, it is true, murdered any senator they could find anywhere in the city outside of the stronghold of the Capitol, which was the only place that was defended anyway. But at least they sold life in exchange for gold to those who had dug themselves in on that hill—despite the fact that they could certainly have drained their life away by siege, even though they were unable to snatch it away at one blow of the sword. And the Goths, in fact, spared so many senators that the wonder is that they killed any at all.

In contrast, Sulla set himself up as victor, while Marius still lived, in the very Capitol that had remained safe from the Gauls. It was from there that he issued his murderous decrees; and when Marius escaped by fleeing (though he would shortly return even more ferocious and bloodthirsty), Sulla in the Capitol deprived many persons of life and property, even making use of senatorial decrees to do so. Then, in Sulla's absence, was there anything Marius's faction regarded as sacred or to be spared? They did not even spare Mucius, a citizen, senator, and pontiff, clinging piteously to the very altar where, so they say, the fate of Rome resides. And lastly, to say nothing of countless other deaths, Sulla's final list of proscriptions put more senators to death than the Goths were even able to plunder.

30. How can people be so shameless, then, so rash, so impudent, so foolish—or, rather, so utterly mad—that they do not blame their own gods for all these past evils, and yet do blame our Christ for any present evils?[51] Those ruthless civil wars, as their own authors admit, were more bitter than all their foreign wars, and they are judged not merely to have distressed the republic but to have entirely destroyed it. But they began long before the coming of Christ, and, by a chain of criminal causes, they led from the wars of Marius and Sulla

49. [GWL] Augustine develops his point that the Romans inflicted worse damage on one another than they suffered from external enemies.

50. Augustine is referring here to the sack of Rome in 410 that led to the writing of *City of God.*

51. [GWL] A reiteration of Augustine's thesis in Book 3. The Romans blame Christianity for the sack of Rome without acknowledging the severe disasters, including civil wars, that they suffered before Christ.

to the wars of Sertorius and Cataline (the former proscribed by Sulla, the latter nurtured by him), then to the war of Lepidus and Catulus (of whom the one desired to rescind, the other to defend the enactments of Sulla), and then to the wars of Pompey and Caesar (Pompey had been a partisan of Sulla and had equaled or even exceeded his power; Caesar could not bear Pompey's power, but only because he did not have it himself, and yet, after Pompey was defeated and killed, he surpassed it). And finally they led to another Caesar, afterwards called Augustus, during whose reign Christ was born.

Civil Wars in the Time of Augustus

For Augustus himself also waged civil wars with a number of enemies, and in those wars, too, many distinguished men perished, including Cicero, articulate and skilled as he was in the art of governing a republic.[52] It is true that Gaius Caesar, the one who defeated Pompey, showed genuine clemency in exercising his victorious powers and granted both life and civic honors to his opponents. But a conspiracy made up of certain noble senators, claiming to act in defense of the liberty of the republic, murdered him in the very senate house itself on the grounds that what he really wanted was to be king. Then Antony, a man of very different moral character, stained and corrupted by every vice, was seen to be striving for Caesar's power; and Cicero fiercely resisted him in the name of that same liberty of the homeland. At this point there emerged a young man of extraordinary qualities, that other Caesar, the adopted son of Gaius Caesar, who, as I said, was afterwards called Augustus. This young Caesar was favored by Cicero in order that his power might be nurtured against Antony. What Cicero hoped was that, once Antony's dominance had been repulsed and suppressed, this Caesar would restore the republic's liberty—which shows how blind and how incapable of foreseeing the future Cicero was! For that young man, the very one whose career and power Cicero had been promoting, permitted Cicero himself to be slain by Antony under the provisions of a kind of pact of alliance with the latter, and he brought firmly under his own rule the very liberty of the republic for which Cicero had spoken out so forcefully.

---

52. [GWL] Augustine's treatment of Augustus Caesar concentrates on Augustus's wars against other Romans, including his role in the assassination of Cicero. These themes contrast with common depictions of Augustus as the emperor who brought peace and unity around the Mediterranean. See Clark, *Comm. 1–5*, 129.

31. So then, let those who are ungrateful to Christ for his great benefits blame their own gods for these great evils. It is beyond doubt that, when these evils took place, the divinities' altars were "warm with Sabean incense and fragrant with fresh garlands,"[53] their priesthoods were honored, their shrines were resplendent, their sacrifices were made, their games were held, there were frenzies in their temples—and all this at a time when the blood of so many citizens was being shed everywhere by citizens, not just in other places but even in the midst of the very altars of the gods. Cicero did not choose to flee to a temple, because Mucius had already found that it did no good to make that choice. But those who, with much less reason, now hurl abuse at these Christian times either fled on their own to places most especially dedicated to Christ or were even led to those places by the barbarians themselves, in order to save their lives.

These Evils All Occurred Prior to Christianity, When the Gods Were Still Worshiped

Now—omitting the many other instances I have already cited, as well as the many more I decided it would take too long to relate—I am certain of one thing, and anyone who judges impartially will readily acknowledge the point: if the human race had received the teaching of Christ prior to the Punic Wars, and if a vast devastation had followed, such as that which afflicted Europe and Africa in those wars, there is not one of those who now berate us who would have blamed those evils on anything but the Christian religion. And their outcries would have been all the more intolerable if—speaking only of what pertains to the Romans—the reception and spread of the Christian religion had come before the invasion of the Gauls, or the flooding of the Tiber, or the fires that laid waste to Rome, or the worst evil of all, the Civil Wars.

There were other evils as well, evils so incredible when they occurred that they were counted as prodigies. And if these had happened in Christian times, who would have been blamed for them, as if they were crimes, but the Christian people? I say nothing of those prodigies that were more surprising than harmful: oxen speaking, unborn infants crying out certain words from their mothers' wombs, snakes flying, women turned into men or hens into roosters, and other things of this sort which are recorded in their works, not of fable

53. Virgil, *Aeneid* 1.416–17.

but of history.[54] Whether true or false, such things inflict no harm on human beings; they only evoke astonishment. But when it rained earth, when it rained chalk, when it rained stones (not what we call hailstones, but real stones),[55] these things were certainly able to do serious damage. We have read in their books that the fires of Etna, flowing down from the peak of the mountain to the nearby shore, brought the sea to such a boil that rocks were burned and the pitch melted in ships.[56] And this was clearly more than a little harmful, however incredible and astonishing it was. Again, they write that in the same surge of flame Sicily was buried under such an enormous quantity of ash that the houses of the city of Catana were crushed to ruins under its weight, and the Romans, moved to pity by the disaster, reduced the city's tribute for that year.[57] They also record that in Africa, which was by then a Roman province, there was a swarm of locusts so vast that it was like a prodigy; and once the swarm had consumed all the fruit and leaves of the trees, so they say, it was hurled into the sea in one huge and measureless cloud. When the dead locusts were cast back up on the shore and the air was polluted with them, such a pestilence broke out that in the kingdom of Masinissa alone eight hundred thousand people are said to have perished, and many more in the nearby coastal districts.[58] Of the thirty thousand troops in Utica at the time, they claim that only ten thousand survived.

The kind of nonsense we are faced with, and to which we are forced to reply, would certainly blame all these evils, without exception, on the Christian religion, if it saw them in Christian times. And yet they do not blame such things on their own gods; rather they demand that their gods be worshiped for the sake of escaping the lesser evils of the present, despite the incontrovertible fact that those who used to worship them suffered these far greater evils in the past.

54. [GWL] In the Roman context, "prodigy" referred to an aberration from nature that signaled the anger of the gods. Augustine does not necessarily believe that these incidents occurred. His purpose is to note their presence in Roman literature. These incidents demonstrate the inconsistency of the Romans blaming Christians for the sack of Rome and not blaming the gods for disasters before Christ. See 3.23.

NCP: "Augustine has probably collected these examples of strange but harmless occurrences from a variety of sources, perhaps including hearsay; they and the ones that are mentioned in the next few lines, which had fatal consequences, anticipate the lists of oddities that appear . . . at 14.24 and 21.4–5."

55. See Livy, *History of Rome* 27.37.

56. See Julius Obsequens, *Book of Prodigies* 29.

57. See Julius Obsequens, *Book of Prodigies* 32.

58. See Julius Obsequens, *Book of Prodigies* 30.

Book 4

1–8, 14–16

Together, Books 4 and 5 concentrate on one issue: why God allowed the Romans to expand as an empire and what this had to do with their moral qualities. Before Augustine answers this question in Book 5, he treats a preliminary matter in Book 4—namely, the impossibility of attributing the expansion of Rome's empire to the gods. After introductory chapters (4.1–2), Augustine discusses the general topic of empire, arguing that the size of a people does not establish its happiness (4.3–7). This section includes Augustine's famous remark likening a kingdom without justice to a band of robbers (4.4). It also includes an important but often neglected discussion of Assyria, the first major empire, and Ninus, the first king to conduct war for the sake of securing more territory (4.6). Ninus's rule over Assyria represents the beginning of empires. In the central section of Book 4, Augustine challenges the attribution of Rome's empire to the gods (4.8–32). He stresses the absurdity of Roman religion, especially with the existence of the goddess Felicity (or "happiness"), who rendered the other gods unnecessary (4.18–25). The arguments in this section castigate the pursuit of temporal benefits over virtue; the proliferation of gods reflects the lust for earthly goods. The concluding chapters of Book 4 assert God's rule over all kingdoms (4.33–34).

1. When I set out to speak of the city of God, I thought that I should first reply to its enemies. In their pursuit of earthly joys and their insatiable longing for fleeting goods, these people cry out against the Christian religion, the

117

one true and saving religion, for any sorrows that they suffer on this score. Yet those sorrows come upon them not from God's severity, punishing them, but rather from God's mercy, admonishing them.

Among these enemies of ours, there is the great mass of the uneducated, who are all the more inflamed to hate us by what they suppose is the authority of the learned.[1] In their ignorance, they imagine that the happenings of their own times are quite extraordinary and never occurred before in other eras in the past, and they are encouraged in this view by those who know it to be false but keep their knowledge hidden in order to make it seem that they have good reason to complain about us. It was necessary, therefore, to demonstrate that the truth of the matter is very different from what they think, and to show this from the very books which their own authors wrote to present us with the history of times past. At the same time, it was necessary to make it clear that the false gods whom these people used to worship openly and still worship secretly[2] are nothing but unclean spirits, wholly malignant and utterly deceitful demons, so much so that they delight in crimes—crimes real or crimes imagined, but in either case their own crimes—which they wanted to have celebrated for them at their festivals. What they wanted was to make it impossible for human weakness to be restrained from committing abominable deeds due to the fact that imitating such acts has the support of a supposedly divine authority.

It was not on the basis of my own conjectures that I proved all this. Rather I drew partly on recent memory—for I myself have seen performances of this kind put on for such divinities as these[3]—and partly on the writings of authors who left descriptions of these matters for posterity, not as a reproach to their gods but rather in their honor. Varro, who is reckoned among them as a most learned man and a supreme authority, is an example.[4] He wrote separate books on things human and things divine, assigning some books to things human and others to things divine, according to the dignity of the topic in each case, and he placed the theatrical shows not among things human but among things divine (although, if there had been only good and honorable

1. [GWL] Augustine repeatedly critiques Roman elites for misleading the masses against the Christians. For references to this theme, see essay: "Roman Religion."

2. The gods were being worshiped secretly presumably because paganism had been effectively outlawed by an imperial edict issued in 391. See *Codex Theodosianus* 16.10.10.

3. See *Confessions* 1.19.30; 4.1.1.

4. [GWL] On Varro, see note 4 on Book 19, below. NCP: "Augustine is referring here to his vast work *Human and Divine Antiquities*, which contained several books on the theater."

men in the city, the theatrical shows ought not even to have had a place among things human!). Varro certainly did not do this on his own authority but rather because, himself born and raised in Rome, he found these shows already ranked as things divine.

At the end of the first book I briefly set out the points to be discussed next.[5] In the second and third books I discussed some of these, and I recognize that I must now meet my readers' expectations by taking up the rest.

2. I had promised, then, that I would say something in response to those who blame our religion for the disasters of the Roman republic and that I would recount the evils, as many as might occur to me or as might seem sufficient for the purpose, which the city of Rome, or the provinces belonging to her empire, suffered before their sacrifices were banned. All of which evils, no doubt, the Romans would have blamed on us, if our religion had already shone its light on them at that time or had already put an end to their sacrilegious rites!

These points, I would judge, I have adequately addressed in the second and third books. In the second I dealt with moral evils, which we ought to regard as the only true evils, or certainly as the greatest evils; and in the third I dealt with those evils which are the only ones that fools dread to suffer, namely, evils of the body and of external affairs, evils which good people often suffer as well. For our opponents accept moral evils not just patiently but even with pleasure, despite the fact that these are the evils by which they themselves are made evil.

And yet what a small number of episodes I took from the history of that one city and her empire! I have not even given a full account down to Caesar Augustus.[6] What if I had wanted to recount and to stress not the evils that people do to each other, such as the devastation and destruction of war, but rather the evils that happen in earthly affairs due to the elements of the universe itself![7] Apuleius touches briefly on these in a passage in the book he wrote on the universe.[8] He states that all earthly things are subject to change,

5. [GWL] A reference to 1.36.

6. Caesar Augustus ruled as emperor from 27 BCE to 14 CE.

7. [GWL] Though Book 3 generally concerned physical disasters that Rome experienced before Christ, Augustine concentrated on wars and other evils inflicted by humans on other humans. He did not attend as much to disasters without a human cause, or what philosophers today call "natural evil." For Augustine, both evils inflicted by humans on other humans and so-called natural evils fall under God's providence. See essay: "Providence and Suffering."

8. Apuleius (125–180 CE), better known as the author of *The Golden Ass*, was also the translator of a work, *The Universe* (*De mundo*), falsely attributed to Aristotle. Augustine was among those who considered Apuleius its author.

alteration, and annihilation. For he declares, to use his own words, "in massive tremors of the earth, the ground has burst open and cities have been wiped out with their inhabitants; whole regions have been washed away by sudden cloudbursts; some areas, once part of the mainland, have become islands due to the intrusion of strange floods; and others, once islands, have become accessible by foot due to the receding of the sea; cities have been overthrown by wind and storm; fires have flashed out from the clouds, by which regions of the east have been set aflame and have perished; and, in western lands, certain gushings-up and inundations have brought the same devastation: thus rivers of fire, kindled by the gods, once overflowed from the craters at Etna's peak and ran down the slopes like torrents."[9] If I had wanted to collect historical examples of this kind from wherever I could, when would I ever have finished? And these all happened in periods before the name of Christ had suppressed any of those empty rites of theirs, with all their danger to true salvation.

The Basis for Rome's Expansion

I had also promised that I would show what the morals of the Romans were, and why the true God, who holds all kingdoms in his power, deigned to help them increase their empire—and to show, as well, how little help they got from those whom they count as gods, and how much harm these gods actually did by their trickery and deceit.[10] I see, then, that I must now discuss these points, and especially the growth of the Roman empire. For I have already spoken at length, especially in the second book, of the deadly deceit of the demons, whom they used to worship as gods, and of how much evil they brought into Roman morality. At the same time, in all three of the books now complete I have made clear, whenever the occasion arose, how much

---

9. *Universe* 34.

10. [GWL] This is the topic of both Books 4 and 5, though Augustine's argument is somewhat difficult to track. In 4.3–7, Augustine challenges the Romans' pride in the size of their empire. In 4.8–32, Augustine says the gods were not responsible for the expansion of the empire. He concludes this discussion in 4.33–34 by confessing God as the source of happiness and the ruler of history. In 5.1–10, Augustine says fate cannot account for the expansion of the empire. He concludes this discussion in 5.11 with another affirmation of God's sovereignty over all things. Finally, in 5.12–20 Augustine explains why God allowed the expansion of the empire, concentrating on the Romans' lust for glory. This vice motivated the Romans to display false virtue—which, though false, still benefited those under Roman rule. The last section, 5.21–26, expands on God's sovereignty by treating the rise and fall of emperors. This section includes a discussion on what it means for an emperor to be blessed.

solace God has granted to good and evil alike, even in the midst of war's terrible evils, through the name of Christ, which the barbarians honored so fully, beyond all the customs of war. It is in this way that God *makes his sun rise on both the good and the evil, and sends rain on both the just and the unjust* (Matt. 5:45).[11]

3. Let us now see, then, how it is that they dare to give the credit for the wide expanse and long duration of the Roman empire to those gods whom they claim to have worshiped with honor, despite the fact that their service consisted of the offering of abhorrent shows and the ministry of abhorrent men.

The Evaluation of Empire

First, however, I would like briefly to consider this question: what reason or sense is there in wanting to boast of the size and expanse of an empire when you cannot show that its people are happy?[12] Or why boast of an empire if its people always dwell in the midst of the disasters of war and the spilling of blood—the blood of fellow-citizens or the blood of foreign enemies, but, in either case, human blood—and always live under the dark shadow of fear and in the lust for blood? Any joy they have may be compared to the fragile brilliance of glass: there is always the terrible fear that it will suddenly be shattered.

It will be easier to reach a decision on this point if we are not carried away by empty bombast and do not let the sharp edge of our inquiry be blunted by high-sounding terms when we hear of "peoples," "kingdoms," and "provinces."[13] Instead, let us imagine two individuals, for single individuals, like single letters in a word, are the elements, so to speak, of which a city or a kingdom is made up, no matter how broad the territory it occupies. Let us suppose that one of these two individuals is poor, or rather of moderate means, and the other very rich. But the rich man is tortured by fears, wasted with griefs, aflame with greed, never free from care, always

11. [GWL] Augustine is probably alluding to his discussion of suffering in 1.8–9.

12. [GWL] By definition, empires are large nations. Augustine questions whether nations should seek to expand. What matters is not the size of a nation but its moral character.

13. [GWL] To challenge the grandeur associated with empire, Augustine compares nations to individuals. An individual of moderate means is happier than an individual of great means. So also, nations of moderate means are happier than nations of great means. For similar remarks, see 3.10 and 4.15.

restless and uneasy, out of breath from unending struggles with his enemies. It is true enough that he increases his holdings beyond measure by going through these miseries; but at the same time, thanks to that very increase, he also multiplies his bitter cares. In contrast, the individual of moderate means is satisfied with his small and limited property; he is loved by family and friends; he enjoys sweet peace with his relations, neighbors, and friends; he is devout in his piety, benevolent of mind, sound of body, moderate in his style of life, unblemished in character, and untroubled in conscience. I do not know whether anyone would be so foolish as to have any doubt about which of the two to prefer.[14] It is the same with two families, two peoples, or two kingdoms, as it is with the two individuals. The same rule of equanimity applies. If we are vigilant in using it and make it the rule for our inquiry, we shall have no difficulty in seeing where happiness lies, and where hollow show.

Therefore, if the true God is worshiped and is served with authentic rites and good morals, it is beneficial that good persons should rule far and wide and for a long time; and this is beneficial not so much for the good persons themselves as for those over whom they rule.[15] For as far as they themselves are concerned, their piety and integrity, which are great gifts from God, are enough to bring them the true happiness by which this life is lived well and, thereafter, eternal life is attained. On this earth, then, the reign of the good is not so much of profit to themselves as it is to human society at large. In contrast, the reign of the wicked does harm rather to those who are the rulers.[16] They devastate their own souls due to the wider scope they have for their wickedness, while those placed under them in servitude are not harmed at all,

14. Citing the advantages of poverty vis-à-vis wealth is a romantic notion not uncommon in ancient thought, both pagan and Christian. See, e.g., Lucan, *Pharsalia* 5.527–67; Ambrose, *Hexaemeron* 6.8.52. Augustine initially posits a poor individual but, more reasonably, immediately changes his mind in favor of one of moderate means.

15. [GWL] Augustine believes it is better for all citizens, Christian and non-Christian, if Christians exercise political power. A Christian ruler will exhibit good character, leaven justice with mercy, and destroy false religion, which oppresses the populace. (For similar remarks, see 5.19 and 5.24–26.) Augustine's affirmation of Christians in political power reflects the aftermath of Constantine's conversion to Christianity and Theodosius's establishment of Nicene Christianity as the official religion of the empire. It is difficult to know whether or how Augustine's position on this topic could be appropriated in modern contexts.

16. [GWL] Similar to his treatment of suffering in Book 1, Augustine argues that external harms cannot damage a person so long as they remain virtuous. A wicked ruler is of no consequence to the righteous. Someone legally enslaved can be internally free, while someone legally free can be enslaved to vice. Augustine's argument resonates with Stoic themes (Seneca, *Letter* 47.17), even as it cites 2 Pet. 2:19 and echoes Rom. 6–7. See Clark, *Comm. 1–5*, 184.

except by their own iniquity.[17] Thus the good person is free, even if a slave, and the evil person is enslaved, even if a ruler—enslaved not to one master but, what is far worse, to as many masters as he has vices. It is in reference to these vices that Scripture says, *For people are slaves to whatever masters them* (2 Pet. 2:19).

4. Remove justice, then, and what are kingdoms but large gangs of robbers? And what are gangs of robbers but small kingdoms?[18] The gang, too, is a group of men ruled by a leader's command. It is bound together by a pact of association, and its loot is divided according to an agreed law. If, by constantly adding desperate men, this scourge grows to such an extent that it acquires territory, establishes a home base, occupies cities, and subjugates peoples, it more openly assumes the name of kingdom, a name now publicly conferred on it due not to any reduction in greed but rather to the addition of impunity. For it was a witty and true response that a certain captured pirate made to the famous Alexander the Great. When the king asked the man what he meant by infesting the sea, he defiantly replied, "Just what you mean when you infest the whole world! But because I do it with one tiny ship, I am called a robber; and because you do it with a great fleet, you are called an emperor."[19]

5. I will not ask here what sort of people Romulus gathered together. For, in their case, great care was taken to make sure that, when they left their former way of life and were given a place in the city's community, they would no longer be concerned about the punishments due to them, fear of which was driving them to still greater crimes, so that in the future they would be more peaceful members of society.

The Revolt of the Gladiators

But I do say this—that the Roman empire, when it was already great and had subjugated many peoples and was feared by the rest, was bitterly distressed and greatly alarmed and had no small difficulty in avoiding a major

17. That the good are not hurt by the actions of the wicked is the argument presented at length . . . at 1.10–29.

18. [GWL] One of the most quoted passages in *City of God*. The size of a nation is irrelevant to its worth. An empire without justice is like a band of robbers on a giant scale. The same moral standards govern both large and small communities.

19. See Cicero, *Republic* 3.24. Alexander the Great lived from 356 to 323 BCE; he is referred to as Alexander of Macedon, where he was born, below at 4.7.

catastrophe, when a tiny band of gladiators escaped from their training camp in Campania, gathered a large army, appointed three generals, and savagely laid waste to the whole length and breadth of Italy.[20] So, let them tell us which god it was that helped those men to rise from a small and contemptible gang of robbers into a kingdom which the Romans, for all their forts and forces, still had to fear. Or are they going to deny that the gladiators received divine aid on the grounds that they did not last very long? As if anyone's life lasted all that long! By that reasoning, the gods help no one to rule, for each individual soon dies, and we should not count anything a benefit which vanishes in an instant, like a puff of smoke,[21] for each individual—and so, one by one, for all men together. After all, what does it matter to those who worshiped the gods under Romulus and died long ago that the Roman empire subsequently grew to such vast proportions? Those people are now busy pleading their causes before the gods of the underworld (whether those causes are good or bad is not relevant to the present argument). What we must understand, however, is that the same point applies to all who, in the scant span of their lives, have passed briefly and swiftly through even the imperial office itself, carrying with them the heavy burden of their own deeds (even though the empire itself extends out through great stretches of time, as one generation of mortals dies and another succeeds it).

But if even those benefits which last for only the briefest time are to be ascribed to the gods, then those gladiators clearly received no little help. They broke the chains of their servile condition; they escaped; they evaded their pursuers; they gathered a large and exceedingly strong army; and, in their obedience to the plans and orders of their kings, they struck fear into the lofty power of Rome. They proved invincible to a number of Roman generals; they seized much plunder; they gained many victories; they took their pleasure where they would; what desire suggested, they did; and, in short, they lived like kings until their eventual defeat, which was only achieved with the greatest difficulty. But let us come to matters of more import.

20. [GWL] This insurrection was led by the general Spartacus and his lieutenants, Oenomaus and Crixus, in 73–71 BCE. It is the Servile War Augustine mentioned in 3.26. By treating it here, Augustine illustrates how a band of robbers can retain immoral character even as it expands to become a kingdom. He also mocks the attribution of earthly blessing to the gods, who in this case would have favored insurrectionists over the Romans.

21. See Pss. 37:20; 102:3.

The Gods and the Rise and Fall of Assyrian Rule

6. Justinus, who followed Trogus Pompeius[22] in writing Greek or rather foreign history not only in Latin, as Trogus did, but also in abbreviated form, begins his work in this way: "At the beginning of the history of tribes and nations, power was in the hands of kings, who rose to this peak of authority not by courting popular support but because their moderation was recognized among good men. The peoples were not kept in check by any laws; it was the custom to defend rather than to extend the boundaries of one's rule; and kingdoms were confined each within the limits of its own homeland. Ninus,[23] king of the Assyrians, was the first to change the ancient and, as it were, ancestral custom of the peoples due to his novel lust for empire. He was the first to make war on his neighbors; and, subduing peoples still untrained to resist, he extended his rule all the way to the borders of Libya."[24] And a little later Justinus says, "Ninus secured the vast dominions he had won by constantly adding to them. Thus, strengthened by the new forces he gained from subjugating his neighbors, he went on to attack others, and each new victory became the instrument of the next until he subdued all the peoples of the east."[25]

Now, whether or not Justinus or Trogus wrote reliable accounts (for other more trustworthy accounts show that they lied about some matters), it is agreed among other writers that Ninus extended the kingdom of the Assyrians far and wide.[26] And the Assyrian kingdom lasted so long that the Roman empire has not yet reached the same age. For those who have studied the chronology of history write that, starting from the first year of Ninus's reign, it endured for 1240 years until it passed to the Medes. But to make war on one's neighbors, to go on from there to further attacks, to crush and

22. Marcus Junianus Justinus was a third-century CE historian, while Pompeius Trogus wrote in the early first century CE. Trogus's history has not survived except in the abbreviated form produced by Justinus.

23. [GWL] This reference to Ninus is important for Augustine's narration of empires. Relying on Eusebius's *Chronicle* (see essay: "Eusebius's *Chronicle*"), Augustine identifies Ninus as the first ruler to pursue war for the sake of gaining territory and not just for self-defense (16.3, 10, 17; 18.2, 22). Ninus was the founder of Nineveh and the progenitor of the Assyrian empire, which Augustine often pairs with Rome as the two dominant nations of human history. The Assyrian empire was eastern, earlier, and lasted longer than the Roman empire had at the time of Augustine's writing. The Roman empire was western and followed the Assyrian empire. Empire is the political expression of the earthly city.

24. Justinus, *Epitome of the Philippic History of Pompeius Trogus* 1.1.

25. Justinus, *Epitome of the Philippic History of Pompeius Trogus* 1.1.

26. See Diodorus Siculus, *Library of History* 2.1–2.

subjugate peoples without provocation, all out of mere lust for dominion—
what else are we to call this but armed robbery on a grand scale?[27]

7. And if this Assyrian kingdom became so large and lasted so long without the help of the gods, why is it that the wide extent and lengthy duration
of Rome's rule are ascribed to the Roman gods? Whatever caused the one is
surely also the cause of the other. But if people claim that the Assyrian success is, in fact, to be ascribed to the gods' help, then I ask, which gods? For
the other nations that Ninus subdued and subjugated did not then worship
other gods. Or if the Assyrians did have special gods of their own—who were
more highly skilled, as it were, in building and maintaining an empire—had
these gods died when the Assyrians lost their empire? Or did they prefer to
go over to the Medes because their back wages had not been paid, or because
they had the promise of higher pay? And then on to the Persians, when Cyrus
enticed them with the promise of a still better deal?[28] The Persians, after all,
ever since the very large but very brief kingdom of Alexander of Macedon,
have maintained their rule right down to the present over no inconsiderable
territory in the east.

If this is true, either the gods are faithless, abandoning their own people
and going over to the enemy, something that even the man Camillus did not
do when, after storming and taking a city which was a bitter enemy, he felt the
sting of Rome's ingratitude, the very Rome for which he had won the victory;
instead he later forgot the wrong done to him and, with only his homeland
in mind, saved it a second time from the Gauls.[29] Or else the gods are not as
strong as gods ought to be, if they can be defeated by mere human plans or
mere human strength. Or if, perhaps, when the gods wage war against each
other, they are defeated not by human beings but by other gods who are
the special gods of specific cities, then they obviously have enmities among
themselves, which each takes up on behalf of his own faction. And it follows
that no city should worship its own gods more than others, from whom its
own gods might receive aid and support.

Finally, whatever may or may not be true about this transfer or flight or
migration or desertion in battle on the part of the gods, it is certainly true
that the name of Christ had not yet been preached in those eras or in those

27. [GWL] An allusion to 4.4: "Remove justice, then, and what are kingdoms but large gangs
of robbers? And what are gangs of robbers but small kingdoms?"
28. Cyrus the Great ruled Persia for about thirty years and died in 530 BCE.
29. See . . . 3.17.

regions of the earth when those kingdoms were lost through incalculable military disasters and passed into other hands. For if, when their kingdom was taken from the Assyrians after more than twelve hundred years, the Christian religion had already been proclaiming another eternal kingdom and had already put an end to the sacrilegious worship of false gods, what would the foolish people of that nation have said? What else but that a kingdom which had endured so long could only have perished for one reason: because it had abandoned its own cults and embraced Christianity! Our opponents should see themselves mirrored in that foolish claim (which, after all, might well have been made), and, if there is any shame in them, they should be too embarrassed to make similar complaints of their own.

The Roman empire, however, is simply afflicted, not changed into something else. The same thing has happened to it in other eras, before Christ's name was proclaimed, and it has recovered from such affliction. There is no need, then, to despair of recovery now. For who knows God's will in this regard?[30]

Which of the Gods Aided the Expansion of Rome?

8. Next let us ask, if you like, which god or which gods, from the whole throng that the Romans worshiped, they believe did the most to extend and preserve their empire.[31] For they obviously do not dare to ascribe any part in a work of such grandeur and so replete with nobility to Cloacina, or to Volupia, who gets her name from pleasure, or to Lubentina, whose name comes from lust, or to Vaticanus, who presides over the wails of infants, or to Cunina, who

30. The relevant note in Bibliothèque Augustinienne 33.550 cites 2.29 . . . and makes the observation that "Saint Augustine cannot prevent himself from believing, like his contemporaries, in the eternity of the empire." The section cited, however, cannot be used to show that Augustine so much as hoped for, never mind believed in, the eternity of the empire; in fact it clearly contrasts earthly Rome with heavenly eternity. When Augustine says, "For who knows God's will in this regard?" he is not holding out any hope for the eternity of Rome but rather pointing to the inscrutability of God's judgment, which is an ongoing theme of his. See, e.g., . . . 3.1 ("the most hidden and most just judgment of God"), . . . 4.17 ("his purpose may be hidden, but it can never be unjust"), and 21.13 ("his just, if hidden, judgment").

31. [GWL] Here begins Augustine's extended critique of the gods, which challenges the incoherence of Roman religion and the frivolity of the gods it incorporated. Many of the gods named in this section are obscure. Some are known only through *City of God*. It is not necessary to know much about them to grasp Augustine's general argument. NCP: "The following chapters are reminiscent of Tertullian, *Apology* 25 and, much more extensively, of Arnobius, *Against the Nations* 4."

looks after their cradles.[32] But how can I possibly list the names of all their gods and goddesses in just one passage of this book? They themselves were hardly able to include them all in the huge volumes in which they marked out the specific responsibilities and individual areas of all their divinities. They did not think that responsibility for the land should be entrusted to just one god. Rather they assigned rural areas to the goddess Rusina and mountain ridges to the god Jugatinus, and they put the goddess Collatina in charge of hills and Vallonia in charge of valleys.[33]

They could not even find one single Segetia to whom they would entrust the corn once and for all. Rather they wanted the goddess Seia in charge as long as the seed-corn was still under the ground, and the goddess Segetia in charge once the shoots began to sprout and to form corn; and when the corn had been harvested and stored away, they set the goddess Tutilina over it to keep it safe.[34] Who would not have thought that just the one Segetia would suffice, just so long as the corn actually made it all the way from the initial grassy shoots to the final stored, dry ear? But one was not enough for people who so loved a multitude of gods that each wretched soul spurned the pure embrace of the one true God and prostituted itself with a throng of demons. Therefore, they put Proserpina in charge of the germinating seeds, the god Nodutus in charge of the knots and nodes of the stems, the goddess Volutina in charge of the coverings of the follicles, and the goddess Patelana in charge when the follicles open so that the ears may emerge.[35] When the corn stood level in the field, with new ears, they put the goddess Hostilina in charge (since the ancients' word for "make level" was *hostire*); when the corn was in flower, the goddess Flora; when it was milky, the god Lacturnus; when it ripened, the goddess Matuta; and when it was reaped, that is, taken from the field, the goddess Rucina.[36]

---

32. Cloacina, from *cloaca*, meaning "sewer"; Volupia, from *voluptas*, meaning "pleasure"; Lubentina, from *libido*, meaning "lust"; Vaticanus, from *vagitus*, meaning "wailing"; Cunina, from *cuna*, meaning "cradle."

33. Rusina, from *rus*, meaning "rural area"; Jugatinus, from *jugum*, meaning "mountain ridge"; Collatina, from *collis*, meaning "hill"; Vallonia, from *valles*, meaning "valley."

34. Segetia, from *seges*, meaning "corn"; Seia, from *sata*, meaning "seed corn"; Tutilina, from *tutum*, meaning "safe."

35. Proserpina, from *proserpere*, meaning "to come forth imperceptibly"; Nodutus, from *nodus*, meaning "node" or "knot"; Volutina, from *involumenta*, meaning "coverings"; Patelana, from *patescere*, meaning "to open." Of these divinities, Proserpina, or Persephone, the daughter of Jupiter and Ceres, was a major and universally respected figure.

36. Hostilina, from *hostire*, meaning "to level"; Flora, from *flora*, meaning "flower"; Lacturnus, from *lactosus*, meaning "milky"; Matuta, from *maturescere*, meaning "to ripen"; Rucina, from *runcare*, meaning "to reap."

I do not mention them all, for the whole business bores me, despite the fact that it does not make the Romans ashamed. The very few instances I have listed, however, should make it clear that they certainly do not venture to claim that these were the divinities that established, increased, and preserved the Roman empire. Each of these deities was so involved with his particular duties that nothing was assigned as a whole to any one of them. How, then, could Segetia care for the empire? She was not even allowed to take care of corn and trees at the same time. How could Cunina think about weaponry? Her oversight of infants was not permitted to go beyond their cradles. How could Nodutus help in war? He was not even concerned with the follicle of the ear, but only with the node of the stalk. Everyone appoints a single doorkeeper for his house, and, because the doorkeeper is a man, that is quite enough. But the Romans appointed three gods for the task: Forculus for the doors, Cardea for the hinges, and Limentinus for the threshold.[37] Forculus, no doubt, was simply incapable of guarding the hinges and threshold at the same time as the door!

◆

Victory, Just War, and Foreign Iniquity

14. In this regard, I first ask why the empire itself is not one of the gods. Why should empire not be a god, if Victory is a goddess? For that matter, what need is there for Jupiter to be involved, if Victory is favorable and propitious and always goes to those whom she wishes to be the victors? So long as this goddess was favorable and propitious, even if Jupiter was on vacation or busy doing something else,[38] what nations would remain unconquered? What kingdoms would not submit? But perhaps good men get no pleasure from waging wholly wicked and unrighteous war or from provoking, by deliberate aggression, peaceful neighbors who are doing them no harm, for the sole purpose of extending their dominion. If this is their view, I certainly approve and applaud.

15. Let them consider, then, whether it is really appropriate for good men to rejoice at the extent of their rule. For it was the iniquity of those against

37. Forculus, from *fores,* meaning "door" or "doors"; Cardea, from *cardo,* meaning "hinge"; Limentinus, from *limen,* meaning "threshold."
38. See Elijah's mockery of the priests of Baal in 1 Kings 18:27.

whom they waged just wars that helped the empire to grow.[39] In fact, the empire would undoubtedly have remained small if its neighbors had been peaceful and just, never provoking them into war by doing them any injury. And, in that case, human affairs would have been happier. All kingdoms would have been small, rejoicing in concord with their neighbors, and so there would have been fully as many kingdoms among the peoples in the world as there are now houses among the citizens in a city.[40] Thus, making war and extending their rule by subjugating other peoples may look like happiness to the wicked, but to the good it only looks like a necessary evil. But since it would be still worse for the unjust to rule over those who are relatively more just, even this necessity is not inappropriately called a kind of happiness. There is no doubt, however, that it is a greater happiness to live in concord with a good neighbor than to subjugate a bad neighbor who makes war. It is a bad prayer, then, to want to have someone to hate or to fear in order to have someone to conquer.

If, therefore, it was by waging just rather than irreligious and unjust wars that the Romans were able to acquire such a vast empire, perhaps they should even worship Foreign Iniquity as a goddess. For we see how much she has helped in giving the empire its great extent by making others unjust so that there would be peoples against whom just wars might be waged and the empire be enlarged. And why should not Iniquity—or, at least, the iniquity of foreign peoples—be a goddess, if Fear and Terror and Fever all deserved to be Roman gods? It was due, then, to these two—that is, to Foreign Iniquity and the goddess Victory—that the empire grew, even when Jupiter was on holiday. Iniquity stirred up causes for wars, and Victory brought those wars to a happy conclusion. As for Jupiter, what part would he have to play? Any benefits that might be supposed to come from him were themselves held to be gods, themselves named as gods, and themselves invoked for the sake of the parts they played on their own. Of course, Jupiter might have had some part to play here, if he were called Empire in the same way that the goddess

39. [GWL] Augustine is alluding to a common strategy among Roman thinkers, who defended Rome's early expansion by presenting it as a response to unjust attacks. Augustine seems to affirm it as a "necessary evil." See 3.10; Clark, *Comm. 1–5,* 141–42, 197; and essay: "War." "Necessary evil" should be translated "necessity" (necessitas). Arguably at least, Augustine does not affirm the possibility of necessary (moral) evils.

40. [GWL] Augustine's ideal for the relation between nations. The lust for domination fuels kingdoms' desire for expansion; empires are the natural result. It would have been better for kingdoms to remain small and exist harmoniously with other kingdoms.

is called Victory. Or, if empire is, in fact, a gift of Jupiter, then why should not victory also be considered his gift? And it certainly would be considered a gift if it were not some stone on the Capitol[41] but rather the true *king of kings and lord of lords* (Rev. 19:16) that people knew and worshiped.

16. The Romans assigned separate gods to every single thing and to almost every single mode of activity. They invoked the goddess Agenoria, who stirs people to action; the goddess Stimula, who spurs people to overdo; the goddess Murcia, who does not move a person to outdo himself but rather, as Pomponius[42] says, makes a person *murcidus*, that is, extremely lazy and inactive; and the goddess Strenia, who makes people strenuous. And to all these gods and goddesses they took it on themselves to offer public worship. But what really surprises me is that they refused to take on public worship of the goddess they called Quies, who brings rest,[43] even though she had a temple outside the Colline gate.[44] Was this the indication of a restless mind? Or did it signify, rather, that one who persisted in worshiping that throng—clearly a throng not of gods but of demons—could not possibly have the rest to which the true physician calls us when he says, *Learn from me, for I am gentle and humble of heart, and you will find rest for your souls* (Matt. 11:29).

41. A stone known as the *Iupiter lapis*, or stone of Jupiter, was kept in the temple of Jupiter on the Capitoline Hill in Rome and was used as an object on which to swear when oaths were taken.

42. This is Lucius Pomponius, the first-century BCE author of dramas known as Atellan Fables, of which only fragments survive.

43. [GWL] It is tempting to see here a reference to *Confessions* 1.1.1, where Augustine says, "Our heart is unquiet [*inquietum*] until it rests [*requiescat*] in you [i.e., in God]." If *Confessions* narrates the loves of one individual (Augustine), *City of God* narrates the loves of nations and empires.

44. See Livy, *History of Rome* 4.41. The Colline Gate, or Porta Collina, was an ancient Roman landmark, located near several temples.

——————— Roman Religion ———————

Gregory W. Lee and Avyi Hill, with Sarah Duke

Religion was embedded in every aspect of Roman society and inseparable from politics and civic life. Roman religion concentrated on properly performed ceremonies to maintain the favor of the gods (*pax deorum*). Practices were stressed over doctrines or moral teachings; there were no authoritative texts explaining the purpose and reasoning behind Roman rituals. The central ritual was animal sacrifice, accompanied by prayer, when the gods would communicate messages of approval or disapproval through the animal entrails. Other important rituals included spectacles (see essay: "Roman Spectacles"), which encompassed various performances and games, and the triumph, a processional for victorious generals or emperors—who, for the day, were made to resemble Jupiter—that culminated at the Temple of Jupiter Optimus Maximus.

Roman mythology identified Numa Pompilius, the second king, as the founder of Rome's most venerable religious institutions. Roman religion was structured by colleges of priests responsible for discrete tasks. The college of pontiffs (*pontifices*) oversaw the Roman calendar, which specified the dates of religious festivals, as well as matters of family and property law. This college included a lead pontiff (*pontifex maximus*) and the Vestal Virgins, who guarded a perpetual fire on Rome's sacred hearth. Other colleges included the augurs, who interpreted the will of the gods through "auspices," like the flight of birds; the diviners (*haruspices*), who interpreted the "prodigies," or unnatural events representing warnings from the gods; the fetials, who oversaw rituals concerning war and diplomacy; and the "fifteen men for sacred actions" (*quindecimuiri sacris faciundis*; originally two men), who guarded collections of oracles called the Sibylline Books (see *City of God* 18.23). These colleges advised the senate on religious matters, at the senate's request.

Outside civic contexts, Romans exhibited piety in their personal lives. Domestic religion was led by the father of the household (*paterfamilias*), who performed daily prayers and sacrifices at the *lararium*, or household shrine. These rituals included requests for health and harvest, the veneration of deceased ancestors, and the commemoration of important life events. Roman religious life also included the mystery religions, which were practiced in secret, intimate communities.

From as early as can be discerned, Roman religion drew from a variety of traditions. Rome continued to absorb local deities and practices as it expanded across the Mediterranean. Some gods, like Jupiter, Juno, and Mars, were associated with important traditions and responsibilities. Others were confined to narrow functions, as with the many gods assigned to grain and wine production. Still others were deified abstractions like Liberty, Felicity, or Victory. There was no unified system for coordinating the gods.

By Augustine's time, Roman religion was in significant decline. This shift began with Constantine's conversion to Christianity. There was legislation against sacrifices as early as 341, and the practice had largely ceased by 385. In the 370s to 380s, the emperor Gratian removed the Altar of Victory from the senate house, withdrew public funds from the temples, and renounced the office of *pontifex maximus*, a title that emperors had claimed for themselves since Augustus Caesar. Shortly thereafter, in the early 390s, Theodosius would ban sacrifice and extinguish the Vestal flame. By this point, few elite officials openly espoused traditional Roman religion. Symmachus, who opposed Ambrose in the Altar of Victory controversy, was a notable exception.

Given these circumstances, some scholars have found Augustine's denunciation of Roman religion anachronistic. *City of God* relies on a (now lost) text by Varro, *Divine Antiquities*, which was written centuries earlier and bore questionable relevance to Augustine's time. Multiple explanations have been suggested for Augustine's polemic. Despite the bans on temples and sacrifices, these prohibitions were inconsistently enforced. Local festivals continued, and the spectacles remained popular. Augustine seems to have considered Roman religion a live threat. In addition, the sack of Rome stirred nostalgia for Rome's religious past among educated elites. Varro's work remained authoritative for such readers, offering a suitable target for Augustine's attacks against the gods (see the discussion of *Letters* 16–17 in Clark, *Comm. 6–10*, 10–11).

City of God's treatment of Roman religion adopts arguments developed by earlier Christian writers like Tertullian, Arnobius, and Lactantius. Augustine mocks the incoherence of Roman religion, which assigns an array of gods to minute and overlapping responsibilities (4.8, 11; 6.9; 19.17) and cannot be justified by more philosophical, naturalistic explanations (7.5–28). Augustine also critiques the immorality of Roman religion, both for its absence of moral instruction and for its dishonorable rites. He is especially disgusted by those concerning the Great Mother (*Magna Mater*), whose priests castrated themselves (2.7; 6.7; 7.24–28) and whose shows he attended as a young man in Carthage (2.4). The Romans worship the gifts of God rather than the one true God, who alone provides earthly goods (4.23, 33). Many of the "gods" are demons who seek to be worshiped and to make the Romans as immoral as themselves; many others are people who were deified after death (18.2–24). Finally, Augustine claims that the elites promulgated religious practices they themselves knew to be false, misleading the masses to preserve civic concord and to safeguard their own power. He especially critiques Varro, Seneca, Scaevola, Cicero, and Porphyry for such knowing deceptions (2.3; 3.4; 4.1, 26–27, 29–32; 6.*preface*–10; 7.5, 24, 34–35; 8.5; 10.9–11, 26–28).

Bibliography

Beard, Mary, John North, and Simon Price. 1998. *Religions of Rome*. 2 vols. Cambridge: Cambridge University Press.

Brodd, Jeffrey. 2017. "Roman Religion." In *Augustine in Context*, edited by Tarmo Toom, 129–36. Cambridge: Cambridge University Press.

Dodaro, Robert. 1993. "*Christus Sacerdos*: Augustine's Polemic against Roman Pagan Priesthoods in *De Ciuitate Dei*." *Augustinianum* 33, no. 1: 101–35.

———. 1994. "Eloquent Lies, Just Wars and the Politics of Persuasion: Reading Augustine's *City of God* in a 'Postmodern' World." *Augustinian Studies* 25: 77–138.

Fortin, Ernest L. 1980. "Augustine and Roman Civil Religion: Some Critical Reflections." *Revue d'Études Augustiniennes et Patristiques* 26: 238–56.

Hammer, Dean. 2021. "Books 4 & 5: Roman Religion and Just Power." In Meconi, *COG*, 81–101.

North, J. A. 2000. *Roman Religion*. Cambridge: Cambridge University Press.

Rebillard, Éric. 2015. "Dialogue or Conflict? Augustine on Roman Religion." In *Kampf oder Dialog? Begegnung von Kulturen im Horizont von Augustins "De ciuitate dei,"* edited by Christof Müller, 279–92. Würzburg, Germany: Augustinus bei Echter.

Rives, James B. 2007. *Religion in the Roman Empire*. Oxford: Blackwell.

Rives, J. B. 2024. *Animal Sacrifice in the Roman Empire (31 BCE–395 CE): Power, Communication, and Cultural Transformation*. Oxford: Oxford University Press.

Rüpke, Jörg. 2007. *The Religion of the Romans*. Cambridge: Polity.

Scheid, John. 2003. *An Introduction to Roman Religion*. Translated by Janet Lloyd. Orig. 1998. Bloomington: Indiana University Press.

Book 5

PREFACE, 1, 12–20, 24–26

Book 5 continues the discussion Augustine began in Book 4 on why God allowed the Romans to expand as an empire and how this related to their moral qualities. Book 4 broached this topic by arguing, first, that the size of a people does not guarantee its happiness (4.3–7) and, second, that Rome's expansion cannot be attributed to the gods (4.8–32). Book 5 starts by rejecting the attribution of Rome's expansion to "fate," whether this is defined in terms of astrology (5.1–7) or an impersonal chain of causes (5.8–10). God rules all things, including human kingdoms (5.11). These earlier discussions (4.3–32; 5.1–11) build suspense for the second half of Book 5, which includes some of the most-discussed texts in City of God. *In 5.12–13, Augustine attributes Rome's expansion as an empire to its lust for glory, a unique vice that seeks the appearance of virtue. Since apparent virtue is better than open vice, God preferred that the nations be ruled by Rome rather than by openly wicked peoples. As Augustine continues his discussion of the lust for glory (5.14–20), he offers an extended treatment of Rome's heroes (5.18) and contrasts the lust for glory and the lust for domination (5.19–20). After these sections, Augustine asserts again that God rules the kingdoms (5.21–23). He then treats the topic of Christian emperors (5.24–26). This last section includes an influential description of the ideal emperor (5.24) and an important discussion of Theodosius (5.26).*

Preface. It is clear, then, that happiness is the fulfillment of all that we ought to desire. It is not a goddess but a gift of God, and therefore no god should be worshiped by men except one who can make them happy.[1] Thus, if happiness itself were a goddess, there would be good reason to say that she alone should be worshiped. But God can also bestow the goods which even those who are not good—and therefore are not happy—can possess. Let us now see, then, why God willed the Roman empire to become so large and to last so long.[2] For we have already stated at length that the throng of false gods whom the Romans worshiped were not the ones who did this, and we shall make the same point again wherever it seems appropriate.

Neither Chance nor Fate Caused Rome's Greatness

1. The cause of the Roman empire's greatness, then, was neither chance nor fate.[3] Such a view might accord with the judgment or opinion of people who say that things happen by chance when they have no cause at all, or no cause that arises from an intelligible order, and that things happen by fate when they occur not by divine will or by human will but by virtue of some order governed by necessity.[4] It is beyond doubt, however, that human kingdoms are established by divine providence. If anyone ascribes them to fate because he uses the term "fate" to mean the will and power of God, let him hold to his meaning but correct his terminology. Why not say at the outset what he will say later on, when someone asks him what he means by fate? For, when people hear this word as it is ordinarily used, they understand it to mean nothing other than the influence of the position of the stars at the time when

---

1. [GWL] The word "happiness" is *felicitas*. Augustine is referring to his discussion of the goddess Felicity in 4.18–25. Happiness is that which is sought for its own sake and for the sake of which all other things are sought. If Felicity provides happiness, she renders the other gods superfluous, since she can supply whatever the other gods offer. Felicity thus proves the incoherence of Roman religion. Augustine follows classical philosophical traditions in identifying happiness as the goal of human life. So defined, happiness is not a matter of pleasant feelings but of virtue and a life well lived.

2. [GWL] This is the overarching topic of Books 4 and 5, announced earlier in 1.36 and 4.2. Augustine will not get to his core argument until 5.12.

3. [GWL] This is the topic of 5.2–11, which refutes the conceptions of fate as astrology (5.1–7) and fate as a chain of causes (5.8–10). This discussion concludes in 5.11, which asserts God's sovereignty over all things. Augustine's refutation of fate parallels his refutation of the gods in 4.8–34. Neither the gods (4.8–32) nor fate (5.1–10) can account for the expansion of the Roman empire. It is God who causes all things (4.33–34; 5.11).

4. See Pseudo-Plutarch, *On Fate* 8–9.

a person is born or conceived. Some consider this to be quite separate from the will of God;[5] others insist that it depends on the will of God.[6]

Against Astrological Fatalism: The Case of Twins

But those who hold the opinion that, quite apart from the will of God, the stars determine what we shall do, what goods we shall have, or what evils we shall suffer, should be refused a hearing by everyone—not only by those who hold the true religion but also by those who worship gods of any kind, no matter how false. For what can this opinion mean except that there is no reason to worship or pray to any god at all? Our present argument is directed not against people who take this view but rather against those who oppose the Christian religion for the sake of defending what they think are gods.

As for those who make the position of the stars depend on God's will but hold that the stars somehow determine what sort of person each will be and what good or evil will come his way, they do heaven a grave injustice if they suppose that the supreme power of God has handed over to the stars the power to decide these things any way they want. They imagine, in effect, that heaven's luminous senate, meeting in its lustrous senate house, so to speak, decrees that crimes are to be committed, crimes so horrible that, if any earthly city had decreed them, the whole human race would decree that it should be destroyed. And further, what place is left for God's judgment on human actions—and God is himself, after all, the Lord of both stars and men—if celestial necessity is applied to the acts human beings do? Alternatively, if they claim that the stars received from the supreme God not the power to decree these crimes on their own but only to fulfill his commands in imposing such necessities on human beings, are we then to take a view of God himself that it seemed utterly unworthy to hold of the will of the stars?

On the other hand, it might be said that the stars only signify these things but do not cause them, so that their position merely functions as a kind of announcement which predicts future events but does not bring them about, and people of no ordinary learning have held exactly this view.[7] But this simply is not the way that astrologers usually speak. They do not say, for instance,

5. See Diogenes Laertius, *Lives of Eminent Philosophers* 8.27.
6. See Plato, *Timaeus* 41d–e.
7. See Plotinus, *Enneads* 2.3.7.

"Mars in this position signifies murder" but rather "causes murder."[8] Let us concede, however, that the astrologers do not speak as precisely as they should, and that they ought to take from the philosophers the accurate form of words for declaring what they think they find in the position of the stars. Even granting this, however, how is it that the astrologers have never been able to explain why the lives of twins—their actions, their histories, their professions, their trades, their honors, their involvement with all the other circumstances of human life, and even their deaths—often show such differences that, in these respects, many complete strangers resemble them far more closely than they resemble each other? And this holds true despite the fact that only the smallest interval of time separated the birth of the one twin from the birth of the other, and despite the fact that they were conceived at the very same moment in a single act of intercourse.[9]

◆

Roman Love of Glory and Roman Virtue

12. Let us consider, then, the moral qualities of the Romans and see why the true God, in whose power earthly kingdoms are also included, deigned to help them to extend their empire.[10] It was to set the stage for a fuller discussion of this matter that I wrote the preceding book, showing that their gods, whom they thought should be worshiped even in trifling matters, have no power at all in this regard. For the same reason I wrote the preceding part of the present book, up to this point, in order to dispose of the question of fate. I certainly did not want anyone who is now persuaded that the Roman empire was not extended and preserved by the worship of those gods to attribute this instead to some sort of fate rather than to the all-powerful will of the supreme God.

8. See Plotinus, *Enneads* 2.3.6.

9. The supposed effect of the stars on twins, as well as on persons born at exactly the same time from different mothers, is also discussed in *Confessions* 7.6.8–7.6.10. See likewise *Teaching Christianity* 2.22.33–2.22.34.

10. [GWL] We finally arrive at Augustine's core argument in Books 4 and 5. The remainder of Book 5 presents some of the most important sections in *City of God*. Augustine pursues two central questions: Why did God allow the Romans to expand their empire? and, What does this have to do with Rome's moral qualities? (The Latin word for "moral qualities" is *mores*, which refers to the customs or practices that Romans considered to be the foundation of their nation.) Augustine's answers to these questions are thoroughly theological. In explaining the expansion of the empire, he appeals not to Rome's military prowess but to God's purposes in history.

The ancient and earliest Romans—like all the other nations, with the one exception of the Hebrew people[11]—worshiped false gods and sacrificed victims not to God but to demons, but even so, as their own history teaches and stamps with approval, "they were eager for praise, generous with their money, and longed for boundless glory and riches with honor."[12] This glory they loved with a passion. It was for its sake that they wanted to live and for its sake that they did not hesitate to die. Their boundless desire for this one thing kept all their other desires in check. In short, since they considered it shameful for their country to serve, but glorious for it to dominate and rule, what they desired with all their hearts was first for it to be free and then for it to be dominant. It was for this reason that, unable to bear the rule of kings, "they limited command to a year and appointed two commanders for themselves,"[13] who were called consuls (from serving as counselors) rather than kings or lords (from reigning or lording over others).[14] In fact, however, it would seem better to derive "king" from "to rule" rather than from "to reign";[15] just as "kingdom" derives from "to reign," so "king"—as was said—derives from "to rule."[16] At any rate, the Romans regarded royal haughtiness not as the order imposed by a ruler or the benevolence offered by a counselor but rather as the arrogance of a despot.[17]

Thus, when King Tarquin had been expelled and the consuls established,[18] there followed a period which this same author ranks among the glories of

11. [GWL] Augustine identifies the Jews as the one people that did not worship multiple gods. The Jews belong to the earthly city, but unlike the rest of the earthly city, they worship the one true God. See essay: "Jews and Judaism."

12. [GWL] This quotation is from Sallust, *Catiline Conspiracy* 7. As in 2.17–19, Augustine relies heavily on Sallust to assess the Romans' moral character. Sallust presents lust for glory as a defining quality of the Roman people. Glory is praise for right actions, especially in service to the nation (see Cicero, *Philippics* 1.29). As Augustine will explain, lust for glory is a vice, but it is a unique vice that restrains other offenses for the purpose of appearing virtuous. This feature brings social and political goods. For instance, the Romans were generous with their money because they desired the praise of other people. Although their motives were sinful, their generosity benefited others. For political communities, at least, apparent virtue is preferable to outright vice. Augustine's discussion reflects his general position on pride (*Confessions* 10.36.58–10.39.64). There are some sins that are obvious, like murder or idolatry. But pride is difficult to discern because it can motivate externally good deeds. Pride is a uniquely deceptive sin that cannot be perceived from actions alone.

13. Sallust, *Catiline Conspiracy*, 6.

14. See Varro, *On the Latin Language* 5.14.

15. "King . . . to rule . . . to reign": *rex . . . regere . . . regnare.*

16. [GWL] It is difficult to perceive the literalism of Augustine's argument in English. "King" is *rex*, and "to rule" is *regere*; "kingdom" is *regnum*, and "to reign" is *regnare*. There is not much at stake in this discussion. Augustine is simply offering an etymological remark.

17. See Sallust, *Catiline Conspiracy* 6.

18. See . . . 3.15–16.

the Romans. "Once the city gained its liberty," he says, "it is incredible to relate how much and how quickly it grew, so great was the longing for glory that had taken hold."[19] It was, therefore, this eagerness for praise and longing for glory that accomplished so many wondrous things—things which were, beyond doubt, praiseworthy and glorious in human estimation.

The same Sallust also praises Marcus Cato and Gaius Caesar as great and eminent men of his time.[20] He says that for a long time the republic had no one of outstanding virtue, but that within his own memory there were these two of great distinction, although quite different in character. In his praise of Caesar, he notes that he longed for a great command, an army, and a new war in which his virtue could shine out. Thus it came to be that the chief wish of men of outstanding virtue was for Bellona[21] to stir up miserable peoples to war and urge them on with her blood-stained scourge just so that there might be an opportunity for their virtue to shine. This is what came of their famous eagerness for praise and longing for glory! First, then, from love of liberty, and then from love of domination, as well as from longing for praise and glory, they accomplished many great things.[22] Their famous poet bears witness to both points. With regard to the first, in fact, he says, "When Porsenna ordered banished Tarquin to be restored, and pressed the city with a great siege, then, for the sake of liberty, Aeneas's sons rushed to

19. [GWL] This quotation is from Sallust, *Catiline Conspiracy* 7. It refers to the transition from the time of the kings to the Roman republic, which was governed by consuls. Augustine treats this period in 3.15–16. In their earlier history, the Romans desired liberty from the tyranny of the kings, which was a legitimate concern. After the Romans gained freedom and established the republic, they sought to dominate other peoples. This is an impulse Augustine condemns. In both contexts, the Romans were driven by lust for glory. Thus, Rome's desire for liberty was compromised by sinful motivations too.

20. NCP: "Marcus Portius Cato (95–46 BCE), also known as Cato the Younger, was esteemed for his integrity and for his resistance to Gaius Julius Caesar (100–44 BCE), the great general who was assassinated as Roman dictator."

[GWL] Sallust depicts both Caesar and Cato as virtuous men. Augustine's engagement with Sallust stresses two points. First, it is better to pursue virtue than glory. Whereas Caesar wanted to appear virtuous for the sake of glory, Cato received glory without pursuing it. Cato was more virtuous than Caesar. Second, despite its celebration of Caesar and Cato's virtue, Sallust's history demonstrates that Rome was never virtuous. Most of Rome's history was characterized by discord and oppression, and Rome's greatest accomplishments were the result of a few exceptional individuals and not of its citizens as a whole.

21. I.e., the goddess of war.

22. [GWL] Augustine is summarizing the history of Rome that he has narrated. The Romans were first ruled by kings, whom they cast off for the sake of liberty and governance by consuls. This political transition occurred with the expulsion of King Tarquin. The Romans then sought domination by conquering neighboring peoples. Throughout these major phases of Roman history, the Romans were driven by the lust for glory.

arms."[23] At that time, then, the great thing for the Romans was either to die bravely or to live free.

But, once liberty was won, such a longing for glory took hold of them that liberty alone was not enough unless they were also seeking domination, and what the same poet says, as if the words came from the mouth of Jupiter himself, was taken as a great thing: "Even savage Juno, who now torments sea and land and sky with terror, will be of better mind and, with me, will favor the Romans, the people of the toga, the masters of all the earth. That is my will. In time an age will come when the house of Assaracus will bring Phthia and famed Mycenae to servitude, and have dominion over vanquished Argos."[24] Virgil, of course, represented Jupiter as predicting the future; but, in fact, this is Virgil himself recalling the past and picturing the present state of things. My purpose in quoting these lines, however, is to show that, after liberty, the Romans valued dominion so highly that they ranked it among their greatest glories. Thus, in the following lines, the same poet ranks above the arts of other nations the specifically Roman arts of ruling and commanding peoples, of subjugating and subduing them: "Others may forge the bronze more delicately to breathing life, and may, I grant, carve living faces out from stone. They may plead cases at law with greater skill, and with compass chart the sky or tell the rising of the stars. But remember, Roman, that these will be your arts: to rule peoples by your command, to impose the ways of peace, to spare the conquered and subdue the proud."[25] The Romans practiced these arts with the greater skill when they were the less devoted to pleasure and to the enervation of mind and body that comes from pursuing and amassing wealth. Through wealth, however, they corrupted their morals by plundering their miserable citizens and lavishing gifts on degenerate actors.

But, at the time when Sallust was writing his prose and Virgil composing his verse, people of this sort had already come to prevail and abound, due

23. Virgil, *Aeneid* 8.646–48. Lars Porsenna was an Etruscan king to whom Tarquin appealed for help after his expulsion.

24. Virgil, *Aeneid* 1.279–85. Assaracus was a mythical king of Dardania whose descendents included the founders of Rome. Hence "the house of Assaracus" represents Rome itself.

25. [GWL] Virgil, *Aeneid* 6.847–53. This is the same passage Augustine quotes in the preface to Book 1. Its reappearance here signals the importance of this section of *City of God*. As Virgil comments, other peoples (like the Egyptians or the Greeks) were more gifted in art, law, or astrology. But the Romans were especially gifted at war. They imposed their rule on other nations, sparing the conquered and subduing the proud. In 1.*preface*, Augustine contrasts this language with James 4:6, where it is God—and not Rome—who "resists the proud but gives grace to the humble." Virgil's remarks illustrate Rome's pride, which arrogates for itself authority that belongs to God.

to Rome's moral decline, and it was no longer by these Roman arts that men sought honor and glory but rather by guile and deceit. That is why Sallust says, "At first it was ambition rather than avarice that stirred men's minds, a vice that, even so, comes close to being a virtue. For the good and the worthless alike seek glory, honor, and power for themselves, but the former strive on the true path, while the latter, lacking any good arts, compete by guile and deceit."[26] And the "good arts" that he has in mind are these: to attain honor, glory, and power through virtue and not through ambition cloaked in deceit. The good and the worthless alike want honor, glory, and power for themselves, but the former—that is, the good—strive by the true path. And that path is virtue, by which they strive for the goal they want to attain and possess—by which they strive, that is, for glory, honor, and power.

How deeply this view was ingrained in the Romans is shown also by the fact that the two temples of the gods which they established closest to each other were those of Virtue and Honor[27] (for they took as gods what are actually gifts from God). From this we can see what they wanted virtue to culminate in, and what the good among them correlated virtue with, namely, honor. For the evil among them had no virtue, despite the fact that they wanted to have honor and tried to attain it by evil arts, that is, by guile and deceit.

Cato is given higher praise. Of him, in fact, Sallust says, "The less he sought glory, the more it followed him."[28] Glory, which the Romans burned with desire to have, is simply the judgment of men holding other men in high regard, and therefore virtue is better, since it is not content with mere human testimony apart from the witness of its own conscience. That is why the Apostle says, *For this is our glory, the testimony of our own conscience* (2 Cor. 1:12); and in another passage, *But let each test his own work, and then he will have glory in himself alone, and not in another* (Gal. 6:4). Therefore virtue should not follow on the glory, honor, and power which the Romans desired for themselves and which the good among them strove to attain by "good arts." Instead, glory, honor, and power should follow on virtue. For there is no true virtue except the virtue that is directed toward the end where man's good is actually found, the good than which there is no better. In truth, then, Cato

26. [GWL] *Catiline Conspiracy* 11. In this passage, Sallust contrasts two kinds of people: those who pursue glory through the "the true path" and those who pursue it by "guile and deceit." The true path is associated with virtue. Augustine will quote this passage again in 5.19.

27. See Livy, *History of Rome* 27.25.

28. *Catiline Conspiracy* 54.

ought not to have sought even the honors that he did seek. Rather, the city ought to have bestowed them on him, unsought, in recognition of his virtue.

But even though there were two Romans of great virtue at that time, Caesar and Cato, it seems that Cato's virtue came much closer to true virtue than did Caesar's. For let us see what the state's condition was at that time, and what it had been earlier, according to Cato's own judgment. "Do not imagine," he says, "that it was by force of arms that our ancestors made the republic great from its small beginnings. If that were true, we would have a far more excellent republic now than they did then. Indeed, we are far better supplied with allies and citizens, and with arms and horses, than they were. But it was other qualities that made them great, qualities which are wholly lacking in us: diligence at home, just rule abroad, and an independent spirit in counsel, addicted neither to crime nor to lust. Instead of these, what we have is self-indulgence and greed, public impoverishment and private wealth. We praise riches, we live for idleness, we make no distinction between good people and bad, and raw ambition usurps all the rewards that virtue ought to have. And it is no wonder—when each of you takes thought only for himself, when you are slaves to pleasure at home and to money and favor here in public—that any assault would come on a republic that has no defenses."[29]

Anyone who hears these words of Cato (or rather of Sallust) would presume that all or most of the ancient Romans were like the ones he praises. But that is not true. If it were, the things which Sallust himself writes, the things I quoted in the second book of this work,[30] would be wrong, where he says that the oppressive actions of the powerful, and the resulting alienation of the common people from the patricians, along with other domestic discords, were present from the very beginning, and that, after the kings were expelled, people acted in keeping with just and moderate law only so long as they were still afraid of Tarquin, that is, only up to the end of the grievous war with Etruria that was undertaken on his account.[31] After that, the patricians treated the commoners like slaves, abused them in the manner of kings, drove them

29. *Catiline Conspiracy* 52.
30. See above at 2.18.
31. [GWL] Augustine is summarizing his argument from 2.18–19, where he used Sallust's history of Rome to challenge Sallust's characterization of the Roman people. Sallust identified two main periods when the Romans exemplified virtue: the early years of the republic, following the expulsion of King Tarquin, and the time between the Second and Third Punic Wars. As Augustine argues, even during these periods of apparent virtue, the Romans were motivated less by love for justice than by political and military fear.

from their lands, excluded all others, and exercised sole power. These discords, with the one group bent on domination and the other resisting enslavement, came to an end only with the second Punic War. For at that point a deep fear began to weigh on Rome once again. A new and greater anxiety reined in their restless spirits from these disturbances and called them back to civic concord.

Even so, great matters were managed by a certain few, who were good in their own way, and, when those evils had been endured or alleviated by the foresight of a few good men, the republic grew. The same historian says that, as he read or heard of the many outstanding exploits performed by the Roman people at home and on the battlefield, on sea and on land, he liked to consider what special quality it was that carried through such great affairs. For he knew that, time and time again, a small band of Romans had fought against great legions of the enemy, and he also knew that wars had been waged with few resources against wealthy kings. He said that, after much deliberation, he came to the conclusion that it was the exceptional virtue of a few citizens that had accomplished all this, and it was due to this that poverty vanquished wealth and the few defeated the many.[32] "But conversely," he adds, "once the state had been corrupted by luxury and idleness, the republic by its very size gave free rein to the vices of its generals and magistrates."[33] It was, therefore, the virtue of only a few—the few who strove for glory, honor, and power by the true way, that is, by virtue itself—that Cato praised. From their virtue came the diligence at home that Cato speaks of, the diligence that worked to enrich the public treasury and keep private fortunes slim. And so, in contrast, he sets it down as a vice that, when morals have been corrupted, we find public impoverishment and private wealth.

The Divine Gift of Empire to Rome: An Earthly Reward for Earthly Virtue

13. Thus, at a point when illustrious kingdoms had long existed in the east, God willed that there should arise in the west an empire which, although later in time, would be even more illustrious in its extent and grandeur.[34] And

32. [GWL] Augustine is downplaying Roman virtue. The Romans' reputation for virtue was due to only a few exceptional men, even according to Sallust, and Augustine has already questioned the motivations of these men.

33. Sallust, *Catiline Conspiracy* 52.

34. [GWL] For the eastern kingdoms, Augustine is thinking especially of Assyria, but also of Media, Persia, and Macedonia (Clark, *Comm. 1–5*, 242). For the western empire, Augustine is referring to Rome. See 4.6–7, where he first describes Rome succeeding Assyria as the dominant

in order to counteract the terrible evils of many other peoples, he granted it to the kind of men who, for the sake of honor, praise, and glory, served the good of the country in which they sought their own glory and did not hesitate to put its well-being above their own. For the sake of this one vice—that is, the love of praise—these men suppressed the love of riches and many other vices.[35] For the most reasonable view is to admit that even the love of praise is, in fact, a vice. This is a point which did not escape the poet Horace, who says, "Do you swell with love of praise? There are certain rites of expiation which can restore you to health if, in purity, you read the little book three times."[36] And in a lyric poem, seeking to curb the lust for domination, the same author sings, "You will rule more widely by taming ardent greed than if you join Libya to distant Gades and thus make the two Punic peoples serve one master."[37] Nevertheless, it is for the better that people who do not restrain their baser lusts by the pious faith and the love of intelligible beauty that are given by the Holy Spirit at least do so by their desire for human praise and glory. They certainly are not saints, but at least they are less vile. Cicero, too, was unable to conceal this point. In the books he wrote *On the Republic*, where he speaks of the training of the civic leader—who, he says, ought to be nourished on glory—he goes on to add that his own ancestors did many marvelous and illustrious things due to their desire for glory.[38] Thus not only did they not resist this vice; they even supposed that it should be aroused and kindled, precisely because they considered it to be beneficial for the republic. Not even in his philosophical works does Cicero conceal this pestilential view. Instead, he admits it there as plain as day. For, in speaking of the endeavors which should be pursued for the sake of the true good rather than for the sake of the winds of human praise, he introduced this universal generalization: "Honor nourishes the arts. Everyone is fired in his efforts by the thought of glory, but things that people hold in low esteem always lie neglected."[39]

14. Beyond doubt, therefore, it is better to resist this desire for praise than to yield to it. For each person is more like God the more pure he is of this impurity. And even if it is never fully eradicated from the heart in this life,

---

empire in the world. For his depiction of Rome as the second Babylon, see 16.17; and 18.2, 21–22. Augustine tends to conflate Assyria and Babylon (18.2, 22; 19.24).

35. That vainglory keeps other vices at bay is also expressed in Cassian, *Conferences* 5.12.

36. Letter 1.1.36–1.1.37.

37. *Odes* 2.2.9–2.2.12.

38. This reference to Cicero's *Republic* is found only here.

39. *Tusculan Disputations* 1.4.

since it never ceases to tempt the minds even of those who are making good progress, the desire for glory may at least be surpassed by the love of righteousness. In that case, if things that people hold in low esteem lie neglected at any point—presuming that those things are good, presuming that they are right—even the love of human praise itself will feel embarrassed and will yield to the love of truth. For when desire for glory holds a greater place in the heart than fear or love of God, this vice is so opposed to godly faith that the Lord said, *How can you believe when you look for glory from each other and do not seek the glory which comes from God alone* (John 5:44)? And again, with regard to certain persons who had believed in him but were afraid to confess it openly, the evangelist says, *They loved human glory more than they loved the glory that comes from God* (John 12:43).

The holy apostles were not like this.[40] They preached the name of Christ not only in places where it was held in low esteem (as Cicero says, "Things that people hold in low esteem always lie neglected") but even where it was held in the deepest loathing. They held fast to what they had heard from the good teacher[41] who is also the physician of minds,[42] *If anyone denies me before men, I will deny him before my Father who is in heaven* (Matt. 10:33), or *before the angels of God* (Luke 12:9). In the midst of curses and reviling, in the midst of terrible persecutions and cruel punishments, they were not deterred from preaching human salvation, no matter how great the frenzy of human hatred. By their godly deeds and words, and by the godly lives they lived, they somehow conquered hard hearts and instilled the peace of righteousness in them, so that great glory followed them in the Church of Christ. But they did not rest content with that glory as if it were the end and goal of their virtue. Rather they referred that glory to the glory of God, by whose grace they were the kind of people they were, and with that same spark they kindled those in their care to love for the one by whom they also might become the same kind of people. For, in order to teach them not to be good only for the sake of human glory, their Master had said, *Beware of*

40. [GWL] Augustine contrasts Rome's military heroes with the apostles and the martyrs. The apostles and the martyrs performed good deeds for God's sake and not for human praise, while the Romans performed good deeds to be admired by others. Augustine's comparison relies on the Sermon on the Mount, using Jesus's critique of the Pharisees against the Romans.

41. See Luke 18:18.

42. "Physician of minds": *medico mentium*. The theme of Christ as physician or healer is an important one in Augustine. See Rudolph Arbesmann, "The Concept of 'Christus Medicus' in St. Augustine," in *Traditio* 10 (1954) 1–28.

practicing your righteousness before men in order to be seen by them, for then you will have no reward with your Father who is in heaven (Matt. 6:1). But again, to keep them from interpreting this in the wrong way and, for fear of pleasing men, making themselves of less use by hiding the fact that they were good, he showed them the purpose for which they ought to become known: *Let your works shine before men so that they may see your good deeds and glorify your Father who is in heaven* (Matt. 5:16)—not *in order to be seen by them*, therefore, that is, not with the aim that you want them to be turned toward you, for you are nothing in your own right, but rather *that they may glorify your Father who is in heaven* and, now turned toward him, may become what you are.

The apostles were followed by the martyrs, who surpassed men like Scaevola and Curtius and the Decii not by inflicting pain on themselves but by enduring the pain inflicted on them by others, as well as by their true virtue—true virtue because rooted in true piety—and also by their vast numbers. But since these Romans belonged to an earthly city, and since the goal set before them in all their services on its behalf was to secure its safety and to gain a kingdom not in heaven but on earth, not in eternal life but in a life where the dying pass away and are succeeded by those who are going to die in turn, what else was there for them to love but glory? And what glory but the glory by which they yearned to find a life after death, as it were, on the lips of those who praised them?[43]

15. God was not going to grant to people such as these eternal life with his holy angels in his heavenly city.[44] What leads to that society is true piety, the piety that offers religious service—what the Greeks call *latreia*—only to the one true God. Thus, if God had not at least granted them the earthly glory of supreme empire, no reward at all would have been allotted to their good arts, that is, the virtues by which they strove to attain such an impressive glory. For it is with reference to men such as these, men who seem to do something good for the sake of being glorified by men, that the Lord himself says, *Truly I say to you, they have received their reward* (Matt. 6:2). So also the Romans disregarded their private interests for the sake of the common good, that is,

43. [GWL] The lust for glory derives from a failure to believe in life after death. Those who do not believe in heavenly reward seek a semblance of it through earthly praise. Augustine connects lust for glory with lust for earthly goods, which is what makes the earthly city earthly.

44. [GWL] Rome's military heroes will not receive eternal life because they never sought it; they were consumed with earthly gain. Again, Augustine applies to the Romans what Jesus originally said about the Pharisees: "They have received their reward" (Matt. 6:2).

for the sake of the republic, as well as for the public treasury. They resisted greed, and they advised their homeland with independent counsel, addicted neither to crime (according to its laws) nor to lust. By all these arts, as if by a true way, they strove for honors, power and glory. They were honored among almost all peoples; they imposed the laws of their empire on many peoples; and even today they are glorious among almost all peoples in history and literature. They have no grounds for complaint against the justice of the supreme and true God: *they have received their reward.*

16. Far different, however, is the reward of the saints, who here below endure taunts and insults for the sake of God's truth, which is hateful to those who love this world. That city is eternal. There no one is born because no one dies. There is found true and full happiness, not a goddess but rather a gift from God.[45] From that city we have received the pledge of our faith to hold on to while we yearn for its beauty during our pilgrimage on earth. There the sun does not rise on the good and the evil alike; rather, the sun of righteousness protects only the good.[46] There no great diligence will be required to enrich the public treasury and constrain private wealth, for the treasury of truth is common to all. And, in fact, the Roman empire was not expanded to the full dimensions of human glory simply in order to provide a due reward to such men as they were. This also happened for the benefit of the citizens of the eternal city while they are on pilgrimage here below.[47] It happened so that they might carefully and soberly contemplate the Roman examples, and might see how great a love they owe to their supernal homeland for the sake of eternal life, if the earthly city was so greatly loved by its citizens for the sake of mere human glory.

17. For, as far as this mortal life is concerned, which passes and is over in a few days, what difference does it make under whose rule a person lives who is soon to die, just so long as those who rule do not compel him into anything ungodly and wicked?[48] Did the Romans really do any harm to the peoples whom they

---

45. The goddess Felicity, discussed . . . at 4.18–25, is being referred to here.

46. [GWL] Matthew 5:45 is cited also in 1.8, where Augustine introduces his theology of suffering. Augustine contrasts this temporal condition, where good and evil people receive both temporal good and temporal evil, with the eternal condition, where good people receive only eternal good while evil people receive only eternal evil. See essay: "Providence and Suffering."

47. [GWL] Augustine pivots to a second explanation for why God allowed the rise of the Roman empire. The valor of their military heroes, exhibited for the sake of an earthly city, should inspire Christians to even greater virtue for the sake of the heavenly city.

48. [GWL] A provocative comment. Augustine claims that the oppressed should not worry about who rules them so long as they are not coerced into immoral behavior. This judgment

subdued and on whom they imposed their own laws, apart from the fact that this involved the vast slaughter of war? If they had prevailed by harmonious agreement, that would obviously have been a greater success (but then there would have been no glory of triumph). For the Romans themselves lived under the laws that they imposed on others. And if this imposition had happened without Mars and Bellona—so that Victory, too, had no place (since no one is victor where no one has fought)—would not the Romans and the other peoples have been in exactly the same condition? And this would have been especially true if the Romans had immediately taken the most gracious and humane action that they took later on, when they granted civic standing to all who belonged to the Roman empire so that they would be Roman citizens.[49] Thus what had previously been the privilege of a few would have been common to all. The one exception was that the Roman populace, since they had no lands of their own, would live at the public expense. But this provision would not have been extorted from the vanquished; instead, and more gracefully, it would have been furnished by common consent through good administrators of the republic.

But with regard to security and good morals, the true notes of human dignity, I utterly fail to see what difference it makes that some are conquerors and others conquered, apart from the utterly empty arrogance of human glory.[50] It is in human glory that the men who burned with unstinted desire for glory and spread the flames of war have received their reward. Do not their lands pay tribute? Are they allowed to learn anything that is not allowed to others? Are there not many senators in other lands who do not know Rome even by sight? Take away their boasting and what are all men, after all, but men? But even if the perversity of this age actually allowed the better men to receive the higher honors, human honor still should not be considered of any great significance. It is nothing but smoke without weight.

---

aligns with Augustine's discussion of temporal suffering in 1.8–28, including his treatment of rape in 1.16–28 (see essay: "*City of God* 1.16–28: Rape of Christian Women"). In the context of this chapter, Augustine's purpose is to trivialize the glory that the Romans so avidly sought. Arguably, though, he also trivializes the experience of imperial oppression. We will all die anyway, so what does it matter who rules over us? Augustine's argument here is worth pausing on for critical analysis.

49. [GWL] Augustine is referring to a decree in 212 CE by the emperor Caracalla granting Roman citizenship to all freeborn inhabitants of the empire, a move that was intended to increase the empire's tax base. Augustine will proceed to mention the reliance of the urban poor on a regular ration from the empire.

50. [GWL] As above, the purpose of this paragraph is to criticize Rome's obsession with glory. For Augustine, there is no real benefit in being conqueror as opposed to conquered. Glory is "smoke without weight." Again, his argument risks dismissing the plight of the oppressed.

The Roman Example: An Antidote to Christian Pride

Even in this respect, however, we may profit from the kindness of the Lord our God. Let us keep in mind how much those Romans disdained, what sufferings they endured, what passions they suppressed, all for the sake of human glory.[51] They deserved to receive human glory as their reward for virtues of this sort. And let this thought take such hold on us that it stifles any pride on our part: the city in which it is promised that we shall reign is as far removed from this Rome as heaven is from earth, as eternal life is from temporal joy, as solid glory is from empty praise, as the society of angels is from the society of mortals, as the light of the one who made the sun and moon is from the light of the sun and moon themselves. The citizens of such a marvelous homeland should not think that they have done anything remarkable if, for the sake of attaining it, they performed some good work or endured some few evils, given that the Romans did so much and suffered so much for the sake of an earthly country which they possessed already. And this point is especially noteworthy because the remission of sins, which gathers citizens for the eternal homeland, has a kind of likeness, a sort of shadow, in the asylum established by Romulus, where impunity for every sort of crime brought together the multitude that was to found the city of Rome.[52]

18. Is it any great thing, then, to despise all the enticements of this world, no matter how alluring they may be, for the sake of the eternal and heavenly homeland, when, for the sake of his temporal and earthly country, Brutus was even able to kill his own sons?[53] This is something which the heavenly country compels no one to do. But it is clearly more difficult to kill one's sons

---

51. [GWL] Augustine will now develop the idea he introduced in 5.16, that God allowed the rise of the Roman empire to provide Christians examples to exceed.

52. [GWL] Augustine presents Romulus's offer of asylum as a kind of prefiguration of the forgiveness offered by Christianity. See 1.34, where Augustine compares Romulus's offer with the mercy that the Visigoths displayed during the sack of Rome.

53. [GWL] Lucius Junius Brutus, treated in 3.16, was the first Roman consul following the expulsion of King Tarquin (509 BCE). He had his sons executed for participating in a conspiracy to restore Tarquin to the throne. In this chapter, Augustine draws on a Roman tradition of celebrating examples of virtue (*exempla virtutis*) to imitate. These examples were often military heroes from the republican period who embodied valor in their commitment to Rome. They provided alternatives to the immoral gods for imitation. While there was no official catalog of *exempla*, Augustine cites well-known figures in Roman literature and history.

This chapter is difficult to interpret. Augustine seems to admire Rome's heroes while also using their stories as an argument from the lesser to the greater. If the Romans performed such deeds for the sake of earthly reward, how much more should Christians do for the sake of heavenly reward? See essay: "Pagan Virtue."

than it is to do what the heavenly country does require—either to give to the poor the possessions that it seemed right to accumulate and preserve for one's sons[54] or, if some trial should arise which compels us to do so for the sake of faith and righteousness, to lose those possessions entirely. For earthly riches do not make either us or our children happy; they will either be lost while we are still alive or will pass, after our death, to someone we do not know or even to someone we do not want. Rather, it is God who makes us happy, for he is the true wealth of the mind. And as for Brutus, because he killed his sons, even the poet who praises him bears witness to his unhappiness, for he says, "For the sake of fair liberty, the father will call his own sons to punishment when they instigate new wars—unhappy man, no matter how posterity may celebrate his deeds." In the following line, however, the poet offered the unhappy man this consolation: "Love of country wins the day, and boundless lust for praise."[55]

These, then, are the two things which spurred the Romans to their extraordinary feats: liberty and lust for human praise. And if a father could kill his sons for the sake of liberty for men who were going to die in any case, and for the sake of desire for the praises that we gain from mortal men, is it any great thing if, for the sake of the true liberty which sets us free from the dominion of iniquity and death and the devil, we do not kill our sons but simply count Christ's poor among our sons? It is not from desire for human praise that we do this but from love of setting people free—free not from a King Tarquin but from the demons and from the prince of demons.

Another Roman leader, named Torquatus, also killed his son.[56] He did not kill him because his son had fought against his country. Rather, he killed him because, even though he fought for his country, he fought in disobedience to the orders which his father, as general, had issued. Challenged by the enemy, he fought with all the ardor of youth, and yet, even though he was victorious, his father put him to death, fearing that the evil in the example of insubordination would outweigh the good in the glory of slaying an enemy.[57] And if Torquatus could do this, why should Christians boast if, for the laws of their immortal country, they disdain all earthly goods which, after all, are loved far less than sons?

54. See Matt. 19:21 par.
55. Virgil, *Aeneid* 6.820–23.
56. [GWL] Augustine treats Torquatus in 1.23, contrasting his willingness to kill his son with Cato the Younger's refusal to do the same.
57. See above at 1.23.

After Furius Camillus had cast off from the neck of his country the yoke of the Veii, its most bitter enemy, he was condemned and banished by his rivals; and yet he liberated his ungrateful country once again, this time from the Gauls, because he had no better country where he could live with greater glory.[58] And if Furius Camillus could do this, why should anyone be extolled, as if he had done something grand, if he happens to suffer dishonor and grave injury at the hands of carnal enemies in the Church and yet does not go over to its enemies, the heretics, or even himself establish some heresy in opposition to it, but instead defends the Church with all his might against the heretics' deadly depravity—doing this not because there is no other place where he may live in human glory but because there is no other place where he may gain eternal life?

Mucius, at the time when King Porsenna was pressing the Romans hard in a bitter war, was not able to kill Porsenna himself and, by mistake, killed another man instead.[59] In these circumstances, in order to bring about peace with Porsenna, he reached out and put his right hand in the fire that was burning on an altar before the king's eyes, saying that there were many more men such as the king saw him to be who had sworn to kill him. Appalled at Mucius' fortitude and horrified at the thought of a conspiracy of such men, the king made peace without a moment's hesitation and withdrew from that war.[60] And if Mucius could do this, who will figure that his merits earn him the kingdom of heaven, even if, for its sake, he gives not just one hand but his whole body over to the flames—not acting, however, of his own free will, but rather under duress by order of a persecutor?

Curtius, fully armed, spurred on his horse and hurled himself into a gaping chasm in the earth, in obedience to the oracles of his gods. For they had ordered that the best thing the Romans possessed should be cast into that chasm, and the Romans could see no other interpretation than that, since they excelled in men and in arms, the orders of the gods required that a fully armed man be hurled headlong into that destruction.[61] And if Curtius could

---

58. [GWL] After destroying the Veii in 396 BCE, Camillus was exiled on the charge of misappropriating the spoils. According to tradition, he was recalled from exile to liberate the Romans from the Gauls (390 BCE). Augustine's reference to heretics in this paragraph is probably an allusion to the Donatists (on whom, see the introduction, above). NCP: "See above at 2.17 and 4.7."

59. [GWL] On Mucius, Curtius, and the Decii, see 4.20.

60. See Livy, *History of Rome* 2.12–13.

61. See . . . 4.20.

do this, who is going to say that he has done any great thing for his eternal homeland if he should die at the hands of some enemy of his faith, not by hurling himself into such a death of his own free will but rather by being cast into it by the enemy, especially when he has received from his Lord, the king of his homeland, a far more certain oracle: *Do not fear those who kill the body but cannot kill the soul* (Matt. 10:28)?

The Decii devoted themselves to death, consecrating themselves in a sense by means of certain words, to the end that, when they fell and appeased the anger of the gods with their blood, the Roman army should be saved.[62] And if the Decii could do this, the holy martyrs will by no means turn proud, as though they had done something worthy of winning participation in that homeland where there is true and eternal happiness, if they did battle, even to the point of shedding their blood, in the faith of love and the love of faith—loving not only their brothers for whom their blood was shed, but also, as commanded, the very enemies by whom it was shed.[63]

When Marcus Pulvillus was dedicating the temple of Jupiter, Juno, and Minerva, men of ill will brought him a false report of his son's death, hoping that, in his distress, he would withdraw and his colleague would receive the glory of the dedication. He viewed the matter with such disdain, however, that he even ordered his son's body to be cast out unburied.[64] That is how completely the desire for glory had vanquished the grief of loss in his heart. And if Pulvillus could do this, how will that person say he has done anything great for the preaching of the holy gospel, by which the citizens of the supernal homeland are delivered from their various errors and gathered up, to whom the Lord said, when he was anxious about burying his father, *Follow me, and let the dead bury their dead* (Matt. 8:22)?

In order not to break the oath he had sworn to his ruthless enemies, Marcus Regulus returned to them from Rome.[65] He did so because, as he is reported to have told the Romans when they urged him to stay, he could no longer have the standing of an honorable citizen after being a slave to the Africans. And,

62. See 4.20.
63. See Matt. 5:44.
64. When dedicating the temple of Jupiter on the Capitoline Hill in 509 BCE, the consul Marcus Horatius Pulvillus was told that his son had died and that consequently he was not in a ritual position to perform the dedication ceremonies; he then ordered his son to be buried and resumed the dedication. See Livy, *History of Rome* 2.8. Augustine's account differs considerably from that of Livy.
65. [GWL] Marcus Regulus receives extended attention in 1.15, where he constitutes an important case for Augustine's understanding of "pagan virtue" (see essay: "Pagan Virtue").

because he had spoken out against them in the senate, the Carthaginians put him to death with the most horrible tortures.[66] And if Regulus could do this, are there any tortures that should not be despised for the sake of keeping faith with the homeland to whose blessedness faith itself leads? *Or what shall we render to the Lord for all that he has rendered to us* (Ps. 116:12), if, for the sake of keeping the faith owed to the Lord, a person suffers such things as Regulus suffered for the sake of keeping the faith he owed to his deadliest enemies?

How will a Christian dare to take pride in choosing voluntary poverty in order to walk less encumbered, during the pilgrimage of this life, on the path that leads to the homeland where God himself is the true wealth?[67] How will he dare to do this, that is, when he hears or reads that Lucius Valerius, who died while holding the office of consul, was so poor that his burial had to be paid for by public subscription?[68] Or when he hears or reads that Quintius Cincinnatus, when he owned less than two acres of land and was tilling them with his own hands, was taken from the plow to be made dictator, an office of far greater honor than consul, and yet, after defeating the enemy and gaining untold glory, remained in exactly the same poverty?[69]

Again, how will anyone proclaim that he has done something extraordinary in refusing to be lured away from the society of the eternal homeland by any of this world's rewards, when he learns that Fabricius could not be torn away from the city of Rome by even the most extravagant gifts of Pyrrhus, king of Epirus—who promised him as much as a quarter of his kingdom—but instead preferred to remain in his poverty as a private citizen?[70]

For despite the fact that they had a republic—that is, the common good of the people, of the homeland, of the community[71]—of the greatest wealth and opulence, the Romans themselves were so poor in their own homes that one of them, who had already twice been consul, was expelled from that senate of poor men by the censor because he was discovered to own silver vessels of a mere ten pounds in weight. Such was the personal poverty of the very men whose triumphs enriched the public treasury. There are Christians who put their riches into a

---

66. See above at 1.15.

67. Cincinnatus and Fabricius, named below, are also mentioned in *Letter* 104.6 as models of pagan Roman poverty.

68. See Eutropius, *Abridgement of Roman History* 1.11.

69. See Livy, *History of Rome* 3.26.

70. See Plutarch, *Pyrrhus* 20. Gaius Fabricius Luscinus, consul in 282 and 278 BCE, was often cited as a model of probity; he was said to have been unable to be bribed by Pyrrhus.

71. See above at 2.21.

common holding with a more noble purpose. In accord with what is written in the Acts of the Apostles, they pool their wealth so that what they have may be distributed to each according to his need, and no one calls anything his own, but rather all is held in common.[72] But do they not all understand that they have no reason to swell with pride on this account? They do this, after all, to obtain a place in the company of the angels, while those Romans did something very similar for no greater reason than to preserve the glory of Rome.

How would these feats, and any others of the same kind that may be found in their writings, ever have become so widely known or have been proclaimed with such renown if the Roman empire had not spread far and wide and grown large through its magnificent successes?[73] It is thanks to that empire—so widespread, so long-lasting, so famous and glorious for the virtues of men such as those I have named—that those men received the reward that they sought in their efforts; and it is thanks to that empire that we have their examples set before us as a necessary admonition. If, for the sake of the most glorious city of God, we do not hold fast to the virtues of which they held to a kind of likeness for the sake of no more than the glory of the earthly city, we should be pierced with shame. And if we do hold fast to them, of course, we should not swell up with pride, for, as the Apostle says, *The sufferings of this present time are unworthy of the future glory which will be revealed in us* (Rom. 8:18). In contrast, the lives of those Romans were judged worthy enough of human glory in this present age.

Thus it was entirely right that the Jews, who killed Christ, were given over to the glory of the Romans just when the New Testament was revealing what lay hidden in the Old[74]—that the one true God is to be worshiped not for the sake of earthly and temporal goods, which divine providence grants to the good and the evil alike, but rather for the sake of eternal life, and everlasting gifts, and the society of the supernal city itself.[75] So it was, then, that those who sought and attained earthly glory by their virtues—virtues of a sort—conquered those who by their great vices killed and rejected the giver of true glory and of the eternal city.

72. See Acts 2:44–45; 4:34–35.

73. [GWL] A summary of Augustine's thesis, first presented in 5.16. Rome's expansion enabled its military heroes to be celebrated for their exploits. These stories serve as an admonition to Christians to do even more glorious things for the sake of heavenly reward.

74. See *Instructing Beginners in Faith* 4.8 for a similar formula.

75. [GWL] Following the *adversus Iudaeos* (against the Jews) tradition among early Christian writers, Augustine blames the death of Christ on the Jews. He then interprets the Romans' destruction of the Jerusalem temple in 70 CE as divine punishment for killing Christ. See essay: "Jews and Judaism."

The Difference between the Desire for Glory and the Desire for Domination

19. There is, of course, a difference between the desire for human glory and the desire for domination.[76] For, even though it is all too easy for anyone who takes excessive delight in human glory to slip over into an ardent pursuit of domination, it remains true that those who desire true glory, even if only the glory of human praise, will take care not to displease people of sound judgment. For there are many good qualities of character, and there are many who judge those qualities well, even though not many actually have them. And it is by means of these good qualities of character that the men strive for glory and power and domination of whom Sallust says, "But he strives by the true path."[77] In contrast, anyone who wants domination and power, but lacks the desire for glory that makes a person afraid to displease people of sound judgment, will generally seek to obtain what he loves by even the most blatantly criminal acts. The person who yearns for glory, therefore, will either strive by the true path or "compete by guile and deceit,"[78] wishing to seem good when he is not.

To one who possesses the virtues, then, it is a great virtue to despise glory, for his contempt for glory is seen by God, even if it is not apparent to human judgment. For no matter what he may do before human eyes to show that he holds glory in contempt, if people think that he is only trying to gain greater praise (that is, greater glory), there is no way that he can prove to the senses of those who suspect him that their suspicions have no basis. But the person who despises the judgment of those who praise him will also despise the temerity of those who suspect him. If he is truly good, however, he will not despise their salvation, for so great is the righteousness of the person whose virtues come from the Spirit of God that he loves even his enemies. In fact, he loves them so much that he wants those who hate and belittle him to be set right, and he longs to have them as fellow citizens not in an earthly but in the heavenly homeland. As for those who praise him, although he sets little store by their praise, he most certainly does not set little store by their love. And, precisely because he does not want to deceive those who love him, he does not want

76. [GWL] Augustine distinguishes between lust for glory and lust for domination. Lust for glory generates false virtue, which brings some earthly good. Lust for domination involves outright cruelty. The former is far preferable, but it can easily degenerate into the latter.

77. *Catiline Conspiracy* 11.

78. See *Catiline Conspiracy* 11.

to mislead those who praise him. Therefore he eagerly entreats them to give their praise not to him but rather to the one from whom we receive whatever in us is truly worthy of praise.

In contrast, the person who despises glory but is avid for domination outdoes even the beasts in the vices of cruelty and of self-indulgence. Some Romans were like this. They had lost any concern for their good name but suffered no lack of desire for dominance. History tells us that there were many like this, but it was Nero Caesar who first reached the summit and, so to speak, the citadel of this vice. He went so far in self-indulgence that one might have thought there was nothing hard-fisted to fear from him, and yet he went so far in cruelty that one might have believed, if one did not know better, there was nothing flabby about him.[79] But even in the case of men such as this, the power to dominate is given only by the providence of the supreme God, when he judges that the state of human affairs deserves such overlords. The voice of God is clear about this, where the Wisdom of God declares, *By me kings reign, and by me tyrants hold the earth* (Prov. 8:15). It might be supposed that the word "tyrant" here means not evil and unjust kings but rather strong rulers, as in the ancient sense in which Virgil says, "It will be a part of peace for me to have touched the tyrant's right hand."[80] But to exclude this sense, Scripture most clearly says of God in another passage, *He causes the hypocrite to reign on account of the perversity of the people* (Job 34:30).

As best I could, then, I have explained why the one true and just God aided the Romans in attaining the glory of such a great empire, for they were good men within the context of the earthly city.[81] It is possible, of course, that there is another more hidden reason, better known to God than to us, which has to do with the diverse merits of humankind. But even so, let it be agreed among all who are truly godly that no one can possibly have true virtue without true godliness—that is, without true worship of the true God—and that virtue is not true virtue when it is put to the service of human glory. But let it also

79. See Tacitus, *Annals* 15.37; Suetonius, *Lives of the Twelve Caesars*, Nero.
80. *Aeneid* 7.266.
81. [GWL] A summary of Augustine's argument from 5.12 to this point. God allowed the Romans to expand because their lust for glory generated external acts of righteousness, which bore earthly benefits. Roman heroism also furnished examples for Christians to emulate and exceed. Augustine acknowledges, however, that his explanation is speculative and that a better explanation might be found. This passage exhibits the ambiguities of Augustine's posture toward Roman virtue. Despite his polemic against Roman history and culture, he acknowledges that some Romans, at least, "were good men within the context of the earthly city."

be agreed that those who are not citizens of the eternal city (which is called the city of God in our sacred Scriptures[82]) are more useful to the earthly city when they at least have the kind of virtue that serves human glory than when they do not.

As for those who are endowed with true godliness and who lead good lives, if they also have the skill of governing peoples, there is no happier state of human affairs than when, by God's mercy, they hold power.[83] Such men attribute their virtues, so far as they are able to have virtue in this life, only to the grace of God, for it is God who has given them these virtues in response to their willing, their believing, and their entreating. At the same time, they understand how far they fall short of perfect righteousness as it is found in the company of the holy angels, for which they are striving to prepare themselves. And so, no matter how much we may praise and proclaim the virtue which, lacking true godliness, serves the end of human glory, it is in no way to be compared with even the tiniest first steps of the saints, who have put their hope in the grace and mercy of the true God.

The Proper End of Virtue: Neither Pleasure nor Human Glory

20. There are some philosophers who make virtue itself the highest good for human beings.[84] They like to heap shame on some other philosophers who, while they certainly approve of the virtues, take them as means to the end of bodily pleasure, which they think should be sought for its own sake, but the virtues only for its sake.[85] To make them ashamed, then, they are accustomed to paint a kind of picture in words. They show Pleasure sitting on a royal throne like some spoiled and willful queen, with the virtues as her handmaidens, waiting on her beck and call to do whatever she commands.[86] She orders Prudence to stay alert in seeking how Pleasure may reign and keep her reign secure. She orders Justice to bestow any benefits she can, in order

---

82. See Pss. 46:4; 48:1, 8.

83. [GWL] Augustine affirms the earthly benefit of having Christian rulers. His position differs from the "separation of church and state" commonly affirmed in the modern West. See also 4.3 and 5.24–26.

84. These are the Stoics, as described in Diogenes Laertius, *Lives of Eminent Philosophers* 7.

85. [GWL] Augustine draws on the Stoics' critique of the Epicureans to critique the Romans. Whereas the Epicureans made virtue a servant to pleasure, the Romans made virtue a servant to glory. NCP: "See Epicurus, *Epistle to Menoeceus*, cited in Laertius, *Lives of Eminent Philosophers* 10.122–35."

86. See Cicero, *On the Ends of the Good and the Evil* 2.69.

to gain the friendships necessary for bodily comfort, and to wrong no one for fear that, if laws are broken, Pleasure would not be able to live in security. She orders Fortitude, in the case of any bodily pain that does not bring death in its train, to keep her mistress—that is, Pleasure—firmly in mind so as to dull the sting of present pain by the recollection of previous delights. She orders Temperance to take only just so much food, no matter how delightful it tastes, for fear that the harm of excess might interfere with health and thus Pleasure (which the Epicureans consider to lie most especially in bodily health) be gravely distressed. Thus the virtues, with all the glory of their worth and dignity, will be the slaves of Pleasure, as of some domineering and disreputable little female.[87] Nothing, they say, is more disgraceful and degraded than this picture, and nothing more unbearable to the eyes of the good. And what they say is true.

But even if another such picture were painted, this time with the virtues in the service of human glory, I still do not think it would have the beauty it should. For although Glory is no spoiled little woman, she is still puffed up and swollen with vanity. And it is not right for the firm and solid virtues to serve her, so that Prudence foresees nothing, Justice bestows nothing, Fortitude endures nothing, and Temperance restrains nothing except for the sake of pleasing men and serving the empty wind of glory.

There are people who, even though they spurn the judgments of others as if they really despised glory, still consider themselves wise and are pleased with themselves, but they also have no defense against the ugliness of this picture. For their virtue, if they have any virtue, is simply put at the service of human praise in another way, for the man who pleases himself is still nothing else than a man. But the person who, with true godliness, believes and hopes in God, whom he loves, attends more to those things in which he is displeasing to himself than to those, if any, which are pleasing not to himself but rather to the Truth. Nor does he attribute what can now be found pleasing in him to anything other than the mercy of the one whom he fears to displease, giving thanks for what has been healed and pouring out his prayers for what still needs to be healed.

———————◆———————

87. In *The Catholic Way of Life* 15.25 Augustine defines the four cardinal virtues (prudence, justice, fortitude and temperance) in terms of love, just as he does here in terms of pleasure—there favorably, but here, of course, unfavorably.

The Good Christian Emperor

24. As for us, if we call certain Christian emperors happy, the reason is not that they had longer reigns or that they died peacefully and left sons ruling after them; it is not that they subdued the republic's enemies or that they were able to guard against and suppress insurgencies against them by hostile citizens.[88] After all, even some worshipers of demons, who do not belong to the kingdom of God to which these emperors belong, have deserved to receive these and other gifts and consolations of this troubled life. And this happened by the mercy of God, to keep those who believe in him from desiring to receive such things from him as if they were the highest goods.

Rather,[89] we call Christian emperors happy if they rule justly; if they do not swell with pride among the voices of those who honor them too highly and the obsequiousness of those who acclaim them too humbly, but remember that they are only human beings; if they make their power the servant of God's majesty, using it to spread the worship of God as much as possible; if they fear, love, and worship God; if, more than their own kingdom, they love the one where they do not fear to have co-rulers; if they are slow to punish and quick to pardon; if they enforce punishment only as necessary for governing and defending the republic, not to satisfy their personal animosities; if they grant pardon not to let wrongdoing go unpunished but in the hope of its being corrected; if they compensate for the harsh decisions they are often compelled to make with the leniency of mercy and the generosity of beneficence; if the more they are in a position to give free rein to self-indulgence the more they hold it in check; if they prefer to govern their own base desires more than to govern any peoples; if they do all this not out of a craving for empty glory but rather out of love for eternal happiness; and if, for their sins, they do not

---

88. [GWL] In 5.24–26, Augustine treats the qualities of a blessed ("happy") emperor. These chapters arise often in discussions of Augustine's political theology. Emperors are not blessed just because they enjoy earthly benefits like a long reign and a peaceful death; true blessing requires virtue. Augustine's ideal ruler is a Christian, which means he models humility, favors mercy over justice, and promotes proper worship. These themes appear also in *Letters* 138; 153; and 155. In 5.26, Augustine presents Theodosius as an exemplary Christian ruler. For context on the material that follows, see "Background," in the introduction; and see essay: "History of the Romans."

89. The section that begins here is a so-called "mirror for princes" and, albeit brief, is the first Christian example of that genre, unless, with less justification, one were also to include Eusebius of Caesarea's writings on Constantine [see note 93 below] in that category. The purpose of a "mirror for princes" was to provide instruction to rulers to help them rule wisely, although wise rule was not always understood as virtuous rule, as exemplified in Niccolo Machiavelli's *Prince*, the most famous work of its type.

neglect to offer their true God the sacrifice of humility and compassion and prayer. It is Christian emperors such as this that we say are happy. For the present, they are happy in hope; hereafter, they will be happy in reality, when that to which we now look forward has actually arrived.

25. For God, in his goodness, did not want people who believe that he should be worshiped for the sake of eternal life to imagine that no one, thinking that spirits have great power in such matters, could attain earthly kingdoms and the heights of power without offering worship to demons.[90] And so he heaped worldly gifts, beyond anyone's most audacious wishes, on the emperor Constantine, who offered no worship to demons but worshiped the true God alone.[91] God even granted him the founding of a city to share in Roman rule—the daughter, so to speak, of Rome itself, but wholly without any temple or image of the demons.[92] He had a long reign, and, as sole Augustus, he held and defended the whole Roman world. He was supremely victorious in the wars that he directed and waged, and in every case was successful in crushing tyrants. He died of sickness and old age after a long life, and he left sons to rule after him.[93]

But on the other hand, to keep any emperor from becoming Christian simply to gain Constantine's happy success—since no one should be Christian except for the sake of eternal life—God removed Jovian far more quickly than he did Julian,[94] and he allowed Gratian to be killed by a usurper's sword.[95]

90. [GWL] This argument matches Augustine's theology of suffering in 1.8–9 (see essay: "Providence and Suffering"). Good and evil emperors experience temporal goods and temporal evils. One cannot base judgments about an emperor's blessedness on the quality of his temporal experiences.

91. [GWL] Constantine was the first Roman emperor to convert to Christianity. Following his victory over Maxentius at the Milvian Bridge (312), he and his co-emperor, Licinius, issued the Edict of Milan (313) legalizing Christianity throughout the empire. Constantine would go on to establish the city of Constantinople, formerly called Byzantium, as the new capital of the empire. After defeating his political rivals, Constantine ruled as sole emperor from 324 to his death in 337. With the exception of Julian (sometimes called "the Apostate"), all of Rome's subsequent emperors were Christian.

92. I.e., the city of Constantinople, founded in 330.

93. In composing this section on Constantine, Augustine must have been influenced, at least indirectly, by Eusebius of Caesarea's fulsome encomiums of the emperor—namely, his *Life of Constantine* and *Praises of Constantine* 1–10. Augustine could not have known, for example, that Constantine had his wife Fausta and his son Crispus murdered in 326, that he was generally cruel to his enemies, or that he was baptized only on his deathbed by Eusebius of Nicomedia, an Arian sympathizer.

94. [GWL] Jovian was a Christian who ruled for less than a year, from 363 to 364. This was even shorter than the reign of Julian (361–63), who sought to restore traditional Roman religion and undermine Christianity (5.21). There is no simple correlation between emperors' moral character and the lengths of their reigns.

95. Gratian co-ruled the empire from 367 to 383. The usurper was the Roman general Magnus Maximus, who ruled from 383 to 388 and who was not directly responsible for the

In a sense, however, Gratian's death was far less harsh than that of Pompey the Great, who did worship the supposed gods of Rome. For Pompey could not be avenged by Cato, whom he had left, in a manner of speaking, as his heir in the civil war, but Gratian—although godly souls require no such consolations—was avenged by Theodosius, whom he had made his co-ruler despite the fact that he had a little brother of his own. For Gratian was more eager to have a faithful colleague than to pile up an excess of power.

The Emperor Theodosius

26. Thus Theodosius kept faith with Gratian not only while he was alive but also after his death. For when Gratian's little brother Valentinian was banished by Maximus, Gratian's murderer, Theodosius, as a Christian, took him under his protection in his part of the empire and watched over him with fatherly affection.[96] Because Valentinian was destitute of all resources, Theodosius could easily have removed him, if he had been fired more by the desire to extend his rule than by the love of doing good. Instead he took Valentinian under his wing, preserved his imperial dignity, and consoled him with kindness and graciousness. Then, even though Maximus' success had made him a terror, Theodosius, despite all his anxious cares, did not lapse into sacrilegious and illicit superstitions. Instead he sent to John, a hermit established in the Egyptian desert.[97] For Theodosius had learned, due to John's growing

---

emperor's death. A few lines later Augustine refers to Gratian as one of the "godly souls" (*piae animae*)—undoubtedly because of his support of orthodox Christianity and his close relationship with Ambrose of Milan.

96. NCP: "Theodosius I ('the Great') was co-emperor or emperor from 379 to 395. His friendship with Ambrose and his establishment of orthodox Christianity as the state religion were surely what won Augustine's high approval. Valentinian II was born ca. 371 and became co-emperor in 375; he was either murdered or committed suicide in 392."

[GWL] Despite Maximus's usurpation of Gratian, Theodosius recognized Maximus's rule over Gaul until 387, when Maximus invaded Italy and expelled the young Valentinian II. Valentinian II was the emperor in Milan when Augustine was there (*Confessions* 6.6.9). In *Confessions* 9.7.15, Augustine describes Valentinian II's mother, Justina, as an Arian who persecuted Ambrose. On Augustine's depiction of Theodosius here, see Yves-Marie Duval, "L'éloge de Théodose dans la *Cité de Dieu* (V, 26, 1): Sa place, son sens et ses sources," *Recherches augustiniennes* 4 (1966): 135–79.

97. NCP: "This was John of Lycopolis, one of the most famous of the Desert Fathers. His correspondence with Theodosius is mentioned in Palladius, *Lausiac History* 35.2; Cassian, *Institutes* 4.23; Cassian, *Conferences* 24.26.17."

[GWL] Theodosius supported Valentinian II after Maximus's invasion of Italy. Before counterattacking, Theodosius sought assurance from John of Lycopolis that his military effort

fame, that this servant of God was gifted with the spirit of prophecy. From John he received a most certain assurance of victory. He soon destroyed the tyrant Maximus and, with the greatest mercy and veneration, restored the boy Valentinian to the part of the empire from which he had been forced to flee. When Valentinian was killed soon afterwards, whether by treachery or by some other plot or by accident, another tyrant, Eugenius, was illegally intruded as emperor in his place.[98] Once again Theodosius received a prophetic response and, made confident by his faith in it, crushed the tyrant. It was more by prayer than by sword that he fought against Eugenius's formidable army. Soldiers who were there have told me that the javelins they were throwing were ripped from their hands by a fierce wind blowing from Theodosius's position toward the enemy, and not only did this wind hurl their weapons toward the enemy at amazing speed but it also twisted the enemy's javelins back around toward their own bodies.[99] Thus even the poet Claudian, although a stranger to Christ's name, still says in praise of Theodosius, "O dearly beloved of God, for whom the very air does battle, and the winds, your sworn allies, come at the trumpet's call!"[100]

Being now the victor, as he had believed and predicted he would be, Theodosius threw down the statues of Jupiter which had been consecrated against him by rites of some kind and set up in the Alps. Those statues held thunderbolts made of gold; and when the emperor's couriers (as the joy of the occasion allowed) made a joke about them, saying that they would not mind being struck by that kind of thunderbolt, Theodosius kindly gave the

---

would be successful. John was famed for his ability to see the future. After John foresaw Theodosius's victory, Theodosius attacked and defeated Maximus. After this defeat, Valentinian II began ruling Gaul.

98. [GWL] Four years after Valentinian II was restored, he died under suspicious circumstances, perhaps through the machinations of his military commander, Arbogast. Arbogast installed Eugenius as new co-emperor in 392. Though Eugenius was nominally Christian, he was sympathetic toward traditional Roman religion and restored an altar to the goddess Victory in the Roman senate house. Theodosius defeated Arbogast and Eugenius at the Battle of Frigidus (394). This moment has sometimes been called "paganism's last stand" against Christianity, though scholars have criticized this narrative. See Alan Cameron, *The Last Pagans of Rome* (Oxford: Oxford University Press, 2011). During the two-day battle, Theodosius received a vision of the apostles John and Philip assuring him of success. Augustine stresses Theodosius's reliance on this prophecy and the miraculous character of the victory. The fierce winds mentioned by Augustine also appear in other early Christian texts.

99. See Orosius, *Histories against the Pagans* 7.35.

100. [GWL] Augustine is quoting Claudius Claudianus, *The Third Consulship of Honorius* 96–98 (396). Augustine's attribution is mistaken, however, as Claudius is not addressing Theodosius but Theodosius's son, Honorius. See Clark, *Comm. 1–5*, 259.

thunderbolts to them with a laugh. The sons of his enemies, whose fathers
had been killed—not by his command—in the violence of war, took refuge
in a church, even though they were not yet Christians.[101] Seizing the occasion, Theodosius wished them to become Christians; and he loved them with
Christian charity, not depriving them of their property but rather adding to
their honors. Following the victory, he gave no opening for private animosities against anyone. He was not like Cinna and Marius and Sulla and other
such men, who did not want to end the civil wars even after those wars had
ended.[102] Instead, rather than wishing the war's end to bring harm to anyone,
Theodosius grieved that the war had ever begun.

In the midst of all these happenings, Theodosius did not cease, from the
very beginning of his reign, to help the Church in her struggles against the
ungodly by issuing the most just and merciful legislation.[103] The heretic Valens had favored the Arians and had grievously afflicted the Church.[104] But
Theodosius took more joy in being a member of the Church than in ruling
the world. He ordered the destruction of pagan statues everywhere, for he
knew full well that even earthly rewards do not lie in the power of demons
but rather in the power of the true God. And what was more admirable than
his devout humility when he punished the people of Thessalonica for their
terrible crime? At the intercession of the bishops, he had at first promised
that he would be lenient, but the uproar of certain persons close to him forced
him to take vengeance on the people. But then, corrected by the discipline of
the Church, he did penance with such deep humility that the people, as they
prayed for him, felt more grief at seeing the imperial majesty lying prostrate
than they felt fear of the imperial wrath against sin.[105]

101. These were the sons of Eugenius and Arbogast.

102. [GWL] Note the lengthy treatments of Marius and Sulla in 2.23–24 and 3.27–30.

103. [GWL] In 380, Theodosius issued an edict in Constantinople requiring all citizens to
accept Nicene Christianity. In 391, he banned sacrifices to the gods and ordered the temples
closed. Theodosius was the emperor who convened the Council of Constantinople in 381, which
articulated early Christians' understanding of the Trinity and resulted in what is typically called
the Nicene Creed (short for the Niceno-Constantinopolitan Creed). Theodosius's support for
Nicene Christianity and opposition to Roman religion accords with Augustine's description of
the ideal emperor in 5.24. Augustine seems to be exaggerating Theodosius's aggression when he
claims, a few lines later, that the emperor "ordered the destruction of pagan statues everywhere."

104. NCP: "Valens, the brother of Valentinian I, ruled as co-emperor from 364 to 378."
[GWL] In the latter years of his rule, Valens supported Arian Christians against supporters
of Nicene trinitarian theology. He was killed by the Goths in the momentous Battle of Adrianople (378).

105. The "terrible crime" occurred in the summer of 390, when a mob of Thessalonians
killed Botheric, the military commander of Thessalonica, in retaliation for the imprisonment

These deeds, and others like them, which it would take too long to tell, are the good works that Theodosius took with him from the fog of this temporal life which, no matter how sublime and elevated, is still no more than fog. The reward for these works is eternal happiness, which God gives only to the truly devout. All the other things of this life, whether its high points or its bare necessities, God bestows on the good and the evil alike: such things as the world itself, light, air, land, water, and the fruits of the earth, as well as the soul, body, senses, mind, and life of man himself. And included among these things is also the scope of empire, no matter how great or how small, which God dispenses in accord with his governance of the ages.[106]

I see, however, that we must also respond to those people who, although they have been shown by the most obvious proofs that the throng of false gods is of no help whatsoever in obtaining the temporal goods which are the only goods that foolish people desire to have, still try to claim—even after they have been disproved and refuted on this score—that the gods are to be worshiped not for any benefit in this present life but rather for the sake of the life which is to come after death.[107] For I judge that I have already given an adequate reply in these five books to the people who, as friends of this world, want to worship mere vanities and complain that they are not allowed to follow their childish notions in this regard.

When I had published the first three books and they had begun to circulate widely, I heard that certain persons were preparing some sort of written response to them.[108] Then I was told that they had already written the response but were waiting for a time when they could publish it without risk. My advice to these persons is that they not wish for what is not in their interest. It is easy for anyone who will not keep quiet to seem to have given a response. What, after all, is more talkative than sheer folly? But the fact that folly, if it

---

of a popular but immoral charioteer. Theodosius was enraged and ordered the massacre of the population. Ambrose of Milan tried to prevent this exceedingly disproportionate punishment but was apparently overruled by the emperor's courtiers. Several thousand Thessalonians were killed, and Ambrose in response briefly excommunicated Theodosius and required that he perform public penance. See Ambrose, Letter 51; Paulinus of Milan, *Life of Saint Ambrose* 24. Augustine's sympathies clearly lie with the emperor and not with the Thessalonians; it is strange that he does not mention Ambrose by name but refers instead to unnamed bishops.

106. [GWL] A brief summary of Books 4–5. It is God (not the gods or fate) who allows empires to expand.

107. [GWL] This will be the topic of Books 6–10.

108. The written response to the three books seems not to have survived. Augustine is unusually harsh in describing his critics, but his apparently willing publication of an unfinished work put him in a somewhat compromised position.

wishes, can shout louder than truth does not mean that it is able to do what truth does. Let them consider the whole matter with care. Perhaps, if they can judge without partisan prejudice, they will see that there are some arguments which can be scoffed at, but cannot be overthrown, by impudent babble and the frivolity of satire and mime. If so, let them keep their nonsense in check and choose rather to be corrected by the prudent than to be praised by the impudent. For if they are waiting for a time not of liberty to speak the truth but of license for slander, I certainly hope they do not find themselves in the same position as a certain man of whom Cicero speaks; this man was called fortunate in virtue of his license to sin, but Cicero exclaims, "O wretched man, who had license to sin!"[109] Anyone who counts himself fortunate in having license to slander would be far more fortunate if he had no such license at all. In that case, he could put aside his empty boasting and, even at this late date, could pose any objections he wants, as one eager for discussion, and, in turn, he could hear what he needs to hear from those who, in friendly exchange, respond to his questions honestly, seriously, and candidly as best they possibly can.

109. See *Tusculan Disputations* 5.55. The citation is not verbatim.

Book 10

1–8, 16, 19–20

In Books 8–9, Augustine analyzed the Platonists' understanding of mediating spirits, especially concerning the alleged relationship between humans, demons, and the so-called gods. Following this lengthy discussion, Book 10 contrasts the Roman gods, who are really demons, and the good angels attested in Scripture. Though Book 10 is difficult to follow, its thesis is straightforward. The Roman gods cannot be trusted because they want humans to worship them. By contrast, the angels can be trusted because they direct us to worship God. Book 10 begins with the nature of worship: true sacrifices are defined by love for God and neighbor (10.1–7). Augustine then surveys the miracles of the Old Testament, which were produced by angels to direct humans to God (10.8–19). This section includes a critique of Porphyry's support for theurgy (10.9–11). The high point of Book 10 is a celebration of Jesus, who offered and received the sacrifice of himself (10.20). Augustine also celebrates the martyrs for refusing to sacrifice to demons (10.21–22). Book 10 concludes with a refutation of Porphyry, who misled the masses about the purification of the soul and failed to discover the universal way of salvation (10.23–32).

1. In the view of everyone who is at all capable of using reason, it is a certainty that all people want to be happy.[1] But when, in their mortal weakness, they ask who is happy or what makes them happy, they give rise to a whole host of

---

1. See *The Happy Life* 2.10; *De Trinitate* 13.4.7.

major controversies on which the philosophers have exhausted their energies and consumed their leisure. To bring in those controversies and discuss them at this point would take too long, and, in any case, it is not necessary. We dealt with this matter in the eighth book, when we were selecting the philosophers with whom to discuss the issue of the life of happiness that comes after death.[2] There we asked whether this life is to be attained by directing our religion and sacred rites to the one true God, who is the maker of the gods, or to many gods; and, if the reader will recall what I said there, he will not expect me to repeat the same points here, especially because, if he has forgotten, he can read them again to refresh his memory. We chose the Platonists, who are deservedly the most renowned of all the philosophers, because they were able to see that the human soul, even though it is immortal and rational or intellectual, can only be happy by participation in the light of the God by whom both it and the world were made. Thus they deny that anyone will attain what all human beings desire—that is, the life of happiness—unless he clings with all the purity of a chaste love to the one supreme good which is the immutable God.

But even these philosophers—either because they gave in to popular error and folly or because, as the Apostle says, *they became futile in their thinking* (Rom. 1:21)—thought, or wanted others to think, that we should worship many gods. As a result, some of them went so far as to hold that the divine honors of rites and sacrifices should even be offered to demons. To these we have already replied in no small measure. The present issue, however, concerns the immortal and blessed beings who are established in heavenly thrones, dominions, principalities, and powers,[3] the beings whom the Platonists call gods and to some of whom they give the name either of good demons or, with us, of angels.[4] And what we must now consider and discuss is how we ought to believe that these beings want us to observe religion and piety—that is, to speak more plainly, whether they wish us to offer worship and sacrifices, and to consecrate in religious rites some part of our possessions or our very selves, to themselves also or only to their God, who is also our God.[5]

---

2. [GWL] See 8.5–12, where Augustine says the Platonists defined happiness as the enjoyment of God. Augustine commends them as the best of the philosophers, though he also criticizes them for supporting the worship of many gods. Augustine often cites Rom. 1 with reference to the Platonists' failure. He will return to the question of happiness (or the final good) in Book 19. See essay: "Platonists and Platonism."

3. See Col. 1:16.

4. See Porphyry, *Letter to Anebo*, fragment 10.

5. [GWL] This is the central question of Book 10, where Augustine investigates whether the gods encourage humans to worship God or themselves. Augustine will contrast the angels,

The Terminology of Religion and the Worship Due to God Alone

For this is the worship which is due to divinity or, if we must speak more directly, to deity.[6] To signify this worship in a word—since no wholly satisfactory Latin term occurs to me—I will insert a Greek word where necessary to say what I mean.[7] It is quite true, of course, that wherever the term *latreia* is found in Holy Scripture, our translations employ the word "service."[8] But the kind of service owed to human beings (the kind of service which the Apostle has in mind when he enjoins slaves to be subject to their masters[9]) is ordinarily designated by another term in Greek.[10] *Latreia*, in contrast, according to the usage of those who put down God's words in writing for us, is always—or virtually always—used for the service which pertains to the worship of God.[11] Consequently, if we were simply to use the word *cultus*,[12] this would not seem to be owed to God alone. For we are also said to "cultivate" human beings when we regularly honor them either in our memory or by our presence. Nor is it only things to which we subject ourselves in devoted humility that we are said to "cultivate" but also some things which are subject to us. For from this word we get the words for farmers, colonists, and inhabitants; and the gods themselves are called *caelicolae* for no other reason than that they "cultivate" the heavens[13]—not, of course, by worshiping the heavens but rather by dwelling there as if they were some sort of colonists of the heavens. They are not called "colonists" in the sense of those who owe their condition to the fact that they are bound by birth to the soil and must cultivate it under the dominion of its owners, but rather in the sense in which a great master

---

who direct humans to worship God, with the Roman gods, who seek to be worshiped. As Augustine argues throughout *City of God*, the Roman gods are really demons. See essay: "Angels and Demons."

6. The same distinction is made . . . at 7.1.

7. [GWL] The following paragraphs concentrate on terminology for "worship." Augustine surveys Greek and Latin options and struggles to find the right Latin word for the concept. The Greek *latreia* is exclusively oriented to God, but the Latin word that is usually used to translate it, *servitus* ("service"), can be used with reference to human beings. *Cultus* also has too broad of a range. Similar challenges arise for "religion" (Latin: *religio*; Greek: *thrēskeia*) and "piety" (Latin: *pietas*; Greek *eusebeia*). Augustine eventually settles on "worship of God" (Latin: *cultus Dei*; Greek: *theosebeia*) and stresses that *cultus* is due to God alone.

8. See Exod. 12:25; Matt. 4:12; Luke 4:8.

9. See Eph. 6:6; Col. 3:22.

10. I.e., some form of *doulia*.

11. See Plato, *Phaedrus* 244e.

12. "Worship . . . *cultus*": *colendum . . . cultus*.

13. "Farmers, colonists . . . inhabitants . . . they 'cultivate' the heavens": *agricolae . . . coloni . . . incolae . . . caelum colant*. See Virgil, *Aeneid* 6.554.787.

of Latin eloquence says, "There was an ancient city held by colonists from Tyre."[14] He did not call them colonists because they farmed the land but because they inhabited this city. It is in this sense, too, that cities founded by swarms of people—hiving off, as it were, from larger cities—are called colonies. It is perfectly true, then, that *cultus*, in one proper meaning of the term, is owed to God alone; but, because this term is also used in relation to other things, it is not possible to signify the worship owed to God alone by means of a single Latin word.

Again, the term "religion" itself might seem to signify more precisely not just any worship but specifically the worship of God, and that is why our translators used this word for what is called *thrēskeia* in Greek.[15] But in ordinary Latin usage—and not the usage merely of the ignorant but also of the most highly educated—we say that *religio* should be observed in human relationships, affinities, and ties of all kinds. As a consequence, even this word does not eliminate ambiguity when the point at issue is the worship of the deity. For we cannot genuinely say that *religio* means nothing but the worship of God, since the word would then seem to have been brazenly denied its role in signifying the observances of human relationships.

"Piety," too, which the Greeks call *eusebeia*, is usually understood in its proper sense as the worship of God.[16] But the word is also used of the duties that we owe to parents. And, in common speech, it often refers to works of mercy.[17] This has come about, I think, because God especially commands us to do such works and assures us that they please him more than or instead of sacrifices.[18] From this manner of speaking, it has also come about that God himself is called *pius*.[19] The Greeks, however, never call God *eusebēs* in any usage of theirs, even though, in their case as well, popular speech has adopted *eusebeia* to mean "mercy." In some passages of Scripture, therefore, in order to make the distinction stand out more sharply, they have preferred to use not *eusebeia*, a composite term derived from "good worship," but *theosebeia*, a composite derived from "worship of God."[20] We, however, are unable to express either of these in a single word.

14. Virgil, *Aeneid* 1.12.
15. Augustine means the translators of the New Testament from Greek into Latin. See Col. 2:18; James 1:26–27.
16. See Sophocles, *Philoctetes* 1440–44.
17. See 2 Pet. 3:11.
18. See Matt. 9:13; 12:7.
19. See Sir. 2:13.
20. See 1 Tim. 2:10.

That which in Greek is called *latreia*, then, is called *servitus* in Latin, but it is specifically the service by which we worship God. That which in Greek is called *thrēskeia* is called *religio* in Latin, but it is specifically the religion directed from us to God. And what the Greeks call *theosebeia* we cannot express in a single word, but we can call it the worship of God, and this we say is due only to the God who is the true God and who makes his worshipers gods.[21] Whoever the immortal and blessed beings in their heavenly habitations may be, then, if they do not love us and do not wish us to be blessed, they are certainly not to be worshiped.[22] On the other hand, if they do love us and do want us to be blessed, they clearly want us to attain our blessedness from the same source from which they attain theirs. For it could hardly be true that they have one source of blessedness and we another.

The One Source of Happiness, Both Human and Angelic

2. But there is no conflict between us and these more eminent philosophers on this issue.[23] They saw, and in their writings they affirmed in many ways and at great length, that these beings gain their happiness from the same source that we do—a certain intelligible light shed over them, which is their God, and which is something other than themselves. By this they are illuminated so that they shine bright with light and, by participation in it, exist in a state of perfection and of blessedness.

In explaining Plato's views, Plotinus often stresses that not even the soul which they believe to be the soul of the universe gains its blessedness from any other source than our soul does. It too gains its blessedness from a light which is other than itself, by which it was created, and by whose intelligible illumination it gleams with intelligible light.[24] Plotinus also draws an analogy between these incorporeal beings and the splendid corporeal bodies that we see in the heavens, likening God to the sun and the soul to the moon; for the Platonists suppose, of course, that the moon is illuminated by the light of the

21. See Ps. 82:6.
22. [GWL] After the discussion of terminology, Augustine returns to his thesis. If the gods have our best interests in mind, they will not want us to worship them.
23. [GWL] A reference again to the Platonists. In what follows, Augustine explains why the Platonists are the greatest of philosophers. They affirm a transcendent God and define happiness as participation in God. Augustine believes these positions correspond to what Christians confess. See essay: "Platonists and Platonism."
24. See Plotinus, *Enneads* 5.1.2–5.1.3.

sun shed over it.[25] This great Platonist affirms, then, that the rational soul (or the intellectual soul, as we ought rather to call it)—and he includes in this class the souls of the immortal and blessed beings who, he has no doubt, dwell in heavenly habitations—has no nature above it except the nature of God, who fashioned the world and by whom the rational soul itself was made. Nor, he says, are the life of blessedness and the light by which the truth is understood granted to these supernal beings from any other source than the source from which they are also granted to us.[26] Thus he agrees with the gospel, where we read, *There was a man sent from God, whose name was John. He came as a witness, in order to bear witness to the light, so that all might believe through him. He was not himself the light, but he came to bear witness to the light. This was the true light that enlightens everyone who comes into this world* (John 1:6–9).[27] This distinction shows quite clearly that the rational or intellectual soul, such as John had, cannot be its own light but shines rather by participation in another light, the true light. And John himself acknowledges this when, in bearing witness to God, he says, *From his fullness we have all received* (John 1:16).

3. This being so, if the Platonists (or any others who shared their views), knowing God, had glorified him as God and given thanks to him—if they had not become futile in their thinking,[28] sometimes themselves instigating popular error and sometimes simply being too timid to resist it—they would certainly have confessed that the one God of gods, who is both our God and theirs, is the God who should be worshiped both by those immortal and blessed beings and by us as well, in our mortality and misery, so that we too may be able to attain immortality and blessedness.[29]

It is to this God that we owe the service which is called *latreia* in Greek, whether enacted in certain sacraments or in our very selves.[30] For we are all

25. See Plotinus, *Enneads* 5.6.4.

26. See Plotinus, *Enneads* 5.1.10.

27. [GWL] Augustine believes the Platonists agree with the Gospel of John about the pre-incarnate divine Word. See *Confessions* 7.9.13–7.9.15, which also invokes John to affirm Platonist views about God. Augustine's criticism of the Platonists concentrates on their rejection of the incarnation. The Platonists denied that God could assume flesh.

28. See Rom. 1:21.

29. [GWL] As in *Confessions* 7.9.15, Augustine invokes Rom. 1 in his criticism of the Platonists. Some Platonists knew that Roman religion was false, yet they supported the worship of the gods because they feared to speak the truth against popular superstition.

30. [GWL] These two paragraphs deserve careful attention for Augustine's description of proper worship, which ultimately consists of love for God and neighbor.

collectively his temple and individually his temples,[31] since he deigns to dwell both in the concord of all and in each individual. And he is no greater in all than he is in each, for he is neither enlarged by addition nor diminished by division.[32] Our heart, when lifted up to him, is his altar.[33] It is with his only-begotten Son as our priest that we propitiate him. To him we sacrifice bleeding victims when we fight for his truth to the point of shedding blood. We honor him with the sweetest incense when, in his sight, we burn with devout and holy love. To him we vow and return both his gifts in us and our very selves. To him we dedicate and consecrate the memory of his benefits in solemn feasts and on appointed days, lest ungrateful forgetfulness creep in as time goes by.[34] To him we offer, on the altar of the heart, the sacrifice of humility and praise, kindled by the fire of love. In order to see him, as he can be seen, and to cling to him, we are cleansed of every stain of sin and evil desire and are consecrated in his name. For he is the source of our happiness, and he is the end of all desire. In electing him—or rather in re-electing him, for we had lost him by neglecting him—in re-electing him, then (and the word "religion" is also said to be derived from "re-elect"[35]), we set our course toward him in love, so that, when we reach him, we may be at rest, blessed because made perfect by the one who is our ultimate end. For our good, the final good about which there is so much dispute among the philosophers, is nothing other than to cling to him by whose incorporeal embrace alone, if one can speak of such a thing, the intellectual soul is filled and made fertile with true virtues.

We are enjoined to love this good with all our heart, all our soul, and all our strength. To this good we ought to be led by those who love us, and to it we ought to lead those whom we love.[36] In this way are fulfilled those two

---

31. See 1 Cor. 3:16–17.

32. [GWL] God is immaterial, which means God does not have a body or take up space. God is thus equally present in all things, regardless of their physical size. For a similar discussion, see *Confessions* 7.1.1–7.1.2.

33. A similar spiritual approach to sacrifice, as expressed here, is found in Tertullian, *On Prayer* 28.

34. On the idea that external observances foster an interior awareness see *Letter* 130.9.18.

35. "'Religion' . . . 're-elect'": *religio . . . religentes*. For the etymology of "religion" as Augustine gives it here, see Cicero, *On the Nature of the Gods* 2.28.72. In *Revisions* 1.13.9 Augustine notes two different etymologies—the present one and another that relates it to the word *religare*, meaning "to bind" (to God).

36. [GWL] Humans' greatest good is to love God with all their heart, soul, mind, and strength. This is also what we should want for our neighbors and what our neighbors should want for us. Thus, we can test whether someone loves us by assessing whether they want us to love God. By this test, the Roman gods fail. This passage displays Augustine's emphasis on love for God and neighbor as the core of the Christian life.

commandments on which all the law and the prophets hang, *You shall love the Lord your God with all your heart, and with all your soul, and with all your mind, and You shall love your neighbor as yourself* (Matt. 22:37.39). For, in order that a person may know what it means to love himself, an end has been appointed for him to which he is to refer everything he does so that he may attain happiness, for he who loves himself wants nothing other than to be happy. And this end is precisely to cling to God.[37] Therefore, when a person who now knows what it means to love himself is commanded to love his neighbor as himself, what else is he commanded to do but, so far as possible, to urge his neighbor to love God?[38] This is the worship of God, this is true religion, this is genuine godliness, this is the service due to God alone.

Sacrifice Is Due to God Alone

If any immortal power, then, no matter how great the strength with which it is endowed, loves us as itself, it wants us to be subject, so that we may attain blessedness, to the very one to whom it also is subject and so is blessed.[39] If it does not worship God, it is miserable precisely because it is deprived of God; and if it does worship God, it certainly does not want to be worshiped itself in place of God. Rather, it favors and promotes, with all the force of its love, the divine declaration where it is written, *Whoever sacrifices to any god but to the Lord alone shall be destroyed* (Exod. 22:20).

4. For—to mention nothing else that pertains to the religious service by which God is worshiped—there is no one who would dare to deny that sacrifice is due only to God.[40] There are, of course, many features that have been taken over from divine worship and misapplied to honoring human beings, due either to excessive humility or to dangerously misdirected adulation. Even so, however, those to whom these features are applied are still held to be only human beings. They are said to be worthy of worship and of veneration and even, if still more is credited to them, of adoration. But who ever thought that sacrifice should be offered to any other than to one whom he knew or

---

37. See Ps. 73:28.

38. See *Teaching Christianity* 1.22.21.

39. [GWL] If the gods love us, they will want us to be subject to God, just as they are subject to God.

40. [GWL] Augustine embarks here on a discussion of sacrifice. Sacrifice does not ultimately concern animal offerings but love for God and neighbor.

supposed or imagined to be God? Moreover, the two brothers Cain and Abel, of whom God rejected the sacrifice of the older, but looked with favor on the sacrifice of the younger,[41] show clearly enough just how ancient the practice of worshiping God by sacrifice is.

5. But who would be such a fool as to think that the things offered to God in sacrifice are necessary to him or that he needs them for any use of his own? Divine Scripture makes this clear in any number of passages; but, to avoid going on at length, let it suffice to cite this brief text from the Psalm: *I said to the Lord, You are my God, for you have no need of my goods* (Ps. 16:2). We must believe, therefore, that God not only has no need of cattle or any other corruptible and earthly thing but does not even need a person's righteousness itself. Rather we must hold that everything done in rightly worshiping God is of benefit not to God but to man. For no one would say that he had served the interests of a fountain by drinking from it, or that he had served the interests of a light by using it to see.

The Significance of the Sacrifices Commanded under the Old Law: The Self Directed to God in Love

Nor are those other sacrifices offered by the patriarchs of old with animal victims,[42] which the people of God now only read about but do not perform, to be understood in any other way than this: their role was to signify what is now done among us for the purpose of clinging to God and helping our neighbor to the same end.[43] Sacrifice, therefore, is the visible sacrament of an invisible sacrifice; that is, it is a sacred sign. That is why the penitent in the prophet, or perhaps the prophet himself, in seeking God's forgiveness for his sins, says, *If you had desired sacrifice, I would certainly have given it; you take no delight in burnt offerings. The sacrifice to God is a contrite spirit; a contrite and humbled heart God will not despise* (Ps. 51:16–17).

Note how, in the very place where he said that God does not desire sacrifice, he showed that God does desire sacrifice. The sacrifice that he does not want, then, is the sacrifice of a slaughtered animal, and the sacrifice that

41. See Gen. 4:2–7.
42. See, e.g., Gen. 8:20.
43. [GWL] Augustine's discussion of sacrifice requires him to address the question of Old Testament sacrifices, which involved offering animals to God. As Augustine explains, these sacrifices were a visible sign of the invisible sacrifice we offer now—love for God and neighbor.

he does want is the sacrifice of a contrite heart. Thus, the sacrifice that the
prophet said God does not want signifies the sacrifice that he went on to
say that God does want. And so, what he said was that God does not want
such sacrifices in the way in which fools suppose that he wants them, that is,
as if for his own pleasure. For if he did not want the sacrifices that he does
desire—of which there is only one, a contrite heart, humbled by the sorrow
of repentance—to be signified by the sacrifices he was once thought to desire
for his own delight, he most certainly would not have commanded in the old
law that the latter were to be offered. And the reason why those sacrifices had
to be changed, at the opportune and pre-established moment, was precisely
to keep people from believing that such sacrifices in themselves, rather than
the things they signified, were desirable to God or at least acceptable in us.[44]
Thus, in another passage from another Psalm, God says, *If I were hungry, I
would not tell you, for the world and all its fullness are mine. Shall I eat the
flesh of bulls or drink the blood of goats?* (Ps. 50:12–13). It is as if he were
to say, "Even if I needed such things, I certainly would not ask you for what
I have in my own power." Then, going on to make clear what these things
signify, he says, *Offer to God a sacrifice of praise, and pay your vows to the
Most High; and call upon me in the day of trouble, and I will deliver you,
and you shall glorify me* (Ps. 50:14–15).

Again, in another prophet, it says, *How shall I reach out to the Lord, and
how shall I receive my God, the Most High? Shall I reach out to him with burnt
offerings, with calves a year old? Will the Lord be pleased with thousands of
rams or with tens of thousands of fatted goats? Shall I give my firstborn for
my transgression, the fruit of my loins for the sin of my soul? Has he told
you, O man, what is good? Or what does the Lord require of you but to do
justice, and to love mercy, and to be ready to walk with the Lord, your God?*
(Mic. 6:6–8). In the words of this prophet, too, the two kinds of sacrifice are
distinguished, and it is declared quite plainly that God does not require for
their own sake the sacrifices which are meant to signify the sacrifices that
God does require. In the epistle inscribed to the Hebrews[45] it says, *Do not
forget to do good and to share what you have, for such sacrifices are pleasing*

44. [GWL] The Old Testament sacrifices were signs of a greater reality. The New Testament
ended the sacrifices to demonstrate that the sacrifices were not meant for their own sake but
to foreshadow Jesus. For further discussion of this point, see *De Doctrina Christiana* 3.5.9.

45. Augustine seems to employ a circumlocution here in order to avoid mentioning the
author of the Epistle to the Hebrews; he acknowledges . . . at 16.22 that there is some dispute
as to whether or not it was written by Paul.

to God (Heb. 13:16). Accordingly, where Scripture says, *I desire mercy rather than sacrifice* (Matt. 9:13; 12:7), we must understand it simply to mean that one kind of sacrifice is preferred to another. For the kind of sacrifice that everyone calls sacrifice is a sign of the true sacrifice. And mercy is the true sacrifice, which is why the passage I just cited states, *for such sacrifices are pleasing to God*. All the commands that we read were given by God in relation to the many modes of sacrifice offered in the ministry of the tabernacle or the Temple refer back, therefore, as signs, to the love of God and neighbor. For *on these two commandments*, as Scripture says, *hang all the law and the prophets* (Matt. 22:40).

6. The true sacrifice, then, is every act done in order that we might cling to God in holy fellowship, that is, every act which is referred to the final good in which we can be truly blessed.[46] Thus, even the mercy which we extend to human beings is not a sacrifice if it is not done for God's sake. For, even though sacrifice is made or offered by man, it is still a divine matter, and so the ancient Latins, too, called it by this very term. Thus a person who is consecrated in the name of God and is vowed to God, insofar as he dies to the world so that he may live to God, is himself a sacrifice. For this, too, pertains to mercy, the mercy which a person extends to himself. And so it is written, *Have mercy on your soul by pleasing God* (Sir. 30:24 Vulg.).

Our body also is a sacrifice when we discipline it by temperance, if we do this, as we ought, for God's sake, so as not to present our members to sin as weapons of wickedness but rather to God as weapons of righteousness.[47] It is in exhorting us to this end that the Apostle says, *I appeal to you therefore, brothers, by the mercy of God, to present your bodies as a living sacrifice, holy and pleasing to God, which is your reasonable service* (Rom. 12:1). And so, if the body, which, because it is inferior, the soul uses as a servant or instrument, is a sacrifice when its good and right use is directed to God, how much more does the soul itself become a sacrifice when it directs itself to God so that, aflame with the fire of love for him, it loses the form of worldly desire and, now subject to him, is reformed to him as to an unchanging form, thus pleasing him by receiving its beauty from his beauty![48] It is precisely this point that the same Apostle goes on to make in the next part of the passage: *And do not be conformed to this world,*

---

46. [GWL] A clear definition of sacrifice as Augustine understands it.

47. See Rom. 6:13.

48. [GWL] Though Augustine believes the body is inferior to the soul, he also affirms the goodness of the body, against the Platonists. See essay: "Body."

but be reformed by a renewal of your mind, so that you may discern what is the will of God, what is good and genuinely pleasing and perfect (Rom. 12:2).

Therefore, since true sacrifices are works of mercy, whether shown to ourselves or shown to our neighbors, which are directed to God; and since works of mercy are performed with no other object than that we might be delivered from misery and so become blessed—which only happens by means of that good of which it is said, *But for me the good is to cling to God* (Ps. 73:28)—it obviously follows that the whole redeemed city, that is, the congregation and fellowship of the saints, is offered to God as a universal sacrifice through the great priest who, in his passion, offered himself for us in the form of a servant,[49] to the end that we might be the body of such a great head.[50] For it was this servant form that he offered, and it was in this form that he was offered, because it is according to this form that he is the mediator, in this form that he is the priest, and in this form that he is the sacrifice. Thus, after the Apostle had exhorted us to present our bodies as a living sacrifice, holy, pleasing to God, our reasonable service, and not to be conformed to this world, but to be reformed in a renewal of our mind so that we might discern what is the will of God, what is good and genuinely pleasing and perfect, the whole of which sacrifice is we ourselves, he went on to say, *For by the grace of God given to me, I say to everyone among you not to think more of yourself than you ought to think, but to think temperately, as God has assigned to each his measure of faith. For just as in one body we have many members, and not all members have the same functions, so we, although many, are one body in Christ, and individually members of one another, having diverse gifts according to the grace given to us* (Rom. 12:3–6). This is the sacrifice of Christians: *although many, one body in Christ*. And this is the sacrifice that the Church continually celebrates in the sacrament of the altar (which is well known to the faithful), where it is made plain to her that, in the offering she makes, she herself is offered.[51]

7. As for those immortal and blessed beings who dwell in heavenly habitations and together rejoice in participation in their creator, who are constant

49. See Phil. 2:7.

50. This is the city of God in its purest sense, as Augustine understands it in its earthly instantiation—namely, the whole body of the saved with Christ as its head. In the following section (7) he points out that the city in its entirety consists of both human beings and angels.

51. It seems from Augustine's phrasing that "the sacrament of the altar," which is the eucharist or the sacramental body of Christ, is secondary to the sacrifice that is "we ourselves." But it would be correct to say that the sacrifice of the eucharist subsumes or represents the sacrifice of the body of Christ that is the faithful, or "we ourselves." This theme, in any event, is now temporarily left aside, to be resumed below at 10.20.

by virtue of his eternity, certain by virtue of his truth, and holy by virtue of his gift—because, in their mercy, they love us miserable mortals and wish us also to become immortal and blessed, they rightly do not want us to sacrifice to themselves but rather to God, for they know that, together with us, they are themselves his sacrifice.[52] For, along with them, we are the one city of God, to which it is said in the Psalm, *Glorious things are spoken of you, O city of God* (Ps. 87:3).[53] Part of this city, our part, is on pilgrimage far from home; and part, their part, gives us its help. It is from that supernal city, where God's intelligible and immutable will is law, from that supernal court, so to speak (for it shows care[54] for us), that there descended to us through the ministry of the angels the holy Scripture which reads, *Whoever sacrifices to any god but to the Lord alone will be destroyed* (Exod. 22:20). This Scripture, this law, and such commandments as this, have been attested by such great miracles that it is perfectly clear to whom these immortal and blessed beings, who desire for us what they have themselves, want us to sacrifice.[55]

The Miracles That Confirm the Command to Sacrifice to God Alone

8. If I recount events from far back in the too distant past, I will seem, no doubt, to take much longer than needed in reviewing the miracles which were done to confirm the promises of God, the promises in which he foretold to Abraham, thousands of years ago, that all peoples were going to receive a blessing in his seed.[56] But who would not be amazed that a barren wife bore this same Abraham a son at an advanced age, when not even a fertile woman could still give birth?[57] Or that, when this same Abraham offered sacrifice, a flame from heaven passed

52. [GWL] A key transition sentence. Having treated the general question of sacrifice, Augustine asserts that the angels encourage us to sacrifice to God and not to themselves. This demonstrates their love for us. The angels love us as themselves by desiring for us the same good in which they participate—namely, God. Augustine will soon contrast the goal of angels with the goal of the Roman gods.

53. [GWL] The city of God is composed of both angels and humans. Humans constitute that part of the heavenly city which still resides on earth.

54. "Court . . . care": *curia . . . cura*. See Varro, *On the Latin Language* 6.6. There is, however, no etymological connection between these words.

55. [GWL] This sentence introduces the overarching argument of 10.8–19: the angels' miracles in the Old Testament directed humans to worship God. The angels' example contrasts with the practice of theurgy, which Augustine will refute in 10.9–11.

56. See Gen. 18:18.

57. See Gen. 18:9–14; 21:1–7.

between the pieces of the victims?[58] Or that the fire from heaven that would descend on Sodom was foretold to this same Abraham by angels—angels whom he had welcomed as guests in human form and through whom he had received God's promises about the offspring he was going to have?[59] Or that, when the fire was about to strike Sodom, the same angels would miraculously save Abraham's nephew Lot, whose wife looked back on the way and was immediately turned into a pillar of salt,[60] which was a great sacrament warning us that no one who has set out on the way of salvation should yearn for his past life?[61]

Then, too, there were all the extraordinary miracles performed through Moses for the purpose of rescuing God's people from the yoke of servitude in Egypt, where the sorcerers of Pharaoh—that is, the king of Egypt, who was oppressing that people by his domination—were permitted to perform certain miracles of their own only so that they might be vanquished even more miraculously. They achieved their effects by the sorceries and magical incantations to which the evil angels (that is, the demons) are devoted; but Moses, as much more powerful as he was more righteous, easily overcame them in the name of God, who made heaven and earth, with the angels' help. In short, the sorcerers gave up at the third plague, but, through Moses, the full ten plagues were brought to completion in a great array of mysteries. The result was that the hard hearts of Pharaoh and the Egyptians yielded, and they let God's people go. But they immediately regretted it, and, when they tried to overtake the departing Hebrews, who were passing through the divided sea on dry ground, they were engulfed and overwhelmed by water flowing back together from both sides.[62]

And what shall I say of the miracles that came one after another, by amazing divine power, while that same people was being led through the wilderness? What of the waters that could not be drunk but lost their bitterness and satisfied the thirsty when, as God commanded, a piece of wood was thrown into them?[63] What of the manna which came from heaven when they were hungry,

58. See Gen. 15:17. In *Revisions* 2.43(70).2 Augustine corrects himself by saying that this qualifies not as a miracle but as a vision. This is one of only two (very minor) corrections that he makes in his vast work; the other occurs in reference to 17.5.

59. See Gen. 18.

60. See Gen. 19:15–26.

61. Not restricting himself to the later, medieval, understanding of a set number of sacraments, Augustine uses the term "sacrament," as do many other Fathers, in the sense of any object or action that somehow conveys grace. Here the word, which is applied somewhat unusually to the pillar of salt, points to the grace of admonition.

62. See Exod. 7:1–15:19.

63. See Exod. 15:22–25.

but, since a limit had been set for those gathering it, got worms and went bad when anyone gathered more than the limit, and yet when a double supply was gathered on the day before the sabbath—since gathering on the sabbath was not lawful—it did not go bad at all?[64] What of the birds which, when they longed for meat, and it seemed that nothing could possibly supply so vast a people, filled up their camp and quenched their burning desire with the disgusted satiety that comes from having eaten too much?[65] What of the enemies they encountered, who blocked their path and attacked them, but who were laid low without the loss of a single Hebrew when Moses prayed with his arms outstretched in the shape of a cross?[66] What of the rebels who rose up among God's people and set themselves against the divinely ordained fellowship, but were swallowed alive by the gaping earth as a visible example of invisible punishment?[67] What of the rock struck by a rod that poured forth a flow of water ample for all that great multitude?[68] And what of the deadly serpent-bites—a most just punishment for sinners—which were healed at the sight of a brazen serpent that was held up on a wooden pole not only to bring relief to an afflicted people but also to provide a sign of the destruction of death by death in the likeness, so to speak, of death crucified?[69] Later, when this same serpent, which had been preserved in memory of this deed, began to be worshiped as an idol by the erring people, King Hezekiah, using his power in the service of God and religion, broke it to pieces, winning great praise for his godliness.[70]

Angels, Miracles, and the Worship of God

16. Which set of angels, then, do you think that we ought to believe with regard to eternal and blessed life?[71] Those who themselves want to be worshiped

64. See Exod. 16:14–26.
65. See Num. 11:18–23, 31–33.
66. See Exod. 17:8–13.
67. See Num. 16:1–3, 23–33.
68. See Num. 20:2–11.
69. See Num. 21:6–9. The bronze serpent as an image or type of the crucified Christ is as ancient as the New Testament (see John 3:14) and became a commonplace in patristic literature, beginning with *The Epistle of Barnabas* 12 and Justin Martyr, *1 Apology* 60.
70. See 2 Kings 18:4.
71. [GWL] This chapter presents the clearest contrast in Book 10 between the angels and the demons.

with religious rituals, insisting that mortals offer them rites and sacrifices? Or those who say that all this worship is due only to the one God, the creator of all things, and instruct us to direct it with true godliness to him in contemplation of whom they themselves are now blessed and promise that we also will be blessed in the future? That vision of God is a vision of such beauty and is worthy of such love that Plotinus has absolutely no doubt about saying that, without it, a person is utterly wretched, no matter how abundantly endowed with any other kinds of goods.[72] Since, therefore, some angels prompt us by miraculous signs to worship (in the sense of *latreia*) the one God and others prompt us to worship themselves, and since the former forbid us to worship the latter, but the latter do not dare to forbid the worship of the one God, which of the two should we believe?[73] Let the Platonists answer, let the philosophers in general answer, let the theurgists—or rather the meddlers in magic,[74] for that is what all these arts really deserve to be called—answer. In short, let people in general answer, if there still lives in them any sense that they were created rational in nature. Let them answer, I say, and let them tell us whether we ought to sacrifice to those beings, whether gods or angels, who enjoin us to sacrifice to themselves, or rather to the one God to whom we are enjoined to sacrifice by those who forbid us to sacrifice either to themselves or to the others.

Even if neither of these performed any miracles but only gave commands—the ones ordering us to sacrifice to themselves, the others forbidding this, but commanding sacrifice to the one God alone—piety itself should be enough to determine which of these commands comes from arrogant pride and which from true religion. I will go even further: even if only those beings who seek sacrifice for themselves used miracles to influence human souls, while those who forbid this and enjoin sacrifice only to the one God never stooped to perform any visible miracles at all, it would still be true that the authority of the latter should be preferred not on the basis of the body's senses but on the basis of the mind's rationality. In fact, however, God has acted to make the pronouncement of his truth all the more persuasive by performing, through those immortal messengers who proclaim not their own arrogance but his

72. See *Enneads* 1.6.7.

73. [GWL] The demons do not forbid worship of God because they fear to do so. Their diffidence on this matter underscores the credibility of angels over demons.

74. Augustine uses the neologism *periurgi*, which reflects the Greek word *perierga* ("curious arts") in Acts 19:19 and is translated here as "meddlers in magic."

majesty, miracles that are greater, more certain, and more celebrated.[75] His purpose was to prevent those who seek sacrifice for themselves from easily persuading the weak in faith to embrace false religion merely by showing them wonders that astound the senses. Who, then, is so enamored of folly that he will not choose the truths to follow where he also finds there are more miracles to marvel at?

There are also the miracles of the gods of the nations which history reports to us. I am not thinking, however, of the ominous events that occur from time to time due to hidden causes that belong to this world but are actually ordained and determined by divine providence—such things as freakish births of animals or unusual phenomena in the heavens or on earth, whether merely frightening or actually harmful as well, which are said (due to the demons' cunning deceit) to be averted or alleviated by demonic rites. Rather I am thinking of things that seem clearly enough to be due to these gods' might and power. For instance, it is reported that the images of the household gods which Aeneas took with him when he fled from Troy moved on their own from place to place;[76] that Tarquin cut a whetstone with a razor;[77] that the serpent of Epidaurus attached itself to Aesculapius and accompanied him on his voyage to Rome;[78] that the ship which brought the statue of the Phrygian mother to Rome remained stuck fast, despite all the efforts of men and oxen, but was set in motion and drawn along by one mere woman, using her girdle as a towline, in order to give proof of her chastity;[79] that a Vestal virgin whose purity was in doubt settled the issue when she filled a sieve with water from the Tiber and none leaked out.[80] But such things as these are by no means to be compared in power and magnitude to those that we read were performed among the people of God. How much less, then, can we compare to them things that

75. [GWL] In principle, people should adjudicate between angels and demons on the basis of their teachings. The angels would be more credible than the demons even if they never performed miracles and the demons performed impressive ones. Yet God has accommodated the weakness of human faith by empowering the angels to perform miracles that are greater than those of the demons. Clark, *Comm. 6–10*, 208, suggests that Augustine is thinking of Volusian's criticism, relayed by Marcellinus in Letter 136.1, that Roman magicians performed greater wonders than Christ.

76. See Valerius Maximus, *Memorable Deeds and Words* 1.8.7.

77. See Livy, *History of Rome* 1.36.

78. See Livy, *Epitome* 11.

79. See Ovid, *Festivals* 4.295–325. The Phrygian mother is the so-called Great Mother. See [*City of God, Books 1–10*, 40n6].

80. See Valerius Maximus, *Memorable Deeds and Words* 8.1.5.

were judged worthy of being forbidden and punished by the laws of the very people who worshiped such gods, namely, works of magic or theurgy! Most of these are mere appearances that deceive the human senses by tricks of illusion, such as the drawing down of the moon "until," as Lucan says, "from near at hand she sprays her dew upon the grass below."[81] And even if certain of these miracles do seem to equal some of the deeds of the devout, at least so far as the work itself is concerned, it is still true that the two are distinguished by the ends they serve, and this shows that ours are incomparably the better.[82] For theirs only go to show that the many gods are the less deserving of sacrificial worship the more they strive to get it. But ours point to the one God who, both by the testimony of his Scriptures[83] and by his later abolition of these very sacrifices, demonstrates that he has no need at all for such sacrifice.

If, then, there are angels who seek sacrifice for themselves, we must prefer to them the angels who seek it not for themselves but for God, the creator of all things, whom they serve. In this, they show how genuinely they love us, for they want us, through sacrifice, to be subject not to themselves but to him in the contemplation of whom they themselves are blessed, and they want us to arrive at him from whom they themselves have never departed. And if there are angels who want sacrifices to be made to many gods rather than to one, but want these sacrifices not for themselves but for the gods whose angels they are, we must still prefer to them those who are the angels of the one God of gods. These angels enjoin sacrifice to the one God and forbid sacrifice to any other. But none of those other angels forbid sacrifice to the one God whose angels command us to sacrifice to him alone. And if, as their arrogant deceitfulness suggests, those others are in fact neither good angels nor the angels of good gods but evil demons who want sacrificial worship to be offered not to the one, sole, and supreme God but to themselves, what better defense against them can we choose than the protection of the one God whom the good angels serve—the angels who command us to serve with sacrifice not themselves but him whose sacrifice we ourselves ought to be?

◆

81. See *Pharsalia* 6.506.82.
82. [GWL] Augustine concedes that the demons have performed impressive miracles. But the demons should still be rejected for failing to promote proper worship.
83. See Ps. 50:9–15.

Sacrifice, the Angels, and the Worship of God

19. Some people suppose that visible sacrifices are appropriate for other gods, but that God—since he is invisible, greater, and better—should be offered invisible, greater, and better sacrifices, sacrifices such as the service of a pure mind and a good will. These people, however, obviously do not understand that these visible sacrifices are signs of invisible sacrifices in the same way that spoken words are signs of things.[84] Therefore, just as in the case of prayer and praise we direct to God words that signify and offer to him the things in our hearts that are signified by our words, so also we should understand that, in the case of sacrifice, visible sacrifice is to be offered only to God and that, in our hearts, we should present our very selves as an invisible sacrifice to him. That is when the angels, and all the higher powers whose strength is due to their very goodness and devotion, favor us, rejoice with us, and help us with all their might to do this very thing. But if we desire to offer these sacrifices to the angels themselves, they are not willing to receive them, and, when they are sent to men in a way that allows us to perceive their presence, they explicitly forbid it. There are examples in Holy Scripture.[85] Some people have thought that, by adoration or by sacrifice, they should give to angels the honor that is due to God, but they were prohibited by the angels' own admonition and commanded to offer it only to him to whom the angels know that it can be offered without blasphemy. And the example of the holy angels was followed by holy men of God. For, in Lycaonia, Paul and Barnabas were taken for gods when they performed a miracle of healing, and the Lycaonians wanted to sacrifice victims to them, but in humble piety they refused the honor and proclaimed to them the God in whom they should believe.[86]

The only reason why those deceitful spirits arrogantly demand sacrifice for themselves is that they know it is due to the true God. For, in very truth, it is divine honors that make them rejoice, not—as Porphyry says, and as many think—the odors of dead bodies.[87] After all, they have odors in great abundance on all sides and, if they wanted more, could easily provide more

---

84. [GWL] Augustine transitions to a positive vision for Christian sacrifice. Augustine's treatment of sacrifice relies on his understanding of signs (*signa*), which direct us to more fundamental realities (*res*). This distinction is most fully developed in *De Doctrina Christiana* (1.2.2; 2.1.1–2.5.6; and throughout Books 2–3).

85. See Judg. 13:16; Rev. 19:10; 22:9.

86. See Acts 14:6–15.

87. See . . . 10.11.

themselves. Thus, any spirits who arrogate divinity to themselves actually take delight not in the fumes of some body but in the soul of a suppliant whom they have deceived, subjugated, and brought under their dominion.[88] They bar that person's way to the true God, and they keep him from becoming a sacrifice to God for as long as he sacrifices to anyone other than God.

20. In the form of God, then, the true mediator—since, by taking the form of a servant,[89] he became the mediator between God and man, the man Jesus Christ[90]—receives sacrifice together with the Father, with whom he is one God.[91] In the form of a servant, however, he chose to be a sacrifice rather than to receive sacrifice, and he did so in order to keep anyone from thinking that sacrifice should be offered, even in this case, to any creature at all. At the same time, he is also the priest, himself making the offering as well as himself being the offering. And he wanted the sacrifice offered by the Church to be a daily sacrament of his sacrifice,[92] in which the Church, since it is the body of which he is the head,[93] learns to offer its very self through him. The sacrifices of the saints of old were the manifold and varied signs of this true sacrifice, for this one sacrifice was prefigured by many, just as one thing may be expressed by a variety of words, in order to recommend it highly but not monotonously. To this supreme and true sacrifice all false sacrifices have now given way.

88. [GWL] The real reason the demons want people's sacrifices is that they want to dominate people's souls. Augustine's reference to "fumes" and "bodies" concerns the animal sacrifices that the Romans would offer to their gods.

89. See Phil. 2:6.

90. See 1 Tim. 2:5.

91. [GWL] This paragraph is the climax of Book 10 and deserves pause for Augustine's understanding of sacrifice. As God, Jesus received the sacrifice that he himself offered as a man. For this image, Augustine relies on Phil. 2:6–11, his favorite passage on the divinity and humanity of Christ. The church's practice of the eucharist signifies Christ's ultimate sacrifice. See essay: "Eucharist."

92. Although Augustine refers here to the daily offering of the sacrifice—i.e., the eucharist—he acknowledges in Letter 54.2.2 that it is not offered each day in every place. It is not entirely clear from his own writings whether or not the eucharist was celebrated daily in Hippo.

93. See Eph. 4:15; Col. 1:18.

Platonists and Platonism

Gregory W. Lee and Avyi Hill, with Samuel Cho

Confessions 7.9.13–7.9.15 recounts Augustine's discovery of "some books by the Platonists" prior to his conversion. These books affirmed the immutable and incorporeal God, and their analysis of evil helped Augustine renounce Manicheism (*Confessions* 7.11.17–7.16.22). Scholars agree that these books were the writings of Neoplatonic thinkers, whether Plotinus (the founder of Neoplatonism), Porphyry (Plotinus's greatest student), or both. The writings were translated from Greek into Latin by Marius Victorinus, a philosopher and rhetorician who figures prominently in the story of Augustine's conversion (*Confessions* 8.2.3–8.5.10). Augustine had little, if any, direct knowledge of Plato's writings. For Augustine, Plotinus's philosophy was so similar to Plato's that Plato should be regarded as having lived again in him (*Answer to the Academics* 3.18.41; see also *City of God* 9.10; *Letter* 6.1).

Platonism was a prominent philosophy from the third century BCE to the mid-sixth century CE. It was characterized by a distinction between the intelligible (eternal, nonbodily) realm and the sensible (temporal, bodily) realm. Neoplatonism, a variation of Platonism, was initiated by Plotinus (ca. 205–70) and developed by Porphyry (ca. 232–305) and Iamblichus (ca. 245–325). It divided reality into four principles: the One, the Intellect (*nous*), the Soul (*psychē*), and the material world. The One is the original, transcendent, infinite, and undivided Good. Though it is eternal, it emanates timelessly to generate the lower principles, which are characterized by increasing multiplicity. The human soul can mystically ascend from the material world to the Soul, to the Intellect, and finally to the One.

Augustine seems to have reread Plotinus and Porphyry as he was writing *City of God*. It is the work in which he quotes them the most, including many passages he had not quoted before. Augustine ranks the Platonists as the best of the philosophers and the closest to Christianity (8.9). According to Augustine, they affirmed God as the transcendent, incorporeal source of all things (8.1, 6–8; 10.1); acknowledged God's providence in the world (10.14); and even had something like a doctrine of the Trinity (10.23, 29). They also defined happiness in terms of participation in God (8.5; 10.2; see also 9.17).

187

At the same time, Augustine charges the Platonists with several errors. They thought history was cyclical rather than linear (12.14, 21); denied the resurrection of the body (13.16–19; 22.25–28); and thought souls returned after death into different bodies, even animal bodies (10.30; 12.27; 13.19; 22.12, 27). Even worse, they rejected the incarnation (10.29), claiming lower spirits could mediate between humans and God and promoting the worship of false gods (8.14–22; 9.8–18; 10.9–11, 26–29). Augustine attributes these errors to pride (10.24). Although the Platonists knew God, they did not worship him properly (8.6, 10, quoting Rom. 1:20–21). In short, the Platonists offer no path to happiness, proving the thesis of Books 6–10 that the gods are of no value for eternal life.

Scholars have long debated how to characterize Augustine's relationship with Neoplatonism, particularly in his later years as bishop. This question is a proxy for the wider question of the relationship between Christianity and Hellenistic culture. In general, though Neoplatonism is evident in Augustine's work, he rejects many of its teachings on the basis of his understanding of Scripture.

Bibliography

Armstrong, A. H. 1972. "St. Augustine and Christian Platonism." In *Augustine: A Collection of Critical Essays*, edited by R. A. Markus, 3–37. Garden City, NY: Anchor Books.

Bowery, Anne-Marie. 1999. "Plotinus, *The Enneads*." In *AttA*, 654–57.

Crouse, Robert. 2000. "*Paucis Mutatis Verbis*: St. Augustine's Platonism." In *Augustine and His Critics: Essays in Honour of Gerald Bonner*, edited by Robert Dodaro and George Lawless, 37–50. London: Routledge.

Edwards, Mark J. 1999. "Neoplatonism." In *AttA*, 588–91.

Gerson, Lloyd P. 1994. *Plotinus*. London: Routledge.

———, ed. 1996. *The Cambridge Companion to Plotinus*. Cambridge: Cambridge University Press.

Rist, J. M. 1967. *Plotinus: The Road to Reality*. Cambridge: Cambridge University Press.

Van Fleteren, Frederick. 1999. "Plato, Platonism." In *AttA*, 651–54.

van Oort, Johannes. 2013. *Jerusalem and Babylon: A Study of Augustine's "City of God" and the Sources of His Doctrine of the Two Cities*. Orig. 1991. Leiden: Brill, 235–44.

Angels and Demons

Gregory W. Lee,
with Christopher Iacovetti and Kyle Carter

Augustine lived in a context that assumed the active involvement of angels and demons in human affairs. As the eminent scholar Peter Brown once commented, Augustine's contemporaries felt the presence of demons "quite as intensely as we feel the presence of myriads of dangerous bacteria" (Brown 2000, 30). Besides *City of God*, Augustine's most significant discussions of angels and demons appear in *Demonic Divination, Expositions of the Psalms, Literal Meaning of Genesis*, and *De Trinitate* 2–4. Augustine's treatment of angels and demons sharpens his contrast between the two cities, encouraging virtue and proper worship.

City of God is suffused with angels and demons. These beings are not abstractions or myths but personal agents constituting the first citizens of the heavenly and earthly cities before humans were created (11.34). Still, there are only two cities and not four (12.1). Christians belong to that part of the heavenly city which is on pilgrimage on earth; the other part is angelic (1.*preface*; 10.7, 25; 11.9; 12.9; 14.28). The number of redeemed humans will match and perhaps exceed the number of fallen angels (14.23, 26; 22.1; see also *Enchiridion* 9.29; 16.62; for a later discussion, see Anselm of Canterbury, *Why God Became Man* 1.16–18). After Christ's return, the human part of the heavenly city will join the angelic part to form the full city of God (*City of God* 10.25; 12.23, 28; 22.1, 29). The human part of the earthly city will join the demons in eternal punishment.

The angels were created on the first day as the light of which God said, "Let there be light" (*City of God* 11.9). They generated time through an alternating motion by which they first gained knowledge of creation (evening, since knowledge of created beings pales in comparison with knowledge of the creator), then directed this knowledge to God (day), and then attended to creation again (11.7; 12.16; see also *Literal Meaning of Genesis* 4.22.39–4.32.50). The fall of the evil angels also occurred on the first day, when God separated the light (good angels) from the darkness (bad angels) (*City of God* 11.19–20). The fallen angels were not created sinful by nature but fell by their free choice, pridefully turning from God to themselves (11.13–15; 12.6–9). The fall of angels

189

thus mirrors the fall of humans in important respects. To explain why some angels fell and others did not, Augustine suggests that God may have granted the angels different degrees of grace—even as the evil angels fell by their own will (12.9; see essays: "Providence and Suffering"; "Predestination and the Will").

Following the angelic fall, the good angels received the security of eternal blessedness such that they would never fall away (*City of God* 11.11–13, 32; 12.9; cf. 12.22; 14.10). They have direct, eternal knowledge of God, which they mediate as God's messengers to humans (9.22; 10.15; 11.29; 16.6). They are not, however, coeternal with God, nor did they create the world, though they witnessed and may have aided God's creation in some way (11.32; 12.16, 26; *Literal Meaning of Genesis* 4.24.41–4.26.43; 5.19.37–5.19.39; 9.15.26–9.16.30). The demons became fixed in their damnation, with no opportunity for future redemption (*City of God* 11.33; 21.10, 23–24). On this matter, Augustine departs from the third-century theologian Origen, who allegedly claimed that the devil would be redeemed (*City of God* 21.17, 23). Differing also from the Platonists, Augustine does not distinguish between good demons and bad demons (8.14–22; 9.1–23). All demons are angels who fell from righteousness.

Augustine's narrative suggests a major difference between the fall of angels and the fall of humans (*Enchiridion* 9.28). The angelic fall occurred after many angels already existed, and it resulted in an irreversible distinction between the faithful angels and the fallen demons. By contrast, Adam and Eve fell as the only members of the human race, infecting all their progeny with original sin. From this mass of damnation, God has chosen some to join the heavenly city (see essays: "Original Sin"; "Predestination and the Will"). Humans thus receive an opportunity for redemption that fallen angels do not (*City of God* 22.30). The angels have no story of salvation.

Both the angels and the demons intervene in human affairs, though for opposite purposes. The angels encourage humans to love and worship God, the final good for humans and angels alike (*City of God* 10.3, 7, 12, 16; cf. *De Doctrina Christiana* 1.30.31–1.30.33). They were especially active during the Old Testament period (*City of God* 7.32; 10.8, 12–17). In *De Trinitate* 2–4, Augustine develops this perspective with respect to the Old Testament theophanies. Breaking from previous interpreters, Augustine identifies the theophanies not with the pre-incarnate Son but with the work of angels, who produced miraculous phenomena to prepare humanity for the incarnation (*De Trinitate* 2.8.14–2.9.15; 3.9.19–3.11.27; 4.1.2). He rarely speaks of angels as personal protectors of humans.

In contrast to the angels, the demons seek to corrupt humans by manipulating them into vice and demanding to be worshiped (*City of God* 2.10, 14, 22, 24–25; 3.10; 9.7, 15; 10.19). Having fallen from heaven, the devil envies humans and wants to keep them from heaven too (14.11; *Expositions of the Psalms* 139.8). Moral corruption is the greatest harm demons can inflict on humans (*City of God* 10.22). The demons inflame the sinful impulses of those who already desire to sin (2.14; 3.10; 6.4; 7.22; 10.22). This strategy is most evident in the theater, where the actors tell immoral stories of the gods that lend religious legitimacy to foul behavior (see essay: "Roman Spectacles").

Though demons can produce astonishing phenomena, Augustine cares less about their intellectual or physical abilities than their moral deficiencies (*City of God* 8.14–22; 9.9–18; *Demonic Divination* 3.7–4.8; *Expositions of the Psalms* 77.28–30; *De Trinitate* 3.7.12–3.9.18; see also *Enchiridion* 15.57–59; *To Orosius* 11.14; *De Trinitate* 3.10.21). In *Expositions of the Psalms*, Augustine warns often against the devil's attacks, but he identifies these attacks with the ordinary temptations of hatred, greed, and pride (7.2–3; 34.1.4; 54.4–6; 58.1.4; 69.2; 90.1.1–90.1.2; 103.4.6–103.4.7; 139.8). Demons can act only to the extent that God permits (*City of God* 2.23; 3.10; 10.21–22; 18.18), and Christ has already defeated the devil (*De Trinitate* 13.12.16–13.18.23).

Bibliography

Brown, Peter. 2000. *Augustine of Hippo*. New ed. Orig. 1967. Berkeley: University of California Press.
Ivanovska, Inta. 2011. "The Demonology of Saint Augustine of Hippo." PhD diss., Saint Louis University.
Klein, Elizabeth Anne. 2018. *Augustine's Theology of Angels*. Cambridge: Cambridge University Press.
Muehlberger, Ellen. 2013. *Angels in Late Ancient Christianity*. Oxford: Oxford University Press.
Strand, Daniel DeForrest. 2015. "The Gods of the Nations: St. Augustine's Apocalyptic Political Theology." PhD diss., University of Chicago.
Wetzel, James. 2021. "Books 11 & 12: Angels and Demons: The Eternal Framing of the Two Cities." In Meconi, *COG*, 145–66.
Wiebe, Gregory D. 2021. *Fallen Angels in the Theology of St Augustine*. Oxford: Oxford University Press.

 Eucharist

Gregory W. Lee and Avyi Hill, with Philip Lindia

Christians in North Africa participated in the eucharist throughout the week, sometimes daily (*City of God* 10.20; *Confessions* 5.9.17; *Homilies on the Gospel of John* 26.15; *Letters* 54.2.2; 54.3.4; 228.6; *Sermons* 56.9–10; 58.5, 12; 229D.2). Adults in good standing could participate, as could baptized infants (*Letter* 98.4; *Unfinished Work in Answer to Julian* 2.30), and the eucharist was sometimes offered on behalf of the dead (*Confessions* 9.11.27; 9.13.37; *Enchiridion* 29.110; *Sermon* 172.2). Those who had not received baptism were not permitted to witness the ritual (*Expositions of the Psalms* 103.1.14; *Sermons* 131.1; 132.1; 307.3). The liturgy of the eucharist included the giving of alms (*Confessions* 5.9.17; *Sermon* 56.10–11); the kiss of peace, exchanged on the lips as a sign of love (*Sermons* 227; 229.3); and the Lord's Prayer, when participants would beat their chests as they asked for the forgiveness of their debts (Matt. 6:12; see *Expositions of the Psalms* 140.18; *Letter* 149.2.16; *Sermons* 29.2; 29B.2; 58.12; 351.6).

Augustine did not write a treatise on the eucharist. The topic was not controversial in his time. His theology of the eucharist is most clearly articulated in his sermons, especially his Easter homilies for the newly baptized (*Sermons* 227; 228B; 229; 229A; 272), and his expositions of Jesus's discourse on the bread of life (*Homilies on the Gospel of John* 25–27). Augustine's exclamation "O sacrament of piety, O sign of unity, O bond of charity!" (*Homilies on the Gospel of John* 26.13; see also *Sermon* 272) would become a standard definition of the eucharist for Roman Catholic theology. Scholars have disagreed on the extent to which Augustine affirmed the real presence of Christ in the eucharist. They tend to agree, however, that Augustine offered no sustained analysis of the matter and that he stressed the reality signified by the bread and the wine as opposed to the elements themselves.

Augustine encourages his congregants to "recognize in the bread what hung on the cross, and in the cup what flowed from his side" (*Sermon* 228B.2). He also preaches, "This bread and wine, when the word is applied to it, becomes [*fit*] the body and blood of the Word" (*Sermon* 229.1; see also *Sermon* 229.3). At the same time, the reality and power of the sacrament reside in what it signifies, not in what does the signifying. In the elements, "one thing is seen, another is to be understood. What can be seen has a bodily appearance, what is to be understood provides spiritual fruit" (*Sermon* 272; see also *Sermon* 227). Jesus's teaching about the bread from heaven "refers to the grace of the sacrament, not the sacrament that we can see; to those who eat inwardly, not outwardly, who eat in the heart, who do not just chew with the teeth" (*Homilies on the Gospel of John* 26.12, quoting John 6:50). Jesus was not offering "helpings of his body" to be "finished off in mouthfuls" (*Homilies on the Gospel of John* 27.3; see also *Expositions of the Psalms* 98.9; *Homilies on the Gospel of John* 27.5; *Sermon* 131.1).

Most distinctively, Augustine identifies the body of Christ with Christ's *ecclesial* body, the church. Augustine preaches to his congregants that, as members of Christ's body, "you are yourselves what you receive" (*Sermon* 227; see also *Sermons* 57.7; 228B.2–4; 229.1; 229A.1). Indeed, Christians are on the eucharistic altar. "So if it's you that are the body of

Christ and its members, it's the mystery meaning you that has been placed on the Lord's table; what you receive is the mystery that means you" (*Sermon* 272; see also *Sermon* 229.2). To develop this point, Augustine relies on 1 Corinthians 10:17: "We, being many, are one loaf, one body" (*Sermons* 227; 228B.4; 229A.1; 272). To make one loaf, individual grains must be ground (fasting and exorcism), joined together with water (baptism), and baked with fire (anointing with oil, the sacrament of the Holy Spirit) (*Sermons* 227; 229.1; 229A.2; 272). This unity embraces Christians everywhere. "However many loaves there may be on Christ's altars throughout the world, it's *one loaf*" (*Sermon* 229A.1).

Given the importance of unity, do the benefits of the eucharist extend to those who have separated from the Catholic Church (the Donatists) or to those who externally belong to the church but do not internally belong to Christ (false Christians)? No. Drawing on 1 Corinthians 11:27–29, Augustine claims they eat and drink as a testimony against themselves. Though they may take the sacrament externally, they do not receive Christ internally (*City of God* 21.25; *Expositions of the Psalms* 103.1.9; *Homilies on the Gospel of John* 26.18; *Letter* 185.11.50; *Sermons* 228B.4; 229.2; 272).

City of God 10 contains some of Augustine's most cited passages on the eucharist. These passages arise in his discussion of sacrifice, which he defines in terms of love for God and neighbor (10.3–6). The Old Testament sacrifices prefigured Christ's true sacrifice. As God, Christ receives sacrifice; as man, he is a sacrifice; and as priest, he is the one who offers himself (10.20). The heavenly city is a "universal sacrifice" as the body of Christ's head (10.6). In the eucharist, the church offers a "daily sacrament" of Christ's sacrifice, offering itself through him (10.20).

Bibliography

Bonner, Gerald. 1987. "The Church and the Eucharist in the Theology of St Augustine." In *God's Decree and Man's Destiny: Studies on the Thought of Augustine of Hippo*, 448–61. London: Variorum.

———. 1994. "Augustine's Understanding of the Church as a Eucharistic Community." In *Saint Augustine the Bishop: A Book of Essays*, edited by Fannie LeMoine and Christopher Kleinhenz, 39–63. New York: Garland.

Burns, J. Patout, Jr. 2001. "The Eucharist as the Foundation of Christian Unity in North African Theology." *Augustinian Studies* 32, no. 1: 1–23.

———. 2022. *Augustine's Preached Theology: Living as the Body of Christ*. Grand Rapids: Eerdmans, 105–31.

Burns, J. Patout, Jr., and Robin M. Jensen. 2014. "Word and Eucharist in Augustine's Time." In *Christianity in Roman Africa: The Development of Its Practices and Beliefs*, 261–87. Grand Rapids: Eerdmans.

Cavadini, John C. 2011. "Eucharistic Exegesis in Augustine's *Confessions*." *Augustinian Studies* 41, no. 1: 87–108.

Di Berardino, Angelo. 2017. "Augustine on the Eucharist." *Revista Caritas Veritatis* 2: 25–59.

Jackson, Pamela. 1999. "Eucharist." In *AttA*, 340–44.

Lienhard, Joseph T. 2013. "*Sacramentum* and the Eucharist in St. Augustine." *The Thomist* 77, no. 2: 173–92.

Schlesinger, Eugene R. 2016. "The Sacrificial Ecclesiology of *City of God* 10." *Augustinian Studies* 47, no. 2: 137–55.

Book 12

22–23, 28

These selections concentrate on the creation of humanity. They arise in the context of Books 11–14, which trace the origins of the two cities. In Book 11 and Book 12.1–9, Augustine covers the creation and fall of angels. In 12.10–21, he addresses the idea that humanity is eternal, refuting theories of repeated cycles according to which the world is created and destroyed and created again. In 12.22–28, he turns to the creation of humans. Humans are the most social of all animals and are meant for harmony with one another. If they had persisted in faithfulness, they would have passed into the eternal blessedness of the angels. Against the Platonists, Augustine also asserts that humans were created by the one true God and not by lesser gods (12.24–27).

God's Creation of the Human Race from One Man

22 (21).[1] As far as I could, then, I have explained the exceedingly difficult question regarding God's eternity and how he creates new things without any change of will. In this light, it is not hard to see that what took place—namely, that God multiplied the human race from one man whom he created first—was much better than if he had started it from several.[2] For, while

---

1. [GWL] There is some discrepancy between different editions of *City of God* in how the chapters in Book 12 are numbered from chapter 10 onward. The numbers in the parentheses represent the alternative chapter numbers. They are not commonly cited in studies of *City of God*.
2. [GWL] As this paragraph illustrates, Augustine sees pedagogical purpose in humanity's origins. All humans descended from Adam and Eve and are literally related to one another. And

195

God created some animals that are solitary and, preferring solitude, keep to themselves, such as eagles, kites, lions, wolves, and the like, he created others that are gregarious and would rather gather together and live in flocks, such as doves, starlings, deer, fallow-deer, and so forth.[3] But he did not propagate either of these kinds from single individuals; rather, he ordered many of them into existence all at once. Man, however, whose nature was in a manner to be intermediate between the angels and the beasts, God created in such a way that, if he submitted to his creator as his true Lord, and, if he kept God's commandments in devout obedience, he would, without dying, obtain a blessed and unending immortality and pass over into the company of the angels; but, if he offended the Lord his God by using his free will proudly and disobediently, he would be given over to death and would live like the beasts, a slave to lust and destined for eternal punishment after death.[4] And in this case he created one single individual, but not so that man would be left alone, bereft of human society. Rather, God's purpose was that the unity of human society and the bond of human intimacy would be all the more strongly commended to human beings if they were linked to one another not only by likeness of

since Eve was taken from Adam's side, all humans come from one original man. By creating all humanity through one man, God was teaching humans to value unity with one another (see also *Literal Meaning of Genesis* 9.9.15). Augustine contrasts the origin of humans with the origin of animals. Animal species were created from multiple progenitors. The world's population of lions, e.g., is not traceable to one original lion. Of all the species among creatures, only humans are all kin with one another. NCP: "On the kinship of human beings through the first parents, a theme repeated below at 12.28, see also *The Catholic Way of Life* 30.63; *The Excellence of Marriage* 1.1. For this commonplace see as well Lactantius, *Divine Institutes* 6.10; John Chrysostom, Sermon on 1 Timothy 12.4."

3. The same distinction between solitary and gregarious animals is made below at 19.12.

4. [GWL] Humans are composed of body and rational soul. Angels have rational souls, but they do not have bodies. Nonhuman animals have bodies, but they lack rational souls. Humans are thus created between animals and angels (cf. 11.16). Augustine's position reflects his wider understanding of the order of being, in which different things are ranked lower or higher according to their participation in God (*De Doctrina Christiana* 1.8.8; see essay: "Evil as Privation").

Augustine contrasts humanity's condition before the fall and its condition in heaven. Before the fall, humanity was created good but not perfect, since Adam and Eve were able to sin (*posse peccare*) and thus able to die (*posse mori*; see 22.30). In heaven, humanity will not be able to sin or to die (*non posse peccare*; *non posse mori*). This final condition is blessed immortality. Because of the fall, Christians receive this blessedness only after death. If humans had not sinned, they would have received blessed immortality through a different path. By obeying God's command to "be fruitful and multiply" (Gen. 1:28), they would have reached the population God determined for the heavenly city, at which point they would have passed into perfection (see also *Literal Meaning of Genesis* 9.6.10; *Unfinished Work in Answer to Julian* 6.30). At various points, Augustine indicates this population would have matched or exceeded the number of fallen angels, thus restoring the full number of citizens in the heavenly city (see essay: "Angels and Demons").

nature but also by the sense of kinship. In fact, he did not even create the woman who was to be united with the man in the same way that he chose to create the man himself; instead he created her out of that man, so that the human race might be wholly derived from just one man.[5]

23 (22). God knew full well, however, that man was going to sin and that, having become subject to death, he would propagate men who were themselves going to die. He knew, too, that mortals would go to such savage lengths in sinning that even beasts lacking any rational will, the beasts that came in teeming numbers from the waters and the earth, would live together more securely and more peacefully with their own kind than would human beings, whose race was produced from a single individual precisely in order to encourage harmony among them. For not even lions or dragons have ever waged such wars among themselves as have human beings.[6] But God also foresaw that, by his grace, a godly people would be called to adoption and that, justified by the Holy Spirit, with their sins forgiven, they would be united with the holy angels in eternal peace, when the last enemy, death, had been destroyed.[7] And he knew that this people would benefit from reflecting on the fact that God started the human race from a single individual for the express purpose of showing men how much he prizes unity among many.[8]

◆

Humanity's Social Character

28 (27). It is with good reason, then, that true religion acknowledges and proclaims that the creator of the whole world is also the creator of all living beings, that is, of both souls and bodies. Preeminent among those on earth is man, whom God created in his own image,[9] and, for the reason I have mentioned (although some other and greater reason may lie hidden from us),

5. See Gen. 2:21–22.
6. [GWL] A memorable line. Animals, though less social and less rational than humans, have not committed such atrocities against their own kinds as humans have against one another.
7. See 1 Cor. 15:26.
8. [GWL] Augustine reiterates his point that God created all humanity through Adam to teach humans the importance of unity. Augustine's emphasis on unity contrasts with the earthly city's lust for domination and its history of oppression and war, including civil wars. Unity is also a central concern in Augustine's writings against the Donatists, whom he accuses of dividing the church.
9. See Gen. 1:26.

he was created one, a single individual, but he was not left alone. For there is nothing more contentious by virtue of its fault than the human race, but also nothing more social by virtue of its nature.[10] Nor is there anything more appropriate for human nature to do to counter the vice of contentiousness, whether to keep it from arising in the first place or to heal it after it has arisen, than to recall our first parent. For God chose to create him as one for the propagation of a multitude precisely for the purpose of admonishing us that we should maintain unity and concord even when we are many. And the fact that the woman was made for him from his own side[11] also signifies just how precious the union between husband and wife should be.

These works of God are extraordinary, of course, because they came first. And those who do not believe in them ought not to believe in any marvels at all, for not even these would be called marvels if they had occurred in the usual course of nature. But is there anything, under the supreme governance of divine providence, which occurs to no purpose, even if the reason for it remains hidden? One of the sacred Psalms declares, *Come and see the works of the Lord, what marvels he has placed upon the earth* (Ps. 46:8). In another place, then, I shall discuss—so far as I have God's help—why the woman was made from the man's side and what this first marvel prefigured.[12]

For the present, however, since I must bring this book to a close, let us reckon that in this first man, who was created in the beginning, there arose—not yet in plain sight, of course, but already in the foreknowledge of God—two societies, like two cities, in the human race. For it was from him that all human beings were to come, some to be joined with the evil angels in their punishment, and others to be joined with the good angels in their reward, according to the hidden but always just judgment of God. For, because Scripture says, *All the ways of the Lord are mercy and truth* (Ps. 25:10), his grace cannot be unjust, nor can his justice be cruel.

---

10. [GWL] A summary of Augustine's remarks in 12.22–23. Humans are good by nature, sinful by fault. Humans are also social by nature and contentious by fault. God created humanity through one man to encourage humans to live in unity with one another. Augustine's statement here relies on his understanding of evil as a privation. Since God created humans good, humans are good by nature, even though they have turned from God to sin. Sin has no being but is a kind of nothingness and corruption of good things. Humans are able to sin because they were created from nothing (*ex nihilo*). Unlike humans, God is ultimate being and cannot sin. See essay: "Evil as Privation."

11. See Gen. 2:21–22.

12. See . . . 22.17.

Book 13

1–8, 12–15

In Books 13–14, Augustine treats the fall of humanity. Book 13 concentrates on the nature of death, which separates the body and the soul. After delineating three kinds of death (13.2), Augustine asks why Christians die physically, given that death is a punishment for sin, and Christians' sins have been forgiven (13.3–8). He answers that death encourages faith—most visibly through the martyrs, whose faith when confronted with death was their glory. The following chapters (13.9–11) investigate linguistic perplexities concerning the word "death." Augustine then treats the fall of Adam and Eve, which brought all three kinds of death (13.12–15). The next section challenges the position of the philosophers that the soul's separation from the body is a blessing (13.16–20a). The final section contrasts Adam and Eve's original, earthly bodies with the heavenly bodies that Christians will receive in the resurrection (13.20b–24).

1. Now that we have addressed the very difficult questions of the origin of our world and the beginning of the human race, the right order of things requires that our line of discussion turn next to the fall of the first human being—or, rather, of the first human beings—and to the origin and propagation of human death. For God did not create men like the angels; that is, he did not make them completely incapable of dying, even if they sinned.[1] Rather he made them in

---

1. [GWL] Humans die because of the fall. When the angels fell, they were sealed in their condemnation, but they did not die. Augustine treats the angelic fall at length in 11.9–21 and 12.1–9.

such a way that, if they fulfilled their duty of obedience, angelic immortality and a blessed eternity would follow without any intervening death, but, if they disobeyed, they would most justly be condemned to the punishment of death. But I have already made this point in the preceding book.[2]

The Meanings of Death

2. I see, however, that I need to discuss a little more fully the kind of death that is in question here.[3] For, although the human soul is rightly said to be immortal, it does suffer a kind of death of its own. The soul is called immortal because it never wholly loses all life and feeling, and the body is called mortal because it can be wholly abandoned by life and cannot live at all on its own. The death of the soul occurs, then, when it is abandoned by God, just as the death of the body occurs when it is abandoned by the soul. And the death of the two together—that is, the death of the whole human being—happens when the soul, itself abandoned by God, abandons the body. For, in that case, neither does the soul draw life from God nor the body from the soul.

This death of the whole human being is followed by what the authority of Divine Scripture calls the second death. This is the death to which the savior referred when he said, *Fear him who has the power to destroy both body and soul in hell* (Matt. 10:28). But, since this second death only occurs after the soul and body have been so tightly bound together that nothing can pull them apart, it may seem strange that the body is said to be destroyed by a death in which it is not abandoned by the soul but rather undergoes torment precisely because it retains both its soul and its feeling. For, in that final and eternal punishment (which I shall have to discuss more fully in its proper place[4]), we can rightly speak of the death of the soul, since it will draw no life from God. But how can we speak of the death of the body, since it will draw life from the soul? For without the soul it could not feel the bodily torments that will beset it after the resurrection. Perhaps it is because life of any sort is a good, while pain is an evil, that we ought not to say that the body is alive when its soul is present not for the sake of giving it life but only for the sake of giving it pain.

2. See above at 12.22.

3. [GWL] Augustine will distinguish between three kinds of deaths: (1) the death of the soul: abandonment by God; (2) the death of the body: abandonment by the soul; and (3) the second death: body and soul together experiencing eternal condemnation. The phrase "second death" is taken from Rev. 2:11; 20:6, 14; and 21:8. It refers to the eternal punishment of hell.

4. See Book 21.

The soul, then, draws life from God when it lives rightly, for it can only live rightly when God works what is good in it.[5] The body, on the other hand, draws life from the soul when the soul lives in the body, whether or not the soul itself draws life from God. For the life in the bodies of the ungodly is not the life of their souls but the life of their bodies, and even dead souls— that is, souls that have been abandoned by God—can confer such life on bodies, since their own life, by virtue of which they are immortal, no matter how slight it may be, does not end. In the final damnation, however, it is not without reason that life is called death rather than life. For at that point, although man continues to have feeling, his feeling is made neither delightful by pleasure nor beneficial by rest but, rather, punitive by pain. And this is called the second death because it comes after the first, in which there takes place a separation of conjoined natures, whether of God and the soul or of the soul and the body. Thus it can be said of the first death, the death of the body, that it is a good for those who are good and an evil for those who are evil. But the second death, since it happens to no one who is good, is obviously not a good for anyone at all.[6]

Death as Punishment

3. But here a question arises that we must not gloss over—whether it is really true that the death by which soul and body are separated is a good for those who are good. If this is true, how can we maintain that this death is also the punishment for sin? If the first human beings had not sinned, they most certainly would not have suffered this death. How, then, can it be a good for those who are good, when it could only happen to those who are evil? And, if it could only happen to those who are evil, it ought not to be a good for

5. [GWL] There are two senses in which a soul has life. The first concerns the existence of the soul, which Augustine thinks is immortal and persists after the death of the body. Even in hell, the soul will continue to exist and experience suffering. The second sense is moral. The soul is morally alive when it is living rightly, by participation in God. The sin of Adam and Eve resulted in the death of the soul, according to which the soul is abandoned by God and no longer lives rightly. The death of the soul leads to the death of the body (what we typically mean by "death"). These two deaths (the death of the soul and the death of the body) lead to the second death, in which the soul and the body exist eternally in torment.

6. [GWL] A summary of what Augustine will argue in the next chapters. Though the death of the body is a temporal evil, it serves a good purpose by encouraging Christians' faith. The martyrs offer the paradigmatic example of such faith (13.4). Christians do not experience the second death, hell, which is an eternal evil and serves no restorative purpose.

those who are good but rather ought not to happen to them at all. For why should there be any punishment for those in whom there is nothing that deserves to be punished?

Consequently we must acknowledge that the first human beings were, in fact, so created that, if they had not sinned, they would not have experienced any kind of death. But we must also acknowledge that, as the first sinners, these same human beings were punished with death in such a way that whatever sprang from their stock would also be held liable to the same penalty.[7] For what was born from them was no different than what they themselves were. In keeping with the sheer magnitude of their offense, their condemnation changed their nature for the worse, and, as a consequence, what first came about as punishment for the first human beings who sinned now occurs naturally in all people who are born.

For man does not come from man in the same way that man came from the dust.[8] Dust was the material for the making of man, but man is the parent for the begetting of man. Flesh is not the same as earth, even though flesh was made from earth, but the human offspring is the same as the human parent. Thus the entire human race, which was going to pass through the woman and become its progeny, was present in the first man when that couple received the divine sentence of condemnation; and what man became—not when he was created but when he sinned and was punished—is what man begot, so far as the origin of sin and death is concerned.[9]

The first man was not reduced by sin or its punishment to the infantile weakness and helplessness of mind and body that we see in little children. God wanted these to be, as it were, the first stages of the whelps whose parents he had cast down to life and death at the level of the beasts. For, as Scripture says, *Man, when he was in honor, did not understand; he was paired with the beasts that have no understanding and became like them* (Ps. 49:12, 20). In fact, however, we see that infants are weaker in the use and movement of their limbs, and in their sense of desire and aversion, than even the most vulnerable newborns of the other animals. It is as if human powers distinguish themselves all the more in their excellence over the other animals just to the

7. [GWL] A reference to Augustine's doctrine of original sin, which he is developing against the Pelagians at the same time he is writing this book of *City of God*. Augustine believes all humanity inherits the consequences of Adam and Eve's sin, including the corruption of human nature, the guilt of Adam and Eve's sin, and the penalty of death. See essay: "Original Sin."

8. See Gen. 2:7.

9. [GWL] Another statement of Augustine's doctrine of original sin.

extent that their release is delayed, like an arrow drawn all the way back when the bow is fully bent.

The first man, then, neither slid back nor was pushed back to the rudimentary stage of infancy as a result of his unlawful presumption and his just condemnation. Human nature was so vitiated and changed in him, however, that he suffered the rebellious disobedience of desire in his members and was bound over to the necessity of dying, and so he gave birth to what he himself had become as a result of his fault and his punishment, that is, to children subject to sin and death. But, if infants are released from the bonds of sin through the grace of Christ the mediator, they can suffer only the death that separates the soul from the body.[10] Set free from the hold of sin, they do not pass on to the punishment of that second unending death.

4. If anyone is troubled as to why those whose guilt is removed by grace should suffer even the first death, since it too is a punishment for sin, this question has already been discussed and resolved in another of my works, *The Baptism of Little Ones*. There I state that the soul's experience of separation from the body remains, even after its link with guilt has already been removed, for this reason: if the sacrament of regeneration[11] were immediately followed by the immortality of the body, the very nerve of faith would be cut.[12] For faith is only faith when we look forward in hope to what we do not yet see in reality.[13]

And it was by the strength of faith and the contest of faith, at least in earlier times, that even the fear of death had to be overcome, and this was especially clear in the case of the holy martyrs. There obviously would have been no victory and no glory in this contest—since there would have been no contest at all—if, after the washing of regeneration,[14] the saints were already incapable

10. [GWL] Augustine is referring to infant baptism, which he associates with the salvation of infants. Since infants are born with original sin, they would receive condemnation if they died without baptism.

11. I.e., baptism.

12. [GWL] If those who received baptism did not die, others would pursue baptism for the wrong reasons. Christianity would become a kind of magical religion sought only to avoid physical death. Such a religion could not foster faith, which aims toward what we do not yet see. Augustine's account of why Christians die despite having received baptism aligns with his general theology of suffering, according to which God allows temporal goods and evils to come upon good and bad people for the sake of building up faith. See essay: "Providence and Suffering."

13. See *The Punishment and Forgiveness of Sins and the Baptism of Little Ones* 2.31.50–2.31.51. Augustine is alluding to Heb. 11:1. "Hope . . . reality": *spe . . . re*—a frequent wordplay in Augustine.

14. See Tit. 3:5.

of suffering bodily death. In that case, who would not run to the grace of Christ, along with the children who were to be baptized, just to avoid being parted from the body? Thus, faith would not be tested by virtue of having an invisible prize. In fact, it would no longer be faith at all, if it immediately expected and received the reward for its work.

As it is, however, by the greater and more wondrous grace of the savior the punishment of sin has itself been turned to the service of righteousness.[15] Then it was said to man, "If you sin, you shall die."[16] Now it is said to the martyr, "Die to keep from sinning." Then it was said, "If you break the commandment, you shall surely die." Now it is said, "If you refuse to die, you will break the commandment." What was once to be feared so that we would not sin is now to be accepted so that we do not sin. Thus, by the ineffable mercy of God, the very penalty of vice turns into the armor of virtue, and the punishment of the sinner becomes the merit of the righteous. Then death was incurred by sinning, now righteousness is fulfilled by dying. This is true in the case of the holy martyrs, whom the persecutor confronts with the alternative of either forsaking their faith or suffering death. For the righteous would rather suffer for their belief what the first sinners suffered for their disbelief. If the latter had not sinned they would not have died, but the former will sin if they do not die. It is because the latter sinned, then, that they died, and it is because the former die that they do not sin. By the latter's guilt they incurred punishment; by the former's punishment they do not incur guilt. It is not that death, which was previously an evil, has now become a good; it is rather that God has bestowed such wondrous grace on faith that death—which everyone agrees is the opposite of life—has become the means of passing into life.

5. When the Apostle wanted to show how much harm sin has the power to do unless grace intervenes with its help, he did not hesitate to say that the very law which prohibits sin is itself the power of sin. *The sting of death*, he says, *is sin, and the power of sin is the law* (1 Cor. 15:56). And this is entirely true. For prohibition only increases the desire for an illicit act if love for righteousness is not strong enough to overcome the desire for sin by delighting in it, and it is only by the help of divine grace that we love and delight in true

15. [GWL] This paragraph rewards a patient read as a display of Augustine's rhetorical gifts. On Augustine and martyrdom, see Adam Ployd, *Augustine, Martyrdom, and Classical Rhetoric* (Oxford: Oxford University Press, 2023).

16. See Gen. 2:17.

righteousness. But to keep us from thinking that the law itself is evil, since it is called the power of sin, the Apostle says in another place, where he is dealing with a similar question, *So the law is holy, and the commandment is holy and just and good. Did what is good, then, bring death to me? By no means! But sin, that it might appear as sin, worked death in me through what is good, so that through the commandment the sinner or the sin might go beyond measure* (Rom. 7:12–13). He says *beyond measure* because the transgression is magnified when, due to an increased desire for sin, even the law itself is held in contempt.

Why did we think we ought to mention this?[17] Because, just as the law is not an evil even when it increases the sinner's desire, neither is death a good even when it increases the sufferer's glory—that is, either when the law is abandoned for the sake of wickedness and it produces transgressors, or when death is accepted for the sake of truth and it produces martyrs. Thus, the law is indeed good, because it is the prohibition of sin, and death is in fact evil, because it is the wages of sin.[18] But, just as unrighteousness makes bad use not only of things that are evil but also of things that are good, so righteousness makes good use not only of things that are good but also of things that are evil. And so it happens both that the evil make evil use of the law, even though the law itself is good, and that it is a good for the good to die, even though death itself is evil.

6. Thus, so far as the death of the body is concerned—that is, the separation of the soul from the body—it is not a good for anyone when it is suffered by those who we say are dying. For the very force that tears apart the two that were conjoined and intertwined in the living person produces an anguished feeling that is contrary to nature and that lasts until all feeling is gone, which was present precisely due to the joining of soul and flesh. Sometimes all this distress is cut short by a single blow to the body or a snatching away of the soul which, coming so suddenly, keeps it from being felt at all. But, whatever it is that with such a feeling of anguish deprives the dying of all feeling, it increases the merit of patience when it is endured with faith and piety. It does not, however, erase the term "punishment." For death is undoubtedly the punishment

---

17. [GWL] This paragraph contrasts the law with physical death. The law was a good that resulted in evil in that it incited humanity's desire to sin (Rom. 7:12–13). Death is an evil that results in good in that it glorifies the faithfulness of Christians who would rather be killed than renounce their faith.

18. See Rom. 6:23.

of all who are born in unbroken succession from the first man. But, if it is undergone for the sake of godliness and righteousness, it becomes the glory of those who are born again; and so, even though death is the retribution for sin, it sometimes ensures that there is no retribution for sin.

The Death of the Saints

7. For, when anyone dies for confessing Christ, even if he has not received the washing of regeneration, this counts just as fully for the remission of his sins as if he had been washed in the sacred font of baptism.[19] It is true that Christ said, *No one will enter the kingdom of heaven unless he is born again of water and the Spirit* (John 3:5), but in another saying he made an exception for this case, where he says in no less general terms, *Everyone who acknowledges me before men, him I also shall acknowledge before my Father who is in heaven* (Matt. 10:32). And in another place he states, *Whoever loses his life for my sake will find it* (Matt. 16:25).

It is for this reason that Scripture says, *Precious in the sight of the Lord is the death of his saints* (Ps. 116:15). For what is more precious than a death by which all a person's sins are forgiven and his merits immensely increased? Even those who were baptized when they could no longer defer death, and so departed this life with all their sins wiped clean, are not equal in merit to those who did not defer death, even though they could have done so, because they preferred to end their life by confessing Christ rather than, by denying him, to live long enough to receive his baptism. Even if they had denied Christ due to their fear of death, however, this too would certainly have been forgiven them in the washing of baptism, in which even the monstrous crime of those who killed Christ was forgiven.[20] How, then, could the martyrs possibly have loved Christ so much that they were unable to deny him, despite the fact that they faced such mortal peril and despite the fact that they had such a sure hope of forgiveness, without the overflowing grace of that Spirit which *blows where it chooses* (John 3:8)?

Precious, therefore, is the death of the saints, for whom Christ's death had already paid the price in advance with such overwhelming grace that they did not hesitate to pay the price of their own death in order to gain him. Their

19. See Titus 3:5. Martyrdom was recognized as a substitute for water baptism as early as the end of the second century in Tertullian, *On Baptism* 16.
20. See Acts 2:23, 36–41.

death showed that what had originally been established for the punishment of sin has been put to such use that from it was born the more abundant fruit of righteousness. But, even so, death should not be considered a good just because it has been turned to such advantage—not on its own strength but thanks to the divine bounty—that what was formerly set before us as a thing to be feared lest sin should be committed is now set before us as a thing to be endured, with the result that no sin is committed and, even if sin has been committed, it is blotted out, and in either case the palm of righteousness, which is owed for a great victory, is awarded.

8. For, if we consider the matter more carefully, we see that, even when a person dies a faithful and praiseworthy death, he is guarding against death. He accepts one aspect of death in order to avoid the whole of death and, beyond that, in order to escape the second death which has no end. He accepts the separation of the soul from the body in order to avoid having God separated from the soul when the soul is itself separated from the body and as a result—with the first death, the death of the whole person, complete— incurs the second, eternal death. Therefore, as I have said,[21] death is not a good for anyone when it is being suffered by the dying and is bringing about their death, but it is praiseworthy to endure death for the sake of maintaining or attaining the good. In the case of those who are called dead because they have already died, however, it is not absurd to say that death is an evil for the evil and a good for the good. For the souls of the godly that are separated from the body are at rest, while those of the ungodly suffer punishment; and this remains true until their bodies are revived—those of the godly to eternal life and those of the ungodly to eternal death, which is called the second death.

◆

The Threat of Death

12. If it is asked, then, which death God threatened to inflict on the first human beings if they should break the commandment they had received from him and should fail to continue in obedience—whether the death of the soul, the death of the body, the death of the whole man, or the death that is called the

21. See above at 13.6.

second death—the answer must be: all of these.[22] For the first death consists of two of these, and total death consists of all of them. For, just as the earth as a whole consists of many lands, and the Church as a whole consists of many churches,[23] so death as a whole consists of all deaths. For the first death consists of two, one of the soul and the other of the body; and so the first death is the death of the whole man, when the soul without God and without the body undergoes punishment for a time. And the second death is when the soul without God, but with the body, undergoes eternal punishment. Thus, when God spoke about the forbidden fruit to the first man, whom he had established in paradise, and told him, *On whatever day that you eat of it you shall die the death* (Gen. 2:17), this threat included not only the first part of the first death, in which the soul is deprived of God, and not only the second part of the first death, in which the body is deprived of the soul, and not only the whole first death, in which the soul, separated both from God and from the body, undergoes punishment, but all that belongs to death, right down to the last death, called the second death, after which there is no further death.

13. For, immediately after the first human beings disobeyed the commandment, divine grace abandoned them, and they were made ashamed by the nakedness of their bodies. Thus they used fig leaves, which were perhaps the first things they found in their distress, to cover their shameful members,[24] which were, of course, the same members as before but previously were no source of shame. They felt, then, a new stirring of their disobedient flesh as a punishment in turn for their own disobedience.[25]

For the soul, now rejoicing in its own freedom for perversity and disdaining to serve God, was itself stripped of the body's former service to it, and, because it had by its own will deserted its Lord above, it no longer controlled its servant below by its own will. Nor did it have the flesh fully submissive to it, as it could always have had if it had itself remained submissive to God. It was at that point, then, that the desires of the flesh began to oppose the

22. [GWL] See 13.2 for Augustine's three kinds of death: (1) the death of the soul, (2) the death of the body, and (3) the second death. The first two together constitute the "first death." Upon their sin, Adam and Eve immediately experienced the death of the soul. Later, they also experienced the death of the body. All who do not receive salvation eventually experience the second death. God's warning to Adam and Eve encompassed all three deaths.

23. Augustine is referring here not to church buildings but rather, as in *Letter* 54, to different locales or dioceses, each with its own customs.

24. See Gen. 3:7.

25. [GWL] Augustine provides a more extensive account of this matter in 14.16–26. On that material, see essay: "Body."

spirit;[26] and we are now born with this conflict, drawing with us the origin of death and carrying in our members and in our vitiated nature, as a result of the first transgression, its combat against us or rather its victory over us.

14. For God created man righteous; he is the author of natures, not of vices.[27] But man, willingly depraved and justly condemned, gave birth to depraved and condemned offspring. For we were all in that one man, since we all were that one man who fell into sin through the woman who was made from him prior to sin. The specific forms in which we were individually to live as particular individuals had not yet been created and distributed to us, but the seminal nature from which we would all be propagated was already present. And, once this nature was vitiated on account of sin, and bound by the chain of death, and justly condemned, man could not be born of man in any other condition. And so from the evil use of free will there arose a series of calamities which led the human race by a succession of miseries from its depraved origin, as from a corrupt root, right through to the final ruination of the second death, which has no end, and the only exceptions are those who are delivered through the grace of God.

15. But since God's threat said, *You shall die the death* (Gen. 2:17), not "You shall die the deaths," let us take it to refer only to the death that occurs when the soul is abandoned by its own life, which is God. It is not, however, that the soul was first abandoned by God and then, as a result, abandoned him; rather, it first abandoned him and then, as a result, was abandoned by him. For the soul's will comes first with respect to its evil, but its creator's will comes first with respect to its good, whether in making it when it did not exist or in remaking it when it had fallen and perished. But, even if we take it that this was the death God threatened when he said, *On the day that you eat of it you shall die the death* (Gen. 2:17)—as if he said, "On the day that you disobediently abandon me, I shall justly abandon you"—it is surely true that, in this death, there was also the threat of the other deaths that were undoubtedly going to follow it.

For, in the fact that a disobedient stirring arose in the flesh of the disobedient soul, on account of which the first human beings covered their shameful

26. See Gal. 5:17.

27. [GWL] Augustine affirms the goodness of human nature, which must be good because God created it and God is good. Sin is a privation that corrupts human nature and arises from humans' misuse of their will. Thus, God is not the author of sin. It was humans who exercised their will for evil instead of good. See essay: "Evil as Privation."

members, one death was experienced, wherein God abandons the soul. It was signified by the words that God spoke when he said to the man, who was out of his mind with fear and desperately hiding himself, *Adam, where are you?* (Gen. 3:9). Plainly God was not asking this in ignorance but rather was admonishing him, as a rebuke, to take note of where he was now that God was not in him. But, when the soul itself abandoned the body, now broken down by time and wasted with old age, another death entered human experience, the death of which God had spoken when, still punishing human sin, he said, *You are earth, and to earth you shall go* (Gen. 3:19). And with these two deaths, the first death, which is the death of the whole man, was complete, and, unless man is delivered by grace, it is followed in the end by the second death. For the body, which is from the earth, would not return to earth except for its own death, which occurs when it is abandoned by its own life, which is the soul. Thus Christians who truly hold the catholic faith are agreed that even the death of the body was not inflicted on us by any law of nature, for God did not create any death for man in this sense, but rather was justly inflicted on us for sin. For it was in punishing sin that God said to the first man, in whom we were all then present, *You are earth, and to earth you shall go.*

Original Sin

Gregory W. Lee, with Kyle Carter

Augustine forged his understanding of original sin against Pelagius, a lay monk and theologian in Rome well known among the elites who fled to Carthage following the sack of Rome. Pelagius had himself left Rome for Africa, arriving in Augustine's Hippo in 410 before continuing to Carthage. Though they never interacted in person, Augustine saw Pelagius once or twice in Carthage before the council against the Donatists. (Concerning Augustine's earliest interactions with Pelagius, see *Deeds of Pelagius* 22.46; 26.51–29.53; *Letter* 146; and *Sermon* 348A.5–7 in vol. III/11 of the New City Press series). He was thus exposed to Pelagius's teachings in the same context that prompted his writing *City of God*. Indeed, Augustine and Pelagius were both concerned about the same spiritual threat—namely, the growing corruption of the church as Christianity became the religion of the empire.

Whereas Augustine developed a theology of the mixed body, according to which the visible church would include both Christians and non-Christians (*City of God* 1.35), Pelagius emphasized moral reform through the rigorous pursuit of purity and perfection. Augustine claims that well before the two of them began writing against each other, Pelagius had heard a bishop read a prayer from *Confessions*—"Give what you command, and then command whatever you will" (10.29.40; 10.31.45; 10.37.60)—and had become enraged to the point of a heated altercation (*Gift of Perseverance* 20.53).

Pelagius stressed the possibility of good works, claiming that the ability to live sinlessly was inherent to human nature. He also claimed this position was compatible with divine grace. Humans received grace through their innate ability to will and do good, God's law and teaching, the example of Jesus Christ, and God's forgiveness for sins (*Grace of Christ and Original Sin* 1.3.4–1.14.15; 1.37.40–1.38.42). What Pelagius denied was the grace by which sinful natures are transformed. Human nature did not need to be transformed because it was not corrupted by Adam and Eve's sin in the first place.

For Augustine, by contrast, Adam and Eve's sin inflicted catastrophe on the human race. He develops this position in *The Punishment and Forgiveness of Sins and the Baptism of Little Ones* (1.9.9–1.15.20) by expositing Romans 5:12–21. While Pelagius attributed the ubiquity of sin to imitation (*imitatio*), as individuals follow the behavior of others, Augustine attributes it to propagation (*propagatio*), according to which Adam's sin infected all his descendants with the same. *Punishment and Forgiveness of Sins* is the first work where Augustine uses "original sin" in a hereditary sense (1.9.9).

Augustine offers two explanations for the transmission of Adam's sin. The first is that all subsequent humans were "in" Adam when he sinned (*City of God* 13.14; 16.27; *Punishment and Forgiveness of Sins* 3.7.14; *Unfinished Work in Answer to Julian* 6.22). Given the genealogical descent of all humans from Adam, there is a literal sense in which they sinned when he sinned. Augustine's position on this matter derives, at least in part, from mistranslations in his Latin text of Romans 5:12: "[Sin] was passed on to all human beings in whom [*in quo*] all have sinned" (*Punishment and Forgiveness of Sins* 1.9.9; see also *Answer to the Two Letters of the Pelagians* 4.4.7). By comparison, one modern translation reads, "*Death* spread to all *because* all have sinned" (NRSVue, emphasis added).

The second explanation concerns sex. For Augustine, lust is necessary to perform the sex act (see essay: "Body"). Procreation thus requires a corrupted will. The sin involved with sex infects the progeny of the act, such that all humans are born into sin. The one exception is Jesus, who was born of the virgin Mary (*Answer to Julian* 2.10.33; *Marriage and Desire* 1.24.27; *Unfinished Work in Answer to Julian* 4.79; see also *Nature and Grace* 36.42, where Augustine suggests Mary could have been sinless too). The rest of humanity is a damned mass (*massa damnata*), from which God chooses some but not all to receive salvation (*City of God* 14.26; 15.1, 21; 21.12; see essay: "Predestination and the Will").

The transmission of sin includes both the corruption of human nature and the guilt of Adam and Eve. The first consequence is widely affirmed in Christian tradition; humans are not born a tabula rasa but with a disposition to sin. The second consequence is more particular to Western, Augustinian theologies. Augustine distinguishes the guilt of personal sins, which individuals accrue for their own offenses, from the guilt of original sin, which they accrue for Adam and Eve's offense. Both require forgiveness. Personal sins can be forgiven through ritual acts of reconciliation, including the recitation of the Lord's Prayer; almsgiving; fasting; and in the case of major sins, public penance (*Enchiridion* 17.65; *Letter* 153.3.6; *Sermons* 9.17–18; 58.6–7). The remedy for original sin is baptism, which washes away the guilt of original sin without removing the desire to sin (*Answer to Julian* 6.14.42; 6.17.51–6.17.52; *Marriage and Desire* 1.23.25; 1.25.28; *Punishment and Forgiveness of Sins* 1.39.70).

To defend this position, Augustine appeals to infant baptism, a widespread practice in his context (*Marriage and Desire* 1.20.22; *Punishment and Forgiveness of Sins* 1.16.21–1.19.25; 1.35.65–1.35.66). Since baptism confers the forgiveness of sins, and infants are too young to commit personal sins, the forgiveness of infant baptism must be for original sin (*Answer to Julian* 1.7.33; *Nature and Origin of the Soul* 1.11.14; *Punishment and Forgiveness of Sins* 1.16.21–1.19.25). Infants who die before receiving baptism will receive condemnation, though they will suffer less than those who have committed personal sins (*Punishment and Forgiveness of Sins* 1.16.21). The damnation of unbaptized infants is a position that causes even Augustinians to demur. Augustine himself struggled to explain it (*Sermon* 294.7; see also *City of God* 21.16, where Augustine acknowledges that infants and children cannot be held fully responsible for obeying God's commands).

Julian of Eclanum, Pelagius's later defender, would attribute Augustine's pessimistic account of human nature to Manicheism. Augustine found this accusation inconceivably insulting, given his repudiation of the sect (*Unfinished Work in Answer to Julian* 1.1–2, and throughout). For Augustine, original sin is crucial to a theology of grace. Sinful humans require the transformation of the Holy Spirit, who is the love of God poured into their hearts (Rom. 5:5; *Grace of Christ and Original Sin* 1.30.31).

Bibliography

Beatrice, Pier Franco. 2013. *The Transmission of Sin: Augustine and the Pre-Augustinian Sources*. Translated by Adam Kamesar. Oxford: Oxford University Press.

Bonner, Gerald. 2002. *St. Augustine of Hippo: Life and Controversies*. Orig. 1963. Norwich, UK: Canterbury, 312–93.

Burns, J. Patout. 1980. *The Development of Augustine's Doctrine of Operative Grace*. Paris: Études Augustiniennes.

Burns, J. Patout, Jr., and Robin M. Jensen. 2014. *Christianity in Roman Africa: The Development of Its Practices and Beliefs*. Grand Rapids: Eerdmans, 333–54.

Couenhoven, Jesse. 2013. *Stricken by Sin, Cured by Christ: Agency, Necessity, and Culpability in Augustinian Theology*. Oxford: Oxford University Press.

Kantzer Komline, Han-luen. 2020. *Augustine on the Will: A Theological Account*. Oxford: Oxford University Press.

Pagels, Elaine. 1988. *Adam, Eve, and the Serpent*. New York: Vintage.

Rees, B. R. 1998. *Pelagius: Life and Letters*. Orig. 1988 and 1991. Woodbridge, UK: Boydell.

Rigby, Paul. 1999. "Original Sin." In *AttA*, 607–14.

Wetzel, James. 1992. *Augustine and the Limits of Virtue*. Cambridge: Cambridge University Press.

Book 14

1–15, 28

Book 14 continues Augustine's treatment of the fall of humanity. The book begins with an important description of the two cities: the earthly city lives according to the flesh, and the heavenly city lives according to the spirit (14.1). It then investigates the meaning of "flesh," which refers not to the physical body but to the self (14.2–4). Citizens of the earthly city live according to the flesh in that they live according to themselves. The body is not to blame for human sin. As Augustine defends the goodness of the body, he also defends the legitimacy of emotions, which are good if the will is good, and bad if the will is bad (14.5–9). The next section recounts the fall of Adam and Eve, concentrating on their abandonment of God for self (14.10–15). The punishment for their disobedience was disobedience itself—namely, humans' inability to obey God even when they want to do so. The following section treats the insubordination of the sexual organs to the will as emblematic of humanity's enslavement to sin (14.16–24). Augustine then summarizes his treatment of the fall (14.25–27) and the contrast between the two cities (14.28). The earthly city was created by love for self, and the heavenly city was created by love for God.

1. As we have already said in the preceding books,[1] God chose to give human beings their start from a single person. He did this, as we said, so that the human race would not only be joined in a society formed by likeness of nature

1. See above at 12.22–28.

but would also be bound together in unity and concord by the tie of kinship, mutually linked by the bond of peace. And the individual members of this race would not have been subject to death if the first two—one of whom was created from nothing,[2] and the other from him[3]—had not merited death by their disobedience. So terrible was the sin of these two that, due to their sin, human nature was changed for the worse and was also transmitted to their posterity under the bondage of sin and the necessity of death.

The reign of death held such dominion over human beings that it would have pitched them all headlong into the second unending death, as the punishment they deserved, if the undeserved grace of God had not delivered some of them from its hold. And so it has happened that, even though there are a great many peoples spread across the world, living under various religious rites and moral customs and distinguished by a wide variety of languages, weaponry, and dress, there are actually only two types of human society; and, following our Scriptures, we may rightly speak of these as two cities.[4] One is the city of those who wish to live according to the flesh, the other of those who wish to live according to the spirit.[5] Each desires its own kind of peace, and, when it finds what it seeks, each lives in its own kind of peace.

Living according to the Flesh and Living according to the Spirit

2. First, then, we need to see what it means to live according to the flesh and what it means to live according to the spirit.[6] For anyone who takes only a superficial view of what I have said, without remembering or without paying attention to how Scripture expresses itself on this matter, could easily go

2. See Gen. 1:27.

3. See Gen. 2:21–22.

4. [GWL] This sentence is an important summary of Augustine's theology of the two cities. Since the fall, all humanity has been divided into two great peoples, the earthly city and the heavenly city. As treated in 13.2, the "second death" refers to hell. Christ's deliverance has rescued the heavenly city from this fate. NCP: "On the variety to be found in the two cities, despite the fact that they remain only two, see below at 19.17."

5. [GWL] Augustine is signaling a major argument in Book 14, which coordinates the contrast between the earthly and heavenly cities with Paul's contrast between the flesh and the spirit. The earthly city consists of those who live according to the flesh (which Augustine will define as self), and the heavenly city consists of those who live according to the spirit.

6. [GWL] As Augustine clarifies, he will not be using "flesh" as a reference to the body or "spirit" as a reference to the mind. Though the Epicureans place happiness in the body and the Stoics place happiness in the mind, they both live according to the "flesh" as Augustine is using the term, following Paul.

wrong. He could think, for example, that the Epicurean philosophers clearly live according to the flesh, simply because they have taken bodily pleasure as man's highest good;[7] and he could think the same of any other philosophers who hold, in one way or another, that the good of the body is man's highest good. He could also think that this is true of the whole range of ordinary people who follow no philosophic teaching but show a propensity for lust and find delight only in the pleasures grasped by the bodily senses. And, on the other hand, he might suppose that the Stoics live according to the spirit, simply because they place the highest human good in the mind.[8] For what is the mind, if not spirit? In fact, however, it is clear that, as Scripture uses these expressions, all of these live according to the flesh.

For it is not only the body of an earthly and mortal creature that Scripture calls flesh.[9] That is the meaning, for example, when it says, *Not all flesh is the same, but there is one flesh for human beings, another for animals, another for birds, and another for fish* (1 Cor. 15:39). But there are many other ways in which Scripture uses the sense of this term; and, among these various modes of expression, it often uses *flesh* to designate man himself, that is, the nature of man. This is an example of the mode of expression which represents the whole by a part. For instance, *No flesh shall be justified by the works of the law* (Rom. 3:20). For what does *no flesh* mean here except "no man"? This is stated more clearly a little later, where the Apostle says, *No one is justified by the law* (Gal. 3:11), and, again, in his epistle to the Galatians, *Knowing that a man is not justified by the works of the law* (Gal. 2:16).

It is in this sense, too, that we understand *and the Word became flesh* (John 1:14) to mean that the Word became man. Certain people have misunderstood this passage and have supposed that Christ had no human soul.[10] But just as, when we read Mary Magdalene's words in the Gospel where she says, *They have taken away my Lord, and I do not know where they have laid him* (John 20:13), we understand that the whole stands for the part, since she was actually speaking only of Christ's flesh, which she thought had been taken from

7. See Diogenes Laertius, *Lives of Eminent Philosophers* 10.128–29.

8. See Laertius, *Lives of Eminent Philosophers* 7.87.

9. [GWL] Augustine here begins a discussion of the word "flesh," which seems to refer to the physical body but has a wider meaning in Paul's writings.

10. Apollinaris of Laodicea (ca. 310–ca. 390) and his followers held that the Word, or the *Logos*, took the place of a human soul or mind in Christ. See also . . . at 10.27 [*City of God, Books 1–10*, 336n129] and below at 14.9. There is a brief description of Apollinarianism in *Heresies* 55.

the tomb where it was buried, so also the part may stand for the whole, as in the instances cited above, where only the flesh is mentioned but the entire man is meant.

Divine Scripture, then, uses *flesh* in a variety of ways, and it would take too long to collect and examine them all. Therefore, to explore what it means to live according to the flesh—which is clearly evil, even though the nature of the flesh is not in itself evil—let us carefully examine the passage in the epistle which the apostle Paul wrote to the Galatians where he says, *Now the works of the flesh are obvious: fornication, impurity, licentiousness, idolatry, sorcery, enmity, strife, jealousy, anger, dissension, heresies, envy, drunkenness, carousing, and the like. I am warning you, as I warned you before, that those who do such things will not gain the kingdom of God* (Gal. 5:19–21).

This whole passage from the Apostle's epistle, when considered as fully as our present purpose seems to require, will be able to resolve the question of what it means to live according to the flesh.[11] For, among the works of the flesh which he said were obvious and which he listed and condemned, we find not only those that have to do with the pleasures of the flesh (such as fornication, impurity, licentiousness, drunkenness, and carousing) but also those that represent vices of the mind and have nothing to do with fleshly pleasure. For who does not see that idolatry, sorcery, enmity, strife, jealousy, anger, dissension, heresies, and envy are all vices of the mind rather than of the flesh? It may actually happen that a person holds back from bodily pleasures for the sake of serving an idol or due to some heretical error; and yet even then, despite the fact that the person seems to restrain and repress the desires of the flesh, he is convicted, on the Apostle's authority, of living according to the flesh. By the very fact that he is abstaining from the pleasures of the flesh he is shown to be doing the works of the flesh!

Does anyone feel enmity except in the mind? Or does anyone talk in such a way that he says to an enemy, whether real or imagined, "Your flesh is set against me" rather than "Your mind is set against me"? Finally, anyone who heard of "carnalities"—to coin a term—would undoubtedly ascribe them to the flesh; and, by the same token, no one doubts that animosities pertain to the mind.[12] Why, then, does the *teacher of the gentiles in faith and truth*

11. [GWL] This paragraph presents Augustine's central argument. "Flesh" does not refer to the physical body alone but also includes the mind.

12. "Carnalities . . . flesh . . . animosities . . . mind": *carnalitates . . . carni . . . animositates . . . animum.*

(1 Tim. 2:7) call all these, and the like, *works of the flesh*? Plainly that is because, using the figure of speech in which the part signifies the whole, he means the word *flesh* to stand for the very man himself.[13]

The Meaning of "Flesh"

3. Now, someone may claim that the flesh is the cause of every sort of vice in moral failure, since it is due to the influence of the flesh on the soul that the soul lives that kind of life.[14] But anyone who says this obviously has not given careful consideration to the whole nature of man. It is true that *the corruptible body weighs down the soul* (Wis. 9:15). But the same Apostle, in discussing this corruptible body, after saying, *Even though our outer man is undergoing corruption* (2 Cor. 4:16), then went on to say a little later, *We know that if the earthly dwelling we inhabit is destroyed, we have a building from God, a dwelling not made with hands, eternal in the heavens. For in this dwelling we groan, longing to be clothed with our dwelling from heaven, if only we shall not be found naked once we have put it on. For we who are in this dwelling groan under its weight not because we want to be stripped of it but because we want to be clothed over, so that what is mortal may be swallowed up by life* (2 Cor. 5:1–4). We are, then, weighed down by the corruptible body; but, because we know that the cause of this weight is not the very nature and substance of the body but rather its corruption, we want not to be stripped of the body but instead to be clothed with its immortality. For at that point, too, the body will still be there; but, because it will no longer be corruptible, it will not weigh us down. Now, therefore, *the corruptible body weighs down the soul, and this earthly dwelling presses down the mind that thinks many thoughts* (Wis. 9:15). Those who hold that all the evils of the soul stem from the body, however, are wrong.

It is true enough that Virgil seems to set forth the Platonic view in glorious verse when he says, "Heavenly is the origin of these seeds, and fiery their force,

---

13. [GWL] Augustine deftly makes "man" synonymous with "flesh." The word translated for "man" is *homo*, which could perhaps have been translated with the gender-neutral "human" or "self." Augustine is linking Paul's "flesh" with the earthly city, which consists of those who live according to self instead of God (14.4). On the translation of *homo*, see William Babcock, introduction to *City of God, Books 1–10*, lii.

14. [GWL] Again, Augustine argues that "flesh" does not always refer to the physical body. In Paul, living according to the flesh means living according to self instead of God. In Wis. 9:15, it is the corruption of the body, as opposed to the body itself, that weighs down the soul. Christian faith does not hope for an escape from the body but for an immortal, perfected body.

were they not held back by harmful bodies and slowed by earthly limbs and death-bound members."[15] And, because he wants us to recognize that the body is the source of all four of the well-known passions of the mind—desire, fear, joy, and grief[16]—as if these were the origins of all sins and vices, he goes on to add, "Hence they fear and they desire, they grieve and they rejoice. They do not look upward to the sky but are confined in darkness, held captive in a blind prison."[17] But our faith holds otherwise. For the corruption of the body, which weighs down the soul, is not the cause of the first sin but rather its punishment. It was not the corruptible flesh that made the soul sinful but the sinful soul that made the flesh corruptible.[18]

Although some incitements to vice and even some vicious desires themselves may stem from this corruption of the flesh, it would still be quite wrong to ascribe all the vices of a wicked life to the flesh. To do so would be to absolve the devil, who has no flesh, from all these vices. For, even though we cannot say that the devil is guilty of fornication or drunkenness or any other sort of evil that has to do with the pleasures of the flesh (despite the fact that he is the one who secretly persuades and incites us to such sins), he is still proud and envious in the highest degree. And these vices have taken such hold of him that, because of them, he is destined to eternal punishment in the prison of this murky air of ours.

And the Apostle attributes the vices that hold dominion over the devil precisely to the flesh, even though it is certain that the devil has no flesh. For he says that enmity, strife, jealousy, animosity, and envy are works of the flesh,[19] and the source and origin of all these evils is pride, which reigns in the devil even though he has no flesh. For who is more inimical to the saints than the devil? Who is found to show more strife, more animosity, more jealousy, and more envy toward them? But he has all these vices without having flesh. How, then, can they be works of the flesh? Only and precisely because they are the works of man, for whom, as I have said, the Apostle uses the term *flesh*.

For it is not by having flesh, which the devil does not have, that man has become like the devil; it is rather by living according to self, that is, according

15. *Aeneid* 6.730–32.

16. See Cicero, *Tusculan Disputations* 3.10.22–3.11.25.

17. [GWL] Virgil, *Aeneid*, 6.733–34. Augustine's quotation of this passage foreshadows 14.5–9, where he will defend the legitimacy of emotions and treat the emotions of fear, desire, grief, and joy.

18. [GWL] A clear statement of Augustine's position.

19. See Gal. 5:20–21.

to man. For the devil chose to live according to self when he did not stand fast in the truth; and so the lie that he told came not from God but from himself. Thus the devil is not only a liar but the very father of lies.[20] He was, in fact, the first to lie; and falsehood, like sin, began with him.

Living according to Man, or Self, and Living according to God

4. It is, then, when man lives according to man and not according to God that he is like the devil.[21] For even an angel should not have lived according to an angel but rather according to God, so as to stand fast in the truth and to speak God's truth rather than his own lie. For in another passage the Apostle says, *But if through my falsehood God's truth abounds* (Rom. 3:7). Thus, in the case of man that falsehood is ours, but that truth is God's.

When man lives according to truth, then, he does not live according to self but according to God. For it is God who said, *I am the truth* (John 14:6). But when he lives according to himself—that is, when he lives according to man and not according to God—he most assuredly lives according to a lie. This is not because man himself is falsehood, for his author and creator is God, who is certainly not the author and creator of falsehood. It is rather because man was created upright, to live according to his creator and not according to himself—that is, to do God's will rather than his own. Not to live as he was created to live, then, is to live a lie.

Man obviously wills to be happy, even when he is not living in a way that makes it possible for him to attain happiness. And what could be more false than such a will? It is no mere empty words, then, to say that every sin is a falsehood. For sin only takes place due to our willing either that things should go well for us or that they should not go badly for us. Thus the falsehood is this: we sin so that things may go well for us, and instead the result is that they go badly; or we sin so that things may go better for us, and instead the result is that they get worse. What is the reason for this except that a man's wellbeing can only come from God, not from himself? But he forsakes God by sinning, and it is precisely by living according to himself that he sins.

Thus my assertion that two different and mutually opposed cities came into existence due to the fact that some people live according to the flesh and

20. See John 8:44.
21. [GWL] A pithy contrast between the city of God and the "city of man." As already noted, Augustine's "according to man" (*secundem hominem*) is not gendered.

others according to the spirit can also be put in this way: it is due to the fact
that some live according to man and others according to God.[22] Paul shows
this very clearly when he says to the Corinthians, *For as long as there is jeal-*
ousy and strife among you, are you not of the flesh and walking according to
man? (1 Cor. 3:3). To walk according to man, then, is exactly the same as to
be of the flesh, for the flesh—that is, a part of man—stands for man himself.

In fact, the very people whom Paul here calls *of the flesh* he had earlier
called *animal*. Here is what he said: *For what man knows the things of a man*
except the spirit of the man which is in him? So also no one knows the things
of a God except the Spirit of God. Now we have received not the spirit of this
world but the Spirit that is from God, so that we may know the gifts given
to us by God. And we speak of these things in words taught not by human
wisdom but by the Spirit, presenting spiritual things to those who are spiri-
tual. But the animal man does not receive the things of the Spirit of God,
for to him they are mere foolishness (1 Cor. 2:11–14). Again, it is to just such
people—that is, to animal men—that he says a little later, *And I, brethren,*
could not speak to you as spiritual people, but rather as people of the flesh
(1 Cor. 3:1). In both cases he uses the same mode of expression, that is, the
figure of speech in which the part stands for the whole. For both the soul[23] and
the flesh, which are parts of man, can signify the whole that is man. And so
the animal man is not one thing and the man of flesh another; rather, both
are one and the same—man living according to man. Similarly, whether where
we read, *No flesh will be justified by the works of the law* (Rom. 3:20), or
where it is written, *Seventy-five souls went down with Jacob into Egypt* (Gen.
46:27), what is signified is simply men. For in the first case *no flesh* means
"no man," and in the second *seventy-five souls* means "seventy-five men."

By the same token, when the Apostle said, *In words taught not by human*
wisdom, he could just as well have said, "In words taught not by the wisdom
of the flesh"; and, when he said, *You are walking according to man*, he could
just as well have said, "You are walking according to the flesh." This comes
out more clearly in what he goes on to say: *For when one says, I belong to*
Paul, and another, I belong to Apollos, are you not mere men? (1 Cor. 3:4).

22. [GWL] Again, Augustine connects Paul's contrast between flesh and spirit with the
conflict between the city of man and the city of God.

23. "Soul": *anima*, hence "animal" (*animalis*), meaning "ensouled." "Soul," which could be
understood by itself as something neutral, is taken in this context to mean the vivifying principle as abstracted from the influence of the Spirit, and hence is understood in negative terms.

Earlier he said, *You are animal* and *You are of the flesh*, but here he is more explicit in stating his meaning: *You are men*—that is, you are living according to man, not according to God, for, if you were living according to God, you would yourselves be gods.

The Flesh, or the Body, Is Not Evil

5. With regard to our sins and vices, then, there is no reason to insult the creator by putting the blame on the nature of the flesh, which in fact is good in its kind and in its order.[24] But it is not good to forsake the good creator and live according to a created good, whether one chooses to live according to the flesh, or according to the soul, or according to the whole man, who consists of soul and flesh and can, as a consequence, be signi-fied either by "soul" alone or by "flesh" alone. For anyone who praises the nature of the soul as the highest good and blames the nature of the flesh as something evil is undoubtedly fleshly in both his attraction to the soul and his flight from the flesh, since his view is based on human folly rather than divine truth.

The Platonists, of course, are not as foolish as the Manicheans. They do not detest earthly bodies as the very nature of evil.[25] Rather, they ascribe all the elements from which this visible and tangible world is put together, along with their properties, to God as their maker. But they still take the view that souls are so influenced by earthly limbs and death-bound members that these are the source of the soul's diseased desires and fears and joys and sorrows.[26] And these four disturbances (as Cicero calls them[27]) or passions (the usual term, taken directly from the Greek[28]) include all the vices of human immorality.

If this is true, however, why is it that, in Virgil, when Aeneas hears from his father in the underworld that souls will return again to bodies, he is amazed at this belief and cries out, "O father, are we to believe that some exalted souls rise up from here to heaven and then return to listless bodies? What dread

---

24. [GWL] To denigrate the body is to denigrate God, who created bodies. Scripture does not condemn creation but worshiping creation, whether one worships the body, the soul, or both together.

25. For the Manicheans, matter in general was evil.

26. [GWL] The next chapters expand on these four "disturbances" (*perturbationes*) or "pas-sions" (*passiones*), first noted in 14.3.

27. See *Tusculan Disputations* 4.5.10.

28. See . . . 8.17.

desire for life holds them in such misery?"[29] Is it true that this dread desire, deriving from earthly limbs and death-bound members, is still present in that purity of souls which we hear so much about? Does Virgil not assert that souls have in fact been purified from all such bodily plagues, as he calls them, prior to the point at which they begin to desire a return to bodies?[30]

Thus, even if it were true that departing and returning souls go through an unceasing round of purification and defilement (although, in fact, this is a completely baseless notion), we would still conclude that it cannot, in truth, be said that all their culpable and vice-ridden emotions stem from their earthly bodies. In fact, according to the Platonists themselves, that dread desire—as their renowned spokesman calls it—is completely unrelated to the body; for, entirely on its own, it impels the soul back to the body even after the soul has been fully purified from every bodily plague and fully separated from all bodies. By the Platonists' own admission, then, it is not exclusively due to the influence of the flesh that the soul feels desire and fear, joy and grief. It can also be disturbed by these emotions arising not from the flesh but from itself.

The Will, the Passions, and Love

6. The important factor here is the quality of a person's will.[31] If it is perverse, these emotions will be perverse; but, if it is right, they will be not only blameless but even praiseworthy. The will is involved in all of them; or, rather, they are all nothing more than modes of willing. For what are desire and joy but the will consenting to things that we want? And what are fear and grief but the will dissenting from things that we do not want? When the consent takes the form of seeking the things that we want, it is called desire; and when it takes the form of enjoying the things that we want, it is called joy. Similarly, when we dissent from something that we do not want to have

29. [GWL] Virgil, *Aeneid* 6.719–21. Augustine quotes this passage for the phrase "dread desire." Desire is one of the four passions the philosophers consider immoral and associate with the body. In this passage, however, the souls that desire to return to their bodies are disembodied. Since the souls are disembodied, the desire cannot come from the body. The philosophers are thus wrong to blame the body for the passions.

30. See *Aeneid* 6.730–51. See also . . . 10.30 and . . . 22.26.

31. [GWL] Augustine's thesis. Emotions are not inherently bad; they reflect the will, and they are good or bad according to whether the will is good or bad. In the lines that follow, Augustine delineates the four emotions. Desire and joy are oriented to desirable things. Fear and grief are oriented to undesirable things. For both pairs, the former is anticipatory (desire and fear), while the latter concerns a present condition (joy and grief).

happen, it is called fear; and when we dissent from something that actually does happen to us against our will, it is called grief. And in general, as a person's will is attracted or repelled in accord with the diversity of things that are pursued or avoided, so it is changed and turned into emotions of the one sort or the other.

Therefore, the person who lives according to God and not according to man must be a lover of the good, and it follows that he will hate the evil. And, since no one is evil by nature, but whoever is evil is evil due to some fault, the person who lives according to God owes a perfect hatred to those who are evil[32]—that is, he will neither hate the person because of the fault nor love the fault because of the person but will rather hate the fault and love the person.[33] For, once the fault is cured, all that he should love will remain, and nothing will remain that he should hate.

7. When a person is resolved on loving God and on loving his neighbor as himself,[34] not according to man but according to God, it is undoubtedly on account of this love that he is called a person of good will.[35] This disposition is more commonly called charity in Holy Scripture, but according to the same sacred writings it is also called love.[36] For the Apostle teaches that the person chosen to rule the people ought to be a lover of the good.[37] And the Lord himself, when questioning the apostle Peter, asked, *Do you cherish me more than these?* (John 21:15). And Peter answered, *Lord, you know that I love you* (21:15). And the Lord again asked not whether Peter loved him but whether he cherished him, and Peter again answered, *Lord, you know that I love you* (21:16). But when Jesus asked for a third time, he himself did not ask, "Do you cherish me," but rather, *Do you love me?* (21:17). At this point the evangelist observes, *Peter felt hurt because he said to him for the third time, Do you love me?* (21:17). In fact, however, it was not three times but only once that the Lord asked, *Do you love me?* The other two times he

---

32. See Ps. 139:21.

33. [GWL] "Hate the sin, love the sinner." This phrase reflects Augustine's understanding of evil as privation, according to which human nature is good by virtue of its participation in God's goodness and being but can be corrupted by sin, which involves an absence of being. Corruption presupposes the goodness of the nature that has been corrupted. See essay: "Evil as Privation."

34. See Matt. 22:37–39 par.

35. [GWL] Augustine defines a good will according to love for God and neighbor. The following paragraphs review different terms in Scripture for love and conclude there is no significant distinction between them.

36. "Charity . . . love": *caritas . . . amor.*

37. "Lover": *amator.* See Titus 1:8.

asked, *Do you cherish me?*[38] From this we can see, then, that even when the
Lord asked, *Do you cherish me?* what he meant was no different from when
he asked, *Do you love me?* Peter, however, did not change the word he used
for the same thing but replied the third time, *Lord, you know everything; you
know that I love you* (21:17).

I thought that I should mention this because some people suppose that
cherishing and charity are different from love.[39] They claim that cherishing
is to be taken in a good sense and love in a bad sense. It is quite certain,
however, that not even the writers of secular literature spoke in this way.
And so the philosophers will have to see for themselves whether and on
what grounds they can make such a distinction. Their books, at any rate,
indicate clearly enough that they place a high value on love when it is concerned with good things and directed toward God himself. But the point
I wanted to make is that the Scriptures of our religion, whose authority
we rank above all other writings, make no distinction between love and
cherishing or charity. For I have already shown that they speak of love in
a good sense.

Nor should anyone think that, while love can be used in both a good and a
bad sense, cherishing can be used only in a good sense. Note what the Psalm
says, *Anyone who cherishes iniquity hates his own soul* (Ps. 11:5). Note,
too, the words of the apostle John, *If anyone cherishes the world, there is
no cherishing of the Father in him* (1 John 2:15). In this case, in one and the
same passage, cherishing has both a good and a bad sense. And if anyone
wants an instance of love in a bad sense (since I have already shown that it
has a good sense), let him read what is written: *For people will be lovers of
themselves, lovers of money* (2 Tim. 3:2).

A right will, therefore, is a good love, and a perverse will is an evil love.[40]
Thus, love longing for what it loves is desire, and love actually possessing and
enjoying what it loves is joy. Love seeking to escape what opposes it is fear,
and love experiencing what opposes it, when it actually happens, is grief.

---

38. "Love . . . cherish": forms of the verbs *amare* and *diligere* respectively.

39. "Cherishing . . . charity . . . love": *dilectionem . . . caritatem . . . amorem. Dilectio, caritas* and *amor* are the principal terms that Augustine uses for love. Sometimes he gives different
weights to them, emphasizing either positive or negative possibilities. But at other times, as
here, he treats them all as positive and as practically indistinguishable. See also . . . 15.22, where
dilectio is translated as "affection."

40. [GWL] An important summary statement. Augustine defines the four emotions (or
wills) in terms of love.

These feelings are all bad, then, when the love is bad, and they are all good when the love is good.[41]

Let us now prove the point from Scripture.[42] The Apostle desires *to depart and be with Christ* (Phil. 1:23), and *My soul desired to long for your judgments* (Ps. 119:20), or, to put it more aptly, "My soul longed to desire your judgments," and *The desire for wisdom leads to a kingdom* (Wis. 6:20).[43] Customary usage has it, however, that, when the words for desire[44] are used without specifying their object, they can only be understood in a bad sense. Joy has a good sense: *Have joy in the Lord and exult, O righteous* (Ps. 32:11), and *You have put joy in my heart* (Ps. 4:7), and *You will fill me with joy in your presence* (Ps. 16:11). Fear has a good sense in the passage where the Apostle says, *Work out your own salvation with fear and trembling* (Phil. 2:12), and *Do not become high-minded but stand in fear* (Rom. 11:20), and *But I fear that, as the serpent deceived Eve by its cunning, so your minds will be led astray from the purity that is in Christ* (2 Cor. 11:3). As for grief— which Cicero, instead, calls "distress"[45] and which Virgil calls "pain" where he says, "They feel pain and gladness,"[46] but which I have preferred to call "grief" because distress and pain are more commonly used in relation to the body—it is not easy to say whether an example of grief used in a good sense can be found.

8. In place of three of these passions the Stoics wanted to claim that there are in the mind of the wise man three dispositions which are called *eupatheiai* in Greek[47] and which Cicero calls "constant dispositions" in Latin[48]—will in place of desire, gladness in place of joy, and caution in place of fear.[49] They

41. This recalls Augustine's translation of the cardinal virtues into forms of love in *The Catholic Way of Life and the Manichean Way of Life* 1.15.25.

42. [GWL] Augustine now investigates Scripture for passages that present "desire," "joy," "fear," and "grief" as good emotions. He finds examples for the first three but not for "grief." At the end of 14.8, however, he finds "grief" used positively in 2 Cor. 7:8–11.

43. Forms of the verb *concupiscere* and of the noun *concupiscentia* are used in these four instances.

44. Augustine mentions the nouns *cupiditas* and *concupiscentia*.

45. "Distress": *aegritudinem*. See *On the Ends of the Good and the Evil* 3.35.

46. *Aeneid* 6.734.

47. Diogenes Laertius, *Lives of Eminent Philosophers* 7.116. *Eupatheiai* might be translated as "appropriate passions."

48. "Constant dispositions": *constantias*, or "constants." See *Tusculan Disputations* 4.6.11–4.6.14.

49. [GWL] The Stoics affirm positive and allegedly more stable versions of the first three emotions, though they use different terms for each. "Desire," "joy," and "fear" (*cupiditas, laetitia,* and *metus*) become "will," "gladness," and "caution" (*uoluntas, gaudium,* and

denied, however, that there could be anything in the mind of the wise man that corresponds to distress or to pain, which, to avoid ambiguity, we have preferred to call "grief."

Will, they say, pursues the good, which is what the wise man does; gladness comes from attaining the good, which the wise man invariably attains; and caution avoids evil, which is what the wise man ought to avoid. But because grief arises from an evil that has already happened, and because the Stoics hold that no evil can happen to the wise man, they maintain that there can be nothing in his mind that corresponds to grief. In effect, then, they are saying that only the wise man can have will, gladness, and caution, while the foolish can feel only desire, joy, fear, and grief. The first three are constant dispositions, and the latter four are disturbances, as Cicero calls them, or passions, as most call them. As I have said, however, the first three are called *eupatheiai* in Greek, and the latter four *pathē*.[50]

When I was examining, as carefully as I could, whether these expressions are in keeping with Holy Scripture, I came across this saying of the prophet: *There is no gladness for the wicked, says the Lord* (Isa. 57:21 LXX).[51] This suggests that the wicked can feel joy over things that are evil, but not gladness, because gladness properly belongs to the good and the godly alone. Again, a passage in the Gospel says, *Whatever you will that others should do to you, this do also to them* (Matt. 7:12); and this seems to suggest that no one can will but can only desire something in an evil or sordid way. In fact, due to customary usage, some translators have added the words "good things" to the passage, translating it this way: "Whatever good things you will that others should do to you." Their aim was to guard against anyone's willing people to do disreputable things for him—such as giving him extravagant banquets (not to mention anything more sordid)—and then thinking that he would fulfill the commandment if he did the same for them. But in the Greek Gospel, from which the Latin translation comes, we do not find the words "good things." The passage simply reads, *Whatever you will that others should do to you, this do also to them.* The reason for this, I believe, is

---

cautio). The latter are legitimate dispositions for the virtuous "wise man." The fourth emotion, grief (*tristitia*), finds no Stoic analogue, for the virtuous person will supposedly not feel grief about anything. See essay: "Stoics and Stoicism."

50. *Pathē* is usually translated simply as "passions."

51. [GWL] The next paragraphs investigate Scripture and classical authors for the terms "will" and "gladness" and conclude that they are ascribed to both good and bad people. The Stoics are wrong to ascribe them only to the virtuous "wise man."

that the evangelist meant the word *will* to imply "good things," for he does not use the word "desire."[52]

There is no reason, however, that these niceties of meaning should always govern our speech; they are to be used, rather, as the occasion requires. And, when we are reading the writers whose authority it is ungodly to reject, they must be brought into play in cases where it would not otherwise be possible to find the true sense, as in the instances I have just cited, one from the prophet and one from the Gospel. For everyone knows that the ungodly exult with joy, and yet *there is no gladness for the wicked, says the Lord*. How can this be true unless "gladness" has a different meaning when the word is used in a specific and designated sense? Again, no one would deny that it is wrong to teach people to do to others whatever they desire that others do to them, lest they would then regale each other with sordid and illicit pleasures. And yet there is no more salutary and true commandment than this, *Whatever you will that others should do to you, this do also to them*. And how can this be true unless *will* is used in this passage with a specific meaning that cannot be taken in a bad sense. On the other hand, if there were no such thing as an evil will, Scripture certainly would not follow the more familiar usage, which is especially common in ordinary speech, as it does where it says, *Do not will to utter any lie* (Sir. 7:13). The depravity of an evil will is distinguished, then, from the will that the angels proclaimed when they said, *Peace on earth to men of good will* (Luke 2:14). For it would have been superfluous to add the word good here if the will can only be good. And again, when the Apostle says that love does not feel glad in wrongdoing,[53] would that be any great praise of love if it were not for the fact that malice *does* feel gladness in wrongdoing?

A similarly undifferentiated use of these terms is also found in authors of secular literature. For the very distinguished orator Cicero says, "I desire, conscript fathers, to be merciful."[54] Here he uses "desire" in a good sense, and who would be so perversely pedantic as to argue that he ought to have said "I will" rather than "I desire." Again, in Terence, there is the disgraceful young man who, out of his mind with burning desire, says, "I will nothing but Philumena."[55] But that his will was in fact desire is made quite clear in

---

52. Augustine also comments on the two versions of Matt. 7:12 in *The Lord's Sermon on the Mount* 2.22.74.
53. See 1 Cor. 13:6.
54. *Against Catiline* 1.4.
55. *Andria* 2.306.

the response given by his saner slave at this point. The slave says to his master, "It would be far better for you to take yourself in hand and put this love out of your mind, instead of chattering on about it and stupidly inflaming your desire all the more."[56] And the great Virgil himself attests that these authors also used "gladness" in a bad sense. In the very verse where, with supreme brevity, he lists the four passions, he says, "Hence they fear and they desire, they grieve and they are glad."[57] And the same author also speaks of "the evil gladness of the mind."[58]

Will, caution, and gladness are common, then, to both the good and the evil; and, to say the same thing in other words, desire, fear, and joy are also common to both the good and the evil.[59] But the good have these emotions in a good way and the evil in a bad way, just as the human will is either rightly directed or wrongly directed. And even grief itself, despite the fact that the Stoics thought that they could find nothing corresponding to it in the mind of a wise man, is found in a good sense, especially in our writers.[60] For the Apostle praises the Corinthians for feeling grief in a godly way. Perhaps, however, someone will observe that the Apostle congratulates them for feeling the grief of repentance, the sort of grief that can only be felt by those who have sinned. For this is what he says: *I see that my letter grieved you, though only briefly. Now I rejoice, not because you were grieved but because your grief led to repentance. For you felt a godly grief, so that you suffered no damage from us in any way. For godly grief produces a repentance that leads to salvation and brings no regret, but worldly grief produces death. For see what earnestness this godly grief has produced in you* (2 Cor. 7:8–11).

This makes it possible for the Stoics, on their part, to respond that grief does seem to serve a useful purpose in leading to repentance for sin, but that there can be no grief in the mind of the wise man because, in his case, there is no sin for which he might grieve and repent, nor does he endure

56. *Andria* 2.307–9.
57. *Aeneid* 6.733.
58. *Aeneid* 6.278–79.
59. [GWL] Augustine's conclusion concerning the Stoics' three dispositions.
60. [GWL] Augustine now addresses the fourth emotion, grief, which the Stoics reject as an option for the wise man. In 2 Cor. 7, Paul uses "grief" positively, claiming those who fail morally should experience grief over their failure. For the Stoics, this response would make no sense for the wise man, who by definition does not fail morally. Augustine's discussion raises one of his central disagreements with the Stoics. According to Augustine, everyone (except Jesus) fails morally in this life.

or experience any other evil that might lead him to grieve. For a story is told about Alcibiades (if my memory has not deceived me about the man's name). To himself he seemed to be happy, but when Socrates, by argument, proved to him how miserable he was because he was foolish, he burst into tears.[61] In his case, then, foolishness was the cause of this useful and desirable grief, the grief of a person who laments that he is what he ought not to be. But it is not the fool, the Stoics claim, but the wise man who cannot feel grief.

The Passions in the City of God

9. With regard to this question of the disturbances of the mind, however, I have already given my response to these philosophers in the ninth book of this work,[62] showing that they are more eager for controversy than for truth on this issue, which is far more a dispute over words than over reality. Among us Christians, in contrast, the citizens of the city of God, who live according to God during the pilgrimage of this life, feel fear and desire, pain and gladness,[63] in accord with Holy Scripture and sound doctrine; and, because their love is right, they have all these emotions in the right way.

They fear eternal punishment, and they desire eternal life. They are pained in reality because they are still groaning inwardly while they wait for adoption, the redemption of their bodies,[64] and they are gladdened in hope because *the saying that is written shall be fulfilled: Death is swallowed up in victory* (1 Cor. 15:54). Again, they fear to sin, and they desire to persevere. They are pained by their sins, and they are gladdened by their good works. That they may fear to sin, they are told, *Because iniquity will abound, the love of many shall grow cold* (Matt. 24:12). That they may desire to persevere, Scripture tells them, *The one who perseveres to the end shall be saved* (Matt. 10:22).

61. See Cicero, *Tusculan Disputations* 3.32.77.
62. See . . . 9.4–5.
63. [GWL] Virgil, *Aeneid* 6.733. This is an allusion to the same passage Augustine quotes in 14.3, 7, and 8. (See also 21.3, 13.) The second half of the quotation (*dolent gaudentque*) is not translated consistently. The reader might therefore miss how Augustine develops his argument around a single passage. In 14.3, the translation reads, "They grieve and they rejoice." In 14.7, it reads, "They feel pain and gladness." In 14.8, it reads, "They grieve and they are glad." The phrases "feel pain" and "grieve" translate the same words, as do "feel gladness" and "rejoice." In what follows, Augustine explains how Christians experience the four emotions, citing passages from Scripture corresponding to each one.
64. See Rom. 8:23.

That they may be pained by their sins, they are told, *If we say that we have no sin, we deceive ourselves, and the truth is not in us* (1 John 1:8). That they may be gladdened by good works, they are told, *God loves a cheerful giver* (2 Cor. 9:7).

Again, depending on how weak or strong they are, they fear to be tempted or desire to be tempted, and they are pained at being tempted or gladdened at being tempted. That they may fear to be tempted, they are told, *If a person is detected in any sin, you who are spiritual should set him right in a spirit of gentleness, taking care that you yourselves are not tempted as well* (Gal. 6:1). On the other hand, that they may desire to be tempted, they are told of a certain strong man of the city of God who said, *Prove me, O Lord, and tempt me; test my heart and my mind by fire* (Ps. 26:2). That they may be pained at being tempted, they see Peter in tears.[65] That they may be gladdened at being tempted, they hear James saying, *Consider it all gladness, my brothers, when you meet with various temptations* (James 1:2).

Nor is it only on their own account that the citizens of the city of God are moved by these feelings. It is also on account of those whom they desire to see delivered and fear to see perish, and over whom they are pained if they do perish and gladdened if they are delivered. We who have come into Christ's Church from the gentile world should most especially keep in mind that best and strongest of men who glories in his own weaknesses,[66] the teacher of the gentiles in faith and truth, who worked harder than all his fellow apostles[67] and who taught the people of God in his many epistles, not only those whom he saw at the time but also those whom he foresaw in the future. He was an athlete of Christ, taught by him,[68] anointed by him, crucified with him,[69] glorying in him.[70] In the theater of this world, where he became a spectacle to both men and angels,[71] he fought a great fight according to the rules and pressed on toward the prize of his heavenly calling.[72] With the eyes of faith, the citizens of God's city gladly watch him rejoicing with those who rejoice, weeping with those who

65. See Matt. 26:75.
66. See 2 Cor. 12:19. The encomium of the apostle Paul that begins here attests to the high place that he occupied in the thought of Augustine, not only as a theological but also as a moral inspiration, and is typical of the early Church's attitude in his regard.
67. See 1 Cor. 15:10.
68. See Gal. 1:12.
69. See Gal. 2:19.
70. See Rom. 15:17
71. See 1 Cor. 4:9.
72. See Phil. 3:14; 2 Tim. 4:7–8.

weep,[73] facing battles without and fears within,[74] desiring to depart and be with Christ,[75] longing to see the Romans in order to reap some harvest among them also, as he had among the rest of the gentiles.[76] They gladly watch him feeling jealousy for the Corinthians and, in this very jealousy, fearing that their minds might be led astray from the purity that is in Christ.[77] They gladly watch him feeling deep grief and unceasing anguish of heart for the Israelites[78] because, being ignorant of God's righteousness and willing to establish their own, they have not submitted to the righteousness of God;[79] and they gladly watch him declaring not only his pain but also his mourning for some who had previously sinned and had not repented of their impurity and fornication.[80]

If these emotions and feelings, which spring from love of the good and holy charity, are to be called vices, then we might as well allow real vices to be called virtues. But, since these emotions are in accord with right reason when they occur where they ought properly to occur, who would dare to call them diseased or vice-ridden passions in this case?[81] For this reason, even the Lord himself,[82] when he condescended to live a human life in the form of a servant[83] (although wholly without sin[84]), showed these emotions where he judged that they ought to be shown. For there was nothing fake about the human emotion of one who had a true human body and a true human mind.[85] It is certainly not false, therefore, when the Gospel reports that he was grieved and angered at the Jews' hardness of heart,[86] or that he said, *For your sake I am glad so that you may believe* (John 11:15), or that he even shed tears when

73. See Rom. 12:15.
74. See 2 Cor. 7:5.
75. See Phil. 1:23.
76. See Rom. 1:11–13.
77. See 2 Cor. 11:2–3.
78. See Rom. 9:2.
79. See Rom. 10:3.
80. See 2 Cor. 12:21.
81. [GWL] Though Augustine affirms the legitimacy of emotions (*affectiones*), he believes they should accord with "right reason" (*rectam rationem*), which involves experiencing the right emotion with the right intensity.
82. [GWL] Having treated Paul's emotional life, Augustine turns to Jesus's emotions. For Augustine, the reality of Jesus's emotions corresponds to the reality of the incarnation. Jesus experienced emotions because he was human.
83. See Phil. 2:7.
84. See Heb. 4:15.
85. This is perhaps said in view of Apollinarian doctrine. See [*City of God, Books 11–22*, 100n7 // above, Book 14n10].
86. See Mark 3:5.

he was about to raise Lazarus,[87] or that he desired to eat the Passover with his disciples,[88] or that his soul was grieved when his passion drew near.[89] Rather, for the sake of his fixed purpose, he took on these emotions in his human mind when he willed, just as he became man when he willed.

The Emotions and the Future Life

Even when we have these emotions in the right way and according to God, however, we have to acknowledge that they belong to this life, not to the future life that is our hope, and that we often give way to them against our will. Sometimes, then, even though we are moved not by blameworthy desire but by praiseworthy charity, we still weep even when we do not want to.[90] In our case, then, it is due to the weakness of the human condition that we have these emotions. But that is not true of the Lord Jesus, for even his weakness was an expression of his power. So long as we bear the weakness of this life, however, we certainly would not be living rightly if we did not feel these emotions at all. For the Apostle berated and denounced certain people who were, he said, unfeeling.[91] And a holy Psalm blames those of whom it says, *I looked for someone to grieve with me, but there was none* (Ps. 69:20). For, so long as we are in this place of misery, to live entirely without pain—as one of this world's men of letters saw and said—"comes only at the high price of an inhuman mind and an unfeeling body."[92]

In this regard, let us consider what is called *apatheia* in Greek, which, if it could be put into Latin, would be called "impassibility."[93] If we are to

87. See John 11:35.
88. See Luke 22:15.
89. See Matt. 26:38.
90. As an example of Augustine's sensitivity on this issue, see *Confessions* 9.12.33.
91. See Rom. 1:31.
92. Cicero, *Tusculan Disputations* 3.6.12.
93. In what follows Augustine briefly discusses the controversial topic of *apatheia*, which had already been addressed with less nuance by Jerome at about the same time in his Letter 133.1–3. Augustine may have this letter in mind (like Jerome, he translates *apatheia* as *impassibilitas*, or "impassivity"), as well as Jerome's *Answer to the Pelagians*, in which he argues that the Stoic notion of *apatheia* forms part of the basis of Pelagian doctrine, which allows for the possibility of sinlessness in this life. Augustine distinguishes between two kinds of *apatheia*—complete control of the emotions (*affectus*) that disturb the mind, which equates with sinlessness and which, though desirable in this life, is attainable only in eternal life; and the elimination of all the emotions, which may be possible in this life (as Augustine seems to allow theoretically) but neither desirable nor, when it comes to such emotions as love and gladness, possible or desirable in eternal life.

understand this to mean living without those emotions which come upon us against reason and disturb the mind—for *apatheia* obviously refers to the mind, not to the body—then it is clearly a good and is much to be desired, but it does not belong to this life.[94] For it is not in the voice of just any sort of people, but in the voice of those who are most godly and are most righteous and holy, that Scripture says, *If we say that we have no sin, we deceive ourselves, and the truth is not in us* (1 John 1:8). This *apatheia*, then, will come only when there is no sin in man. In this present life, however, we do well if we live without censure. And if anyone thinks that he lives without sin, he succeeds only in forfeiting forgiveness, not in avoiding sin.

But if *apatheia* means that no emotion at all can touch the mind, who would not regard this stupor as worse than all the vices?[95] There is nothing absurd, then, about saying that perfect happiness will be free from the pangs of fear and from all forms of grief; but only a person wholly shut off from the truth would say that it will feel no love and gladness. Again, if *apatheia* means that no fear terrifies us and no pain hurts us, then we must certainly shun *apatheia* in this life if we want to live rightly, that is, if we want to live according to God. But, in the life of happiness which, it is promised, will be eternal, it is clearly something that we should hope for.

There is the kind of fear of which the apostle John says: *There is no fear in love, but perfect love casts out fear, for fear has to do with punishment, and whoever feels fear is not perfect in love* (1 John 4:18).[96] But this is not the same kind of fear as Paul's fear that the Corinthians might be led astray by the serpent's cunning.[97] Paul's fear is the kind of fear that love feels; and, in fact, it is only love that feels this fear. But the other kind of fear, which love does not feel, is the fear of which the apostle Paul himself says, *You did not receive a spirit of slavery to fall back into fear* (Rom. 8:15). On the other hand, the fear that is *pure, enduring forever* (Ps. 19:9)—if it will be present in the world to come (and how else can it be understood to endure forever?)—is not the kind of fear that frightens a person away from an evil

94. [GWL] Here is the first problem with the Stoics. They believe it is possible to avoid irrational emotions in this life. Augustine challenges this perspective in 19.4, which criticizes the philosophers, and especially the Stoics, for claiming happiness is possible in this temporal existence.

95. [GWL] Here is the second problem with the Stoics. They consider the absence of emotions good. Augustine challenges this position in 19.6–8.

96. [GWL] The next two paragraphs distinguish between different kinds of fear, enlisting passages from Scripture that use the word "fear."

97. See 2 Cor. 11:3.

that might occur but rather the kind that holds him to a good that cannot be lost.[98]

For, where the love of a good already attained is immutable, there, surely, any fear of an evil to be avoided is a fear without anxiety (if we can say such a thing). For fear that is pure signifies the will whereby we shall necessarily will not to sin and shall necessarily will to guard against sin, not from any anxiety that in our weakness we might fall into sin but with the utter tranquility of love. Or, if no fear of any kind will be present in the total security of our unending and blissful joys, then to say *The fear of the Lord is pure, enduring forever* (Ps. 19:9) is like saying *The patience of the poor shall not perish forever* (Ps. 9:18). For it is not that patience itself will last forever, because there is no need for patience where there are no evils to be endured. It is rather that the goal reached through patience will endure for all eternity. And perhaps it is in this sense that this pure fear is said to endure forever, that is, in the sense that the goal to which it leads will endure forever.

All this being so, since we must lead a right life to reach a happy life, it follows that a right life will have all these emotions in the right way, and a perverse life will have them in a perverse way. But the life that is both happy and eternal will have a love and a gladness that are not only right but also assured, and it will have no fear or grief at all. And so it is now clear what qualities the citizens of the city of God ought to have during this pilgrimage here on earth in living according to the spirit and not according to the flesh, that is, in living according to God and not according to man; and it is clear, too, what qualities they will have in the immortality toward which they are traveling.

In contrast, the city, that is, the society, of the ungodly—who live not according to God but according to man, and, in their very worship of false divinity and contempt for true divinity, follow the teachings of men or of demons—is racked by perverse forms of these emotions as though by diseases and disruptions. And, if this city has any citizens who appear to control and in some way to temper these emotions, they are so proud and puffed up in their impiety that, for this very reason, the tumors of their pride expand as the pangs of their pain shrink.[99] And, if some of these,

---

98. On the two types of fear see also *Homilies on the First Epistle of John* 9.4–8; Cassian, *Conferences* 11.13.

99. [GWL] A polemical statement about the Stoics, with a wordplay: *maiores tumores, quo minores dolores.*

with a vanity as monstrous as it is rare, are so enamored of their own self-restraint that they are not stirred or excited or swayed or influenced by any emotion at all, the truth is that they are losing all humanity rather than gaining real tranquility. For the fact that something is difficult does not make it right, nor does the fact that something has no feeling mean that it is in good health.

Emotion in the First Human Beings

10. But what of the first man—or rather of the first human beings, since there was a married pair?[100] It is not unreasonable to ask whether they felt in their animal bodies prior to sin the kinds of emotion that we shall not feel in our spiritual bodies when all sin has been purged and ended. If they did, how could it be true that they were genuinely happy in that memorable place of happiness, that is, in paradise? For who can truly be called happy if he is afflicted by fear or grief? But what possible reason could they have had for fear or for grief in the midst of such a marvelous abundance of such marvelous goods, where there was no death or any bodily illness to fear, and where nothing was absent that a good will might acquire and nothing was present that might do harm to either the flesh or the mind of a person living in happiness?

The pair lived in faithful and unalloyed fellowship, and their love for God and for each other was undisturbed. And from this love came great gladness, for what they loved was always present to be enjoyed. There was a tranquil avoidance of sin, and, as long as this lasted, no evil broke in from any side to bring them sorrow. Or did they, perhaps, desire to touch the forbidden tree and eat its fruit but were held back by fear of dying? In that case both desire and fear were already troubling them, even in that place. By no means, however, should we imagine that this was true where there was no sin whatsoever. For it plainly counts as sin to desire what the law of God prohibits and to abstain from it only from fear of punishment rather than from love of righteousness. By no means, I say, should we imagine that, prior to all sin, there was already present in paradise such sin that they felt with regard to a tree exactly what the Lord said with regard to a woman, *If anyone looks*

---

100. That Adam and Eve were married is a noteworthy affirmation on the part of Augustine, inasmuch as this was not universally accepted in the early Church. See, e.g., Tertullian, *On Monogamy* 5; Gregory of Nyssa, *On Virginity* 12.4.

at a woman with lust for her, he has already committed adultery with her in his heart (Matt. 5:28).[101]

How fortunate, then, were the first human beings! No disturbances of mind upset them; no distresses of body afflicted them. And all human society would have been just as fortunate if only the first pair had not committed the evil that would be transmitted to their posterity, and if only none of their stock had sown in iniquity what they would reap in damnation. This felicity would have continued until, through the blessing that said, *Be fruitful and multiply* (Gen. 1:28), the number of the predestined saints was completed; and then another and greater felicity would have been granted, which was granted to the most blessed angels, where there would already have been the certain assurance that no one would sin and no one would die, and where the life of the saints, without any prior experience of toil, pain, or death, would already have been what it will be, after going through all these experiences, when incorruption is restored to the body at the resurrection of the dead.[102]

The First Evil Will

11. But, because God foreknew all things and therefore could not have been unaware that man was going to sin, what we say about the city of God ought to correspond with his foreknowledge and design rather than with imaginings that could not actually have come to our knowledge because they were not actually in God's design. In fact, there was no way in which man could upset the divine purpose by his sin—as if he could have compelled God to change what he had determined! For God in his foreknowledge had anticipated both how evil man, whom he had created good, would become and what good,

101. [GWL] Augustine claims there were no evil desires in paradise prior to the fall. Yet he will also say the open disobedience of Adam and Eve was preceded by their evil desires. At some juncture, then, following the temptation of the serpent, Adam and Eve experienced evil desires that they had never experienced before. How could Adam and Eve have experienced evil desires if they were sinless? Augustine offers no complete answer. Indeed, he denies the possibility of explaining the first evil will. "An evil will is the efficient cause of an evil act, but nothing is the efficient cause of an evil will" (12.6). Though this quotation refers to the fall of the angels, it applies also to the fall of humanity.

102. [GWL] See 12.22. If humans had not fallen, they would have reproduced until their population matched the number God had predestined for the heavenly city. At that juncture, they would have entered blessed immortality. Augustine invokes here his standard comparison between life before the fall and life in heaven. Before the fall, Adam and Eve were able to sin and able to die (*posse peccare, posse mori*). In heaven, humans will be unable to sin and unable to die (*non posse peccare, non posse mori*).

even so, he would himself bring forth from man. And, even if God is said to change his decrees (for we even read in Scripture, in a figurative expression, that God repented[103]), such statements are made from the point of view of human hopes and expectations or with respect to the orderly course of natural causes, not from the point of view of almighty God's foreknowledge of what he was going to do. As it is written, then, God *made man upright* (Eccles. 7:29) and therefore possessed of a good will. For man would not have been upright if he did not have a good will. A good will is, then, the work of God, since man was created with it by God.

In contrast, the first evil will, since it preceded all evil works in man, was a kind of defection from God's work to the will's own works rather than being any sort of work in its own right, and the will's own works were evil because they were willed according to self and not according to God.[104] Thus the will itself—or rather man himself, insofar as his will was evil—was, so to speak, the evil tree that bore these works as its evil fruit.[105] Furthermore, although an evil will, because it is a fault, is contrary to nature rather than in accord with nature, it still belongs to the nature in which it is a fault, for a fault cannot exist except in a nature. But it can only exist in a nature which the creator created out of nothing, not in a nature which he begot out of himself in the way that he begot the Word through whom all things were made.[106] For, although God fashioned man from the dust of the earth,[107] the earth itself and all earthly matter come from nothing whatsoever, and the soul which God gave to the body when man was made was also created out of nothing.

Evil things, however, are overcome by good things. This is in fact so true that, although evil things are allowed to exist in order to show how the creator's all-foreseeing justice can use even these for the good, good things can exist without the evil, as can the true and supreme God himself, and as can

---

103. See Gen. 6:6; 1 Sam. 15:11.

104. [GWL] Although sin entered the world with Adam and Eve's action, their action must have been preceded by an evil will. Otherwise, Adam and Eve's actions would not have represented their desires, in which case their actions would not have counted as sin. Augustine says Adam and Eve were capable of sinning because they were created out of nothing. This origin contrasts with that of Jesus, the divine Son, who was eternally begotten of the Father. (Consider the Nicene Creed, which confesses that the Son was "begotten, not made.") Augustine's argument depends on his understanding of evil as privation (see essay: "Evil as Privation"). Since humans were created from nothing, they were created with the capacity (but not the necessity) of sinning. Augustine discusses this matter more fully in 14.13.

105. See Matt. 7:17–18.

106. See John 1:3.

107. See Gen. 2:6.

all heavenly creatures, invisible and visible, above this murky air of ours. But evil things cannot exist without the good, for the natures in which they inhere, insofar as they are natures, are most certainly good. What is more, evil is eliminated not by removing the nature which it had entered or by removing any part of that nature but rather by healing and rectifying the nature that had become vitiated and depraved.

The will's choice, then, is only truly free when it is not enslaved to vices and sins. That is how it was given by God. But what it lost by its own fault can only be restored by the one who was able to give it in the first place. That is the reason why the Truth says, *If the Son sets you free, you will be free indeed* (John 8:36). And this is the same as if he said, "If the Son makes you saved, you will be saved indeed." For he is our liberator in precisely the same way that he is our savior.

The Human Fall

Thus, man lived according to God in a paradise both corporeal and spiritual. It was not a merely corporeal paradise providing good things for the body without also being spiritual to provide good things for the mind. Nor was it a merely spiritual paradise for man to enjoy through his inner senses without also being corporeal for him to enjoy through his outer senses. It was plainly both, and it plainly provided for both. But then came that proud and therefore envious angel who, through his pride, had turned away from God and had turned to himself. With a tyrant's disdain, so to speak, he chose to rejoice at having subjects rather than to be a subject himself; and so he fell from the spiritual paradise.[108] As best I could, I have discussed his fall—and that of his companions who, from being angels of God, were turned into his angels—in the eleventh and twelfth books of this work.[109] After his fall, he sought to worm his way into the heart of man by cunning and false counsel, for, after his own fall, he was consumed with envy of the still unfallen human beings. To this end he chose as his mouthpiece a serpent in the corporeal paradise

---

108. [GWL] Jealousy prompted the devil to tempt Adam and Eve into sin. The devil is constitutionally superior to humans in that he is more intelligent, he has a superior body, and he can perform miraculous feats (11.16–17). He could not bear that humans were morally superior to him, given that he had fallen and they had not. He thus tempted humanity to fall into the same corruption as himself. Since the devil cannot reverse his condemnation, he seeks to bring down with him as many people as possible. See essay: "Angels and Demons."

109. See . . . 11.13–15, 33; and 12.6, 9.

where, along with the two humans, the male and the female, there lived all
the other terrestrial animals, tame and harmless. This slippery animal, which
moves in twists and coils, was obviously suitable for his work. By his angelic
presence and his superior nature, he made the serpent his subject in spiritual
wickedness, and, misusing it as his instrument, he had deceitful conversation
with the woman. He began, that is, with the lower lesser part of the human
couple so that, by stages, he might reach them both, presuming that the man
would not be so easy to dupe and could not be deceived into erring himself
but would fall prey to another's error.[110]

That is what happened in Aaron's case when the people went astray. He
did not consent to make an idol because he was convinced; instead he gave
in because he felt constrained.[111] Nor is it credible that Solomon made the
error of thinking that he ought to serve idols; it was rather by the enticements
of women that he was compelled into such a sacrilegious act.[112] And it was
the same with that man and his wife. They were alone with each other, two
human beings, a married couple; and we must believe that it was not because
he thought she was speaking the truth that he was seduced into transgressing
God's law but because he yielded to the tie that bound them together. It was
not without reason, then, that the Apostle said, *Adam was not deceived, but
the woman was deceived* (1 Tim. 2:14). For she accepted what the serpent
said to her as if it were true, while he was unwilling to be separated from his
only companion, even when it came to sharing in sin. He was no less guilty
on that account, however, if he sinned knowingly and deliberately. That is
why the Apostle does not say that Adam did not sin but that *Adam was not
deceived*. For he is plainly referring to Adam when he says, *Through one man*

---

110. [GWL] Augustine's treatment of Adam and Eve draws from the assertion in 1 Tim. 2:14
that Eve was deceived but Adam was not. Whether this section assumes women are more gullible
than men is a question worth discussing. Augustine's writings on this topic are inconsistent,
and he wonders in one text if Eve had not yet developed full rationality when she was deceived
(*Literal Meaning of Genesis* 11.42.58). As he explains here, Adam was deceived too, but in a
different way than Eve. Eve was deceived in that she believed the serpent and did not think it
would be a sin to eat from the tree of the knowledge of good and evil. (In Gen. 2:16–17, God's
command is to Adam. Eve is not present because she has not yet been created.) By contrast,
Adam did not believe what the serpent said. He ate from the tree, knowing full well this was sin,
to avoid separation from Eve. Adam thus acted like Aaron, who made an idol because he was
pressured by the Israelites, and like Solomon, who worshiped idols because he was pressured by
his wives. Still, Adam was deceived in the sense that he underestimated the seriousness of the
sin and thought it would be pardonable. Ultimately, Adam and Eve "were both taken captive
by sin and entangled in the devil's snares." See essay: "Women."

111. See Exod. 32:1–5.

112. See 1 Kings 11:1–8.

sin came into the world (Rom. 5:12), and again, more explicitly, when he says a little further on, *Like the transgression of Adam* (Rom. 5:14).

The Apostle wanted us to understand that the "deceived" are those who do not think that what they are doing is sin. But Adam knew. Otherwise, how could it be true that *Adam was not deceived*? Since he was still unacquainted with God's severity, however, he could have been mistaken in believing that he had committed a pardonable offence. Thus, while he was not deceived in the same way that the woman was deceived, he was still mistaken about how his excuse would be judged when he said, *The woman whom you gave to be with me, she gave me fruit from the tree, and I ate* (Gen. 3:12). What need, then, to say more? They were not both deceived by credulity, but they were both taken captive by sin and entangled in the devil's snares.

12. Someone may want to ask why human nature is not changed by other sins in the same way that it was changed by the transgression of the first two human beings.[113] As a result of their sin it was made subject to all the corruption that we see and feel and, through this, to death as well. At the same time, it was disturbed and tossed about by a flood of powerful and conflicting emotions; and so it became very different from what it had been in paradise prior to sin, even though man then had an animal body just as he does now.

As I say, if anyone is concerned about this, he should not think that the sin committed was minor or trivial just because it only had to do with food, and a food that was not even evil or harmful, except that it was forbidden. For God certainly would not have created or planted anything evil in that place of preeminent felicity. What was at stake in God's precept, however, was obedience, and this virtue is in a way the mother and guardian of all virtues in a rational creature. For the rational creature was so made that it is beneficial for it to be subject to God but ruinous for it to follow its own will rather than the will of its creator. Furthermore, where there was such an abundance of other foods, a command prohibiting the eating of one kind of food was as easy to observe as it was simple to remember, especially when desire was not yet at odds with the will (which only came later, due to the

---

113. [GWL] Why was the sin of Adam and Eve so significant as to have corrupted human nature? As Augustine answers, the tree of the knowledge of good and evil was not inherently evil, since God could not create anything evil. It represented a test of Adam and Eve's obedience. Given how easy God's command was to obey, Adam and Eve's disobedience signaled their principled rejection of God's authority. What corrupted humans was not the fruit itself, but their refusal to obey God as God.

punishment of the transgression).[114] Thus the injustice of violating the command was all the greater precisely because it would have been so very easy to observe and keep it.

The Evil Will Precedes the Evil Act

13. It was actually in secret, however, that the first human beings began to be evil, and it was as a consequence of this that they subsequently slipped into open disobedience. For there would have been no evil act unless there had first been an evil will.[115] And what could have been the beginning of their evil will except pride? For *pride is the beginning of all sin* (Sir. 10:13).[116] And what is pride but an appetite for perverse exaltation? For it is perverse exaltation to abandon the principle to which the mind ought to adhere and instead, as it were, to become and to be one's own principle. This happens when a person is overly pleased with himself, and he is overly pleased with himself when he defects from that immutable good which ought to please him far more than he pleases himself. And this defection is voluntary. For, if the will had remained steadfast in love for the higher and immutable good by which it was illumined with the light to see and kindled with the fire to love, it would not have turned away from that good in order to please itself; and it would not have been so darkened and chilled as to allow the woman to think that the serpent had spoken the truth or allow the man to put his wife's will ahead of God's command and to imagine that it was a pardonable transgression if he did not forsake his life-companion even when it came to sharing in sin.

Thus, the evil act—that is, the transgression of eating the forbidden food— was committed by people who were already evil, and it would not have been committed if they had not already been evil. For only an evil tree would have produced that evil fruit. Furthermore, it happened contrary to nature that

114. [GWL] A concise statement on why the command was so easy to obey. Besides the simplicity of the command, Adam and Eve did not even have a sinful nature disposing them to disobedience. The fall is what corrupted humanity, making God's commands impossible to obey without the grace of Christ.

115. [GWL] See 14.11, which also teaches that Adam and Eve's sinful act was preceded by a sinful will and that they were able to sin because they were created out of nothing.

116. The best Hebrew and Greek manuscripts indicate that this verse should read *The beginning of pride is sin* rather than *Pride is the beginning of all sin*. See W. W. Green, "*Initium omnis peccati superbia*: Augustine on Pride as the First Sin," in *University of California Publications in Classical Philology* 13 (1949): 413. Augustine had before him a Latin version of the text that reversed the order; it is also reversed in both the Septuagint and the Vulgate.

the tree was evil, for it certainly would not have happened without a fault of will, which is contrary to nature. But only a nature created out of nothing could have been perverted by a fault. That it is a nature, therefore, is due to the fact that it was created by God, but that it fell away from what it was is due to the fact that it was created out of nothing.

But man did not fall away so completely as to lose all being and cease to exist; rather, in turning to himself, he became less than he was when he still clung to the one who supremely exists.[117] Thus, to abandon God and to exist in oneself—that is, to be pleased with oneself—does not mean that one immediately loses all being but rather that one veers toward nothingness. That is why, according to Holy Scripture, the proud are also given another name and are called *self-pleasers* (2 Pet. 2:10). For it is good to lift up your heart[118]— not to self, however, which is due to pride, but to the Lord, which is due to obedience. And obedience can belong only to the humble.

Humility and Pride

Surprisingly, then, there is in humility something that lifts up the heart, and there is in exaltation something that brings down the heart.[119] It certainly seems somewhat paradoxical that exaltation should bring down and humility should lift up. Devout humility, however, makes the heart subject to what is superior to it. But nothing is superior to God, and so the humility that makes the heart subject to God actually exalts it. In contrast, exaltation expresses a fault, and, for that very reason, it spurns subjection and falls away from him who has no superior. As a result, it brings the heart down, and what is written comes to pass: *You cast them down while they were being exalted* (Ps. 73:18). It does not say "when they had been exalted," as if they were first exalted and then cast down. Rather, it says that they were cast down exactly while they were being exalted. In itself, then, to be exalted is already to be cast down.

For this reason humility is especially commended in the city of God and to the city of God in the present, while it is on pilgrimage in this world; and

---

117. [GWL] By defecting from God, who is being itself, humanity loses its being, yet not to the point of total nonbeing. See essay: "Evil as Privation."

118. Augustine is alluding here to a liturgical formula—"Lift up your hearts"—that is part of the dialogue which precedes the preface of the eucharistic liturgy and which dates to at least the early third century. See Hippolytus (?), *Apostolic Tradition* 4.

119. [GWL] A rich paragraph contrasting humility and pride, the qualities that separate the heavenly and earthly cities.

humility is especially proclaimed in its king, who is Christ. At the same time, Sacred Scripture teaches that the opposite of this virtue, the vice of exaltation, is especially dominant in his adversary, who is the devil. Here, certainly, is the great difference that distinguishes the two cities of which we are speaking, one a company of the godly, the other a company of the godless, each including the angels that belong to it: in one the love of God comes before all else and in the other love of self.

The devil, therefore, would not have ensnared man in the open and obvious sin of doing what God had forbidden if man had not already begun to be pleased with himself. For it is precisely because he had begun to be pleased with himself that he was also delighted to hear *You shall be like gods* (Gen. 3:5). But they would have been better able to be like gods if they had clung to the true and supreme principle in obedience, instead of taking themselves as their own principle in pride.[120] For created gods are not gods by virtue of any truth of their own but by virtue of participation in the true God. By grasping for more, then, a person becomes less when, in choosing to be self-sufficient, he defects from the only one who is truly sufficient for him.

The first evil, then, is this: when man is pleased with himself, as if he were himself light, he turns away from the light which, if it pleased him, would have made him light himself. This evil came first, in secret, and its result was the evil that was committed in the open. For what Scripture says is true: *Before a fall the heart is exalted, and prior to honor it is humbled* (Prov. 18:12). In short, the fall that takes place in secret precedes the fall that takes place in full view, even though the former is not counted as a fall.[121] For who thinks of exaltation as a fall, despite the fact that it already includes the defection by which a person turns away from the Most High? On the other hand, who fails to see that there is a fall when an obvious and unmistakable transgression of a commandment takes place?

It was for this reason that God prohibited an act that, once committed, could not possibly be defended under any pretense of righteousness. And I

---

120. "Principle": *principium*. The Latin word usually means "beginning" or "source"—in this case the source of being.

121. [GWL] Adam and Eve disobeyed when they ate of the forbidden tree. Their act was an open sin. However, this act was preceded by the secret fall of their pride. Augustine's insistence that the evil act followed an evil will reflects his interest in the motivations behind human behavior. NCP: "The notion of a hidden fall in paradise that preceded the open fall is found also in Origen, *On Prayer* 29.18."

dare say that it is beneficial for the proud, who had already fallen by being pleased with themselves, to fall into some open and obvious sin which might lead them to be displeased with themselves. Peter, after all, was better off in being displeased with himself when he wept than he was in being pleased with himself when he was overconfident. And the holy Psalm says, *Fill their faces with shame, so that they may seek your name, O Lord* (Ps. 83:16)—that is, so that those who were pleased with themselves when they were seeking their own name might be pleased with you when they seek your name.

14. But still worse and more damnable is the pride that tries to take refuge in an excuse, even when the sins are perfectly obvious. That is what the first human beings did when the woman said, *The serpent deceived me, and I ate* (Gen. 3:13), and the man said, *The woman whom you gave to be with me, she gave me fruit from the tree, and I ate.* No plea for pardon sounds here, no entreaty for healing. Although, unlike Cain,[122] they did not deny what they had done, their pride still tried to shift its own wrongful act onto another, the woman's pride blaming the serpent and the man's pride blaming the woman. But, where the transgression of the divine command is so obvious, their words serve more as an accusation than as an excuse. For the fact that the woman acted on the serpent's instigation and the man on the woman's invitation does not mean that they themselves were not the ones who acted—as if anything ought to take priority over God when it comes either to believing someone's words or yielding to someone's suggestion!

The Punishment of Sin

15. Thus, man scorned the command of God, who had created him,[123] who had made him in his own image,[124] who had set him above the other animals,[125] who had established him in paradise,[126] who had provided him with an abundance of all things for his wellbeing,[127] and who had not burdened him with numerous oppressive and difficult commandments but had given him one very brief and easy command to guide him in wholesome obedience.[128] By this commandment God sought to impress on his creature, for whom free service

122. See Gen. 4:9.
123. See Gen. 1:27; 2:7.
124. See Gen. 1:26–27.
125. See Gen. 1:28; 2:19–20.
126. See Gen. 2:8.
127. See Gen. 1:29; 2:16.
128. See Gen. 2:17.

is a benefit and an advantage, that he is Lord. And because man scorned this commandment, the condemnation that followed was just. The consequence of that condemnation was that man, who would have become spiritual even in his flesh by keeping the commandment, instead became fleshly even in his mind; and man, who had become pleased with himself due to his pride, was now given over to himself due to God's justice.[129] He was not given over to himself, however, in such a way that he was fully his own master. Rather, he was at odds with himself, and, in place of the freedom he desired, he lived a life of harsh and bitter slavery under the one to whom he had given his consent by sinning.[130] By his own will, he was dead in spirit, and, against his own will, he was going to die in body as well.[131] He had forsaken eternal life, and, unless delivered by grace, he was condemned to eternal death.

If anyone considers this kind of condemnation either excessive or unjust, he obviously has no idea how to gauge the sheer wickedness of sinning where it was so easy not to sin at all. For, just as Abraham's great obedience is celebrated—and not without reason—because he was commanded to do something extremely difficult—namely, to kill his own son[132]—so in paradise the disobedience was all the greater because what was commanded was not difficult at all. And, just as the obedience of the second Adam is the more laudable because he *became obedient unto death* (Phil. 2:8), so the disobedience of the first Adam was the more detestable because he became disobedient unto death. For, where the punishment appointed for disobedience is so great and the creator's command so easy, who can adequately convey how grave an evil it is not to obey when something so simple has been commanded by such a great power under the threat of such a terrifying punishment?

To put it briefly, then, in the punishment of that sin the retribution for disobedience was simply disobedience itself.[133] For what is man's misery if not

129. [GWL] If humans had kept God's commands, they would have been glorified in their physical bodies and entered blessed immortality (see 12.22). By sinning, they became fleshly (sinful) even in their minds. Augustine's language here recalls 14.2–4, which claims Paul's "flesh" refers not to the body alone but to the self.

130. See Gen. 3:18–19.

131. See Gen. 3:19.

132. See Gen. 22:2.

133. [GWL] There is an organic relationship between sin and sin's punishment. When humans sin, they fall so deeply into sin that they cannot stop sinning even when they want to do so. Sin thus becomes its own punishment. Augustine derives this point from Rom. 7:14–25. For Augustine's account of his own bondage to sin, see *Confessions* 8.5.10–8.5.12. See also essay: "Providence and Suffering."

his own disobedience to himself, with the result that, because he would not do what he could, he now cannot do what he would?[134] In paradise, before he sinned, even though he could not do everything, he did not will to do anything that he could not do, and so he was able to do everything that he willed to do. Now, however, as we see in his offspring, and as Divine Scripture attests, *Man has become like vanity* (Ps. 144:4). For who can count all the many things that man wills to do but is unable to do, now that he is disobedient to himself— that is, now that his very mind and even his lower part, his flesh, do not obey his will? For it is against his will that his mind is often distressed and that his flesh experiences pain and grows old and dies and suffers anything else that we would not suffer against our will if our nature were only obedient to our will in every way and in all its parts.

But perhaps the flesh suffers from some condition that keeps it from serving us? What difference does it make how this comes about? The key point is simply that, through the justice of God the Lord, whom we refused to serve as his subjects, our own flesh, which was once subject to us, now brings us distress by not serving us, although we, by not serving God, are only able to bring distress on ourselves, not on God. For he does not need our service to him as we need the body's service to us, and so what we receive is punishment for us, but what we did was no punishment for him. Besides, the so-called pains of the flesh are actually pains of the soul which are experienced in the flesh and from the flesh.[135] For what pain or desire does the flesh feel on its own, apart from the soul?

When the flesh is said to feel desire or pain, it is actually either the man himself, as I have said,[136] or some aspect of the soul that is affected by what happens to the flesh, whether something harsh that produces pain or something gentle that produces pleasure. In fact, the pain of the flesh is nothing but a kind of distress of the soul arising from the flesh, and a kind of aversion to what is happening to the flesh, just as the pain of the mind, which is called grief, is an aversion to what has happened to us against our will.[137] And grief is usually preceded by fear, which itself is something in the soul, not in the

---

134. See Rom. 7:15–20; Terence, *Andria* 2.1.305–2.1.306.

135. Augustine is drawing on and slightly altering Plotinus's notion of the immobility of the soul, which reflects the divine immobility (see *Enneads* 5.1.6) and which cannot be moved by the body but which can move the body. See . . . 21.3; *On Music* 6.5.9–6.5.10; *De Trinitate* 11.1.1–11.5.9.

136. See above at 14.2.

137. [GWL] This paragraph assumes the fourfold delineation of emotions first mentioned in 14.3: fear, desire, grief, joy.

flesh. For the pain of the flesh is not preceded by any sort of fear on the part of the flesh, that is, a fear felt in the flesh prior to the pain. Pleasure, on the other hand, is preceded by a kind of appetite that is felt in the flesh as a desire of its own—hunger, for example, or thirst, or what is usually called lust in the sexual organs, although lust is actually a general term for desire of any kind.[138]

The ancients even defined anger as nothing but the lust for revenge, despite the fact that people often get angry at inanimate objects which certainly cannot feel any revenge that we take out on them, as when, in a rage, we smash a stylus or break a reed pen that writes badly.[139] But even this, although quite irrational, is still a kind of lust for revenge; in a sense, one might say, it is a kind of shadow of retribution's insistence that those who do evil should suffer evil. There is, then, the lust for revenge that is called anger. And there is the lust for money, called avarice, the lust to win at any cost, called obstinacy, and the lust for glory, called self-promotion. There are many different kinds of lust, some of which have names of their own and some of which do not. For it is not easy to say what the lust for domination should be called, even though civil wars show just how powerfully it grips the minds of tyrants.

———— ◆ ————

Two Loves Have Made Two Cities

28. Two loves, then, have made two cities.[140] Love of self, even to the point of contempt for God, made the earthly city, and love of God, even to the point of contempt for self, made the heavenly city. Thus the former glories in itself, and the latter glories in the Lord. The former seeks its glory from men, but the latter finds its highest glory in God, the witness of our conscience. The former lifts up its head in its own glory; the latter says to its God, *My glory, and the one who lifts up my head* (Ps. 3:3). In the former the lust for domination dominates both its princes and the nations that it subjugates; in

---

138. "Pleasure . . . lust . . . desire": *voluptas . . . libido . . . cupiditas.*

139. [GWL] The reference to lust signals Augustine's longer treatment of this topic in the rest of Book 14. Augustine will detail various kinds of lusts before concentrating on the lust of sexual desire. On that material, see essay: "Body."

140. What follows is probably the best-known passage in *City of God*, which serves as a concise summary of the entire work. There are similar passages in *Literal Meaning of Genesis* 11.15.20 and *Exposition of Psalm* 64.2 (where the two cities are symbolized by Jerusalem and Babylon).

the latter both leaders and followers serve one another in love, the leaders by their counsel, the followers by their obedience. The former loves its own strength, displayed in its men of power; the latter says to its God, *I love you, O Lord, my strength* (Ps. 18:1).

In the former, then, its wise men, who live according to man, have pursued the goods either of the body or of their own mind or of both together; or, at best, any who were able to know God *did not honor him as God or give thanks to him, but they became futile in their thinking, and their foolish heart was darkened. Claiming to be wise*—that is, exalting themselves in their own wisdom, under the domination of pride—*they became fools; and they changed the glory of the incorruptible God into the likeness of an image of a corruptible man or of birds or of four-footed beasts or of serpents*—for in adoring idols of this kind they were either leaders or followers of the people—*and worshiped and served the creature rather than the creator, who is blessed forever* (Rom. 1:21–23, 25). In the latter, in contrast, there is no human wisdom except the piety which rightly worships the true God and which looks for its reward in the company of the saints, that is, in the company of both holy men and holy angels, in order *that God may be all in all* (1 Cor. 15:28).

——————— Body ———————

Gregory W. Lee,
with Philip Lindia and Michael Contreras

Augustine's writings on the body reflect a philosophical context in which the goodness of the body was contested and the soul was understood to be independent of the body and superior to it. Though his earliest writings denigrated the body, Augustine's theology developed toward a stronger affirmation of the body and its centrality for human identity. He was one of the first Christian thinkers to integrate these themes systematically with the doctrines of creation, incarnation, and resurrection. Yet he continued to associate sex with sin.

In his earliest writings, Augustine urged readers to flee the things of the body (*Soliloquies* 1.14.24), presented death as the soul's escape from the body (*Magnitude of the Soul* 33.76), and claimed, somewhat ambiguously, that the resurrection body would not be "flesh" (*Faith and the Creed* 10.24; see also *Answer to Adimantus* 12.5; *Christian Combat* 32.34; *Miscellany of Eighty-Three Questions* 47; *Music* 6.4.7). At the end of his career, Augustine repudiated his earlier assertions, lamenting the similarity between these positions and the perspective of Porphyry (*Revisions* 1.4.3; 1.11.2; 1.17; 1.22.3; 1.26; 2.3; see essay: "Porphyry").

As Augustine's theology evolved, he came to affirm the soul's union with the body and the continuity between humans' present and future bodies. The soul and body are united in one person, as divinity and humanity are united in the one person of Christ (*Letter* 137.3.11). "Nobody has ever hated his own flesh"; people hate the burdens of the body and not the body itself (*De Doctrina Christiana* 1.24.24, quoting Eph. 5:29; see also *Expositions of the Psalms* 141.17). The soul has a natural desire to be united with the body and cannot receive eternal blessedness without it (*Literal Meaning of Genesis* 7.25.36–7.27.38; 12.35.68; *Letter* 140.6.16). Christ has ensured that Christians' bodies will rise from corruption (*Homilies on the Gospel of John* 23.6). The bodies to rise at Christ's return will be the same bodies that were buried after death (*Answer to Faustus* 11.3; see also *City of God* 22.26–28). In 1 Corinthians 15:42–54, Paul says Christians will receive "spiritual" bodies in the resurrection. These bodies will indeed be physical, while also incorruptible and obedient to the spirit (*Literal Meaning of Genesis* 6.19.30–6.28.39; 9.3.6; 9.10.16–9.10.17; 12.7.18; *City of God* 13.20, 22–23; for Augustine's earlier interpretation of 1 Corinthians 15, see *On Genesis: A Refutation of the Manichees* 2.8.10).

City of God represents Augustine's mature perspective on the body. Though Paul speaks against "the works of the flesh," he does not mean the body is bad (14.2–5, referring to Gal. 5:19–21). "Flesh" refers to self. To live according to the flesh is to live according to oneself instead of the spirit. Death is not the soul's liberation from the body; it is an evil that ruptures the union between body and soul (13.6). The souls of the departed saints desire to be united with their bodies, not because they have forgotten the former miseries of their bodies but because they remember the promise of the bodily resurrection (13.20, alluding to Luke 21:18). Augustine castigates Porphyry for claiming the body should be fled, a position that does not align even with Plato's teaching that the gods have immortal bodies (10.29; 13.16; 22.26; see also *Sermon* 241.7).

The fates of both the righteous and the unrighteous require the body's indissoluble union with the soul, a transformation all will experience upon Christ's return. Hell is defined by the eternal suffering of the body, which will never be consumed and which the soul cannot escape (21.3). Heaven involves an eternal union between body and soul that enables humans to see God through their bodies (22.29). To imagine Christians' resurrection body, Augustine extrapolates from the blessings of the present body (22.12–21, 24; see also *Enchiridion* 23.84–91; *Sermons* 240–43; essay: "Last Things"). Augustine's speculations are the most vivid evidence of how strongly he had come to affirm the body.

For some time, Augustine wondered whether sex was a function of the fall (*Excellence of Marriage* 2.2). He would eventually conclude that humans would have had sex without the fall, but he continued to associate sex with sin. As presented in *City of God* 14.16–26, Augustine's mature perspective is as follows (see also *Answer to the Two Letters of the Pelagians* 1.16.32–1.17.35; *Literal Meaning of Genesis* 9.3.6; 9.10.18; 11.31.41–11.32.42). If humans had not fallen, they would have procreated without lust. Men would have been able to control their penises as they control their other limbs, producing erections on demand. Because of the fall, men have no control over their penises, which produce erections in response to sexual desire even when men do not desire them, or fail to produce erections when they are desired. The insubordinate penis manifests the body's rebellion against the mind. Erections have become a response to lust. Adam's shame at this new phenomenon is the reason he covered himself with fig leaves. (Augustine offers minimal explanation for Eve's covering herself, claiming only that her body was aroused in a "hidden motion." See *Answer to the Two Letters of the Pelagians* 1.16.32. For Augustine's tendency to associate sexual desire with men, see *Marriage and Desire* 2.15.30. See also *Marriage and Desire* 2.13.26.)

Since it is not possible to have sex without an erection, lust always accompanies sex. This lust taints the progeny of sexual union such that all children are born with original sin. The mechanism that generates children thus ensures their corruption. Sex brings death even as it brings life. (See essay: "Original Sin.") Though sex for procreation is not a sin, sex not for procreation is a sin, even in the context of marriage. Still, non-procreative sex between spouses is not a mortal sin. It is only a venial sin, one forgivable by the good of marriage (*Excellence of Marriage* 6.6–7.6; see also *Letter* 6*.5), and Augustine has never heard of anyone abstaining from it (*Excellence of Marriage* 13.15). While Augustine's position on sex may appear negative by modern standards, he was something of a moderate in his context for defending marriage at all.

Bibliography

Brown, Peter. 1988. *The Body and Society: Men, Women, and Sexual Renunciation in Early Christianity*. New York: Columbia University Press, 387–427.

Burnell, Peter. 2005. *The Augustinian Person*. Washington, DC: Catholic University of America Press.

Cavadini, John C. 2005. "Feeling Right: Augustine on the Passions and Sexual Desire." *Augustinian Studies* 36, no. 1: 195–217.

Clark, Elizabeth. 1986. "'Adam's Only Companion': Augustine and the Early Christian Debate on Marriage." *Recherches Augustiniennes* 21: 139–62.

Hunter, David G. 2007. *Marriage, Celibacy, and Heresy in Ancient Christianity: The Jovinianist Controversy*. Oxford: Oxford University Press.

———. 2012. "Augustine on the Body." In Vessey, *Blackwell Companion*, 353–64.

Lawless, George. 1990. "Augustine and Human Embodiment." *Augustiniana* 40: 167–86.

McGlothlin, Thomas D. 2024. "Augustine's Resurrection Framework: Clarifying and Connecting Senses of 'Resurrection.'" *Augustinian Studies* 55, no. 1: 25–42.

Miles, Margaret Ruth. 1979. *Augustine on the Body*. Missoula, MT: Scholars Press.

———. 1996. "Corpus." In *AugLex*, 2:6–20.

Reisenauer, Augustine M. 2023. *Augustine's Theology of the Resurrection*. Cambridge: Cambridge University Press.

Rist, John M. 1994. "Soul, Body and Personal Identity." In *Augustine: Ancient Thought Baptized*, 92–147. Cambridge: Cambridge University Press.

Rombs, Ronnie J. 2006. *Saint Augustine and the Fall of the Soul: Beyond O'Connell and His Critics*. Washington, DC: Catholic University of America Press.

van Bavel, Tarsicius Jan. 1995. "'No One Ever Hated His Own Flesh': Ephesians 5:29 in Augustine." *Augustiniana* 45: 45–93.

Women

Gregory W. Lee and Avyi Hill

Augustine's writings on women have generated wide differences of interpretation. His theology is indisputably androcentric, and he frequently characterizes women as sources of temptation. Yet he is distinct among his contemporaries for affirming that humanity exhibited sexual differentiation before the fall and that women will retain their sex in heaven. Arguably at least, his personal interactions with women exhibit courtesy and admiration.

Augustine believes sexual differentiation was a blessing of creation, intended for procreation (*City of God* 14.22; *Literal Meaning of Genesis* 9.3.5; 9.5.9; cf. *On Genesis: A Refutation of the Manichees* 1.19.30 and *Revisions* 1.10.2). His position on this matter is often contrasted with that of Gregory of Nyssa, who associated procreation and sexual differentiation with the fall, as a mechanism to extend humanity's existence after the entrance of death into the world (Nyssa, *On the Making of the Human* 16–17, 22).

Augustine claims Eve was deceived by the serpent into violating God's command, whereas Adam sinned knowingly because he did not want to be separated from Eve (*City of God* 14.11; *Expositions of the Psalms* 83.7). Augustine's formulation of this position appeals to 1 Timothy 2:14: "Adam was not deceived, but the woman was deceived." At one juncture, he speculates that Eve was deceived because she had not yet received the mature rationality she would eventually attain as the image of God (*Literal Meaning of Genesis* 11.42.58). Eve's sin was reversed by Mary and those who discovered the empty tomb: "Because mankind fell through the female sex, mankind was restored through the female sex; because a virgin gave birth to Christ, a woman proclaimed that he had risen again. Through a woman death, through a woman life" (*Sermon* 232.2; see also *Sermons* 45.5; 51.3; 229L.1).

According to Augustine, though Eve was ruled by Adam before the fall, this relationship was characterized by affection and service. After the fall, male rule became a form of domination (*City of God* 15.7; *Commentary on the Epistle to the Galatians* 28; *Confessions* 13.32.47; *Excellence of Marriage* 1.1; *Expositions of the Psalms* 143.6; *Literal Meaning of Genesis* 8.23.44; 9.5.9; 11.37.50; *Marriage and Desire* 1.9.10; *Questions on*

254

the Heptateuch 1.153; *Unfinished Work in Answer to Julian* 6.26). In Christ, husbands
and wives are called to mutual affection even as they observe the rule of husbands over
wives (*The Catholic Way of Life and the Manichean Way of Life* 1.30.63). Augustine goes
so far as to encourage the slavery of wives to their husbands (*Answer to Faustus* 22.31;
Confessions 9.9.19; *Sermons* 332.4; 392.4). Properly ordered concord is necessary for
domestic peace (*City of God* 19.14; *Homilies on the Gospel of John* 2.14).

Challenging Roman custom, Augustine holds husbands and wives to the same sexual
standards, forbidding husbands and not just wives from sexual activity outside marriage
(*Adulterous Marriages* 2.8.7; 2.20.21; *Answer to Faustus* 22.31; *Letter* 259; *Sermons*
9.3; 132.2; 153.6; 224.3; 332.4; 392.4–5). He also extends this prohibition to sexual activity with slaves (*Sermon* 9.4, 12). The men in Augustine's congregation seem to have
resented these restrictions, even grousing that the church instigated their wives against
them. Beyond his concentration on sex and procreation, Augustine acknowledges the
value of friendship and love in marriage (*Excellence of Marriage* 1.1; *Expositions of the
Psalms* 55.17). Scholars dispute the degree to which he stresses these goods.

Augustine often describes women as the weaker sex (*Literal Meaning of Genesis*
9.13.23)—an unfortunately common assumption in his context. In some instances,
Augustine seems to mean women are physically weaker than men (*Sermons* 159A.11;
280.1; 281.1; 282.2, though these instances stress the courage and "manly spirit" of the
female martyrs Perpetua and Felicity). In one passage, he claims women are rationally
inferior to men (*Questions on the Heptateuch* 1.153). Still other passages suggest, at
least for the sake of argument, that women are morally weaker too (*Adulterous Marriages*
2.20.21; *Miscellany of Eighty-Three Questions* 61.5; *Sermons* 9.12; 132.2). As Augustine
contends, though women experience bodily desires, they can remain sexually chaste.
How much more should men?

Scholars have critiqued Augustine's tendency to associate women with carnal desires.
Often cited in this regard are his admonition to nuns against flirting with their eyes (*Letter*
211.10–11), his warning to "avoid Eve in any woman" (*Letter* 243.10), his expectation
that wives provide for their husbands' sexual needs (*Letter* 262), and his commendation
of the husband who "loves [his wife] insofar as she is a human being but hates the fact
that she is a wife" (*Lord's Sermon on the Mount* 1.15.41, explaining Jesus's remark that
those who wish to be his disciples must "hate" their families).

Despite these passages, Augustine also affirms women as the intellectual and spiritual
equals of men (*Answer to Faustus* 24.2; *Confessions* 13.32.47; *Lord's Sermon on the
Mount* 2.2.7; *De Trinitate* 12.7.12). Though men and women are distinct in body, they
have the same rationality, both bearing the image of God in the mind (*Literal Meaning
of Genesis* 3.22.34). Christ was a man, but he was born of a woman, thus honoring both

sexes (*Christian Combat* 22.24; *Faith and the Creed* 4.9; *Miscellany of Eighty-Three Questions* 11; *Sermons* 51.3; 72A.4; 184.2; 190.2; *True Religion* 16.30). In Christ, women are capable of the same virtue as men (*Expositions of the Psalms* 26.2.23; *True Religion* 41.78). Augustine especially celebrates his mother, Monica, for her philosophical wisdom (*Happy Life* 2.10; *Order* 1.11.31–1.11.32). He also describes God as both father and mother: "our father because he created us, because he calls us, gives orders and rules us"; and "our mother because he cherishes us, nourishes us, feeds us with milk, and holds us in his arms" (*Expositions of the Psalms* 26.2.18). Because sexual differentiation is a good of creation and not a consequence of the fall, women will retain their female bodies in the resurrection. Female sexual organs will no longer serve the purposes of intercourse and childbearing, nor will they evoke male lust. They will be transformed with new beauty, evoking praise to God (*City of God* 22.17).

One of Augustine's most controversial statements about women appears in *De Trinitate* 12.7.9–12.7.12 (see also *City of God* 14.22; *Literal Meaning of Genesis* 3.22.34; 6.7.12; *On Genesis: A Refutation of the Manichees* 2.14.20–2.14.21; *De Trinitate* 12.3.3; *Work of Monks* 32.40). This passage seeks to reconcile Genesis 1:27–28, which ascribes the image of God to both men and women, with 1 Corinthians 11:7, which says "[the man] is the image and glory of God" and "the woman is the glory of the man." Augustine interprets Paul's words as a figurative reference to the human mind. Men symbolize a higher rational faculty, *sapientia* ("wisdom"), which contemplates God. Women symbolize a lower rational faculty, *scientia* ("knowledge"), which administers material things. Whereas *sapientia* by itself bears God's image, *scientia* bears God's image only with *sapientia*. It must also submit to *sapientia* to avoid being diverted to inferior realities. Augustine claims that both men and women have both *sapientia* and *scientia*. Scholars debate whether he claimed that women bear God's image only in their union with men. Some have observed the asymmetry in Augustine's arguments. He never suggests, even figuratively, that men represent the image of God only with women.

As for Augustine's interactions with women, scholars refer especially to his relationship with his mother, Monica, whom Augustine presents as a model of Christian piety (*Confessions* 9.8.17–9.9.22). Shortly before her death, she and Augustine participated together in a mystical ascent (*Confessions* 9.10.23–9.10.26). Augustine's concubine (sometimes called his "common-law wife") has also been the subject of much discussion. Augustine claims to have been faithful to her throughout their relationship, an arrangement that may have lasted fifteen years (*Confessions* 4.2.2). Some scholars have stressed Augustine's affection for her, noting his sorrow at their separation (*Confessions* 6.15.25) and his positive allusions to her in various texts (*Excellence of Marriage* 5.5; *Faith and Works* 19.35; cf. *Excellence of Marriage* 14.16). Others have stressed his brusque termination of the relationship so that he could marry an elite Roman woman.

In his correspondences as a bishop, Augustine wrote twenty-four extant letters to women. These letters are written to widows, monastic communities, and Roman nobility, and they cover a range of theological and personal topics. Some scholars have seen in these letters evidence of Augustine's respect for women. Others have observed in them a distant tone in comparison with the affection Augustine exhibits toward his male interlocutors. Unlike his contemporaries Jerome and Chrysostom, Augustine never developed a close group of monastic women friends. According to his first biographer, Augustine avoided the company of women (Possidius, *Life of Augustine* 26–27). Following a common practice, he avoided visiting monasteries of women except in exigent circumstances. Not even his sister or nieces were allowed to stay at his home, lest they or their companions become stumbling blocks for the men who were staying there.

Bibliography

Børresen, Kari Elizabeth. 1990. "In Defence of Augustine: How 'Femina' Is 'Homo.'" *Augustiniana* 40: 411–28.

Clark, Elizabeth. 1986. "'Adam's Only Companion': Augustine and the Early Christian Debate on Marriage." *Recherches Augustiniennes* 21: 139–62.

Cooper, Kate. 2023. *Queens of a Fallen World: The Lost Women of Augustine's "Confessions."* New York: Basic Books.

Matter, Ann. 1999. "Women." In *AttA*, 651–54.

———. 2005. "*De cura feminarum*: Augustine the Bishop, North African Women, and the Development of a Theology of Female Nature." *Augustinian Studies* 36, no. 1: 87–98.

McWilliam, Joanne. 2007. "Augustine's Letters to Women." In *Feminist Interpretations of Augustine*, edited by Judith Chelius Stark, 189–202. University Park: Pennsylvania State University Press.

Meconi, David Vincent. 2000. "*Gratia Sacris Angelis*: Gender and the *Imago Dei* in Augustine's *De Trinitate* XII." *American Catholic Philosophical Quarterly* 74, no. 1: 47–62.

Miles, Margaret. 2007. "Not Nameless but Unnamed: The Woman Torn from Augustine's Side." In *Feminist Interpretations of Augustine*, edited by Judith Chelius Stark, 167–88. University Park: Pennsylvania State University Press.

Power, Kim. 1996. *Veiled Desire: Augustine on Women*. New York: Continuum.

Rist, John M. 1994. *Augustine: Ancient Thought Baptized*. Cambridge: Cambridge University Press, 112–21.

Ruether, Rosemary Radford. 2007. "Augustine: Sexuality, Gender, and Women." In *Feminist Interpretations of Augustine*, edited by Judith Chelius Stark, 47–67. University Park: Pennsylvania State University Press.

Shaw, Brent. 1987. "The Family in Late Antiquity: The Experience of Augustine." *Past and Present* 115, no. 1: 3–51.

Stark, Judith Chelius. 2007. "Augustine on Women: In God's Image, but Less So." In *Feminist Inter- pretations of Augustine*, edited by Judith Chelius Stark, 215–41. University Park: Pennsylvania State University Press.

Truax, Jean A. 1990. "Augustine of Hippo: Defender of Women's Equality?" *Journal of Medieval History* 16: 279–99.

van Bavel, T. J. 1989. "Augustine's View on Women." *Augustiniana* 39, no. 1/2: 5–53.

Weaver, F. Ellen, and Jean Laporte. 1981. "Augustine and Women: Relationships and Teachings." *Augustinian Studies* 12: 115–31.

—————— Evil as Privation ——————

Gregory W. Lee and Avyi Hill

Augustine's understanding of evil was central to his conversion and shaped his theology of God, humanity, sin, conversion, and the Christian life. As a Manichean, Augustine had espoused a dualist conception of the universe, according to which good and evil were cosmic forces at war with each other, and the material world was evil. *Confessions* recounts Augustine's discovery of Neoplatonist writings that helped him conceive of evil as a privation, an absence of good (3.7.12; 7.1.1–7.5.7; 7.9.13–7.17.23; see essay: "Platonists and Platonism"). This insight resolved the last of Augustine's intellectual doubts about Christianity, preparing him for his eventual conversion.

For Augustine, God is ultimate being or substance: "I AM WHO I AM" (Exod. 3:14; *De Trinitate* 5.2.3). God is not one being among others but being itself; God simply *is*. All created things have being by their participation in God. God does not *have* being, as if being were distinct from and possessed by God; God *defines* and *is* being. God is also ultimate goodness. As with being, God is not simply good but goodness itself. All created things are good by their participation in God, who does not have goodness but defines it. For God, being and goodness are identical. To affirm God as ultimate being is to affirm God as ultimate goodness.

Turning to the created order, everything that exists must be good, since all things participate in both God's being and God's goodness. At the same time, different things participate in God to different degrees. Augustine espouses an order of being that ranks created things according to their participation in God (*City of God* 11.16, 22; 12.1–5; *De Doctrina Christiana* 1.8.8). This order begins with inanimate things (rocks) and proceeds to animate things (trees), sentient things (nonhuman animals), and rational things (humans and angels). Though lower things participate in God's goodness less than higher things do, even the lowest things are good, simply by virtue of their existence, which is a participation in God's being and thus in God's goodness. God does not belong on the order of being, since again, God is not one being among others but being itself.

Based on this framework, evil cannot relate to creation in the same way that goodness does. Whereas goodness corresponds to being, evil is a distortion of being. Evil is not a substance but a perversion of substance. To describe evil's harm on a substance is to assume the goodness of that substance. Harming something means depriving it of goodness, and nothing can be harmed if it did not have goodness in the first place (*Confessions* 7.11.17–7.17.23). Goodness is the stuff of creation; evil is parasitic.

This perspective shapes Augustine's narration of humanity's fall (*City of God* 14.10–15). Since the tree of the knowledge of good and evil was created by God, it could not be evil (13.20). Adam and Eve were not corrupted by the tree itself, as if it contained some spiritual poison to taint partakers. What corrupted Adam and Eve was their choice to partake. By disobeying such an easy command, Adam and Eve declared their refusal to obey God, despite all God's provisions for them. This is why their action wrought such serious consequences on humanity (14.12; see essay: "Original Sin"). Though Augustine says Adam and Eve's evil action was preceded by their evil will, he does not explain how they could have willed evil when they were created good. There is no efficient cause for evil. Looking for a cause is like trying to see darkness or hear silence (12.6–8; 14.11).

By defining evil as privation, Augustine does not deny evil's effects in the world. Suffering is not illusory, as *City of God* makes clear (19.4–10; 22.22–23). For Augustine, the concept of privation is a tool for conceptualizing the relationship between God and creation. Philosophically, Augustine's understanding of sin and nonbeing might support an annihilationist position according to which those who reject God will cease to exist after death. Augustine does not adopt this position, however, affirming the reality of a hell in which bodies suffer eternal torment (see essay: "Last Things").

Sin arises from a disorderly attraction to good, when humans love lower things too much. Lower things are attractive precisely because they participate in God's goodness. (See *Confessions* 2.4.9–2.9.17, which reflects on this theme in light of Augustine's childhood theft of pears.) Yet they must be sought appropriately, according to properly ordered loves (*De Doctrina Christiana* 1.27.28). Christians are commanded to love God with all their heart, soul, and mind and to love their neighbor as they love themselves (Matt. 22:37–39). It would be inappropriate for them to love their neighbor with all their heart, soul, and mind or to love God only as much as they love themselves. God alone is the final object of love; no human merits this status (*De Doctrina Christiana* 1.22.20–1.22.21).

In describing Adam and Eve's turn from God to self, *City of God* speaks of their losing being—not to the point of nonexistence, but such that they became "less" than they were when they clung to God (14.13). This language may seem strange, since one might think things either exist or do not exist; there is no in-between. For Augustine, however, being and goodness are identical in God, which means humans participate less in being as they participate less in goodness. In contrast to the Son, who is eternally begotten from the Father (Nicene Creed), humans were created from nothing, *ex nihilo* (14.11). When humans turn from God to self, they abandon the source of all being for nothingness, becoming shells of what they were made to be. Even today, we use the words "shallow," "hollow," or "empty" to describe envious, hateful, scheming people. We also use the words "depth," "substance," or "integrity" for those who radiate humility, love, and truth. For Augustine, sin literally prevents people from being their best selves. Yet sin never fully defines sinners, who still were created good and continue to participate in God's goodness, at least to some extent. We can thus hate the sin and love the sinner (14.6).

Confessions exhibits the significance of evil as privation for Augustine's understanding of conversion. In their pursuit of happiness, humans turn from God to lower goods that fail to satisfy their deepest longings. Instead of returning to God, sinners pursue lower goods more, even as their selves disintegrate and waste away (2.1.1). As this pattern hardens into a habit, they become addicted to sin, incapable of breaking free by their own will (8.5.10–8.5.12). Only the grace of Christ liberates them to love rightly and to find their rest in God (1.1.1; 8.11.25–8.12.29; 10.27.38).

Bibliography

Cress, Donald A. 1989. "Augustine's Privation Account of Evil: A Defense." *Augustinian Studies* 20: 109–28.

Evans, G. R. 1982. *Augustine on Evil*. Cambridge: Cambridge University Press.

Kantzer Komline, Han-luen. 2020. "Augustine and the Limits of Evil: From Creation to Christ in the *Enchiridion*." In *Evil and Creation: Historical and Constructive Essays in Christian Dogmatics*, edited by David J. Luy, Matthew Levering, and George Kalantzis, 67–83. Bellingham, WA: Lexham.

King, Peter. 2019. "Augustine on Evil." In *Evil: A History*, edited by Andrew P. Chignell, 155–93. Oxford: Oxford University Press.

Wetzel, James. 2012. "Augustine on the Origin of Evil: Myth and Metaphysics." In Wetzel, *COG*, 167–85.

Williams, Rowan. 2016. "Insubstantial Evil." In *On Augustine*, 79–105. Orig. 2000. London: Bloomsbury.

Book 15

1–7

Book 15 commences the next major unit of City of God, *Books 15–18, on the development of the two cities. Before starting this story, Augustine discusses the identity of Israel, a unique part of the earthly city that signifies the heavenly city (15.2–3). His narrative of the two cities then begins with Cain and Abel (15.4–7). Cain was the founder of the earthly city, and his fratricide of Abel inaugurated the earthly city's persecution of the heavenly city. In the next section, Augustine digresses to address questions about the genealogies in Genesis (15.8–16). He then resumes the narrative. Cain's line of descent corresponded to the earthly city, and Seth's line of descent corresponded to the heavenly city (15.17–20). After the two cities became intermingled (15.21–23), God punished humanity with the flood, preserving only Noah and his family (15.24–27).*

1. Many opinions have been held, and much has been said and written, about the felicity of paradise, about paradise itself, about the life there of the first human beings, and about their sin and punishment. We too have spoken about these matters in the preceding books, following Holy Scripture and presenting either what we read directly in Scripture or what we could draw from Scripture in accord with its authority. To pursue these issues in more detail, however, would give rise to a great number and variety of discussions that would take more volumes to unravel than this work requires or our time permits. We do not have the leisure to linger over every puzzle that might

be raised by people who have time on their hands and want to go into every detail, the kind of people who are more ready to pose questions than they are capable of understanding the answers.

All the same, I think that I have already dealt adequately with the great and difficult questions concerning the beginning of the world, of the soul, and of the human race itself. We have divided the human race into two groups, one consisting of those who live according to man and the other of those who live according to God.[1] Speaking allegorically, we also call these two groups two cities, that is, two human societies, one predestined to reign with God for all eternity, the other to undergo eternal punishment with the devil.[2] But this is their final end, which is to be discussed later.[3] At this point, since enough has been said about the rise of these two cities, whether in the angels, whose number is beyond our knowing, or in the two first human beings, it seems to me that I should now undertake to trace the course that each has followed from the point at which the first two human beings began to have children down to the point at which humans will cease to have children.[4] For the course followed by the two cities that we are discussing runs through this whole period, or age, in which the dying pass away and the newborn take their place.

Cain and Abel, the Earthly City and the Heavenly City

Cain, then, was the first child born to those two parents of the human race,[5] and he belonged to the city of men. Abel was born later,[6] and he belonged to the city of God. Now, in the case of a single individual we find, in the words of

---

1. See above at 14.28.

2. Although Augustine may be accused here, as well as . . . at 22.24, of teaching double predestination (i.e., predestination from eternity not only to heaven but also to hell), it should be noted that there is an asymmetry to his teaching on this score. On the one hand, those condemned to eternal punishment are condemned on the basis of their own moral failing, both as participants in and as co-agents of Adam's sin and (except in the case of infants who die before achieving the status of moral agents) for their own personal sin. On the other hand, those elected to eternal salvation are chosen by the sheer grace of God, utterly without regard to any good or evil that they may previously have done.

3. See [Books 21 and 22].

4. [GWL] Having treated the origins of the two cities in Books 11–14, Augustine turns to the development of the two cities. Books 15–17 walk through the Old Testament, tracing the heavenly city before Christ. Book 18 ties up loose ends, including the history of the earthly city from the time of Abraham to Christ.

5. See Gen. 4:1.

6. See Gen. 4:2.

the Apostle, that *it is not the spiritual that is first, but the animal, and then the spiritual* (1 Cor. 15:46), and that is why each one of us, since he comes from a condemned stock, is of necessity first evil and carnal due to Adam, but, if he advances by being reborn in Christ, will afterwards be good and spiritual.[7] And it is just the same in the case of the whole human race. When those two cities began to run their course of birth and death, the first to be born was the citizen of this world, and only after him was there born the pilgrim in this world, who belonged to the city of God, predestined by grace and chosen by grace—by grace a pilgrim below and by grace a citizen above. So far as he himself is concerned, he comes from the same lump that was wholly condemned[8] at the start; but, like a potter (and the Apostle uses this image not to be insolent but to be apt), God made *from the same lump one vessel for honor and another for dishonor* (Rom. 9:21).[9] The vessel for dishonor, however, was made first, and then the vessel for honor. For in the individual case also, as I have already said, the unworthy comes first. That is where we have to start, but that is not where we have to stay. Afterwards comes the worthy, which we may approach by advancing towards it and where we may remain once we have reached it. It is certainly not true, then, that every evil person will be good, but it is certainly true that no one will be good who was not previously evil. And the sooner a person changes for the better, the faster he will take on the name for what he has gained and cover over the earlier term with the later one.

Scripture states, then, that Cain founded a city;[10] but Abel, as a pilgrim, did not. For the city of the saints is on high, even though it brings forth citizens

7. [GWL] Augustine frequently cites 1 Cor. 15 to this effect. All humans enter the world corrupted by original sin. Those who receive new life in Christ will be glorified with resurrection bodies. This is the moment when humans' "animal" bodies will become "spiritual" bodies. Augustine's contrast between "animal" (*animale*) and "spiritual" (*spiritale*) does not correspond to a contrast between bodily and nonbodily. Christians' "spiritual" existence will still be bodily; their bodies will simply become glorious and immortal. By "animal" body, Augustine means a body enlivened by a soul (*anima*). This "ensouled" (animal) body will be transformed into the "enspirited" (spiritual) body of the resurrection. Augustine's discussion relies on 1 Cor. 15:45, which itself relies on Gen. 2:7: "Thus it is written, 'The first man, Adam, became a living soul [*animam uiuentem*].' The last Adam became a life-giving spirit [*spiritum uiuificantem*]." See 13.22–23; and essay: "Body."

8. "Lump . . . condemned": *massa . . . damnata*. See also . . . 14.26 [and *City of God, Books 11–22*, 135n123] and . . . 15.21 and 21.12.

9. [GWL] This passage reflects Augustine's doctrine of predestination, which relies heavily on Rom. 9. Because of Adam and Eve's sin, all humanity is a mass of damnation. From this corrupt lump, God chooses some but not others for salvation. See essays: "Original Sin"; "Predestination and the Will."

10. [GWL] Gen. 4.17. Note Augustine's attention to scriptural detail and the elegance of his comparison. Cain, the founder of the earthly city, founded the first city on earth.

here below, in whom it is on pilgrimage until the time of its kingdom arrives. Then it will gather them all together as they rise again in their bodies, and the promised kingdom will be given to them, where, with their prince, the *king of the ages* (1 Tim. 1:17), they will reign for time without end.

Israel: The Earthly Image of the Heavenly City

2. There was, to be sure, a kind of shadow and prophetic image of this city which served to signify it here on earth, although not to make it actually present, at the time when it needed to be made manifest.[11] And this shadow was also called the holy city by virtue of the fact that it was an image signifying the truth, even though not presenting it as distinctly as it would come to be. The Apostle is speaking of this subservient city, and of the free city that it signifies, when he says to the Galatians, *Tell me, you who desire to be under the law, have you not heard the law? For it is written that Abraham had two sons, one by a slave woman and one by a free woman. But the one born of the slave was born according to the flesh, and the one born of the free woman was born through the promise. These things are an allegory. These women are two covenants. One woman, in fact, is from Mount Sinai, bearing children for servitude; this is Hagar. For Sinai is a mountain in Arabia, and it corresponds to the present Jerusalem, which is in servitude with her children. But the Jerusalem above is free, and she is our mother. For it is written, Rejoice, you barren one who bears no children, exclaim and shout, you who are not in labor, for the children of the desolate woman outnumber those of the married woman. But we, brothers, are children of the promise, like Isaac. But, just as at that time the child who was born according to the flesh persecuted the child who was born according to the Spirit, so it is now. But what does Scripture say? Cast out the slave and her son, for the son of the slave shall*

11. [GWL] This section is significant for Augustine's theology of Israel, which he treats here to introduce his narration of the Old Testament. Israel was the main locus where citizens of the heavenly city resided before Christ. But Israel was not itself the heavenly city; it was a part of the earthly city that foreshadowed the heavenly city. There is thus a distinction between Old Testament Israel and the New Testament church. Augustine associates the New Testament church closely with the heavenly city (scholars disagree as to the degree of identification). He does not do the same for Old Testament Israel, which only foreshadows the heavenly city. That said, according to Augustine, Israel occupies a special place in God's plan for redemption as a unique people that worships the one true God, possesses the Scriptures that speak of Christ, and will experience a massive restoration at the end of time. None of these qualities can be ascribed to other nations. See essay: "Jews and Judaism."

not be heir with the son of the free woman. So then, brothers, we are children not of the slave but of the free woman, by virtue of the freedom with which Christ has set us free (Gal. 4:21–5:1).

This mode of interpretation, which comes down to us by apostolic authority, shows us how we ought to understand the Scriptures of the two covenants, the old and the new.[12] For one part of the earthly city, because it signifies not itself but another, was made an image of the heavenly city, and it is therefore in servitude. For it was not established for its own sake but for the sake of signifying another city; and, since it was itself preceded by a prior sign, the prefiguring image was itself prefigured. For Hagar, Sarah's slave, together with her son, was a kind of image of this image. But the shadows were to pass away when the light came, and that is why Sarah, who was free and who signified the free city—which the prior shadow, Hagar, served to signify in another way—said, *Cast out the slave and her son, for the son of the slave shall not be heir with my son Isaac* (Gen. 21:10), or, as the Apostle puts it, *with the son of the free woman* (Gal. 4:30).

The Earthly City and the Heavenly City, Born of Nature and Born of Grace

In the earthly city, then, we find two features, one pointing to its own presence, the other serving by its presence to signify the heavenly city. What gives birth to citizens of the earthly city, however, is a nature vitiated by sin, and what gives birth to citizens of the heavenly city is grace liberating that nature from sin.[13] Consequently, the former are called *vessels of wrath* (Rom. 9:22) and the latter are called *vessels of mercy* (Rom. 9:23). This is also signified in Abraham's two sons. For one of them, Ishmael, was born of the slave named Hagar according to the flesh; and the other, Isaac, was born of Sarah, the free woman, according to the promise. Both sons, obviously enough, came

12. [GWL] Galatians 4 is crucial for Augustine and other early Christian writers as the only text in the New Testament that uses the word "allegory." Paul presents Sarah as an image of the church—a radical interpretation in his context, given that Sarah was the genealogical ancestor of the Jews. By contrast, Hagar is an image of Israel, which Augustine associates with the earthly city. As Augustine reasons, since Hagar was an image of Israel, and Israel was an image of the heavenly city, Hagar was an image of an image.

13. [GWL] Grace is what distinguishes the heavenly city from the earthly city. Only the former receives grace for liberation from original sin. To support this position, Augustine cites Rom. 9 on the difference between "vessels of wrath" and "vessels of mercy." See essay: "Predestination and the Will."

from Abraham's seed, but the one was begotten in the ordinary way, showing how nature works, while the other was given by the promise, signifying divine grace. In the one case, human practice is displayed; in the other, divine beneficence is acclaimed.

3. Sarah, plainly, was barren, and, in her despair of having children, she wanted at least to have from her slave what she realized that she could not have from herself. So she gave her slave to be made pregnant by her husband, with whom she had wanted to have children herself but could not.[14] In this way, then, she exacted her due from her husband, exercising her own right in another's womb.[15] Ishmael was born, therefore, in the ordinary human way, by sexual intercourse according to the regular course of nature. That is why it says that he was born *according to the flesh* (Gal. 4:23). It is not that such things are not benefits that come from God, or that they are not the work of God, whose creative wisdom *reaches mightily*, as Scripture says, *from one end to the other, and arranges all things sweetly* (Wis. 8:1). But, when it was a matter of signifying an unmerited gift of God, freely bestowed on humankind by divine grace, it was right for a son to be given in a manner that did not follow the usual course of nature. For nature denies children to the kind of sexual intercourse of husband and wife that was possible for Abraham and Sarah at their age; and, besides, because Sarah was barren, she was not even able to have children when the root of the problem was not that she had passed the age of fertility but that she lacked the fertility appropriate to her age.

The fact that no fruit of posterity was owed to a nature in this condition signifies, then, that human nature—vitiated by sin and therefore justly condemned—did not deserve any true happiness for the future. Thus Isaac, who was born through the promise, is rightly taken to signify the children of grace, who are citizens of the free city and who share in eternal peace, where there is no love for one's personal and, so to say, private will, but rather a love that rejoices in the common and immutable good and joins many hearts into one, namely, a love which is perfectly at one in the obedience of charity.[16]

14. See Gen. 16:1–3.
15. See Rom. 7:3–4.
16. [GWL] Again, grace distinguishes the heavenly city from the earthly city. Note also the contrast between love for one's personal or private will (*propriae ac priuatae . . . uoluntatis*) and love for the common good (i.e., God). Human sin involves a fall from God to self. As individuals follow their personal desires, they become estranged from one another. By contrast, citizens of the heavenly city enjoy unity and harmony with one another because of their shared love for God, who is common to all.

The Goods of the Earthly City and the Conflicts to Which They Give Rise

4. The earthly city, in contrast, will not be everlasting, for, when it is condemned to its final punishment, it will no longer be a city. It has its good here on earth, and its joy—such joy as can be had from things of this sort—comes from sharing in this good. And, since its good is not the sort of good that brings no anxieties to those who love it, the earthly city is often divided against itself by lawsuits, wars and conflicts, and by seeking victories that either bring death or are themselves doomed to be short-lived.[17] For, if any part of it rises up in war against another part, it seeks to be the victor over nations when it is itself the prisoner of its vices; and if, when it triumphs, it is puffed up with pride, its victory brings death. But, if it takes the human condition and all its vicissitudes into account and is more distressed by the adversities that may occur than elated by its present prosperity, then its victory is at best short-lived.[18] For it will not be able to rule for long over those whom it was able to subdue in the moment of victory.

It would be wrong, however, to say that the things which this city desires are not goods; for even this city, in its own human fashion, is better when it has them.[19] For it desires a sort of earthly peace for the sake of the lowest goods, and it is that peace which it wants to achieve by waging war. For, if it triumphs and there is no one left to resist it, there will be peace, which the opposing parties did not have so long as they were fighting each other, in their wretched need, over things that they could not both possess at the same time. It is for this peace that grueling wars are fought, and it is this peace that supposedly glorious victory obtains.

And, when the victory goes to those who were fighting for the more just cause, who can doubt that the victory deserves to be celebrated or that the resulting peace is very much to be desired?[20] These are goods, and they are

17. [GWL] An important description of the earthly city, whose lust for earthly goods naturally results in violence. Those who conquer their enemies in battle may themselves be prisoners to vice. Even as the earthly city seeks to dominate others, it is dominated by its lust for domination (1.*preface*).

18. [GWL] If the conquering party considers its situation soberly, it will realize that its victories will not last forever. Material prosperity is only temporary.

19. [GWL] Despite his critique of the earthly city, Augustine acknowledges the importance of earthly goods. Augustine expands on this point in 19.17.

20. [GWL] Though Augustine never developed a theory of war, he believes it is better for the more righteous nation to gain victory. See essay: "War." NCP: "On the possibility of a just war see above at 1.21 and [*City of God, Books 1–10*, 24n65 // above, Book 1n71]."

undoubtedly gifts from God. But, if the higher goods are neglected, which belong to the city on high, where victory will be secure in supreme and eternal peace, and if these lower goods are desired so much that people believe them to be the only goods or love them more than the goods that they believe to be higher, then misery will necessarily follow, and their previous misery will only be made worse.[21]

5. So it is that the first founder of the earthly city was a fratricide; for, overcome by envy, he killed his own brother, who was a citizen of the eternal city on pilgrimage on this earth.[22] It is no wonder, then, that this first example—or archetype, as the Greeks call it—was reflected by an image of the same kind at the founding, long afterwards, of the city that was to be the head of the earthly city of which we are speaking and which was to rule over so many peoples. There also, as one of the poets says in telling of the crime, "the first walls dripped with a brother's blood."[23] For this is how Rome was founded when, as Roman history attests, Remus was killed by his brother Romulus.[24] These two, however, were both citizens of the earthly city. Both wanted the glory of founding the Roman republic, but, as cofounders, they could not both have as much glory as only one would have as the single founder of Rome. For the rule of anyone wishing to glory in his own dominion would obviously be less if his power were diminished by the presence of a living coruler. Therefore, in order for one to have total domination, his colleague was removed, and what would have been kept smaller and better by innocence grew into something larger and worse by crime.

In contrast, the brothers Cain and Abel did not both have the same desire for earthly gains. Nor did the one who killed the other feel envious of his brother because his own dominion would be restricted if they both held rule

21. [GWL] Augustine attributes war to improperly ordered loves. Those who love earthly more than heavenly goods will necessarily enter into conflict with one another. Violence and strife are thus endemic to the earthly city, though the earthly city fails to secure even the temporal goods that it seeks.

22. [GWL] Augustine likens Cain's murdering his brother Abel to Romulus's murdering his brother Remus. Cain was the founder of the earthly city, and Romulus was the founder of Rome, the greatest instance of the earthly city (at least on my interpretation of *City of God*). Though Cain and Romulus both committed fratricide, there is a difference between their stories. Both Romulus and Remus belonged to the earthly city, whereas Cain and Abel belonged to different cities. Abel's death at Cain's hands epitomizes the relation between the earthly and heavenly cities: the first is defined by violence, while the second is defined by peace. Persecution and martyrdom are characteristic experiences of the heavenly city.

23. Lucan, *Pharsalia* 1.95.

24. See . . . 3.6; Livy, *History of Rome* 1.7.

at once, for Abel did not want to have dominion in the city founded by his brother. Cain's envy was rather the diabolical envy that the evil feel toward the good simply because they are good, while they themselves are evil. For a person's possession of the good is by no means diminished when another comes or continues to share in it. On the contrary, goodness is a possession that spreads out more and more widely insofar as those who share it are united in undivided love. In fact, anyone who is unwilling to share this possession will find that he does not possess it at all, but, the more he is able to love the one who shares it with him, the greater he will find that his own possession of it becomes.

Conflict between the Two Cities: The Flesh and the Spirit

Thus, the conflict that arose between Remus and Romulus showed how the earthly city is divided against itself, and the conflict between Cain and Abel demonstrated the antagonism between the two cities themselves, the city of God and the city of men. The evil, then, fight against each other, and, likewise, the evil and the good fight against each other. But the good, if they have attained perfection, cannot fight against each other. While they are making progress, however, but have not yet attained perfection, they can fight against each other in that someone who is good may fight against another due to that part of him by which he also fights against himself. Even in the case of a single individual, *what the flesh desires is opposed to the spirit, and what the spirit desires is opposed to the flesh* (Gal. 5:17). Thus, one person's spiritual desire can fight against another's carnal desire, and his carnal desire can fight against another's spiritual desire, in the same way that the good and the evil fight against each other. And the carnal desires of two good people who have not yet attained perfection can obviously fight against each other in just the same way that the evil fight against each other, at least until the health of those who are in the process of being healed is brought to its ultimate triumph.[25]

6. Now, infirmity of this kind—that is, the disobedience which we discussed in the fourteenth book[26]—is the punishment for the first disobedience. It is

---

25. [GWL] Augustine acknowledges that members of the heavenly city experience conflict with one another. Since Christians continue to struggle with earthly desires, they will harm and be harmed by one another. They are thus encouraged to correct, endure, and forgive one another, as the next paragraphs stress.

26. See above at 14.1, 11–15.

not, therefore, a matter of nature but rather of moral fault, and this is why it is said to the good who are making progress and are living by faith during this pilgrimage, *Bear one another's burdens, and in this way you will fulfill the law of Christ* (Gal. 6:2). And elsewhere it is said, *Correct the unruly, comfort the fainthearted, support the weak, be patient with everyone. See that no one repays evil for evil* (1 Thess. 5:14–15). And again, in another passage, *If anyone is caught in some sin, you who are spiritual should instruct such a person in a spirit of gentleness, taking care that you yourself are not tempted* (Gal. 6:1). And elsewhere, *Do not let the sun go down on your anger* (Eph. 4:26). And in the Gospel, *If your brother sins against you, correct him between yourselves* (Matt. 18:15). Again, in the case of sins which he feared might become a stumbling block for many, the Apostle says, *As for those who sin, rebuke them in front of everyone, in order to instill fear in the rest* (1 Tim. 5:20).

It is for this reason, too, that so many precepts are given about forgiving one another and about the great care that we must take to maintain peace, without which no one will be able to see God.[27] Just think of the terrifying experience of the slave who, because he did not forgive his fellow slave a debt of a mere hundred denarii, was ordered to repay a debt of ten thousand talents that had previously been forgiven to him.[28] And, when the Lord Jesus had told this parable, he went on to say, *So your heavenly Father will also do to you, if you do not each forgive your brother from your heart* (Matt. 18:35). It is in this way that the citizens of the city of God are healed while they are pilgrims here on earth, longing for the peace of their homeland above. And the Holy Spirit works inwardly to give effect to the medicine that is applied outwardly. Otherwise, even if God himself makes use of a creature subject to him to speak to the human senses in some human form, whether to the bodily senses or to the very similar senses that we have when asleep, but does not rule and direct the mind with his inward grace, no preaching of the truth will be of any use.

But this is in fact what God does, distinguishing the *vessels of wrath* from the *vessels of mercy* according to a deeply hidden and yet fully just dispensation known only to himself.[29] For God helps us in wondrous and secret ways,

27. See Heb. 12:14.
28. See Matt. 18:23–34.
29. That God's judgments are often obscure but nonetheless just is an idea that appears frequently in *City of God*. See [3.1; 14.17; 18.18; and 21.13].

and when, as the Apostle teaches, the sin that dwells in our members (which is now, rather, the punishment of sin) no longer reigns in our mortal bodies to make us obey its desires, and when we no longer present our members to it as weapons of wickedness,[30] we are changed in mind. Under God's rule, a person's mind no longer consents to his own impulses to evil. For the present, he will have his mind exercising its rule with greater tranquility, and later, when he attains full health and receives immortality, he will himself reign without any sin at all in eternal peace.

Cain's Sacrifice and Its Rejection

7. But, with regard to the very point which I have just explained as best I could, what use was it to Cain when God spoke to him in his usual way of speaking with the first human beings, that is, by means of a creature subject to him, taking on an appropriate form as if he were himself one of the creatures?[31] When Cain killed his brother, did he not carry out the crime he had conceived, even after God had warned him against it? For, when God distinguished between the sacrifices of the two brothers, honoring the one but despising the other, it is not to be doubted that the testimony of some visible sign made it possible to tell the difference. And God did this precisely because Cain's works were evil, but his brother's good. But Cain went into a sulk, and his countenance fell. For it is written, *And the Lord said to Cain, Why are you sulking, and why has your countenance fallen? If your sacrifice is rightly offered but is not rightly divided, have you not sinned? Be quiet, for it shall return to you, and you shall master it* (Gen. 4:6–7).

In this admonition or warning that God gave to Cain, it is not clear why or on what basis the passage says, *If your sacrifice is rightly offered but is not rightly divided, have you not sinned?* (Gen. 4:7). As a consequence, the obscurity of the passage has given rise to many interpretations, as each commentator on Divine Scripture has tried to explain it according to the rule of faith.[32] Obviously a sacrifice is rightly offered when it is offered to the true

30. See Rom. 6:12–13.

31. In fact Scripture does not indicate that God spoke to Cain otherwise than directly. See Gen. 4:6–15. But Augustine insists in *Literal Meaning of Genesis* 8.27.49–8.27.50 that, in cases such as when he spoke to Cain, he must have done so through a creature.

32. On the "rule of faith" (*regula fidei*) see also . . . 15.26 and [*City of God, Books 1–10*, 330n111].

God, to whom alone we should offer sacrifice. But it is not rightly divided when we do not rightly select the places or times of sacrifice, or the thing offered in sacrifice, or the one who makes the offering or the one to whom it is made, or those to whom the sacrificed victim is distributed to eat. Here, then, we understand *divided* to refer to a selection of this sort. An offering may be made at a place where it should not be made, or it may be an offering that should not be made in that place but in another place; or an offering may be made at a time when it should not be made, or it may be an offering that should not be offered at that time but at some other time; or an offering may be made which should not be made at any place or at any time whatsoever; or a person may keep for himself choicer parts of the same kind of thing than those that he offers to God; or someone profane may partake of the offering, or someone who may not lawfully partake of it.

It is not easy, however, to discover in which of these ways Cain displeased God. But the apostle John, in speaking of these brothers, says, *Do not be like Cain, who was from the evil one and murdered his brother. And why did he murder him? Because his own deeds were evil and his brother's righteous* (1 John 3:12). We are given to understand, then, that the reason why God did not honor Cain's gift is that it was wrongly divided in the sense that, although he gave something of his own to God, he gave himself to himself.[33] And this is precisely what is done by all those who follow their own will rather than God's—that is, who live in perversity of heart rather than righteousness of heart—and yet still offer gifts to God. They suppose that, by means of these gifts, they are buying God's help not in healing their debased desires but rather in fulfilling them. And this is characteristic of the earthly city: to worship a god or gods with whose help it might reign in victory and earthly peace, not from love of caring for others but rather from the lust to exercise dominion over others. For the good make use of the world in order to enjoy God, but the evil, in contrast, want to make use of God in order to enjoy the world.[34] This is true, at least, of those who still believe that there is a God and that he cares about human affairs, for those who do not believe even this are in a far worse state. Thus, when Cain saw that God had honored his brother's sacrifice but

33. [GWL] The Bible does not explain why Cain's gift counted as a sin. Augustine's explanation is that Cain used God for the sake of earthly goods instead of using earthly goods for the sake of God.

34. Augustine contrasts enjoying (*frui*) and using (*uti*) here as he does . . . at 8.8 and elsewhere. See [*City of God, Books 1–10*, 252n40].

not his own, he ought surely to have changed his ways and imitated his good brother rather than standing on his pride and envying his brother. In fact, however, he went into a sulk, and his countenance fell. This sin—sulking over another's goodness, and a brother's goodness at that—is one that God most especially rebukes, and it was precisely to rebuke it that God questioned Cain, asking, *Why are you sulking, and why has your countenance fallen?* (Gen. 4:6). For God saw that he envied his brother, and that is what he rebuked.

To human observers, from whom the hearts of others are hidden, it might seem doubtful or even completely uncertain whether Cain was sulking over his own malice, by which, as he had just learned, he had displeased God, or over his brother's goodness, which pleased God when God honored his sacrifice. But God himself gave the reason that he refused to accept Cain's offering, and he did this with the aim that Cain should rightly be displeased with himself rather than wrongly displeased with his brother. For, although Cain was unrighteous in not dividing rightly—that is, in not living rightly— and so was unworthy of having his offering approved, God showed how much more unrighteous he was in hating his righteous brother for no reason. Even so, however, God did not dismiss Cain without giving him a command that was holy, righteous, and good. *Be quiet,* he said, *for it shall return to you, and you shall master it* (Gen. 4:7). Did he say, "You shall master him," that is, "your brother"? Not at all! What, then, is he to master if not sin?[35] For God said, *Have you not sinned?* And it was then that he added, *Be quiet, for it shall return to you, and you shall master it.* And the fact that there must be a return of sin to the man himself can certainly be understood to mean that he should know that he ought to ascribe his sin to no one but himself.

For this is a health-bringing medicine of repentance and a plea for pardon that is by no means unfitting. And so, when God says, *For it shall return to you,* we should understand this to mean not "it shall" in the sense of a prediction but rather "it should" in the sense of a prescription. For a person masters sin only if he does not give it dominion over himself by defending it but instead makes it subject to himself by repenting of it. Otherwise, if he always defends it when it occurs, he will be its slave, and it will be his master.

But sin may also be understood to mean the very carnal desire of which the Apostle says, *What the flesh desires is opposed to the spirit* (Gal. 5:17). Among the fruits of this flesh he mentions envy,[36] and it was certainly envy

---

35. The Latin *illius* allows for either "him" (Cain's brother) or "it" (Cain's sin).
36. See Gal. 5:21.

that goaded and sparked Cain to destroy his brother. On this understanding, then, the verb is rightly understood to mean "it shall," that is, *For it shall return to you, and you shall master it.* For this is what may happen when the carnal part is itself aroused, the part which the Apostle calls *sin* in the passage where he says, *It is no longer I that do it, but sin that dwells in me* (Rom. 7:17). There are also some philosophers who say that this part of the soul is perverse, and that it ought not to drag the mind after it but ought rather to be under the mind's control and to be restrained by reason from illicit acts. At any rate, when this part is aroused to commit some wrongful act, if we are quiet and obey the words of the Apostle, *Do not present your members to sin as weapons of wickedness* (Rom. 6:13), it returns to the mind, subdued and vanquished, with the result that it is subject to reason, and reason masters it.

This is the very command that God gave to Cain, who was inflamed with the fires of envy against his brother and wanted to do away with the very one whom he ought instead to have taken as his model. *Be quiet*, God said, keep your hands away from crime, do not let sin reign in your mortal body to make you obey its desires, do not present your members to sin as weapons of wickedness.[37] *For it shall return to you*—just so long as you do not help it along by loosening your hold but instead rein it in by being quiet—*and you shall master it.* For, if it is not permitted to act outwardly, it will become accustomed, under the control of the ruling and benevolent mind, to remain unstirred inwardly as well.

Something of this sort was also said concerning the woman in the same divine book. After their sin, when God questioned the sinners and judged them, they each received sentences of condemnation, the devil in the form of the serpent, and the woman and her husband in their own right. For, after God told the woman, *I will multiply your sorrows and groaning many times over, and, in sorrows you shall bring forth children*, he then added, *you shall return to your husband, and he shall be master over you* (Gen. 3:16). What was said to Cain concerning sin, or the perverse desire of the flesh, is said in this passage concerning the sinful woman; and in this case it is to be understood that the man, in ruling his wife, should be like the mind in its rule over the flesh.[38] It is for this reason that the Apostle says, *He who loves his wife loves himself, for no one ever hated his own flesh* (Eph. 5:28–29).

37. See Rom. 6:12–13.
38. NCP: "I.e., the mind (*animus*) is symbolized by the husband and the flesh (*caro*) by the wife." [GWL] This passage reflects patriarchal assumptions Augustine held with other writers of his time. See essay: "Women."

We ought, then, to be healed of these sins, accepting them as our own rather than condemning them as if they were someone else's. But Cain received God's command like a transgressor. In fact, the vice of envy grew stronger within him, and he laid his plans and killed his brother. Such was the founder of the earthly city. Cain also signifies the Jews, by whom Christ was killed, the shepherd of the flock of men, who was himself prefigured by Abel, the shepherd of the flock of sheep. But because this is a matter of prophetic allegory, I say no more about it here. I recall, however, that I discussed it in my *Answer to Faustus, a Manichean.*[39]

39. [GWL] Faustus was a Manichean bishop who played an important, though inadvertent, role in Augustine's conversion. His failure to address Augustine's questions about Manichean beliefs resulted in Augustine's leaving the religion (*Confessions* 5.3.3–5.7.13). Though Faustus was unable to defend Manichean theology, he raised difficult critiques of the Old Testament that would trouble Augustine for some time. *Answer to Faustus* defends the Old Testament through a line-by-line refutation of Faustus's (now lost) work, *The Chapters. Answer to Faustus* is by far the longest of Augustine's anti-Manichean works, and he wrote it after Faustus was dead. This text represents Augustine's mature position on the relation between the Old and New Testaments, a topic to which he will return in Book 17. For Augustine's treatment of Cain, see *Answer to Faustus* 12.9–13. See also essay: "Jews and Judaism."

———— Predestination and the Will ————

Gregory W. Lee and Avyi Hill, with Philip Lindia

Augustine's understanding of predestination is one of the most studied areas of his theology and one of the clearest examples of how his thought developed throughout his career. The contours of his positions would shape Western theological discourse for centuries, even for those who disagreed with him.

In his earliest writings, Augustine attributed the beginning of faith to humans and claimed election was based on God's foreknowledge of individuals' faith (*Commentary on Some Statements in the Apostle's Epistle to the Romans* 60; see *Revisions* 1.23.2). He then repudiated these positions in *Miscellany of Questions in Response to Simplician* (written in 396/97, shortly before *Confessions*), where he asserted that election is utterly gratuitous, based solely on divine mercy and, therefore, not a response to God's foreknowledge of human deeds (1.2.8). His new conclusions relied heavily on Romans 9, where Paul explains God's election of Jacob instead of Esau in terms of divine mercy (1.2.5–1.2.7).

Several years later, Augustine returned to these topics in a controversy with Pelagius, a monk and theologian in Rome. From 411 to 418, Augustine wrote against Pelagius and two of his supporters, Caelestius and Rufinus, who held that human nature was not corrupted by Adam and Eve's sin. Following Pelagius's condemnation in 418, Augustine would direct his attention against Julian of Eclanum, his most formidable opponent in the controversy. A final stage began in 426, when Augustine confronted objections from monks in Hadrumetum and Gaul. Inaccurately labeled semi-Pelagian, these monks worried Augustine's theology undermined the importance of good works.

In the course of his writings, Augustine's views on predestination evolved in several ways. He developed his doctrine of original sin, according to which all humanity suffers the curse of Adam and Eve's fall (see essay: "Original Sin"). He attributed salvation exclusively to divine mercy, which does not require the cooperation of the human will but operates efficaciously and irresistibly on it. And he stressed the ongoing effects of sin on Christians, who will continue to struggle with temptation in this life. Emblematic was Augustine's new interpretation of Romans 7. Though he once understood this text as a description of someone under the law, apart from the liberation of Christ (*Miscellany of*

276

Questions in Response to Simplician 1.1.11), he came to read the passage as the experience of those under grace (*Answer to the Two Letters of the Pelagians* 1.8.13–1.11.24; *Predestination of the Saints* 4.8).

Augustine defines predestination as the preparation for grace by which God bestows salvation (*Predestination of the Saints* 10.19; *Gift of Perseverance* 14.35). God extends this grace only to the elect. Why God chooses some and not others is a mystery of providence. On this matter, Augustine repeatedly cites Paul: "How inscrutable are his judgments and unsearchable are his ways!" (*Rebuke and Grace* 8.17–19, quoting Rom. 11:33). The damned display God's justice, making God's mercy to the elect shine more brightly. Scholars generally do not think Augustine held to double predestination, according to which God not only predestines the elect for salvation but also reprobates the non-elect for damnation. Augustine attributes predestination to God's active involvement; he does not do the same for reprobation. Still, only the elect will receive salvation; everyone else will be damned (*Enchiridion* 24.95; *Grace and Free Choice* 23.45; *Sermon* 26.13; see also *Enchiridion* 26.100 and *Nature and Origin of the Soul* 4.11.16, where Augustine speaks of predestination to punishment without espousing reprobation).

God's grace not only prompts faith and conversion but also sustains subsequent good works. Not all who receive the beginning of faith will persevere in faith until death (*Gift of Perseverance* 1.1; 8.19). The reason some persevere and others do not is that God has chosen only some and not all to persevere. Augustine's explanation for this disparity is the same as his answer concerning the beginning of faith: God's providence is inscrutable, Christians should not question it, and the damnation of those who fail to persevere encourages Christians' reliance on God's grace (*Gift of Perseverance* 8.16; 9.21; 11.25). Augustine's position on this topic differs from what later Protestants would call "perseverance of the saints." He does not believe all who presently have faith will persevere. At the same time, he attributes this disparity between believers to providence as opposed to free will.

Despite the apparent determinism of Augustine's theology, he encourages pastors to preach predestination without fatalism (*Gift of Perseverance* 22.57–23.64). Pastors cannot know the state of their congregants' souls. Some who lack faith may be granted it. Those who trust in themselves will fall into despair. "'It is better to trust in the Lord rather than to trust in human beings'" (*Gift of Perseverance* 22.62, quoting Ps. 118:8). The ultimate example of predestination is Jesus Christ, who was chosen to be perfect without regard for his prior merits (*Predestination of the Saints* 15.30–31; *Gift of Perseverance* 24.67). In his own preaching, Augustine encouraged Christians to recognize God's work within them as a sign of their election—a grace that is "impossible to explain" but "easy to feel" (*Homilies on the Gospel of John* 40.5, trans. from Miles 2024, 67).

Bibliography

Bonner, Gerald. 2002. *St. Augustine of Hippo: Life and Controversies*. Orig. 1963. Norwich, UK: Canterbury, 312–93.

———. 2007. *Freedom and Necessity: St. Augustine's Teaching on Divine Power and Human Freedom*. Washington, DC: Catholic University of America Press.

Burns, J. Patout. 1980. *The Development of Augustine's Doctrine of Operative Grace*. Paris: Études Augustiniennes.

Drecoll, Volker Henning. 2019. "Praedestinatio." In *AugLex*, 4:826–37.

Harrison, Carol. 2006. *Rethinking Augustine's Early Theology: An Argument for Continuity*. Oxford: Oxford University Press.

Kantzer Komline, Han-luen. 2020. *Augustine on the Will: A Theological Account*. Oxford: Oxford University Press.

Miles, Margaret R. 2024. "Augustine on God's *Intus* Activity." *Augustinian Studies* 55, no. 1: 67–82.

Wetzel, James. 1992. *Augustine and the Limits of Virtue*. Cambridge: Cambridge University Press.

Book 17

1–4A, 5–7

In Book 16, Augustine treated the development of the two cities from Noah to Abraham and the development of the heavenly city from Abraham to David. (Augustine will return to the time of Abraham in Book 18 to trace the subsequent history of the earthly city.) In Book 17, Augustine recounts the era of the prophets, beginning with Eli, Samuel, Saul, and David. This book opens with general remarks on prophecy (17.1–3). It then treats the replacement of Eli by Samuel and the replacement of Saul by David (17.4–7). Each of these events signifies the replacement of the old covenant by the new covenant. The rest of Book 17 treats the promises to David (17.8–13), the psalms of David (17.14–19), and the prophecies of later kings (17.20–24). This last section covers the exiles of the Northern and Southern Kingdoms of Israel and the cessation of prophecy after the restoration of Judah from Babylon. Since Augustine cannot treat the later prophets in this book, he promises to discuss them in the next one (17.24).

1. As for the promises God made to Abraham—to whose seed, as we have learned, we owe both the Israelite people according to the flesh and all peoples according to faith, in accord with God's promise—the course of the city of God through the ages will indicate how these are being fulfilled. And, since the end of the previous book brought us down to the reign of David, we will now touch on what came after his reign so far as seems sufficient for the work we have undertaken.

The Age of the Prophets

The entire period that extends from the point at which the holy Samuel began to prophesy[1] down to the time when the people of Israel were taken as captives to Babylonia, and then down to the point at which, after the return of the Israelites seventy years later, the house of God was restored as prophesied by the holy Jeremiah,[2] constitutes the age of the prophets.[3] Of course, we can—and not without reason—give the name of prophet both to the patriarch Noah himself, in whose time the whole earth was wiped out by the flood,[4] and to others before and after him, right down to the present era when there began to be kings among the people of God. For certain future events having to do with the city of God and with the kingdom of heaven were signified or foretold through them in one way or another, and in fact we read that several of them, such as Abraham and Moses, were expressly called prophets.[5] It remains true, however, that the period chiefly and principally termed "the days of the prophets" starts with the earliest prophecies of Samuel, who at God's command first anointed Saul as king[6] and then, when Saul was repudiated,[7] anointed David himself,[8] from whose stock all the following kings succeeded each other, so long as it was fitting for such a succession to last.

It would be an unending task, however, if I wanted to compile everything that the prophets foretold about Christ during this time, as the city of God was running its course and the generations of its members came and went, one dying out and the next coming to birth. This is due to the fact, first of all, that Scripture itself—which seems, in presenting its ordered account of the kings and their deeds and their fates, to have been chiefly concerned with historical accuracy in its narration of events—is found, when considered and interpreted with the help of God's Spirit, to be even more intent (or, certainly, no less intent) on foretelling things to come in the future than it is

1. See 1 Sam. 3:19–20.
2. See Jer. 25:11–12.
3. [GWL] Augustine believes David's time, beginning with Samuel, inaugurates more open prophecies about Christ and his church. Much of Book 17 will concentrate on the psalms, which are associated with David. The time of the prophets ends with Israel's restoration from Babylon. After the prophecies associated with that event, Israel does not receive further prophecies until the time of Christ (17.24).
4. See Gen. 6:11–9:17.
5. For Abraham see Gen. 20:7; for Moses see Deut. 34:10.
6. See 1 Sam. 10:1.
7. See 1 Sam. 15:10–34.
8. See 1 Sam. 16:13.

on relating things that happened in the past.[9] And who, if he gave the matter even a little thought, could fail to see how laborious and interminable it would be to trace all this out and present it in full detail, not to mention how many volumes it would require? In addition, there is the fact that even the passages that unambiguously count as prophecies relating to Christ and the kingdom of heaven, which is the city of God, are so numerous that it would require a longer discussion to present them all than the scope of this work allows. If I can, therefore, I shall keep my pen firmly under control so that I say neither anything more nor anything less than is needed to bring this work to its completion, according to God's will.

2. In the previous book we said that two things were promised to Abraham from the start.[10] The first was that his seed was going to possess the land of Canaan, and this was signified where Scripture said, *Go to the land that I shall show you, and I will make of you a great nation* (Gen. 12:1). But the second, and by far the more important, concerned not his carnal but rather his spiritual seed, because of which he is the father not simply of the one Israelite people but of all the peoples that follow in the footsteps of his faith, and this promise begins with these words: *And in you all the tribes of the earth shall be blessed* (Gen. 12:3). And we have shown by many testimonies that these two promises were kept in full measure. Thus, Abraham's seed according to the flesh—that is, the people of Israel—were now in the promised land and had now begun to rule there, not only by taking and holding the cities of their enemies but also by having kings. God's promises concerning this people, then, had already been fulfilled in large part—not only those made to the three patriarchs, Abraham, Isaac, and Jacob, and to others of their time, but also those made through Moses himself, through whom this same people was delivered from their Egyptian servitude, and through whom all the past promises were revealed in his time, when he led the people through the wilderness.

God's promise that the land of Canaan would extend from a certain river of Egypt all the way to the great river Euphrates,[11] however, was not fulfilled

9. [GWL] Though Augustine affirms the historicity of Old Testament events, he thinks Scripture's intent in recounting them is not simply to narrate the past but to direct readers to Christ and the church. See essay: "Figurative Interpretation of Scripture."

10. [GWL] See 16.16. Throughout his treatment of Abraham in Book 16, Augustine asks whether a given promise to Abraham should be interpreted literally, concerning the land of Canaan, or spiritually, concerning the church from all nations.

11. See Gen. 15:18.

through the illustrious leader Joshua the son of Nun, who led that people into the promised land, defeated its inhabitants, divided it among the twelve tribes as God had commanded, and then died.[12] Nor was it fulfilled after him, during the whole period of the judges, even though it was no longer prophesied of the distant future but rather was expected to be fulfilled at any moment. This promise was fulfilled, however, through David and through his son Solomon, whose rule extended over all the area that had been promised, for they subdued all those lands and made them pay tribute.[13] Under these kings, therefore, Abraham's seed according to the flesh was so fully established in the promised land—that is, in the land of Canaan—that nothing of God's earthly promise remained to be fulfilled except that the Hebrew people should continue in this same land, secure and unshaken so far as temporal prosperity is concerned, through the successive generations of their posterity right down to the end of this mortal age, just so long as they obeyed the laws of the Lord their God.[14] But, since God knew that they would not do this, he also made use of his temporal punishments both to train the few among them who remained faithful to him and to admonish those who were later going to be spread among all peoples. For it was right that those in whom he was going to fulfill his second promise, when the new covenant was revealed through the incarnation of Christ, should be admonished.

3. Thus, like the divine oracles granted to Abraham, Isaac, and Jacob, and like any other prophetic signs or sayings given in the earlier sacred writings, the rest of the prophecies, those given during the time of the kings, also refer partly to Abraham's people according to the flesh and partly to the seed of Abraham in which all peoples are blessed, as coheirs of Christ through the new covenant, for the sake of gaining eternal life and the kingdom of heaven.[15] Partly, then, they refer to the maidservant whose children are born into servitude, that is, to the earthly Jerusalem, which is in servitude together with her children; and partly they refer to the free city of God, that is, the true

---

12. See Josh. passim.
13. See 1 Kings 4:21.
14. [GWL] At the literal level, the promises to Abraham were fulfilled through Israel's taking the land of Canaan and through Israel's expansion under David and Solomon. At the spiritual level, the prophecies would be fulfilled in the church, which encompasses all nations.
15. [GWL] As with the prophecies to Abraham, Isaac, and Jacob, the prophecies beginning with Samuel involve two levels of fulfillment, one concerning physical Israel and the other concerning the church. Drawing on Gal. 4:21–5:1, Augustine likens earthly Jerusalem to the maidservant, Hagar, and the heavenly Jerusalem to the free woman, Sarah (see 15.2–3). As Augustine continues, some prophecies simultaneously refer to both Israel and the church.

Jerusalem, eternal in heaven, whose children are those who live according to God and are on pilgrimage here on this earth.[16] At the same time, however, there are some among these prophecies that we understand to refer to both at once, to the maidservant in their literal sense, and to the free woman in their figurative sense.

The Types of Prophecy

We find, then, that the sayings of the prophets are of three types: some have to do with the earthly Jerusalem, some have to do with the heavenly Jerusalem, and others have to do with both. I see, however, that I need to support what I say with examples.[17] The prophet Nathan was sent to charge King David with a grievous sin and to foretell the future evils that would follow.[18] And who doubts that these statements and others like them referred to the earthly city, whether they were spoken publicly, that is, for the welfare and benefit of the people in general, or privately, as when someone receives divine words relating to his own affairs through which he learns something of the future for use in his temporal life? In contrast, when we read, *See, says the Lord, the days are coming when I will make a new covenant with the house of Israel and the house of Judah. It shall not be like the covenant that I made with their ancestors, when I took them by the hand to lead them out of the land of Egypt, for they did not continue in my covenant, and I despised them, says the Lord. But this is the covenant that I will make with the house of Israel after those days, says the Lord: I will put my laws in their minds, and I will write them on their hearts, and I will look to them, and I will be their God, and they shall be my people* (Jer. 31:31–33), there is no doubt that this prophecy refers to the Jerusalem on high, whose reward is God himself and whose supreme and total good is to possess him and to be his.

But when Jerusalem is called the city of God, and it is prophesied that the house of God will be located there, this refers both to the earthly and to the heavenly Jerusalem. For we see that this prophecy was fulfilled when King Solomon

16. See Gal. 4:22–26.
17. [GWL] The two levels of fulfillment correspond to three categories of prophecy: (1) literal alone, (2) spiritual alone, and (3) both literal and spiritual. As examples of each, Augustine names (1) Nathan's prophecy to David, (2) Jeremiah's prophecy about the law being written on human hearts, and (3) references to Jerusalem as the city of God.
18. See 2 Sam. 12:1–14.

built his celebrated Temple.[19] But this was not only a historical event in the earthly Jerusalem; it was also a figure of the heavenly Jerusalem. This third type of prophecy—in which the other two are, as it were, mixed and mingled together—is of great importance in the ancient canonical books that narrate historical events, and it has greatly exercised (and continues greatly to exercise) the abilities of those who study Sacred Scripture with the aim of discerning which of the things that we read were foretold about and fulfilled in Abraham's seed according to the flesh were also things that allegorically signified something to be fulfilled in Abraham's seed according to faith.[20] In fact, some have even thought that there is nothing that was prophesied or enacted in these books, or that was enacted without being prophesied, which does not carry some figurative significance that is to be referred to the heavenly city of God and to the children of that city who are pilgrims in this life.

If this is so, however, then the discourse of the prophets will be of only two types, not three; or, rather, this will be true of all the Scriptures that are included in the Old Testament. For, if whatever is said in the Old Testament about the earthly Jerusalem or in relation to it, and is fulfilled, also signifies something that refers to the heavenly Jerusalem and allegorically prefigures it, then there will be nothing in the Old Testament that refers only to the earthly Jerusalem. And, in that case, there will be only two kinds of prophecy, one referring to the free Jerusalem, and the other referring to both.

In my view, however, just as people are badly mistaken when they think that the events recorded in writings of this kind signify nothing more than the mere event itself, so people are far too rash when they insist that everything recorded there carries allegorical significance.[21] That is why I have said that the prophecies are of three types and not merely of two. In holding this view, however, I do not condemn those who have been able to devise a spiritual meaning for each historical event recorded there, just so long as,

19. See 1 Kings 6:1–7:51.
20. [GWL] For Augustine, untangling the two levels of meaning is perhaps the greatest challenge of interpreting Scripture. A given passage can jump back and forth between references. *De Doctrina Christiana* 3.30.42–3.37.56 delineates patterns according to which the prophecies switch referents. See essay: "Figurative Interpretation of Scripture."
21. [GWL] Probably a reference to the third-century theologian Origen. Origen claimed all Scripture had a spiritual meaning but not all of it had a literal meaning (*First Principles* 4.3.5). Although Augustine embraces spiritual interpretation, he stresses the historicity of the events in Scripture. Augustine's affirmation of the historical, literal sense of the text develops throughout his career. While he affirms allegory in his mature writings, his allegorizing tends to be more restrained there than in his earlier writings.

first of all, they preserve the truth of the history itself. On the other hand, with regard to any statements that cannot possibly apply to any historical event, whether divine or human, whether past or future, no person of faith can doubt that there must have been some good reason for making them.[22] Anyone who could, would certainly interpret them in a spiritual sense; or, at the very least, he would grant that they should be interpreted in a spiritual sense by someone who can.

4. Thus, when the city of God had followed its course down to the period of the kings, it reached the point at which Saul was repudiated and David first took such a firm hold on the kingdom that, from then on, his descendants ruled in the earthly Jerusalem in enduring succession.[23] Now, these events had figurative significance. For they signified and foretold something that must not be passed over in silence. They pointed to the change that was to take place in the future with respect to the two covenants, the old and the new, when the priesthood and the monarchy were transformed by the new and eternal priest and king who is Christ Jesus. For, when Eli the priest was rejected and Samuel was substituted for him in the service of God, functioning both as priest and as judge,[24] and when Saul was deposed and King David was established in the kingship,[25] these happenings prefigured the change I am talking about.[26]

◆

The Transformation of the Priesthood: The Prophecy to Eli

5. But this transformation is expressed more clearly by the man of God who was sent to the priest Eli himself. Scripture does not tell us his name, but his

22. [GWL] There are some texts that have no historical reference and can have only spiritual meaning. In the next chapter, for instance, Augustine treats 1 Sam. 2:5, which says, "The barren woman has given birth to seven." Since, according to 1 Sam. 2:21, Hannah had only five children, the "seven" must refer to the "full perfection of the Church."

23. [GWL] An important paragraph indicating the argument of the next chapters, especially 17.5–7. The replacements of Saul by David, as king, and of Eli by Samuel, as priest, signify the establishment of Christ's kingship and priesthood. Christ's new covenant also enacts the replacement of Israel by the church as the locus of God's saving activity. See essay: "Jews and Judaism."

24. See 1 Sam. 2:27–4:1.

25. See 1 Sam. 16:1–13.

26. [GWL] In the following section, omitted for the purposes of this volume, Augustine provides an extended analysis of Hannah's prayer (1 Sam. 2:1–10) as a prophecy of Christ and the church.

office and ministry make it plain, beyond any doubt, that he was a prophet. For this is what Scripture says: *And a man of God came to Eli and said, Thus says the Lord, Truly, I revealed myself to the house of your father, when they were slaves in the house of Pharaoh, and I chose the house of your father out of all the tribes of Israel to serve as my priest, to go up to my altar, to burn incense, and to wear the ephod. And I gave to the house of your father all the offerings by fire of the children of Israel to be their food. Why, then, have you looked with insolent eye on my incense and my sacrifice and glorified your sons more than me, to bless the firstfruits of every offering in Israel in my sight? Therefore, thus says the Lord, the God of Israel, I declared that your house and the house of your father should walk before me forever. But now the Lord says, By no means, for I will glorify those who glorify me, and I will despise him who despises me. See, the days are coming when I will banish your seed and the seed of your father's house, and you shall not have an elder in my house all your days; and I will banish the male of your house from my altar, so that his eyes fail and his soul melts away. Every one of your house who survives shall die by the sword of men. And this shall be a sign to you, which shall come upon your two sons, Hophni and Phinehas: they shall both die on the same day. And I will raise up for myself a faithful priest, who does all that is in my heart and all that is in my mind; and I will build a sure house for him, and he shall walk before my anointed all his days. And it shall come to pass that everyone who is left in your house shall come to bow down to him for a piece of silver and shall say, Let me have a part in your priesthood, so that I may have bread to eat* (1 Sam. 2:27–36).

It is not the case that this prophecy, where the transformation of the old priesthood is announced with such clarity, may be said to have been fulfilled in Samuel.[27] For, even though Samuel was not from a tribe other than the one that had been appointed by the Lord to serve the altar, still he was not one of the sons of Aaron, whose offspring had been set aside as those from whom priests should come.[28] As a consequence, in the event too there was a fore-

---

27. [GWL] This chapter claims the replacement of Eli by Samuel signifies the replacement of the Levitical priesthood by Christ's priesthood. Augustine will also argue that the replacement of Saul by David signifies the replacement of Israel's kingship by Christ's kingship.

28. See *Revisions* 2.43(70).2, where Augustine corrects his text of *City of God* for a second and final time (the first time with reference to 10.8 above): "What was said of Samuel, 'He was not one of the sons of Aaron,' should instead have been 'He was not the son of a priest.' It was a more legitimate custom, in fact, for the sons of priests to succeed the dead priests. For Samuel's father is numbered among the sons of Aaron, but he was not a priest, nor is he [listed] among Aaron's sons as though he himself had begotten him, but he was like all of that people, who

shadowing of the same transformation that was going to take place through Christ Jesus, and the prophecy itself pertained literally to the old covenant (with respect to the event) but figuratively to the new (with respect to the words), for it signified by means of the event what was said to the priest Eli by means of the prophet's words. For in fact there were priests from Aaron's line in later times, such as Zadock[29] and Abiathar[30] during David's reign, and others after them, until the right time came for the transformation of the priesthood, foretold so long before, to be accomplished through Christ. But must not anyone who views the matter with the eyes of faith see that what was foretold has now been fulfilled? For now there is no tabernacle, no temple, no altar, and no sacrifice, and therefore there is no priest remaining for the Jews, despite the fact that they were commanded by God's law to appoint priests from Aaron's seed.[31]

And this point is indicated here, where the prophet says, *Thus says the Lord, the God of Israel, I declared that your house and the house of your father should walk before me forever. But now the Lord says, By no means, for I will glorify those who glorify me, and I will despise him who despises me* (1 Sam. 2:27, 30–31). For, when he speaks of the house of your father, he is referring not to Eli's immediate father but rather to the Aaron who was installed as the first priest and from whose offspring all later priests were to come. This is made quite clear by the prophet's earlier words, where he says, *I revealed myself to the house of your father, when they were slaves in the house of Pharaoh; and I chose the house of your father out of all the tribes of Israel to serve as my priest* (1 Sam. 2:27–28). For which of Eli's fathers was in that servitude in Egypt and was then, after they were delivered from Egypt, chosen for the priesthood? Only Aaron. It was, therefore, of Aaron's line that the prophet was speaking in this passage, when he said that the time would come when they would no longer be priests, and we now see this fulfilled. Let faith be on the alert. The facts are right in front of us, they are plain to see, they are in our possession, they are forced upon the eyes even of those who have no wish to see them. *See*, he says, *the days are coming when I will*

are called sons of Israel." Scripture does not in fact number Samuel's father Elkanah among the sons of Aaron.

29. See 1 Kings 1:8, 38.

30. See 2 Sam. 15:24; 1 Kings 1:7; 2:26.

31. [GWL] Augustine interprets the destruction of the Jewish temple in 70 CE as proof that Israel has been replaced by the church. This is a common perspective among early Christian writers. See essay: "Jews and Judaism."

banish your seed and the seed of your father's house, and you shall not have an elder in my house all your days; and I will banish the male of your house from my altar, so that his eyes fail and his soul melts away (1 Sam. 2:31–33). See, the days that were foretold have now arrived. There is no priest according to the order of Aaron; and whenever a man from his line sees the sacrifice of the Christians prevailing throughout the entire world, and sees the great honor that was his taken from him, his eyes fail and his soul melts away in a flood of grief.

What comes next, however, refers literally to the house of Eli, to which it is addressed: *Every one of your house who survives shall die by the sword of men. And this shall be a sign to you, which shall come upon your two sons, Hophni and Phinehas: they shall both die on the same day* (1 Sam. 2:33–34). This took place, then, as a sign of the transfer of the priesthood from the house of Eli; by this sign, however, it was also signified that the priesthood of the house of Aaron was to be transformed. In fact, what the death of Eli's sons signified was not the death of any human beings but rather the death of the very priesthood itself that had belonged to the sons of Aaron.[32] And what follows refers to that priest whom Samuel prefigured when he succeeded Eli, for the words are spoken of Christ Jesus, the true priest of the new covenant: *And I will raise up for myself a faithful priest, who does all that is in my heart and all that is in my mind; and I will build a sure house for him* (1 Sam. 2:35). This house is, of course, the eternal and heavenly Jerusalem. *And he shall walk before my anointed all his days* (1 Sam. 2:35). Here *he shall walk before* means "he shall dwell with," just as it did above, when he said of the house of Aaron, *I declared that your house and the house of your father should walk before me forever* (1 Sam. 2:30).[33] When it says, *he shall walk before my anointed*, however, we should understand the subject to be the *sure house*, not the priest who is Christ himself, the mediator and savior. The meaning is, then, that his house will walk before him. It is also possible, however, to take *he shall walk before* to mean "he will pass," that is, "he will pass" from death to life during *all his days* spent in this mortal condition down to the end of this world. Again, when God says that his faithful priest will do *all that is in my heart and all that is in my mind*, we should not imagine that God has a soul, for he is the creator of the soul. This is not said of God literally but

---

32. [GWL] A strong statement on the end of the Levitical priesthood.

33. "Shall walk before . . . dwell with . . . should walk before": *transibit . . . conversabitur . . . transibunt.*

rather in a figure of speech, in the same way that we speak of God's hands or feet or other parts of the body.[34] Furthermore, to keep us from believing, on the basis of such expressions, that it is in the shape of his body that man is made in the image of God,[35] Scripture also speaks of God's wings—and human beings obviously do not have wings! For example, it is said to God, *Hide me in the shadow of your wings* (Ps. 17:8). People should understand, then, that such expressions are used of God's ineffable nature not in the literal but rather in a figurative sense of the words.

The prophet then says, *And it shall come to pass that everyone who is left in your house shall come to bow down to him* (1 Sam. 2:36). In the literal sense, however, this does not refer to the house of Eli himself but rather to the house of Aaron, whose line lasted down to the advent of Christ and in fact continues even today. For it had already been said above, with respect to the house of Eli, *Every one of your house who survives shall die by the sword of men*. And, if it is true that no one of his line was to survive the avenging sword, how could it also be true to say here, *And it shall come to pass that everyone who is left in your house shall come to bow down to him*? We are to understand, then, that this applies not to the line of Eli in particular but rather to the line of the whole priesthood according to the order of Aaron. This statement refers, then, to that predestined remnant of whom another prophet said, *A remnant shall be saved* (Isa. 10:22), and the Apostle also says, *So too at the present time there is a remnant, chosen by grace* (Rom. 11:5); and, since it is well understood that *everyone who is left in your house* must belong to that remnant, it is obvious that they will believe in Christ. And, in fact, just as a great many from that race believed in Christ, so even now there are some, although very few, who believe in him. This fulfills, then, what the man of God immediately went on to say, *shall come to bow down to him for a piece of silver* (1 Sam. 2:36). Bow down to whom, if not to the high priest who is also God? For not even under the priesthood according to the order of Aaron did people come to the Temple or to the altar of God to bow down to the priest. And why does he mention *a piece of silver* if not to point to the

34. Here and in what follows Augustine expresses concern about the danger of anthropomorphism. See *Letter* 148.4.13–148.4.14.

35. See Gen. 1:26. This text was, for anthropomorphists, an important proof for a God with the features of a human body. In discussing Gen. 1:26 in his *Fragments on Genesis* (PG 12.93), Origen traces anthropomorphism to the late-second-century Melito of Sardis, "who left writings asserting that God was corporeal." There is a poignant example of the verse's anthropomorphic use in the late fourth century in Cassian, *Conferences* 10.3.

brevity of the word of faith, with regard to which the Apostle cites this say-ing, *The Lord shall complete his word and cut it short upon the earth* (Rom. 9:28; Isa. 10:23). Again, there is also a Psalm that attests the use of the word "silver" for speech, where it chants, *The words of the Lord are pure words, silver refined in fire* (Ps. 12:6).

And, when he comes to bow down to the priest of God and to the priest who is God, what does he say? *Let me have a part in your priesthood, so that I may have bread to eat* (1 Sam. 2:36). That is, I do not want to be elevated to the honored status of my fathers; that is now gone. Instead let me have a part in your priesthood. For *I would rather be lowly in the house of my God* (Ps. 84:10). What I want is to be a member of your priesthood, no matter how small or how insignificant. Here he clearly uses priesthood to mean the people itself, that is, the people whose priest is the *mediator between God and men, the man Christ Jesus* (1 Tim. 2:5). It is this people whom the apostle Peter calls *a holy people, a royal priesthood* (1 Pet. 2:9). There are some translators who have put *your sacrifice* in place of *your priesthood*,[36] but this translation still signifies the same Christian people. This is the basis on which the apostle Paul says, *We, being many, are one bread and one body* (1 Cor. 10:17). Thus, when the prophet added *bread to eat*, he expressed beautifully the very nature of this sacrifice, of which the priest himself says, *The bread that I will give for the life of the world is my flesh* (John 6:51). *Let the reader understand* (Matt. 24:15): this is the sacrifice not according to the order of Aaron but accord-ing to the order of Melchizedek. What we have here, then, is a confession, which is marked by brevity and salutary humility: *Let me have a part in your priesthood so that I may have bread to eat.* This confession is itself the *piece of silver*, for it is brief and is the word of the Lord, who dwells in the heart of the believer. Earlier God had said that he had given food to the house of Aaron from the sacrifices of the old covenant, *I gave to the house of your father all the offerings by fire of the children of Israel to be their food* (and these were, of course, the sacrifices of the Jews); here, therefore, he said *bread to eat*, and this bread, in the new covenant, is the sacrifice of the Christians.

6. But, even though all this was foretold at that time in such profound terms and now shines forth with such obvious clarity, it is not without reason that a person might still feel moved to ask how we can be sure that everything whose coming was foretold in those books is actually going to come about.

---

36. The Greek original is *hierateion*, which can mean either "priesthood" or "sacrifice."

For one of the things that was declared by God in this passage clearly could not happen in fact—*that your house and the house of your father should walk before me forever* (1 Sam. 2:30). For we see that that priesthood has been replaced, and there is no hope that what was promised to that house can ever be fulfilled, for what is now proclaimed as eternal is what succeeded it, after it was rejected and replaced.[37] Anyone who says this, however, does not yet understand, or does not recollect, that the priesthood according to the order of Aaron was itself instituted as a kind of shadow of the eternal priesthood that was to come. Thus, when eternity was promised to it, it was not promised to the shadow or figure itself but rather to what was shadowed and prefigured by it. And so, to keep people from thinking that the shadow itself was going to endure, its replacement had to be prophesied as well.

The Transformation of the Kingship: Saul and Samuel

In the same way, the kingdom of Saul, who was himself repudiated and rejected, was the shadow of a future kingdom that was going to endure for all eternity.[38] In fact, the oil with which he was anointed, by virtue of which he was called the anointed, must be taken in a mystical sense and must be understood as a great mystery.[39] David himself was so much in awe of this mystery in Saul's person that, with stricken heart, he trembled in fear when, while hiding in a cave that Saul also entered to answer the call of nature, he sneaked up behind him and secretly cut off a tiny piece from his garment in order to have proof that he had spared Saul when he could have killed him.[40] David's aim was to remove from Saul's mind the suspicion due to which he was hunting down the holy David, thinking him to be his enemy. But David was terrified for fear that he might be guilty of having violated so great a mystery in Saul's person simply by touching his clothing in this way. For this is what Scripture says, *And David was stricken to the heart because he had cut off a corner of Saul's cloak* (1 Sam. 24:5). And to the men who were with

---

37. [GWL] Another strong statement on the end of the Old Testament priesthood. The Latin for "rejected and replaced" is *reprobato mutatoque*. Augustine will proceed to call the Old Testament a shadow of New Testament realities. This recalls the language of 15.2, a touchstone text for the relation between Israel and the church.

38. [GWL] Having treated the replacement of Eli by Samuel, Augustine turns to the replacement of Saul by David.

39. "Great mystery": *magnum sacramentum*. Similarly in the next few lines.

40. See 1 Sam. 24:3–4.

him, who were urging him to kill Saul since he had been given into his hands, David said, *The Lord forbid that I should do this thing to my lord, the Lord's anointed, to raise my hand against him, for he is the Lord's anointed* (1 Sam. 24:6). Such great reverence was shown for this shadow of the future, however, not for its own sake but rather for the sake of what it prefigured.

Again, there is what Samuel said to Saul: *Because you have not kept my commandment, which the Lord commanded you, just as the Lord had once prepared your kingdom to last forever over Israel, now your kingdom shall not endure for you, and the Lord shall seek out for himself a man after his own heart, and the Lord shall command him to be a ruler over his people, because you have not kept what the Lord commanded you* (1 Sam. 13:13–14). And again, we must not take this as if God had prepared Saul himself to rule forever and then refused to keep his promise after Saul sinned, for God certainly was not ignorant of the fact that Saul was going to sin. Rather, he had prepared Saul's kingdom as a prefiguration of the eternal kingdom. That is why he went on to say, *Now your kingdom shall not endure for you* (1 Sam. 13:14). Thus, what was signified by his kingdom did endure and will endure, but it will not endure for him, because he himself was not going to rule forever. And neither were his offspring, so that it would not appear that the *forever* might be fulfilled through his descendants as they succeeded one another. *And the Lord*, he says, *shall seek out for himself a man* (1 Sam. 13:14), here signifying either David or the *mediator of the new covenant* (Heb. 9:15) himself, who was prefigured in the chrism with which both David himself and his descendants were anointed.[41] Of course, it is not that God did not know where the man was and so had to look for him. It is rather that, in speaking through a man, he speaks in the way we human beings speak, and it is precisely by speaking in our human way that he seeks us out. For we were already so thoroughly known not only to God the Father but also to his only-begotten Son, who came to seek what was lost,[42] that we were chosen in him even before the foundation of the world.[43] Therefore, *he shall seek out* means "he shall take as his own." Thus, in Latin this word takes on a prefix and, from "he seeks out," becomes "he acquires,"[44] and what this signifies is plain enough. Even

---

41. "Prefigured in the chrism" because both "Christ" and "chrism" have the same root. Augustine himself mentions the relationship between the two words . . . at 17.16. See also [*City of God, Books 11–22*, 248nn34–35].

42. See Luke 19:10.

43. See Eph. 1:4.

44. "He seeks out . . . he acquires": *quaeret . . . acquirit.*

without the prefix, however, "to seek out" may mean "to acquire," and it is on this basis that profits are sometimes called "acquisitions."[45]

7. Saul again sinned through disobedience, and Samuel again said to him, in the word of the Lord, *Because you have spurned the word of the Lord, the Lord has spurned you, that you may not be king over Israel* (1 Sam. 15:23).[46] And again, in relation to the same sin, when Saul confessed it and prayed for forgiveness and asked Samuel to return with him to placate God, Samuel said, *I will not return with you, for you have spurned the word of the Lord, and the Lord shall spurn you, that you may not be king over Israel. And Samuel turned away to depart, and Saul caught hold of the hem of his robe and tore it. And Samuel said to him, The Lord has torn the kingdom from Israel out of your hand this day and shall give it to a neighbor of yours, who is good above you, and Israel shall be divided in two. And he shall not change his mind or repent, for he is not like a man, that he should repent, who issues a threat and does not stick to it* (1 Sam. 15:26–29).

In fact, however, the one to whom it is said, *The Lord shall spurn you, that you may not be king over Israel* and *The Lord has torn the kingdom from Israel out of your hand this day* (1 Sam. 15:28), actually ruled over Israel for forty years,[47] for as long a time, that is, as David himself, and yet it was in the first part of his reign that he heard these things. They were said, therefore, so that we should understand that no one from Saul's line was going to rule, and so that we should instead look to David's line, from which came, according to the flesh, *the mediator between God and men, the man Christ Jesus* (1 Tim. 2:5).

We should also note that in this passage Scripture does not have the reading that appears in most of the Latin versions: *The Lord has torn the kingdom of Israel out of your hand*; instead it has what we find in the Greek version, just as we have reproduced it: *The Lord has torn the kingdom from Israel out of your hand*. And it is worded in this way in order to make it clear that *out of your hand* means the same thing that *from Israel* means. Figuratively speaking, then, Saul represented the person of the people of Israel, the people that was going to lose the kingdom when Christ Jesus our Lord came to rule, not carnally but spiritually, through the new covenant.[48] And when it goes on

45. "Acquisitions": *quaestus*.

46. [GWL] Having treated 1 Sam. 13:13–14 in the previous chapter, Augustine turns to 1 Sam. 15.

47. See Acts 13:21.

48. [GWL] A clear statement that Saul's deposition as king signified Israel's loss of its kingdom because of Christ's new covenant.

to say, *and shall give it to a neighbor of yours* (1 Sam. 15:28), this refers to kinship in the flesh, for Christ, according to the flesh, was from Israel, as was Saul. What comes next—*who is good above you* (1 Sam. 15:28)—can in fact be understood to mean "who is better than you," and some have translated it in this way. It is preferable, however, to take *good above you* to mean that, because he is *good*, he is therefore *above you*. This accords with that other prophetic saying, *Until I put all your enemies beneath your feet* (Ps. 110:1). For Israel, too, is one of those enemies, and it was from Israel, as his persecutor, that Christ took away the kingdom. Even then, however, there was also the Israel in whom there was no guile,[49] like a bit of grain among all the chaff.[50] For the apostles certainly came from Israel, as did any number of martyrs, of whom Stephen was the first,[51] as well as any number of churches, which the apostle Paul mentions as glorifying God for his conversion.[52]

I have no doubt that what comes next is to be understood with reference to this distinction: *And Israel shall be divided in two* (1 Sam. 15:28), that is, into the Israel that is the enemy of Christ and the Israel that adheres to Christ, the Israel that belongs to the maidservant and the Israel that belongs to the free woman.[53] For these two peoples were at first together, just as Abraham still adhered to the maidservant until the barren woman, now made fertile by the grace of Christ, cried out, *Cast out the maidservant and her son* (Gen. 21:10). We know, of course, that, due to Solomon's sin, Israel was divided in two during the reign of his son Rehoboam, and that the division persisted, with each part having its own kings,[54] until the whole people was overthrown with great devastation by the Chaldeans and carried away into captivity. But what did this have to do with Saul? For, if any such thing was to be threatened, the

49. See John 1:47.
50. [GWL] Luke 3:17. Augustine acknowledges the presence of faithful Jews among Israel. In *De Doctrina Christiana* 3.6.10–3.7.11, he even claims that the first Jewish Christians, who already worshiped the one true God, were more receptive to the Holy Spirit than the first gentile Christians, who formerly worshiped idols. Only the Jewish Christians sold all their possessions to share with the poor (Acts 4:32–35).
51. See Acts 7:58–60.
52. See Gal. 1:22–24.
53. [GWL] Gal. 4:22. Augustine is referring to the division among the Jews between those who accept Christ and those who reject him. Though the prophecy of Israel's division initially seems to refer to the separation of the northern and southern tribes under Jeroboam and Rehoboam, Augustine observes that the Jews of his time are not divided into two peoples but scattered among the nations. He thus refers the prophecy to the deeper separation between those who are enemies of Christ and those who adhere to him. Augustine's reference to Hagar and Sarah recalls 15.2.
54. See 2 Chron. 10.

threat should properly have been addressed to David himself, since Solomon was his son. And at the present time the Hebrew people is not divided into two parts but is rather scattered indiscriminately across the earth in a single society of shared error. But the division with which God threatened the kingdom and people in the person of Saul, who personified them, was shown to be eternal and immutable by what came next: *And he shall not change his mind or repent, for he is not like a man, that he should repent, who issues a threat and does not stick to it* (1 Sam. 15:29). That is, a man issues a threat and does not stick to it, but not God, who, unlike a man, does not repent. For, when we read that God repents, this only signifies a change in events, while the divine foreknowledge remains immutable. Thus, when it is said that God does not repent, the meaning is that he does not change.[55]

We see, then, that the divine sentence issued in these words with regard to this division of the people of Israel was completely indissoluble and wholly permanent.[56] For any who have gone over to Christ from that people, or are now going over to Christ, or will go over to Christ, were not actually from that people according to God's foreknowledge, nor were they from them according to the one common nature of the human race. In fact, any Israelites who adhere to Christ and persevere in him will never be together with those Israelites who persist as his enemies to the end of this life; rather, they will remain forever divided by the division that is foretold here. For the old covenant *from Mount Sinai, bearing children for slavery* (Gal. 4:24), is only of benefit because it points to the new. Otherwise, so long as Moses is read, a veil is placed over their hearts, but, when any of them go over to Christ, the veil is removed.[57] It is for this reason that the great prophet Samuel took the action he did in the period before he had anointed Saul as king. It was when he cried out to the Lord for Israel, and the Lord heard him; and, as he was offering a burnt offering, the foreigners drew near to attack the people of God, but the Lord thundered against them, and they were thrown into confusion, and they were routed before Israel.[58] Then Samuel took a stone and set it up between the old and the new Mizpah and called it Ebenezer, which in Latin means "the stone of the helper," and he said, *To this point the Lord has*

---

55. See *Miscellany of Questions in Response to Simplician* 2.2.4.

56. [GWL] Israel will be permanently divided between those who receive and those who reject Christ. This paragraph is crucial for Augustine's theology of the Jews and Judaism. See essay: "Jews and Judaism."

57. See 2 Cor. 3:12–16.

58. See 1 Sam. 7:7–11.

helped us (1 Sam. 7:12). Mizpah means "watchfulness."[59] And "the stone of the helper" is the mediation of the savior, through whom one must go over from the old Mizpah to the new—that is, from the watchfulness that looks for false, carnal happiness in the carnal kingdom to the watchfulness that looks for the supremely true spiritual happiness in the kingdom of heaven. And, since there is nothing better than this, the Lord helps us *to this point*.

59. See Jerome, *Interpretation of Hebrew Names*, 4 Kingdoms, s.v. Massephat. According to Jerome the word means "speculation or contemplation." The Hebrew meaning is "watchtower."

– Figurative Interpretation of Scripture –

Gregory W. Lee, with Kathleen Taylor

Like many early Christians, Augustine believed the Old Testament prefigured the New Testament, and he interpreted Scripture according to both literal and figurative senses. (Augustine sometimes calls the figurative sense "allegorical," though that is not his preferred term.) Even the New Testament bears spiritual meanings, as with the parable of the good Samaritan, who must ultimately be Christ (*Questions on the Gospels* 2.19). Though Augustine's approach to the Old Testament develops throughout his life, *City of God* represents his mature interpretation of the text.

Confessions recounts Augustine's discovery of Manicheism, a variation of Christianity with strong Zoroastrian and Buddhist themes (3.6.10–3.10.18). Augustine would become a Manichean for several years before repudiating it for Catholic Christianity. The Manicheans rejected the Old Testament on the grounds that it ascribed physical characteristics to God and endorsed immoral practices like polygamy and animal sacrifice. Ambrose's figurative interpretation of the Old Testament offered a strategy for addressing these criticisms, a crucial factor in Augustine's conversion (5.14.24; 6.3.3–6.5.8).

In *De Doctrina Christiana*, Augustine frames the figurative reading of the Old Testament according to a distinction between signs (*signa*) and things (*res*, the root for "realities"). Whereas *res* encompasses all things in as much as they exist, *signa* concern things in as much as they signify other things (1.2.2). Augustine presents Scripture as a book of signs composed of words that refer to objects in the world (2.4.5–2.5.6). He also believes the Old Testament is composed of figurative signs, according to which a word signifies a thing, which signifies another thing. For instance, the word "sacrifice" signifies an animal or agricultural sacrifice, which signifies Christ's sacrifice (3.5.9). Augustine casts the literal interpretation of figurative signs as a characteristically Jewish error. Many Jews rejected Jesus because they failed to see how the Old Testament signified him. (See essay: "Jews and Judaism.")

Augustine acknowledges the difficulty of discerning when a sign is literal or figurative. Indeed, he believes God intended the difficulty to exercise and please readers' minds (*De Doctrina Christiana* 2.6.7–2.6.8; see also *Expositions of the Psalms* 140.2). Augustine thus offers a list of patterns according to which Scripture bears multiple or shifting referents (*De Doctrina Christiana* 3.30.42–3.37.56). He derives this list, awkwardly, from Tyconius, a former Donatist who rejected aspects of Donatist theology without joining the Catholic communion. Among Tyconius's rules, Augustine concentrates most on the principle according to which a part (*species*) represents a whole (*genus*). This principle accounts for Old Testament prophecies that switch imperceptibly between references to the nation of Israel and references to the church of all nations (*De Doctrina Christiana* 3.34.47–3.34.49). Augustine relies on this principle throughout *City of God* 16–17.

Augustine's ultimate hermeneutical principle is love. As he writes, any passage that does not promote love for God and neighbor should be interpreted figuratively (*De Doctrina Christiana* 3.10.14; 3.15.23–3.16.24). Since love is the final purpose of Scripture, any interpretation that does not promote love constitutes a failure, whereas readings that misinterpret the author's meaning yet promote love require only mild correction (*De Doctrina Christiana* 1.35.39–1.36.41). There will be no need for Scripture in heaven because Christians will embody perfect love (*De Doctrina Christiana* 1.39.43; *Sermon* 57.7). Augustine's emphasis on love is christological. All Scripture directs readers to Jesus, who came to inspire their love for God and neighbor by his own example (*Instructing Beginners in Faith* 3.6; 4.8). The texts in which Augustine most clearly identifies love with Jesus are his *Expositions of the Psalms*. These sermons also exhibit Augustine's principle of *totus Christus*, according to which the words of the psalmist can represent the words of Christ, the head, or of the church, his body (*Expositions of the Psalms* 140.3–6).

As Augustine matures, he develops stronger confidence in the literal sense. He also affirms the historicity of the literal sense, claiming any apparent discrepancies should be attributed to defective manuscripts, translation errors, or interpretive failures (*Answer to Faustus* 3.5; 11.5; *Letter* 82.1.3). Yet his understanding of the literal sense is more expansive than that of modern interpreters. In *Literal Meaning of Genesis*, he claims that Adam and Eve were actual people and that the tree of life and the tree of the knowledge of good and evil were actual trees (8.1.1–8.7.14). He does not, however, interpret the six days of creation as twenty-four-hour blocks of time (4.18.33; 4.26.43–4.28.45; 4.35.56; 5.1.1–5.3.6). He treats them instead as immaterial, causal principles (*rationes seminales* or *causales*) that were created simultaneously by God and would determine the development of all created things (5.5.12–5.5.16; 5.11.27–5.12.28; 5.23.44–5.23.46; 6.10.17–6.11.19; 6.14.25–6.18.29).

Augustine affirms pursuing the intent of Scripture's human authors as a means of discerning God's intent in the text (*De Doctrina Christiana* 2.5.6). Yet he thinks the human authors may have intended multiple meanings and the Spirit may have intended meanings of which the human authors were unaware (*Confessions* 12.23.32; 12.30.41–12.32.43;

Literal Meaning of Genesis 1.21.41). Readers can profit from any of these interpretations so long as they lead to truth. The gospel writers cared more about meaning than about exact words (*Agreement among the Evangelists* 2.12.28; 2.66.128).

Bibliography

Arnold, Duane W. H., and Pamela Bright, eds. 1995. *De doctrina christiana: A Classic of Western Culture*. Notre Dame, IN: University of Notre Dame Press.

Bonner, Gerald. 1970. "Augustine as Biblical Scholar." In *The Cambridge History of the Bible*. Vol. 1, *From the Beginnings to Jerome,* edited by P. R. Ackroyd and C. F. Evans, 541–63. Cambridge: Cambridge University Press.

Bright, Pamela, ed. and trans. 1999. *Augustine and the Bible*. Notre Dame, IN: University of Notre Dame Press, based on *Bible de tous les temps*. Vol. 3, *Saint Augustin et la Bible*, edited by Anne-Marie La Bonnardière. Paris: Beauchesne, 1986.

Byassee, Jason. 2007. *Praise Seeking Understanding: Reading the Psalms with Augustine*. Grand Rapids: Eerdmans.

Cameron, Michael. 2012a. "Augustine and Scripture." In Vessey, *Blackwell Companion*, 200–214.

———. 2012b. *Christ Meets Me Everywhere: Augustine's Early Figurative Exegesis*. Oxford: Oxford University Press.

Dodd, C. H. 1961. *The Parables of the Kingdom*. Orig. 1935. Glasgow: Collins. (See pp. 13–14 for Dodd's famous critique of Augustine's allegory of the good Samaritan.)

Kannengiesser, Charles. 2006. *Handbook of Patristic Exegesis: The Bible in Ancient Christianity*. Leiden: Brill, 1149–233.

Van Fleteren, Frederick, and Joseph C. Schnaubelt, eds. 2001. *Augustine: Biblical Exegete*. New York: Peter Lang.

Williams, Rowan. 2016. "Language, Reality and Desire: The Nature of Christian Formation." In *On Augustine*, 41–58. Orig. 1989. London: Bloomsbury.

Book 18

1–2, 27, 46–51, 54E

Book 18 is by far the longest book in City of God. *Though difficult to follow, it is crucial to the structure of Augustine's work. To complete Books 15–18, on the development of the two cities, Augustine has to tie up several loose ends. Most significantly, he has not traced the development of the earthly city from the time of Abraham to the Roman empire. He thus backtracks to cover this material in 18.2–26, which begins with Ninus of Assyria, the first king to pursue empire. In 18.27–36, he treats later prophets of the Old Testament, a topic he could not squeeze into Book 17. The next two sections defend the superiority of Scripture over the philosophers (18.37–41) and the inspiration of the Septuagint (18.42–44), the Greek translation of the Old Testament. Augustine then returns to his narrative, concentrating on the Jews and the church from the cessation of the Old Testament prophets to the present time (18.45–54). His treatment of the New Testament is quite brief, as is his treatment of Constantine and the conversion of the emperors.*

1. I promised that, with the help of God's grace, I would refute the enemies of the city of God, who prefer their own gods to Christ its founder and who detest the Christians with a spite and malice that are far more destructive to themselves than to anyone else, and I did this in the first ten books.[1] I also

1. [GWL] Augustine reviews and explains the structure of his work. While he promised in 1.35 to treat the origins, development, and ends of the two cities, he left the length of each

promised that I would then go on to write about the origin, the course, and the destined ends of the two cities, one of which is the city of God and the other the city of this world, in which the city of God dwells so far as its human element is concerned, but only as a pilgrim. With respect to the three parts of this last promise, I offered an account of the origins of the two cities in the four books following the tenth book; and then, in one book, the fifteenth of this work, I gave an account of the course that the two cities followed from the first man down to the flood. Again, from the flood down to Abraham, the two cities ran their course both in time and in our account; but, from Abraham down to the time of the Israelite kings, where we ended the sixteenth book, and then down to the coming of the savior himself in the flesh, where the seventeenth book reaches its close, it is clear that my pen traced only the course of the city of God.[2] In reality, however, this city did not run its course all alone in this world; rather, just as both cities began together, so both experienced the variations of time together in human history. I wrote as I did, however, so that the city of God might stand out the more clearly—without any opposing intrusion on the part of the other city—as it ran its course from the time when God's promises first began to be more open and apparent down to his birth from the virgin, in which the earlier promises were due to be fulfilled. For, up to the revelation of the new covenant, it ran its course not in broad daylight but in shadow. Now, therefore, I see that I must make up for my omission by giving an account of the course followed by that other city from the time of Abraham on down, and the account should at least be full enough to allow the reader to consider the contrast between the two cities.

---

section undefined. Here he specifies that he treated the origins of the two cities in Books 11–14 and their development in Books 15–18. This material follows Augustine's delineation of history according to the days of creation. See essay: "Last Things."

2. [GWL] From Book 15 through 16.11, Augustine treated the two cities concurrently. At 16.12, when Augustine came to Abraham, he turned exclusively to the heavenly city, whose story corresponds with the Old Testament. Augustine completed most of that material in Book 17. In Book 18, he moves backward in history to the earthly city from Abraham's time on. Abraham lived during the time of Ninus, the founder of Nineveh and the progenitor of the Assyrian empire (4.6). Augustine thus begins with Ninus in 18.2. As Book 18 proceeds, Augustine fills in gaps from the earlier books and moves the story forward: 18.2–26 treats Ninus to the beginning of Rome; 18.27–44 treats prophets from later in Israel's history; and 18.45–54 treats the cessation of the prophets, the history of the Jews under foreign rulers, the incarnation, the scattering of the Jews, and the early church to Augustine's time. Book 18 ends its history of the earthly city with the beginning of Rome because Book 3 already treated the rest of Rome's history through Christ. Augustine's discussion of the incarnation is surprisingly brief (18.49), perhaps because he already treated it in Book 10. For more on the structure of *City of God*, see above: "Interpretation," in the introduction.

The Divisions in Human Society

2. The society of mortals, then, was spread everywhere across the earth, and, despite all its different locations, it was still bound together by a kind of fellowship in one and the same nature, even though each group pursued its own advantage and followed its own desires.[3] What people want, however, is never enough for anyone, or at least not for everyone, because they do not all want the same thing; and so human society is largely at odds with itself, and, whenever one part gains a position of strength, it oppresses another. For the vanquished submit to the victor, and they prefer to have peace and security at any price rather than power or even liberty.[4] And this is so universally true that it is a source of astonishment whenever anyone would rather die than lose his liberty. For, in almost all peoples, the voice of nature has somehow declared that those who suffer defeat should prefer to be subject to the victors than to be wholly eradicated by the devastation of war. And so it happened—although not apart from the providence of God, in whose power it lies to determine who falls under another's rule in war and who imposes his rule on others—that some peoples were endowed with kingdoms and some were subjected to the rule of others. But among the many kingdoms on earth into which the society that pursues earthly advantage and follows earthly desire has been divided—the society to which we give the all-embracing name of "the city of this world"—we see that two have come to stand out far more sharply than the rest: first that of the Assyrians, and then that of the Romans.[5] These two are related to and distinguished from each other in terms of both time and space. For, just as the one arose earlier and the other later, so the one arose in the east and the other in the west; and, finally, the beginning of the latter came immediately

3. [GWL] Perhaps a reference to Gen. 11 and the tower of Babel, after which the nations were scattered across the earth. Because citizens of the earthly city pursue their own "advantage" and "desires" (*utilitates et cupiditates suas quibusque sectantibus*), i.e., earthly goods, the earthly city tends toward competition and conflict. Oppression is a near universal feature of the earthly city, as the more powerful kill or enslave the less powerful. This section is one of the most important descriptions of the earthly city in *City of God*, summarizing the history Augustine has recounted to this point.

4. See Lucan, *Pharsalia* 4.577–79.

5. [GWL] Augustine pairs Rome and Assyria, which he conflates with Babylon, as the two dominant empires in world history. Toward the end of 18.2, he will even call Rome a "second Babylon" and Babylon a "first Rome." See also 4.6–7; 5.13; and 18.22. Augustine's history reflects his understanding of the earthly city as a community that spans time and space. The earthly city is defined not by historical era or physical territory but by moral qualities.

after the end of the former.[6] And I would say that all other kingdoms and kings are like appendages of these.

Assyria as the "First Rome" and Rome as the "Second Babylon"

When Abraham was born in the land of the Chaldeans, then, Ninus was already ruling as the second king of the Assyrians, in succession to his father Bel, the first king of that kingdom.[7] At that time, there was also the extremely small kingdom of the Sicyonians,[8] and, because this kingdom was so ancient, Marcus Varro, a man of great learning in all fields, began his work *On the Race of the Roman People* with an account of it.[9] From the kings of Sicyon, he turns to the Athenians, and then to the Latins, and finally to the Romans. But the powers that he mentions prior to the founding of Rome are of little account in comparison with the kingdom of the Assyrians. This is true despite the fact that even the Roman historian Sallust admits that the Athenians gained the highest standing in Greece, although more in reputation than in reality.[10] For in describing them he says, "The achievements of the Athenians, in my view, were great and glorious enough, but still rather less than their reputation suggests. But, because writers of great genius emerged in that city, the deeds of the Athenians are celebrated throughout the world as the greatest accomplishments. Thus the valor of those who performed these deeds is considered to equal the ability of writers of genius to praise them in words."[11] It is also true that this city won no little glory from literature and philosophy, for such studies flourished there to a remarkable degree. So far as imperial rule is concerned, however, there was no greater power in early times than that of the Assyrians, and none that extended so far and wide. In fact King Ninus, Bel's son, is reported to have subjugated all Asia as far

6. See below at 18.27.

7. [GWL] Ninus was the king of Assyria at the time of Abraham. He was the first ruler to pursue war for the sake of acquiring territory and not just for self-defense. As the first king of an empire, he is thus a paradigm for later rulers. See 4.6–7 and 16.17.

8. See . . . 16.17 and [*City of God, Books 11–22*, 207n76].

9. For Augustine's lengthy encomium of Varro's scholarship see . . . 6.2. His work *On the Race of the Roman People* exists only in fragments.

10. [GWL] Augustine stresses the importance of Assyria and downplays Greece. Though the Greeks were not an especially powerful people, their writers produced and preserved their outsized reputation.

11. *Catiline Conspiracy* 8.

as the borders of Lydia,[12] and Asia is counted as one of the three parts of the whole world, although in geographical extent it is actually found to cover half of the world.[13] The truth is that the only people in the regions of the east that Ninus did not bring under his rule were the Indians, and even they were attacked after his death by his wife Semiramis.[14] Thus, it came about that all the peoples and kings in those lands submitted to the rule and authority of the Assyrians and did whatever the Assyrians commanded them to do.

Abraham, then, was born in that kingdom, among the Chaldaeans, in the time of Ninus. But Greek history is much better known to us than Assyrian history, and those who have investigated the ancient origins of the race of the Roman people have traced a chronological sequence that runs through the Greeks to the Latins and then to the Romans, who themselves are also Latins.[15] As a consequence, we must provide the names of the Assyrian kings, where necessary, in order to show how Babylon—the first Rome, as it were—runs its course along with the city of God on its pilgrimage in this world. At the same time, however, the points that we need to bring into this work for the sake of comparing the two cities—that is, the earthly and the heavenly—we should take rather from Greek and Latin history, in which Rome itself is like a second Babylon.[16]

The Earthly Kingdoms and Their Gods from Abraham to the Exodus

When Abraham was born, then, two second kings were ruling, Ninus over the Assyrians in succession to Bel, and Europs over the Sicyons in succession to Aegialeus.[17] But by the time when, after Abraham had departed from Babylonia, God promised him that a great people would come from him and that all peoples would be blessed in his seed,[18] the Assyrians had their fourth king and the Sicyonians their fifth. For the son of Ninus ruled over the Assyrians

12. See . . . 4.6 and 16.17.
13. See . . . 16.17 and [*City of God, Books 11–22*, 207n78].
14. See Eusebius, *Chronicles* 1.15.
15. [GWL] Augustine's account of the earthly city will focus disproportionately on Greece, despite its insignificance compared to Assyria. This discrepancy reflects the sources available to Augustine. He has much more material on the Greeks than the Assyrians.
16. See Rev. 14:8.
17. [GWL] From this point through 18.27, Augustine coordinates developments in the earthly city with developments in the heavenly city, relying on Eusebius's *Chronicle* (see essay). The narrative Augustine develops should not be taken as historically accurate or complete.
18. See Gen. 17:3–8.

after his mother Semiramis. It is said that Semiramis was killed by her son because she, his mother, had dared to defile him by incestuous intercourse.[19] Some people even think that Semiramis actually founded Babylon, and she could in fact have rebuilt the city.[20] But I have already indicated when and how Babylon was founded in the sixteenth book.[21] Further, the son of Ninus and Semiramis, who succeeded his mother in rule, is himself also called Ninus by some, although others call him Ninyas,[22] a name derived from that of his father. At this point, the kingdom of the Sicyonians was held by Telxion. During his reign, the times were so mild and pleasant in Sicyon that, at his death, people worshiped him as a god, offering sacrifices and celebrating games which they say were first instituted in his honor.[23]

◆

The Hebrew Prophets: Hosea, Amos, Isaiah, Micah, Jonah, and Joel

27. So that we can turn to the era of the prophets, then, let us step back a bit in time.[24] At the beginning of the Book of Hosea the prophet, who is placed first among the twelve,[25] it is written, *The word of the Lord that came to Hosea in the days of Uzziah, Jotham, Ahaz, and Hezekiah, kings of Judah* (Hos 1:1). Amos, too, writes that he prophesied in the days of King Uzziah, and he adds the name of Jeroboam, king of Israel, who also ruled in those days.[26] Again, Isaiah, the son of Amos (whether of the prophet just mentioned or, as is more widely held, of another man of the same name who was not a prophet), also lists at the start of his book the same four kings that Hosea had

---

19. See Eusebius, *Chronicles* 1.15.
20. See Eusebius, *Chronicles* 1.15.
21. See . . . 16.4.
22. See Eusebius, *Chronicles* 1.14.
23. NCP: "There is no record in Augustine's surviving sources of these honors paid to Telxion (or Thelxion)." [GWL] In the chapters that follow, Augustine names many dead people from non-Christian and non-Roman history who were deified. These individuals were not truly gods; people just worshiped them as such. Though the following chapters are not included in this book, they serve an important purpose in *City of God* by recounting the history of the earthly city to the founding of Rome. As this history reveals, the earthly city has persistently been defined by idolatry. See above: "Interpretation," in the introduction; and essay: "Roman Religion."
24. [GWL] This chapter locates the later prophets in the history Augustine has been recounting. Hosea, Amos, Isaiah, Micah, Jonah, and Joel all prophesied around the same time.
25. I.e., the twelve so-called "minor prophets," whose designation is explained . . . at 18.29.
26. See Amos 1:1.

named, and he says that he prophesied in their days.[27] Micah, too, indicates that he prophesied in the same times, after the days of Uzziah. For he names the three following kings, whom Hosea had also named—Jotham, Ahaz, and Hezekiah.[28] From their own writings, then, we find that these men all prophesied in the same period. To them are added Jonah, during the reign of the same King Uzziah, and Joel, who prophesied during the reign of Jotham, the successor of Uzziah. But we could only discover the dates of these two prophets in *The Chronicles*[29] rather than in their own writings, which say nothing about when they prophesied. The period of these prophets extends, then, from Procas, king of the Latins, or his predecessor Aventinus, down to Romulus, now king of the Romans, or even down to the start of the reign of Numa Pompilius, Romulus's successor, since Hezekiah, the king of Judah, reigned until that date. And so we see that these men all erupted together, like fountains of prophecy, at the point when the Assyrian kingdom faded out and the Roman kingdom began.[30] Thus, just as in the first days of the kingdom of the Assyrians Abraham appeared, and to him were given the most manifest promises that in his seed all peoples would be blessed,[31] so also at the first rise of the western Babylon,[32] during whose rule Christ was to come, in whom those promises would be fulfilled, the lips of the prophets were opened to testify to this great future event not only in speech but also in writing. For, although the people of Israel had hardly ever been without prophets from the moment when they began to have kings, those prophets were only for their benefit, not for the benefit of the peoples at large. But, when the prophetic Scriptures were being more openly established, which would ultimately be of benefit to the nations at large, it was appropriate that this should start at the very point when the city that would rule the nations was also being established.

------◆------

27. See Isa. 1:1.
28. See Mic. 1:1.
29. I.e., in the work of that title by Eusebius.
30. [GWL] Augustine correlates the writings of the later prophets with the rise of the Romans, during whose rule Christ would come. The alignment of these events resembles another alignment—that between the promises to Abraham and the rise of the Assyrians. There was intense prophetic activity at the beginnings of both Assyria and Rome, the two greatest empires. Augustine perceives these interconnections as communications of divine providence. God uses prophecies to signal major developments in world history.
31. See Gen. 12:2–3; 15:5; 17:4; 18:18; 22:17–18.
32. I.e., Rome, as it is also referred to in Rev. 17:5 and thereafter.

The Coming of Christ in Fulfillment of Prophecy

46. During the reign of Herod in Judea,[33] then, and when, after the change in the republic's status,[34] Caesar Augustus had become emperor[35] and brought peace to the world, Christ was born in Bethlehem of Judah in accord with the earlier prophecy.[36] Outwardly he was human, a man born from a human virgin; hiddenly he was God from God the Father. For this is what the prophet had foretold: *See, a virgin shall conceive in her womb and bear a son, and they shall call him Emmanuel, which means God with us* (Isa. 7:14; Matt. 1:23). And, in order to show himself as God, he performed many miracles, of which the scriptural Gospels contain as many as seemed sufficient to proclaim him. The first of these is that he was born in such a miraculous way, and the last is that he ascended into heaven with his body, which had itself been raised from the dead. But the Jews, who put him to death and would not believe in him (since it was necessary for him to die and rise again), suffered even more miserable devastation at the hands of the Romans.[37] They were utterly uprooted from their kingdom, where they were already under the dominion of a foreign power, and were scattered through the world.[38] In fact there is no place in the world where they are not present. Through their own Scriptures, then, they bear witness for us that we did not make up the prophecies about Christ. In fact a great many of them, reflecting on those prophecies both before his passion and most especially after his resurrection, have come to believe in him, and these are the Jews of whom it was foretold, *Though the number of the children of Israel were like the sand of the sea, a remnant of them shall be saved* (Isa. 10:22).[39] The rest, however, were made blind, and of them it was foretold, *Let their table become a trap before them*

---

33. See Matt. 2:1.

34. [GWL] Augustine is referring to Rome's transition from a republic to an empire under the leadership of Octavian, Augustus Caesar.

35. See Luke 2:1.

36. See Mic. 5:2.

37. [GWL] It was common in early Christianity to interpret the destruction of the Jewish temple in 70 CE as a punishment against the Jews for crucifying Jesus.

38. [GWL] Like other early Christian authors, Augustine conflates the destruction of the temple (70 CE) and the Bar Kokhba revolt (135 CE). After the latter event, the Jews were banned from Jerusalem and scattered around the empire. Augustine sees this scattering as providential, for the Jews took with them their Scriptures (what Christians call the "Old Testament"), which speak of Christ. This is Augustine's Jewish "witness doctrine," according to which Jews provided inadvertent testimony to Jesus. See essay: "Jews and Judaism."

39. [GWL] Augustine acknowledges that many Jews at the time of Jesus believed in him and received salvation. He will also assert, however, that the rest of the Jews were made "blind" in

*and a retribution and a stumbling block; let their eyes be darkened to keep
them from seeing and their backs be always bent over* (Ps. 69:22–23). Thus,
when they do not believe our Scriptures, their own Scriptures, which they read
with blind eyes,[40] are fulfilled in them. Someone might say, of course, that the
Christians made up the prophecies about Christ that are cited under the name
of the Sibyl or under the name of others—if any—who do not belong to the
Jewish people. For us, however, the prophecies that come from the books of
our enemies are enough, for we recognize that it is precisely for the sake of
bearing this testimony, which they unwillingly provide for us simply by having
and preserving those books, that they were themselves scattered through all
peoples, wherever the Church of Christ spreads.

For this very thing was itself prophesied in advance in the Psalms, which
they also read, where it is written, *My God, his mercy shall go before me.
My God has shown me with regard to my enemies: do not kill them, lest
they some day forget your law; scatter them in your power* (Ps. 59:10–11).[41]
Thus God has shown the Church the grace of his mercy with regard to her
enemies the Jews, for, as the Apostle says, *Their sin is the salvation of the
gentiles* (Rom. 11:11). Thus the reason why God did not kill them—that is,
the reason why he did not put an end to their being as Jews, despite the fact
that they were conquered and oppressed by the Romans—is precisely so that
they would not forget the law of God and, as a result, be unable to bear the
testimony that we are discussing here. That is why it was not enough for the
Psalm to say, *Do not kill them, lest they some day forget your law*, without
also adding *scatter them* (Ps. 59:11). For if the Jews, with the testimony that
they bear from Scripture, were only in their own land and not everywhere,
then the Church, which is everywhere, obviously could not have them as witnesses in all nations to the prophecies that were given in advance about Christ.

47. As a consequence, if it has come or should come to our attention that
any foreigner—that is, anyone not born of Israel and not accepted by that
people into the canon of Sacred Scripture—is read to have prophesied something about Christ, he can be cited by us as additional confirmation. It is not

---

that they could not see that their own Scriptures were fulfilled in Christ. According to Augustine,
their rejection of Jesus was itself foretold in their Scriptures (Ps. 69:22–23).

40. See 2 Cor. 3:15.

41. [GWL] Augustine interprets this passage as a prophecy of the Jews from the time of
Christ. First, God has protected the Jews from destruction so that they might guard the Scrip-
tures that testify to Christ. Second, the Jews have been scattered so that they would testify to
Christ around the empire.

that we have need of any such outside testimony, even if it were lacking. It is rather that there is nothing inappropriate in believing that there were also people in other nations to whom this mystery was revealed and who were also driven to proclaim it.[42] This is so regardless of whether they participated in the same grace from God or whether, quite apart from that grace, they were taught by evil angels—who, as we know, confessed Christ when he was present, even though the Jews did not acknowledge him.[43] For I do not think that even the Jews themselves dare to claim that, from the very beginning of Israel's line, after the rejection of his older brother,[44] no one other than the Israelites has ever belonged to God. It is quite true, of course, that there was no other people that could properly be called the people of God, but the Jews still cannot deny that there were also some people in other nations who belonged, not by earthly but by heavenly association, to the true Israelites who are citizens of the homeland above.[45] For, if they deny this, there is nothing easier than to refute them by referring to the holy and extraordinary man Job, who was neither a native-born Israelite nor a proselyte (that is, an outsider admitted into the people of Israel).[46] He came rather from the race of Edom,[47] and that is where he was born as well as where he died. But he is so highly praised in the divine discourses that no one of his time is his equal so far as righteousness and piety

42. [GWL] Augustine affirms the possibility of revelation from non-Christian sources. These sources could still be untrustworthy, though, like the demons who sometimes spoke truth about Jesus. See 18.23, where Augustine claims the Erythraean Sibyl prophesied of Christ; and see essay: "Roman Religion."

43. See, e.g., Matt. 8:29 par.; Mark 1:24.

44. See Gen. 27:1–40.

45. A thought similar to that which Augustine develops here and in the following lines can be found in Justin Martyr, 1 Apology 46.

46. [GWL] If Job was not an Israelite, he proves the heavenly city before Christ was not restricted to the nation of Israel. Augustine also defends the possibility of salvation before Christ outside Israel in Letter 102.12–15 and Sermon Dolbeau 26.36–38 (included as Sermon 198 in vol. III/11 of the New City Press series). In later writings, he stresses that these individuals received revelation of Christ, who spoke in visions before the incarnation, and that salvation was granted according to God's determination and not just foreknowledge of humans' response. See Grace of Christ and Original Sin 2.24.28; Letters 164.1.1; 164.2.4; 164.4.12–164.4.13; 164.6.17–164.6.18; and Predestination of the Saints 9.17–10.19, which quotes Letter 102 and qualifies its appeal to foreknowledge. For examples besides Job, Augustine names Melchizedek and the Ninevites who repented at Jonah's preaching. For further discussion, see Aimé Solignac, "Le salut des païens d'après la prédication d'Augustin," in Augustin prédicateur (395–411): Actes du Colloque International de Chantilly (5–7 septembre 1996), ed. Goulven Madec (Paris: Études Augustiniennes, 1998), 419–28; Robert Dodaro, "Agostino d'Ippona, Sermo Dolbeau 26 e la questione della salus extra ecclesiam," Lateranum 68, no. 2/3 (2002): 259–66; and Dodaro, "The Secret Justice of God and the Gift of Humility," Augustinian Studies 34, no. 1 (2003): 83–96, esp. 84–87.

47. Job is said in Job 1:1 to have come from Uz, which is identified with Edom in Lam. 4:21.

are concerned.[48] And, although we do not find his dates in *The Chronicles*, we gather from his book—which the Israelites accepted into their authoritative canon on its merits—that he came in the third generation after Israel.[49]

I have no doubt that it was due to divine providence that, by virtue of this one man, we know that there could also be people of other nations who lived according to God, were pleasing to him, and belonged to the spiritual Jerusalem. We should not believe, however, that this was granted to anyone to whom there was not revealed *the one mediator between God and man, the man Christ Jesus* (1 Tim. 2:5), whose coming in the flesh was foretold to the saints of old, just as his having come was announced to us; and so the result is that, through him, one and the same faith leads to God all who are predestined for the city of God, the house of God, the temple of God. It remains possible, however, to suppose that any prophecies about the grace of God through Jesus Christ[50] that come from other sources were actually concocted by the Christians; and so there is no surer way of convincing outsiders, if they argue this point (and of making them ours, if they show good sense) than to cite the divine predictions about Christ that are written in the books of the Jews. It is, then, due to the expulsion of the Jews from their own homes and their dispersal throughout the entire world to bear this testimony that the Church has everywhere grown and increased.[51]

48. This house of God is of greater glory than was that former house built of wood and stone and other precious materials and metals.[52] Thus, the prophecy of Haggai[53] was not fulfilled by the rebuilding of that former Temple. For that Temple can never be shown to have had as much glory after it was rebuilt as it had in the time of Solomon. On the contrary, the diminished glory of that house is shown first by the cessation of prophecy and then by the terrible disasters that came upon the people themselves, right down to the final destruction inflicted by the Romans, as the events we mentioned above all testify. But this house, which belongs to the new covenant, is certainly of

48. See Job 1:1; Ezek. 14:14–20; James 5:11.
49. Nothing in the book of Job suggests this.
50. See Rom. 7:25.
51. [GWL] Augustine returns to the witness doctrine.
52. [GWL] A reference to 18.45, where Augustine interpreted Haggai's prophecy of a new "house" as a reference to the church and not to the Jewish temple. The temple built by Solomon was destroyed by the Babylonians and subsequently rebuilt. According to Augustine, this rebuilt temple was not as glorious as Solomon's original temple, and its rebuilding was followed by the cessation of prophecy and by subjugation to foreign nations. Far more glorious is the church, the new temple God has established in Christ.
53. See Hag. 2:9.

greater glory, in that *living stones* (1 Pet. 2:5) are better. For it is built of people, who believe and have been made new.[54] It was signified by the rebuilding of that former Temple, however, because the rebuilding of that Temple itself signified by prophetic discourse another covenant, which is called the new covenant. Thus, when God said, through the prophet just mentioned, *And I will give peace in this place* (Hag. 2:9), we should understand that the word place stands for that which it signifies. And so, because what was rebuilt in that place signified the Church, which was going to be built through Christ, we should take *I will give peace in this place* to mean nothing other than "I will give peace in the place which this place signifies." For anything that signifies something else seems in a sense to play the part of the thing that it signifies. For instance, the Apostle said, *The rock was Christ* (1 Cor. 10:4), because the rock of which he spoke undoubtedly signified Christ. Thus, the glory of this house, the new covenant, is greater than the glory of the former house, the old covenant; and it will appear even greater when it is dedicated.[55]

For that is when *the one desired by all peoples shall come* (Hag. 2:7), as the Hebrew reads. His first coming was not yet desired by all peoples, for they did not know the one whom they ought to desire, since they had not yet believed in him. That is also when, according to the translators of the Septuagint (and this too has a prophetic sense), *the Lord's elect shall come from all peoples* (Hag. 2:7 LXX).[56] For then it is only the elect that will come, of whom the Apostle says, *Just as he chose us in him before the foundation of the world* (Eph. 1:4). And the master builder himself, who said, *Many are called, but few are chosen* (Matt. 22:14), is going to show us a house built not of those who were called but only came in such a way that they were thrown out of the feast[57] but rather of the elect—a house that will have no fear of downfall from then on. For now, however, while the churches are full of those whom the winnowing will separate out as though on a threshing floor,[58] the glory of this house is not yet as fully apparent as it will be when everyone who is there will be there forever.[59]

54. I.e., in baptism.
55. [GWL] Augustine is interpreting the dedication of the temple as a reference to Christ's return, when he will finally establish his people by separating true Christians from false Christians.
56. [GWL] The word "elect" runs throughout this paragraph, a point this translation somewhat obscures. Eph. 1:4 could read, "Just as he elected [*elegit*] us in him," and Matt. 22:14 could read, "Many are called, but few are elected [*electi*]." On election, see essay: "Predestination and the Will."
57. See Matt. 22:11–13.
58. See Luke 3:17.
59. [GWL] Here and in the next paragraph, Augustine speaks of false Christians within the church who claim to have faith but do not belong to the heavenly city. The church will remain

49. In this malignant world, then, and in these evil days, the Church is preparing through her present humiliation for her future exaltation. She is being schooled by the stings of fear, by the torments of sorrow, by the hardships of toil, and by the dangers of temptation, and it is only in hope that she rejoices,[60] when her rejoicing is well founded.[61] Many of the reprobate are mixed in with the good. Both are gathered, so to speak, in the nets of the Gospel, and in this world, as in the sea, both swim about without distinction, enclosed in those nets until drawn to shore, where the evil will be separated from the good[62] and *God may be all in all* (1 Cor. 15:28) in the good as in his temple. We now recognize, in fact, that the words are fulfilled of the one who spoke in the Psalm and said, *I have announced and have spoken; they are multiplied beyond number* (Ps. 40:5). This is now coming to pass, and it has been coming to pass from the moment when, first through the mouth of his forerunner John and then through his own mouth, he announced and spoke, saying, *Repent, for the kingdom of heaven has come near* (Matt. 3:2; 4:17).

He chose disciples (whom he also called apostles[63]) of low birth, without honor or learning, so that, if they were or did anything great, it would be he himself who was or did that great thing in them.[64] He included one among them who was evil[65] but whom he used for good, both to fulfill his destined suffering and to give his Church an example of bearing with the evil.[66] And,

---

a mixed body until the return of Christ, who will separate the wheat (true Christians) from the chaff (false Christians). Only then will the full glory of the church be revealed. Augustine's position on this matter was central to his arguments against the Donatists. See 1.35.

60. See Rom. 12:12.

61. [GWL] A striking passage given the ascendance of imperial Christianity under Constantine and his successors. Despite this political reality, Augustine describes the present time as an era of suffering and temptation that the church must endure until Christ's return.

62. See Matt. 13:47–50.

63. See Luke 6:13.

64. [GWL] Augustine's treatment of the incarnation in this paragraph is surprisingly short, given the length he dedicates to other topics in *City of God*. This may be because Book 10 already treated Christ's identity as mediator between God and humanity, and that discussion concluded an extended analysis of mediation in Books 8–9. See John C. Cavadini, "Epilogue: The Architectonic Plan of *The City of God*," in Meconi, *COG*, 297–320.

65. I.e., Judas Iscariot. See Matt. 10:4 par.

66. [GWL] Judas Iscariot's presence among the disciples furnishes a powerful example of the church's character as a mixed body. As Augustine writes elsewhere, Jesus shared the bread and the wine with Judas Iscariot at the very institution of the Lord's Supper (*Answer to the Writings of Petilian* 2.22.50; *Expositions of the Psalms* 10.6; *Letters* 43.8.23; 44.5.10; 93.4.15; *Sermon* 266.7). Jesus's willingness to "bear with" (root word: *tolerare*) Judas is a model for how Christians should bear with false Christians in the church.

when he had sowed the holy Gospel, so far as it was right for him to sow it through his bodily presence, he suffered, died, and rose again, showing by his passion what we ought to endure for the sake of the truth and by his resurrection what we ought to hope for in eternity (to say nothing of the profound mystery[67] in which his blood was shed for the remission of sins[68]). He remained on earth for forty days with his disciples, and then, before their eyes, he ascended into heaven.[69] Ten days later he sent the Holy Spirit,[70] as he had promised,[71] and the greatest and most compelling sign of the Spirit's coming into those who believed was that each of them spoke in the tongues of all peoples,[72] signifying that the unity of the Catholic Church would embrace all peoples and thus would speak in all languages.

The Spreading of the Church: Persecutions and Consolations

50. Then came the fulfillment of the prophecy, *The law shall go forth from Zion and the word of the Lord from Jerusalem* (Isa. 2:3); and the fulfillment of the Lord Christ's own predictions when he appeared to his amazed disciples after his resurrection and *opened their minds to understand the Scriptures, and he said to them, Thus it is written, that the Christ was to suffer and to rise from the dead on the third day, and that repentance and forgiveness of sins is to be proclaimed to all peoples, beginning from Jerusalem* (Luke 24:45–47); and again, when he replied to those who were asking about his final coming and said, *It is not for you to know the times that the Father has put in his own power, but you shall receive the power of the Holy Spirit when it comes upon you, and you shall be my witnesses in Jerusalem, in all Judea and Samaria, and to the very ends of the earth* (Acts 1:7–8).[73]

67. "Mystery": *sacramenti.*
68. See Matt. 26:28 par. Augustine is referring here both to Christ's suffering and death and to the eucharist.
69. See Acts 1:3–9.
70. See Acts 2:1–4.
71. See John 14:16–17:26, esp. 15:26.
72. See Acts 2:6–11.
73. [GWL] Each of these passages (Isa. 2:3; Luke 24:45–47; and Acts 1:7–8) refers to the gospel's spread from Jerusalem to all nations. This was another point of contention against the Donatists, who tended to restrict the church to Roman Africa on the grounds that the churches in fellowship with Caecilian were tainted. According to Augustine, this position entailed rejecting the catholic communion around the Mediterranean and denying Christ's promise that the gospel would be proclaimed among all peoples.

For the Church first spread out from Jerusalem, and, when a great many in Judea and Samaria had believed, it then went on to other peoples, as the Gospel was proclaimed by those whom Christ himself had prepared by his word, like lamps, and had set alight by the Holy Spirit. For he had said to them, *Do not fear those who kill the body but cannot kill the soul* (Matt. 10:28), and, so that they would not be frozen with fear, they burned with the fire of love. Finally, the Gospel was proclaimed throughout the entire world, not only by those who had seen and heard Christ both before his passion and after his resurrection but also, after their death, by their successors, in the midst of dreadful persecutions, all sorts of torture, and the deaths of the martyrs. And God himself bore witness by signs and prodigies and various displays of power and by the gifts of the Holy Spirit, so that the peoples of the nations, believing in him who was crucified for their redemption, might venerate with Christian love the very blood of the martyrs that they had shed in devilish fury, and so that the rulers by whose laws the Church was being ravaged might savingly become subject to the very name that they had ruthlessly tried to erase from the face of the earth, and might begin to persecute the false gods for whose sake the worshipers of the true God had been persecuted before.[74]

51. But when the devil saw that the temples of the demons were deserted and that all humanity was rushing to the name of the mediator who sets men free, he stirred up heretics who call themselves Christian but oppose Christian teaching.[75] As if heretics could be contained indiscriminately in the city

74. [GWL] A reference to Constantine and his successors. Augustine's treatment of this period is sparse and muted. He affords it only a few lines. This is partly because he already treated the Christian emperors in 5.24–26. It is also because he qualifies their theological significance. The Christianization of the empire is not the culmination of history, nor does it augur Christ's return. Roman history cannot be conflated with redemptive history. Augustine supports this point in 18.52 when he affirms the possibility of the church suffering persecution again before the last things.

75. [GWL] Since the devil could no longer attack the church using outside enemies, he raised up enemies from within the church—namely, those who promoted false teachings. Augustine calls these individuals "heretics." He probably means groups like the Arians, Eunomians, Sabellians, Photinians, Donatists, and Pelagians (*Sermons* 182–83). For Augustine, heresy involves more than doctrinal error; it is also a stubborn refusal to receive correction. Augustine's position on heresy is complex, and it changed throughout his career. During the final years of his life, he began a work called *Heresies* in which he stated that heresy is very difficult, perhaps impossible, to define (*preface*.7). He died before completing the work or attempting a new definition. For more on Augustine and heresy, see Robert Dodaro, "'Omnes haeretici negant Christum in carne uenisse' (Aug., *serm.* 183.9.13): Augustine on the Incarnation as Criterion for Orthodoxy," *Augustinian Studies* 38, no. 1 (2007): 163–74; Maureen A. Tilley, "When Schism Becomes Heresy in Late Antiquity: Developing Doctrinal Deviance in the Wounded Body of Christ," *Journal of Early Christian Studies* 15, no. 1 (2007): 1–21; Erika T. Hermanowicz, *Possidius of Calama: A Study of the North African Episcopate at the Time of Augustine* (Oxford: Oxford University Press,

of God without any correction, in the same way that the city of confusion[76] indiscriminately contained philosophers who took different and mutually opposed positions! Thus, if anyone in the Church of Christ holds diseased and depraved opinions and, when corrected to bring him to sound and right views, resists and stubbornly refuses to revise his pernicious and deadly teachings but instead persists in defending them, he becomes a heretic; and, when he leaves the Church, he is counted among the enemies who put the Church to the test. Such people even turn out to benefit the true and catholic members of Christ by their very wickedness, for God puts even the evil to good use, and *all things work together for good for those who love God* (Rom. 8:28). In fact all the Church's enemies, no matter how blinded by error or corrupted by malice, serve a useful purpose. If they have the power of inflicting bodily harm on the Church, they train it in patience; if they oppose it only by holding evil opinions, they train it in wisdom; and, in addition, whether it is with persuasive doctrine or with strict discipline that the Church addresses them, they train it in benevolence, or even in beneficence, so that even its enemies are loved.[77]

Thus, even the devil, the prince of the ungodly city, is not allowed to do any harm to the Church when he stirs up his own vessels against the city of God on its pilgrimage here in this world. Beyond doubt, divine providence provides that city with both the consolation of prosperity, so that it is not broken by adversity, and the discipline of adversity, so that it is not corrupted by prosperity;[78] and each is so tempered by the other that we recognize that the saying in the Psalm—*According to the multitude of my heart's sorrows, your consolations have cheered my soul* (Ps. 94:19)—arises from no other source. And the words of the Apostle have the same basis: *Rejoicing in hope, patient in suffering* (Rom. 12:12).

In fact no one should think that there is any time when another saying of the same teacher fails to apply: *All who want to live a godly life in Christ*

2008), 92–93, 128–32; Todd S. Berzon, *Classifying Christians: Ethnography, Heresiology, and the Limits of Knowledge in Late Antiquity* (Oakland: University of California Press, 2016), 218–45.

76. I.e., Babylon, which means "confusion" and which symbolizes the earthly city. See . . . 16.4.

77. [GWL] Augustine approves stern measures to address heretics, including excommunication. Discipline is ultimately benevolent, since it intends the spiritual wellbeing of those who receive it. This perspective shapes Augustine's writings on several challenging topics, including war, capital punishment, slavery, and the coercion of the Donatists. On church discipline, see Tarsicius van Bavel, "Discipline," in *AttA*, 273–76; Allan D. Fitzgerald, "Penance," in *AttA*, 640–46; J. Patout Burns Jr. and Robin M. Jensen, *Christianity in Roman Africa: The Development of Its Practices and Beliefs* (Grand Rapids: Eerdmans, 2014), 333–54.

78. [GWL] A concise summary of Augustine's theology of suffering, most clearly articulated in 1.8–9. See essay: "Providence and Suffering."

suffer persecution (2 Tim. 3:12). Even when those on the outside do not rage, and there appears to be, and really is, tranquility, which is a great consolation, especially to the weak, there are still some on the inside—indeed, there are many—who by their dissipated morals torment the hearts of those who live pious lives.[79] They cause the name of "Christian" and "Catholic" to be blasphemed, and, the more precious this name is to those who want to live a godly life in Christ, the more deeply they are pained that, due to the wicked on the inside, it is less loved than the minds of the godly desire. And the heretics as well, since they are thought to have the Christian name and sacraments and Scriptures and creed, cause great pain in the hearts of the godly. For many who want to become Christians are compelled to hesitate due to the heretics' dissensions, and many revilers also find in them some ground for blaspheming the Christian name, since even the heretics are called Christians in one sense or another. It is due to these, and to other such depraved morals and human errors, that those who want to live a godly life in Christ suffer persecution, even when no one attacks or mistreats them in the body. For they suffer this persecution not in their bodies but in their hearts, and that is why the Psalm says *according to the multitude of my heart's* sorrows rather than "my body's."

At the same time, because the divine promises are considered immutable, and because the Apostle says, *The Lord knows those who are his* (2 Tim. 2:19), *for those whom he foreknew he also predestined to be conformed to the image of his Son* (Rom. 8:29), none of the elect can perish. And that is why the Psalm goes on to say, *Your consolations have cheered my soul.* In fact the very sorrow that strikes the hearts of the godly when they are persecuted by the misdeeds of evil or false Christians is actually of benefit to those who feel it. For it stems from a love due to which they do not want such people either to perish themselves or to be an obstacle to the salvation of others. Above all, great consolations come from the correction of these people, which flood the souls of the godly with a joy as great as were the sorrows that tormented them at the prospect that these people might be lost. And it is in this way that the Church runs its course on its pilgrimage in this world, in these evil days, amid the persecutions of the world and the consolations of God, not simply from the time of the bodily presence of Christ and his apostles but all the way

---

79. [GWL] Augustine is probably referring here to those who have received baptism yet continue to participate in immoral Roman practices like the spectacles. He frequently condemns such behavior in his sermons. See essay: "Roman Spectacles."

from Abel himself, the first righteous man,[80] who was killed by his ungodly brother,[81] and ultimately on down to the end of this age.[82]

54e.[83] Now, however, let us at last bring this book to a close.[84] Up to this point, we have discussed and demonstrated, as far as seemed sufficient, the mortal course of the two cities, the heavenly and the earthly, which are mingled together from start to finish. One of them, the earthly city, has made for itself whatever false gods it wanted, creating them from anything at all, even from human beings, and serving them with sacrifices. The other, the heavenly city, which is on pilgrimage here on earth, does not make up false gods but is itself created by the true God and is itself his true sacrifice. Both alike make use of temporal goods, and both alike are afflicted by temporal evils.[85] But their temporal lives are directed by different faiths, different hopes, and different loves, until at last they are separated by the final judgment and each receives its own end, of which there is no end.[86] It is these ends that we must now discuss.

80. See Matt. 23:35.

81. See Gen. 4:8.

82. [GWL] A summary of the relation between the two cities. The conflict between them began with Cain's murdering Abel (15.5–7). The earthly city will continue to persecute the heavenly city until Christ's final return.

83. [GWL] This selection presents only the last paragraph of 18.54. In the previous chapters, not included in this book, Augustine addressed two theories about the ongoing history of the heavenly city. One was that the church would not experience further persecution until the time of the antichrist. Augustine's rejection of this idea reflects his rejection of *tempora christiana*, the notion that the Christianization of Rome marked the culmination of God's plans in history. It is possible that the church will suffer persecution again; there may be non-Christian kings before Christ's return. For comment, see R. A. Markus, *Saeculum: History and Society in the Theology of St. Augustine*, 2nd ed. (orig. 1970; Cambridge: Cambridge University Press, 1988), 54. The second, obscure theory was that Peter used sorcery to prophesy that Christ's name would be worshiped for only 365 years. According to this theory, the gods were permitting the rise of Christianity for a season, after which they would bring it to an end. Augustine lambasts this theory for its impiety and its predictive failure, given the persistence of Christianity well after it was supposed to end.

84. [GWL] In this final paragraph, Augustine concludes Book 18, which has treated the earthly city from the time of Abraham through Augustine's present time. Book 18 also completes the larger unit of Books 15–18 on the development of the two cities. Augustine stresses two differences between the two cities: their religion and their posture toward temporal goods. Despite these differences, both cities rely on temporal blessings and are afflicted by temporal suffering.

85. A similar idea, typical of early Christian apologetic literature, is expressed in *Letter to Diognetus* 5; Tertullian, *Apology* 42.

86. [GWL] A reference to the Pauline triad: faith, hope, and love (1 Cor. 13:13). The earthly city directs its faith, hope, and love toward temporal goods while the heavenly city directs its faith, hope, and love toward eternal goods. Augustine's reference to the "end" of each city indicates the topic of the next major unit, Books 19–22, which treats the ends of the two cities.

Eusebius's *Chronicle*

Gregory W. Lee and Avyi Hill

Augustine's narration of the earthly city in Book 18 relies on an account of the history of humanity called the *Chronicle* (or *The Chronicles*, as the NCP text and notes have it). This work was produced by Eusebius of Caesarea and revised by Jerome. The contrast between Eusebius's and Augustine's histories illuminates Augustine's theology of the two cities, which broke sharply from Eusebius's attribution of Rome's expansion as an empire to God's final purposes in the world.

Eusebius (ca. 260–339 CE) is most famous for his work *Ecclesiastical History* (sometimes called *History of the Church*), which remains scholars' most important source for the earliest centuries of Christianity. Probably born in Caesarea Maritima, a port city in Palestine, Eusebius spent many of his early years curating the works of Origen (ca. 186–255), an influential theologian who spent the last decades of his life in the city and died only years before Eusebius was born.

Eusebius presided as bishop of Caesarea from around 313 until his death. His life spanned some of the most dramatic events in early Christianity, including the sudden persecution of Christians under the emperor Diocletian after Christianity had been tolerated for forty years, the conversion of Constantine, and the Council of Nicaea, which Eusebius personally attended (despite his earlier support for Arius, whom the council would declare a heretic). Though Eusebius had limited access to Constantine, he established a reputation as the emperor's great panegyrist through two speeches, *Treatise on the Holy Sepulcher* and *Oration in Praise of Constantine* (or *Tricennial Oration*), together with his work *Life of Constantine*, which records the story of Constantine's conversion prior to the Battle at the Milvian Bridge.

The *Chronicle* was written before *Ecclesiastical History* and furnished material for it (*Ecclesiastical History* 1.1.6). Though scholars differ on the *Chronicle*'s compositional history, the first edition was likely written between 306 and 313/14, before or shortly after the end of Diocletian's persecution. Given this range of dates, the *Chronicle* does not represent Eusebius's later theology of Constantine. It seems to have been written for apologetic reasons, against Porphyry (see essay: "Porphyry"). Eusebius revised the

Chronicle on at least one occasion, extending his history to 325, Constantine's twentieth year as emperor. Jerome would further extend this history to 378, ending with the reign of Valens. Produced in 380/81, Jerome's revision would become the basis for later Western chronicles.

Eusebius's *Chronicle* was composed of two parts, typically called the *Chronography* and the *Chronological Canons*. The *Chronography* provided excerpts and historical details on ancient civilizations, covering fifteen kingdoms. Eusebius acknowledged uncertainty on many details, especially for the history before Abraham. The Chaldean and Egyptian sources recounted implausible durations of time and impossible myths. The accounts given in different versions of the Bible (Hebrew, Septuagint, Samaritan) could not be fully reconciled with one another. Jerome did not include the *Chronography* in his revision.

The *Canons* presented a visual history of the world on a single timeline (see fig. 18.1). The histories of the kingdoms were arranged in parallel columns, demarcated by decades, and synchronized with one another. Columns appeared and disappeared as kingdoms rose and fell. The space between the columns was filled with details about various rulers, events, and authors. In its structure and scope, the *Canons* was unprecedented. It was likely inspired by Origen's *Hexapla*, a massive work that laid out different manuscripts of the Bible in parallel columns for comparison.

The *Canons* began with Abraham and four columns: the Assyrians, the Hebrews, the Sicyonians, and the Egyptians. The column for the Hebrews split into two with the division between the Northern and Southern Kingdoms; each column disappeared, in turn, through captivity. With the Maccabean revolt, a column for the "Jews" emerged. (From the exile in Babylon, Eusebius no longer uses the word "Hebrews.") The Romans then absorbed the other columns until only the Romans and the Jews remained. After the destruction of the Jerusalem temple (70 CE), the table consisted of only one column, illustrating the Romans' rule over all the nations. When Constantine converted to Christianity, so did this single column. The *Canons* thus presented a visual theology of history culminating in the dominance of the Roman empire and the rise of Christianity.

Augustine seems to have secured a copy of Jerome's edition of the *Chronicle* as he was writing *City of God*. Nearly every king or god mentioned in 18.2–27 can be found in Jerome's work. The *Chronicle* also supplied the synchronisms Augustine used to coordinate the histories of the earthly and heavenly cities. As with the *Chronicle*, Augustine's history of the earthly city begins with the time of Abraham, who was born during the reign of Ninus of the Assyrians, son of Bel and founder of Nineveh (18.2). Ninus had already featured prominently in 4.6 as the first king to conduct war to seize territory (see also 16.3, 10, 17; 18.22). He was thus the progenitor of empire. Following the *Chronicle* again, Augustine coordinates the beginning of the Romans with Hosea, Amos,

THE KINGDOM OF THE ASSYRIANS	THE BEGINNING OF THE NATION OF THE HEBREWS	THE KINGDOM OF THE SICYONIANS	THE KINGDOM OF THE EGYPTIANS
Ninus, the son of Bel, was the first to rule all Asia, except for India. He reigned fifty-two years. In the forty-third year of his reign, Abraham was born.	During Ninus's reign, Abraham was born among the Hebrews. When Abraham was one hundred years old, he begat Isaac.	In Greece, Europs, the second king of the Sicyonians, ruled for forty-five years. In the twenty-second year of his reign, Abraham was born.	The Egyptians were in their sixteenth government, which they call dynasty. During this time, the Thebes reigned for 190 years.
a Ninus founded the city Ninus in the land of the Assyrians. The Hebrews call this city Nineveh.	Abraham **b** While Ninus was reigning over the Assyrians, at the end of his time, Abraham was born.	**e** While Ninus was reigning over the Assyrians, Aegialeus, the first king of the Sicyonians, ruled for fifty-two years. What is now called Peloponnese was named Aegialeia after him. Following him was the second king, Europs, who was also distinguished by name.	**f** While Ninus was reigning over the Assyrians, the Thebes were ruling the Egyptians.

Assyrians	Hebrews	Sicyonians	Egyptians
XLIII	I	XXII	I — 2016 BC*
XLIIII	II	XXIII	II
XLV	III	XXIIII	III
XLVI	IIII	XXV	IIII
XLVII	V	XXVI	V — 2012
XLVIII	VI	XXVII	VI
XLVIIII	VII	XXVIII	VII
L	VIII	XXVIIII	VIII
LI	VIIII	XXX	VIIII
<u>XLII</u>	<u>X</u>	<u>XXXI</u>	<u>X</u> — 2007
I	XI	XXXII	XI
II	XII	XXXIII	XII
III	XIII	XXXIIII	XIII
IIII	XIIII	XXXV	XIIII
V	XV	XXXVI	XV — 2002
VI	XVI	XXXVII	XVI
VII	XVII	XXXVIII	XVII
VIII	XVIII	XXXVIIII	XVIII — 1999

Assyrians notes:
c The magician Zoroaster, king of the Bactrians, is renowned. Ninus fought against him.
The second ruler of the Assyrians, Semiramis, reigned forty-two years.

Hebrews notes:
d Abraham spent his youth among the Chaldeans in the nation of Chaldea.

Sicyonians notes:
g Semiramis, the wife of Ninus, ruled the Assyrians. Innumerable things are told about her. She also held Asia, and she built mudbanks because of a deluge, restoring much of the city of Bablyon.

Fig. 18.1. Sample of Eusebius's *Chronicle*. Translated and adapted from *Eusebius Werke*, ed. Rudolf Helm, vol. 7, *Die Chronik des Hieronymus/Hieronymi Chronicon* (Berlin: Akademie-Verlag 1956), 20a–b.

*The numbers in this column represent years. Though this timeline distinguishes between years before and after Christ, it dates the year of Christ's birth as 1 BC, unlike modern calendars, which date it as AD 1.

Isaiah, Micah, Jonah, and Joel, whose prophecies were oriented toward the nations and not just Israel (18.27). The two great empires, Assyria and Rome, thus rose in tandem with God's promises to all peoples. The Assyrians rose when God promised to bless the nations through Abraham, and the Romans rose when the prophets started speaking of God's blessings to the nations.

Despite Augustine's reliance on Eusebius and Jerome for chronological details, his theology of history departed from the *Chronicle*'s. For Augustine, history did not culminate in the dominance of Rome over other nations. Since Adam and Eve, all humanity could be divided into two columns, the heavenly city and the earthly city; differences between the nations were of secondary importance (14.1). The history of the earthly city was defined by idolatry and violence. The gods were a device to manipulate the masses and secure temporal goods, and empire is the aim of those who are dominated by the lust for domination (1.*preface*; 18.2). The heavenly city is not a nation among others but a sojourning people enduring captivity until Christ's return.

Bibliography

Adler, William. 1992. "Eusebius' *Chronicle* and Its Legacy." In *Eusebius, Christianity, and Judaism*, edited by Harold W. Attridge and Gohei Hata, 467–91. Detroit: Wayne State University Press.

Barnes, Timothy D. 1981. *Constantine and Eusebius*. Cambridge, MA: Harvard University Press.

Burgess, R. W. 1997. "The Dates and Editions of Eusebius' *Chronici Canones* and *Historia Ecclesiastica*." *Journal of Theological Studies* 48, no. 2: 471–504.

Burgess, R. W., and Michael Kulikowski. 2013. *Mosaics of Time: The Latin Chronicle Traditions from the First Century BC to the Sixth Century AD*. Vol. 1, *A Historical Introduction to the Chronicle Genre from Its Origins to the High Middle Ages*. Turnhout, Belgium: Brepols, 99–131.

Chesnut, Glenn F., Jr. 1975. "The Pattern of the Past: Augustine's Debate with Eusebius and Sallust." In *Our Common History as Christians: Essays in Honor of Albert C. Outler*, edited by John Deschner, Leroy T. Howe, and Klaus Penzel, 69–95. New York: Oxford University Press.

Grafton, Anthony, and Megan Williams. 2006. *Christianity and the Transformation of the Book: Origen, Eusebius, and the Library of Caesarea*. Cambridge, MA: Belknap.

Hollerich, Michael J. 2021. *Making Christian History: Eusebius of Caesarea and His Readers*. Berkeley: University of California Press.

Jeanjean, Benoît, and Bertrand Lançon, ed. and trans. 2004. *Saint Jérôme, "Chronique": Continuation de la "Chronique" d'Eusèbe, années 326–378*. Rennes, France: Presses Universitaires de Rennes.

Lee, Gregory W. 2011. "Republics and Their Loves: Rereading *City of God* 19." *Modern Theology* 27, no. 4: 553–81.

Jews and Judaism

Gregory W. Lee, with Henry Prinz

Beginning in the second century CE, many early Christian authors produced writings against the Jews and Judaism, forming what scholars have called an *aduersus Iudaeos* ("against the Jews") tradition. These writings stressed the moral and theological deficiencies of Judaism and the superiority of Christianity. They also blamed the Jews for crucifying Jesus and claimed God had punished them through religious and political devastation.

Supposedly, God's judgment was evident in two events, which the authors often conflated: the destruction of the Jerusalem temple in 70 CE, under the military commander Titus and the emperor Vespasian (Titus's father), and the expulsion of the Jews from Jerusalem in 135 CE, following an uprising against the Romans spearheaded by a Jewish revolutionary named Bar Kokhba. In comparison with this tradition, Augustine has generally been considered more affirming of the Jews and Judaism. Yet his writings on the topic include many elements that modern readers have found troubling.

City of God treats Old Testament Israel in two contrasting ways. On the one hand, Israel was set apart from the nations to bear witness to Christ and the church (7.32; 10.32; 15.8; 16.3). Israel was also the main nation where members of the heavenly city could be found before Christ (though Augustine also acknowledges some individuals outside Israel, like Job and Melchizedek, who belonged to God; see 18.47 and Book 18n46). In contrast to the other nations' idolatry, Israel worshiped the one true God (4.31, 34; 5.12; 19.23). In their Scriptures, the Jews possessed wisdom greater than that of the philosophers (18.41).

On the other hand, Israel was a slave people that belonged to the earthly city, a prophetic image that signified the heavenly city without making it present (15.2). Augustine's position on this matter draws on Paul's contrast between the slave woman Hagar and the free woman Sarah (Gal. 4:21–5:1). It also reflects a distinction Augustine develops in *De Doctrina Christiana* between signs (*signa*) and things (*res*), according to which signs exist for the purpose of referring to (or "signifying") other realities (1.2.2–1.4.4). Though *De Doctrina Christiana* applies this schema to all Scripture, which is a book of

word-signs signifying the intent of its authors (2.3.4–2.5.6), Augustine applies it especially to the Jews by claiming that Israel and its practices were signs of New Testament
realities (3.5.9–3.6.10; see essay: "Figurative Interpretation of Scripture").

In his interpretation of the Old Testament, Augustine wrestles with whether prophecies refer to ethnic Israel or to the church from all nations. In *City of God*, this concern
especially arises with the promises to Abraham (16.16, 18, 21, 23, 26; see 17.2–3).
According to Augustine, some of these prophecies refer to Abraham's physical descendants, others to his spiritual descendants, and still others to both. In some instances,
the referent is not clear.

Book 17 presents the strongest statements in *City of God* concerning the replacement
of Israel by the church, an idea scholars call "supersessionism." Augustine concentrates
on two events: the rejection of Eli as priest, to be replaced by Samuel (17.5), and the
rejection of Saul as king, to be replaced by David (17.6–7). For Augustine, these events
involved more than the succession of one individual by another. They signified the rejection of Israel's priesthood and monarchy, which would give way to Christ's priesthood
and rule. To support this point, Augustine uses a common argument from the *aduersus
Iudaeos* tradition: the Jews no longer have a temple, altar, or priest (17.5). Since the
incarnation, Israel has been divided between those who accept Christ and those who
reject him (17.7).

Scholars disagree on whether Augustine believed Israel would be restored at the end
of time. There is evidence in *City of God* indicating he did (18.28; 20.29, 30; drawing
respectively on Hosea 3:5; Mal. 4:5–6; and Zech. 12:9–10). These passages do not claim
that every Jew will receive salvation or that the Jews will receive salvation without Christ.
Yet they still affirm a massive Jewish conversion to Christ at his return. The conversion
of the Jews is one of the major events Augustine includes among the last things (20.30).

The most distinctive feature of Augustine's theology of Judaism is his "witness doctrine" (18.46; see also *Agreement among the Evangelists* 1.26.40; *Answer to Faustus*
12.9–13; *Expositions of the Psalms* 58.1.21–58.1.22; *Letter* 149.1.9). This doctrine correlates the scattering of the Jews among the nations with the nations' conversion to
Christian faith. By bearing Scriptures that prophesy to Christ, the Jews offer inadvertent testimony for the truth of Christianity, proving that Christians did not invent these
prophecies. To support this perspective, Augustine appeals to Psalm 59:11: "Do not kill
them, lest they some day forget your law; scatter them in your power." As Augustine
interprets this passage, God's not "killing" the Jews means God has preserved the Jews
in their Jewish identity, despite the persecution of other nations. God has "scattered"
them for the sake of Christian witness.

Scholars have differed on how to assess the Jewish witness doctrine. Some have noted its significance in the Middle Ages, when Christians relied on Augustine's arguments to deter violence against the Jews. Others have objected to Augustine's treating the Jews as instruments in service of the church. Either way, scholars agree that Augustine's depiction of the Jews is largely theoretical, reflecting his theological interests as opposed to interactions with actual Jews. In the only known instance in which Augustine interacts with an actual Jew, a legal dispute between a Jewish landowner and a Christian bishop, he sides with the former (*Letter* 8*).

Bibliography

Cohen, Jeremy. 1999. *Living Letters of the Law: Ideas of the Jew in Medieval Christianity*. Berkeley: University of California Press.

Fredriksen, Paula. 2010. *Augustine and the Jews: A Christian Defense of Jews and Judaism*. New Haven: Yale University Press.

Harkins, Franklin T. 2005. "Nuancing Augustine's Hermeneutical Jew: Allegory and Actual Jews in the Bishop's Sermons." *Journal for the Study of Judaism* 36, no. 1: 41–64.

Hood, John Y. B. 2019. "Did Augustine Abandon His Doctrine of Jewish Witness in *Adversus Judaeos*?" *Augustinian Studies* 50, no. 2: 171–95.

Lee, Gregory W. 2016. "Israel between the Two Cities: Augustine's Theology of the Jews and Judaism." *Journal of Early Christian Studies* 24, no. 4: 523–51.

Signer, Michael. 1999. "Jews and Judaism." In *AttA*, 470–74.

Unterseher, Lisa A. 2009. *The Mark of Cain and the Jews: Augustine's Theology of Jews and Judaism*. Piscataway, NJ: Gorgias.

Book 19

Book 19 is the most studied text in Augustine's political thought and has been included here in full. It commences Books 19–22, the final unit of City of God, on the ends of the two cities. The next three books will address the major events to conclude human history: final judgment (Book 20), hell (Book 21), and heaven (Book 22). Book 19 treats a philosophical question: What is humanity's final good? In the first chapters (19.1–3), Augustine methodically delineates six questions philosophers have sought to answer about the final good. The next block of material provides Augustine's answers to these questions (19.4–20). The longest discussion by far concerns whether happiness is social (19.5–17). This section includes a celebrated digression on peace (19.10–17). The final section of Book 19 is a kind of appendix in which Augustine returns to an earlier discussion of Cicero's definition of a republic (19.21–28). This section includes Augustine's own definition of a republic (19.24), a topic that has received much attention in modern scholarship.

The Ends of the Two Cities: The Supreme Good and the Supreme Evil

1. I see, then, that I must next discuss the due ends of these two cities, the earthly and the heavenly. And first I have to set out, so far as the scheme of this work allows, the arguments by which mortals have tried to contrive happiness for themselves in the midst of all the unhappiness of this life.[1] I do this in

---

1. [GWL] The purpose of Book 19 is to refute the philosophers' understanding of happiness, which they believe is attainable in this temporal life. Augustine argues that happiness can be secured only in eternity.

order to make clear how different their empty views are both from our hope, which God has given us, and from the reality itself,[2] the true happiness which God will give us; and I shall proceed not only by appealing to divine authority but also, for the sake of unbelievers, by appealing to reason as far as possible.

Now, the philosophers have engaged in much and many-sided debate about the supreme ends of good and evil, and they have given this question their fullest attention in an effort to discover what it is that makes a person happy.[3] For our final good is that for the sake of which other things are to be desired, while it is itself to be desired for its own sake; and the final evil is that for the sake of which other things are to be avoided, while it is itself to be avoided for its own sake. Thus, when we speak of the "end" of good in this context, we do not mean "end" in the sense that the good is finished and gone, so that it no longer exists; rather, we mean "end" in the sense of the culmination in which the good is brought to its full realization, so that it is wholly fulfilled. And again, when we speak of the "end" of evil, we do not mean "end" in the sense that evil ceases to exist but rather "end" in the sense of the culmination to which evil leads in doing its harm. These two ends, therefore, are the supreme good and the supreme evil. Now, as I have said, those who have devoted themselves to the pursuit of wisdom in the midst of the vanity of this world have worked hard to discover what each of these is and to attain the supreme good in this life while avoiding the supreme evil. And, although they have gone wrong in various ways, the limits imposed by nature kept them from veering too far from the path of truth. Thus, there are none who did not locate the ultimate good and the ultimate evil either in the soul or in the body or in both together. Starting from this threefold classification of general positions, Marcus Varro, in his work *On Philosophy*, identified by subtle and diligent analysis such a large variety of views that, by bringing certain distinctions to bear, he easily reached a total

2. "Hope . . . reality": *spes . . . res*. A frequent wordplay in Augustine. See also below at 19.20.

3. [GWL] Happiness is also called the "final good" (*summum bonum*). However it is defined, it is that which is sought for its own sake, and for the sake of which everything else is sought. Augustine's identification of happiness as humanity's final goal resides firmly within classical philosophical tradition. He also treats happiness according to his distinction in *De Doctrina Christiana* 1 between enjoyment and use. To enjoy (*frui*) something is to pursue something for its own sake. To use (*uti*) something is to pursue something for the sake of some other thing (1.3.3–1.4.4). Happiness consists of eternal life in God, who alone is to be enjoyed. Everything else is to be used. A valuable study of Augustine on use and enjoyment is Rowan Williams, "Language, Reality and Desire: The Nature of Christian Formation," in *On Augustine* (orig. 1989; London: Bloomsbury, 2016), 41–58.

of two hundred and eighty-eight philosophical sects—not sects already in existence but possible schools of thought.[4]

Varro: Possible Positions on the Supreme Good

To show this briefly, I need to begin with the fact that in the above-mentioned book Varro himself observes and posits that there are four things which human beings seek naturally, that is, without a teacher, without the aid of instruction, without conscious effort, and without acquiring the art of living (which is called virtue and which, beyond doubt, is learned).[5] These four are pleasure, by which bodily sense is moved with delight; repose, the state in which a person feels no bodily distress; the combination of these (which Epicurus nevertheless calls by the one name of pleasure[6]); or, comprehensively, the primary goods of nature, which include the first three in addition to others, whether in the body (such as the integrity of its members and its health and wellbeing) or in the mind (such as the abilities, small or great, which are found in the innate capacities of human beings). Now, these four—pleasure, repose, the combination of these, and the primary goods of nature—are in us in such a way that

4. [GWL] Marcus Terentius Varro (116–27 BCE) was a Roman praetor and scholar who wrote nearly five hundred works on a great range of topics. Quoting Cicero, Augustine calls Varro the most learned mind from antiquity (6.2). In Books 6–7, Augustine critiques Varro for feigning belief in Roman religion and for his naturalistic explanations of the gods. These books rely on Varro's lost work *Divine Antiquities*. Book 19 is structured according to Varro's six categories of philosophical disagreement, as delineated in his *On Philosophy*, which is also lost and is known only through *City of God*. For analysis of *On Philosophy*, see Thomas Tarver, "Varro and the Antiquarianism of Philosophy," in *Philosophia Togata II: Plato and Aristotle at Rome*, ed. Jonathan Barnes and Miriam Griffin (Oxford: Clarendon, 1997), 130–64.

The six categories are as follows: (1) whether to seek pleasure, repose, a combination of the two, or primary goods of nature (*prima naturae*, also called *primigenia*); (2) whether these things are beneath, above, or equal to virtue; (3) whether to seek virtue for one's own sake or for the sake of others; (4) whether knowledge is certain or uncertain; (5) whether to follow the lifestyle of the Cynics or those of other philosophers; (6) whether to pursue a life of leisure, activity, or both. Augustine treats questions 1 and 2 in 19.4, question 3 in 19.5–17 (note the disproportionate length of this section), question 4 in 19.18, and questions 5 and 6 in 19.19. He summarizes his positions in 19.20.

In 19.1–2, Augustine explains how Varro multiplied potential answers to these questions to produce 288 combinations (4 x 3 x 2 x 2 x 2 x 3 = 288). This total does not represent actual schools of philosophy but theoretical possibilities that could be derived from the answers. The notes that follow track the multiplication of possibilities, but these details are not crucial for understanding Augustine's argument.

5. [GWL] The first question. There are four options.

6. See *Letter to Menoeceus*, cited in Diogenes Laertius, *Lives of Eminent Philosophers* 10.128–32.

either virtue (which teaching implants in us at a later point) is to be sought
for their sake, or they are to be sought for the sake of virtue, or both they and
virtue are to be sought, each for its own sake.[7] Thus we get twelve sects, since
each of the first four is tripled by means of this consideration.

Once I have demonstrated this point in one case, it will not be difficult
to see it in each of the others. Since, therefore, bodily pleasure may either
be subordinated to virtue of mind, or preferred to virtue of mind, or set on
the same plane with it, we get a threefold division of sects.[8] Bodily pleasure
is subordinated to virtue when it is brought into the service of virtue. For
example, it belongs to the office of virtue both to live for one's country and
to produce sons for the sake of one's country, neither of which can be done
without bodily pleasure. For it is impossible to eat and drink (in order to live)
or to have sexual intercourse (in order to generate children) without bodily
pleasure. On the other hand, when bodily pleasure is preferred to virtue, it is
sought for its own sake, and it is believed that virtue should be brought into the
service of bodily pleasure. It is believed, that is, that the only point of virtue
is to gain or to sustain bodily pleasure. This is certainly a deformed kind of
life, where virtue becomes the slave of domineering pleasure (although in fact
this should not be called virtue at all), but, even so, this horrible and degrading
view has some philosophers who support and defend it.[9] Again, pleasure is
set on the same plane with virtue when neither is sought for the sake of the
other but both are sought, each for its own sake. Thus, pleasure gives us three
sects, depending on whether it is subordinated to virtue, preferred to virtue,
or set on the same plane with virtue; and, in exactly the same way, repose,
the combination of pleasure and repose, and the primary goods of nature
are each found to give rise to three sects. According as human opinions vary,
each of these ends is sometimes subordinated to virtue, sometimes preferred
to virtue, and sometimes set on the same plane with virtue. And so we reach
a total of twelve sects.

But this number is itself doubled when a further distinction is brought into
play, namely, social life.[10] Anyone who follows any of these twelve sects does so
either for his own sake alone or for the sake of others as well, for whom he is
obligated to will the same good that he wills for himself. Thus, there are twelve

7. [GWL] The second question. There are three options. 4 x 3 = 12.
8. [GWL] This discussion continues Augustine's analysis of the second question.
9. E.g., Aristippus. See Laertius, *Lives of Eminent Philosophers* 2.65–104.
10. [GWL] The third question. There are two options. 4 x 3 x 2 = 24.

sects of those who suppose that whichever view they take is to be held for the sake of oneself alone, and twelve others of those who maintain that this philosophy or that philosophy should be held not only for one's own sake but also for the sake of others, whose good they seek just as much as their own. And these twenty-four sects are again doubled, to make forty-eight, when a distinction drawn from the New Academy is introduced.[11] On the one hand, a person may hold and defend the views of any one of those twenty-four sects as being certain (in the same way that the Stoics defended their claim that the human good, by which a person attains happiness, consists only of virtue of soul[12]). But, on the other hand, someone else may hold his views as uncertain (in the way that the New Academics defended views that to them seemed not certain but still probable[13]). Thus, we get twenty-four sects made up of those who maintain that their views are to be followed as certain, because they are true, and another twenty-four made up of those who maintain that their views are to be followed, even though they are uncertain, because they are probable. Again, because one person who follows any one of these forty-eight sects may adopt the mode of life of most other philosophers, but another may adopt the mode of life of the Cynics,[14] the number is again doubled on the basis of this distinction, and we get ninety-six sects.[15] And, finally, each of these sects can be followed and upheld either by people who love the life of leisured retirement, like those who only wanted and valued being free to study their sect's teachings; or by those who love the active life, like those who, while engaged in philosophy, were still fully occupied with the administration of the republic and governing human affairs; or by those who love a combination of both forms of life, like those who have alternately devoted themselves to learned leisure on the one hand and to necessary business on the other.[16] And, on the basis of this distinction, the number of sects can again be tripled, getting us up to two hundred and eighty-eight sects.

11. [GWL] The fourth question. There are two options. $4 \times 3 \times 2 \times 2 = 48$. Varro contrasts the New Academy (or skepticism), which holds to the uncertainty of knowledge, with the Old Academy, which he associates with the Academy of Plato. Augustine describes his brief attraction to the New Academy, which he discovered through Cicero, in *Confessions* 5.10.19 and 6.11.18. He also writes an early work against this school of philosophy, *Answer to the Academics* (386/387).

12. See . . . 9.4.

13. See *Answer to the Academics* 2.5.11–2.6.15.

14. As explained later in this section, Cynicism is characterized less by philosophical ideals than by style of life; what one ate or how one dressed, for example, was a matter of indifference.

15. [GWL] The fifth question. There are two options. $4 \times 3 \times 2 \times 2 \times 2 = 96$.

16. [GWL] The sixth and final question. There are three options. This brings us to the total number of possibilities: $4 \times 3 \times 2 \times 2 \times 2 \times 3 = 288$.

Varro's Position on the Supreme Good and the Life of Happiness

I have set out these points from Varro's book as briefly and as clearly as I could, expressing his views in my own words. Now, he goes on to refute all these sects but one, which he wants to be that of the Old Academy. This sect was founded by Plato and continued down to Polemo, who was, after Plato, the fourth head of the school which was then called the Academy.[17] Varro wants it to appear that this school held its doctrines as certain; and, on this basis, he distinguishes it from the New Academy, which holds that all things are uncertain and which began with Arcesilaus, Polemo's successor. Varro also considers this sect—that is, the Old Academy—to have been as free from error as it was from doubt. It would take too long to follow out Varro's argument in all its detail, but his reasoning should not be wholly omitted.

First, then, he removes all the distinctions which multiplied the number of sects, and the reason he thinks that these distinctions should be taken away is that they have nothing to do with the issue of the supreme good.[18] In his opinion, no position should be called a philosophical sect unless it differs from the others in having a distinctive view of the supreme good and supreme evil. For there is no reason to pursue philosophy except in order to be happy, and what makes for human happiness is precisely the ultimate good. There is no reason to pursue philosophy, therefore, except the supreme good, and so a sect which does not have its own distinctive view of the ultimate good should not to be called a philosophical sect at all. When, therefore, it is asked whether the wise man ought to embrace the social life, so that he wants and cares about the supreme good, which makes a person happy, as much for his friend as for himself, or whether he does what he does solely for the sake of his own happiness alone, this is not a question about the ultimate good itself.[19] Rather, it is only a question about including or not including a companion to participate in that good with oneself, and doing so not for one's own sake but for the sake of the companion, so that one rejoices as much in one's companion's good as one does in one's own. Again, if it is asked,

17. The writings of Polemo, or Polemon (died ca. 270 BCE), have not survived. See Diogenes Laertius, *Lives of Eminent Philosophers* 4.16–20.

18. [GWL] Augustine now explains how Varro reduces the philosophical categories. In the end, Varro reduces disagreement about the supreme good to disputes over the second question, whether happiness resides in the primary goods of nature (corresponding to the body), in virtue (corresponding to the soul), or in both.

19. [GWL] The third question.

with regard to the New Academy, to which all things are uncertain, whether this is the view we ought to take of the matters that philosophy should deal with or whether, like other philosophers, we ought to hold them as certain, this is not a question about what should be pursued as the ultimate good.[20] Instead, the question is whether or not we should have doubts about the truth of the good it seems we should pursue. In other words, to put it more plainly, the question is whether the supreme good is to be pursued in such a way that the one pursuing it should say that it is true, or rather in such a way that the one pursuing it should say that it seems true to him, even though it may possibly be false. In either case, however, one and the same good is being pursued. Again, with regard to the distinction which has to do with the customs and mode of life of the Cynics, what is at issue is not the ultimate good.[21] Rather, what is at issue is whether the person pursuing the true good—whatever it is that may seem true to him and rightly to be pursued—ought to follow those customs and that mode of life. There were, after all, people who pursued different ultimate goods (some pursued virtue, and some pleasure) but still adopted the same customs and the same mode of life as the Cynics, and so they were all called Cynics. Thus, whatever it is that distinguishes the Cynics from other philosophers, it obviously makes no difference with regard to their choice of and support for the good by which they sought to gain happiness. For, if it did make any difference, the same mode of life would require pursuit of the same end, and a different mode of life would exclude pursuit of the same end.

2. Again, in the matter of those three kinds of life—one spent not in mere idleness but in leisured contemplation of the truth or leisured inquiry into the truth, another spent in the business of managing human affairs, the third in a combination of both—when it is asked which of these should be chosen, the supreme good itself is not at issue.[22] At issue is only which of these three makes it either difficult or easy to attain or retain the ultimate good. When a person achieves the supreme good, it at once makes him happy; but no one is immediately made happy simply by living a life of educated leisure or of public business or of both by turns. For many can live in any one of these three ways and still go wrong in seeking the supreme good that brings human happiness.

20. [GWL] The fourth question.
21. [GWL] The fifth question.
22. [GWL] The sixth question.

Thus, the question of the ultimate good and evil—the question which makes a philosophical sect a sect in its own right—is one thing, and the questions of the social life, the doubtfulness of the Academy, the food and dress of the Cynics, and the three kinds of life (the leisured, the active, and the combination of the two) are quite another. None of these involves any points of dispute about the supreme good and evil. Now, it was by using these four distinctions—that is, the social life, the New Academy, the Cynics, and the three kinds of life—that Marcus Varro arrived at his two hundred and eighty-eight sects (plus any others that could be added by similar calculations). Accordingly, once he removed them all on the grounds that they have nothing to do with the issue of the ultimate good to be pursued, and so give us nothing that either is or should be called a sect, he dropped back to those twelve sects in which what is at issue is the human good (the attainment of which brings happiness) in order to show that one of them is true, the others false. For, if the distinction based on the three kinds of life is taken away, two-thirds of the total are eliminated, and ninety-six sects remain. Again, if the distinction drawn from the Cynics is taken away, that number is reduced by half, which leaves forty-eight. And, if we exclude the distinction drawn from the New Academy, again only half remain, that is, twenty-four sects. Similarly, if we exclude the distinction which he brought in concerning the social life, only twelve sects remain—the number which that distinction had doubled, to make twenty-four.

As for the remaining twelve, then, nothing can be said against taking them as genuine sects, for their point of inquiry is in fact nothing other than the ultimate good and evil. And further, once you discover the ultimate good, you immediately have the ultimate evil as its contrary. Now, to get these twelve sects, four things are each multiplied by three: pleasure, repose, the combination of both, and the primary goods of nature, which Varro calls "innate goods." These four are each sometimes subordinated to virtue, so that they appear worthy of being sought not for their own sake but for the sake of their role in serving virtue. They are each sometimes preferred to virtue, so that virtue is considered necessary not for its own sake but simply for the sake of acquiring and holding onto them. And they are each sometimes put on the same plane as virtue, so that it is believed that both they and virtue are to be sought, each for its own sake. In this way the number four is tripled, and we get twelve sects. From these four things, however, Varro subtracts three, namely, pleasure and repose and the combination of both. He does this not because he rejects them but because the primary goods of nature already include both pleasure and repose.[23] What need is there, then, to turn these two into three— that is, two when pleasure and repose are sought separately, each apart from the other, and a third when both are sought at the same time—especially when the primary goods of nature already include both of these and many other things as well? For Varro, then, there are only three sects that must be examined with care to see which should be chosen in preference to the others. For sound reason does not allow more than one to be true, whether it is one of these three or some other not included among them, as we shall see later on. In the meantime, however, let us set out as briefly and clearly as we can how Varro chooses one of the three. And there are three sects because either the primary goods of nature are to be sought for the sake of virtue, or virtue is to be sought for the sake of the primary goods of nature, or both virtue and the primary goods of nature are to be sought, each for its own sake.

3. Here, then, is how Varro tries to convince us as to which of these three sects is the one that is true and to be followed.[24] First, since the ultimate good that philosophy seeks is not that of a tree or of an animal or of God but of human beings, he holds that we must start by asking what human beings themselves are. He maintains that, in human nature, there are two elements, body and soul, and he has no doubt that, of these two, the soul is the better and far and away the more excellent. But is the soul by itself the human being, so that the body is only related to the man as a horse to its rider? For the rider is not both the man and the horse but only the man, and he is called a rider only because he is related to the horse in a certain way. Or is the body by itself the human being, standing in some such relation to the soul as that of a cup to the drink it contains? For it is not the cup and the drink together that are called the cup, but only the cup itself—even though it is called a cup precisely because it is meant to hold a drink. Or, again, is it neither the soul by itself nor the body by itself that is the human being, but rather both at once, the soul and the body each being a part, but the whole requiring both if it is to be a human being? It is in this sense that we call two horses harnessed together a pair. The near horse and the off horse are both parts of the pair,

23. [GWL] The first question. By grouping pleasure, repose, and their combination under the primary goods of nature, Varro can concentrate on the second question.

24. [GWL] Varro's main interest is the second question. His own position is that happiness involves both virtue and the primary goods of nature. Happiness thus includes the wellbeing of both the soul and the body.

but, no matter how they are connected to each other, we do not call either one of them a pair by itself but only both at once.

Of these three possibilities, Varro chose the third and concluded that a human being is neither the soul by itself nor the body by itself but the soul and the body together. Therefore, he says, the ultimate human good, which makes a human being happy, consists in the goods of both, that is, of both the soul and the body. As a consequence, he holds that the primary goods of nature are to be sought for their own sake, and so is virtue, which teaching implants in us as the art of living and which is the most excellent of all the goods of the soul. Accordingly, when this virtue—that is, the art of conducting one's life—takes its place with the primary goods of nature, which were present prior to virtue (and in fact were present prior to any teaching whatsoever), it seeks all of these for their own sake, and, at the same time, it also seeks itself for its own sake.[25] Thus, virtue makes use of all these, and also of itself, to the end that it may delight in and enjoy them all. This enjoyment may be greater or less, according as each of these goods is itself greater or less. But virtue still rejoices in them all, although, if necessity requires, it may disdain some of the lesser ones for the sake of gaining or keeping greater ones. Of all these goods, however, whether of the soul or of the body, there is absolutely none that virtue ranks above itself. For it is virtue that makes right use both of itself and of the other goods that make for human happiness. And, where virtue itself is lacking, no matter how many other goods are present, they are of no good to the one whose goods they are, and in fact they should not really be called his "goods" at all, for they cannot possibly be of use to one who uses them wrongly.

This, then, is the human life that is properly called happy, the life that enjoys both virtue and the other goods of soul and body without which virtue cannot exist. But, if a life also enjoys any or many of those other goods without which virtue can exist, it is happier still; and, if it enjoys all goods, so that no good whether of soul or of body is lacking to it, it is happiest of all. For

25. [GWL] Virtue was a central concept in classical philosophy that stood for moral excellence in the human life. On this conception, virtuous people do not just perform moral acts; they are disposed to virtuous behavior, and they act virtuously for virtuous reasons. Virtue is constitutive of true happiness. Classical philosophy understood temperance, prudence, justice, and fortitude to be the most important ("cardinal") virtues. Augustine treats each in turn in 19.4. The philosophers also debated whether happiness required bodily goods in addition to virtue. Varro answers yes, as does Augustine. For Augustine, however, neither bodily goods nor virtue can be secured in this life. Happiness is possible only in the life to come.

life is not identical with virtue, since not every life counts as virtue but only a life lived wisely. And there can, of course, be life of some sort without any virtue at all, even though it is impossible for virtue to exist without any life at all. I might say the same of memory and reason and any other such human faculties. For these are present prior to teaching, but without them there can be no teaching; and without them, therefore, neither can there be virtue, which is certainly learned through teaching. But to run well, to be beautiful in body, to prevail by great strength, and other things of this sort can obviously be present without virtue, just as virtue can be present without them. But they are goods all the same, and, according to these philosophers, virtue loves even these goods for their own sake and uses and enjoys them in a way that accords with virtue.

This happy life, these philosophers claim, is also social; it loves the good of friends for its own sake in the same way that it loves its own good, and, for their own sake, it wants for them precisely what it wants for itself.[26] And this is true whether these are friends at home, such as one's spouse and children and other members of one's household; or friends in the place where one lives, such as a city, as are those called one's fellow-citizens; or friends in the world at large, as are those united with us by common membership in human society; or friends in the very universe itself, which is collectively called heaven and earth, as are those whom they call gods and want to count as a wise man's friends but whom we more usually call angels. In addition, they deny that there is any room for doubt with regard to the ultimate good and its opposite, the ultimate evil; and this, they assert, is what distinguishes them from the New Academy. Nor does it make any difference to these philosophers whether anyone who pursues philosophy adopts the Cynics' dress and diet or some other mode of life in seeking the ends which they hold to be true. Finally, with regard to those three kinds of life—the leisured, the active, and the combination of both—they insist that they prefer the third. Varro asserts that the Old Academy held and taught these things, and he bases his

---

26. [GWL] The philosophers agree that happiness is social (the third question). They also divide social life into four spheres: home (*domus*), city (*urbs*), world (*orbis*), universe (*mundus*). In 19.5–9, Augustine will argue that happiness is impossible in each of these social spheres: home (19.5), city (19.6), world (19.7–8), universe (19.9). The rest of this paragraph summarizes the positions of the Old Academy, which Varro favors, on the remaining questions. Briefly, the positions are as follows: (1) pleasure, repose, and its combination are included in the primary goods of nature; (2) happiness involves both the body and the soul; (3) happiness is social; (4) knowledge is certain; (5) it does not matter whether one follows the Cynics' lifestyle; (6) a combination of leisure and activity is best.

claim on the authority of Antiochus, Cicero's teacher and his own (although, in fact, Cicero seems to think that, on many points, Antiochus was more a Stoic than a follower of the Old Academy).[27] But what does that matter to us? For we ought to judge on the basis of the facts themselves rather than setting any great store on knowing what anyone else has thought about them.

The Supreme Good and the Supreme Evil according to the City of God: Eternal Life and Eternal Death

4. If, then, we are asked what the city of God would respond when questioned on each of these points, and, first, what view it holds about the ultimate good and evil, its response will be that eternal life is the ultimate good and eternal death the ultimate evil, and that to attain the one and avoid the other we must live rightly.[28] That is why Scripture says, *The just person lives by faith* (Rom. 1:17). For we do not yet see our good, and, as a consequence, we must seek it by believing. Nor is it in our power to live rightly by our own efforts unless we are helped in believing and praying by the one who gave us the very faith by which we believe that we must have his help.

Happiness, the Supreme Good, Cannot Be Found in This Life

But those who have imagined that the ultimate good and evil are to be had in this life, whether they place the ultimate good in the body or in the soul or in both together—or, to speak more explicitly, whether they place it in pleasure or in virtue or in both of these, or in repose or in virtue or in both of these, or in the combination of pleasure and repose or in virtue or in both of these, or in the primary goods of nature or in virtue or in both of these—have wanted, with astonishing folly, to be happy in this life and to become happy by their own efforts.[29] The Truth scoffed at these people in the words of the prophet, *The Lord knows the thoughts of men* (Ps. 94:11)—or, as the

---

27. Antiochus of Ascalon (ca. 159–ca. 86 BCE) was a Greek philosopher whose lectures Cicero followed in Rome and to whom he often referred in his writings.

28. [GWL] This section begins Augustine's response to Varro's six questions. Augustine challenges the philosophers' starting point, which is to imagine that happiness can be found in this life. By contrast, Christians pursue eternal reward. The *summum bonum* is eternal life, and the *summum malum* is eternal death.

29. [GWL] Regardless of how philosophers have answered their questions, they have all supposed that happiness is attainable in this life.

apostle Paul cites this passage, *The Lord knows the thoughts of the wise, that they are folly* (1 Cor. 3:20).

For who, no matter how wonderful the flow of his eloquence, can find words to portray the miseries of this life?[30] Cicero lamented them as best he could in his *Consolation* on the death of his daughter,[31] but what did his best amount to? When, where, and how can what are called the primary goods of nature be so securely possessed in this life that they are not tossed about by uncertain chance?[32] Is there any pain, the contrary of pleasure, or any distress, the contrary of repose, that cannot strike the wise man's body? The amputation or crippling of his limbs destroys his physical wellbeing, deformity ruins his beauty, sickness his health, weakness his strength, torpor or listlessness his mobility. And is there any one of these that is not perfectly capable of attacking the flesh of the wise man? The posture and movement of the body, when attractive and fitting, are numbered among the primary goods of nature. But what if some dire disease causes the limbs to shake with a tremor? What if a person's spine is so bent over that he drags his hands on the ground, making him a kind of human quadruped? Will this not put an end to all the beauty and grace of the body's posture and movement?

And what about the innate goods, as they are called, of the mind itself?[33] The two ranked highest are sensation and intellect, because they are the ones that enable us to comprehend and perceive the truth. But how much sensation remains, and what kind, if a person becomes deaf and blind (to say nothing of other possibilities)? And where do reason and intelligence withdraw, where do they slumber, when a person is driven mad by some disease? The insane say and do all sorts of absurd things at odds with, or rather directly contrary to, their own good intentions and character; and, when we consider this or see it with our own eyes, if we are serious about

---

30. Augustine discusses the miseries of this life again . . . at 22.22.

31. This work, written to memorialize Cicero's daughter Tullia, is no longer extant.

32. [GWL] Following Varro's answer to the first question, Augustine assumes the primary goods of nature encompass pleasure, repose, and the combination of the two. The primary goods of nature concern the body. Augustine then treats the second question, whether happiness concerns the body (primary goods of nature), the soul (the seat of virtue), or both. In this paragraph, he says the primary goods of nature cannot be secured in this life. The implication is that happiness cannot be secured in this life either, since no one who suffers greatly in the body can be considered happy. For Augustine, happiness involves the body, but this happiness can be secured only in eternity.

33. [GWL] It is also impossible to secure the goods of the mind in this life. Again, the implication is that happiness cannot be secured in this life, since no one who suffers greatly in the mind can be considered happy.

it, we can hardly hold back our tears, or perhaps cannot hold them back at all. And what shall I say about people who suffer attacks from demons? Where does their own intelligence lie hidden and buried while the malign spirit makes use of their soul and body for its own purposes? And who has any certainty that this evil cannot strike the wise man in this life? Again, what sort of perception of the truth do we have in this flesh, and how much, when, as we read in the truth-bearing Book of Wisdom, *The corruptible body weighs down the soul, and this earthly habitation presses down on the mind that thinks many things* (Wis. 9:15)? And again, with regard to the drive or impulse to action (if this is the right way to designate in Latin what the Greeks call *hormē*)—for they count this, too, among the primary goods of nature—is it not this very impulse that produces, when sensation is deranged and reason asleep, those pitiable motions and actions of the insane that horrify us so?[34]

The Struggle of the Virtues against the Vices: Temperance, Prudence, and Justice

And what about virtue itself, which is not one of the primary goods of nature, since it comes in later, brought in by teaching?[35] Even though it claims the topmost place among human goods, what is its role here in this world but to do perpetual battle against the vices—and these not external but internal, not other people's but clearly our own? This is especially true of the virtue which the Greeks call *sophrosyne* and the Latins call temperance, which reins in the desires of the flesh to keep them from gaining the consent of the mind and drawing it into every sort of degrading act.[36] For it is certainly not true that there is no vice, when, as the Apostle says, *The desires of the flesh oppose the spirit* (Gal. 5:17). To this vice, however, there is an opposing virtue, when, as the same Apostle says, *The desires of the*

---

34. [GWL] *Hormē* is an important term in Stoic philosophy. Augustine assumes this "drive or impulse" can produce action without rationality. See Sarah Catherine Byers, *Perception, Sensibility, and Moral Motivation in Augustine: A Stoic-Platonic Synthesis* (Cambridge: Cambridge University Press), 217–18.

35. [GWL] Having treated body and mind, Augustine turns to the virtues. The next paragraphs walk through the "cardinal" virtues: temperance, prudence, justice, and fortitude. Each of these virtues presupposes temporal suffering, proving that even perfect virtue cannot secure happiness in this life. Augustine especially advances this case against the Stoics, who believe that happiness can be secured through virtue alone, regardless of the suffering one experiences during this life.

36. [GWL] The treatment of temperance.

spirit oppose the flesh, for these two are opposed to each other so that you do not do what you will to do (Gal. 5:17). But what is it that we will to achieve when we will to be made perfect by the ultimate good, unless it is precisely that the desires of the flesh should not oppose the spirit and that we should not have this vice in us for the desires of the spirit to oppose? But, since we are unable to achieve this in this present life, no matter how much we may will it, we can at least see to it, with God's help, that we do not give in to the desires of the flesh that oppose the spirit or allow the spirit to be overcome, and that we are not drawn into committing sin by our own consent. God forbid, then, that we should imagine, so long as we are caught up in this internal warfare, that we have attained the happiness we wish to reach by our victory. And who is so fully wise that he no longer has to engage in any struggle against his fleshly desires?

What of the virtue called prudence?[37] Does it not take all the vigilance that prudence can muster to distinguish the good from the evil, so that no error creeps in as we try to pursue the one and avoid the other? Thus, prudence itself bears witness that we dwell in the midst of evils and that there are evils dwelling in us. For prudence teaches us that it is evil to consent to the desire to sin and good not to consent to the desire to sin. But neither prudence, which teaches us not to consent to evil, nor temperance, which keeps us from consenting to evil, has the effect of removing that evil from this life.

What of justice, whose function is to assign to each his due—as a result of which a certain just order is established in man himself, so that the soul is set under God, and the flesh is set under the soul, and thus both the soul and the flesh are set under God?[38] Does not justice, in performing this very function, show that it is still laboring at its task rather than resting because its task is done? For the less the soul focuses on God in all its thinking, the less it is set under God, and the more the flesh's desires oppose the spirit, the less the flesh is set under the soul. And so, as long as we have in us this infirmity, this plague, this torpor, how can we dare to claim that we are already saved? And, if we are not saved, how can we dare to claim that we are already happy with that ultimate happiness?

37. [GWL] The treatment of prudence.
38. [GWL] The treatment of justice. According to a hierarchy Augustine will repeat often, the flesh (or body) submits to the soul (*anima*), and the soul submits to God. In 19.21, Augustine will support this schema with a quotation from Cicero.

Fortitude and the Question of Suicide

Then there is the virtue called fortitude.[39] No matter how much wisdom it is coupled with, however, it bears the most evident witness to human evils, for it is precisely these evils that it is compelled to endure with patience. It is astonishing to me that the Stoic philosophers have the gall to argue that these evils are not really evils.[40] For at the same time they admit that, if these evils become so severe that a wise man could not or should not endure them, he would be compelled to put himself to death and take leave of this life.[41] These men, who suppose that the supreme good is to be found in this life and imagine that they can attain happiness by their own efforts, are so stupefied with pride that their wise man (as they describe him in their incredible folly)—even if he goes blind, deaf, and dumb; even if he is disabled in limb and tortured with pain; even if he is stricken with every other evil that can be described or imagined, so that he is compelled to put himself to death—feels no shame in calling this life, set in the midst of these evils, a happy life.[42] What a happy life! It seeks death's help to bring about its own end! If it is really a happy life, let the wise man remain in it. How can those things not be evils when they vanquish the good of fortitude and compel that same fortitude not only to give in to them but even to become so delirious that, at one and the same time, it both calls this life happy and insists that the wise man should flee from it. Who is so blind as not to see that, if this life is happy, it is not a life one ought to flee from? But their admission that it should be fled from is an open expression of weakness. Is there any reason, then, why they should not also give up their stiffnecked pride and go on to admit that this life is actually wretched? Was it out of patience, I ask you, that Cato killed himself, or out of impatience? For he would not have done this if he had not been so impatient that he could not

39. [GWL] The treatment of fortitude.

40. [GWL] Augustine challenges the Stoics, who claim that perfect virtue suffices for happiness in this life. This requires them to disregard the reality of temporal evils. Yet they also claim that a "wise man" should commit suicide to avoid overwhelming suffering. This is a contradiction, since on their terms, the wise man should be happy regardless of his suffering. See Veronica Roberts Ogle, "Therapeutic Deception: Cicero and Augustine on the Myth of Philosophic Happiness," *Augustinian Studies* 50, no. 1 (2019): 13–42. This chapter's discussion of the wise man provides important background for the discussion of torture in 19.6.

41. The issue of suicide, which is discussed here, is treated at greater length above at 1.17–27.

42. See Cicero, *Tusculan Disputations* 4.4.7–4.38.84.

endure Caesar's victory.[43] Where, then, was his fortitude? It clearly gave in; it clearly succumbed; it clearly was so thoroughly defeated that it forsook, abandoned, and fled from this "happy life." Or was it no longer a happy life? In that case it was wretched. How, then, were those things not evils which made his life wretched and made it something to flee from?

Those who admitted, therefore, that these things are evils, as did the Peripatetics[44] and the Old Academy (the sect that Varro defends), speak in a more acceptable way. But even they fall into astonishing error, when they argue that in the midst of these evils—even if they are so severe that a person who suffers them is right to flee from them by self-inflicted death—this life is still happy. "The torments and agonies of the body," Varro says, "are evils; and, the worse they are, the more evil they are. To be free of them, one should flee from this life." "From which life?" I ask. "From this life," he asserts, "which is weighed down by such evils." It is definitely happy, then—this life in the midst of the very same evils on account of which you say that we ought to flee from it? Or do you call it happy, rather, precisely because it is permissible for you to escape these evils by death? What if, by some divine judgment, you had to remain in these evils and were not permitted to die or ever allowed to exist without them? Surely in that case, at least, you would say that such a life was miserable. What keeps it from being miserable, then, is the fact that it is quickly abandoned, since, if it lasted forever, even you yourself would consider it miserable! What keeps it from being miserable, then, is the fact that, since the misery does not last long, it should apparently not count as misery—or, what is even more absurd, the fact that, since the misery does not last long, it should be called happiness!

What tremendous power there is in these evils, which compel a man— and, according to these philosophers, even a wise man—to rob himself of the very fact that he is a man![45] For they say, and say rightly, that the first and greatest urging of nature, so to speak, is that a man should be at one with himself and therefore should instinctively flee from death, that he should be so thoroughly a friend to himself that he vehemently wishes and desires

43. Cato the Younger (95–46 BCE), after having opposed Julius Caesar both politically and militarily, committed suicide rather than live under Caesar's rule. On the events surrounding his suicide see Plutarch, *Lives*, Cato the Younger 66–70.

44. I.e., members of the school founded by Aristotle.

45. [GWL] By locating happiness exclusively in virtue, the Stoics deny the integrity of the human as a body-soul unity. Humans cannot be considered happy when they experience great physical suffering, regardless of their possession of virtue.

to be alive, a living being, and to stay alive in this conjunction of body and soul.[46] What tremendous power there is in these evils, which overthrow this natural impulse, in virtue of which we use our every strength and effort to avoid death—and overthrow it so completely that what was once avoided is now chosen and desired and, if it cannot come in any other way, is inflicted on a man by the very man himself! What tremendous power there is in these evils, which make fortitude a murderer—if in fact it should still be called fortitude when it is so completely defeated by these evils that it is not only unable to safeguard, through patience, the person whom, as a virtue, it is supposed to rule and protect but is itself compelled to put him to death. It is true, of course, that the wise man ought to bear even death with patience, but the death he ought to bear with patience is death that comes from some other source. If, however, he is compelled—as these philosophers claim—to inflict death on himself, surely they must admit that the things which compel him to commit this act are not only evils but are in fact unbearable evils.

The life, therefore, which is weighed down by the burden of such great and severe evils, or is subject to the chance that such great and severe evils might afflict it, should by no means be called happy. And it would not be called happy if the people who say this, when they are defeated by sound reasoning, would just condescend to give in to the truth in their search for the happy life, just as, when they are defeated by the growing press of evils, they give in to unhappiness in their self-inflicted death. In that case they would not imagine that there is any rejoicing in the ultimate good to be had here in this mortal condition. In this condition the very virtues themselves—than which nothing better or more beneficial is found in man here on earth—attest all the more clearly to its miseries precisely because they are our best helps against its perils, hardships, and pains. In fact, if they are true virtues, which can only be present in those who have true godliness, they make no claim to be able to guard the people in whom they are present from suffering misery. What they do claim is that human life, which is compelled to be miserable by all the terrible evils of this age, is happy by reason of hope for the age to come, just as it is also saved by hope. For how can a life be happy which is not yet saved? That is why the apostle Paul—speaking not of people who had no prudence or patience or temperance or justice but rather of those who live according to true piety and whose virtues are therefore true virtues—says, *For we are*

---

46. See Cicero, *On the Ends of the Good and the Evil* 3.5.16; 5.9.24.

saved by hope. But hope that is seen is not hope. For why would a person hope for what he already sees? But, if we hope for what we do not see, then we look forward to it with patience (Rom. 8:24–25). Just as it is by hope that we are saved, therefore, so it is by hope that we are made happy; and, just as we do not yet possess salvation in the present but look forward to salvation in the future, so we do not yet possess happiness in the present but look forward to happiness in the future, and we do this *with patience*. For we are in the midst of evils, which we ought patiently to endure until we attain those goods where everything will afford us inexpressible delight and there will be nothing left that we have to endure. Such is the salvation which, in the world to come, will itself also be our ultimate good. But these philosophers refuse to believe in this happiness because they do not see it; and precisely for this reason they try to contrive for themselves, here in this life, an utterly false happiness based on a virtue which is as fraudulent as it is arrogant.[47]

The Miseries of Social Life: The Household and the City

5. The philosophers also hold that the life of the wise man is social, and this is a view that we much more fully approve.[48] For we now have in hand the nineteenth book of this work on the city of God, and how could that city either make its start or proceed on its course or reach its due end if the life of the saints were not social? But who could possibly enumerate all the grinding evils with which human society abounds here in this mortal condition? Who is adequate to weigh them all up? These people should listen to a character in one of their own comedies, who expresses what everyone thinks and agrees with: "I took a wife. What misery I found! Children were born. More cares!"[49] What about the tribulations of love, listed off by that same Terence: "Injuries, suspicions, hostilities and war, then peace again."[50]

47. [GWL] A summary of Augustine's argument against the philosophers, and especially the Stoics. Happiness cannot be secured in this life.

48. [GWL] Here commences Augustine's extended discussion of happiness as a social good (Varro's third category). This section runs through 19.17 and challenges the Stoics' claim to be social. By claiming the "wise man" is self-sufficient, able to attain happiness regardless of others' suffering, Stoicism is fundamentally anti-social. Augustine concentrates first on miseries in the home (the first sphere of social life). This chapter rewards a slow reading. Augustine laments our inability to see the hearts of others, a condition that contrasts with his vision of heaven, where we will see one another's minds (22.29). He also observes the bitterness of betrayal by our closest companions.

49. Terence, *Adelphoi* 867–68.

50. *Eunuch* 59–61.

Have these tribulations not filled up human affairs everywhere we look? Do we not find them, as often as not, even in the case of honorable love between friends? Are not human affairs everywhere full of these evils? We count injuries, suspicions, hostilities and war as certain evils. But we count peace as no more than an uncertain good, for we do not know the hearts of those with whom we wish to be at peace, and, even if we could know their hearts today, we still would not know what they might be like tomorrow.[51] Again, who usually are—or ought to be—more friendly with each other than those who live in the same household? But who feels secure about this, when such terrible evils so often arise from the secret treacheries of people who live together? And the sweeter the peace that was thought to be true—when it was actually no more than a clever disguise—the more bitter these treacheries are. That is why Cicero's words touch all our hearts so deeply that they compel us to weep: "There are no more insidious treacheries than those which hide behind a pretense of friendliness or under the name of kinship. For you can easily steer clear of an open enemy, simply by being on guard, but this hidden evil, being internal and domestic, not only arises but even overwhelms you before you so much as have a chance to detect and expose it."[52] That is also why it is with such deep sadness of heart that we hear the divine saying, *And one's foes will be the members of one's own household* (Matt. 10:36). For, even if someone is strong enough to bear these evils with composure or alert enough to guard against the plots of false friendship with prudence and foresight, it is still true that, if he himself is good, he cannot help but feel terrible pain at the evil of his betrayers when he discovers just how evil they are. And this is so whether they were always evil and merely pretended to be good or whether they underwent some change from goodness to their subsequent malice. And, if not even the home is safe, our common refuge amid the evils of mankind, what of the city?[53] The larger the city, the more its forum teems with lawsuits, both civil and criminal, and this is true even when a city is not disturbed by the turbulence, or more often the bloodshed, of sedition and civil war. For cities may sometimes be free from such events, but they are never free from the risk of them.

51. See *Letter* 73.3.6–73.3.10, addressed to Jerome, in which Augustine alludes poignantly to the erstwhile friendship of Jerome and Rufinus of Aquileia, shattered by a dispute over Origen, and expresses the same sentiments.

52. See *Against Verres* 2.1.15.

53. [GWL] This sentence transitions to miseries in the city (the second sphere of social life).

6. What about the verdicts pronounced by men on men, which no city can do without, no matter how fully at peace it is? How miserable, how lamentable we consider them to be, such as they are! For those who judge obviously cannot see into the consciences of those whom they judge. As a result, they are often compelled to seek the truth by torturing innocent witnesses in a case that has nothing to do with them.[54] And what about torture applied to a person in his own case? The question here is whether or not he is guilty. But he is tortured even if he is innocent; and so, for a crime that is uncertain, he suffers an all too certain punishment—not because he is found to have committed the crime but because it is not known that he did not commit it. For this reason the ignorance of the judge is most often a calamity for the innocent. And what is still more intolerable—and still more to be lamented and, if only it were possible, to be washed away in a flood of tears—is the fact that, when the judge tortures the accused in order to keep from unknowingly putting an innocent person to death, it may happen that, as a result of his wretched ignorance, he puts to death, both tortured and innocent, the very person whom he had tortured in order to keep from putting an innocent person to death. For if, following the wisdom of these philosophers, the accused chooses to flee from this life rather than to endure those torments any longer, he admits that he committed a crime he did not commit.[55] And, when he has been condemned and put to death, the judge still does not know whether it was a guilty or an innocent man that he put to death, even though the very reason he tortured him was to keep from unknowingly putting an innocent man to death. Thus, he has both tortured an innocent man in order to learn the truth and put him to death without learning it.

54. [GWL] Torture was a standard practice in the Roman judicial system. This chapter is Augustine's fullest treatment of torture, and it is often interpreted as a defense of the practice. In my judgment, Augustine's purpose is to prove the miseries of life in the city on the Stoics' own terms. Though Augustine does not explicitly condemn torture, he does not approve it either. In practice, Augustine opposes torture in every instance where someone he knows is at risk of suffering it. See essay: "Stoics and Stoicism." My interpretation of this chapter follows Veronica Roberts Ogle, "Sheathing the Sword: Augustine and the Good Judge," *Journal of Religious Ethics* 46, no. 4 (2018): 718–47. NCP: "While lamenting the necessity of torture in the following lines, Augustine does not denounce it as an immoral practice."

55. [GWL] Augustine is referring to the Stoics, whom he critiqued in 19.4 for claiming that the "wise man" who experiences overwhelming suffering should commit suicide. According to the Stoics, those who are being tortured should falsely confess guilt so that they can die. As Augustine argues, this creates a problem for judges, who will never know whether they have tortured and killed an innocent person.

In the midst of these dark shadows of the social life, will the wise man
serve as a judge or will he shrink from doing so?[56] Clearly he will serve.
The claim of human society, which he finds it unthinkable to ignore, constrains him and draws him to this duty. For he does not find it unthinkable
that innocent witnesses are tortured in cases that have nothing to do with
them, or that the accused are very often overcome by the force of pain and
make false confessions and are punished despite their innocence. Nor does
he find it unthinkable that, even if not sentenced to death, they very often
die under torture or due to torture, or that those who bring charges—moved,
perhaps, by the desire to benefit society by seeing to it that crimes do not go
unpunished—are sometimes themselves condemned by an unknowing judge
in cases where witnesses lie and the guilty man himself adamantly refuses to
crack under torture and confess, so that the plaintiffs are unable to prove their
charges even though the charges are true. He does not count all these grievous evils as sins, for the wise judge does not do these things from any will to
inflict harm but rather from the inescapable necessity of ignorance—but also,
however, because human society demands it, due to the inescapable necessity
of judging. All this certainly shows, therefore, the human misery of which I
am speaking, although not any malice on the part of the wise man serving as
judge.[57] But, since it is due to the inescapable necessity of ignorance and the
inescapable necessity of judging that he tortures the innocent or punishes the
innocent, is it not enough for him that he is not counted guilty? Must he also
be counted happy? How much more perceptive it would be, how much more
worthy of a human being, for him to recognize the human misery laid bare
by those necessities, to detest that misery's grip on him, and, if he is devout
in his wisdom, to cry out to God, *Deliver me from my necessities* (Ps. 25:17)!

The Miseries of Social Life: The World

7. After the city or town comes the world, which the philosophers posit as the
third level of human society.[58] They start with the household, go from there
to the city, and come finally to the world. And the world, like a confluence of

56. [GWL] The "wise man" here also seems to refer to the Stoic ideal.
57. [GWL] In principle, Augustine seems to acknowledge, the judge who tortures does not
sin by doing so. But he can hardly be considered happy, which proves the emptiness of Stoic
philosophy in asserting the possibility of happiness in this temporal existence.
58. [GWL] From city to world: a transition to the third sphere of social life.

waters, is the more full of dangers due to its greater size. In the first place, the diversity of languages estranges people from each other. If two people meet, neither knowing the other's language, and are compelled by some necessity to stay together rather than moving on, it is easier for dumb animals, even if of different species, to associate together than it is for these people, even though they are both human beings. For, when people cannot communicate their thoughts to each other, because of nothing more than the diversity of their languages, their likeness of nature is of so little use in bringing them together that a man would rather be with his dog than with a foreigner. It is true enough that, for the sake of social peace, the imperial city has taken pains to impose on her subjugated peoples not only her yoke but also her language, so that there is not only no lack of interpreters but even an abundant supply.[59] But at what a cost this was achieved: all those terrible wars, all that human slaughter, all that human bloodshed!

Those wars themselves are now over, but there is still no end to the misery of their evils. For, although there was not and is not any lack of enemy foreign nations, against which wars have always been waged and are still being waged, yet the very extent of the empire has given birth to even worse kinds of wars, namely, social and civil.[60] By these the human race is even more miserably battered, either because the wars are actually being fought for the sake of eventual peace or because people are living in fear that war may break out again. If I wanted to describe, with words worthy of the reality, these many evils, these manifold disasters, these harsh and dire necessities, even though I could not possibly measure up to the reality itself, when would my discourse ever come to an end?

But the wise man, they say, will wage just wars.[61] Surely, however, if he remembers that he is a human being, it is far more true that he will grieve at being faced with the necessity of waging just wars. If they were not just, he would not have to wage them, and so there would be no wars for the wise man. For it is the iniquity of the opposing side that imposes on the wise man the

59. [GWL] Augustine sees benefit in Rome's imposition of Latin on those it conquered, since it reverses the diversity of languages separating humans from one another since Babel. Yet he laments the bloodshed of Rome's wars.

60. [GWL] Recall Book 3, where Augustine recounts Rome's history of wars, including its social and civil wars.

61. [GWL] The "wise man," again, seems to refer to the Stoic ideal, as described in 19.4. Even if someone is waging war justly to combat others' iniquity, the iniquity is itself tragic. This proves that happiness cannot be found in this life. See essay: "War."

obligation of waging just wars; and this iniquity should certainly be lamented by human beings, even if no necessity of waging war arises from it, for the very reason that it is the iniquity of human beings. Let everyone, therefore, who reflects with sorrow on such vast, such horrendous, such savage evils as these, acknowledge our misery. And, if anyone suffers such evils, or even just thinks about them, without anguish of soul, he is even more miserable, for it is only because he has lost all human feeling that he thinks himself happy.

8. In the miserable circumstances of this life it often happens that we believe an enemy is actually a friend or that a friend is actually an enemy. But, if we do not fall prey to this ignorance, akin to madness, what greater consolation do we have in this human society, riddled with errors and anxieties, than the unfeigned faith and mutual love of true and good friends? The more friends we have, however, and the more places we have them in, the more widespread is our fear that some evil may happen to them out of all the accumulated evils of this world.[62] Not only are we anxious lest they be afflicted by famine or war or disease or captivity (fearing that in slavery they may undergo sufferings more terrible than we can imagine), but also, with a far more bitter fear, we are anxious lest their friendship turn into betrayal, malice, and villainy. And, when such a thing does happen—and the more friends we have, the more often it happens—and comes to our knowledge, who but the one who has had this experience can really know the burning pain that scorches our heart? In fact we would rather hear that our friends were dead, although we also could not hear this without grief.

For, if their life delighted us with the comforts of friendship, how could it possibly happen that their death would bring us no sadness?[63] Anyone who forbids such sadness must forbid, if he can, all friendly conversation; he must ban or banish all mutual affection; he must with unfeeling savagery sever the bonds of all human relationships; or else he must stipulate that they are only to be used in such a way that the soul gets no pleasure from them. But, if this is utterly impossible, how could it be that the death of a person whose life was

---

62. [GWL] This discussion extends Augustine's analysis of the third sphere of social life, the world. The more friends we have around the world, the more we worry about them. This, too, is proof that happiness cannot be found in this life.

63. [GWL] These poignant sentences are worth pausing on. It is the delights of friendship that cause us such sadness when our friends die. The only way to protect ourselves from sadness is to avoid emotion altogether, but this is to deny our own humanity. NCP: "See Augustine's description of his own reaction to the death of a young friend, and his later regret at having been so inconsolable, in *Confessions* 4.4.7–4.7.12."

sweet to us should not be bitter to us? This is why the grief of a heart that is not inhuman is like a wound or a sore, for whose healing we offer our kind words of consolation. Nor should we think that there is no healing involved just because, the more refined a soul is, the more quickly and easily it is healed.

Thus, even though the life of mortals is pained, sometimes more gently, sometimes more harshly, by the death of those most dear to us, and especially of those whose responsibilities are essential to human society, we would still rather hear of, or even see, the death of those whom we love than hear or see that they have fallen away from faith or virtue, that is, that they have died in their very soul.[64]

The earth is full of this vast store of evils. That is why Scripture says, *Is not human life on earth a trial?* (Job 7:1 LXX). And that is why the Lord himself says, *Woe to the world because of stumbling blocks* (Matt. 18:7); and again, *Because iniquity has abounded, the love of many shall grow cold* (Matt. 24:12). As a result, we feel thankful at the death of good people who are our friends, for, even though their death saddens us, it at least offers us this more certain consolation: that they have been spared the evils by which, in this life, even good persons are either crushed or corrupted or put at risk of both.

The Miseries of Social Life: The Angels and the Demons

9. Then there is the society of the holy angels.[65] The philosophers who wanted to claim that the gods are our friends placed this on a fourth level, moving up from the earth to the universe at large so as to include, in some sense or other, even heaven itself. In this case it is certainly true that we have no fear that such friends will ever sadden us by dying or by becoming depraved. The angels, however, do not mingle with us on the familiar footing that human beings do, and this in itself is one of the tribulations of this life. Furthermore, as we read, Satan sometimes transforms himself into an angel of light[66] in order to tempt those who need this sort of training or who deserve to be deceived in this way. God's great mercy is needed, therefore, to keep anyone

64. [GWL] Augustine considers moral failure a worse fate than physical death. The death of the soul is more devastating than the death of the body. Despite his critique of the Stoics, Augustine's valorization of the soul over the body retains Stoic influences.

65. [GWL] The fourth sphere of social life is the universe, which involves angels and demons. NCP: "See *Teaching Christianity* 1.30.31–1.30.33, where Augustine asserts that angels may be understood to be neighbors, as the term is used in Matt. 22:39 par."

66. See 2 Cor. 11:14.

from supposing that he has good angels as friends when he actually has evil
demons as false friends, and thus to keep him from suffering harm at the
hands of these enemies. For, the more sly and deceitful they are, the more
harm they do. And what is it that makes God's great mercy so necessary
if it is not the great human misery which is so encumbered with ignorance
that it is easily taken in by the demons' dissembling? In fact it is absolutely
certain that the philosophers of the ungodly city who claimed that the gods
were their friends had actually fallen into the hands of the malign demons
to whom that city is totally subject and with whom it will endure eternal
punishment. For the character of the beings who are worshiped in that city
is made quite clear by the sacred—or, rather, the sacrilegious—rites by which
its citizens suppose that they are to be worshiped and by the obscene shows,
celebrating their crimes, by which its citizens suppose that they are to be
propitiated. For the demons themselves are the ones who authorized and
exacted all these vile indecencies.

10. But not even holy and faithful worshipers of the one true God are safe
from the deceits and the many temptations of the demons. For, in this place of
infirmity and in these evil days, anxiety on this score is not without its uses; it
leads them to seek with more fervent longing that state of security where peace
is completely full and assured.[67] There the gifts of nature—that is, the gifts
bestowed on our nature by the creator of all natures—will be not only good
but also eternal, and this will be true not only for the soul, which is healed by
wisdom, but also for the body, which will be renewed by resurrection. There
the virtues will not do battle against any vices or against any evils at all but
will have eternal peace as the reward of victory, a peace which no adversary
will ever disturb. For this is the ultimate happiness, this the final perfection,
which will have no end to bring it to an end. Here on earth, it is true, we are
called happy when we have peace—the little peace, that is, which it is possible
to have here on earth in living a good life. But this happiness is found to be
sheer misery when compared to the happiness that we call ultimate. Thus,
when we mortals, if we live rightly, have such peace as it is possible for human
beings to have in mortal affairs, virtue makes right use of its goods; and, when
we do not have that peace, virtue makes good use even of the evils a person
suffers. But virtue is true virtue only when it directs all the goods of which
it makes good use, and directs all that it does in making good use of both

---

67. [GWL] Augustine's reference to peace gestures toward his thesis, in 19.11, that happiness is eternal peace.

goods and evils, and directs itself as well, to the end where our peace will be so unsurpassed that it could not possibly be better or greater.

The Meanings of Peace

11. We may say of peace, then, as we have said of eternal life, that it is our ultimate good, and we may say this most especially because of what is said to the city of God (which is the subject of this very toilsome discourse of ours) in the holy Psalm: *Praise the Lord, O Jerusalem; praise your God, O Zion. For he has strengthened the bars of your gates; he has blessed your children within you; he has made your borders peace* (Ps. 147:12–14). For, when the bars of her gates are strengthened, then no one will enter her, nor will anyone go out from her. Thus, we should understand here that her borders are that final peace which I am now trying to set forth. For, as I have also said before, this city's mystic name, Jerusalem, means "vision of peace."[68]

But, since the term "peace" is also often used in relation to merely mortal affairs, where there obviously is no eternal life, I have preferred to call the ultimate end of this city, the end where its supreme good will be found, eternal life rather than peace. Of this end the Apostle says, *But now, having been set free from sin and made servants of God, you have your fruit in sanctification, and the end is eternal life* (Rom. 6:22). On the other hand, those who are not familiar with Sacred Scripture may presume that the life of the wicked is also eternal life. They may think this because, even according to some of the philosophers, the soul is immortal;[69] or they may think this because, even according to our own faith, the punishment of the ungodly is endless. After all, how could the ungodly go through torments for all eternity if they did not live for all eternity? Consequently, in order that everyone might more easily understand what we mean, we really ought to call the end of this city, in which it will gain its supreme good, either "peace in life eternal" or "eternal life in peace."[70] For peace is such a great good that, even in earthly and mortal affairs, no other word evokes more gratitude, nothing else is

68. See *Exposition of Psalm* 64.2. The Hebrew does not seem to allow for this understanding, although it had some currency among both Jewish and early Christian writers. See Jerome, *Interpretation of Hebrew Names*, Galatians, s.v. Jerosolyma. "Foundation of peace" may be the most likely meaning.

69. See Plato, *Phaedrus* 245b–246a; *Meno* 81c; Plotinus, *Enneads* 4.3.5.

70. [GWL] Here is Augustine's definition of the supreme good, eternal peace—a definition that challenges philosophical accounts of happiness.

desired more intensely, and, in short, nothing better can possibly be found. And, if I choose to linger on the subject a little longer, I shall not, I think, be imposing any burden on my readers, both because peace is the ultimate end of the city we are discussing and because of the very sweetness of peace itself, which is dear to all.[71]

The Universal Desire for Peace

12. Anyone who, with me, makes even a cursory examination of human affairs and our common human nature will realize how sweet peace is. For, just as there is no one who does not wish to have joy, neither is there anyone who does not wish to have peace.[72] In fact, even those who want war want nothing other than victory; what they desire, then, in waging war is to achieve peace with glory. What is victory, after all, but the subjugation of those fighting against us? And, when this is achieved, there will be peace. It is with the aim of peace, therefore, that wars are waged, even when they are waged by men who are eager to exercise the martial virtues in command and in battle. It is plain, then, that peace is the desired end of war. For everyone seeks peace, even in making war, but no one seeks war by making peace. Even those who want to disrupt the state of peace they currently have do not despise peace; rather, they want that peace to be changed for one they like better. What they want, therefore, is not no peace but rather the peace that they wish to have. And, even if they separate themselves from others by sedition, they cannot achieve their aim unless they maintain some sort of peace with their co-conspirators and confederates. Even robbers, in order to assault the peace of others both more ferociously and more safely, want to have peace with their own comrades.

71. [GWL] Augustine is announcing a digression on peace. This treatise on peace, which runs through 19.17, is one of the richest and most challenging sections in *City of God*.

72. [GWL] Peace is similar to happiness in that it is something people cannot help wanting. Peace is the social fabric of being. It is necessary to the created order in a way that war is not. Augustine's understanding of peace reflects his understanding of goodness and being. There is a metaphysical primacy to goodness and being, in contrast to evil (which is nonbeing or privation). See *Confessions* 10.8.12–10.23.34, where Augustine presents similar contrasts between memory and forgetting, happiness and unhappiness, and truth and falsehood. See also essay: "Evil as Privation."

In this chapter (19.12), Augustine offers several examples demonstrating the significance of peace: in war; for robbers; in the story of Cacus; among animals; among all human relations; and within the body—even when it dies, whether it is preserved or decomposes into the earth. The first examples (war, robbers, and Cacus) may allude to Rome. In 19.13–17, Augustine offers a more structured treatment of peace at different levels of being and social complexity.

Even in the case of a single bandit, who is so powerful on his own and so cautious about going in with others that he will not ally himself with anyone at all but rather works entirely alone, lying in wait, overwhelming his victims, and taking his booty from those he has overpowered and killed, it is still true that he maintains at least a shadow of peace with those whom he cannot kill and from whom he wishes to conceal his deeds. And in his own home, surely, he takes pains to be at peace with his wife and children and other members of his household. No doubt, in fact, he takes delight in having them serve his every beck and call. For, if this does not happen, he is outraged. He rebukes and punishes, and, if necessary, he even takes harsh measures to impose on his household a peace which, he believes, cannot exist unless all the other members of the same domestic society are subject to one master—who, in his own home, is himself. Thus, if he were offered the servitude of a larger group—of a city, say, or of a whole people—who would serve him in the same way he wishes to be served at home, he would no longer lurk in hiding like a robber but would exalt himself like a king for all to see.[73] But exactly the same avarice and malice would still remain in him. All men desire, then, to have peace with their own subjects, whom they want to live according to their dictates. And, if they can, they even want to make those on whom they wage war their subjects and to impose on them the laws of their own peace.

But let us imagine such a creature as poetry and fable portray, a creature so anti-social and wild that people have preferred to call him not human but half-human.[74] Even though his kingdom was the solitude of an ominous cave; even though his wickedness was so singular that he was given a name reflecting this fact (for the Greek word for "evil" is *kakos*, which is what he was called); even though he had no wife with whom to exchange expressions of love, no children to play with when they were little or to govern as they grew older, and no friends with whom to enjoy conversation, not even his father Vulcan (the only respect, but not an insignificant one, in which he was happier than his father was that he did not beget any monster such as himself); and, even though he gave nothing to anyone but rather took what he wanted from everyone he could whenever he could, it is still true that in his own

73. See above at 4.4 for the exchange between Alexander the Great and an anonymous pirate.
74. [GWL] Cacus was a mythical figure from Virgil's *Aeneid* (8.184–279) who lived on Rome's Aventine Hill and thus represented Rome before it was founded. According to Augustine, though Cacus was solitary and violent, he still desired peace in that he did not want to be disturbed by others, and he sought to pacify his own appetites. See Andrew Hofer, "Book 19: The Ends of the Two Cities: Augustine's Appeal for Peace," in Meconi, *COG*, 243–44.

solitary cave ("the floor of which," as it is described, "was always warm with fresh kill"[75]), all he wanted was a peace in which no one would trouble him and no violence, or fear of violence, from any side would disturb his quiet. Beyond this, he desired to be at peace with his own body; and, so far as he had this, all was well with him. His limbs obeyed his commands, and, when his mortal nature rebelled against him out of need and stirred up the sedition of hunger with its threat of separating and excluding the soul from the body, he acted with all possible speed to pacify that nature: he plundered, he killed, he devoured. Thus, for all his cruelty and savagery, he was, by these cruel and savage means, solicitous of the peace of his life and of his wellbeing. And so, if he had only been willing to have the same peace with others that he was determined to have in his cave and with himself, he would not be called evil or monstrous or half-human. Or, if it was actually his bodily appearance and his belching of black flames that scared away human companions, perhaps it was not the desire to do harm that made him so savage but rather the need to preserve his own life. But perhaps he never existed at all or, more probably, was not anything like what poetic fantasy describes. For, if Cacus had not been painted so black, Hercules would have gotten too little praise.[76] As in the case of many figments of the poets' imagination, then, we should give no credence to the existence of such a man or, better, such a half-man.

For even the most savage wild animals, from whom Cacus drew a part of his wildness (for he was also called half-wild[77]), preserve their own kind by a sort of peace: they mate, they reproduce, they give birth, they nurse and nourish their young. And this is true even when, as in most cases, they are anti-social and solitary—that is, like lions, wolves, foxes, eagles, and owls, rather than like sheep, deer, doves, starlings, or bees.[78] For what tigress does not purr softly over her young and caress them with her ferocity kept at peace? What kite, no matter how solitary in hovering over its prey, does not couple with its mate, build a nest, keep the eggs warm, feed the chicks, and maintain with the mother of the family, as it were, as peaceful a domestic society as he can? How much the more, then, is a human being drawn by the laws of his nature, so to speak, to be social and to maintain peace with all human beings, so far as it lies in his power? Even the wicked wage war to ensure the peace of their own

---

75. Virgil, *Aeneid* 8.195–96.
76. I.e., for slaying him. See Virgil, *Aeneid* 8.247–79.
77. See Virgil, *Aeneid* 8.267.
78. The same distinction between solitary and social animals is made above at 12.22.

people and would want, if they could, to make all men their own, so that all men and all things might serve one master. But how could this happen unless they all consented to that master's peace, either out of love or out of fear?

And so pride is a perverse imitation of God.[79] For it hates a society of equals under God and instead wishes to impose its own domination on its fellows in place of God's rule. Therefore, it hates the just peace of God and loves its own unjust peace. But it is quite impossible for it not to love some kind of peace. No one's vice is so completely contrary to nature that it destroys even the last vestiges of nature.

Thus, anyone who knows enough to prefer right to wrong and the well-ordered to the perverse sees that, in comparison to the peace of the just, the peace of the unjust ought not to be called peace at all.[80] But even what is perverted must of necessity be at peace in or from or with some part of the order of things in which it exists or of which it consists. Otherwise it would not exist at all. If someone hangs upside down, for example, the position of his body and the arrangement of his limbs are certainly perverted. What nature requires to be above is actually below, and what nature intends to be below is actually above. This perversity disturbs the peace of the flesh and therefore puts it under stress. But, even so, the soul is at peace with its body and is concerned for its wellbeing, and that is why the person feels pain. But, even if the soul is driven out of the body by its distress and leaves the body behind, what is left is still not without a kind of peace among its parts, so long as the structure of the limbs remains, and that is why there is still someone hanging there. And, because the earthly body pulls down toward the earth and pulls against the chain that holds it up, it tends toward the position of its own peace, and, by the voice of its own weight, so to speak, it begs for a place where it may find rest. Even now, then, when it is lifeless and wholly without sensation, it does not depart from the peace that is natural to its ordered place, either when it holds to or when it tends toward that peace. For if treatments and preservatives are applied, which keep the corpse's form from disintegrating and dissolving, a kind of peace still joins one part to another and holds the whole mass in its earthly place, its fitting place, and therefore its place of peace.[81]

79. [GWL] An important paragraph that connects pride, domination, and (unjust) peace, all of which characterize the earthly city as Augustine depicts it in *City of God*.

80. At this point, and continuing on to [chapter] 20, the discussion of peace gradually develops into a discussion of order as well, which had been debated at length at the beginning of Augustine's career in *Order*, especially at 1.3.6–1.3.8; 2.4.11–2.5.14.

81. See *Confessions* 13.9.10 for a meditation on place and peace.

But, if no preservative treatment is applied and the body is simply left to nature's course, there is for a while a kind of tumult of exhalations that are disagreeable and offensive to our senses (for it is this that we smell in cases of such decay). This lasts until the body merges with the elements of the world and, little by little, particle by particle, is dispersed into their peace. In this process, however, nothing whatsoever falls outside the laws of the supreme creator and ruler by whom the peace of the universe is arranged and directed. For, even if tiny animals are born in the carcass of a larger animal, all those little bodies, by the same law of the creator, serve their little souls in the peace of their wellbeing; and even if the flesh of dead animals is devoured by other animals—no matter where it is taken, no matter what it is mixed with, no matter what it is transformed and changed into—it still finds itself under the same laws, which are spread out through all things for the wellbeing of each mortal species, matching, in peace, what is suitable with what is suitable.[82]

Peace and Order

13. The peace of the body is, then, the properly ordered arrangement of its parts;[83] the peace of the irrational soul is the properly ordered satisfaction of the appetites; the peace of the rational soul is the properly ordered accord of cognition and action; the peace of body and soul together is the properly ordered life and wellbeing of a living creature; peace between mortal man and God is properly ordered obedience, in faith, under eternal law; peace among men is the properly ordered concord of mind with mind; the peace of

82. [GWL] Peace is essential to all existence. Even when a living creature dies, its body decomposes into a kind of peace with the earth. If insects appear in the carcass or other animals eat it, all these creatures also act according to a desire for peace.

83. [GWL] The following list outlines the topics Augustine will address in 19.14–17. The topics move in roughly ascending order from lower to higher beings and from smaller to larger social units: (1) peace of the body; (2) peace of the irrational soul (especially in animals, who are sentient but lack rationality); (3) peace of the rational soul (in humans and angels); (4) peace between the body and the soul; (5) peace between humans and God; (6) peace among humans; (7) peace of the household; (8) peace of the city; (9) peace of the heavenly city. Augustine treats topics 1–6 in 19.14, topic 7 in 19.14–16, and topics 8 and 9 in 19.17. He closely connects peace with order. He also identifies two contexts that require command and obedience: the household (topic 7) and the city (topic 8). Augustine's treatment of the household concentrates on the head of the household's responsibility to discipline his slaves in order to preserve peace. His treatment of the city discusses the importance of laws in the earthly city.

The NCP translation of (6) could have been gender-neutral and adds the phrase "mind with mind," which is not in the Latin. An alternate translation might be "peace among humans is properly ordered concord."

a household is the properly ordered concord, with respect to command and obedience, of those who are living together; the peace of a city is the properly ordered concord, with respect to command and obedience, of its citizens; the peace of the heavenly city is perfectly ordered and wholly concordant fellowship in the enjoyment of God and of each other in God.[84] The peace of all things is the tranquility of order,[85] and order is the arrangement of things equal and unequal that assigns to each its due place.

Therefore, the wretched—since, insofar as they are wretched, they are certainly not at peace—lack the tranquility of order, which is free of all disturbance. Even in their very wretchedness, however, they do not and cannot fall outside the reach of order, for their wretchedness itself is just and deserved. They are obviously not united with the blessed, but it is precisely by the law of order that they are set apart from them. And, when they are free of disturbance, they are adapted to their circumstances with at least some degree of suitability, and, as a result, there is in them at least something of the tranquility of order, and therefore at least something of peace. But they are still wretched simply because, although they are to some degree free of care and pain, they are not in the place where they ought to be wholly without care or pain. And they would be still more wretched if there were no peace at all between them and the law by which the natural order is directed. For, when they are in pain, their peace is disturbed because of the part in which they feel pain, but there is still peace in the part in which no pain burns and the bodily structure itself is not dissolved. Just as there can be life without pain, therefore, but no pain without at least some degree of life, so there can be peace without war but no war without at least some degree of peace.[86] This is due not to the nature of war itself but to the fact that it is waged by

84. [GWL] The peace of the heavenly city involves enjoying God and one another in God. This language departs from *De Doctrina Christiana* 1.22.20–1.22.21, where Augustine says we are to enjoy God alone and thus to use other humans. As Oliver O'Donovan has surmised, Augustine may have been uncomfortable with the language of using humans. In later writings, Augustine adopts the formulation that humans should enjoy one another, though always with reference to God, who alone is to be enjoyed as our final good. Oliver O'Donovan, "*Usus* and *Fruitio* in Augustine, *De Doctrina Christiana* I," *Journal of Theological Studies* 33, no. 2 (1982): 361–97.

85. This thumbnail definition of peace as the tranquility of order has achieved classic status. See, e.g., Thomas Aquinas, *Summa Theologiae* II-II.29.1.

86. [GWL] This discussion parallels Augustine's treatment of being and evil. War is parasitic on peace in the same way that evil is parasitic on being and goodness. See essay: "Evil as Privation."

or within persons who are in some sense natural beings, for they would not exist at all if they did not subsist by virtue of some sort of peace.

There is, then, a nature in which there is no evil and in which in fact it is impossible for evil to exist, but it is not possible for there to be a nature in which there is no good. Not even the nature of the devil himself is evil, insofar as it is a nature.[87] It is perversity that makes it evil. Thus, he did not stand in the truth,[88] but he did not escape the judgment of the truth. He did not remain in the tranquility of order, but even so he did not evade the power of the orderer. The goodness of God, which is his with respect to his nature, does not remove him from the justice of God, by which he is ordained for punishment. Nor does God punish the good which he created but rather the evil which the devil committed. For God does not take away all that he gave to that nature. Rather, he removes something and, at the same time, he leaves something, so that there is something left to feel pain over what is taken away. And this very pain attests both to the good that was taken away and to the good that was left, for, if no good had been left, there could be no pain over the good that was lost. A person who sins is even worse if he rejoices in the loss of righteousness; but a person in torment, even if he gains no good from it, at least feels pain at the loss of salvation. And since both righteousness and salvation are good, and since we ought to feel pain rather than joy at the loss of any good (as long as there is no greater good compensating for the loss, as, for instance, righteousness of soul is a greater good than health of body), it is obviously more fitting for the unjust to feel pain in punishment than to feel joy in sin. Thus, just as feeling joy in sin due to the good that one has forsaken is evidence of an evil will, so feeling pain in punishment due to the good that one has lost is evidence of a good nature. For anyone who feels pain at the lost peace of his nature feels this due to some remnant of that peace by virtue of which his nature still shows its care for itself. In the final punishment, then, it is right that, in their torments, the wicked and the ungodly should lament the loss of their natural goods, knowing that those goods were taken from them by the supremely just God, whom they despised when he was their supremely generous benefactor.

God is, therefore, the supremely wise creator and the supremely just orderer of all natures. He established the mortal human race as earth's highest ornament, and he bestowed on human beings certain goods suited to this

87. See the more extended discussion on the devil . . . at 11.13–15.
88. See John 8:44.

life, namely, a temporal peace appropriate to the brief measure of a mortal life, consisting in bodily health and soundness, and the society of one's own kind, as well as whatever is necessary to maintain or recover this peace (such as those things which are readily and conveniently on hand for our senses—light, speech, air to breathe, water to drink—and whatever is suited to feeding, clothing, healing, and adorning the body). He did this, however, on the wholly just condition that any mortal who makes right use of such goods, which are meant to serve the peace of mortals, will receive fuller and better goods, namely, the peace of immortality and the glory and honor appropriate to it, in an eternal life meant for the enjoyment of God and of one's neighbor in God, but that anyone who uses them wrongly will not receive these eternal goods and in fact will lose those temporal goods.[89]

Earthly Peace and Eternal Peace

14. In the earthly city, then, all use of temporal things is directed to the enjoyment of earthly peace; in the heavenly city, in contrast, it is directed to the enjoyment of eternal peace. Thus, if we were no more than irrational animals, we would seek nothing more than the properly ordered arrangement of the body's parts and the satisfaction of the appetites, that is, nothing more than the comfort of the body and a good supply of pleasures, so that the peace of the body might promote the peace of the soul.[90] For, if the peace of the body is lacking, the peace of the irrational soul is also impeded, because it cannot achieve the satisfaction of its appetites. Together, however, these two kinds of peace promote the peace which the soul and the body have with each other, that is, the peace of properly ordered life and wellbeing.[91] For, just as animals show their love for the body's peace by fleeing pain and their love for the soul's peace by pursuing pleasure in order to meet the demands of their appetites, so they indicate clearly enough, by fleeing death, how much they love the peace by which soul and body are harmoniously united with each other.

89. [GWL] An allusion to *De Doctrina Christiana* 1, where Augustine distinguishes between use and enjoyment. See above: Book 19nn3, 84.

90. [GWL] A reference to (1), peace of the body, and (2), peace of the irrational soul. On the numbered topics in this and the following notes, see above: Book 19n83.

91. [GWL] A reference to (4), peace between the body and the soul. Augustine reverses the order of (4) and (3), the only break of sequence from the list of topics in 19.13.

But, because man has a rational soul, he subordinates everything that he has in common with the beasts to the peace of the rational soul, and this is so that he may picture something with the mind and act in accord with what he has pictured so as to bring about that properly ordered accord of cognition and action which we have called the peace of the rational soul.[92] And for this reason he should will to be neither distressed by pain nor disturbed by desire nor dissolved by death, so that he may arrive at some useful knowledge and may shape his life and moral character in accord with that knowledge. But because, in his very eagerness for knowledge, he may fall into some deadly error due to the weakness of the human mind, he has need of divine guidance, which he may obey with certainty, and divine help, so that he may obey it freely. And further, so long as he is in this mortal body, he is on pilgrimage far from God, and he walks by faith, not by sight.[93] That is why he directs all these forms of peace, whether of the body or of the soul or of both together, to the peace which mortal man has with the immortal God, so that he may have a properly ordered obedience, in faith, under eternal law.[94]

Now, since God, our teacher, teaches two chief precepts, love of God and love of neighbor,[95] in which man finds three things to love—God, himself, and his neighbor; and since one who loves God does not go wrong in loving himself, it follows that he also wants his neighbor to love God, since he is commanded to love his neighbor as himself.[96] And so he wants this for his wife, for his children, for his entire household, and for anyone else he can, and he wants his neighbor to have the same concern for him, if he happens to be in need of it. As a result, he will be at peace with all men, so far as it is in his power, with that peace among men which is the properly ordered concord of man with man; and this concord's order is, first, to harm no one and, second, to help anyone that one can.[97] First of all, then, his care will be for his own people, for, by the order of nature or of human society itself, he obviously

92. [GWL] A reference to (3), peace of the rational soul.
93. See 2 Cor. 5:6–7.
94. [GWL] A reference to (5), peace between humans and God.
95. See Matt. 22:36–40 par.
96. [GWL] Love for God and neighbor is at the heart of Augustine's ethics. There is no need for a command to love self, since all humans do this anyway. There are thus two love commandments but three objects of love. NCP: "Ideas similar to those expressed in the following lines are developed more fully in *Teaching Christianity* 1.22.20–1.29.30."
97. [GWL] A reference to (6), peace among humans. See above: Book 19n83.

has a readier and more immediate opportunity to care for them.[98] That is why the Apostle says, *Anyone who does not provide for his own, and especially for the members of his household, has denied the faith and is worse than an unbeliever* (1 Tim. 5:8). It is here, therefore, that domestic peace takes its rise, that is, the properly ordered concord, with respect to command and obedience, of those who are living together.[99] For it is those who exercise care that give the commands, as husbands to wives, parents to children, and masters to servants, and it is those who are cared for that obey, as wives their husbands, children their parents, and servants their masters. In the household of the just person who lives by faith[100] and is still on pilgrimage far from the heavenly city, however, even those who give commands are at the service of those whom they appear to command.[101] For they do not give their commands out of any desire for domination but rather out of dutiful concern for others, not out of any pride in ruling but rather out of compassion in providing for others.

Sin and Slavery

15. This is what the order of nature prescribes; this is the way God created man. For he said, *Let him have dominion over the fish of the sea and the birds of the air and every creeping thing that creeps on the earth* (Gen. 1:26). He did not want a rational creature, made in his own image,[102] to have dominion except over irrational creatures—not man over man but man over beasts.[103] That is why the first righteous men were established as shepherds

98. [GWL] Augustine is transitioning to (7), peace in the household. Augustine believes we have special obligations to those in close proximity to us. See *De Doctrina Christiana* 1.28.29.

99. [GWL] Note the reference to "command and obedience," the phrase that distinguishes relations within the household and the city from other relations. The section that follows is the fullest discussion of slavery in Augustine's corpus. See essay: "Slavery."

100. See Rom. 1:17.

101. See Matt. 20:25–26 par. Augustine touches on this theme with respect to the relationship between bishops and their flocks in *Sermons* 340.1; 340A.1–3.

102. See Gen. 1:26.

103. [GWL] This passage is often cited for Augustine's understanding of political authority. According to a common interpretation of Augustine, humans were not originally created with political authority over one another. Political authority is a function of the fall and inherently coercive, yet it is necessary to establish order and peace among immoral people. Augustine's position is often contrasted with that of Thomas Aquinas, who is understood to affirm the inherent goodness of political society (*Summa Theologiae* I.96.4). These interpretations have been contested. For further discussion, see R. A. Markus, "Two Conceptions of Political Authority: Augustine, *De Civitate Dei*, XIX. 14–15, and Some Thirteenth-Century Interpretations," *Journal of Theological Studies* 16, no. 1 (1965): 68–100; Paul J. Weithman, "Augustine and Aquinas on Original Sin and

of flocks rather than as kings of men,[104] so that in this way, too, God might indicate what the order of created beings requires and what the fault of sinners demands. For we recognize it is on sinners that the condition of slavery is justly imposed.[105] That is why we do not read of any slave in Scripture until the just man Noah[106] punished his son's sin with this designation.[107] His son deserved the name, then, not by nature but by fault. In Latin, the origin of the word for "slaves" is believed to stem from the fact that those who might have been killed under the laws of war were instead sometimes preserved by the victors and became slaves; thus they were called slaves due to the fact that they were preserved.[108] But even this does not hold good apart from the just deserts of sin. For, even when a just war is waged, the opposing side is fighting in defense of its sin; and every victory, even when it goes to the wicked, is a humiliation imposed on the vanquished by divine judgment either to correct or to punish their sins.[109] Daniel, a man of God, is a witness on this score: when he was taken captive, he confessed his own sins and the sins of his people to God, and in devout sorrow he testified that this was the cause of his captivity.[110] The first cause of slavery, therefore, is sin, with the result that man is made subject to man by the bondage of this condition, which can only happen by the judgment of God, in whom there is no unrighteousness and who knows how to assign different punishments according to the merits of the offenders.

As the Lord on high says, *Everyone who commits sin is a slave of sin* (John 8:34). Thus, although there are many godly men who are the slaves of unrighteous masters, this does not mean that the masters they serve are

---

the Function of Political Authority," *Journal of the History of Philosophy* 30, no. 3 (1992): 353–76; Eric Gregory and Joseph Clair, "Augustinianisms and Thomisms," in *The Cambridge Companion to Christian Political Theology*, ed. Craig Hovey and Elizabeth Phillips (Cambridge: Cambridge University Press, 2015), 176–95; and Katherine Chambers, "Slavery and Domination as Political Ideas in Augustine's *City of God*," *Heythrop Journal* 54, no. 1 (2013): 13–28.

104. See Gen. 4:2.

105. As becomes clearer from what follows, Augustine does not intend to say that a particular slave's sinfulness is responsible for the fact that he is enslaved but rather that the very existence of slavery is the result of human sinfulness in general. As with his discussion of torture above at 19.6, Augustine regrets the existence of slavery but does not denounce it.

106. See Gen. 6:9.

107. See Gen. 9:25–26, where Canaan, the son of Ham, is called a slave.

108. "Slaves . . . preserved": *servi . . . servando*. Augustine's etymology is incorrect.

109. [GWL] See 1.8–9, where Augustine introduces the idea of suffering as a form of divine pedagogy. See essays: "Providence and Suffering"; "War."

110. See Dan. 9:3–19.

themselves free men, *for a person is a slave to whatever masters him* (2 Pet. 2:19). Clearly it is a happier lot to be enslaved to a man than to be enslaved to lust; in fact it is the very lust for domination itself, to mention no others, that ravages the hearts of mortals by exercising the most savage kind of domination over them.[111] And, within that order of peace by which some men are subject to others, while humility is beneficial to those who serve, pride is harmful to those who rule.

By nature, then, as God first created man, no one is a slave either to man or to sin. But it is also true that the punishment of slavery is ordained by precisely the same law which commands that the natural order is to be preserved and forbids it to be disturbed, for, if nothing had been done in violation of that law, there would be nothing for the punishment of slavery to keep under constraint. It is for this reason that the Apostle admonishes slaves to be subject to their masters and to serve them from the heart with a good will,[112] so that, if they cannot be freed by their masters, they can at least make their own slavery free in a sense, that is, by serving their masters not with cunning fear but with faithful love, until all unrighteousness passes away, all human rule and power are brought down,[113] and God is all in all.[114]

16. Thus, even though our righteous fathers had slaves, and even though they managed their domestic peace in such a way as to distinguish between the status of their children and the condition of their slaves with regard to temporal goods, they still showed equal affection in their care for all the members of their household with regard to the worship of God,[115] in whom we are to place our hope for eternal goods.[116] This is what the order of nature prescribes, with the result that this is the origin of the name *paterfamilias*,[117] which is now so widely and commonly used that even those who rule unjustly delight to be called by the name.[118] But the true fathers of their families are those who are just as much

111. [GWL] The worst form of slavery is not to another person but to sin. For similar remarks, see 5.17.

112. See Eph. 6:5–8; Col. 3:22–24; Titus 2:9–10.

113. See 1 Cor. 15:24.

114. See 1 Cor. 15:28.

115. See, e.g., Exod. 12:44.

116. [GWL] The head of the household was to rule his children and slaves so as to direct them to proper worship. Doing so was an act of love and service, which he extended to his slaves as well as to his children.

117. I.e., "father of the family" or "head of the household." *Familia*, often translated as "family," had a broader connotation in Roman society than it does today and could include all the members of a household.

118. See Seneca, *Letter* 47.14.

concerned for all in their households as they are for their children when it comes to worshiping God and living worthily of him. They desire and pray that they will all come to the heavenly home where the duty of commanding mortals will no longer be necessary, because the duty of caring for others will no longer be needed when they have all attained the happiness of that immortality. Until that home is reached, however, fathers have a greater obligation to put up with being masters than slaves do to put up with being slaves.

If anyone in the household disrupts domestic peace by his disobedience, he is corrected by word or blow or some other just and legitimate kind of punishment, to the extent that human society allows.[119] This is, however, for the benefit of the person corrected, and its aim is that he may be brought back into line with the peace from which he had broken away. For, just as there is nothing kind about helping a person if it causes him to lose a greater good, neither is there anything blameless about sparing a person if it allows him to fall into graver evil. To be blameless, then, we are obliged not only to do no evil to a person but also to restrain him from sin or to punish his sin, either so that the one who is punished may be corrected by his experience or so that others may be deterred by his example.

Since, therefore, a man's household ought to be the beginning, or a small part, of the city, and since every beginning is directed to some end appropriate to its own kind, and since every part is directed to the integrity of the whole of which it is a part, it seems to follow clearly enough that domestic peace is directed to civic peace; that is, the properly ordered concord, with respect to command and obedience, of those who are living together is directed to the properly ordered concord, with respect to command and obedience, of citizens.[120] So it is that the father of a family should draw his precepts from the law of the city, and he should so rule his household by those precepts that it is fully in accord with the peace of the city.

Earthly Peace and the Two Cities

17. But a household of people who do not live by faith pursues an earthly peace based on the goods and advantages of this temporal life.[121] In contrast,

---

119. [GWL] Augustine supports corporal punishment in the household. Augustine's position on this matter reflects the wider principle of benevolent severity, according to which external harshness can express internal love. See essay: "War."

120. [GWL] Augustine transitions from (7), peace of the household, to (8), peace of the city. Each sphere is to be governed by the same principles, whether by the *paterfamilias* or by political officials. Each requires command and obedience to preserve order and peace.

121. [GWL] This chapter is one of the most studied passages in Augustine's political theology, in part because it leaves so ambiguous the nature of the heavenly city's cooperation with the

a household of people who live by faith looks to the eternal goods which are promised for the future.[122] It makes use of earthly and temporal things like a pilgrim. It is not captivated by them, nor is it deflected by them from the path that leads toward God, but it is sustained by them so that it may more easily bear the burdens of the corruptible body that weighs down the soul[123] and may at least keep those burdens from getting any worse. Thus, use of the things necessary to this mortal life is common to both kinds of people and to both kinds of household, but each uses them for its own very different end.

So also the earthly city, which does not live by faith, seeks an earthly peace, and it establishes a concord of command and obedience among its citizens in order to bring about a kind of accommodation among human wills with regard to the things that pertain to this mortal life.[124] And the heavenly city—or, rather, that part of it which is on pilgrimage in this mortal existence and which lives by faith—must of necessity make use of this peace as well, at least until this mortal existence, for which such peace is necessary, passes away.[125] Consequently, for as long as it leads its pilgrim life as a captive, so to speak, in the earthly city, even though it has already received the promise of redemption and the gift of the Spirit as a pledge of that redemption, it does not hesitate to obey the laws of the earthly city, by which the things needed for sustaining this mortal life are administered. For, since this mortal existence is common

---

earthly city. Scholars differ on how to interpret and apply Augustine's remarks. Some see Augustine encouraging Christian participation in pluralist contexts and stress the value of Christian civic engagement. Others focus on Christians' status as captives in the earthly city and stress the church's identity as an alternate society distinct from the world. For analysis, see R. A. Markus, *Saeculum: History and Society in the Theology of St. Augustine*, 2nd ed. (orig. 1970; Cambridge: Cambridge University Press, 1988); Oliver O'Donovan, "The Political Thought of *City of God* 19," in *Bonds of Imperfection: Christian Politics, Past and Present*, ed. Oliver O'Donovan and Joan Lockwood O'Donovan (orig. 1987; Grand Rapids: Eerdmans, 2004), 48–72; and Rowan Williams, "Politics and the Soul: Reading the *City of God*," in *On Augustine* (orig. 1987; London: Bloomsbury, 2016), 107–29. For my approach, see Gregory W. Lee, "Republics and Their Loves: Rereading *City of God* 19," *Modern Theology* 27, no. 4 (2011): 553–81.

122. [GWL] Augustine begins this chapter by contrasting the earthly household and the heavenly household. He then invokes the distinction between use and enjoyment, taken from *De Doctrina Christiana* 1.

123. See Wis. 9:15.

124. [GWL] Following his comparison between the earthly and heavenly households, Augustine compares the earthly and heavenly cities. The earthly city tries to coordinate conflicting human desires toward an agreement on earthly things necessary for this temporal life.

125. [GWL] So long as the heavenly city sojourns in this world, it will need the earthly peace of the earthly city. It thus cooperates with the earthly city on many matters. Augustine's reference to pilgrimage, which he associates with captivity, alludes to the exile of the Israelites in Babylon (19.26). His emphasis on obedience reflects his concern for order, which is constitutive of peace (19.13).

to both cities, its obedience serves to maintain a concord between the two with regard to the things that pertain to our mortal life.

But the earthly city has included among its members certain wise men whose views the divine teaching rejects, and these thinkers, due either to their own surmise or to demonic deception, believed that there are many gods whose favor must be gained in human affairs and that various matters fall under the various areas of responsibility that these gods are presumed to have.[126] Thus, the body falls to one god, the mind to another; and, within the body itself, the head falls to one god, the neck to another, and each of the other parts to other gods. Similarly, within the mind, native intelligence falls to one god, learning to another, anger to another, and desire to another. And so on with regard to all the things that bear on our lives: livestock fall to one god, grain falls to another, wine to another, oil to another, woods to another, money to another, navigation to another, wars and victories to another, marriage to another, birth and fertility to another, and so on and so forth.[127] In contrast, the heavenly city knew that the one God is alone to be worshiped, and it insisted with faithful devotion that only this God is to be served with the service which in Greek is called *latreia* and which is due only to God.[128] As a result of this difference, it has been impossible for the heavenly city to have laws of religion in common with the earthly city. Instead, it has of necessity had to dissent from the earthly city at this point and to become an annoyance to those who think differently. As a result it has had to endure their wrath, their hatred, and the assaults of their persecutions, except when it turned back the minds of its foes, sometimes due to their fear of its sheer numbers and always due to God's aid.[129]

So long as this heavenly city is a pilgrim on earth, then, it calls forth citizens from all peoples and gathers together a pilgrim society of all languages. It cares nothing about any differences in the manners, laws, and institutions by which earthly peace is achieved or maintained. But it does not rescind or

126. [GWL] The primary area where the heavenly city cannot cooperate with the earthly concerns religion. This paragraph recalls Augustine's earlier polemic against the gods (especially in Book 4). One interpretive question, which this passage leaves unresolved, concerns the breadth of immoral practices with which a Christian cannot cooperate. Beyond the obvious case of polytheism, could other forms of injustice count implicitly as false religion?

127. See Book 7 passim.

128. For an extended discussion of various religious terms, including *latreia*, see above at 10.1.

129. [GWL] Augustine may be alluding to the Christianization of the Roman empire since Constantine's rule. By Augustine's time, Christians were not being persecuted for their faith. Yet he describes this situation as an aberration to the normal status of Christians in the earthly city.

abolish any of these; rather, it preserves and follows them, provided only that they do not interfere with the religion which teaches that we are to worship the one supreme and true God,[130] for, however different they may be in different nations, they all aim at one and the same thing—earthly peace.[131] Thus, even the heavenly city makes use of earthly peace during its pilgrimage, and, so far as sound piety and religion allow, it defends and seeks an accommodation among human wills with regard to the things that pertain to humanity's mortal nature.[132] At the same time, however, it directs this earthly peace toward the heavenly peace which is so truly peace that, strictly speaking, it alone is to be considered and called the peace of the rational creature, namely, a perfectly ordered and wholly concordant fellowship in the enjoyment of God and of each other in God. When we reach this peace, our life will not be mortal but rather fully and definitely alive, and our body will not be the animal body which, so long as it is corrupted, weighs down the soul,[133] but rather the spiritual body, in need of nothing and wholly subject to the will. So long as the heavenly city is on pilgrimage, it has this peace in faith, and by this faith it lives justly when it directs toward the attainment of this peace every good act it performs for God and—since the life of a city is most certainly social—for neighbor.[134]

The Issues of Certainty and Style of Life

18. As for the distinction which Varro ascribes to the New Academy, that all things are uncertain, the city of God abhors such doubt as madness.[135] With regard to things it apprehends by mind and reason, it has fully certain knowledge, even though that knowledge is circumscribed due to the

130. For the same thought see above at 14.1. This toleration of—or indifference to—diversity in secular matters is consonant with Augustine's attitude toward certain ecclesiastical customs, provided only that the divine law be obeyed. See *Letter* 54.2.2–54.7.10.

131. [GWL] Since peace is an unavoidable desire (19.12), all earthly governments pursue peace of some sort, even when they secure this peace by dominating others.

132. [GWL] A repeat of Augustine's earlier point in this chapter that the heavenly city requires the earthly peace of the earthly city.

133. See Wis. 9:15.

134. [GWL] This concludes Augustine's treatise on peace and his treatment of Varro's third question, whether happiness is social. Augustine affirms that it certainly is.

135. [GWL] A reference to Varro's fourth question on whether knowledge is certain or uncertain.

corruptible body which weighs down the soul,[136] for, as the Apostle says, *We know in part* (1 Cor. 13:9). In every case, too, it trusts the evidence of the senses, which the mind uses by means of the body, for anyone who thinks that the senses are never to be trusted is miserably mistaken. It also believes in the Holy Scriptures, both Old and New, which we call canonical, from which comes the very faith by which the just person lives[137] and by which we walk—without doubting—as long as we are on pilgrimage and away from the Lord.[138] As long as this faith is sound and certain, however, we may, without ground for reproach, have doubts about certain things which we have not perceived by sense or reason, which have not been made clear to us through canonical Scripture and which have not come to our knowledge through witnesses whom it would be absurd not to believe.

19. It makes no difference to the heavenly city what mode of dress or manner of life is adopted by one who follows the faith that leads to God, just so long as it is not contrary to the divine precepts.[139] Consequently it does not compel those philosophers of theirs, when they become Christian, to change either their dress or their customary diet; it only compels them to change their false doctrines. Thus, it does not care at all about the distinction which Varro drew from the Cynics,[140] provided that it involves nothing indecent or intemperate. As for the three kinds of life—the leisured, the active, and the combination of both—it is true that anyone, so long as his faith is sound, can lead his life and attain to eternal rewards in any one of them.[141] It does matter, however, what he holds back in his love of truth and what he pays out in the duty of charity. No one ought to be so completely at leisure that in his leisure he takes no thought for serving his neighbor, nor should anyone be so fully active that he makes no room for the contemplation of God. In the leisured life it is not inert idleness that ought to delight but rather the seeking or the finding of truth, so that each makes progress in this respect and no one jealously keeps from others what he finds. And in the active life it is not honor or power in this life that ought to be prized,

136. See Wis. 9:15.
137. See Rom. 1:17.
138. See 2 Cor. 5:6.
139. [GWL] A reference to Varro's fifth question on whether to follow the practices of the Cynics or those of other philosophers.
140. See above at 19.1 and [*City of God, Books 11–22*, 349n7 // above, Book 19n14].
141. [GWL] A reference to Varro's sixth question on whether to pursue a life of leisure, activity, or both.

since everything under the sun is vanity;[142] instead, what ought to be prized is the task accomplished by means of that honor and power, just so long as the task is accomplished rightly and helpfully, so that it truly contributes to the wellbeing of those set under us. This is what accords with God, as we have discussed above, and it is for this reason that the Apostle says, *Anyone who desires the episcopate desires a good work* (1 Tim. 3:1). He wanted to explain what *episcopate* means, for it is the name of a task, not an honor. It is a Greek word, and it derives from the fact that a person who is set over others superintends them, that is, bears the responsibility of caring for them. For *skopos* means "intention," and so, if we wish, we may translate *episkopein* into Latin as "superintend." Thus, a person who loves being preeminent rather than helpful should understand that he is no bishop. No one, therefore, is barred from eagerness to know the truth, which is what makes the leisured life praiseworthy. But it is not seemly to seek out a high position, without which no people can be governed, even if that position is held and administered in a seemly fashion.

It is the love of truth, then, that seeks holy leisure, and it is the drive of love that takes on righteous activity. If no one imposes that burden on us, we ought to devote our free time to discerning and contemplating the truth, but, if that burden is imposed on us, we must accept it due to the drive of love. Even then, however, delight in the truth should by no means be abandoned, lest its pleasure be taken from us and that drive leave us swamped.

20. The supreme good of the city of God is, then, eternal and perfect peace, not the peace through which mortal men pass on their way from birth to death but rather the peace in which they remain as immortals and no longer suffer any adversity at all.[143] Who, therefore, would deny that this is the supremely blessed life? Or who would not judge that, in comparison with it, the life which we lead here on earth, no matter how filled it may be with the goods of soul and body and external things, is utterly miserable? Nevertheless, if anyone uses this life in such a way that he directs it to that other life as the end which he loves with ardent intensity and for which he hopes with unwavering faithfulness, it is not absurd to call him happy even now, although happy in

---

142. See Eccles. 1:14.
143. [GWL] A summary statement on the *summum bonum*. Happiness is eternal peace, and it cannot be found in this temporal life.

that hope rather than in this reality.[144] Without that hope, in fact, this reality is only a false happiness and a great misery. For it does not make use of the true goods of the soul, because no wisdom is true wisdom if it does not direct its intention—in everything that it discerns with prudence, bears with fortitude, constrains with temperance, and distributes with justice—to the end where God will be all in all[145] in assured eternity and perfect peace.

The Definition of a Republic

21. Here, then, is the place for me to fulfill, as briefly and as clearly as I can, the promise I made in the second book of this work.[146] There I promised to show, according to the definitions Scipio uses in Cicero's book, *The Republic*, that there never was a Roman republic. For, in brief, he defines a republic as "the common good of a people."[147] But, if this definition is true, there never was a Roman republic, because it never was "the common good of a people," which is the definition Scipio wanted to use for a republic. For he defined "a people" as "a multitude joined together by a common sense for what is right and a community of interest."[148] And in the course of the discussion he explains what he means by "a common sense for what is right," showing on this basis that a republic cannot be maintained without justice. Thus, where there is no true justice there can be no right. For what is done rightly is obviously done justly, while what is not done justly cannot possibly be done rightly. Thus, unjust human institutions should neither be called nor be considered right, for even the philosophers say that right is what flows from the fount of justice,[149] and they insist that it is false to say, as some wrongheaded thinkers do, that right is in fact the interest of the stronger.[150]

---

144. [GWL] There is a qualified way in which people can be happy now, though only by hope and not in reality. This contrast between hope (*spes*) and reality (*res*) is standard in Augustine.
145. See 1 Cor. 15:28.
146. [GWL] After seventeen books, Augustine finally returns to Cicero's definition of a *res publica*, first treated in 2.21. To review that discussion, a *res publica* ("republic" or "commonwealth") is a *res populi* ("common good of a people" or "weal of a people"). A *populus* ("people") is not just any assembly, but an assembly characterized by a "common sense for what is right." The phrase "what is right" translates *ius*, which is the root word for *iustitia* ("justice" or "righteousness").
147. *Republic* 1.39.
148. *Republic* 1.39.
149. "Right . . . justice": *ius . . . iustitiae*.
150. See Plato, *Republic* 338c.

Where there is no true justice, then, there can be no gathering of persons "joined together by a common sense for what is right," and therefore there can be no people according to the definition used by Scipio and Cicero. And, if there is no people, there is no "common good of a people" but only of a multitude of some sort that is not worthy of the name "people." Thus, if a republic is "the common good of a people," and if a group which is not "joined together by a common sense for what is right" is not a people, and if there is no right where there is no justice, it follows beyond any doubt that where there is no justice there is no republic. Furthermore, justice is the virtue which gives to each his due. What sort of justice is it, then, that takes a person away from the true God and gives him over to demons?[151] Is this to count as giving to each his due? Are we going to call a person unjust if he takes a piece of property away from the one who bought it and gives it to someone else who has no legal claim to it, but call a person just if he takes himself away from the Lord God who made him and instead serves evil spirits?

Now, in that same work, *The Republic*, an exceedingly strong and forceful argument is put forth on behalf of justice and against injustice. But first an argument was mounted on the side of injustice against justice, and the claim was made that without injustice it is impossible for a republic to stand and to be governed. It was taken as the strongest point in this argument that it is unjust for men to serve other men who hold dominion over them, but, unless an imperial city, the head of a great republic, takes up precisely this injustice, it cannot rule its provinces.[152] But the response on the side of justice was that in fact this is just, because servitude is in the interest of such people; and, when it is established in the right way, it is established in their interest, that is, when its establishment takes the freedom to do harm away from the wicked.[153] In that case, the subjugated people will be better off precisely because they were worse off before they were subjugated. And here a notable example was brought in, as if drawn from nature, to confirm this reasoning: "Why is it that

151. [GWL] In this passage, Augustine is defining justice not in terms of equitable relations between humans but as proper worship. Worshiping demons instead of God is unjust since it fails to honor God as God is due, and it ascribes honor to demons that they do not deserve.

152. [GWL] "You can't make an omelet without breaking some eggs." This is not Augustine's position but an opinion that Cicero presents and rejects.

153. [GWL] Augustine seems to affirm this position, following his general commitment to order and benevolent severity. A war is just when it prevents some population from doing wicked things. This population will be prevented from doing wicked things when it comes under the subjugation of another nation. Subjugation is good for the defeated group when the victors are just. See essay: "War."

God rules man, the soul rules the body, and reason rules the sensual desires and the other vice-ridden parts of the soul?"[154] By this example it was shown plainly enough that servitude is beneficial for some, and that in fact serving God is beneficial to all.

For, when it serves God, the soul rules the body rightly, and in the soul itself the reason that is subject to God as Lord rightly rules sensual desire and the other vices. When a person does not serve God, then, what justice are we to think there is in him?[155] For, when the soul does not serve God, it can by no means rule the body justly, nor can reason rule the vices justly. And, if there is no justice in such a person, it is beyond doubt that there is no justice in a human gathering that is made up of such persons.[156] Here, then, there is nothing of that "common sense for what is right" which makes a human multitude into a people, whose common good is called a republic.[157] And what shall I say about that "community of interest" by virtue of which, according to this same definition, a human gathering is also called a people? If you look closely, in fact, you will see that nothing is in the interest of those who live impiously, as do all those who do not serve God but rather serve demons, who are all the more ungodly in that they want sacrifices made to them as gods, when in fact they are nothing but unclean spirits. But I think that what we have already said about a "common sense for what is right" is enough to make it clear that, by this definition, no people in which there is no justice may properly be called a republic.[158]

154. NCP: "Cited also in *Answer to Julian* 4.12.61, where Augustine says that the quotation is taken from the third book of *The Republic*; the passage is known only from Augustine's citation."
[GWL] Augustine will refer to this schema multiple times in the chapters that follow. Justice entails the body submitting to the soul and the soul submitting to God. This hierarchy also appears in Augustine's treatment of justice in 19.4.

155. [GWL] Again, Augustine defines justice in terms of proper worship. No person can be just without worshiping God.

156. [GWL] This sentence presents communities as the sum of their parts (and not, apparently, more than this). A community is just if the individuals that compose it are just. Augustine does not entertain here the possibility of communities being composed of both just and unjust individuals or of communities embodying a collective identity that exceeds the aggregate contributions of individuals.

157. [GWL] Another reference to Cicero's treatment of *res publica*. Consensus on what is right or just (*ius*) is what makes a "people" (*populus*) or a "republic" (*res publica*). The upshot is that justice is essential for republics.

158. [GWL] Following Cicero's definition, a community cannot be called a *res publica* unless it is defined by justice. Since Rome serves demons instead of God, it lacks justice, and it is not a *res publica*. Augustine is taking Cicero's argument to its logical conclusion.
NCP: "At this point Augustine interrupts his discussion on the nature of a republic with a lengthy digression on the true God and Porphyry's understanding of him. The discussion is resumed below at 19.24."

Justice and the True God: Against Porphyry

And, if they claim that it was not unclean spirits that the Romans served in their republic but good and holy gods, must we repeat all over again the very same things we have already said so often, so very often? For how could anyone, after reading the earlier books of this work up to this point, still doubt that the Romans served evil and impure demons, unless, of course, he is just exceedingly stupid or obnoxiously argumentative? But, to say nothing of the kind of gods the Romans worshiped with their sacrifices, it is written in the law of the true God, *Whoever sacrifices to any gods but to the Lord alone shall be destroyed* (Exod. 22:20).[159] It is quite clear, then, that the one who gave this command, and backed it with such a dire threat, did not want us to sacrifice to any gods at all, whether good or evil.

22. Now, it could be said in reply, "Who is this God, and how is he shown worthy to be the one whom the Romans ought to have obeyed, worshiping no other god but him with their sacrifices?" But anyone still asking who this God is must be utterly blind! He is the very God whose prophets foretold the things that we now see with our own eyes.[160] He is the very God from whom Abraham received the answer, *In your seed all peoples shall be blessed* (Gen. 22:18). And this is exactly what took place in Christ, who sprang from Abraham's seed according to the flesh. Even those who have remained hostile to his name acknowledge this, whether they like it or not. He is the very God whose divine Spirit spoke through the men whose prophecies, fulfilled in the Church that we now see spread through the whole world,[161] I cited in the preceding books.[162] He is the very God who Varro, the most learned of the Romans, thought was Jupiter, although he did not know what he was saying.[163] I still thought it worth noting, however, that a man of such learning found that he could neither consider this God non-existent nor reduce him to insignificance

159. [GWL] In Books 1–10, Augustine argued at length that the gods were demons. But even if they were good gods, Scripture forbids sacrificing to anyone but the one true God. Augustine bases this argument on Exod. 22:20, which he quotes several times in his critique of Porphyry in 19.23.

160. [GWL] A reference to the fulfillment of the Old Testament in the New. This might be taken as an argument for Christianity against the Jews.

161. [GWL] Augustine commonly used the church's expansion throughout the world (catholicity) as an argument against the Donatists, whom he accused of restricting the church to Africa.

162. See . . . Books 15–18, especially 18.27–50.

163. [GWL] Having challenged the Jews and the Donatists, Augustine turns to the Romans. NCP: "For Augustine's summary of Varro's view of God (although Jupiter is not mentioned) see . . . 4.31."

but rather believed him to be the same as the supreme god. Finally, he is the very God who Porphyry, the most learned of the philosophers,[164] although the most bitter enemy of the Christians, acknowledges is a great god, even according to the oracles of those he takes to be gods.[165]

23. In the book that he calls *Philosophy from Oracles*,[166] in which he collects and compiles supposedly divine oracular responses on matters related to philosophy, Porphyry says (to use his own words, although translated from Greek into Latin), "To someone who inquired what god he should appease in order to recall his wife from Christianity, Apollo[167] gave this response in verse."[168] Then come these words, as if from Apollo himself: "You would be more able, perhaps, to inscribe letters on water or to spread light wings and fly through the air like a bird than to recall a defiled and ungodly wife to her senses. Let her go on as she likes, persevering in her empty delusions and singing laments for a god who died in his own delusions, condemned by right-thinking judges and executed in full public view by the worst sort of ironbound death." Then, following these verses from Apollo (here translated into Latin prose), Porphyry goes on to say, "In these verses Apollo made it clear that the views of the Christians are incurable, saying that the Jews uphold God better than they do." See how, in demeaning Christ, he gives preference to the Jews over the Christians, asserting that it is the Jews who uphold God. For he explains the verses of Apollo, where the god says that Christ was killed by right-thinking judges, as if Christ actually deserved to be punished and as if those judges actually were just in their judgment. But as to what Apollo's lying seer said about Christ and Porphyry believed, or perhaps what the seer

---

164. NCP: "Porphyry (234–ca. 305) was one of the greatest Neoplatonic philosophers and a notable adversary of the Christian religion. He is cited at length . . . at 10.9–32."

[GWL] It is not clear why Augustine concentrates on Porphyry here. Perhaps Augustine wanted to underscore the church's identity as a sacrifice to the one true God and thus to contrast the church's justice with Rome's injustice. It is also possible that Porphyry's critique of Christianity loomed so large that Augustine wanted to address it somewhere, and this seemed like a convenient location. See essay: "Porphyry."

165. See *On Abstinence from Eating Animals* 2.37.

166. The work has not survived in its entirety but exists in fragments, many of them in *City of God*. It may be identical with Porphyry's *On the Return of the Soul*. See John J. O'Meara, *Porphyry's Philosophy from Oracles in Augustine* (Paris: Études Augustiniennes, 1959).

167. Apollo was the god who uttered oracles at Delphi in Greece.

168. [GWL] The quotation ascribed to Apollo denigrates Jesus as a deluded god who was rightly executed. (Augustine assumes Jesus was executed by the Jews.) Following this quotation, Porphyry claims the Jews are superior to Christians because the Jews are more committed to the one true God. This is the point Augustine seizes in what follows. Porphyry should have rejected the worship of other gods.

did not really say but Porphyry himself simply invented, that is their business. We shall see shortly, however, how consistent Porphyry is with himself or, rather, how consistent he makes those oracles of his with each other.

Here, at any rate, he says that the Jews, as upholders of God, judged rightly in determining that Christ should be tortured by the worst kind of death. Porphyry himself, therefore, bears witness to the God of the Jews, and so Porphyry should have listened when he said, *Whoever sacrifices to any god but to the Lord alone shall be destroyed.*[169] But let us come to more obvious matters; let us hear how great Porphyry says the God of the Jews is. For example, when he asked Apollo which is better, word (that is, reason) or law, he says that Apollo "gave this response in verse." And then he adds Apollo's verses, from which I have selected these as sufficient for our purposes: "In God, the begetter, and the king before all things, before whom tremble heaven and earth, and the sea and the hidden places of the underworld, and from whom the very divinities themselves shrink in dread, whose law is the Father, whom the holy Hebrews greatly honor." In this oracle from his own god Apollo, Porphyry says that the God of the Hebrews is so great that the very divinities themselves shrink from him in dread. And, since it is this very God who said, *Whoever sacrifices to any gods but to the Lord alone shall be destroyed*, I am surprised that Porphyry himself did not shrink from him in dread and was not terrified of being destroyed for sacrificing to other gods.

But this philosopher also has some good things to say about Christ. It is as if he had forgotten that insult of his which we just mentioned, or as if his gods had said nasty things about Christ in their sleep but when awake recognized that he was good and gave him the praise he deserved. For Porphyry says, as if about to announce something marvelous and incredible, "What we are about to say will certainly seem beyond belief to some. For the gods have declared that Christ was most pious and has been made immortal, and that they think of him with favor; but the Christians, they say, are defiled and polluted and entangled in error, and they utter many such blasphemies against them."[170] He then gives examples of supposed oracles in which the gods blaspheme the Christians and goes on to say, "But to those who inquired whether Christ was

169. [GWL] According to Porphyry, Apollo affirmed the greatness of the Jewish God, who caused the other gods to shrink away in dread. Augustine claims Porphyry should have feared God, too, and rejected the gods. Given his affirmation of the Jews for worshiping the one true God, Porphyry should have affirmed Exod. 22:20, first quoted in 19.22.

170. [GWL] Porphyry is quoted here praising Jesus and condemning Christians. These words are at odds with the earlier Porphyry quotation in which Apollo calls Jesus a deluded god.

God, Hecate[171] replied, 'You know that the soul goes on after the body, but when it is cut off from wisdom it always errs. That soul is the soul of a man of outstanding piety; they worship it because the truth is alien to them.'"[172] And, after citing the words of this supposed oracle, he adds his own comments: "Thus Hecate said that he was a most pious man and that his soul, like those of other pious men, was deemed worthy of immortality after death, and the Christians in their ignorance worship his soul. And to those who inquired, 'Why, then, was he condemned?' the goddess replied with this oracle: 'The body, of course, is always faced with debilitating torments, but the souls of the pious take their seat in heaven. But that soul gave to other souls the fatal gift of entanglement in error; these were souls to whom the fates had not granted that they should acquire the gifts of the gods or have knowledge of immortal Jupiter. It is for this reason, then, that they are hated by the gods: because to those who were not fated to know God or to receive the gifts of the gods this man gave the fatal gift of entanglement in error. He himself, however, was pious, and, like other pious men, he passed into heaven. And so you shall not blaspheme him but shall rather pity the madness of men. On his account they face a present and precipitous danger.'"

Who, then, is so dull-witted as not to understand that these oracles were either invented by a devious man, the worst enemy of the Christians, or were the responses of unclean demons with a similar purpose? In praising Christ, of course, what they really want is to convince people that they are telling the truth in demeaning Christians and so, if possible, to close off the way of eternal salvation by which one becomes Christian.[173] They obviously assume that it is no drawback to their malicious and multifarious cunning if they are believed when they praise Christ, just so long as they are also believed when they demean Christians. Their purpose is to ensure that the person who believes them on both counts will praise Christ but have no wish to become a Christian; and so, even though he praises Christ, he will not be delivered by

171. The goddess Hecate was the daughter of Perses and Asteria and had a wide range of powers.

172. [GWL] In the following discussion, Augustine treats a passage from Porphyry in which Hecate praises Jesus and condemns Christians. According to this passage, Hecate said Jesus was a pious man whose soul received immortality after death. Yet Jesus's soul deceived people into worshiping him. He deceived these people because they had not been fated to receive divine gifts or knowledge. Augustine responds to this theory with perplexity and indignation.

173. [GWL] The purpose of Porphyry's false story is to dissuade people from becoming Christians. He does so by condemning Christians. Yet he also praises Christ in order to appear fair, and thus credible, in his condemnation of Christians. Given his duplicity, Porphyry is "the worst enemy of the Christians."

Christ from the domination of these demons. This is especially true because anyone who believes in the Christ they proclaim will not be a true Christian but rather a Photinian heretic[174]—that is, one who acknowledges Christ as a man but does not acknowledge him as God and therefore cannot be saved by him and cannot avoid or escape from the snares of those lying demons.

For our part, we cannot approve either of Apollo's demeaning of Christ or of Hecate's praising of him.[175] Apollo would have it believed that Christ was an unrighteous man, since he says that he was put to death by right-thinking judges; Hecate would have it believed that he was the most pious of men, but only a man. In both cases, however, the intent is the same: to keep people from wanting to be Christian, for, unless people become Christian, they cannot be delivered from the demons' power.

But this philosopher, or, rather, any persons who believe in such so-called oracles against the Christians, must first, if they can, find a way to make Apollo and Hecate consistent with each other in what they say about Christ, so that either both condemn him or both praise him. Even if they were able to do this, however, we ourselves would still turn our backs on deceitful demons, whether demeaning Christ or praising him. But, when their own god and goddess contradict each other about Christ, the one demeaning and the other praising him, people who take a sound view of the matter will not put any stock in their blasphemies against the Christians.

In fact when Porphyry (or Hecate), in praising Christ, declares that he gave himself to Christians as a fatal gift entangling them in error, he also lays bare—so he thinks—the causes of that same error. But before I set out these causes in his own words, I first ask, If Christ gave Christians this fatal gift of entanglement in error, did he give it willingly or unwillingly? If willingly, how could he be just? If unwillingly, how could he be blessed? But now let us hear the causes of that error.[176] "There are in a certain place," Porphyry

174. So called after Photinus, a mid-fourth-century bishop of Sirmium who, among his other unorthodoxies, held that Christ was a mere man. He is closely associated with Paul of Samosata, a bishop of Antioch, who preceded him by nearly a century, because they believed many of the same things. See *Heresies* 44–45. Augustine mentions Photinus in *Confessions* 7.19.25 and indicates that, before he embraced orthodox Christianity, he was drawn to Photinianism.

175. [GWL] Augustine is comparing Hecate's quotation with the quotation by Apollo earlier in this chapter. Though Hecate praises Jesus and Apollo demeans Jesus, both seek to keep people from Christianity.

176. [GWL] According to the following long (and confusing) quotation, Porphyry affirms the existence of the one true God, celestial gods, evil demons, and earthly spirits. Both the Hebrews and the celestial gods directed humans to worship the celestial gods and the one true

says, "very small earthly spirits, subject to the power of evil demons. The wise men of the Hebrews (one of whom was this Jesus, as you have heard from the oracles of Apollo, quoted above) barred religious men from these foul demons and lesser spirits and forbade them to pay them any attention, telling them rather to venerate the celestial gods and most especially to venerate God the father. But the gods also teach this, and we have shown previously how they admonish the mind to turn to God and command it to worship him everywhere. But uninstructed and irreligious natures, who were not fated to obtain gifts from the gods or to have any conception of immortal Jupiter, paying no attention to the gods or to divine men, rejected all the gods; and, far from hating these forbidden demons, they revered them. Although they make a show of worshiping God, they do not do the things by which alone God is adored. For in fact God, as the father of all, is in need of nothing, but it is a benefit to us when we adore him by means of justice, chastity, and the other virtues, making our very life itself a prayer to him by imitating and seeking to know him. For seeking to know him purifies us, and imitation of him deifies us by shaping our disposition to reflect his."

Porphyry certainly did well in proclaiming God as father and in stating the mode of life by which he is to be worshiped; and the prophetic books of the Hebrews are full of such precepts, where the life of holy men is enjoined or praised. But his errors or slanders in speaking of the Christians are everything that the demons (whom he imagines to be gods) would want. It is not difficult, after all, to recall the shameful obscenities enacted in the theaters and temples at the behest of the gods; nor is it difficult, in contrast, to note what is read, said, and heard in the churches, and what is offered to the true God. And so it is not difficult to understand where moral character is built up and where it is brought down to ruin! Who but a diabolical spirit could have told Porphyry, or inspired in him, such a baseless and obvious lie as that the Christians revere, instead of hating, the demons whose worship was forbidden by the Hebrews?[177] In fact the God whom the wise men of the

---

God and to reject the evil demons and earthly spirits. According to Porphyry, Christians instead rejected God and the celestial gods and worshiped the evil demons. Augustine is flabbergasted by Porphyry's accusation and claims Porphyry must have been under the influence of demons. John J. O'Meara speculates that Porphyry was answering charge with counter-charge (*Porphyry's Philosophy from Oracles in Augustine*, 54–58). The Christians had accused Porphyry of worshiping demons, so he was just returning the accusation.

177. [GWL] Against Porphyry, the Christians do not worship other gods, not even the good angels (Book 10). They worship only the one true God, in obedience to Exod. 22:20, cited multiple times already in 19.22–23.

Hebrews worshiped forbids sacrifice even to the holy angels and powers of God in heaven, whom we venerate and love, here in this mortal pilgrimage of ours, as our most blessed fellow citizens. For in God's law, which he gave to his Hebrew people, he declares with thunder and menace, *Whoever sacrifices to any gods shall be destroyed* (Exod. 22:20). Now, someone might think that this command applies only to the foul demons and the earthly spirits whom Porphyry calls lesser or minor spirits. For even these are called gods in Sacred Scripture—not gods of the Hebrews, of course, but gods of the gentiles, as the seventy translators[178] make clear in one of the Psalms, where they say, *For all the gods of the peoples are demons* (Ps. 96:5). To keep anyone from thinking, then, that sacrifice is forbidden only to these demons but is permitted to all or some of the heavenly beings, the command immediately adds, *but to the Lord alone* (Exod. 22:20), that is, to the Lord only. I add this to make sure that no one presumes that *to the Lord alone* means "to the Lord, the Sun";[179] that this is not the meaning is easy to see from the Greek version of the Scriptures.

Thus, the God of the Hebrews, to whom even this preeminent philosopher gives such impressive testimony, gave the law to his Hebrew people, written in Hebrew, a law neither obscure nor unknown but rather spread abroad among all peoples.[180] And in this law it is written, *Whoever sacrifices to any gods but to the Lord alone shall be destroyed.* What need is there, then, to hunt for more passages on this matter in his law and his prophets? In fact, there is no need at all to hunt for them, for the passages are not obscure or rare; there is not even any need to collect and cite the obvious and frequent passages in which it is made clearer than day that the true and supreme God wants there to be no sacrifice whatsoever to any but to himself alone. We have this one passage, spoken briefly but grandly, with menace but with truth, by the God whom their most learned thinkers proclaim so well. Let it be heard, let it be feared, let it be fulfilled, lest destruction come down on the disobedient. *Whoever sacrifices to any god*, he says, *but to the Lord alone shall be destroyed.* This is

---

178. I.e., of the Septuagint.

179. "To the Lord alone . . . to the Lord, the Sun": *Domino soli . . . Dominum solem.* The Latin word for "alone" (*solus*) could in an instance such as this be taken for the word "sun" (*sol*), since the dative case of both words is identical, i.e., *soli.* The sun was almost universally worshiped in antiquity and in Rome, as the god Sol, was often identified with Apollo/Phoebus.

180. [GWL] Augustine expounds further on Exod. 22:20. Nothing could be clearer than Scripture's command to worship God alone, whom Porphyry himself affirmed. On Porphyry's terms, Augustine seems to be arguing, the Romans should have rejected the gods.

not because the Lord is in need of anything but because it is to our benefit to belong to him. For it is to him that the psalmist sings in the Hebrews' sacred writings, *You are my God, for you do not need my goods* (Ps. 16:2). And we ourselves—that is, his own city—are his best and most noble sacrifice, and it is the mystery of this sacrifice that we celebrate in our offerings, which are known to the faithful, as we discussed in the previous books.[181] For it was announced by divine oracles through the Hebrew prophets that the sacrificial victims which the Jews used to offer were going to cease, and that from the rising of the sun to its setting the peoples were going to offer one sacrifice,[182] as we see happening now; and we have already selected a sufficient number of these oracles and presented them at various points throughout this work.[183]

Thus, true justice is found where the one supreme God rules an obedient city, so that there is no sacrifice but to him alone, and where, in consequence, the soul rules the body in all who belong to that city and obey God, and reason faithfully rules the vices in lawful order.[184] Consequently, just as a single just person lives by the faith that works through love,[185] so does the whole company and people of the just. This is the love by which a person loves God as God ought to be loved, and his neighbor as himself.[186] But where there is no such justice, there clearly is no company of persons joined by a common sense for what is right and by a community of interest. And (assuming that this is the true definition of a people) where this is missing, there certainly is no people. And therefore there is no republic, for, where there is no people, there is no common good of a people.

An Alternate Definition of a People

24. But if a people is defined in another way—if we say, for instance, that a people is a multitude of rational beings joined together by common agreement

181. [GWL] This sentence echoes 10.20, the high point of Book 10. The heavenly city sacrifices to God alone. Indeed, the heavenly city is itself a sacrifice to God. Since the heavenly city sacrifices (itself) only to the one true God, it is characterized by justice. By contrast, Augustine seems to imply, the Romans worshiped false gods. Rome is therefore unjust.

182. See Mal. 1:11; Ps. 113:3.

183. See especially . . . 18.35.

184. [GWL] Augustine is coming full circle, returning to his engagement with Cicero in 19.21. Given its worship of false gods, Rome was unjust. According to Cicero's definition, then, it was never a *res publica*.

185. See Gal. 5:6.

186. See Matt. 22:37–39 par.

on the objects of their love—then it is clear that to discover the character of any people we should take a close look at what it loves.[187] No matter what it loves, however, if it is an assembled multitude, not of animals but of rational creatures, and is joined together by common agreement on the objects of its love, it is not absurd to call it a people, and it is clear that, the better the objects of its love, the better the people, and the worse the objects of its love, the worse the people. According to this definition of ours, the Roman people is a people, and its common good is without doubt a republic. As to what that people loved in its first days and what it subsequently came to love, and as to the moral decline by which it fell into bloody seditions and finally into the Social and Civil Wars, thus violating and corrupting the bond of concord which is, so to speak, the health of a people, history bears witness to all this, and we have provided many examples on this score in the previous books.[188] I do not claim on this account, however, that the Roman people is not a people, or that its common good is not a republic, given that there remains some sort of assembled multitude of rational creatures joined together by a common agreement on the objects of their love. I would have it understood, however, that what I have said about Rome's people and republic I also say and maintain about those of the Athenians and any other Greeks, about those of the Egyptians, about the former Babylon of the Assyrians, and about those of any other people, when they exercised imperial rule, great or small, in their republics.[189] For in general the city of the ungodly is not ruled by God and is not obedient to him in offering sacrifice only to him, and in that city, as a

187. [GWL] Here is Augustine's new definition of a *res publica*, first promised in 2.21. Augustine's definition is an alternative to Cicero's, one that replaces justice with love as the defining quality of a *populus*. Though objects of love may be good or bad, the Romans' agreement on certain objects of love is sufficient for Rome to count as a people and thus as a republic. With 19.17, this chapter is among the most cited texts in modern appropriations of Augustine's political thought. For many scholars, Augustine's new definition affirms the legitimacy of non-Christian political societies and thus of Christian participation in the world. Others (including me) have questioned this interpretation and stressed Augustine's criticism of what Rome loves.

188. [GWL] Recall Book 3 on Rome's history of violence. Rome counts as a republic because it is united by common objects of love, but Rome's loves are earthly and generate unending conflict. Rome's status as a *res publica* does not mean that it is moral.

189. [GWL] By grouping Rome with these other nations, Augustine deflates Rome's sense of superiority. The other nations were idolatrous, and Babylon (which Augustine conflates with Assyria) was notoriously vicious. They can be called republics too. Despite this argument, Augustine is not claiming that Rome is as immoral as the other nations. For modern readers, the question is whether and to what degree Christians should participate in immoral political communities that nevertheless count as republics.

consequence, the soul does not rightly and faithfully rule the body, nor does reason the vices. And so it lacks true justice.

25. For, no matter how laudably the soul may appear to rule the body and reason the vices, if the soul and reason do not themselves serve God as God himself has taught that he is to be served, they do not rule the body and the vices rightly at all.[190] What kind of ruler of the body and the vices can the mind be if it does not know the true God and, instead of being subject to his rule, is prostituted to the corrupting influence of the most vicious demons? In fact the very virtues which the mind imagines that it has, and by which it rules the body and the vices for the sake of gaining or keeping whatever is the object of its desire, are themselves vices, and not virtues at all, if the mind does not direct them to God. Some people suppose that the virtues are true and authentic when they are directed to themselves alone and are not sought for the sake of anything beyond themselves.[191] But even then they are puffed up and proud, and so they are not to be counted as virtues but rather as vices. For, just as what causes the flesh to live does not come from the flesh but is rather above it, so what causes a person to live blessedly does not come from the person but is rather above him. And this is true not only of human beings but also of every heavenly dominion and power whatsoever.

Earthly Peace and the City of God

26. Accordingly, just as the life of the flesh is the soul, so the blessed life of human beings is God, of whom the Hebrews' Sacred Scripture says, *Blessed is the people whose God is the Lord* (Ps. 144:15). Wretched, therefore, is the people that is alienated from God. But even this people loves a kind of peace of its own, which is not to be despised. It will not have that peace in the end, because it does not make good use of it prior to the end. In the meantime, however, it is beneficial to us, too, that this people should have its peace in this life, for, as long as the two cities are intermingled, we also make use of

---

190. [GWL] Augustine's treatment of apparent virtue may allude to 5.12–20, where he describes lust for glory as Rome's defining quality and as a unique sin that suppresses open vice for the sake of appearing virtuous. This apparent virtue is false. Rome is not virtuous; it merely pretends to be. See essay: "Pagan Virtue."

191. This was part of the Stoic understanding of virtue, summarized in Seneca, *Letter* 66.

the peace of Babylon.[192] And this is true even though the people of God are so fully set free from Babylon by faith that during this meantime they are no more than pilgrims in its midst. But, because we do make use of the peace of Babylon, the Apostle admonished the Church to pray for its kings and for all in high positions[193] and went on to say, *so that we may live a quiet and tranquil life with all godliness and love* (1 Tim. 2:2). And when the prophet Jeremiah foretold the captivity that was to come for the ancient people of God and commanded them, by divine inspiration, to go obediently into Babylon, serving their God by means of this very patience and endurance, he also admonished them on his own to pray for Babylon, *because in its peace is your peace* (Jer. 29:7).[194] He was referring, of course, to the temporal peace which, in this meantime, is common to the good and the evil alike.

27. The peace that is proper to us, in contrast, we both have now with God through faith and shall have for all eternity with God through sight.[195] But the peace that we have here, whether the peace common to both the good and the evil or the peace proper to us alone, is a solace for wretchedness rather than the joy of blessedness.[196] Our justice, too, although it is true justice because it is directed to the true supreme good, is such that in this life it consists in the forgiveness of sins rather than in the perfection of virtue.[197] The prayer of the whole city of God that is on pilgrimage here on earth bears witness to this point. In all its members it cries out to God, *Forgive us our debts, as we also forgive our debtors* (Matt. 6:12). But this prayer has no efficacy for those

192. [GWL] This chapter presents Augustine's central image for the heavenly city in the world. *City of God*'s many references to pilgrimage (*peregrinatio*) derive from this picture of the Israelites in Babylon. Augustine develops this image more fully elsewhere in his corpus, especially *Expositions on the Psalms*. See the introduction, above.

193. See 1 Tim. 2:1–2.

194. [GWL] Augustine takes Jeremiah's words to legitimate Christians' support for the earthly peace of the earthly city, since this peace furnishes the temporal resources that all persons need during this life. See 19.17, where Augustine develops these ideas more explicitly. The heavenly city will cooperate with the earthly city on many matters, but it will reject the practices of the earthly city when they violate Christian faith. The heavenly city will especially reject the religious practices of the earthly city.

195. See 2 Cor. 5:7.

196. [GWL] Christians can experience a foretaste of heavenly peace now, by faith and not by sight. Both Christians and non-Christians can also experience a measure of earthly peace now.

197. [GWL] In this fallen world, Christians' justice (or righteousness) consists in receiving the forgiveness of sins rather than in living perfect lives. Justice differs from peace in that non-Christians can experience a measure of earthly peace whereas non-Christians cannot be just. Justice is defined by the soul submitting to God and the body submitting to the soul (19.21). Since the earthly city does not worship God, the earthly city cannot be just.

whose faith is without works and dead;[198] it only has efficacy for those whose faith works through love.[199] Prayer of this kind is needed by the righteous because, in this mortal condition and in this corruptible body which weighs down the soul,[200] even though their reason is subject to God, it still does not perfectly rule the vices. For, although reason does indeed rule the vices, it by no means rules them without struggle and resistance on their part. And, in this place of weakness, even if reason fights well or goes on to dominate these enemies by defeating and subduing them, something still creeps in which leads into sin, if not by immediate action, then at least by unconsidered talk or fleeting thought.

As long as it is necessary to rule the vices, then, there is no full and complete peace.[201] This is true both because our battle against the resisting vices is full of peril and because our triumph over defeated vices is still far from secure and effortless; it is only with an anxious and a care-filled rule that we manage to hold them down. We live, then, in the midst of all these trials, which have been succinctly summarized in the divine discourse where it says, *Is not human life on earth a trial?* (Job 7:1). And who will presume that he is living in such a way that he has no need to say to God, *Forgive us our debts* (Matt. 6:12)?[202] Only an arrogant person would be so presumptuous, not someone who is truly great but someone puffed up and bloated with pride, who is justly resisted by the one who pours out his grace on the humble. That is why it is written, *God resists the proud but gives grace to the humble* (James 4:6).[203]

In this life, therefore, justice is only present in each person when the person is obedient to God's rule, when the mind rules the body, and when reason

198. See James 2:17, 26.

199. See Gal. 5:6.

200. See Wis. 9:15.

201. [GWL] Recall the discussion of the cardinal virtues in 19.4.

202. [GWL] This line from the Lord's Prayer is foundational for Augustine's theology and church practice. Augustine's church celebrated the eucharist throughout the week, and the eucharist was associated with the recitation of the Lord's Prayer and the giving of alms. During this line of the Lord's Prayer, parishioners would beat their chests in penitence. Augustine interpreted this practice in light of Jesus's statement to Peter that those who have had a bath (i.e., been baptized) need only to wash their feet (John 13:10). A related passage is 1 John 1:8–9, which encourages Christians to continue confessing their sins and to receive God's forgiveness. For Augustine, those who have received baptism still need to ask daily for their sins to be forgiven, especially in the context of the eucharist. See essay: "Eucharist."

203. [GWL] Recall the reference to this passage in 1.*preface*, which uses the verse to illustrate the Romans' pride in claiming God's authority for themselves. Other references to this passage appear in 11.33 and 17.4.

rules the vices, even when they fight against its rule by subduing or resisting them.[204] Justice is only present when it is from God himself that the person seeks both the grace for meritorious works and the forgiveness for sins, and when he gives full thanks to God for the benefits he receives. In that final peace, however, to which this justice should be directed, and for the attaining of which it should be maintained, our nature will be healed by immortality and incorruption. Then it will have no vices, and there will be nothing at all, whether in ourselves or in anyone else, that fights against us. Thus, there will be no need for reason to rule the vices, because there will be no vices. But God will rule the person, the soul will rule the body, and the delight and ease with which we obey in that final peace will be as great as the happiness with which we live and reign in it. There, for each and every one of us, this will last for all eternity, and its lasting for all eternity will be completely certain and totally assured; and so the peace of this blessedness, or the blessedness of this peace, will be the supreme good.

The Supreme Evil: Eternal Misery

28. For those who do not belong to the city of God, in contrast, there will be eternal misery. This misery is also called the second death,[205] because the soul cannot be said to be alive at that point, since it will be alienated from God, and neither can the body, since it will be subject to eternal torments. And so this second death will be all the harsher, precisely because it cannot come to an end in death. Now, just as misery is the opposite of happiness, and death the opposite of life, it seems that war is the opposite of peace. There is good reason, then, to ask what and what sort of war can be seen in the final state of the wicked in contrast to the peace we have proclaimed and praised in the final state of the good. But anyone who puts this question should take note of what it is that is so harmful and destructive in war, and he will see that it is nothing other than the opposition and conflict of things with each other.[206] What more grievous and bitter war, then, can be

204. [GWL] The image of the body submitting to the mind (*animus*) and the mind submitting to God is Augustine's operative picture of justice in the last chapters of Book 19. For an earlier instance of this image, see 19.4 and the comment at n38.

205. See Rev. 2:11; 20:6, 14; 21:8. For a brief discussion of the second death see above at 13.2.

206. [GWL] As peace is an incomparably great good, conflict is an incomparably terrible evil.

imagined than a war in which the will is so deeply opposed to passion and passion so deeply opposed to the will that their hostility cannot be ended by victory on either side, or a war in which the force of pain conflicts so powerfully with the very nature of the body that neither can give in to the other?[207] In this life, when such conflict occurs, either pain wins and death snuffs out all feeling, or nature wins and health takes away the pain. In the life to come, however, the pain persists to inflict torment, and nature endures to feel the pain. Neither one comes to an end, and so the punishment does not come to an end either.

These, then, are the final ends of the good and the evil, the one to be sought and the other to be avoided. And, since it is as the result of a judgment that the good will pass over to the one and the evil pass over to the other, I shall discuss this judgment, as far as God grants, in the following book.

---

207. [GWL] Augustine here defines hell as unending hostility between the body and the soul. He treats hell at greater length in Book 21.

Stoics and Stoicism

Gregory W. Lee, with Sadie Rynbrandt

Stoicism was a philosophical system in classical antiquity that was founded in Athens by Zeno of Citium around 300 BCE, gained popularity during the Roman imperial period, and persisted through the rule of the philosopher-emperor Marcus Aurelius, who died in 180 CE. Augustine engaged Stoic thought through the writings of Cicero (106–43 BCE), Seneca (4 BCE–65 CE), and other Roman authors.

Stoicism was divided into three branches: physics, logic, and ethics. Among these branches, ethics was the area that Augustine engaged the most. In Stoicism, as in other classical philosophies, happiness (*eudaimonia*) represented the goal (*telos*) of human life. The Stoics also held that happiness depends solely on virtue, as defined by the conformity of human conduct with nature and reason. Stoicism thus conceived of happiness in terms of internal goods as opposed to external factors like health, beauty, wealth, or reputation. The latter belong to the category of "indifferents" (*adiaphora*), which are morally neutral and need not perturb humans. Happiness depends not on the presence or absence of indifferents but on virtue alone.

Though Augustine retains strains of Stoicism in his moral philosophy, *City of God* challenges the Stoics on several major issues. While Augustine shares an emphasis on virtue, he argues in 19.4 that many "indifferents," like disease or insanity, render happiness impossible in this life. Even the virtues assume the miseries of temporal existence, demonstrating that happiness is a future reality. The virtue of fortitude, for instance, involves enduring suffering with patience, which is to assume that suffering exists in this life. The Stoics also claim it is possible to be virtuous by one's own efforts, a position Augustine denies on the grounds that virtue requires divine grace.

Besides these matters, Augustine claims Stoicism is self-centered, concentrating so much on personal virtue that it disregards the suffering of others. This failure reflects deficiencies in Stoicism's account of emotions. Though the Stoics affirmed the legitimacy of emotions, they believed emotions should be disciplined by reason. Emotions that were too intense or lasted too long fell into the category of inappropriate "passions." The Stoics also rejected the emotion of compassion (*misericordia*), which they cast as irrational pity for those who suffer. (For an exception, see Seneca, *De Clementia* 2.6.)

Augustine agrees that emotions are legitimate when they are indexed to reason (14.5–9). Yet he also defends compassion, claiming that a virtuous person should mourn others' physical sufferings and moral failures (9.4–5; 19.8). Augustine's commitment to compassion grounds his opposition to torture (*Letters* 91.9; 104.1.1; 104.2.5; 104.4.17; 133; 134; 10*.3–4; 14*.2; 15*.3–4; *Sermons* 13.7; 277A.1; see also *Sermon* 29A.3). It also suggests that his discussion of torture in 19.6 is not a defense of the practice but a criticism of the Stoics' disinterest in others' suffering.

Scholars debate whether Augustine understood Stoicism accurately and the degree to which his ethic remained influenced by Stoicism. Some have claimed, for instance, that Augustine's treatment of the Stoics in 9.4–5 and 14.8 mischaracterizes their position on emotions.

Bibliography

Boersma, Gerald P. 2017. "Augustine's Immanent Critique of Stoicism." *Scottish Journal of Theology* 70, no. 2: 184–97.

Byers, Sarah Catherine. 2012. "The Psychology of Compassion: Stoicism in *City of God* 9.5." In Wetzel, *COG*, 130–48.

———. 2013. *Perception, Sensibility, and Moral Motivation in Augustine: A Stoic-Platonic Synthesis.* Cambridge: Cambridge University Press.

Colish, Marcia L. 1990. *The Stoic Tradition from Antiquity to the Early Middle Ages.* Vol. 2, *Stoicism in Christian Latin Thought through the Sixth Century.* Orig. 1985. Leiden: Brill, 142–238.

Ogle, Veronica Roberts. 2018. "Sheathing the Sword: Augustine and the Good Judge." *Journal of Religious Ethics* 46, no. 4: 718–47.

———. 2019. "Therapeutic Deception: Cicero and Augustine on the Myth of Philosophic Happiness." *Augustinian Studies* 50, no. 1: 13–42.

Sorabji, Richard. 2000. *Emotion and Peace of Mind: From Stoic Agitation to Christian Temptation.* Oxford: Oxford University Press.

Torchia, N. Joseph. 1999. "Stoicism." In *AttA*, 816–20.

Wetzel, James. 1992. *Augustine and the Limits of Virtue.* Cambridge: Cambridge University Press.

Wolterstorff, Nicholas. 2012. "Augustine's Rejection of Eudaimonism." In Wetzel, *COG*, 149–66.

Slavery

Gregory W. Lee

According to Augustine, "nearly all households" in his context had slaves (*Expositions of the Psalms* 124.7). Slaves were vulnerable to physical harm, including whipping, sexual abuse, torture, and execution, and they lacked legal recourse against their masters. Augustine was familiar with these social realities. He was nursed by a slave as an infant (*Confessions* 1.6.7; 1.7.11), and his mother, Monica, grew up with slaves before marrying into a family with slaves (*Confessions* 9.8.17–9.9.22). After dismissing the mother of his son, Augustine may have turned to a slave-concubine for sexual relations (*Confessions* 6.15.25). Though as a bishop, Augustine did not own slaves, he preached to congregations with both slaves and slave masters.

Augustine affirmed slavery's legitimacy as a social institution, and he incorporated the topic into much of his writing and preaching (*The Catholic Way of Life and the Manichean Way of Life* 1.30.63; *City of God* 18.2; 21.11; *Confessions* 2.6.14; 3.3.5; 3.7.13; 7.21.27; *Excellence of Marriage* 17.20; *Expositions of the Psalms* 122.6–7; *Free Will* 1.4.9; 3.9.27; *Homilies on the Gospel of John* 11.13; 41.4; *Instructing Beginners in Faith* 21.37; *Letters* 185.4.15; 185.6.21; 10*; 24*; *Lord's Sermon on the Mount* 1.19.59; *Sermons* 21.6–7; 114B.12; 199.3; 356.3, 6, 7). In a disturbing passage about Monica and her husband's violent temper, Augustine commends her for encouraging women "whose faces were badly disfigured by traces of blows" to submit to their husbands as slaves to their masters (*Confessions* 9.9.19). One prominent translation of *Confessions*, by Sarah Ruden, has rendered the Latin *servus* "slave" (instead of "servant") and *dominus* "Master" (instead of "Lord"), illuminating Augustine's self-presentation as a rebellious slave who needs his master's benevolent chastisement (*Confessions* 3.3.5; 7.21.27).

City of God 19.14–16 is the most cited passage on slavery in Augustine's corpus. It treats slavery as a divine response to human sin, one instituted as a mechanism for correcting and punishing wrongdoing. Although he attributes slavery to sin, Augustine does not claim particular individuals are enslaved because of sins they have personally committed. All are sinners, but not all are slaves. Why has God chosen some to be enslaved and not others? This is a mystery of providence.

Despite its origins in the fall, slavery accords with the order God has established for creation. In a Roman household, the *paterfamilias* ruled his wife, children, slaves, and other dependents. According to Augustine, the Christian *paterfamilias* will not dominate his subordinates but nurture (*consulere*) them, with concern for their wellbeing. This concern extends to his slaves in addition to his children. He will promote Christian worship and obedience among both groups, correcting them with words and physical punishment as appropriate. Slavery to sin is worse than slavery to a master.

Another much-cited text is *Expositions of the Psalms* 124, where Augustine observes that there are good and evil masters, just as there are good and evil slaves. On the day of judgment, Christ will separate good masters from evil masters, and good slaves from evil slaves. Until then, good slaves should bear the dominance of evil masters (*Expositions of the Psalms* 124.8). Paul did not seek to "turn slaves into free men and women, but bad slaves into good slaves" (*Expositions of the Psalms* 124.7). Nor did Christ liberate slaves from earthly bondage. He commanded them to do their duty, as he himself became a slave and submitted to evil people. Elsewhere, Augustine somewhat mitigates these remarks. Masters are not to hate their slaves, for slaves are also human beings (*Sermon* 159B.4; see *Expositions of the Psalms* 124.7; *Lord's Sermon on the Mount* 1.19.59; and *Sermon* 159.5).

The most salient area where Christian leaders of Augustine's time challenged Roman mores concerning slavery was sex. Augustine and other bishops encouraged monogamy among spouses, if not the total renunciation of sexual activity (see essay: "Women"). This ethic precluded sexual activity with slaves (*Sermons* 9.4, 12; 82.11; 153.6; 224.3; see also *Answer to Julian* 3.11.22). Based on the tone of these admonitions, it does not appear that congregants took them seriously. Arguably at least, early Christians' accommodations to slavery reflected the new realities of imperial Christianity, when Christians came to justify Roman practices instead of challenging them. Augustine's position on slavery raises serious challenges for the modern application of his social writings.

Apart from the question of slavery specifically, *City of God* 19.14–16 is often cited for Augustine's position on political authority, especially his statement that humans were not originally meant to dominate other humans: "The first righteous men were established as shepherds of flocks rather than as kings of men, so that in this way, too, God might indicate what the order of created beings requires and what the fault of sinners demands" (19.15; see above: Book 19n103). According to a common interpretation, this quotation suggests that political authority is a function of the fall, inherently coercive, and thus similar to slavery. Augustine's remark at the end of 19.16 likening command and obedience in the city to command and obedience in the household supports this interpretation. Given his approbation of slavery, Augustine may not have considered this understanding of political authority to be especially negative.

Bibliography

Alimi, Toni. 2024. *Slaves of God: Augustine and Other Romans on Religion and Politics*. Princeton: Princeton University Press.

Clark, Patricia. 1998. "Women, Slaves, and the Hierarchies of Domestic Violence: The Family of St. Augustine." In *Women and Slaves in Greco-Roman Culture: Differential Equations*, edited by Sandra R. Joshel and Sheila Murnaghan, 109–29. London: Routledge.

de Bruyn, Theodore S. 1999. "Flogging a Son: The Emergence of the *pater flagellans* in Latin Christian Discourse." *Journal of Early Christian Studies* 7, no. 2: 249–90.

Elia, Matthew. 2024. *The Problem of the Christian Master: Augustine in the Afterlife of Slavery*. New Haven: Yale University Press.

Elm, Susanna. 2017. "Sold to Sin through *Origo*: Augustine of Hippo and the Late Roman Slave Trade." *Studia Patristica* 98: 1–21.

Garnsey, Peter. 1996. *Ideas of Slavery from Aristotle to Augustine*. Cambridge: Cambridge University Press.

Harper, Kyle. 2011. *Slavery in the Late Roman World, AD 275–425*. Cambridge: Cambridge University Press.

———. 2012. "Marriage and Family." In *The Oxford Handbook of Late Antiquity*, edited by Scott Fitzgerald Johnson, 667–714. Oxford: Oxford University Press.

Markus, R. A. 1965. "Two Conceptions of Political Authority: Augustine, *De Civitate Dei*, XIX. 14–15, and Some Thirteenth-Century Interpretations." *Journal of Theological Studies* 16, no. 1: 68–100.

Ramelli, Ilaria L. E. 2016. *Social Justice and the Legitimacy of Slavery: The Role of Philosophical Asceticism from Ancient Judaism to Late Antiquity*. Oxford: Oxford University Press.

Rist, John M. 1994. *Augustine: Ancient Thought Baptized*. Cambridge: Cambridge University Press, 236–39.

Ruden, Sarah. 2017. Introduction to *Confessions*, by Augustine. Translated by Sarah Ruden. New York: Modern Library. (See xxxi–xxxiii for Ruden's defense of her translation decisions.)

Shaw, Brent. 1987. "The Family in Late Antiquity: The Experience of Augustine." *Past and Present* 115, no. 1: 3–51.

——————————— Porphyry ———————————

Gregory W. Lee, with Sadie Rynbrandt

Augustine calls Porphyry "the most learned of the philosophers, although the most bitter enemy of the Christians" (*City of God* 19.22). Porphyry (ca. 232–305) was a student of Plotinus, the founder of Neoplatonism, and he edited and published Plotinus's *Enneads*.

Porphyry also composed many of his own works, including some that criticized Christianity. Most of Porphyry's writings survive only in fragments because of imperial decrees against his work. Constantine banned Porphyry's *Against the Christians* in 324/25; possession of the work was punishable by death. Though Augustine once refers to this text, he demonstrates no direct knowledge of its contents (*Letter* 102.8). There is disagreement among scholars about how to interpret the titles of works attributed to Porphyry. Some titles may represent stand-alone texts, while others may represent sections of other texts.

Scholars tend to identify Porphyry as one of the Neoplatonic authors Augustine discovered prior to his conversion (*Confessions* 7.9.13). In *City of God*, Augustine commends Porphyry's affirmation of the true God while castigating him for denying the incarnation and the resurrection of the body. (Noteworthy sections include 8.12; 10.9–11, 23–32; 12.21, 27; 13.19; 19.22–23; 22.3, 25–28.) He also criticizes Porphyry's writings about theurgy and the universal way of salvation. Augustine relies on Porphyry's *Philosophy from Oracles, On the Return of the Soul* (which may be a section of *Philosophy from Oracles* instead of a separate work), and *Letter to Anebo*. Since these works are not extant, it is difficult to assess Augustine's depictions of them. Even based on limited evidence, however, Augustine seems to misrepresent Porphyry on many points.

According to Augustine, Porphyry believed in the existence of the supreme God, lower gods, and still lower demons (10.9; 19.23). As for humans, Porphyry distinguished between two faculties within the soul: the intellectual soul, by which we perceive intelligible (nonbodily) things, and the lower, spiritual soul, by which we perceive images of bodily things (10.9). The intellectual soul is capable of returning to God, while the spiritual soul can receive a lower degree of purification through ritual acts. By contrast, "every body is to be escaped" (10.29, my trans.; see also 12.27; 13.17; 22.12, 26; *Sermon* 241.7). Augustine rejects the idea of divine intermediaries and Porphyry's denigration of the body. He also criticizes Porphyry's discussion of theurgy, a Platonic ritual practice for purifying the soul (10.9–11).

In 10.32, Augustine claims Porphyry sought "the universal way of the soul's liberation" but did not discover it. Augustine defines this as the way all souls may be liberated, without which no soul is liberated. For Augustine, of course, the universal way of liberation is Christianity. Porphyry failed to recognize this because Christianity was being persecuted during his life, and he feared the consequences of conversion. Scholars question Augustine's depiction of Porphyry's positions. Porphyry may have imagined different paths to salvation for different classes of people according to their philosophical maturity (Clark, *Comm. 6–10*, 233), and he may have rejected the idea—espoused especially by Christians—that liberation is exclusive in the first place (DeMarco, 274–76, 315).

In 19.22–23, Augustine returns to Porphyry during a discussion about Cicero's definition of a republic. Though it is not clear why this section engages with Porphyry at such length, Augustine seems to claim that Porphyry's criticisms of Christianity inadvertently support Cicero's condemnation of the Romans. Porphyry affirmed the true God, who forbids sacrifice to other gods. Since the Romans sacrificed to many gods, they lacked justice and thus, following Cicero's definition, did not count as a republic.

Bibliography

Barnes, T. D. 1994. "Scholarship or Propaganda? Porphyry *Against the Christians* and Its Historical Setting." *Bulletin of the Institute of Classical Studies* 39, no. 1: 53–65.

Beatrice, Pier Franco. 2023. *The Philosophy of the Few against the Christians: An Inquiry into the Textual Transmission of Porphyry's "Philosophy according to the Chaldean Oracles."* Leiden: Brill.

Bochet, Isabelle. 2010. "The Role of Scripture in Augustine's Controversy with Porphyry." *Augustinian Studies* 41, no. 1: 7–52.

Clark, Gillian. 2007. "Augustine's Porphyry and the Universal Way of Salvation." In *Studies on Porphyry*, edited by George Karamanolis and Anne Sheppard, 127–40. London: Institute of Classical Studies.

Clemmons, Thomas. 2021. "Augustine and Porphyry." In *Augustine and Tradition: Influences, Contexts, Legacy; Essays in Honor of J. Patout Burns*, edited by David G. Hunter and Jonathan P. Yates, 153–79. Grand Rapids: Eerdmans.

DeMarco, David C. 2021. *Augustine and Porphyry: A Commentary on "De ciuitate Dei"* 10. Leiden: Brill.

Edwards, Mark. 2007. "Porphyry and the Christians." In Karamanolis and Sheppard, *Studies on Porphyry*, 111–26.

Johnson, Aaron P. 2013. *Religion and Identity in Porphyry of Tyre: The Limits of Hellenism in Late Antiquity*. Cambridge: Cambridge University Press.

O'Meara, John J. 1959. *Porphyry's Philosophy from Oracles in Augustine*. Paris: Études Augustiniennes.

Simmons, Michael Bland. 2015. *Universal Salvation in Late Antiquity: Porphyry of Tyre and the Pagan-Christian Debate*. Oxford: Oxford University Press.

Van Fleteren, Frederick. 1999. "Porphyry." In *AttA*, 661–63.

Zwollo, Laela. 2021. "Augustine's Motivations for His Refutation of Porphyry and Theurgy in *The City of God*." In *Augustine of Hippo's "De ciuitate Dei": Content, Transmission, and Interpretations*, edited by Anthony Dupont and Gert Partoens, 177–90. Leuven: Peeters.

Last Things

Gregory W. Lee and Avyi Hill

After narrating the origins and development of the two cities, Augustine concludes with their ends in *City of God* 19–22. Whereas Book 19 addresses the philosophical question of humanity's final good, Books 20–22 cover the final events of human history. The last things culminate in an eternal sabbath characterized by humanity's rest in God (22.30; cf. *Confessions* 13.35.50–13.37.52). Central to Augustine's theology of the last things is the distinction between time and eternity. Human history is characterized by ambiguity, such that both righteous and unrighteous people receive temporal blessing and suffering. The future life involves an absolute separation between the righteous and the unrighteous, such that the former will receive only eternal blessing and the latter will receive only eternal suffering (*City of God* 1.8–9; 20.1–2; see essay: "Providence and Suffering").

Augustine's identification of heaven as a sabbath arises from his delineation of history according to the days of creation. Days 3–5 correspond to the time periods in the genealogy of Matthew 1:1–17. Augustine sometimes correlates these days with the stages of human life. (See *Answer to Faustus* 12.8; *City of God* 10.14; 16.24, 43; 18.1; 22.30; *Expositions of the Psalms* 92.1; *On Genesis: A Refutation of the Manichees* 1.23.35–1.24.42; *Homilies on the Gospel of John* 9.6; *Instructing Beginners in Faith* 17.28–24.44; *Miscellany of Eighty-Three Questions* 58.2; *Sermon* 259.2; *De Trinitate* 4.4.7.)

Day 1: Adam to Noah

Day 2: Noah to Abraham

Day 3: Abraham to David

Day 4: David to exile

Day 5: Exile to incarnation

Day 6: Incarnation to Christ's final return

Day 7: Heaven

City of God roughly follows this schema: Books 12–14 treat humanity's creation and fall, Book 15 treats Adam (after the fall) to Noah, Book 16 treats Noah to David, and Book 17 treats David to the time of Christ. Book 18 then backtracks to the earlier history of the earthly city before treating the time of Christ to Augustine's present. With this material complete, Augustine can turn to the last things and conclude *City of God*.

Revelation 20:2-3 describes the millennium as a time when the devil is bound and thrown into the bottomless pit. In some early writings, Augustine interprets this time (which he identifies with the sabbath) as a future age when Christ will reign on earth with his saints (*Answer to Adimantus* 2.2; *Sermons* 259.2; 260C.4). In *City of God* 20.7, Augustine disavows his former position. According to his new interpretation, the millennium is a present reality corresponding to the age of the church. The devil's being bound in Revelation 20 means that he cannot destroy the church, even as he incites the impious (symbolized by the bottomless pit) against Christians. Augustine's interpretation incorporates both literal and figurative readings, an approach that would prove highly influential for medieval theology. Though Augustine affirms the future occurrence of apocalyptic events, including the conversion of the Jews and the antichrist's persecution of Christians (*City of God* 20.30), he rejects speculation about when the world will end (*Letter* 199, cited in *City of God* 20.5).

Relying on John 5:24-29, Augustine distinguishes between the first resurrection (the ongoing regeneration of souls through faith) and the second resurrection, following Christ's return, when the souls of both the righteous and the unrighteous will be reunited with their bodies (*City of God* 20.6). Only those who receive the first resurrection will receive eternal blessing. Everyone else will receive eternal punishment. Though the righteous and the unrighteous will both participate in the bodily resurrection, the righteous alone will be changed for the better, with incorruptible bodies that cannot experience pain (*Letter* 205.14-15; *Sermon* 362.19, 23; both relying on 1 Cor. 15:50-53). Following the final judgment, the world will experience a massive conflagration and be transformed into a new heaven and a new earth (*City of God* 20.14, 16, 18, 30).

Book 21 presents Augustine's theology of hell and addresses objections to the doctrine. In response to those who claim that bodies cannot suffer eternally, Augustine invokes apparently miraculous phenomena in nature—including salamanders that were thought to live in fire and, somewhat famously, the meat of peacocks, which was said to resist putrefaction (*City of God* 21.1-10, specifically 21.4). Another objection concerns the legitimacy of eternal punishment for crimes that were committed in a short period of time (21.11-12). As Augustine argues, the duration of punishment corresponds not to the duration of an offense but to its magnitude. According to human law, for instance, a slave who offends his master briefly might be punished with years of shackles (21.11; see essay: "Slavery").

In the second half of Book 21, Augustine refutes various efforts to mitigate the doctrine of hell, including the proposals that hell is only temporary or that it can be escaped through intercession, baptism, eucharist, perseverance in the Catholic Church, or works of mercy (*City of God* 21.17–27; see also *Enchiridion* 18.67–19.70, much of which is reproduced in *Eight Questions of Dulcitius* 1.10–13). Despite Augustine's defense of eternal punishment, he grants that there are gradations of damnation, such that those who sinned less will suffer less (*City of God* 21.16). God may also alleviate the suffering of the damned at certain intervals of time (*Enchiridion* 29.111–13).

Though individuals enter their eternal fates following the bodily resurrection, they are judged immediately following death, whereupon they experience temporary reward or punishment foreshadowing their eternal reward or punishment (*City of God* 13.8; *Enchiridion* 29.109; *Literal Meaning of Genesis* 12.32.60; *Nature and Origin of the Soul* 2.4.8; *Predestination of the Saints* 12.24). Among those who experience punishment, some will eventually receive eternal life (*City of God* 21.13, 24, 26; *Enchiridion* 29.110). For this position, Augustine relies on Matthew 12:32, which speaks of forgiveness in the world to come. (He hedges on whether 1 Corinthians 3:15, which speaks of the one who "shall be saved, but only as through fire," refers to a temporary period of purification after death.) Augustine's writings on this topic gesture toward later conceptions of purgatory, though scholars disagree as to the degree of alignment. Augustine opposes the Platonic position that all punishment is purgative (*City of God* 21.13). Yet he affirms a category of people neither righteous enough to receive immediate reward nor unrighteous enough to be irredeemably damned. These individuals strengthen their prospects of heaven by giving alms now (21.27, citing Luke 16:9). After death, they can receive aid to eternal blessing through the prayers, eucharistic sacrifice, and alms of living Christians (*Care to Be Taken of the Dead* 1.2; *Sermon* 172.2). In *Confessions* 9.13.34–9.13.36, Augustine prays on Monica's behalf.

Book 22 treats eternal blessing, offering Augustine's most materialist speculations about the resurrection body (see also *Enchiridion* 23.84–91). Drawing on Ephesians 4:13 (Christians will reach "the measure of the age of the fullness of Christ") and Romans 8:29 (Christians will be "conformed to the image of the Son of God"), Augustine suggests that infants and aborted fetuses will be raised as mature humans, with the size they would have had at the age of thirty (*City of God* 22.13–16). Women will retain their sex in heaven, though they will no longer have sex or give birth (22.17; see essay: "Women"). Following the promise that "not a hair of your head shall perish" (Luke 21:18), Augustine claims that all lost hair and nails will be restored, together with any flesh that has been consumed by wild beasts; fire; or, in the toughest case, other people (22.19–21). Heavier and thinner people will be raised with lovely symmetry, and martyrs will retain their scars, though as marks of honor and not deformity. Augustine's discussion exhibits his affirmation of bodily beauty, a good not reducible to utility (*City of God* 22.24 and *Sermon* 243.6, both of which invoke men's useless beards and nipples).

City of God culminates in Augustine's account of the beatific vision and his portrait of heaven (22.29–30). Augustine also addresses a question that has vexed him to this point: Will humans see God through their bodily eyes? He concludes that humans will see God through the bodies of others, as "our thoughts, too, will then lie open to each other" (22.29). As readers may have come to expect, Augustine's account of the beatific vision is thoroughly social.

Bibliography

Boersma, Gerald P. 2018. "Augustine on the Beatific Vision as *ubique totus*." *Scottish Journal of Theology* 71, no. 1: 16–32.

Bonner, Gerald. 1989. "Augustine and Millenarianism." In *The Making of Orthodoxy: Essays in Honour of Henry Chadwick*, edited by Rowan Williams, 235–54. Cambridge: Cambridge University Press.

Bowlin, John. 2012. "Hell and the Dilemmas of Intractable Alienation." In Wetzel, COG, 186–204.

Burrus, Virginia. 1999. "An Immoderate Feast: Augustine Reads John's Apocalypse." *Augustinian Studies* 30, no. 2: 183–94.

Coyle, J. Kevin. 1987. "Augustine and Apocalyptic: Thoughts on the Fall of Rome, the Book of Revelation, and the End of the World." *Florilegium* 9, no. 1: 1–34.

———. 1999. "Adapted Discourse: Heaven in Augustine's *City of God* and in His Contemporary Preaching." *Augustinian Studies* 30, no. 2: 205–19.

Daley, Brian E. 1991. "Signs of a Church Triumphant: Latin Eschatology in the Fifth Century." In *The Hope of the Early Church: A Handbook of Patristic Eschatology*, 124–67. Cambridge: Cambridge University Press.

Hunter, David G. 2021. "Books 21 & 22: The End of the Body; Heaven and Hell in *The City of God*." In Meconi, COG, 276–96.

McGlothlin, Thomas D. 2024. "Augustine's Resurrection Framework: Clarifying and Connecting Senses of 'Resurrection.'" *Augustinian Studies* 55, no. 1: 25–42.

Moreira, Isabel. 2021. "Book 20: The Last Day; Judgment, Purification, and Transformation." In Meconi, COG, 251–75.

Pollmann, Karla. 1999. "Moulding the Present: Apocalyptic as Hermeneutics in *City of God* 21–22." *Augustinian Studies* 30, no. 2: 165–81.

Reisenauer, Augustine M. 2023. *Augustine's Theology of the Resurrection*. Cambridge: Cambridge University Press.

Book 22

6–7, 29–30

Book 22 concludes Books 19–22, on the ends of the two cities, and City of God *as a whole. In the first major section, Augustine defends the resurrection of the body (22.4–11). In the second, he addresses questions about resurrected bodies (22.12–21a). The speculations in this section are somewhat notorious for their specificity. How tall will we be? What will happen to our lost hair and fingernails? Will women retain their sex in heaven? In the last section (22.21b–30), Augustine imagines what the future life will be like, extrapolating from the blessings humans experience already in this present life. He also addresses Platonist positions on the body (22.25–28). According to Augustine's vision of heaven, the future life will be bodily, social, sinless, and suffused with praise and joy, especially for the forgiveness of sins.*

6. In this context let us also call to mind Cicero's surprise at the Roman belief in Romulus's divinity.[1] I cite his words just as he wrote them: "The case of Romulus is the more astonishing because all the other human beings who are said to have become gods lived in ages when people were less educated,

---

1. [GWL] This material has been included for Augustine's remarks on the defense of earthly cities. Augustine's purpose in this chapter is to compare Romulus's alleged deification unfavorably to Jesus's resurrection from the dead. In this context, he also asks whether collective self-preservation is a good that political communities should pursue at all costs. For discussion of this chapter, see Rowan Williams, "Politics and the Soul: Reading the *City of God*," in *On Augustine* (orig. 1987; London: Bloomsbury, 2016), 107–29, esp. 121–23.

when reason was prone to make up fables, and the ignorant were easily led to believe them. But we know that Romulus lived less than six hundred years ago, when literature and education were already well established and all the primitive error of uncivilized life had been erased."[2] A little later he again makes much the same point about Romulus: "From this we can understand that Homer lived a great many years before Romulus, so that in the time of Romulus, when people were educated and the age itself was more advanced, there was hardly any place left for making up fables. Antiquity accepted fables, which were often no more than crude inventions, but this age was already cultured and quick to mock and reject anything that could not actually be true."[3] Marcus Tullius Cicero was one of the most learned of men, and he was the most eloquent of all.[4] He declares that belief in Romulus's divinity is astonishing precisely because the times were already more advanced and would accept no false fables.[5] But who ever believed that Romulus was a god except Rome—and that at a time when the city was small and still at its very beginning?[6] After that, posterity felt obligated to maintain what was handed down from their ancestors; and as a result the city drank in this superstition with its mother's milk, so to speak, as it grew and attained a great empire. And from its position of power, as from a high place, it then flooded the other peoples it came to rule with this belief. Those peoples, of course, did not actually believe that Romulus was a god; they simply said that he was a god in order not to offend the city to which they were subject. They could not afford to give Rome's founder any other title than the one Rome itself—not from a love of error but from an error of love—believed that he should have.

In contrast, although Christ is the founder of the heavenly and eternal city, it was not because this city was founded by him that it believed in him

2. *Republic* 2.18.

3. *Republic* 2.19.

4. Augustine often recalls Cicero's erudition and eloquence when it suits his purposes. See, e.g., . . . 5.9 and 14.8 and . . . 22.20. But he is also capable of slighting him for the same reason. See . . . 2.27 and also [*City of God, Books 1–10*, 67n92].

5. See . . . 18.24.

6. [GWL] Cicero was perplexed that the Romans believed in the divinity of Romulus, for the Romans at the time of Romulus were sophisticated enough to reject such fables. Augustine argues that this story was believed only at the beginning of Rome's history, when the city was still small. From that point forward, the superstition was bequeathed to future Romans and imposed on other peoples as they were incorporated into the empire. These populations did not believe the story about Romulus but had to accept it because of their subjugation to Rome. Augustine's account of the belief in Romulus's divinity offers an example of how falsehoods can attain widespread, intergenerational consensus and yet still be false.

as God; rather, it is because this city believes in him that it must have him as its foundation. It was only after Rome had been built and dedicated that it gave its founder a temple and worshiped him as a god; but this Jerusalem took its founder, Christ, who is God, as the foundation of its faith precisely so that it might be built and dedicated.[7] The former believed Romulus to be a god because she loved him; the latter loved Christ because it believed him to be God. In the case of the former, then, the love came first, and the result was that it willingly believed even a false good of the one it loved. In the case of the latter, however, the belief came first, and the result was that, due to its right faith, it did not rashly love what was false but loved what was true. For, apart from the many great miracles which persuaded it that Christ is God, there were also the divine prophecies that preceded him, which were most worthy of belief. And at this point we no longer believe these prophecies, as our fathers did, as prophecies that are going to be fulfilled in Christ; we believe them, rather, as prophecies that are now demonstrated to have been fulfilled in him.

As for Romulus, we hear and read that he founded Rome and reigned there, but we neither hear nor read that the event was prophesied before it happened. And, as for his reception among the gods, their writings record it as a belief; they do not teach it as a fact.[8] There are certainly no miraculous signs that prove this actually happened to him. Of course, the she-wolf that nursed him might seem to have been a great portent, but is it the kind of portent—or a portent significant enough—to show that he is a god?[9] Even if the she-wolf really was a wild animal and not a prostitute, she nursed both of the twins, and yet Romulus's brother is not held to be a god. And is there anyone who, when forbidden to say that Romulus or Hercules or any other such men are gods, preferred to die rather than to deny it? Again, would any

7. [GWL] Whereas the Romans expressed their affection for Romulus by making him a god, Christ actually is God, which is why Christians love him. In the former case, love (for Romulus) generated a falsehood. In the latter, the truth (of Jesus's divinity) generated love. This discussion reflects Augustine's wider interest in the relation between knowledge and love. See De Trinitate 9–10, which investigates the relation between the Son and the Spirit according to the relation between knowledge and love.

NCP: "The contrast in this section between Christ and the heavenly city on the one hand and Romulus and Rome on the other is a recasting of the better-known contrast between the heavenly city and the earthly city above at 14.28."

8. [GWL] Livy, History of Rome 1.16. Livy records only that the Romans believed Romulus was a god, not that he actually was one. Augustine says, polemically, that Romulus might have been raised by a prostitute rather than by a literal she-wolf.

9. See Livy, History of Rome 1.4.

nation worship Romulus among its gods if not compelled by its fear of the Roman name? In contrast, who could count all the people who have preferred to be put to death in the most cruel and savage ways rather than to deny that Christ is God?[10] Fear of even the mildest indignation on Rome's part, which people thought might otherwise arise in Roman minds, was enough to compel some of the cities under Roman rule to worship Romulus as a god. But no fear—not fear of some mere mild offense to Roman minds, not even fear of vast and varied punishments, and not even fear of death itself, which is feared more than anything else—could keep a whole multitude of martyrs among all the peoples of the world from not only worshiping Christ as God but even openly professing him as God.[11] And the city of Christ, even though it has taken in whole hosts of people while still on its pilgrimage here on earth, never once fought back against its ungodly persecutors for the sake of securing its temporal wellbeing. Instead, it did not fight back at all for the sake of securing its eternal wellbeing. Its people were manacled, imprisoned, beaten, tortured, burned, maimed, slaughtered—and they multiplied. It was not for them to fight for safety's sake, except by disdaining safety for their savior's sake.

I know that Cicero argues (in the third book of *The Republic*, if I am not mistaken) that the best city will not go to war except in defense of its good faith or its safety.[12] What he means by safety, or how he wants safety to be understood, he shows in another passage: "Private individuals often evade those punishments which even the least sensitive must feel—poverty, exile, imprisonment, beatings—when a speedy death is there for the taking. But to

10. [GWL] According to Augustine, no one ever died to defend their belief in Romulus's divinity. By contrast, many Christians have died because of their belief in Jesus's divinity. Augustine's discussion of this topic will lead to another contrast: Christians do not fight to defend themselves, whether for their temporal or eternal wellbeing, whereas non-Christians must defend their political communities because it is in those communities that they have placed their ultimate hope.

11. Martyrdom was sometimes cited as proof of the truth of the Christian religion. See Irenaeus, *Against Heresies* 4.33.9; Tertullian, *Apology* 50; Athanasius, *On the Incarnation of the Word of God* 27.

12. [GWL] Cicero furnishes a working definition of a just war—namely, one in which a city defends its faith or its safety. By "faith" (*fides*), Cicero refers to the honor of a community, especially through fidelity to its promises to other peoples. By "safety" (*salus*), Cicero refers to a community's right to self-defense. *Salus* is also the term that Christians used for salvation. At the end of this chapter, Augustine will offer alternative, Christian understandings of both *fides* and *salus*. Augustine's acknowledgment of uncertainty ("if I am not mistaken") about the reference for Cicero's statement demonstrates the limitations of his access to his sources and his characteristic transparency as an author.

cities death, which seems to rescue individuals from punishment, is itself a punishment. For a city ought to be so constituted that it is eternal. Therefore, death is never natural for a republic as it is for a human being, for whom death is not only inevitable but often desirable. When a city is destroyed, it is erased and extinguished. It is somehow as if—to compare the small to the great— this whole world were to collapse and perish."[13] Cicero said this because, like the Platonists, he thought that the world was never going to perish.[14] It is clear, then, that the safety for which he thought a city should go to war is the safety which ensures, as he says, that it will endure for all eternity, even though its individual citizens successively die and are born, just as the dense foliage of the olive, the laurel, and the other evergreen trees is sustained by the continual fall and renewal of the leaves. In fact, as he says, death is not always a punishment for individual humans, for it very often rescues them from punishment. But it is always a punishment for a whole city. There is good reason, then, to ask whether the Saguntines acted rightly when they preferred to have their whole city perish rather than to break the faith by which they were bound to the Roman republic.[15] They are praised for their action by all the citizens of the earthly republic. But, in truth, I do not see how they could have complied with Cicero's stipulation. He says that war should never be undertaken except in defense of faith or safety, but he does not say which of these to choose if both faith and safety are simultaneously at risk and it is impossible to keep one without losing the other. For it is obvious that, if the

13. [GWL] *Republic* 3, frag. 34b. With other Romans, Cicero held that death was sometimes preferable to other forms of suffering (e.g., poverty, exile, imprisonment, beatings). Yet he related this principle only to individuals and not to cities. Individuals will inevitably die and be replaced by other citizens. By contrast, the death of a society is catastrophic—the destruction of a whole reality. This is the fear that compels the earthly city to defend itself at all costs. The heavenly city does not share such fears because its hope is in eternal reward. It can therefore pursue peace instead of war.

14. *On the Eternity of the World*, by Proclus (412–485), one of the last great representatives of Neoplatonism, reprises the philosophical arguments for the eternity of the world that were current in Augustine's time and before.

15. [GWL] Augustine treats this incident in 3.20. Saguntum was a Spanish city and ally to Rome. Because of this alliance, Hannibal, the Carthaginian general fighting Rome, sieged the city and eventually destroyed it (219 BCE). This event initiated the Second Punic War. Augustine argues that the Saguntines were faced with an impossible choice between their faith (*fides*) to Rome and their wellbeing (*salus*). By remaining faithful to Rome, they were destroyed. Their example demonstrates the inadequacy of Cicero's definition of just war. There are circumstances in which self-preservation (*salus*) requires the violation of faith (*fides*). Collective self-preservation should not be a final end. Earthly communities are only temporal and not eternal goods. Trying to preserve a community at all costs leads to moral compromise.

Saguntines had chosen safety, they would have had to abandon faith; and, if they ought to have kept faith, they would certainly have had to relinquish their safety—which is exactly what happened.

But the safety of the city of God is such that it can only be kept, or rather can only be acquired, with faith and through faith; and, when faith is lost, no one can possibly attain to that safety.[16] It is this thought, lodged in a steadfast and patient heart, that made so many and such noble martyrs. But Romulus did not have, nor could he have had, even one such martyr in the days when he was believed to be a god.

7. It is quite ridiculous, however, to mention Romulus's false divinity when we are speaking of Christ. But, if Romulus lived some six hundred years before Cicero and if that age was already so sophisticated, as we are told, that it rejected everything that could not possibly be true, how much more in Cicero's own time, six hundred years later, and still more in the reigns of Augustus and Tiberius,[17] which were certainly more highly educated times, would the human mind have been unable to accept the resurrection of Christ's flesh and its ascension into heaven if it were something that could not possibly be true! People would have mocked at it and spewed it out of their ears and hearts if the divinity of truth itself, or the truth of divinity, along with the confirming miraculous signs, had not shown both that it could take place and that in fact it had taken place. And so, despite the terror and opposition of so many horrible persecutions, the resurrection and immortality of the flesh—first in Christ, then in all the rest of us, which will follow in the new age—have been both faithfully believed and fearlessly proclaimed. They were sown with the blood of the martyrs to sprout up all the more abundantly throughout the world. For the prior pronouncements of the prophets were read, manifest works of power confirmed them, and the truth—new to custom but not contrary to reason—exercised its persuasive force until the whole world, which once persecuted the truth in fury, now followed it in faith.

———————◆———————

16. [GWL] Here are Augustine's theological alternatives to Cicero's understandings of *fides* (faith) and *salus* (safety). For the city of God, *salus* means eternal salvation, not the preservation of an earthly city; and this salvation, this true *salus*, comes through *fides*. Christians thus face no conflict between *fides* and *salus*. If they are faced with a choice between their integrity and their earthly lives, they will choose the former. This is the logic of Christian martyrdom, which requires hope in eternal and not temporal reward.

17. Augustus ruled from 27 BCE to 14 CE, Tiberius from 14 to 37.

The Eternal Life of the Saints: The Vision of God

29. Now, so far as God grants his help, let us see how the saints will be occupied in their immortal and spiritual bodies, when their flesh is no longer living carnally but now spiritually. To tell the truth, however, I do not know what their activity, or rather their rest and repose, will be like.[18] I have never seen it with my bodily senses; and, if I should say that I have seen it with my mind, that is, with my understanding, what does our understanding amount to, and how far can it take us, in relation to such excellence? Then, as the Apostle says, there will be *the peace of God which surpasses all understanding* (Phil. 4:7). And whose understanding does he mean if not ours, and perhaps even that of the holy angels? It certainly does not surpass God's understanding! If the saints are going to live in the peace of God, then, they are clearly going to live in the peace *which surpasses all understanding*. It obviously surpasses our understanding; there is no doubt of that. If it also surpasses the angels' understanding—and the one who said *all understanding* seems not to have made an exception even of them—then we have to take this saying to mean that neither we nor any of the angels can know the peace of God, whereby God himself is at peace, as God knows it. And so it *surpasses all understanding* except, of course, his own.

But, because we also are made partakers in his peace according to our capacity, we too know supreme peace in ourselves, among ourselves, and with him, insofar as what is supreme is possible for us. Similarly, the holy angels know it according to their capacity. At present, however, human beings know it only to a far lower degree, no matter how outstanding they are in mental progress. For we must keep in mind how great a man it was who said, *For we know only in part, and we prophesy only in part, until that which is perfect comes* (1 Cor. 13:9) and *Now we see in a mirror dimly, but then face to face* (1 Cor. 13:12). This is how the holy angels see already. The holy angels are also called our angels. For we have been rescued from the power of darkness, have received the pledge of the Spirit, and have been transferred to the kingdom of Christ,[19] and so we have already begun to belong to the angels with whom

---

18. [GWL] As Augustine acknowledges, his sketch of the future life is speculative. He has never witnessed our final condition, which is beyond human understanding. Theologically, the value of speculating about heaven resides less in predicting the future than in assessing what is fundamental about human life. Augustine's vision of heaven reveals his central concerns: the beatific vision, the resurrection of the body, community, proper worship, freedom from sin, redemption, and rest.

19. See Col. 1:13.

we shall share the holy and most delightful city of God, about which we have now written so many books.[20] Thus, the angels, who are God's angels, are also our angels in the same way that Christ is both God's Christ and our Christ. They are God's because they did not abandon God, and they are ours because they have begun to have us as their fellow citizens. The Lord Jesus said, *See that you do not despise one of these little ones. For I tell you that in heaven their angels always see the face of my Father who is in heaven* (Matt. 18:10). As they see, then, we also shall see. But we do not yet see in this way. That is why, as I indicated a moment ago, the Apostle says, *Now we see in a mirror dimly, but then face to face.* This vision is being saved for us as the reward for faith, and it is this vision about which the apostle John is speaking when he says, *When he appears we shall be like him, for we shall see him as he is* (1 John 3:2). And by God's face, of course, we must understand his manifestation, not a part of the body similar to the one we have and call by that name.

Will the Saints See God with the Eyes of the Spiritual Body?

Consequently, when I am asked what the saints' activity in the spiritual body will be, I do not say what I already see. I say only what I believe, in keeping with what I read in the Psalm, *I believed, and therefore I have spoken* (Ps. 116:10 LXX). And so I say that the saints are going to see God in the body.[21] But whether they will see him by means of the body—as we now see the sun, the moon, the stars, the sea, the earth, and the things on earth—is no small question. For, on the one hand, it is hard to say that the saints will then have bodies of such a kind that they will not be able to close and open their eyes whenever they want; but, on the other, it is even harder to say that anyone who shuts his eyes there will stop seeing God.

---

20. [GWL] As in the rest of *City of God*, Augustine includes angels in the heavenly city. During this temporal existence, the heavenly city is separated between angels, who already have blessed immortality, and humans, who must persist in pilgrimage until Christ's return. In the life to come, these communities will be joined in everlasting fellowship. See essay: "Angels and Demons."

21. [GWL] The rest of this chapter concentrates on one, somewhat involved, question: How will humans see God in their bodies? Augustine affirms that we will have bodies in heaven, and Scripture says we will see God (1 Cor. 13:12; 1 John 3:2). We will therefore see God *while* we have bodies. But will we see God *through* our bodies, such that our eyes will relay a vision of God to our souls? The challenge with this question is that God is nonbodily. How could we see God through our bodies when God does not have a body to be seen? According to *Revisions* 2.41.68, this chapter in *City of God* resolves Augustine's long-standing struggle to answer this question. For Augustine's earlier treatments of this issue, see *Letters* 92; 147; 148; 162; and *Sermon* 277.

The prophet Elisha, although absent in body, saw his servant Gehazi receiving gifts given to him by Naaman the Syrian, whom the prophet had healed from the deformity of leprosy; and all the while the servant supposed that his wicked act was hidden because his master was not there to see it.[22] How much the more, then, will the saints in their spiritual bodies see all things, not only when their eyes are closed but even when they are not bodily present! For then the *perfect* will have come of which the Apostle speaks when he says, *We know only in part, and we prophesy only in part, but, when that which is perfect comes, that which is only in part shall come to an end* (1 Cor. 13:9–10). Then, in order to show as best he could by means of some simile how different this life is from the life to come—and not just the present life of ordinary people but even of those who are here endowed with outstanding holiness—he says, *When I was a child, I thought like a child, I spoke like a child, I reasoned like a child; but, when I became an adult, I put away childish things. Now we see in a mirror dimly, but then face to face. Now I know in part, but then I shall know even as I also am known* (1 Cor. 13:11–12).

Even in this life, therefore, where the prophetic gift of men with miraculous powers can only be compared to the future life as a child is compared to an adult, Elisha still saw his servant receiving gifts when he himself was far away.[23] Does it make sense, then, to think that—once the perfect has come and the corruptible body no longer weighs down the soul[24] but is incorruptible and offers no impediment at all—the saints will need bodily eyes to see what they are going to see, especially when the absent Elisha had no need of bodily eyes to see his servant? For, according to the Septuagint translation, this is what the prophet said to Gehazi: *Did not my heart go with you when the man left his chariot to meet you and you took the money?* and so on; or, as the priest Jerome has it in his translation from the Hebrew, *Was not my heart present when the man turned from his chariot to meet you?* (2 Kings 5:26). The prophet says, then, that he saw this with his heart, which beyond

22. See 2 Kings 5:19–27.

23. [GWL] Elisha saw his servant, Gehazi, through the eyes of his heart without using the eyes of his body. But Elisha still retained the ability to see through the eyes of his body. This incident suggests that we will see through the eyes of our hearts and through the eyes of our bodies. The question is whether we will see *God* through the eyes of our bodies (and not just through the eyes of our hearts). By "eyes of the heart," Augustine is referring to our internal spirit (*spiritus*), which receives impressions of the external world (like sights and sounds) through the physical senses (like the seeing of eyes and the hearing of ears). In this miraculous instance, Elisha's spirit could see Gehazi without the use of physical eyes.

24. See Wis. 9:10.

doubt was miraculously helped by God. But how much more will all abound in this gift, when God will be all in all![25] Even so, however, the bodily eyes will also be in their place and have their function, and the spirit will make use of them through the spiritual body. For the fact that the prophet did not need his bodily eyes to see his absent servant does not mean that he did not use them to see things present, even though, if he closed his eyes, he could have seen them by the spirit in the same way that he saw absent things when he was not there himself. It would be completely wrong, then, to say that in the life to come the saints will not see God when they have their eyes closed, for they will always see him with the spirit.

But will they also see with their bodily eyes when they have them open? That is the question. If the eyes of the spiritual body, even as spiritual, can see no more than the eyes we have now, there is no doubt that God cannot be seen with them.[26] They will have a far different power, then, if they are to see the incorporeal nature which is not contained in any place but is wholly present everywhere. For the fact that we say that God is present both in heaven and on earth—and God himself says, through the prophet, *I fill heaven and earth* (Jer. 23:24)—does not mean that we also say that one part of him is in heaven and another on earth. Rather, he is wholly in heaven and wholly on earth, not at different times but simultaneously, which is impossible for any bodily nature. The power of those eyes, then, will be far greater than it is now, not so that they can see more sharply than certain serpents or eagles are reported to see (for, no matter how sharp-eyed these animals are, they still can only see corporeal things), but so that they can also see incorporeal things. Perhaps it was this great power of sight that was briefly given to the eyes of the holy man Job, while he was still in this mortal body, when he said to God, *Before I heard you by the hearing of the ear, but now my eye sees you; therefore, I despise myself and melt away and count myself dust and ashes* (Job 42:5–6 LXX). At the same time, however, there is nothing to prevent us from understanding Job to be speaking here of the eye of the heart, of which the Apostle says, *having the eyes of your heart enlightened* (Eph.

25. See 1 Cor. 15:28.

26. [GWL] By definition, it would seem, nonbodily things cannot be physically seen. We certainly cannot see nonbodily things with our bodily eyes now. Yet Augustine wonders whether our resurrected bodies will be able to see nonbodily things. This would require more than an enhancement of our present vision (such as might allow us to see further distances with acuity). Seeing nonbodily things—which are currently impossible for us to see, from any distance—would require a categorically different visual ability.

1:18). And it is certain that, when God is seen, he will be seen with the eyes of the heart; for this is something that no Christian can doubt who faithfully accepts what our God and teacher says, *Blessed are the pure in heart, for they shall see God* (Matt. 5:8).

But the question before us is this: will God also be seen then with the eyes of the body?[27] It is written, *And all flesh shall see God's salvation* (Luke 3:6). But this passage can be understood without difficulty as if it said, "And every person will see God's Christ." For Christ obviously was seen in the body, and he will also be seen in the body when he comes to judge the living and the dead. There are many scriptural passages that show that Christ is God's salvation, but this is declared most clearly in the words of the venerable old man Simeon who, when he took the infant Christ in his arms, said, *Lord, you are now letting your servant depart in peace, according to your word, for my eyes have seen your salvation* (Luke 2:29–30). Again, there is what the above-mentioned Job says, as found in the copies translated from the Hebrew, *And in my flesh I will see God* (Job 19:26). Here, beyond doubt, Job prophesied the resurrection of the flesh. But he did not say that he was going to see God "by means of my flesh." And, even if he had, *God* could still be understood to mean Christ, who will be seen in the flesh and by means of the flesh. As it is, however, the words *in my flesh I will see God* can simply be understood to mean "I shall be in my flesh when I see God." Nor does the Apostle's phrase, *face to face* (1 Cor. 13:12), require us to believe that we shall see God by means of our corporeal face and its bodily eyes, for we shall see him without interruption in the spirit. And, if there were no sense in which the inner man has a face, the same Apostle would not have said, *But we, with unveiled face, beholding the glory of the Lord, are transformed from glory to glory, as by the Spirit of the Lord* (2 Cor. 3:18). This is also the only way we can interpret what the psalmist sings, *Draw near to him, and be illumined, and your faces shall not be ashamed* (Ps. 34:5). For it is by faith that we draw near to God; and faith, as all agree, is a matter of the heart, not of the body. But we do not know how much power the spiritual body will acquire, for we are speaking

---

27. [GWL] In this paragraph, Augustine rules out two easy options: (1) the eyes of our bodies will see God in the sense that they will see Christ in his body, and (2) the eyes of our hearts will see God. Both of these cases involve "like seeing like": a body seeing a body, or an intelligible (i.e., nonbodily) thing seeing something intelligible (see *Letters* 92.3; 147.21.49; 148.1.1–148.1.3). Augustine is interested in the toughest case: whether our *bodies* will see the *nonbodily* God. Though our bodies will be spiritual, they will still be bodily. Is it possible for a body—even a spiritual body—to see God?

about matters of which we have no experience, and for which we have no scriptural authority to guide us that cannot be interpreted in more than one way. It is inevitable, therefore, that what we read in the Book of Wisdom also applies to us: *The thoughts of mortals are timid, and our views of the future uncertain* (Wis. 9:14).

There is, of course, the reasoning of the philosophers, who insist that intelligible things are seen by the vision of the mind and sensible—that is, bodily—things by the senses of the body and, consequently, that the mind is not capable of viewing intelligible things through the body or bodily things through itself alone.[28] If we could be completely sure of this, it would clearly follow that God can in no way be seen through the eyes of even the spiritual body. But both true reason and prophetic authority hold this reasoning up to ridicule. For who has so completely turned his back on the truth that he would dare to deny that God knows corporeal things? Does God have a body, then, the eyes of which make it possible for him to acquire this knowledge? Again, does not what we just said about the prophet Elisha indicate clearly enough that bodily things can be perceived by the spirit, even without the body? When his servant took the gifts, this was obviously a bodily act, but the prophet saw it not by means of the body but by means of the spirit. It is perfectly clear, then, that bodily things are seen by the spirit. Why, then, should the spiritual body not have such power that the spirit may also be seen by the body? For *God is spirit* (John 4:24). Moreover, it is by his inner sense and not by his bodily eyes that a person knows his own life, by which he now lives in the body and animates his earthly members and makes them alive. In contrast, however, it is by means of his body that he knows the life of other persons, despite the fact that it is invisible.[29] For how do we distinguish living bodies from bodies without life except by seeing at one and the same time both the bodies and their life, which we can only see by means of the body?

What we do not see with our bodily eyes, however, is life itself, separate from the body. Consequently, it is possible, and in fact highly probable, that

---

28. [GWL] The principle, mentioned above, of "like seeing like." This principle is clearly false, since nonbodily things can see bodily things. God can see our bodies, and Elisha witnessed Gehazi's actions through the eyes of his heart. Augustine wonders whether the reverse is also the case. Can bodies see nonbodily things?

29. [GWL] Augustine is now approaching his solution. We use bodies to see the "life" (*uita*) of other people. The eyes of our bodies see the bodies of other people, and it is through their bodies that we perceive their life. Though we cannot see their life in a physical sense, we can see their life through their bodies.

in the world to come we will see the corporeal bodies of the new heaven and
the new earth[30] in such a way that, wherever we look, we shall see God with
brilliant clarity, everywhere present and governing all things, including bodily
things—seeing him both through the bodies we shall be wearing and through
the bodies we shall be looking at.[31] It will not be as it is now. Now the invisible
things of God are understood through the things he has made;[32] now they are
seen in a mirror dimly and only in part;[33] now the faith by which we believe
counts more for us than the sight of bodily things that we perceive with our
bodily eyes. Even in this life, however, as soon as we catch sight of the people
among whom we live—living people, showing vital motion—we not merely
believe but actually see that they are alive. Even though we cannot see their
life apart from their bodies, we do see it in their bodies, by means of our
bodies, with no room for any doubt whatsoever. And in the same way, in the
life to come, wherever we look with the spiritual eyes of our bodies, we shall,
even by means of our bodies, behold the incorporeal God ruling all things.

It is possible, then, that God will be seen in this way due to the fact that
the eyes will then have some excellence similar to that of the mind, by which
they will even be able to discern an incorporeal nature.[34] It is difficult, however,
or even impossible to support this view with any examples or testimonies
from Divine Scripture. Alternatively—and this is easier to grasp—God will
be known to us in such a conspicuous way that we shall each see him by the
spirit in ourselves, in each other, in himself, in the new heaven and the new
earth, and in every created thing that will then exist; and, at the same time,
by the body we shall each see him in every body, wherever the eyes of the
spiritual body are directed with their penetrating gaze.[35] Our thoughts, too,
will then lie open to each other; for the words of the Apostle will be fulfilled,
who, after saying, *Do not pronounce judgment before the time*, immediately

30. See Isa. 65:17; 66:22; 2 Pet. 3:13; Rev. 21:1.

31. [GWL] Here is Augustine's solution. We will see God with the eyes of our bodies through
the bodies of other people. This proposal involves two instances of bodily mediation. The first
concerns our minds' perception of others through *our* bodies, while the second concerns our
minds' perception of God through *others'* bodies. Though mediated, our vision of God will
count as sight and not faith. We do not just believe in the life of other people; we see it. The
same will be the case with God.

32. See Rom. 1:20.

33. See 1 Cor. 13:12.

34. [GWL] Augustine briefly entertains, and dismisses, another possibility—namely, that
our spiritual eyes will be similar to our minds in their ability to discern God.

35. [GWL] Augustine returns to his solution in this chapter: we will see God through the
bodies of other people.

added, *until the Lord comes, who shall bring to light the hidden things of darkness and shall make manifest the thoughts of the heart, and then each one shall have praise from God* (1 Cor. 4:5).[36]

The Felicity of the Saints: Seeing, Loving, and Praising God

30. How marvelous that felicity will be, where there will be no evil, where no good will be hidden from sight, where all our time will be given to praising God, who will be all in all![37] For I do not know what else we shall be doing when our activity will neither be halted by idleness nor driven by need. And I am guided, too, by the holy canticle, where I read or hear, *Blessed are those who dwell in your house; they shall praise you for ever and ever* (Ps. 84:4).

All the members and organs of the incorruptible body, which we now see assigned to the various functions that the necessities of life require of them, will contribute to praising God; for then there will be no such necessities but only full, certain, secure, and eternal felicity. All the proportions of bodily harmony, of which I have already spoken[38] and which are now hidden from us, will no longer be hidden. Distributed through all the parts of the body, within and without, they—along with all the other great and wondrous things that will then be seen—will set rational minds on fire with praise for such a great artist from sheer delight in their rational beauty.

What the movements of such bodies will be in the world to come I am not rash enough to try to describe. In fact I cannot even imagine it. But their motion and their rest, like their form itself, will be fitting, for nothing unfitting will be there at all. Where the spirit wills, it is certain, there the body will instantaneously be; nor will the spirit will anything which could possibly be

36. [GWL] One of the richest moments in Augustine's writings. The fall of humanity resulted in our opacity to one another. Instead of seeing one another's thoughts, we were forced to communicate through signs (mostly words). These signs are vulnerable to deception and misunderstanding, which arise when we share or receive signs that do not represent the right thoughts. Human trust and intimacy are severely compromised. In heaven, we will see each other's thoughts again. Since everyone will be holy and suffused with thoughts about God, seeing others' thoughts will be the same as seeing God. This is the opposite of our present condition, in which we would be ashamed if others could see our thoughts. In short, the beatific vision is the fullness of the heavenly community's celebration of God. We will see God through our bodies by seeing God in the bodies of the saints. NCP: "See *Letter* 92.2; *Enchiridion* 32.121."

37. This final chapter of *City of God*, which begins with the words *Quanta erit illa felicitas*, must have been the inspiration for the twelfth-century theologian Peter Abelard's celebrated Saturday vespers hymn, *O quanta qualia*, which repeats several of the chapter's themes and images.

38. See . . . 22.24.

unfitting either for the spirit or for the body. True glory will be there, for no one will be praised in error or in flattery; true honor, for honor will be denied to no one who is worthy and will be awarded to no one who is unworthy, nor will anyone who is unworthy aspire to it, since only the worthy are permitted to be there; and true peace, for no one will suffer opposition either from himself or from others.[39]

The reward of virtue will be God himself, who gave the virtue and who promised himself to it, and than whom there can be nothing better or greater.[40] When he said through the prophet, *I will be their God, and they shall be my people* (Lev. 26:12), what did he mean but "I will be their fulfillment; I will be all that people rightly desire—life, health, sustenance, plenty, glory, honor, peace, and all good things"? This is also the right way to understand what the Apostle says, *That God may be all in all* (1 Cor. 15:28). He will be the end of our desires: he will be seen without end, loved without satiation, and praised without weariness. And this gift, this feeling, this activity, like eternal life itself, will be shared by all.

But who could possibly imagine, much less describe, the grades of honor and glory there will be then, in proportion to the merits deserving of reward?[41] It is not to be doubted, however, that there will be such distinctions. And the blessed city will also see this great good in itself—that no inferior will envy any superior any more than the other angels envy the archangels. No one will wish to be what he has not been given to be, but will be linked by a bond of the utmost peace and concord to the one to whom this has been given—just as, in the body, the finger does not wish to be the eye, since the structure of the body contains both members in peace.[42] Thus, some will have lesser gifts than others, but they will also have the gift of not wanting more.

39. [GWL] Heavenly glory will far exceed the Romans' distorted version. The Romans gained earthly glory through the semblance of virtue. Heavenly glory will reward true virtue. Augustine's reference to glory bookends *City of God*, the first word of which is *gloriosissimam*. This signals the significance of glory as a theme in Augustine's work.

40. [GWL] The presence of God is the center of Augustine's eschatological vision. While sin involves using God for the sake of other things, heaven is characterized by the enjoyment of God as Christians' final end. Against the Romans, who made virtue a goddess (4.20–21), God is the ultimate source of virtue and its ultimate reward.

41. [GWL] Augustine believes there will be differences of honor and glory in heaven. These differences will not cause jealousy, as difficult as this might be to imagine. Jealousy is an antisocial sin in that we feel sad when others experience good, and we feel joy when others experience evil. Our reactions are the opposite of what they should be. In heaven, we will experience joy at others' good, even when their reward exceeds our own.

42. See 1 Cor. 12:14–26.

Sin will no longer be able to give them any delight, but this does not mean that they will have no free will. On the contrary, it will be all the more free, because it will have been so completely set free from delight in sinning that it will take unfailing delight in not sinning. The initial free will, given to man when he was first created righteous, was able not to sin, but it was also able to sin.[43] In contrast, the final free will will be more powerful than the first in that it will not be able to sin, but this will be due to God's gift, not to any capacity of its own nature. For it is one thing to be God and quite another to participate in God. God is by nature unable to sin, but one who participates in God receives it from God that he is unable to sin. In addition, there was a gradation in the divine gift that had to be preserved: man was first given a freedom of will by virtue of which he would be able not to sin, and he was ultimately given a freedom of will by virtue of which he would not be able to sin. The former was suited to acquiring merit, the latter is suited to receiving reward. But, because man's nature sinned when it was able to sin, it is delivered by a more generous gift of grace, so that it may be led to the liberty in which it is unable to sin. For, just as the first immortality, which Adam lost by sinning, consisted in being able not to die and the final immortality will consist in not being able to die, so the first free will consisted in being able not to sin and the final free will will consist in not being able to sin. Thus, it will be just as impossible then to lose the will to godliness and justice as it is impossible now to lose the will to happiness.[44] For in sinning we lost our hold on both godliness and happiness, but, when we lost happiness, we obviously

43. [GWL] As observed above in Book 12n4, the Latin for "able not to sin" is *posse non peccare* and for "not able to sin" is *non posse peccare*. Later in the paragraph, Augustine will also invoke the phrases "being able not to die" (*posse non mori*) and "not being able to die" (*non posse mori*). Augustine uses these phrases throughout his writings to contrast humanity's condition before the fall with humanity's condition in heaven. Though Adam and Eve were created without sin, they still possessed the ability to sin, and thus to die as a punishment for sin. In heaven, we will not be able to sin, which means we will not be able to die either. See *Answer to the Two Letters of the Pelagians* 3.7.17; *Enchiridion* 28.104–105; *Literal Meaning of Genesis* 6.25.36; *Rebuke and Grace* 12.33–34; *Unfinished Work in Answer to Julian* 5.56, 58, 60; 6.10, 12, 25; Han-luen Kantzer Komline, *Augustine on the Will: A Theological Account* (Oxford: Oxford University Press, 2020), 11n39.

44. [GWL] According to Augustine, all humans desire to be happy. Indeed, it is impossible for humans *not* to desire happiness (*Confessions* 10.20.29–10.23.34). Happiness is thus like peace, which is also impossible not to desire (*City of God* 19.12). Despite the universal desire for happiness, not all humans recognize the necessity of godliness and justice for happiness. In heaven, by contrast, happiness and virtue will go together. Everyone will desire virtue in the same way that everyone on earth desires happiness now. For Augustine, this is true freedom. Whereas modern notions of freedom might concentrate on the ability to choose between alternate possibilities, Augustine defines freedom as the ability to obey God perfectly, which entails being *unable* to sin.

did not lose the will to happiness. Then, too, God himself certainly cannot sin. But does that mean we should deny that he has free will?

In the heavenly city, then, there will be freedom of will, one freedom in all and indivisible in each. It will be freed from all evil and filled with all good, enjoying without fail the delight of eternal joys; and it will have no memory of faults or punishments. It will not, however, have forgotten its own liberation, and so it will not be ungrateful to its liberator.[45] As a matter of rational knowledge, then, it will even remember its past evils; but as a matter of felt experience it will not remember them at all—in the same way that a highly skilled physician knows virtually all the diseases of the body as they are known to his art but is ignorant of most of them as they are actually felt in the body, since he has not suffered them himself.

There are, then, two kinds of knowledge of evils, one by virtue of which they are not hidden from the mind's grasp, another by virtue of which they are ingrained in felt experience. Indeed, all the vices are known in one way through the teachings of wisdom, and in quite another through the wicked life of the fool. Similarly, there are two ways of forgetting evils. The person who has education and learning forgets them in one way, the person who has actually experienced and suffered them forgets them in another way—the former when he disregards his knowledge, the latter when he is no longer in misery. It is according to this second kind of forgetting that the saints will have no memory of past evils. For they will now be free from all evils, and they will be completely erased from their feelings. By the great power of knowledge that they will have, however, they will be aware not only of their own past misery but also of the eternal misery of the damned. Otherwise—if they were to have no knowledge at all that they were once in misery—how, as the Psalm says, will they sing the Lord's mercies forever?[46] Nothing will give more joy to that city than this song to the glory of the grace of Christ, by whose blood we are delivered.[47]

45. [GWL] The next couple paragraphs defend the position that we will remember our sins in heaven. We will remember them not so as to be tempted or ashamed by them but so as to celebrate our deliverance from them.

46. NCP: "See Ps. 89.1." [GWL] The central activity in heaven is worshiping God. Humans will worship God by celebrating God's mercies. This blessing is unique to humans. The angels who belong to the heavenly city never fell into sin. The angels who sinned became demons and never received the possibility of redemption. By contrast, humans have fallen into sin and have also received the possibility of redemption. Given this difference, the angels cannot sing of God's redemption as humans can. See essay: "Angels and Demons."

47. See Rev. 5:9.

Then the words of the Psalm will be fulfilled, *Be still and see that I am God* (Ps. 46:10).[48] This will truly be the supreme sabbath, the sabbath which has no evening, the sabbath which the Lord stamped with his approval in the first works of creation, where we read, *And on the seventh day God rested from all his works that he had done. And God blessed the seventh day and sanctified it, because on it he rested from all his works that he had begun to do* (Gen. 2:2). For we shall ourselves be the seventh day, when we have been made full by his blessing and made new by his sanctification. Then we shall be still and see that he is God; then we shall see that he is what we ourselves wanted to be, when we fell away from him, listening to what we heard from the seducer, *You shall be like gods* (Gen. 3:5), and deserting the true God, who would have made us gods by participation in him, not by desertion of him. For what have we done without him except to waste away in his wrath? But, when we are made new by him and are perfected by his greater grace, we shall be still for all eternity and shall see that he is God, and by him we shall be filled when he is all in all.[49]

For it is only when we have come to understand that our good works are actually his, not ours, that they are credited to us so that we may attain this sabbath. If we ascribe them to ourselves, they will be servile works,[50] and it is said of the sabbath, *You shall do no servile work* (Deut. 5:14). For the same reason it is also said through the prophet Ezekiel, *And I gave them my sabbaths as a sign between me and them, so that they might know that I am the Lord, who sanctifies them* (Ezek. 20:12). We shall know this perfectly when we are perfectly still and see perfectly that he is God.

This sabbath will stand out more clearly if we enumerate the ages, as if they were days, according to the divisions of time that we see represented in Scripture, for we shall find that it is the seventh age.[51] The first age, counted as the first day, extends from Adam to the flood, and the second from the flood to Abraham. These two are equal not in length of time but in number of generations, for each turns out to contain ten generations. From Abraham down to the coming of Christ, by the reckoning of the evangelist Matthew,

48. [GWL] The remainder of this chapter treats heaven as our ultimate sabbath, an unending day of blessing and rest. Augustine's emphasis on rest recalls his famous prayer: "Our heart is unquiet until it rests in you" (*Confessions* 1.1.1).

49. See 1 Cor. 15:28.

50. I.e., works done for pay or for a reward.

51. [GWL] Augustine believes human history unfolds in six stages, or "days," and culminates in the seventh. See essay: "Last Things."

there are three ages, each extending across fourteen generations—one from Abraham to David, the second from David to the exile to Babylon, and the third from the exile to Babylon down to Christ's birth in the flesh.[52] These make five ages in all. The sixth age is now in progress, but it is not to be measured by any set number of generations, for Scripture says, *It is not for you to know the times that the Father has put in his own power* (Acts 1:7). After this sixth age God will rest, as on the seventh day; and he will cause this same seventh day—the day that we ourselves shall be—to rest in him.[53] It would take too long, however, to discuss each of these ages in detail now. It is enough simply to point out that this seventh age will be our sabbath, and its end will not be an evening but rather the Lord's Day, as an eighth and eternal day, consecrated by Christ's resurrection, and prefiguring the eternal rest not only of the spirit but also of the body. There we shall be still and see, see and love, love and praise.[54] Behold what will be in the end without end! For what else is our end but to reach the kingdom that has no end?

It seems to me that, with God's help, I have now paid my debt with this huge work.[55] May those who think it too small or too large forgive me; and may those who think it sufficient give joyful thanks not to me but, with me, to God. Amen. Amen.[56]

---

52. See Matt. 1:17.

53. See *Confessions* 13.36.51–13.37.52.

54. [GWL] The sequence here is meaningful. We need to be still (rest) before we can see God. Seeing is closely related to knowing. Since knowledge is the basis for love, seeing God will fuel our love for God. Finally, our love for God will spark praise, humanity's central activity in heaven.

55. [GWL] Augustine recalls the preface of *City of God*, where he introduced the work as a debt he owed to Marcellinus. Marcellinus was no longer alive at the time that Augustine was completing *City of God*, which is presumably why Augustine does not mention him here.

56. [GWL] With these words, Augustine concludes *City of God*. One senses his relief at having completed it—and his perception of its significance.

Appendix

OUTLINE OF *City of God*

∞∞ *Against the Gods: Blessings in This Life* ∞∞

Book 1. The Sack of Rome and the Christian View of Suffering

1. (*Preface*) The city of God will be treated in contrast with the earthly city.
2. (1–7) Many hypocrites who are attacking Christianity found refuge in Christian shrines and basilicas during the sack of Rome. This clemency was unprecedented. These people should thank and not slander God.
3. (8–29) Explaining suffering.
   A. (8–9) God brings temporal blessing and suffering on both good and evil people but for different reasons. Good people are not as affected as evil people by temporal blessing or suffering because they do not put their hope in temporal things.
   B. (10–15) For Christians, all suffering works for good. Christians experienced no ultimate harm during the sack of Rome, despite various forms of suffering (loss of riches, torture, famine, death, lack of burial, captivity).
   C. (16–28) The rape of Christian women.

      i. (16–18) Chastity is a virtue of the mind, so the violation of the body does not merit suicide.

     ii. (19–27) Arguments against suicide, engaging Roman examples and Scripture.

    iii. (28) Perhaps the reason God allowed Christian women to be violated was to discipline their pride.

   D. (29) Summary: Christians endure suffering as pilgrims in this world.

4. (30–34) The Romans attack Christianity only because they want to indulge in vice, especially theatrical performances dedicated to the gods—who are really demons. The demons introduced the shows as a ploy to corrupt the Romans. During the sack of Rome, God still spared Romans who confessed Christ or took refuge in Christian shrines.

5. (35–36) The two cities are interwoven and intermixed in this temporal life. Outline of topics to be addressed in Books 2–10.

Book 2. Rome's Moral Suffering before Christ

1. (1–3) The foolishness of those who criticize Christianity. Summary of Book 1 and introduction to next topic.

2. (4–16) The gods and Rome's immorality.

   A. (4–7) The gods never provided public teaching of morality. The shows are full of obscenities. The philosophers taught truth, despite their errors, and are worthier of worship than the gods.

   B. (8–13) The gods introduced theater to corrupt the Romans and allowed wicked deeds to be ascribed to themselves. Recognizing the immorality of the theater, the Romans forbade the slander of humans in the shows and denied actors civic honors. The Romans should also have rejected the worship of the gods.

   C. (14–15) The Romans were inconsistent in that they denied actors honor while they honored the poets who wrote the shows. Plato condemned the poets and was worthier of worship than the gods.

   D. (16) The gods never provided laws for morality, but rather promoted immorality.

3. (17–21) Rome's immorality according to its own authors.

A. (17–18) Sallust said the Romans were just by nature and not by laws. But his history of the Romans demonstrates that they were always immoral, and they degenerated after the destruction of Carthage.

B. (19–20) The gods have never warned against immorality, and the Romans indulge in vice.

C. (21) Cicero said Rome had become so immoral that it was no longer a republic.

4. (22–27) Instead of preventing Rome's immorality, the gods encouraged it by manipulating the people with temporal goods, signs, criminal examples for imitation, the shows, and secret instruction.

5. (28–29) Christianity promotes virtue. Exhortation for the Romans to become Christian.

Book 3. Rome's Physical Suffering before Christ

1. (1) Introduction.

2. (2–8) The destruction of Troy, first by the Greeks and later by the Romans, cannot be explained by the gods.

3. (9–12) Numa Pompilius enjoyed long peace but established many gods to secure Rome's protection. His successors added even more gods.

4. (13–31) History of Rome's physical disasters.

A. (13–15) The gods did not protect Rome during the period of the kings.

B. (16–18) The gods did not protect Rome from the time of the first consuls through the Second Punic War.

C. (19–21a) The gods did not protect Rome between the Second and Third Punic wars.

D. (21b–31) The period leading to Augustus Caesar.

   i. (21b–22) King Mithridates slaughtered Romans throughout Asia.

   ii. (23–31) Rome's internal wars caused even more suffering than its foreign wars. The war between Marius and Sulla was especially brutal. If Christ had come earlier, the Romans would have blamed him for these disasters, but the Romans do not blame them on their gods.

Book 4. The Expansion of Rome's Empire: A False Explanation

1. (1–2) Review of previous books and next topics.
2. (3–7) Empires and the gods.
   A. (3–4) The expansion of empire is not necessarily a good. Without justice, kingdoms are large bands of robbers.
   B. (5) During the Servile War, a tiny band of gladiators revolted against Rome and grew into a kingdom. The Romans did not attribute this to the gods.
   C. (6–7) Ninus, king of the Assyrians, was the first ruler who sought to expand his territory. The Assyrian kingdom lasted longer than the Roman empire has endured. Assyria's rise and fall cannot be attributed to the gods.
3. (8–32) The expansion of Rome's empire cannot be attributed to the gods.
   A. (8) The minor gods oversee such discrete, minute tasks that they cannot account for the expansion of Rome's empire.
   B. (9–13) The Romans must therefore appeal to Jupiter, king of the gods. Many explanations have been proposed for how to conceive of Jupiter. The only one that makes sense is that he is king of the other gods, each of whom exists and demands worship. According to this explanation, Jupiter was ultimately responsible for Rome's expansion.
   C. (14–17) The goddess Victory renders Jupiter unnecessary, for the former could alone account for the expansion of Rome's empire. It would have been better for all kingdoms to remain small and peaceful as opposed to expanding by war. The expansion of Rome's empire cannot be explained by the gods. Oddly, the goddess Quies (rest) was excluded from public worship, perhaps indicating Rome's restlessness.
   D. (18–25) The goddess Felicity renders all the gods unnecessary, since felicity is that which is desired above all else. It also makes no sense to have goddesses for Fortune or Virtue. Felicity and Virtue are not goddesses but gifts of the one true God.
   E. (26–32) Roman religion was a deceit of the demons and of Roman statesmen who knew the gods were fictions but intentionally misled the people.
4. (33–34) God is the true source of felicity and the ruler of history, including Israel's deliverance from Egypt.

Book 5. The Expansion of Rome's Empire: The True Explanation

1. (*Preface*) Review and introduction.
2. (1–11) Fate cannot account for the expansion of Rome's empire.
   A. (1–7) "Fate," defined as astrology, cannot explain historical events.
   B. (8–10) "Fate," defined as a chain of causes, is not the same as God's will unless this chain is compatible with divine foreknowledge. God's foreknowledge is compatible with human freedom.
   C. (11) God is sovereign over all things.
3. (12–20) Why God allowed the expansion of Rome's empire.
   A. (12–13) God allowed the expansion of Rome's empire because its virtues, though animated by the lust for glory, still benefited its subjects.
   B. (14–18) Lust for glory is a vice that provides no eternal reward. Christians should imitate and exceed the virtues Romans displayed for their earthly empire.
   C. (19–20) Concluding remarks on the desire for glory and the desire for domination.
4. (21–26) God's rule over kingdoms and rulers.
   A. (21–23) God controls the rise of earthly kingdoms and rulers, the duration of wars, and military success.
   B. (24–25) The happiness of Christian emperors is a function of virtue and not material blessing, for God grants material blessing and suffering to good and evil people alike. This is evident in the rule of Constantine and his successors.
   C. (26) Emperor Theodosius was a virtuous emperor.

∞∞ *Against the Gods: Blessings in the Life to Come* ∞∞

Book 6. Critique of Mythical Theology

1. (*Preface*–1) Review and introduction: The gods are of no value for temporal goods or eternal life.
2. (2–9) Varro's inconsistencies.

A. (2–4) Varro was a brilliant and learned man. His *Antiquities* distinguished between human and divine matters and treated the former first. Varro was hinting that the gods are a human fiction.

B. (5–9) Varro condemned mythical theology, commended natural theology, and located civic theology somewhere between the other two without critiquing it. But mythical theology is a part of civic theology, so he should have condemned civic theology too. Varro sought to condemn civic theology but feared doing so openly.

3. (10–11) Seneca openly condemned civic religion but encouraged its practice for the sake of law and custom. He also critiqued Jewish rites.

4. (12) Conclusion.

Book 7. Critique of Civic Theology: The "Select" Gods

1. (1) Introduction: Are the select gods of value for eternal life?

2. (2–4) The select gods are not select because of the greatness of their tasks but because of the greatness of their fame—or rather infamy.

3. (5–28) Varro's naturalistic explanations of the select gods.

A. (5–6) Varro suggests God is the soul of the world and the gods correspond to different parts of the world.

B. (7–8) Varro's naturalistic explanations of Janus, the god of beginnings, make no sense.

C. (9–18) Jupiter.

    i. (9–14) Varro claims Jupiter is the god of all causes and the soul of the world, but he cannot explain Jupiter's relationship with the other gods. Given their tasks, the gods should be identified with Jupiter rather than worshiped as separate gods.

    ii. (15–18) Some have equated the gods with the stars or with different parts of the world. In truth, the gods were once human beings who were then proclaimed as gods by demons and poets.

D. (19–28) Other select gods.

    i. (19–22) Varro's naturalistic explanations fail for Saturn, Ceres, Liber, and Neptune's wives. The rites for these gods are vile.

    ii. (23–26) Varro claims Tellus, the Great Mother, is the goddess of the earth. But there are multiple gods of the earth who are worshiped separately and not just as different names of Tellus. The use of castrated or effeminate men in the worship of Tellus makes her the cruelest of all the gods.

   iii. (27–28) The select gods are renowned for their wicked deeds.

4. (29–35) Christianity and Roman religion.

  A. (29–30) What the naturalistic explanations ascribe to the select gods should, rather, be ascribed to the one true God.

  B. (31–33) God sent the Word to bring us salvation, preparing the way for Christ through signs, angels, and the Hebrew people. True religion has exposed and defeated the demons, including Varro's select gods.

  C. (34–35) Numa discovered the truth about the gods but buried his writings on this matter. The senate later discovered and burned his writings, keeping the people in error.

Book 8. Critique of Natural Theology: Demons

1. (1) Introduction: The Platonists acknowledged truths about God but considered the gods necessary for happiness after death.

2. (2–4) Plato and his predecessors: Socrates turned philosophy from questions about nature to questions about morality. Plato integrated Socrates's teachings with new learning and established three branches of inquiry: moral, natural, and rational.

3. (5–12) The Platonists.

  A. (5–9) Because they affirm a supreme and transcendent God, the Platonists' writings are superior to Varro's theologies and to other philosophies. The Platonists understood God as the source of all things (according to natural philosophy), the criterion of truth (according to rational philosophy), and the highest good (according to moral philosophy). They were the closest among the philosophers to Christians.

  B. (10–12) Even Christians unfamiliar with philosophy will agree with the Platonists on certain points. Plato may have read the Old Testament prophets through an interpreter, though he could not have encountered Jeremiah or read the Septuagint. The best recent philosophers called themselves Platonists: Plotinus, Iamblichus, Porphyry, and Apuleius.

4. (13–22) Apuleius's theory of demons.

   A. (13–17) The nature of demons: Plato said all gods are good even
   though he rejected the shows that the gods commanded. The Platonists, and especially Apuleius, posited a threefold division of gods,
   demons, and humans. According to this hierarchy, the demons are
   superior to humans because the demons have better bodies and
   reside in the air and not on the earth. This position is misguided.
   Superiority is about moral excellence and not the abilities of bodies. Apuleius also claimed the gods have passions, or motions of the
   soul contrary to reason.

   B. (18–22) The mediation of demons: Apuleius said the demons serve
   as intermediaries between the gods and humans, conveying to the
   gods messages produced by humans through immoral magic arts.
   But this still means the gods receive humans' prayers through immoral magic arts, and it suggests good gods are more willing to
   interact with evil demons than with good humans. The gods would
   then care more about (demons') bodily superiority than about (humans') moral superiority. It does not make sense that the gods
   would be ignorant of human affairs, for then the demons could
   deceive the gods. Apuleius's theory of mediation should be rejected.

5. (23–28) Hermes Trismegistus.

   A. (23–26) Hermes [the Greek name for the Egyptian god Thoth]
   taught that humans made gods by uniting images with invisible
   spirits. He foresaw the destruction of the gods, whom he understood
   to be false. Yet he still mourned this future. At least Hermes did
   not espouse Apuleius's theory that the demons are intermediaries
   between the gods and humans.

   B. (27–28) Hermes foresaw Egypt being filled with tombs, a reference to
   the memorials of martyrs, which are replacing the Egyptian temples
   and shrines. Christians do not worship the martyrs but only honor
   them.

Book 9. Further Critique of Natural Theology: "Good Demons"

1. (1–2) Introduction: Some people say there are both bad demons and good
   demons. Could good demons exist and be of benefit for life after death?

2. (3–8) The demons and passions.

    A. (3–4) Apuleius said demons experience irrational passions of the soul. Despite their differences in terminology, the philosophers agree that wise people control their passions by reason.

    B. (5–8) Christians believe passions can be virtuous. In contrast to the Stoics, Christians also affirm the legitimacy of compassion. Given Apuleius's admission that the demons do not control their passions by reason, the demons must be evil.

3. (9–18) The demons are upside-down mediators.

    A. (9–14) On Apuleius's definition, demons have immortal bodies and miserable, vice-ridden souls. In comparison, the gods have immortal bodies and blessed souls, and humans have mortal bodies and miserable souls. The demons are in the worst situation since they will be miserable forever. They cannot serve as mediators for humans.

    B. (15) As both God and man, Christ is the mediator humans need. He became temporarily mortal while remaining permanently blessed to lead miserable mortals to blessed immortality.

    C. (16–18) Apuleius said the gods avoid contact with humans to avoid being contaminated by them. But then the demons are contaminated by humans and unable to purify them, or the demons are less vulnerable to contamination and superior to the gods. Humans do not approach God through bodily ascent but through spiritual ascent.

4. (19–23) The terms "angels" and "demons."

    A. (19) The Scriptures speak of good and bad angels but not of good demons.

    B. (20–22) The word "demons" comes from the Greek word for knowledge. The demons are arrogant because they have knowledge but not love. They fear Jesus's power, but they do not love his righteousness. Good angels care more about loving God than about temporal knowledge, though their knowledge of the future exceeds that of demons.

    C. (23) The Platonists call the angels "gods," which Scripture allows. But the Platonists think it is not angels but demons (or good demons) who mediate between the gods and humans.

Book 10. The Angels and True Worship

1. (1) Review and introduction: Do the gods want us to worship God or themselves?

2. (2–7) True worship.

   A. (2–3) The Platonists affirm that God alone is the source of happiness, both for humans and for the gods (angels). These gods should thus direct humans to worship God and not themselves.

   B. (4–7) Sacrifice is due only to God. The Old Testament sacrifices signified the sacrifice of Christians whereby they love God and neighbor. The whole city of God is a sacrifice to God. The angelic part of the heavenly city directs the human part to sacrifice to God.

3. (8–19) Miracles.

   A. (8) The angels performed miracles during the Old Testament to encourage proper worship.

   B. (9–11) These miracles contrast with theurgy, which cannot purify the soul and involves many absurdities. Porphyry recognized these problems, though he concealed his doubts.

   C. (12–17) God uses miracles to encourage proper worship. Angels performed many miracles in Israel's history, when temporal goods were promised as signs of eternal goods. Angels who direct us to worship God should be trusted above those who seek to be worshiped themselves.

   D. (18–19) Potential objections addressed: (a) the miracles of Scripture did not happen; (b) visible sacrifices should not be offered to the invisible God.

4. (20–22) Christian sacrifice.

   A. (20) Christ is the true mediator, acting as priest, sacrifice, and the one who receives sacrifice.

   B. (21–22) The martyrs refused to sacrifice to demons and defeated them with virtue.

5. (23–32) Porphyry.

   A. (23–24) Porphyry affirmed the existence of "principles" that could purify the soul, but he did not acknowledge Christ as the "principle" made flesh.

B. (25) The Old Testament promised material rewards that signified eternal rewards. Psalm 73 signals the difference between the Old and New Testaments and teaches humans that their greatest good is to cling to God.

C. (26–29) Porphyry knew the problems with theurgy yet hypocritically commended it to the masses. He refused to recognize the incarnation because he despised the flesh. The philosophers reject Christ because he is humble and they are proud.

D. (30–31) Porphyry rightly rejected Plato's ideas concerning the transmigration of souls. Porphyry also said that souls come into being and have not existed eternally. Though Plato said the same, the Platonists interpret his words so as to affirm the eternal existence of souls.

E. (32) Porphyry failed to discover the universal way of liberation, which is Christianity.

∞∞ *The Origins of the Two Cities* ∞∞

Book 11. The Creation and Fall of the Angels

1. (1–3) Introduction.
   A. (1) The city of God introduced. Review and summary of upcoming topics.
   B. (2–3) Christ leads Christians from the temporal to the eternal, teaching Christians through Scripture what they otherwise could not know.
2. (4–6) God created the world. This marked the beginning of time.
3. (7–21) The creation account.
   A. (7–8) Figurative interpretations for the days of creation and for the seventh day.
   B. (9–21) The separation of light and darkness.
      i. (9–13a) The account of God's creating the light refers to the creation of the angels. Some angels fell from God. Happiness consists of the enjoyment of God and the certainty of remaining in God. The evil angels did not enjoy this certainty before their fall, but the good angels do now.

ii. (13b–18) The devil was not sinful by nature but made an evil choice. God uses such evil choices for good.

iii. (19–21) The separation of light from darkness refers to the separation of the good angels from the evil angels. God approved the light, but not the darkness. This approval does not suggest God learned something new.

4. (22–23) Against alternative accounts of creation: Manicheism and Origen.

5. (24–28) Traces of the Trinity in creation.

  A. (24–25) God is Trinity. There are traces of the Trinity in the tripartite divisions of philosophy and of art.

  B. (26–28) Humans were created in the image of the triune God. We exist (Father), we know we exist (Son), and we love this existence and knowledge (Spirit).

6. (29–34) Angels again.

  A. (29) The angels enjoy knowledge of God by direct participation in God.

  B. (30–31) Reflections on the numbers six and seven.

  C. (32–34) Alternate interpretations of the creation account. Perhaps the angels were created prior to what is described in the Genesis account; it is possible that "in the beginning" is not a reference to time but means "in the Word." Perhaps the separation of the angels was seen in the separation of the waters. Regardless, there was a division between two societies of angels, one that loves God and another that loves self.

Book 12. The Cause of the Angelic Fall; The Creation of Humanity

1. (1a) Introduction: Both the cities include both humans and angels. There are only two cities, not four.

2. (1b–9) The cause of the angelic fall.

  A. (1b–5) The evil angels were not sinful by nature but fell by their sinful choice. God is supreme being and goodness, bestowing being and goodness on all things. Those who sin against God corrupt their own natures. Some things are created with lower degrees of being, but they are still good according to the order of nature.

B. (6–9) The angels fell by turning from God, who is supreme being, to themselves, who do not possess supreme being. There is no efficient cause of evil; evil is a deficiency that arises in the rejection of higher goods for lower goods. The good angels cling to God by the love of the Spirit. Together, the good angels and the human part of the heavenly city constitute the one city of God.

3. (10–28) The creation of humanity.

A. (10–14) Some believe that humans have always existed, appealing to various theories concerning eternal cycles of the world. These theories are absurd.

B. (15–21) God created the world as a new act without something new happening in God's mind. Nothing in creation is coeternal with God.

C. (22–28) God created humanity from one man as an inherently social people. Humans would fall into sin and conflict with each other. It was God who created humans, not the lesser gods of the Platonists. From the first man would arise the two cities.

Book 13. The Fall of Humanity: Death and the Body

1. (1) Introduction: If humans had been obedient to God, they would have received blessed immortality without intervening death. They received the punishment of death because of their disobedience.

2. (2–15) Death.

A. (2) Definitions of death. (a) The death of the soul is abandonment by God. (b) The death of the body is abandonment by the soul. This separation of body and soul is the "first death." (c) The union of body and soul for eternal punishment is the "second death."

B. (3–8) Those who have been forgiven in Christ still experience the first death, though not as a penalty for sin but as an encouragement to faith. If Christians did not die, people would pursue baptism just to avoid death. The martyrs conquered death by their confession of Christ. Thus, the penalty for sin became the armor of virtue. Martyrdom ensures the remission of sins.

C. (9–11) Perplexities concerning the term "death." It is difficult to identify when a person is "in death," for someone who is dying is still alive, and someone who has died is "after death."

D. (12–15) The death God threatened Adam and Eve with included all the deaths. Adam and Eve immediately experienced the death of the soul. This would lead to the death of the body and, eventually, to the second (i.e., final) death. Death was passed on to all posterity.

3. (16–24) Questions concerning the body.

A. (16–20a) Refutation of the philosophers, who think separation from the body is a blessing and not punishment. They inconsistently hold that the gods have bodies and are happy.

B. (20b–24) The saints will receive even better bodies than Adam and Eve had before the fall. Adam and Eve were created with earthly, animal bodies capable of death. The resurrected body will be immortal and spiritual, following Paul's teaching in 1 Corinthians 15.

Book 14. The Fall of Humanity: The Abandonment of God for Self

1. (1) Introduction: All humanity can be divided into two main groups, those who live according to the spirit and those who live according to the flesh.

2. (2–9) "Flesh."

A. (2–4) "Flesh" refers not to the body but to the self. Living by the standard of the flesh means living by the standard of humans, not God.

B. (5–9) The philosophers wrongly blame the body for humans' moral failings, which they associate with four "disturbances": desire, joy, fear, and grief. These emotions represent the will, and they are not inherently bad. They are good if the will is good, and bad if the will is bad, and they ultimately represent humans' loves. Christians use emotions rightly, according to the spirit and not the flesh.

3. (10–27) The fall of humanity.

A. (10–15) Adam and Eve enjoyed great happiness before the fall. The devil led Adam and Eve into sin because he was jealous of their unfallen condition and wanted to rule over them. The fall began with pride, the abandonment of God for self. Pride and humility distinguish the earthly and heavenly cities. The punishment of the first sin was disobedience itself. Humans were abandoned to themselves, such that their bodies no longer submitted to their minds.

B. (16–20) Lust involves the insubordination of the sexual organs to the will. This sign of disobedience was fitting retribution for Adam and Eve's sin and the source of their shame after the fall.

C. (21–24) Had humans not fallen, procreation would have occurred without lust, with the sexual organs obedient to the will.

D. (25–27) Summary: Adam and Eve enjoyed happiness before the fall. God foresaw the fall but permitted it to demonstrate the magnitude of human sin and the glory of divine grace.

4. (28) The two cities were created by two loves, one of self and the other of God.

∞ *The Development of the Two Cities* ∞

Book 15. From Cain to Noah

1. (1–3) Introduction.
   A. (1) Review and summary. Cain was of the earthly city, Abel of the heavenly city.
   B. (2–3) Israel was a prophetic image of the heavenly city, according to Paul's allegory in Galatians 4:12–5:1. Ishmael was born naturally, signifying the earthly city, while Isaac was born miraculously, signifying the heavenly city.

2. (4–20) The lines of Cain and Seth.
   A. (4–7) Cain's crime: The earthly city is characterized by violence, as witnessed by the fratricides of Cain and Romulus. Though the heavenly city also experiences conflict, it progresses in its pilgrimage through mutual forgiveness and the help of the Holy Spirit. Cain was rejected because he withheld from God the offering of himself.

B. (8–16) Cain's city: How could Cain have founded a city when there were so few people on earth? The genealogies do not mention everyone who lived, and the earliest people lived long enough to produce offspring for many cities. This position can be defended despite discrepancies in the genealogies between the Hebrew and Greek versions of the Old Testament, and against the suggestion that years were counted differently at that time.

C. (17–20) Cain and Seth became the fathers of two lines of descent, the earthly and heavenly cities. Scripture records these lines to the flood.

3. (21–27) The flood.

A. (21–23) The two lines of descent, Cain's and Seth's, were intermingled when men of the heavenly city were captivated by women of the earthly city and abandoned God.

B. (24–27) God destroyed humanity in the flood, preserving Noah and his family, the only people who did not deserve this punishment. The ark is a figure of the city of God on pilgrimage in this world. The account of the flood should not be treated only historically or only allegorically. The flood was a historical event that prefigured the church.

Book 16. From Noah to David

1. (1–11) The development of humanity to Abraham.

A. (1–3) Noah blessed Shem and Japheth and cursed Ham. Shem signified Jewish Christians, Japheth signified gentile Christians, and Ham signified heretics and false Christians. The lines of descent from Noah's sons.

B. (4–6) The tower of Babel was an instance of pride, which God punished appropriately. God did not literally "come down" to see what the people were doing. God descended through angels.

C. (7–9) All nations have come through Noah, even monstrous nations (if such mythical peoples exist).

D. (10–11) Following the flood, Scripture traces the city of God through Shem's line. But it is probable that all the lines of descent—from Shem, Japheth, and Ham—included members of both the heavenly

and earthly cities. Hebrew was the original language of all humanity. It was preserved in the line of Heber, from whom arose the
descendants of Abraham.

2. (12–17) Abraham and the two cities.

A. (12–16) The family of Abraham's father, Terah, came to Haran
from the territory of the Chaldeans, which was part of the Assyrian
kingdom. Terah's family had been persecuted for worshiping the
one true God. Abraham received the first promise and left Haran
when he was seventy-five, while his father was still alive.

B. (17) There were three great kingdoms at the time of Abraham: the
Sicyonians, the Egyptians, and the Assyrians. The Assyrian kingdom was by far the most powerful.

3. (18–43) The heavenly city from the time of Abraham.

A. (18–34) The life and promises of Abraham. It is not always clear
whether a given promise referred to Israel or to Abraham's spiritual
children from all nations. The later promises more explicitly referred
to Abraham's spiritual children. In particular, the promise of Isaac
and the institution of circumcision signified a people characterized
by grace and not by nature, by regeneration and not by generation.

B. (35–42) The progress of the city of God in Abraham's descendants.
The events of Isaac's and Jacob's lives signified Christ and the church.

C. (43) The history of Israel from Moses to David. Humankind pro-
gressed from infancy (the period from Adam to Noah) to childhood
(the period from Noah to Abraham) to adolescence (the period
from Abraham to David). The imposition of the law gave rise to an
abundance of sins and the beginning of Israel's earthly kingdom.
Yet there remained spiritual people on earth.

Book 17. The Prophets

1. (1–3) There are three ways to interpret prophecies: in terms of earthly
Jerusalem, of heavenly Jerusalem (the city of God), or of both.

2. (4–7) The prophetic significance of Samuel and Saul.

A. (4–5) The rejection of Eli for Samuel signified the transition from the
old covenant to the new, and the establishment of Christ's priesthood.

Hannah's prayer spoke of Christ and the church. The prophecy of Eli's death signified the death of the whole Aaronic priesthood.

B. (6–7) The rejection of Saul as king signified the establishment of Christ's kingship. Saul personified Israel, which would lose its kingdom when Christ established a spiritual kingship under the new covenant. Israel would be irrevocably divided between those who accepted and those who rejected Christ.

3. (8–13) The promises to David.

A. (8) God's promise that David's son would build God a house was a reference to Christ, not Solomon.

B. (9–13) Psalm 89 [88 in Augustine's Latin Bible] speaks of Christ's kingship. Solomon never enjoyed the peace prophesied in these promises.

4. (14–19) The psalms of David.

A. (14–15) David was a musician who wrote psalms that testify to Christ and the church.

B. (16–19) Treatment of specific psalms with reference to Christ.

5. (20–24) Prophecies of later kings.

A. (20) There are scattered prophecies in the writings of Solomon of Christ and the church.

B. (21–23) The kings of the divided kingdom did not utter many prophecies. There were, however, many prophets during that time. Summary of Israel's and Judah's exiles and the return from Babylon.

C. (24) After the return from Babylon and the prophets associated with that time, there were no prophets until the time of Christ.

Book 18. The Two Cities to the Present Time

1. (1–2) Introduction.

A. (1) The previous books were concerned only with the development of the heavenly city from the time of Abraham. The development of the earthly city must now be considered from that earlier time.

B. (2) The earthly city has always been characterized by the pursuit of its own desires and thus by conflict. The two great kingdoms of the earthly city were the Assyrian empire (or Babylon, the first Rome) and the Roman empire (the second Babylon).

2. (3–26) Development of the earthly city: earthly kings and the rise of the gods.

A. (3–7) The earthly city during the time from Abraham to Moses.

B. (8–12) The earthly city during the time from Moses to Joshua.

C. (13–18) The earthly city during the time of the judges and the Trojan War. Stories about the gods, including tales of humans becoming animals. Many of these stories were probably fictitious, though demons do have power to bring about such illusions.

D. (19–23) The earliest days of Rome and the transition from the Assyrian to the Roman empire. There were sibyls who prophesied of Christ.

E. (24–26) The earthly city during the time of Israel's captivity in Babylon.

3. (27–36) Later prophets.

A. (27) Prophets arose during the early days of Rome, as the Assyrian kingdom was waning. They spoke about the hope of the gentiles.

B. (28–36) Prophecies of Christ and the church in these later prophets.

4. (37–44) The superiority of the Old Testament prophets over the philosophers.

A. (37–40) The prophets wrote before the philosophers did.

B. (41) The philosophers disagreed on many matters, whereas the prophets exhibit harmony with one another.

C. (42–44) The translation of the Septuagint was directed by the Holy Spirit. Both the Septuagint and the Hebrew Old Testament are authoritative.

5. (45–54) The cessation of the prophets to the present [i.e., Augustine's time].

A. (45) The prophets ceased after the restoration of the temple following the Babylonian captivity. The Jews were under foreign rule until the time of Christ.

B. (46–49) Jesus came as both man and God but was killed by the Jews in accordance with prophecy. The Jews were devastated by the Romans and scattered throughout the nations, where their Scriptures now serve as a testimony to Christ. The house of the new covenant, the church, is far more glorious than the restored physical temple was. The church is a mixed body. Jesus died, rose again, ascended into heaven, and sent the Spirit.

C. (50–51) The gospel spread from Jerusalem to the world through the apostles and martyrs until the rulers of this world became subject to Christ. Witnessing the abandonment of the temples, the devil stirred up heretics to oppose the church.

D. (52–54) It is not possible to determine how many more persecutions the church will endure. The suggestion that Peter used sorcery to ensure that Christianity would only last 365 years is ridiculous.

∞∞ *The Ends of the Two Cities* ∞∞

Book 19. The Supreme Good

1. (1–3) The questions of philosophy. The supreme good is that which is sought for its own sake and for the sake of which all other things are sought. Varro delineated 288 potential schools of philosophy according to their positions on six questions. The only major difference between these schools concerns the pursuit of virtue and physical goods. Varro held that both should be sought for their own sake.

2. (4–20) Christian responses.

A. (4) Questions 1–2: Whether or not physical goods and virtue should be sought for their own sake, happiness cannot be found in this life. The ultimate good is eternal life, and the ultimate evil is eternal death.

B. (5–17) Question 3.

   i. (5–9) Social life in this present age is characterized by evils at the levels of household, city, world, and universe.

   ii. (10–11) The supreme good is eternal peace.

   iii. (12–17) Discourse on peace.

      a. (12–13) It is impossible not to seek peace of some sort. Peace at every level of being involves the tranquility of order.

      b. (14–16) The peace of the household involves perfectly ordered concord with respect to command and obedience. This includes the discipline of slaves, though slavery is a result of the fall.

    c. (17) Both earthly and heavenly households seek earthly peace, but for different ends; so also with the earthly and heavenly cities. The heavenly city obeys the laws of the earthly city for the sake of earthly peace, except for laws concerning religion.

  C. (18) Question 4: The faith of the heavenly city is certain.

  D. (19) Questions 5–6: Varro's final questions, concerning the Cynics' mode of life and the lifestyles of leisure and activity, are of no importance to the heavenly city.

  E. (20) Conclusion: The supreme good of the city of God is everlasting peace.

3. (21–25) Rome and the definition of "republic."

  A. (21) On Cicero's definition, Rome was never a republic because it was never just. It is unjust to worship demons instead of God.

  B. (22–23) Despite his attacks against Christianity, even Porphyry recognized that God alone is to be worshiped.

  C. (24–25) If "republic" is defined not in terms of justice but in terms of common objects of love, Rome is a republic, though it still lacks justice. The semblance of virtue without submission to God is vice.

4. (26–27) During this life, Christians are like captives in Babylon who use and pray for the temporal peace of the earthly city. They also exhibit some justice, though they are not perfectly virtuous and need to receive the forgiveness of sins.

5. (28) The final end of the heavenly city is eternal peace. The final end of the earthly city is eternal war between passion and the will.

Book 20. Final Judgment

1. (1–3) The final judgment will reveal God's justice, bringing ultimate happiness on the good alone and ultimate unhappiness on the evil alone.

2. (4) Scriptural testimonies of the final judgment will be treated, first from the New Testament, then from the Old Testament.

3. (5–20) New Testament testimonies.

  A. (5–6) The Gospels: Jesus speaks of the coming judgment and the resurrection of the dead. In John, Jesus speaks of two resurrections.

The first concerns souls receiving new life now, and the second concerns the resurrection of the body for final judgment.

B. (7–17) Revelation 20–21: The devil has been bound for a thousand (figurative) years and thrown into a pit, prevented from deceiving the nations that now belong to Christ. At the end of this period, the devil will be released briefly, for the last persecution of the church. The church will persevere. In the second resurrection, Christ will judge everyone according to their deeds. The devil and the wicked will be thrown into eternal fire. The present world will be consumed in a blaze, and the saints will never suffer again.

C. (18–20) Other New Testament testimonies: 2 Peter 3; 2 Thessalonians 2; 1 Thessalonians 4; 1 Corinthians 15.

4. (21–29) Old Testament testimonies.

A. (21–24) Testimonies from Isaiah, Daniel, and Psalms.

B. (25–29) Malachi 3–4: God will purify the righteous, who will offer themselves as sacrifices in righteousness. There will be a separation between the righteous and the unrighteous. Elijah will return to teach the Jews to interpret the law spiritually so that they will believe in Christ.

5. (30) The Old and New Testaments both speak of the coming judgment. The New Testament speaks more explicitly of Christ, but there are many Old Testament passages that also speak of Christ as the final judge. Summary of the events concerning the last judgment.

Book 21. The Punishment of the Wicked

1. (1) The punishment of the damned will involve bodies suffering eternal torment.

2. (2–10) The possibility of eternal bodily suffering.

A. (2–7) Some deny that bodies can experience pain without dying or burn eternally without being consumed, but God can produce remarkable phenomena, as many examples from nature demonstrate.

B. (8–9) God can alter human nature so that the body will burn eternally without being consumed.

C. (10) The demons will also suffer bodily fire even though they are nonbodily spirits.

3. (11–12) Eternal punishment for temporal sins is not unjust. The eternity of punishment corresponds to the gravity of humanity's first sin. All humanity was condemned because of the first sin.

4. (13–16) Not all punishment is purificatory, but only that which results in correction. This life is characterized by suffering, which makes us hope in the future. During this temporal existence, and aided by God's grace, Christians must struggle against vice.

5. (17–22) Errors concerning eternal punishment.

   A. (17) Some suggest punishment will be temporary.

   B. (18) Some suggest punishment can be escaped through the intercession of the saints.

   C. (19–21) Some suggest punishment can be escaped through baptism, eucharist, or perseverance in the Catholic Church, regardless of how one has lived.

   D. (22) Some suggest punishment can be escaped through works of mercy.

6. (23–27) Response to these errors.

   A. (23) If punishment is temporary, the devil also will be saved. But Scripture refutes this position.

   B. (24) If punishment can be escaped through the intercession of the saints, the saints and holy angels should pray for the salvation of evil angels, but they do not. The church does not pray for those whose condemnation is certain.

   C. (25–26) Baptism, eucharist, and perseverance in the Catholic Church do not secure salvation if one commits immorality or heresy. Though 1 Corinthians 3 claims some will be saved "as through fire," Paul is referring to those who fundamentally love Christ above earthly goods.

   D. (27) Works of mercy should be performed, but they do not license sin. Still, there is a type of life that is not righteous enough to merit the kingdom of heaven but righteous enough to receive pardon through almsgiving. It is not clear how this righteousness should be defined.

Book 22. The Reward of the Righteous

1. (1) The final end of the city of God is eternal blessedness.
2. (2–3) The final things will occur according to God's will.
3. (4–11) Addressing objections to the resurrection of the body.
   A. (4–5) Some deny that bodies can be resurrected, but the resurrection of the body is not as incredible as the union of the soul and the body or the fact that the world has come to believe in the resurrection of Christ's body.
   B. (6–7) Cicero was astonished that earlier Romans believed in Romulus's (false) divinity even though they lived in a sophisticated age. It is even more astonishing that the world has believed in Christ's resurrection and true divinity in a much more sophisticated age.
   C. (8–10) Miracles continue to happen today [i.e., in Augustine's time], especially through the martyrs. Many miracles have occurred in association with Saint Stephen. The martyrs' miracles are greater than the demons' and direct us to worship God, not the martyrs.
   D. (11) Against Platonist cosmology, it is possible for earthly bodies to dwell in heaven.
4. (12–21a) Addressing questions about the resurrection of the body.
   A. (12) Summary of the questions.
   B. (13–21a) Responses.
      i. (13) Aborted fetuses might participate in the resurrection of the body.
      ii. (14) Infants will be raised as mature humans.
      iii. (15–16) Humans will be raised in the size that corresponds to the peak of youth (thirty years of age).
      iv. (17–18) Women will retain their sex in heaven.
      v. (19) Humans' hair and nails will be restored, yet without deformity in the body. Heavier and thinner people will exhibit beautiful symmetry. Martyrs will retain their scars as marks of honor.
      vi. (20–21a) God will restore bodies that have been destroyed, including the flesh of those who were cannibalized. Summary of responses concerning the resurrected body.

5. (21b–30) The future life.

A. (21b–24) Speculations about the future life based on the gifts God gives both the good and the evil in this life. This life is full of suffering, particularly in the battle against sin. Yet this life is also full of blessing: procreation, the human mind, the human body, the rest of creation. How much greater will the future life be?

B. (25–28) The philosophers and the resurrection of the body.

   i. (25) The philosophers affirm the future blessedness of the soul but deny the resurrection of the body.

   ii. (26–28) Porphyry held that the purified soul could not return to the miseries of a corruptible body. Plato held that the soul could not exist forever without a body. Varro held that the soul would return to the same body as before. Together, their positions lead to Christian truth. Christians hold that the soul will return to its own body and that this body will be transformed for eternal blessedness.

C. (29–30) Christians will see God with the eyes of the body through the bodies of others. The future life will be marvelous, characterized by true glory, true freedom, praise for God's mercy, and rest.